MARY TODD LINCOLN

A BIOGRAPHY

MARY TODD LINCOLN

A BIOGRAPHY

JEAN H. BAKER

W. W. NORTON & COMPANY

NEW YORK · LONDON

Library of Congress Cataloging-in-Publication Data

Baker, Jean H.
Mary Todd Lincoln.

Bibliography: p.
Includes index.
1. Lincoln, Mary Todd, 1818–1882. 2. Lincoln,
Abraham, 1809–1865—Family. 3. Presidents—United
States—Wives—Biography. I. Title.
E457.25.B35 1987 973.7'092'4{B} 86-23757

ISBN 0-393-30586-4

W. W. Norton & Company, Inc.,
500 Fifth Avenue, New York, N.Y. 10110
W. W. Norton & Company Ltd.,
10 Coptic Street, London WC1A 1PU

7 8 9 0

TO BRICKS

Contents

Illustrations appear following page   167

Acknowledgments

So MANY scholars, librarians, and friends have helped me during the writing of this book that to name some is to overlook others. Still, special thanks to Lincoln scholars Thomas Dyba, James Hickey, Mark Neely, Charles Strozier, Wayne Temple, and Doris Porter. The splendid edition of Mary Todd Lincoln's letters edited by Justin and Linda Levitt Turner has made my task incalculably easier. I am grateful as well to librarians and archivists at Transylvania University, the Lexington (Kentucky) Public Library, the University of Kentucky Library, the Illinois Historical Library, the Chicago Historical Society, and the Library of Congress. Drs. Robinson Baker, Benjamin Baker, Mervyn Carey, William Fitzpatrick, Mel Prosen, William Speed, and Stewart Wolff gave patient instruction on medical matters.

My research has been generously supported by the Elizabeth Connolly Todd Foundation, established in 1970 by George L. and Elizabeth Connolly Todd at Goucher College, where my colleagues in the History Department—Peter Bardaglio, Julie Jeffrey, and Kent

Lancaster—have listened, read, and commented. William S. McFeely offered useful suggestions at a critical time. Steven Forman, my editor at W. W. Norton, has provided valuable editorial assistance.

Finally my family—Susan, Scott, Rob, Jenny, and son-in-law Ethan—have served as a sympathetic (if sometimes captive) audience and to them and my husband, special thanks.

J.H.B.

Introduction

"*I WISH* I could forget myself," Mary Todd Lincoln once lamented. It was a lifelong battle that she often lost, though in the process of remembering herself, she made certain others would, too. And not always favorably. Today Mary Lincoln ranks among the most detested public women in American history, and Americans who do not know her husband's wartime policies or the names of his cabinet officers have unshakable opinions about Mary Lincoln's failings.

Many remember because she demonstrated her husband's humanity. The President who dealt so generously with the afflicted in public affairs learned, in this understanding, to do so through his private life with a shrew. It is, of course, not a solely American idea that men of great mind and sensibility, like Socrates, often endure wives of abominable temper, like Xanthippe. In our national version of this myth Lincoln, the most venerated of all American heroes, daily practiced tolerance of a cantankerous female who was neither his first nor his greatest love. If the great Abraham assures his wife's tainted immortality, the maligned Mary guarantees her husband's nobility.

Mary Todd Lincoln was assigned her role when, during wartime, she tried to transform the White House into a palace. Then, as a widow and thrice-bereaved mother, she violated the nineteenth-century rules of submission to the decrees of Providence. She cried too long and too hard, and in between, she pressed Congress, with unladylike implacability, for money. She retold the horror of Lincoln's assassination too often, and when no one listened anymore, she abandoned the United States for Europe. Having lost the home and husband that were central to her life, for good cause she annulled her maternal relationship with her only surviving son. Disobeying every rule of the anonymity expected of ladies (especially First Ladies, who, as their husbands represented the nation, themselves reflected womanhood), she was seen as lacking the self-control of the pious female. After the Civil War America's Job was bereaved mother and retiring widow. But Mary Todd Lincoln refused this assignment of quiet suffering when the family she idolized was destroyed. As a result, she was easily transformed into the most notorious of shrews, her faults magnified, her virtues forgotten, her neuroses unobserved, and her very sanity questioned.

Of course, popular stereotypes of Mary Lincoln are classic instances of a male-ordered history that is no longer acceptable. But if Mary Lincoln is to be considered on her own terms and not as Mrs. Abraham Lincoln, what is her importance? She left no published work. She joined no reform movements, nor was she a clandestine supporter of unpopular social causes. She said nothing about women's issues and very little about slavery. She did not influence public policy or secretly author Lincoln's speeches, though her prose was occasionally as eloquent as his. Moreover, her status as a well-educated Todd of Lexington and her marriage to a lawyer who became President of the United States removed her from any authentic representation of nineteenth-century womanhood.

Exceptional in many ways, Mary Lincoln nonetheless accepted conventional views about women and held as her ideal "a nice home, a loving husband, and precious child." Wives, she believed, should be what she never was: quiet and submissive and out of the public eye. A miserable childhood made her clamor for acknowledgment early denied, and when a series of catastrophes destroyed her home and family, her behavior departed further from social ideals. Like a flawed marble statue the cracks of which are repeatedly hammered, Mary Lincoln was a victim battered by personal adversity and trapped by destructive conventions of Victorian domesticity.

Hers, then, is a life that illuminates the human conditions of family love and loss, of convention and nonconformity, of pride and humiliation, and of determination and destiny. Mary Lincoln was exceptional not because she married Abraham Lincoln (that was result, not cause) but because of the range of her experience, the persistence of her tragedies, and the means of her survival. Her life was amplified, and her endurance immense. But within these particulars she suffered universal experiences and was, dangerously, ourselves.

At the end of her life Mary Lincoln left the United States and moved to France. Alone, sick, and for a time forgotten by almost everyone except herself, she used to walk along the promenades, observing the gay world in which she had once participated. Because she was unable to forget herself, remembering became an animating, though painful, preoccupation in an empty life. Her memories went back sixty years, longer, in fact, than she liked to admit, to Lexington, Kentucky, in the 1820s.

MARY TODD LINCOLN

A BIOGRAPHY

I

First Family: Parkers and Todds

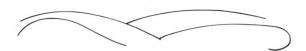

IN the fall Lexington's weather turned wet and dreary, matching the unpleasant economic news. Along Cheapside, the marketplace that served Fayette County, even well-to-do merchants were feeling the effects of the depression that was slowing business after the War of 1812. The decline in hemp prices had forced several owners to close their bagging establishments and offer them for sale, though there were no buyers. A few pessimists spoke of leaving Kentucky to make their fortunes elsewhere. Still, amid the gloom there was some good news. The summer dysentery, especially severe the past season, was over. Palmentier's new tavern had opened on Main Street, and there were plans to "embellish" the courthouse square or at least to complete its bricking. And on Short Street, Eliza Parker Todd and her husband Robert Smith Todd were expecting another baby.[1]

When Eliza Todd's time came, that rainy Sunday in December 1818, she most likely sent down the street for Harriet Leuba, the watchmaker's wife and the best known of Fayette County's midwives. At the time the faculty of Transylvania's medical school—just three blocks up Limestone Road from the Todds—included a specialist in midwifery and the new field of obstetrics. But deliveries, at least normal ones, remained a woman's affair. Not that midwives like Leuba did much. Mostly they let nature take its course, encouraging mothers with talk and sometimes mulled liquor, closing windows to keep out airborne vapors, administering ergot in dilatory cases, and, when the great moment came, catching the baby and tying the umbilical cord.[2]

The setting for this unremarkable nativity was a two-story, nine-room, L-shaped house on Short Street, in the center of Lexington. The Todd residence was typical of those new brick houses admired by travelers who came to Lexington expecting to encounter savage Indians, wild animals, and wooden shacks, but who left admiring the wealthiest, most sophisticated community west of the Alleghenies, excepting, of course, New Orleans. For second-generation Lexington families like the Todds and Parkers, stately Georgian residences measured the distance their community had come from its log cabin beginnings. Foreign travelers agreed with the natives about its elegance, and the city (though it was hardly that until after the Civil War) was featured on many an itinerary. In 1817, the year before Mary Todd's birth, an English merchant described Lexington as the "largest inland town west of the Alleghenies." And for André Michaux, a French traveler, it was the "manor house of Fayette County."[3]

As for its newest resident, there is no record of her looks, weight, and habits. According to the protective superstition of the day, pretty babies grew into ugly women, and if this was true, she was not pretty. After two daughters, both parents certainly hoped for a son, and in this sense their infant girl was a disappointment.[4] They named her Mary Ann after her mother's only sister, although on both sides of the braided Parker-Todd family tree, the name was a popular one. So it was as Mary Ann Todd that the infant entered one of Kentucky's largest, most eminent families.[5]

Her grandfathers, Robert Parker and Levi Todd, had been among a handful of pioneers who had established her birthplace. As a young soldier of the Revolution, Levi, along with his brothers John and Robert, had chosen the name of a distant battle in Massachusetts for what was, in the summer of 1775, no more than a clearing in the wilderness. After the Revolution the Todd brothers returned to the place they had named, and avoiding any mention of the horse thieves, summer sickness, and Indians that kept the timid away, they promoted

Lexington. In a letter to a prospective settler from Maryland, Levi offered the premature—but eventually accurate—prediction that "the People who have been confined to the Forts are now entering the woods and beginning stately houses. In a few years homes will be reared where small log cabbins [*sic*] have stood, wheat fields and meadows where cane brakes now grow."[6]

To others (and his Pennsylvania cousin Robert Parker was one) Levi publicized Lexington as a haven for patriots. To be sure, those who were unwilling to give up the luxuries Todd associated with decadent monarchies had best stay where they were. But to brave republicans, Todd guaranteed "as free a government as the frailties of human nature will admit—and be assured that George the Third is as Little Esteemed here as any other place. And if the citizens of the Eastern waters do not corrupt our principles we shall, I believe, be a free and happy people. Kentucky will be an asylum for liberty."[7]

Even for liberty's sake it took time to settle this western wilderness, and for years Lexington remained no more than a few cabins and a fort where a handful of families huddled behind a stockade fence. There in 1781 Levi and Jane Todd's first child was born and named for Levi's mother. Thereafter the Todds claimed Hannah as their Virginia Dare—the first child of white parents born in Kentucky—though like many Todd stories, the boast was more family advertisement than historical truth. Along with the natural increase in population, outsiders came to Lexington, some attracted by the Todds' optimistic promotion, others by the expectation of good land and pure water, and a few like John, Levi, and Robert Todd's elderly parents, by the renewal of family ties.[8] Hannah and David Todd had emigrated from Ireland to Pennsylvania in 1737. More than forty years later, with all their sons "gone to Kentucky," they uprooted again. Selling their Pennsylvania farm, they joined their sons in the Kentucky wilderness.

Robert Parker and his bride, Elizabeth Porter, migrated for similar reasons. A cousin of the Todds through his maternal grandmother, Parker had grown up with the family in Montgomery County, Pennsylvania, and had heard, through Levi's parents, of the young Todds' adventures on the frontier. Like many other second sons, Parker was willing to exchange the certainties of farming (in his case along the Susquehanna River) for Kentucky's possibilities. Borrowing money for the journey, the Parkers arrived in Lexington in the spring of 1790.

They came to a pioneer community that numbered 843 residents according to the census taken in the fall after their arrival. The year before, George Washington had been inaugurated President of the United States, under a Constitution that guaranteed the formation of new states from territory earlier claimed by the original colonies. In Kentucky there was strong sentiment for independence from Virginia, though the government in Williamsburg continued to encourage settlement through its generous land grants to pioneers in what Virginians knew as Fincastle County. For the time, at least, the Choctaws and Catawbas who had fought tenaciously against the white man's intrusions during the Revolution had moved west into the area around Paducah. As Levi Todd had predicted, the people were indeed leaving the forts to build permanent homes.

At first, having nowhere to live, Elizabeth and Robert Parker stayed in the protective blockhouse outside Lexington on what later became the Richmond Pike. There Parker, the Todd brothers, and a dozen others drew up the citizens' compact that two years later became the basis for a local government run by self-appointed trustees. As veterans of the Revolution both Major Parker and General Todd held warrants and redemption rights that would make them, if Lexington prospered, rich men. But with settlement by neither religious community nor organized group, individuals constantly left the town to take up (for they often did not legally own it) the pastureland outside Lexington. The reason for their coming explained their departure, and by 1800 only half the town's original lot holders remained. Others might move on to clear the land for hemp and grain crops in the surrounding counties, but Robert Parker and Levi Todd stayed in town.[9]

It was typical of the Todds' refined sense of honor that they encouraged the nearby settlement of Frankfort as Kentucky's permanent capital. In view of their extensive holdings, to support their hometown would be, they believed, a conflict of interest. In the building of Lexington they had been exceptionally active, and holding great expectations for its future, they accepted the offices required of founding fathers. "I am," wrote Levi to a friend, "County Lt of a Populous County, Clerk of the Court in the same, a farmer, and at the head of a large family and in addition to this, practice as an attorney in an adjacent county. My life is an active one and I receive hourly calls to various duties and yet I have the assurance to deny that I am anxious or ambitious in search of Honour or Wealth."[10]

Todd may not have been seeking wealth or honor, but in time he got both. As surveyors he and his cousin Robert Parker often had to choose between the devalued eighteenth-century Kentucky currency of land or no payment at all. Soon both men had amassed a planter's estate (spread over three Kentucky counties), though neither was attracted to agriculture. "I believe you have as little taste for farming as myself," Todd once wrote a friend.[11] For some reason—perhaps the restlessness that was characteristic of Parkers and Todds or perhaps the difficult physical labor required to raise an annual crop of grain, corn, or hemp—few family members ever earned their livings from the land. Instead, they used surveying, law, and commerce as levers to establish their prominence, and they served themselves—and Lexington—in a mutually beneficial exchange as churchmen (the Todds gave land to Lexington's first Presbyterian and Episcopalian churches), as trustees of Transylvania University (to which the Todds gave more than 5,000 acres), and as benefactors of schools and other private associations.[12]

Of the two men, the six-foot, 200-pound Levi was the more prominent, in part because his older brother John was an authentic Kentucky hero, who had died, an easy target astride his white horse, defending Lexington from an attacking force of Miamis and Chickasaws during the Battle of Blue Licks in 1782. It was a fitting reward when Kentucky's first governor, Isaac Shelby, appointed the younger brother of such a patriot to the important position of clerk of the Fayette County Court. From 1780 until his death in 1807 Levi Todd took depositions, recorded the relinquishment of dowers, furnished and kept records of road surveys, drew up deeds, made lists of taxable property, issued marriage and tavern licenses, and kept deeds and mortgages. For twenty-seven years Mary Ann Todd's grandfather was a veritable one-man government.[13]

If Robert Parker was not as prominent as Levi Todd, the major was still a well-known surveyor, miller, merchant, and, for a time, clerk of the Lexington Trustees, the city's governing body. In the last capacity he collected four shillings every time a property exchanged hands in Lexington, just as Levi, in a similar annuity, collected a fee on all legal documents processed in Fayette County. Both men, but especially Parker, profited from the provision that the city trustees be given lots out of the 700 acres they controlled.

One measure of the financial success of Mary's grandfathers appeared in their homes, and it is characteristic of these families that Robert Parker built the first brick house in town, while Levi Todd erected the first one in Fayette County. In keeping with family pride, Todd named his house after the small Scottish village where his sixteenth-century Todd ancestors had lived, and he began Ellerslie in the 1790s as a one-room-deep, two-story square residence on thirty acres. When brick-layers and carpenters became available, he hired the best of them to build additional rooms and embellishments until Ellerslie became a well-furnished country villa of more than twenty rooms, decorated by that high Georgian feature of conspicuous consumption, a completely unfunctional belt of bricks around the outside. Inside the house spa-ciousness prevailed in the large hall and square rooms arranged in suites connected by double doors.[14] Outside, among Ellerslie's numer-ous outbuildings, was the stone round house where Todd kept Fayette County's public documents, there being no other place. There angry squatters and tenant farmers whose land tenures were threatened by a court decision came in 1803 to burn the documents that imperiled their property rights. Some said the "mob" even threatened to destroy Ellerslie.[15]

Certainly both Todd and Parker were logical targets for such attacks. In hard times they had bought cheap the land scrip given, in lieu of payment by the government, to veterans of the Revolution. As a result, when Todd died in 1807, he owned 7,000 acres in Fayette and Frank-lin counties. His personal property (exclusive of real estate) was worth more than $6,000, in a society in which more than four-fifths of the households had no property or personal estate at all. Along with silver, china, and leather-bound books (his library included volumes by Wollstonecraft, Burke, and Blackstone), Todd also owned twenty-one slaves, nine horses, other livestock, and a carriage, although he derived his principal income from his clerkship and law practice.[16] Years later, on an anniversary occasion of Lexington, an early resident recalled that "Levi Todd was a father of the Kentucky bar—though I don't expect he was much of a lawyer. He is one of the pioneers of the County—a man of high character and universally esteemed."[17] No doubt Todd himself preferred the epithet on his tombstone in the Lexington Cem-etery: "General Levi Todd—a youthful adventurer to Kentucky and active in its defense in the most perilous time."

Robert Parker died seven years before Todd. A younger man and therefore not as wealthy as Todd, by any standard he, too, was rich, although, in the habit of this society, sometimes land-poor. The fluc-tuations in Parker's economic circumstances emerged in testimony given in a suit brought by the heirs of Levi Todd's profligate brother Robert Todd against Parker's heirs in 1817. (It was typical of the interwoven Parker and Todd clan that in this action, Robert Smith Todd, Mary's father, was both plaintiff through his father's family and defendant through his wife's.) According to Widow Parker's affidavit, in the 1790s her husband could not come up with the forty dollars of gold and silver required to pay off the debt he had contracted when he migrated to Lexington. So he paid in goods rather than cash. Still, he was proud and determined. "I have silver enough to more than discharge my debts but find it impossible to exchange it at this time. I don't want anyone especially one who had so much confidence in me to sustain the smallest loss thereby. Now I am determined that if you think you have I will make ample satisfaction next spring."[18]

Such stringency was temporary and reflected frontier conditions as much as Parker's economic straits. By the time of his death in 1800, from his surveying, from his general store on the corner of Main and Cross streets, and from his mill on the Versailles Road, he had amassed enough cash to put his four sons through professional school and to guarantee his wife's comfort during her half century of widowhood. Shortly before her death in 1850, Elizabeth Parker was taxed on two and a half town lots valued at $4,650, 217 acres on Shannon Run worth $6,500, six slaves, three horses, one carriage, and the inevitable gold watch.[19]

In all their endeavors Parker and Todd benefited from their extensive family connections. Levi Todd had six sons and two brothers; Robert Parker had four sons and three brothers. The marriage of their combined seven daughters and six sisters into other eminent families, such as the Brecks, Todhunters, Richardsons, and Bodleys, produced an interlocking directorate of modern-day corporate proportions with sons, cousins, nephews, and in-laws gradually moving into important posts throughout Kentucky.

IN 1794 Eliza Parker, Robert and Elizabeth Parker's first daughter, was born into this expanding network. Just after her sixth birthday her father succumbed to a long, debilitating illness that may have been cancer. Shortly thereafter her mother sold the family house a few miles out of town and moved back into the center of Lexington. There, on a lot her husband had originally surveyed for the trustees, she built a substantial brick house where she presided for the rest of her life. In time, both to distinguish her from a multiplicity of other Parkers and to recognize her status as Robert Parker's long-surviving relict, she became known as Widow Parker.

While it is difficult to appreciate this today, Widow Parker's lot was part of a planned community based on a grid design ("Penn's plan" some called it) with rectangular one-half-acre lots near the town's center and larger five-acre outlots on the periphery. To ensure development, original lot holders like Widow Parker were required to build, within a prescribed time, "a house equal to an 18 foot square with a brick chimney." If they did not, the lots reverted to the trustees, who used the land to attract residents with essential talents, like the printer John Bradford, who received his lot free in exchange for a promise of permanent settlement. From the second story of their house the Parkers could see most of Lexington, including the expectant eighty-foot-wide Main Street, the brick-pillared courthouse, and Cheapside Market, where Eliza's brothers and uncles ran a dry goods business. Even Lexington's slave markets could be seen and heard from Widow Parker's house.

Of Eliza Parker's early life, little is known. In the will Robert Parker wrote during his long illness he directed that his children "be carefully brought up and well-instructed. Should they appear promising for a professional character I wish them to receive as complete an education as any estate or circumstances will admit."[20] And so his sons did—two became Transylvania-trained doctors of medicine, and one a lawyer—but for his daughters, it was different. While Lexington prided itself on its girls' schooling (the first was held within the stockade), schools for "little misses" usually lasted only a few years. Run by impecunious widows, they taught the rudiments of spelling and reading, avoided the "male" subjects of classics and mathematics, and offered, instead, advanced work in needlework and sewing. Some women—Senator Henry Clay's wife, Lucretia Hart, was one—remained virtually illiterate, even after several years' attendance.

For a time Eliza and her sister Mary Ann Parker probably attended the Lexington Female Academy, where strict, English-born Mary Beck presided over a curriculum of reading, writing, grammar, epistolary correspondence, and, for an extra fee, "fancy work, knitting, painting and embroidery." Mr. Beck, a poet and landscape artist, doubled as the arithmetic teacher. All this cost parents $150 a year, and a card published in the 1806 Lexington papers suggested that most parents were satisfied. "It has long become a matter of complaint that the plan of education for the female mind has generally not been equal to the rank which females hold in all civilized society. Those who had the pleasure of attending Mrs. Beck's examination must rejoice in beholding a foundation laid for removing in great measure this grand complaint." Certainly the rare examples of Eliza Parker's writing suggest that more attention was given to her penmanship than her spelling. But, then, nowhere was nineteenth-century America the great age of spelling.[21]

After Mrs. Beck's, Eliza Parker entered that singular phase of female existence expected of daughters of the gentry. She did nothing. Her mother ran the Parker household; six slaves did its labor. From twelve until her marriage at eighteen Eliza turned her attention to what her famous daughter once called the "gay world." Some days she took the Parker carriage (one of only sixty carriages in Lexington) to the country or on shopping expeditions for the French silks and ribbons displayed in the stores along Cheapside. Other days she participated in the developing ritual of calling on or receiving friends. Often she sewed, for even in elegant Lexington there were no ready-made clothes. Occasionally she read, although a strict prejudice separated girls from the titillation of novel reading, and it is doubtful whether Eliza Parker had much taste for the masculine adventure stories available in Lexington's juvenile library.

Mostly she courted, attending tea parties and cotillions, dancing in the upstairs rooms of Giron's confectionery, watching the performances at Usher's Theater, and gossiping about the doings of Lexington's newly organized Society for Bachelors. Along with her female friends, cousins, and sister she surveyed the Transylvania students. Perhaps it was one of them who composed the sentimental rhyme that appeared in the *Kentucky Gazette:*

> My heart Eliza turns me all to thee,
> To thee sweet girl who has my bosom warmed.

Whether written for Eliza Parker or not, she was acknowledged as "a rising beauty," and by the time she was fifteen gossip linked her name to that of two young students at the university: Stephen Austin and Robert Smith Todd.[22]

In time she would choose and be chosen in that complicated and, for this generation, largely self-willed matrimonial calculus. But for seven years she continued her chaperoned search for the essential vehicle into her future—a husband. Young women of this time and place were taught to worry about being "old maids." Although they had only to look about to see that few Kentucky women remained unmarried (in fact, only 1 in 100 of those who survived to age forty-five,[23] there was always the possibility of an ignominious spinsterhood.

For the time being Eliza Parker and her friends inhabited a slow-paced world of ease and sociability. Just as young girls were often dressed up at Lexington's public events to represent states of the Union or political parties (anything but themselves), so in a less obvious way they served as the best displays of Kentucky's (and the South's) idealized life of leisure and idleness. As one English traveler observed of these flat years of female adolescence, "Lexington's females, however idle, and however great their difficulties, remain at home, with their parents' 'til removed by the great change that all hope for."[24]

WHILE Eliza Parker marked time until the great event of matrimony altered her existence, Robert Smith Todd, the third of Levi's six sons, was growing up at Ellerslie. Like Eliza, he had lost a parent while a child, but unlike Widow Parker, his father, Levi Todd, found a young replacement within two years. In the custom of the day Robert entered Transylvania at fourteen and was graduated four years later after studying mathematics, geography, rhetoric, logic, natural and moral philosophy, and astronomy, "perfecting himself" in Latin, "making considerable progress" in Greek and history, and conducting himself (as all Todds did not) "in a becoming and praiseworthy manner."[25] Perhaps because he was already courting Eliza, Lexington's social life did not distract him as much as it did some others. Wrote one unhappy law student of the period: "Girls and study are incompatible. They excite one's mind beyond the endurance of tame dry reading. One is forever tempted to marry or attempt their virtue."[26]

After Transylvania, Robert Smith Todd set out (some said "like a house afire" so that he might marry Eliza Parker) to become a lawyer, and there is more than a little imitation of his father's career in these early years. First he apprenticed in the office of Thomas Bodley, who was clerk of Fayette County and by marriage a relation of the Parkers. From such a position a young man—whose two older brothers had already carried off the first spoils of family favor—might someday expect to become a county clerk himself. Next Robert Todd studied in Frankfort with the famed Kentucky jurist George Bibb, a chief justice of the state appeals court and later a United States senator. Finally on September 28, 1811, after producing written references and a sufficient amount of information to satisfy his examiners, Robert Smith Todd, aged twenty, was admitted to the Kentucky bar.[27]

He never practiced. Whatever plans Todd had made, the War of 1812 interrupted, and after the war there were too many lawyers even for litigious Fayette County. Actually this overpopulation had always been the case. In 1792, the year that Kentucky became a state, 39 lawyers were admitted to practice in a community of no more than 100 white families. One observer noted that attorneys "collect in Lexington like swarming bees." A few years later a struggling young lawyer complained that "those who follow the bar must hunt buffalo or starve." Robert's brothers, David and Roger Smith, moved to Missouri because there was so little patronage, and by 1822 Robert's name had disappeared from the list of Lexington's lawyers.[28]

Initially Robert gave up the law for patriotism's sake. Elsewhere in the nation it was possible to ignore or even to oppose the War of 1812, but not in Kentucky. The state was close enough to the frontier to support, with men and money, the war against the British and their ally Tecumseh. With Lexington's own Senator Henry Clay leading the way as head of the prowar party, Kentucky became one of the few states whose congressional delegation unanimously supported the declaration of war. In the revolutionary tradition of statesmen-soldiers who serve in peace and war, six members of Kentucky's Washington delegation were in uniform by the fall of 1812.[29]

Even within a community of war hawks the Todds and Parkers stood out for their martial spirit. Before war was declared, Robert Smith Todd had been active in the militia company that was later merged into the Lexington light artillery of the 5th Kentucky Regiment, and in the winter of 1811–1812 he asked one of the Parkers to recommend him to Senator Clay for a commission.[30]

His father would have approved, for military service was a living tradition in a clan that kept as its motto *Oportet vivere*, which the family translated as its militant credo: "it is necessary to live." The first Todds had fought as Scots Covenanters against England at the Battle of Bothwell Bridge in Scotland in 1689. Because they were Presbyterians, they then fled Scotland for Northern Ireland where in the early eighteenth century they resisted the Anglicans in Armagh County. More recently Robert's father, Levi, had served in the American Northwest. The Todds often retold the story of the fall of Kaskaskia and Levi's capture of the Creole commander Rocheblave in 1778. Levi Todd's brother John was a legendary character, ranking with Daniel Boone as a defender of Kentucky. To commemorate his bravery, the Kentucky legislature had bestowed the family surname on a Kentucky county, a fitting testament, in the Todds' estimation, to their family's importance. Indirectly the women of the family participated in this glory, and all the Todds knew about Levi's wife, Jane, who had chosen a Kentucky stockade over Virginia luxury. There, according to family tradition, she ingeniously wove her wedding dress from the weeds and wild flax that were the only textiles available.[31]

Many Americans of this period had similarly heroic traditions. But with that sense of uniqueness that became a birthright, the Todd family raised historical exaggerations to legend. Once instructed, its members never forgot, and this explained why Robert's older sister Hannah chose Todd as the middle name for three of her sons and why Robert named a son after George Rogers Clark, his father's commander during the Revolution. Even as middle-aged civilians Robert and his brother David sought to correct "a false impression of Uncle John's behavior" at the 1782 debacle of Blue Licks, where a Kentucky militia unit had been ambushed by Indians. Defeat might be an orphan, but as the Todds learned, it continued to have many jurors. "Be assured," wrote a concerned David to his brother Robert sixty-six years after the battle, "it is of importance and should not sleep. Is it not monstrous that we suffer such a violation of fact to become a matter of history?"[32] Necessarily the Todd women served as the audience for the retelling of these adventures. In 1880, when Emilie Todd Helm, Robert's seventh daughter, began her family genealogy, she had no trouble recalling the military exploits of her ancestors, though she had difficulty remembering the first names of her great-aunts.[33]

In 1812 history, it seemed to Robert Todd and his generation of Kentuckians, could be made again. Like others of this postrevolutionary age, Todd males suffered in the recollection of their fathers' place in history and hoped for their own chance at glory. When Governor Shelby gave the clarion call, "I will meet you in person. I will lead you into battle," the Todds responded. In July 1812, when the 5th Kentucky Regiment marched out of Lexington attired for British minié balls and national immortality in its eye-catching uniform of light blue with red lacings and red cockades stuck in a black "citizen's" hat (the latter modeled after those of the citizens' army of the French Revolution), eight young Todd cousins and four of Levi's sons were among its troops. Robert's brothers John and David were officers, but Robert had failed to receive his commission. With his younger brother Samuel, he signed on as a private.[34]

Like more soldiers than history ever records, Robert was felled before the battle began. For weeks he lay ill of pneumonia in southern Ohio. When his regiment moved north, he returned home. There he recuperated, and on November 13, 1812, in Widow Parker's drawing room, Robert Smith Todd married Eliza Ann Parker. According to family tradition, the young groom left the next day for the front and participated in the January 1813 fight at Frenchtown, Michigan, and, later in the fall, at the Battle of the Thames near Detroit. Such stories fulfilled family expectations, but they did little to explain the timing of his first child's birth in November 1813.

No matter what Robert's service record, his brothers' exploits continued the Todd narrative that had begun in the sixteenth century. When Sam Todd was wounded on the battlefield at the river Raisin in Michigan, his older brother John removed the minié ball that had penetrated his shoulder—or so the story went. The operation took too long, and the Shawnees captured both men. John escaped after running an Indian gauntlet, but the still-recovering Sam—by all accounts, the handsomest of the Todds with his black hair, slender six-foot frame, and beautiful black eyes—was captured. Later he faced another trial when the tribe demanded that he wed the chief's daughter. This he barely resisted until his loyal brother (Todd legends always had a place for family fidelity) ransomed him for, in one version, the unprincely sum of twenty dollars and, in another version, the popular Todd commodity of a barrel of whiskey.

Like patriots everywhere, the Todds had selective recollections of courage. An English commander in the Northwest considered these Kentucky soldiers especially barbarous and accused them of tomahawking, scalping, and then stripping the skins from their Indian victims; the Indians retaliated with similar brutality at the river Raisin. In any case, Kentuckians (and none more than the Todds and Parkers) mixed their love of state and country with an exaggerated prejudice that Alexis de Tocqueville labeled "a refined egotism which bears the name of patriotism."[35]

The Parkers had their own legends, and some furnished women with wartime roles. In one, Eliza Parker's maternal grandmother had brought food and clothing to her husband, Captain Andrew Porter, during the difficult winter at Valley Forge in 1777. Serving as a canteen and mess mate, she frequently rode out with provisions to the camp, where one day she met an unfamiliar officer who led her to her husband, complimenting her, as they rode through the snow on a bitter cold day, on her devotion to her husband and, through him, the republican cause. The officer was George Washington, who frequently appeared in such tales, and the story, which placed the Todds in touch with the supreme American hero, afforded an example of patriotism for the females of the family to emulate.

Later Eliza's Grandmother Porter caught the eye of another general. This time it was Henry Knox, who was impressed with her husband's uniform during the campaign of 1777, when other officers were in rags. Porter explained that his wife had taken his uniform, turned it inside out, and by stitching all night produced by morning a clean uniform worthy of a patriot.[36] Such models of female valor became a part of Eliza Parker's life, and their instruction was clear: Through sacrificial service to their husbands, American women contributed to the new Republic. Having grown up with such a tradition, when Robert Todd proposed in 1812, Eliza Parker could do no less than accept a soldier's claims to her affection.

To be sure, there were other reasons to marry Robert, and though at eighteen Eliza Parker was slightly younger than average for brides of her time and place, her marriage was entirely in keeping with family expectations. Robert Smith Todd was a blood relative well known to her mother, the indomitable Widow Parker. That she and Robert shared a set of great-grandparents and were second cousins was unremarkable in a clan in which one of the groom's sisters had married a first cousin, as had the bride's mother. In some religions and states, including Pennsylvania where Eliza's parents, Elizabeth Porter and Robert Parker, had married, this was a forbidden degree of consanguinity, though it was not in Kentucky.[37]

Modern society frowns on even such remote incest, but in the early nineteenth century there were compelling reasons for kin to marry. Among the wealthy, family considerations often superseded legal, religious, and even biological prohibitions, though usually they did not override the romantic predilections of the betrothed. For patriarchal families like the Parkers and Todds, consanguinal marriage prevented the dilution of landholdings, assured high stations for sons, and reinforced the link between family and place. And, of course, cousins like Eliza Parker and Robert Todd married because they had only a small pool of approved candidates for the dynastic compact their marriage represented.[38]

After her daughter Eliza had married Robert Todd in 1812, Widow Parker gave the couple the lower half of her lot. Years later, when Widow Parker's death required the division of her assets, no one knew the precise details of this arrangement, though her grandchildren believed that Eliza and Robert had lived for a time with their grandmother before a new house was finished and that their father had been away with Kentucky's volunteer forces for part of that time. In any case it was 1814 before the couple moved into their own house. The result was a family compound with the imposing Widow Parker attending to her own large household (the 1810 census lists five white males, three white females, and six slaves) as well as that of her married daughter.[39]

Certainly eighteen-year-old Eliza Parker Todd could use help, for she was uncertain about the domestic tasks that most young brides took for granted. After six months of marriage she acknowledged her difficulties in a letter to her grandfather General Andrew Porter shortly before his death: "I have been very busy for some time past preparing for house-keeping. I had no idea it was attended with so much trouble, it really is almost enough to deter girls from getting married. We intend residing in Lexington, it would never do for me to go far from Mama as I shall stand so much in need of her instruction."[40] Apparently these fretful warnings convinced her younger sister Mary Ann to delay her marriage until she was in her mid-twenties.

By the time of her daughter Mary's birth in 1818 Eliza had been married six years and had borne three children. Her husband was absent for long periods—a habit that had begun with Todd's military service during the War of 1812 and continued in peacetime with his trips to New Orleans, where he purchased the French brandies, Holland gin, and green coffee he and his partner, Bird Smith, offered for sale to Lexington's carriage trade. Although Robert Smith Todd would have been expected to do little inside the Short Street house, his periodic desertions meant that Eliza had to supervise the traditional male chores—overseeing the carriage, disciplining the slaves, and buying the staples. Sometimes there were economic worries as well. The year Mary Ann was born, business was so bad that Todd made only one trip down the Mississippi to the Louisiana markets. The advertisements for his dry goods store indicated hard times. "Smith and Todd will sell wholesale cheaper than can be imported from the East and by retail a very small profit for cost only."[41] While Todd struggled with a business he eventually gave up as unprofitable, his wife had problems running their expanding household.

In good and bad times Widow Parker helped by sending her slaves down the hill to help with the incessant domestic tasks of cleaning, cooking, washing, and caring for the babies. No matter what the master of the house's convictions about slavery, and Robert Smith Todd came to oppose the institution in theory, his home always depended on slave labor. Usually there were three slaves on loan from Widow Parker. According to the census, all were female. One was under fourteen and probably watched the babies, the second was in her twenties and did the cleaning and washing, and the third, the cook, Mammy Sally, was older and much more experienced than her mistress in the management of domestic affairs.

By the 1820s some wealthy Lexington mothers also used slaves for the most confining of female labors—nursing their numerous offspring. Before the development of artificial nursing preparations, human milk was the only sustenance available. In some households it mattered not who delivered it. Indeed, the number of newspaper advertisements for wet nurses as well as the numerous private inquiries for recent slave mothers must have outnumbered those mothers who had no milk or those who died in childbirth. In this as in other matters, wellborn Lexingtonians imitated the French, as they voluntarily surrendered their maternity. In fact, the practice had become a scandal. One shocked Scottish Presbyterian wrote home about the "number of rich Lexington women who relieve themselves from the drudgery of giving suck to their own children by using recent slave mothers."[42]

Sometimes lonely husbands also encouraged wet nursing. A few were refused by women who believed from folklore (science was as yet silent on the matter) that mother's milk was best. When Joseph Breckinridge insisted that his wife wean the baby and join him for the winter in Frankfort, Eliza Todd's friend Mary Breckinridge demurred. "It is essential," she wrote, "to the preservation of her health through this to keep her at the breast." Eventually this good mother enjoined her husband to get out the trundle bed, for she would come but with her baby.[43]

Considering the ages of her slaves and the spacing of her children, Eliza Todd may have used a wet nurse. In any case she nursed Mary Ann so rarely as to remain fertile and thus lost her only means of natural contraception. Usually nursing mothers became pregnant as they weaned their children to the cup and started ovulating again. It was this fact of life (not what they were calling at the Transylvania Medical School "morbid catamenial cycles") that accounted for the lockstep, two- to three-year intervals between babies.[44]

Eliza Todd was pregnant within a few months of Mary Ann's birth and later that year delivered her first son, a notable occurrence in any nineteenth-century family with three daughters, but an especially important event among the Todds. Mary Ann had spent only a short time as the last among many (and this probably not at her mother's breast), and in 1819 she lost any particularity when Levi, named for his paternal grandfather, took the spotlight. Within months Eliza Todd was pregnant again, and in 1820 Robert Parker Todd arrived. This fifth child then died at fourteen months from one of the bacterial infections that made childhood so perilous in the nineteenth century.

In early Kentucky an infant's death was neither unusual nor unexpected, and few parents raised all their children to maturity. Eliza's friends Henry and Lucretia Clay lost five of their six daughters, and within a single year four of Richard and Margaret Anderson's eight children had died during a cholera outbreak. Although there is no evidence of Eliza and Robert's response to their son's death, such routine departures were nonetheless mourned. But some parents were reluctant to commit unguarded affection to such impermanent objects of love. After it was apparent that his infant daughter would not survive, Dr. Samuel Brown (who later became Mary Todd's stepuncle) explained he "scarcely had the fortitude to indulge my parental affection for my poor dear little Nancy," who shortly thereafter died along with her mother.

Whatever happened, mothers were expected to find comfort in the church, especially in the doctrine of Christian resurrection. Heaven, according to the preachers at McChord's Presbyterian Church, where the Todds were members, was a better place than earth. At least one bereaved parishioner had learned the lesson and recommended faith in God: "The uncertainties of life are so great and eternity so important that to have our dear ones safe is a consolation so great that the more we dwell on their removal, the better we are able to afford the loss." For four-year-old Mary Ann, such theological consolations were no doubt incomprehensible, and the death of this baby brother became the first of a melancholy progression of family abandonments.[45]

Within months of her second son's death Eliza Todd was pregnant again. Anxious to honor a convivial and childless sister, her husband named this fourth daughter Ann. Abruptly Mary Ann was forced to surrender her euphonious double name. Henceforth she was simply Mary Todd. She also gave up her place as the youngest daughter to a newcomer she always resented. Years later she wrote with characteristically implacable judgment and incisive turn of phrase, "Poor unfortunate Ann, inasmuch as she possesses such a miserable disposition and so false a tongue."[46]

Meanwhile, her mother's inexorable fifteen-month cycles of conception, pregnancy, and birth continued. In 1825 a third son was born, Eliza's seventh child in twelve and a half years. Within hours of George Rogers Clark Todd's birth, Eliza was feverish. It was July, and eight residents of Lexington were already dead from cholera and bilious fever. But most likely Eliza was suffering from puerperal sepsis, the post-birth bacterial infection feared by nineteenth-century women as the "childbed fevers."

Women of Eliza Todd's time knew that childbearing was a risky, painful, and unavoidable business; in fact, it was to kill one out of every eight pregnant women in their generation. These women suffered, in the absence of any therapies, not only the pain of labor but perineal tears, prolapsed uteri, vaginal fistulas, and the lethal childbed fevers. They went unaided by the chloroform and ether that were to help their granddaughters. (When the latter was used on Fanny Long-fellow in the 1840s, this Bostonian declared herself "proud to be the pioneer to less suffering for poor weak womankind."[47]) Eliza's friend Mary Breckinridge provided a vivid description of childbirth's trials in an 1823 letter to her husband: "Mrs. Mary Caldwell [of Lexington] was taken ill on Saturday and after suffering all that a woman is capable of enduring had her infant taken from her with instruments. Her shrieks were heard distinctly at the [Transylvania] University for two days without interruption. There was thought no hope for her life after she was delivered, but she is now better."[48]

Charlotte Mentelle, who later became Mary Todd's teacher, confessed that she was expecting "an event I cannot face alone without fright and even with great assistance I still fear this terrible moment." After the safe delivery of her daughter, Madame Mentelle acknowledged that she had expected to die in childbirth.[49] Some women feared the aftermath as much as the delivery, and today's afterbirth depression appeared in the nineteenth century as "bereavement of mind." Although it was generally accepted that some women would be sick "after an event," it was not expected to last long. One Kentucky grandmother expressed irritation that her "dear son William's wife is still in a deplorable condition since the birth of her child last November."[50]

Three doctors were called to the Todd house that July 1825: Dr. Elisha Warfield, Robert Todd's friend, who had been professor of surgery and obstetrics for a brief time at Transylvania; Dr. Benjamin Dudley, the newly appointed professor of anatomy and surgery; and Dr. William Richardson, an expert on diseases of women and children, who was admired by his patients as "competent and agreeable." Such attendance by male doctors was unusual, and it was the nearby medical school that guaranteed Eliza this advanced, though ineffective, care. In Lexington, as in few other places in America, childbirth was a shared enterprise between doctors and midwives. But only during a crisis did males venture into the room set aside for the child's birth. While doctors like Richardson and Dudley agreed that "dame nature was the best midwife," they also believed that in cases like Eliza's, "dame nature" could use the help of male physicians.[51]

Yet the state of their art was too primitive to save their patient. Richardson's work on diseases of the uterus had earned him a national reputation, and while capable of operating on complications during labor, he could not cure the commonplace childbed fever. Holding firmly to the position that "diseases of pregnancy should be treated on the same principles as diseases in other states," he and his colleagues doubtless administered to Eliza heroic doses of calomel—the popular all-purpose chloride of mercury—followed by the classic remedy (also used during labor) of bloodletting and cupping. In a similar case one of Richardson's colleagues explained his therapy: "a dose of calomel, if it hasn't worked, give her 2 of the Black pills every 2 hours. If her fever returns with violence, I wish her to take another puke—[then] you will add a few drops of laudanum to prevent from cramping her." After this, nineteenth-century medicine's all-purpose remedy—bloodletting—was employed. In fact, William Dewees's standard text of midwifery cited one doctor who over a lifetime's practice had drawn 100 barrels of blood from women before, during, and after labor. None of this affected the bacterial infection somehow introduced into Eliza Todd's lacerated birth passage and now festering in her bloodstream, except perhaps to make her feel worse.[52]

Nor had medicine offered her the means of preventing her pregnancy. No one, including the experts at Transylvania, knew much about the timing of conception, and Professor Richardson, who based his theories on his observations of animal reproduction, mislabeled a woman's most infertile period as that time when in fact she was most likely to conceive. Certainly it did not occur to most couples of this generation—especially not to family-proud Todd and Parkers—to limit their pregnancies by abstinence or coitus interruptus. The only protection for women was to delay marriage, but the belief that younger women had a harder time delivering babies served as scant protection. "Those who marry late / Protect their fate/Those who early wed / Make a widower's bed" went the catchpenny wisdom that Eliza had violated.

There is no record of Eliza Todd's deathbed, though women of her generation were expected to go to their graves without protest or complaint. Through their biology the second sex had become natural Calvinists, accepting their fate as a God-given selection. The first lesson of male-prescribed true womanhood in Eliza Parker Todd's Kentucky, as elsewhere in the United States, was neither piety nor domesticity. It was acquiescence, for, in the oft-quoted lines:

> Woman's lot is on you,
> Silent tears to weep,
> And patient smiles to wear,
> Through suffering hours.

The most admired women displayed Christian resignation and were watched on their deathbeds to see if they went quietly into the night. Those who did earned in their obituaries the supreme accolade that they were "patient, contented, and resigned."[53]

Eliza Parker Todd died at the age of thirty-one. During twelve and a half years of marriage she had been pregnant five years and had spent, even with the help of a wet nurse, another five nursing. Few Kentucky women would have found such a life burdensome or unusual. Todd and Parker females were notably fecund, although usually longer-lived. Widow Parker outlived her daughter by twenty-five years and died at eighty-two. Both of Eliza Todd's grandmothers had survived into their sixties. Like them, she had centered her adult years on motherhood and home, and this is what she meant when as a young bride she explained to her grandfather that she wanted to be a good household "economist."[54]

The Lexington papers duly noted the death of Robert Smith Todd's "faithful consort," and in the custom of the day Todd sent printed cards inviting his friends to his wife's burial from "his residence on Short Street this evening at 4 o'clock, July 6, 1825." Those who did not attend would later decline in the same style used to regret a social invitation: "Miss Louisiana Hart returns the compliments to Mr. [Todd] and regrets his polite invitation. She sincerely sympathizes with the family in the sad calamity that befell them and hopes they will be enabled to survive it."[55]

Later Americans raised to elaborate ceremony what was accomplished simply and quickly in this period of Kentucky history. Customarily funerals began with a few prayers at home delivered by a minister—in this case, the new pastor of the McChord's Presbyterian Church, Reverend John Breckinridge. Then the body was carried to the grave on a bier hoisted by strong-backed males, with family, minister, and mostly male friends walking behind. It was not far from the Todds' to the nearby churchyard cemetery. There, at the grave, the minister gave an address "to the living," who included Eliza's mother, husband, sister, four brothers, and six children—from eleven-year-old Elizabeth to four-day-old George Rogers Clark Todd. Often the ceremonies closed with Isaac Watts's lugubrious hymn:

> And must this body die,
> This mortal frame decay,
> And must this active frame of mine,
> Lie mouldering in the clay.[56]

There is no record of the children's reactions to their mother's death, although today we recognize how difficult a time this must have been for all of them. Still, in the early nineteenth century grief was considered a temporary condition, a natural sickness like the summer ague from which everyone (and some in the briefest of times) recovered. As Presbyterians the older Todds were presumably consoled by the understanding that resurrection in heaven was better than life on earth. Still, Presbyterianism restricted heaven to the righteous, and for years the family had listened to Breckinridge's predecessor, the Reverend McChord, preach threatening instructions on who went where and why. "Yonder," McChord had intoned to his congregation the year Mary Todd was born, "stands the throne glittering like the stars, white as the snow under heaven. Yonder around it plays devouring fire. Arise ye dead and come to judgment." Perhaps the Todds benefited from the traditional instruction of Christian mourning. According to one widower after his wife's death, "Nothing less than affliction can sufficiently teach us the futility of every dependence but that which is upon God."[57]

But in the slave community—in the huts along Lexington's back alleys and the kitchens and carriage houses where blacks congregated apart from their masters—there were enough afflictions. Here the consolation that Mary Todd heard from Chaney, Nelson, Mammy Sally, and Patty differed from Christianity's starchy resurrection of the elect. Lexington's slaves never believed death so permanent or life on earth so different from hell. For them a comforting interchange took place between the physical and the spiritual world. In Lexington, as elsewhere in the United States, blacks had kept alive their African spiritualism, mixing it with the required Christianity of the white man. In black folk religion the dead returned, sometimes to see their babies, sometimes (this especially the case with wandering souls) wearing their burial clothes, and sometimes under the direction of a conjurer. A mourner had only to walk backward or rub dead moles' feet at daybreak to help a dead mother return, at least for a visit.[58]

No doubt dependence on God, Christian resignation, and even the spirit world were small comfort for six-and-a-half-year-old Mary Todd, who, given her placement within her family, was neglected after this sudden, painful separation.. Her father probably spent more time sympathizing with his older children, Elizabeth and Frances (who both favored their mother in looks, as Mary and Ann did their father), and arranging for a wet nurse for baby George. Within weeks even the presence of her remaining parent was not available for middle child Mary. Todd was now spending time in Frankfort, and while his grief was not in question, his availability to his children was. Too young to understand either the irreversibility of her mother's death or to accept the divine purposes of God, Mary may have clung to the notion that her mother would return. Children of her age frequently do so. In any case, she was left with a surplus of anxiety and sorrow about Eliza Todd's disappearance.[59]

II

A Second Family

*E*LIZA *TODD* had been dead less than six months when sometime around Christmas 1825, Robert Todd accomplished the necessary. He proposed to and was accepted by Elizabeth Humphreys. Soon after their understanding, Elizabeth left on a long visit to New Orleans, and throughout the following year Robert pressed his claim: "As your feelings in this matter are involved I am determined to be regulated by your decision, but at the same time trust that the period will not be more remote than the one named, nor our marriage postponed one moment longer than you may deem absolutely necessary. I hope it is not necessary to tell you that my situation is irksome." Off to New Orleans went letters and presents, including a miniature of his recent portrait by Lexington's acclaimed artist Matthew Jouett. "This remembrance," wrote Todd, "is a small testimonial of my sincere regard for you," intended, though he did not say so, as a constant reminder of their engagement.[1]

Although Elizabeth Humphreys had grown up in Frankfort, she knew all about the Lexington Todds and

Parkers. Her best friend had married a Todd and, now a widow, was engaged to Robert's friend John Crittenden. One of Elizabeth's brothers lived near Lexington, and two of her uncles taught at Transylvania. Two maternal uncles, James and John Brown, represented Kentucky and Louisiana in the United States Senate. Every ambitious office seeker sought out the Browns, and Robert Smith Todd had done so when he needed support in his campaign for the clerkship of the Kentucky legislature. After his appointment, during the ten weeks of the session, he stayed in a house near the Browns, just across the Kentucky River from the substantial brick mansion of the Humphreys.[2]

Familiar with Robert Todd's background, Elizabeth Humphreys also knew his domestic circumstances. And for any unmarried woman, no matter how smitten, Todd's suit presented difficulties. On her marriage she would become the stepmother of six young children in a house fifty yards away from their maternal grandmother—the formidable matriarch Widow Parker. To make matters worse, Todd had begun courting her within weeks of his wife's burial, and their romance had become the talk of two towns. In fact, Robert had to warn Elizabeth about "persons of ill-will," as he admitted with mysterious candor that he had "done and said many things I wish now had never been done." But so had everyone, he concluded. In any case, for the rest of the year the couple met surreptitiously and, when apart, sent letters only through trusted friends.

Todd was inclined to overlook the gossip "as seized hold of for purposes of detraction and to gratify personal feelings of ill-will." Later he traced the reports to Frankfort and a daughter of Dr. Warfield, one of the physicians who had attended the first Mrs. Robert Smith Todd on her deathbed. Although Todd did not tell his intended bride, Dr. Warfield's daughter was a close friend of his eldest daughters—Elizabeth and Frances—and it was through the children that the "premature disclosure" of his courtship had come to his former mother-in-law, Widow Parker, and to Ann Maria Todd, the unmarried sister now in charge of his Lexington household. In turn, Ann had passed the news of his romance to other relatives, but Todd assured Elizabeth Humphreys that his five sisters were not gossips. Rather, they had "solicitude for my welfare and . . . perhaps some curiosity on the subject." Certainly, he insisted, they were not "prejudiced" against her. Indeed, she would soon come to love these "amiable, kind, and tender" relatives of his. With Elizabeth still uncertain about her reception in Lexington, he added the assurance that his friends were "prepared to be yours without any exception."

Even with such guarantees she delayed, a common practice in this period among young women who recognized losses as well as gains in matrimony. But by early Kentucky standards, Elizabeth Humphreys was uncommonly old for a first marriage and might have been expected to hurry down the aisle. She was at least twenty-five in 1826—well on her way to spinsterhood—and although her success at hiding her age makes it impossible to be certain, she may have been twenty-eight. No doubt in keeping with Elizabeth's intentions, her five daughters omitted her birthdate from her obituary and tombstone, although with their subject beyond earthly embarrassment it was common practice to put it in both places. In fact, it was Elizabeth Humphreys who taught her young stepdaughter Mary Todd that a lady's age was a movable date.[3]

Elizabeth's mother—the redoubtable Mary Brown Humphreys—may have had something to do with her daughter's hesitation. Throughout her life Mary Humphreys ruled Frankfort society. Even at seventy-three, attired in formal satin dress and a lace cap of the sort featured by aristocrats of the Federal period, she led the procession at the town's annual ball. On her death in 1836 she gained the supreme accolade for a Kentucky female. She was, according to her obituary, "constitutionally cheerful and of a fortitude which no affliction nor difficulty could subdue." Mary Humphreys also earned a reputation for upholding etiquette. The daughter of such a proper lady would adhere to social conventions, and Robert Todd found it necessary to encourage his future wife "not to stick to etiquette or ceremony" in her "communications" with him. Today the stern features and unsmiling gaze of Elizabeth's mother suggest a woman unlikely to compromise on such matters as the proper length of time before a daughter's marriage to a widower.[4]

"Would not some day of the month of June suit you and both of us?" implored Todd again in February 1826. From his perspective there was no reason to delay. His own father, Levi Todd, had been a widower less than two years before marrying a woman fourteen years younger than he. But in August Robert Todd was still single. Perhaps his case lacked romance, for though not yet thirty-five, he pleaded with the weary sentiments of middle age, rather than the passionate ardor of youth: "I need to complete my domestic circle where worn down by cares and complexities of the world, I can retire into the sanctuary of the circle and enjoy that repose and happiness which the

world with all its boasted pleasure and engagements can never give."
Before such practical appeals Elizabeth Humphreys (who had become
the more intimate "Betsey" sometime during the summer) relented.

They were married on November 1, 1826, with John Crittenden
and Betsey's friend Maria Todd as attendants. The day of honeymoons
as an established part of wedding customs awaited better transportation, but the bridegroom promised the bride "my time for a few days
either to the purpose of visiting your friends or otherwise as your
inclinations will lead you." These would be among only a few days in
their twenty-three years together that the new Mrs. Robert Smith
Todd would spend alone with her husband.

MARY TODD was nearly eight when Betsey Todd arrived in Lexington
to become her new "ma." (All the stepchildren used the nickname,
and it was a common one in early Kentucky, although grudgingly
applied in this case.) In her short, hectic life Mary had already encountered a series of family disruptions. At less than a year she had been
abruptly weaned and had lost her place as the youngest to a first son.
When she was four, a baby brother died. At five she lost part of her
name, at six her mother died, and now at seven a stranger absorbed
her father's affections. Later, when family abandonments hammered at
her like "blows," Mary Todd Lincoln recalled her childhood as "desolate" and herself as a victim, perhaps amid so many "afflictions" a
deserving one.[5]

In some form many children face similar predicaments. Certainly
five other Todds shared Mary's deprivations, but in age, circumstance,
and temperament she was the most vulnerable. Her older sisters—
Elizabeth and Frances—had already formed the exclusive alliance that
lasted throughout their lives. Ann, the youngest of the four sisters,
was the namesake and favorite of her aunt Ann, who ran the household
after Eliza died. As permanent Todds, Levi and George Rogers held a
particular place in their uncles' and father's affections. Only Widow
Parker stood as Mary's protector, giving to this granddaughter (and to
none of the other Todd sisters) presents and small sums of money for
clothing. Yet this patronage, even from a relative who lived so close,
extended only so far, for Grandmother Parker, now in her mid-fifties,
had other responsibilities, including her own five children, fifteen
grandchildren, and seven slaves. Necessarily, for young Mary her stepmother became the central figure of her next years.[6]

Stepmothering has never been easy family business, and the nine-teenth century, like the twentieth, abounds with testimony of mutual resentments, especially along its female axis. In most nineteenth-century references the stepmother appears, for the first set of children, as what one child called the "destroyer of our peace." Whatever her other virtues, Betsey Todd was singularly unsuccessful at it. With uncompromising intensity, all six of the first Todds despised her. During later visits to Lexington as married women, her stepdaughters preferred to stay with their grandmother Parker, and on brief encounters with "Ma," bad feelings erupted so quickly as to suggest their permanent implantation.[7]

Such antagonism was not entirely Betsey's fault. Widow Parker had prepared the children to reject any substitute for her daughter, especially one installed so close by and in such an indecently short time. Even uninstructed, the children would have resented the differences between Betsey and their dead mother. Eliza Parker Todd had been an uncertain housekeeper, a timid wife, and presumably, a loving mother. She was also, through her grandmother, a Todd in a clan that appreciated the connection.[8]

Betsey was neither timid nor a Todd. She had been too long a single woman to surrender her independence after marriage. She continued to manage property at Buena Vista, using her brother, not her new husband, as an agent, and she ran her new family as well, insisting on standards of elegance unknown in the first Todd household. To this end she installed her mother's well-trained domestic slaves, Judy and Jane. When her patience was tried by her new stepdaughters, as it often was, the new Mrs. Robert Smith Todd quoted her mother's wisdom that it took seven generations to make a lady—time, she made clear, that her disobedient stepdaughters had not had. Betsey Todd's looks matched her personality. In the only surviving portrait of her during these years, the stern gaze, icy blue eyes, and utter lack of frivolity in hair and dress suggest an intimidating presence.[9]

Sometime during the second year after her arrival in Lexington, the first documented conflict between Mary and her stepmother erupted over the classic female terrain of clothing. Mary, who even as a child had an interest in fashion, became, in the words of one household member, "fascinated by the lovely bouffant summer dresses that puffed and swayed so enhancingly on the hoop-skirted ladies." But wearing a hoopskirt was a sign of womanhood, to be adopted, like lipstick for a later generation, only when one became a young lady. No doubt the fastidious Betsey Todd considered her nine-year-old stepdaughter too young for a hoop. Mary thought otherwise. Secretly she improvised two circular skirts from pliant willow reeds, and then, having stretched her white muslin dress tightly over the hoops, appeared, no doubt proudly, with a similarly attired stepniece, before her stepmother. "What frights you are," Betsey Todd is quoted as saying. "Take those awful things off, dress yourself properly and go to Sunday School."[10]

Afterward Mary wept bitter tears, and because her stepmother told the story so often, it became, according to a contemporary source, a standing joke in the family. And no doubt a humiliating one for its young victim, who for her misdoings often suffered Betsey Todd's shaming. In another confrontation, after Mary (who was never defenseless) had put salt in her stepmother's coffee, Betsey pronounced her "a limb of Satan loping down the broad road leading to destruction."[11]

In the new Todd family the epithet "Satan's limb" was so often applied by the wicked stepmother that the children came to use it ironically. Unlike some nineteenth-century parents who relied on guilt to teach good behavior to their children, Betsey Todd depended on disgrace, embarrassment, and the shame conferred by the label "limb of Satan." It was not an unusual style of parenting, though southerners were more likely to control their children in this way than northerners. The impact of shaming on particular individuals is uncertain, but for most it lowers self-esteem. To be shamed and humiliated is to feel a disgrace to the whole self, not just, as with feelings of guilt, to understand that a particular transgression has occurred. If the effect of guilt is anxiety, then that of shame is a diminished psyche, given to quick, defensive anger.[12]

Soon Betsey Todd had her own children to prefer over the ill-behaved first Todds. In 1827 Robert Smith Todd was born, but he died a few days after birth. Then, two years later, Betsey delivered a daughter who survived. Thereafter her cycles of conception, pregnancy, and nursing matched and eventually surpassed her predecessor's. Like Eliza, Betsey Todd was fulfilling what one southerner explained as God's design for humanity: "Women to breed, men to do the work of the world." Obviously neither Betsey nor Robert Todd rationalized the process of reproduction. Only her age (she stopped having children in her mid-forties) limited his second family of nine.[13]

In Betsey Todd's time midwives still superintended most births, and Lexington's best-known *accoucheurs** found it necessary to advertise in the city papers that they had apprenticed with the renowned midwife Harriet Leuba, were of unblemished moral character (which meant they did not attend syphilitic patients), and had read the practical writers on midwifery. During the nineteenth century the exclusively female occupation of midwifery became the male profession of obstetrics. Up the hill at the university, the Transylvania faculty now included a professor of abortion and premature labor, though Dr. Dickson Dedman was rarely called to attend a delivery. [14]

Along with the midwives and doctors, home remedies still flourished, even in medically sophisticated Lexington. Betsey Todd's friend Sophonisba Breckinridge relied on therapies handed down from her mother for discomfort during the latter stages of pregnancy: "Put roots of fennel in a bottle and fill it with wine. Take two or three times a day. Take it, for a month, also have your back sponged with it, and the inside of your thighs. But this should not be done if there is any fear of abortion. Eat a small piece of saltpetre the size of a pea—horse radish as a vegetable is delicious." But in this new age of shared therapeutic authority she cautioned: "[D]on't do anything without the consent of your physician." [15]

No doubt Betsey Todd also used these home remedies, for she was often sick. Her delicate health and frequent, though unspecified, illnesses were surely the result of bearing nine children in fifteen years. Although Betsey lived into her late seventies, her daughter Emilie recalled that on several occasions she did not expect her mother to survive. Some of Betsey's problems may also have been the reaction of an independent, late-married woman to a suddenly circumscribed life with too many children and a busy husband. [16]

Many southern women resented the disappearances of their husbands, and Betsey's antagonism found a natural target in Robert's first set of children, who were not absent enough. Nor did Robert Smith Todd provide the persevering affection that might have overcome such hostility. American fathers of this period took slight interest in the rearing of their children. Most offered neither time nor emotional support. And not even the most dedicated father could give much individual attention to nine daughters, five sons, and a sick wife. In any

---

*The term *accouchement* associated its users with French obstetricians who were considered leaders in the field.

case, Todd carried family scars that may have made him chary of bestowing such affection. He was an unspecial third son; his mother had died when he was a vulnerable eight, and his first wife when he was thirty-three; and the two sons who bore his name had not survived infancy. When he established his second family, he removed himself from emotional encounters by installing Betsey as the "sun" of a domestic universe of which he intended to be "only a part."[17]

INSTEAD, Robert Smith Todd concentrated on his career. By the time he married Betsey in 1826, Todd had abandoned his partnership in the dry goods business. The depression of 1819 convinced him that such ventures were no way to make a living. And he may have agreed with one of his political enemies who called him, in a slur on his growing corpulence and unsuccessful merchandising, "a slender merchant."[18]

Even as a young man Todd mixed politics with business, intending to obtain the kinds of public offices that his father, Levi, had held. First he was elected clerk of the Kentucky House of Delegates; although this post paid less than $1,000 a year, it bestowed the priceless advantage of important contacts. Then, in rapid succession, he moved from councilman, magistrate, and sheriff in Lexington to greater prominence as an assemblyman and senator in the state capital, Frankfort.[19]

But by itself politics could not provide support for a household of fourteen children and ten slaves. Commissioning his cousin Levi Luther Todd to lobby "his pretensions" in Frankfort, Robert Todd next applied for a clerkship in Lexington's Branch Bank of Kentucky. By 1835 he was president of the bank, at the same time that to the disgust of his Democratic opponents, who charged a conflict of interest, he was a state assemblyman assigned to the Banking Committee. During the 1830s Todd also found time and energy to oversee the most profitable of his ventures, part ownership of a manufactory near the Ohio River that made cotton yarn and coarse fabrics.[20]

Throughout he remained a faithful son to his father's principles and refused, at least in his own mind, to become rich. More so than his older brothers, Robert Smith Todd gave lip service to Levi's republican doctrine that the pursuit of wealth must never be the principal purpose of an American citizen's life, and certainly not a Todd's. Such beliefs had fired a self-sacrificing mentality during the Revolution, and although their circumstances were different, some second-generation

Todds still acted on the faith of their fathers. Even as Robert Todd became wealthy, he understated his financial condition, describing himself "as not poor enough to beg my bread, nor so rich as to forget my maker." He declared: "Wealth is sometimes the high road to distinction and honors but rarely to real happiness."[21]

But it was only by comparing himself to those at the top—the Bodleys, the Wickcliffes, the Hunts, and the Brands—that Todd could devalue his own circumstances. By the 1830s he had inherited slaves and land, to which he added income from politics, banking, and manufacturing. A decade later the elegant furnishings of his home would have astonished the Todds of an earlier generation.

Overseeing such enterprises required long absences from Lexington, and Robert Smith Todd's career makes into fiction the notion that the disappearing male is only a twentieth-century phenomenon. Indeed, both Mary Todd's father and husband often spent more than a third of the year away from home. In her father's case, business usually required two trips a year to New Orleans, where after his dry goods store had folded, he bought the cotton yarn and cured bacon that he sold in the Lexington outlet of the Oldham, Todd and Company. Most winters he spent in Frankfort with the legislature.

Time-consuming social obligations accompanied this growing prominence, and Todd made the most of them. In Kentucky it was custom, duty, pleasure, and good business to extend room and board to visitors. On frequent occasions the crowded Todd household included long-staying friends and relatives. Betsey Todd's niece shared a room with Mary for six years, and Betsey's brother John, who spent many summers with the Todds, died there in 1835. In the 1830s Betsey and Robert Todd served as surrogate parents at the wedding of another visitor who had been living with them for two years.

Often the demands of hospitality took priority over family or romance. Prior to his remarriage, Robert postponed a trip to Frankfort in 1826, explaining his delay to Betsey in a way that suggests both appreciated the conventions of sociability: "Having been apprised since my letter that a number of my friends and acquaintances designed visiting my house for the purpose of witnessing the commencement on tomorrow,—I am under necessity of postponing my visit until the last of the week. . . . I am persuaded that you would not under any circumstances wish me to show or seem to show a want of respect to any person determining from me the rights of hospitality and friendship." In time the Todds gained a reputation as genial hosts with the best liquor cellar and mint juleps in Lexington. The supply of liquor was a benefit of Todd's frequent trips to New Orleans, while the bourbon concoctions were the work of Nelson, the Todds' slave coachman.[22]

Public service also required Robert's attention. Appointed a trustee of Transylvania University in 1827, he joined Lexington's most prominent leaders, Henry Clay and Robert Wickcliffe, on the university board. While there was more of the courthouse than the church in his life, Todd was also an active Presbyterian sufficiently interested in religion to exchange the church of his parents for James McChord's charismatic pastorship. Sometime during the 1820s he became an officer of his Masonic lodge, a director of a fire company, and a city magistrate. Such prominence earned him the ultimate accolade of a Kentucky colonelship. Years after his death in 1849 a local who's who listed Robert "as not a man of brilliant talents but one of clear strong mind, sound judgment and an influential and useful citizen." No one assessed his attributes as father and husband. Yet even by nineteenth-century standards, there was restlessness and absenteeism in a life that ranged professionally through law, retailing, manufacturing, banking, and politics and extended geographically from Lexington to New Orleans and Sandersville and Frankfort, Kentucky.[23]

AMONG Todd's many interests was a new school that opened in 1827 under the direction of an Episcopalian clergyman and fellow Mason, John Ward. Residents of Lexington had been surprised to read the list of patrons supporting the new Shelby Female Academy. In the past these same men—Robert Wickcliffe, Dr. John Boswell, W. S. Dallam, and Robert Smith Todd—had sent their daughters to the Lafayette Female Academy, run by Colonel Dunham. But in the fall of 1827, just before the first session of school, the author of an unsigned letter to the *Kentucky Gazette* accused Dunham's of losing its respectability: "Discipline died, then study languished. Emulation slept and virtue fled. The school has become a sentimental farce."[24]

With his daughter Mary ready for school, Robert Todd withdrew his support from the old and occasionally inebriated Colonel Dunham because the latter did not run a sufficiently academic program. Dunham, for example, did not encourage the end-of-term public recitations that were standard in boys' academies. Still disapproved of by Kentucky's conservative old guard, such performances had become acceptable to men like Todd, who refused to believe, as traditionalists

did, that public speaking by girls would replace natural female benev-
olence with male competitiveness. Rather than such mediocrity, Todd
intended for Mary a school that would uphold the "necessity of afford-
ing our daughters as well as our sons the means of acquiring a substantial as well as ornamental education," even if that meant recitations.
Like his friends, he believed that Dunham's "no longer has the same
reputation here as it has abroad. It is not thought to be first rate by
impartial judges." In the ultimate testament to its declining standards, one Lexington father complained that "those who get honors at
Dunham's should be now learning in some country school."[25]

Robert Todd had inherited his concern for education. His family
counted philosophers and astronomers among its forebears, and in the
eighteenth century Robert's great-uncle, the Reverend John Todd,
had become a celebrated scholar. This John Todd not only was a learned
Presbyterian clergyman but ran a classical seminary in Virginia, where
his pupils had included his nephew, Robert's father, Levi. When the
time came, the Reverend Todd willed his Latin and Greek books, as
well as his scientific apparatus, to Transylvania, the institution his
nephews had helped organize. Under the Todds' sponsorship the university became the hub of an educational constellation the reputation
of which extended far beyond Lexington.

By the 1830s it was common practice for upper-class Kentucky
families to insist on classical training in Greek and Latin for their sons.
What made Robert Smith Todd unusual was his support of education
for his daughters—not so much for themselves (no one needed Homer
or Virgil to manage a household) as for the benefit of their children
and, especially through their sons, the nation. Here, extended to
mothers, was the pragmatic republicanism of the founding Todds.
Women would not be called upon to lead armies or execute laws, but
as the headmistress of a distinguished female seminary in Maryland
explained, they would "be called upon to preside over the domestic
circle, to regulate families by wisdom and to guide and enlighten the
youthful."[26]

Girls' schooling was never a farfetched abstraction for Robert Smith
Todd. Ignorant women certainly had no place in the Todd family and
were not considered good marriage partners. His mother, stepmother,
and two wives had attended school in a community where most women
did not. Both Eliza Parker and at least two of Robert's sisters had
attended Mrs. Beck's, where the no-nonsense principal intended her
school "for the cultivation of the mind, not the killing of time." Rob-

ert Smith Todd's first cousin Levi once explained to his aunt that his future bride must display a "practical kind of patriotism. . . . Nor will you be astonished if that I should fall in love with some one of those young ladies whose patriotism and love of country is pure to the blush." Todd ended with a comparison of intelligent, well-schooled Kentucky women to those in ancient Sparta.[27]

Like all of Levi's children, Robert had also been exposed to the English theorist Mary Wollstonecraft's views that education was a natural right for girls. In the thirty-five-volume library at Ellerslie, alongside works by Edmund Burke, William Blackstone, and James Otis, was a copy of Wollstonecraft's *A Vindication of the Rights of Women*.[28] Here Robert discovered another reason for educating his daughters. According to Wollstonecraft, women were humans endowed like men with the reason and virtue that "ignorance veiled and learning unmasked." Superficial schooling in trivial topics fostered frivolity and guaranteed mean-spirited, dull partners unworthy of the intelligent men that the Todds knew themselves to be and expected their sons-in-law to be as well.[29]

Wollstonecraft's argument for the natural right of women to formal education emerged, in the minds of fathers like Todd, as the conviction that wives must not be boring. Todd intended that his daughter's schooling go beyond the training in etiquette, conversation, and the decorative arts that was the pronounced theme of schools like Miss Adele Sigoigne's famous boarding seminary in Philadelphia. There, at an institution attended by several of Mary Todd's friends, even the rudiments of reading, writing, and arithmetic gave way to intense training in something the advertisements described as "social instincts" and "lady-like manners." The aim of Sigoigne's directors was marriageability. With that purpose Todd, the father of nine daughters, would hardly have disagreed. But he and his friends believed intellectual accomplishments attracted better suitors. As the father of a classmate of Mary Todd's advised his daughters, "It is important to cultivate your mind for your mutual prospects and happiness through life, as well as that you must become a housekeeper attending to the substantial realities of life. You will also be more interesting and pleasing. . . . If you should have paid some attention to the most respectable works on the diseases of women and children so much the better."[30]

Unlike sons, daughters once in school could be exhorted to attend to their lessons on domestic grounds. One Kentucky father threatened: "If you do not study hard now, after your marriage your mind will collapse, and you will fail to amuse your husband." Even more terrifying to Mary Todd's generation was the suspicion that if they remained ignorant, they might not attract family-approved husbands at all.[31]

IN the fall of 1827, a year after her father's remarriage, Mary Todd entered the Shelby Female Academy, or, as all Lexington was soon calling it after its director, Ward's. For the next ten years (with one year's absence for a visit to Springfield) she attended school, first at Ward's and then at Madame Mentelle's. She did so at a time when only a few thousand American women had more than four years of formal education. There are no statistics available for Kentucky, but as late as 1860 in well-schooled Massachusetts only a quarter of the state's teenage girls were still in school. Nearly nine, Mary was old by today's standards when she began, but nineteenth-century parents routinely started boys at six or seven, girls a year or two later. In fact, no one paid much attention to age grading, and a typical first reading class, at Ward's and throughout the United States, included pupils aged eight to fourteen.[32]

For the next five years Mary and her stepmother's niece Elizabeth Humphreys (who had come to Lexington because of its schools) trudged the three blocks uphill to the Reverend and Mrs. Ward's two-story brick house at the corner of Second and Market. Classes began early. In the custom of the day the girls went home for the middle-of-the-day dinner favored by Lexingtonians, returning for afternoon recitations. They did so from early September until the first of January (a few days' holiday was given at Christmas) and from the first of March through July. At Ward's Mary Todd learned—and learned well—reading, writing, grammar (although she applied some personal rules to this), arithmetic, history, geography, natural science, French, and religion.[33]

Sometimes Reverend Ward, an ordained but pulpitless Episcopalian minister, used his students as his congregation, and it is a commentary on the Presbyterian Todds' ecumenicism that such High Church indoctrination did not matter to them. More important for a father of fourteen living children was the moderate tuition, $44 per year, with Mary's French lessons $8 extra per session, to be paid, according to the school's catalog, "in advance in gold or silver and with no deduction on account of absence." Unlike some institutions in the North, all students paid the same amount, no matter what their parents' circumstances. While Ward's was not expensive (at the time Transylvania's tuition was $200 per session, Sigoigne's $150 per year plus boarding), it is safe to assume that only the daughters of the well-to-do were in school with Mary Todd.[34]

Ward described his curriculum as a "complete system of female education," and so it was, with the inclusion of those necessary feminine embellishments of French, painting, and plain sewing. For those pupils who did not bring their own books, he provided the sex-specific texts that in the early nineteenth century had multiplied along with girls' schools: *The Young Ladies Class Book, A Mirror for the Female Sex, The Ladies Geography,* and *Miss Swift's Natural Philosophy.* No matter how rigorous the training, Ward recognized that the quickest way to lose his reputation was to trespass the uncertain divide between boys' and girls' education.

Accordingly, while his pupils did not study needlework, ornamental stitching, and conversation, neither were they trained in what nineteenth-century pedagogues termed close reasoning and deep thinking. Even the most patriotic mother or interesting wife did not need logic. Hence Mary Todd studied less mathematics than her brothers and no Greek or Latin. (Parts of Ovid were considered much too titillating for females; besides, women could not go to Transylvania, where the classics were required for admission.) Nor was she given instruction in oratory, though the school did have public recitations, and in every subject her schooling was incidental to her more important future as a wife and mother.[35]

Like all girls' academies, Ward's provided a female authority, in this case Ward's wife and his sister, although unlike the case in some northern seminaries, these women were not the school's directors. Ward's unmarried sister was well known for her European travels, and no doubt she brought her vivid personal experiences to the geography lessons that served as Mary Todd's introduction to the world beyond Kentucky. Ward's wife, Sarah, a native of Lexington, was admired for different reasons. According to a Transylvania professor whose sisters attended the school, she was "imbued with sound science, a knowledge of the more solid and substantial branches of education. What she wants in the more specious and ornamental accomplishments, she more than atones for in her accomplishments with geography, astronomy and History." Not many schools of this period were superintended by such an ideal woman, who, although not adroit in needlework, offered an unusual example of female learning, along with at least one domestic art. For Mrs. Ward was a good cook, and in the late afternoons, while her husband discussed medicine and theology with the Transylvania professors in the parlor, his wife took the girls into the kitchen. There, according to one, they used "her book with many receipts in it for making puddings and custards."[36]

The versatile Mrs. Ward was also in charge of the school's festivals. Such events were usually arranged around a community celebration, such as Andrew Jackson's visit in 1828 or the laying of the first railroad track to Frankfort in 1830. During these affairs Mary Todd and her classmates marched to the square dressed in white, the same outfits they wore at the important May Day Parade, where beauty, not scholarship, received its due. In 1829, according to the *Kentucky Gazette,* "seventy pupils from Ward's all ornamented with chaplets of flowers went in beautiful procession to James Trotter's grove where they erected a May Pole." An outsider from Nicholas County had been selected queen of the May, and "two young ladies held a canopy over her before their elegant procession was escorted back to town with martial music."[37]

On other mornings Ward's classrooms resembled those throughout the United States. Learning proceeded as recitation, with the schoolbook a litany to be memorized and then repeated. Reverend Ward, whom Mary's stepcousin Elizabeth Humphreys considered "a regular martinet," served as a drill sergeant. "The girls," observed Susan Yandell, who boarded at the Wards' during this period, "today commenced historical reading and reciting." Typically such exchanges involved a ritual performance based on question and collective response:

Question by Teacher: What victory soon followed after Trenton?
Answer by Class: The Battle of Princeton.
Question: Who commanded the Americans at Trenton?
Answer: George Washington.[38]

Because this generation of Americans believed that learning depended on memory, which, like a muscle, strengthened from use, pupils learned their lessons "by heart." One of Mary's cousins, Emily Todd of Boone County, somehow mastered 1,373 Bible verses in a year. This accomplishment put her at the head of her class and into the history books, although she probably had little comprehension of what she recited. No effort was made at Ward's or anywhere else to encourage independent thinking. Nor did students create their own compositions. Instead, they traced and retraced homiletics specially designed for females, such as "Love is the essence of our being" and "Evil communications corrupt good manners; gentleness corrects."[39]

No wonder that family members recalled Mary's poring over her books by candlelight. By every account she excelled in school, and years later a classmate remembered her as "far in advance over other girls in education; she had a retentive memory and mind that enabled her to grasp and understand thoroughly that lesson she was required to learn." While her older sisters, Elizabeth and Frances, courted and her younger brother struggled at Transylvania, Mary distinguished herself. One account has her running to school so early and so fast that the Lexington watchman believed that she must be eloping. Only love—in this masculine understanding—could explain such haste.[40]

There is no record of the response of a busy father and unfriendly stepmother to Mary's academic success. Perhaps Betsey and Robert Todd attended the end-of-semester public recitations, where she surpassed her classmates; perhaps they encouraged her to read in the substantial Todd library, which included 124 volumes of the popular *Harper's Family Library* series. No matter how much esteem she gained and no matter how important her father considered the education of his nine daughters, Mary Todd was not engaged in an enterprise of lasting acclaim. Schooling remained incidental to a woman's life for more than a century after Mary Todd's years at Ward's. Sometimes it was even a convenient explanation for female eccentricity. In any case girls' schooling had amateur status. Boys carried to their obituaries the commendation that they had been proficient in their studies. A Kentucky girl who did well in school was as irrelevantly successful as a boy who knew how to make a good burgoo. And this would not be the only time that Mary Todd did the wrong thing well.[41]

IN 1832, when Mary Todd was fourteen, her world changed. That year she entered Mentelle's boarding school, her family moved to a new house in Lexington, and her oldest sister, Elizabeth, married and moved to Illinois. All three events marked her future.

Had she followed the path of most young ladies, including her sisters, Mary Todd would have stopped school after five years at Ward's. In the North, Emma Willard and her sister Almira Phelps were just beginning their campaign for female seminaries, and even in Kentucky there was concern that the empty years of female adolescence encouraged indolence rather than domestic activity. The author of "Hints for Young Ladies" complained in the *Kentucky Gazette* that "young girls waste their time in trivial amusement. . . . After the prime season for improvement, they will come to feel themselves inferior in knowledge, and as mothers feel their own inability to direct and assist the pursuits of their children."[42] Despite such pleas for education in the name of intelligent maternity, only a handful of Lexington's girls attended school for more than four years.

In that generation there were compelling reasons to keep girls at home. Even while parents worried about marrying off torpid, uneducated daughters, they still suspected intellectual women of behaving as shrews who might pursue the women's movement instead of a husband. Somewhere in between were the intelligent amiability and wise pliancy, not the independence associated with scholarship, that Robert Todd intended. To attain it, most of Mary's classmates at Ward's (including her stepcousin Elizabeth) retired from public activities at twelve or thirteen to undertake lives of conspicuous leisure. Before marrying, they idled at home and filled their hours shopping, sewing, talking, paying calls, and listening to their dance partners' orations at Transylvania. Though better educated than most, Mary's mother, stepmother, and sisters all concentrated on what one Lexington graduate of the school of idleness confessed as her central preoccupation during these years: "The only thing I thought of after twelve was dress and getting married."[43]

Instead, Mary Todd stayed in school. She was to return to Ward's in 1838 for a final year, but now almost fourteen, she enrolled in Madame Mentelle's boarding school. There were family reasons to do so. By 1832 nine Todds—from nineteen-year-old Elizabeth to one-year-old Samuel—were trying Betsey Todd's patience. Now she was again "delicate" and David Humphreys Todd, her fourth child in six years, was born late that year. To Betsey it must have seemed as if none of Eliza's children would ever leave the crowded Short Street house to make room for her own babies. Mary's vexed relationship with her stepmother made her a prime candidate for a mutually convenient separation.

But Mary Todd did not go away to school. Rather, she entered an institution no more than a mile and a half from home. Children younger than she walked longer distances, and Mentelle's accepted day students from Lexington, reserving their beds for those who lived farther away. Nelson, the coachman, could have driven her daily, or she might have ridden her pony or one of the family's four horses. Instead, Nelson delivered her on Monday mornings and retrieved her on Friday nights in a peculiar five-day boarding arrangement dictated by discord at home, not distance from school.

By no means was Mary's new school a Kentucky version of Philadelphia's fashionable Sigoigne's, where her friends Margaret Wickcliffe and Isabelle Trotter were now enrolled. Rather, it was academic and very French, although it advertised "an English education" to separate itself from those institutions that gave superficial language instruction to girls who wanted drawing room French. Like so much else in Lexington, Mentelle's was a Todd-sponsored institution, linked to the family through land given by Mary's great-aunt Polly, Mary Todd Russell Wickcliffe, who had donated five and a half acres along the Richmond Road. There Paris-born Augustus Waldemare Mentelle and his wife, Charlotte Victorie Leclere Mentelle, built Rose Hill, a rambling gabled cottage with separate wings for their own six children and their boarding students.[44]

Only in the late nineteenth century did public opinion accept separate housing for boarding girls. In Mary Todd's youth girls stayed in the residence of the proprietor so they could be properly parented, and it was commonly recognized that the majority of patrons would be orphans—or at least motherless girls—as indeed, Mary Todd was. Like other schools of its kind, Mentelle's called itself a "select family school." As such it could expand only to the limits of Rose Hill. This meant no more than a handful of boarding students, and in 1830 the household numbered twenty-two, including slaves and excluding day students. Such an intimate environment had pronounced effects on its pupils, for even without formal instruction living with the Mentelles would have been a special education.[45]

As the aristocratic directors never tired of telling their charges, they had fled from France in 1792 after the September massacres, when hundreds of wealthy Parisians were executed by revolutionary committees. Their early experiences inspired little affection for the United States. They were cheated out of land in Ohio and deserted by the Du Ponts in Delaware. Even after ten years in Lexington, Charlotte Mentelle advised her parents that "Lexington has no amiable virtues—its citizens have terrible manners and will never be friends with Europeans or more exactly with sensitive French people. The more we see of this country the more we love our country." She then admitted that if she and her husband could just command $400 a year in Paris, they would return. "No human link binds us here."[46]

But they never did return. Perhaps the couple grew more tolerant of Kentucky manners as they climbed Lexington's social and economic ladder, running first a dry goods store, next a dance school, then a farm. While her husband served as cashier of the U.S. Bank and there met Robert Todd, Charlotte Mentelle taught at Mrs. Beck's and then opened a French school that became known as Mentelle's for Young Ladies. Sometime in the 1820s she established the boarding school in her house.

Eventually the Mentelle children provided the human link that tied the couple to the United States. After their daughter's marriage to Henry Clay's son Thomas in 1837 (the English traveler Harriet Martineau once described this second son of the great Clay as "a sot"), they had an influential patron to ease their way. Although Madame and Monsieur continued to complain about "the cold and stiff manner in which Americans pretended to amuse themselves," they remained in Lexington.[47]

For its part, Lexington tolerated them as eccentrics. Gustave Koerner, a German-born student who attended Transylvania in the 1830s, remembered Monsieur Waldemare as "an old man of aristocratic air who still wore a small queue, and whose wife was a lively French woman." Madame Charlotte often appeared in student reminiscences as the "singular" Frenchwoman who played the fiddle at dances. The only surviving picture of her—a miniature now displayed in the Mary Todd Lincoln house on Main Street in Lexington—reveals a high-cheeked, angular woman with short-cropped hair, arranged in a more severe style than the soft hairdos favored by nineteenth-century Lexington ladies. Some contemporaries remembered her as a vigorous walker who strode back and forth to town, reading and talking to herself as she enjoyed a physical activity despised by the town's sedentary females.[48]

Charlotte Mentelle was uncommonly active during her Kentucky years; but the boarding school became her special preserve, and during Mary Todd's day she described it in detail to a prospective client: "My price for tuition and boarding is $120 a year paid quarterly in advance. I give no other holydays than one week at Christmas, one day at Easter, and one at Whitsuntide. We teach every branch of good education, French if wanted. The most particular care is taken of morals, temper, and health. Books are for choice by parents. I hope these terms satisfy you sir, as they are certainly more moderate than these hard times seem to justify." On the last point she was correct; several Kentucky boarding schools, including nearby Green Hill, charged $175 a year.[49]

Charlotte Mentelle did not mention any of the outside-the-class-room activities that made her school memorable, but these were an essential part of Mary Todd's life there. Not only did Mentelle's girls act in French plays, dance in the parlor while Madame played the fiddle, and promenade down the Lilac Walk that led to Henry Clay's Ashland, but they also marched in local parades. During Mary Todd's second summer, dressed in white muslin with black sashes and veils, she and her classmates solemnly represented each state in the Union as well as France and America in a final salute to Lexington's special hero, General Lafayette. Just eight years before, the Marquis de Lafayette had visited the county that had taken his name in recognition of his military service during the American Revolution.

All was obedience during such public performances, but when Charlotte Mentelle's charges got out of hand, she used her own life to entertain and to terrify. With sufficient flare to make her stories unforgettable, she told of being the only child of a wealthy Paris merchant who raised her as a son, denying her any girlish frivolities. Her father taught her to ride in infancy and required her to row across the Seine before breakfast. When she displayed a fear of death, Papa Leclere locked her in a closet with the corpse of an acquaintance—or so she said. Madame also included in her repertoire the saga of her flight across France, one step ahead of the bloodthirsty revolutionary mobs that wanted to burn her children at the stake. Told with Gallic hyperbole, her stories disclosed an excitable woman who relished Gothic horror tales. They also mesmerized her pupils, and not surprisingly former students remembered her throughout their lives. Few nineteenth-century Lexington women earned more than a sentence in the newspaper accounts of their deaths, while Charlotte Mentelle's obituary in 1860 ran to four paragraphs.[50]

For Mary Todd, the Mentelle legacy was more than a lifetime fluency in French, a distaste for Lexington, an interest in reading and writing, and an unshakable fascination with royalty. Charlotte Mentelle, a grandmotherly sixty-two when Mary Todd enrolled, also conveyed indelible images of female independence, aristocratic snobbishness, and individual eccentricity. In addition, she passed on a close understanding of the uses of private theater, and it was at Mentelle's that Mary Todd learned to act. Her stepcousin Elizabeth remembered Mary as the "star actress" in a number of school plays, and offstage Mary began her habit of impersonating acquaintances. Mimicry never made her popular, but it became an attention-getting diversion.[51]

SOMETIME during the summer of Mary's first year at Mentelle's her father and stepmother moved to a new house in Lexington. It was especially hot that year, and the din of the seventeen-year locusts made the season nearly unbearable. No matter how crowded the old house on Short Street, Mary probably resented its abandonment. The first set of Todds had deep attachments to a place they associated with their dead mother, and years later Mary's brother Levi returned to live in the Short Street house Eliza's children had loved.

But for Mary's parents, their new brick house on Main Street provided a grander setting. Certainly Robert Smith Todd was well acquainted with what had earlier been Palmentier's Inn before he bought it at a bargain price during a bankruptcy sale. Like most Lexington men, he had attended political meetings in its large public rooms. Both he and Betsey must have appreciated the six large bedrooms as well as the huge two-room nursery that took up all of the upstairs ell. Fashionable Betsey especially liked the elegant downstairs: a well-proportioned dining room, a single parlor on one side of the hall, and an impressive house-length double parlor where the best Todd furniture, including a new piano, was displayed. Perpetually at odds with her stepchildren, Betsey Todd must also have been grateful that she no longer lived fifty yards from Widow Parker. There would never be enough distance between these two women, but now two blocks, two streets, and her own home separated Mary's maternal grandmother and her stepmother.

In time handsome furniture and luxurious decorations filled the new fourteen-room house on Main Street. When Robert Todd died in 1849, the inventory of his possessions ran to four pages, and it is a measure of the change in Lexington that his father's had barely filled two. The latter listed one carpet, a few pieces of silver, six beds, a looking glass, and more than thirty books, while the younger Todd's Main Street house was embellished by astral lamps, two Matthew Jouett paintings valued at $1,500, red damask curtains, and several pieces of imported French mahogany furniture chosen by Robert on his trips to New Orleans. Not only was the entire downstairs and the staircase carpeted (a special Belgian rug covered the floor in the best parlor), but there were nineteen chairs in the downstairs (including a small slipper rocking chair for Mary), more than 200 books in the upstairs sitting room, a bathtub in the back hall, and, in the pantry, the silver forks and soup spoons whose ownership later became the grounds of a court action brought by Mary's brothers Levi and George against their step-mother.[52]

Ironically—for this is the house Americans now associate with her childhood—Mary Todd did not spend much time here. No matter how elegant, anyplace where Betsey presided could be only a house to Mary, who later acknowledged that she found her "true" home at Mentelle's.[53]

LIKE many wealthy Lexingtonians, during the summers the Todds traveled fifty miles south to Crab Orchard Springs, their refuge from the fevers and a health tonic for the delicate Betsey Todd. But school was not yet out the first week of June 1833 when a torrential rain caused the privies to overflow and contaminate the stream that mean-dered through town. The next day a resident of low-lying Water Street became ill with stomach cramps, diarrhea, and vomiting. She was dead by night—of what appeared to be the dreaded Asiatic cholera.[54]

Like a marauding army, the disease had been watched from the time of its first arrival in the United States. Lexington's newspapers had followed its progress across the United States: thousands dead in New York City in the summer of 1832 and, by early 1833, 5,000 dead in New Orleans. Part of Kentucky had experienced its lethal visitations in the summer of 1832, and Mary's aunt Hannah Stuart, her father's oldest sister, had died in that year's epidemic. There was no way to account for its course. Some communities escaped entirely, and this inconsistency led Lexington to consider the disease, in the words of the *Gazette*'s editor, "a providential affliction" that the righteous would avoid, while the sinners suffered, as Mary Breckinridge put it, "God's revenge on the sinful." "Its fatalities," announced the *Kentucky Observer*, "have been experienced almost entirely by the intemperate, squalid, and reckless." By implication good Christians would be spared. The worthy among Lexington's citizens felt themselves further protected by their medical experts, and they were reassured by former Transyl-vania Professor Daniel Drake's conclusion in his recently published *A Practical Treatise on the History, Prevention and Treatment of Epidemic Cholera Designed Both for the Profession and the People* that doctors could now prevent an epidemic.[55]

To no avail. By the end of the first week of June, 10 Lexingtonians were dead, and ten times that number were ill. By the ninth day of the plague there was no newspaper to keep count of the victims. For nearly a month cholera ravaged Lexington, killing more than 500 residents, and not, as the gentry had expected, only the poor and the sinners and the drunkards but the gentlefolk as well: Mrs. Charles Wickcliffe, Dr. Joseph Boswell, Captain Postlewaite, and Mary Todd's school chums from Ward's Emily Houston and Charlotte Wallace. One survivor wrote:

> Never in the course of a life have I spent such a time. I would incomparably prefer a seventh month campaign in a furious war than to undergo another seven days such as these. . . . Our house is a kind of hospital and . . . I have done little else but than nurse the sick and guard the well. And our neighbors nearly all of whom are as badly off as ourselves, and some of them worse, afflict me with their hurried and distracted movements, and not infrequently with their sighs, and groans. The physicians are nearly worn out, nurses cannot be had, the coffin-makers are nearly broken down and the disease still spreading. We are in the hands of God. Let him do what is deemed good. P.S. My mother died at three o'clock.[56]

This generation of Kentuckians, like most Americans, was firmly attached to the miasmatic theory of disease and believed that after originating in putrescent wastes, cholera was carried as a poisonous gas in the atmosphere. To protect themselves, the living heaved the dead through windows quickly reshuttered to keep out airborne germs. In 1833 Lexington had no hospital, only a lunatic asylum that lost one-half its patients to the epidemic. In any case, there was no treatment. The modern understanding of cholera as a bacterial microorganism transmitted through unwashed hands, uncooked fruit and vegetables, and sewage-contaminated drinking water lay half a century away, while the drugs for its cure were a twentieth-century discovery.

In 1833 the few doctors who stayed in the city delivered their all-purpose remedies: calomel, bloodletting, and cupping, which they believed would reduce the painful abdominal spasms of cholera. No doubt some Lexingtonians died of too much mercury chloride, for heroic dosages produced their own casualties, and the victims of metallic poisoning went to their graves with the same symptoms as those who died of cholera. But they did not look the same. Cholera's victims were an unforgettable, unearthly blue, with dark extremities and puckered skin in their feet and hands.[57]

The well-to-do fled the city, but the Todds did not join them. For some reason, perhaps because of a case in their household (although none of Robert Todd's family or slaves died), perhaps because Councilman Todd felt it his duty, or perhaps because it soon became as dangerous to leave as to stay (said one survivor: "[w]hen I thought of flight I knew not where to go for the country was full of cholera too"), the Todds remained. Home from school for a weekend when the epidemic began, Mary, along with the other Todd children, endured three weeks of protective quarantine. They ate neither fruits nor vegetables, drank quantities of beef tea, and, terrified of the outdoors, were nearly out of flour for the beaten biscuits that had become their staple when the epidemic finally ended. They burned tar to destroy the germs in the air, and they put lime everywhere until it was nearly impossible to breathe.

Later Mary Todd described these days in a letter to her stepcousin Elizabeth Humphreys: "When the baby [David Todd] cried, it seemed as if it must be heard all over town. [There was] nothing on the streets, but the drivers and horses of the dead carts with the bodies of those who had just died. Toward the last there were not even coffins. Father had all the trunks and boxes taken out of the attic to serve as coffins." In fact, Old Sol, the town's gravedigger and oddjobber, had already run out of space in the church cemeteries and was now using a hastily dug trench in a new graveyard on the corner of Main and Limestone, a block from the Todds.[58]

ONE Todd escaped the cholera epidemic. In the winter of 1832 Mary's eldest sister, Elizabeth, had married Ninian Edwards. After her husband's graduation from Transylvania's law school the next spring, the couple had moved to Illinois, amid talk that Elizabeth would run the governor's mansion for her widowed father-in-law. (The senior Edwards died of cholera before there was time for this.)

Ninian, Elizabeth's handsome young husband, had impeccable credentials. He had stood first in his class at Transylvania, where in August 1829 he delivered an address in Latin to an audience that no doubt included his future wife and sisters-in-law. Even in that age, when parents no longer controlled their children's choice of mate, their approval, or at least lack of opposition, made a difference. As a Virginia friend of the Todds explained, "I don't believe in interfering with the choice of a husband unless he is utterly objectionable." Certainly Edwards was not. His father had been a well-known Kentucky judge before his appointment as Illinois's territorial governor and his subsequent election as that state's governor and United States senator.[59]

Only the bride's age—Elizabeth was just nineteen—might have troubled her relatives, although Betsy Todd would have encouraged the departure of the eldest of Eliza's children. Certainly some daughters of Lexington's gentry took their vows at younger ages, for by the time they were nineteen they had been contemplating their marriage prospects for seven years. Outsiders, especially those from the North, were shocked at the number of teenage brides in Kentucky, and in the Todd-Parker family most of the women, including Elizabeth's grandmothers and mother, had husbands before they were twenty.[60]

Some of Mary's security faltered when Elizabeth moved to Illinois. For seven years—in fact, since her mother's death—her eldest sister had been more of a mother than the despised Betsey, and so in 1832, Mary was again orphaned. At times these Todd sisters did not even like each other. (Once Mary complained that Elizabeth glorified her children, and in turn, Elizabeth considered Mary impossible). Still, the bonds of sisterly intimacy linked them in a persevering and affectionate relationship of the type that a modern historian has described as the "female world of love and ritual."[61]

Elizabeth had been Mary's guide into the world of Lexington society. Four years older than Frances, her second sister, Elizabeth had entered party life after a few years of schooling. As the eldest girl of nearly forty second- and third-generation Todds living near Lexington, she stood at the center of that extensive cousinry. In a town of 5,000 to be a Todd and Elizabeth's younger sister was to carry, when the time came, a partly filled dance card into the gay world.

Mary Todd had entered this new life with experiences characteristic of her generation. Her earliest years had included informal, mostly out-of-doors contacts with boys: sledding at Walnut Hills, picnics in Fowler's Garden, playing in Elkhorn Creek, picking blackberries along Upper Broadway, and riding ponies out to Ashland. Only Long Bullet—the game played by teams of boys who jerked about a cannonball attached to a rope—and horse racing, were off-limits. And if school was single-sex, Sunday school was not.[62]

As Mary Todd grew up, she was increasingly separated from males. Boys hunted squirrels and caught partridge, went to all boys' academies, such as Locust Grove, and later joined the town's Bachelor Club.

Girls sewed and shopped and went to all girls' schools, spending their days and most evenings with other females. It was not unusual for Betsey Todd to entertain at male dinner parties where the ladies were neither present nor missed. The acid-tongued British visitor Mrs. Trollope marveled at the rarity of mixed dinner parties and the popularity of smoking and drinking rooms for males only. By the time Mary was fourteen her contacts with boys were restricted to formal meetings that took place indoors. There adult supervision was possible, and the Todds' double parlor with its convenient middle doors symbolized this generation's compromise between parental surveillance and young people's privacy.[63]

Of course, constant vigilance by adults was impossible, and the romance of Mary Todd's friends Cassius Clay and Mary Jane Warfield was an example. Unable to meet Mary Jane privately in her own house because her parents and brothers always took up stations in the parlor, Cassius was delighted when "graceful" Mary Jane

> said quietly she was going on a certain day hickory picking with a few girls—In the woods Mary Jane came to me when the others were farthest off, and picking up the nuts, emptied her handkerchief on a pile. I said "Come and help me." She replied, with some tremor in her voice, "I have no seat." Putting my feet closer together as they were stretched out on the ground, I said, "You may sit down here, if you will be mine." She hesitated a moment and then down she came. . . .She just touched me with the skirts of her dress, and said "I am yours." Then she hurried off to mingle with her companions again.[64]

But not for long, for these two married in 1832, with Elizabeth Todd Edwards as one of their attendants.

Away from home, the Todd sisters met young men indoors at tea parties, cotillions, and late-night suppers where the Kentucky stews, buffalo tongues, and hotcakes of Levi Todd's generation had given way to more sophisticated fare—oysters from Maryland, Spanish pickles, and imported herring. At such affairs the Transylvania students, in full dress of dancing pumps, canton crepe trousers, black swallow-tailed coats, stiff shirts, and high-standing collars ("so stiff as to draw the blood from my ears," complained one sufferer) were as uncomfortable as their tight-laced dancing partners.[65]

It was this world to which Elizabeth introduced her sisters before her marriage. Their eldest sister informed Frances, Mary, and Ann of the waltz (as yet untaught in the dancing academies of the town), wedding etiquette, and what to do when one was left without a dance partner. The last concern was especially important, for even in a town the youthful population of which was unbalanced by the annual infusion of 200 or 300 male students, there was sometimes a lack of suitable partners. Gustave Koerner described how female conviviality flourished within that male-dominated society. "Parties followed upon parties, the waltz mania had spread and while quadrilles were the rule, we generally had two or three round dances every time. A great many ladies for want of gentlemen—waltzing with one another."[66]

Elizabeth Todd was living in Springfield when her younger sister became a full-fledged member of this courting world. Certainly Mary had all the necessary requirements for success. Better-looking and more personable than her two older sisters (one family friend found Frances taciturn, cold, and reserved while Mary was pretty and warmhearted), she was all Todd in her plumpness of figure and ruddiness of cheek. She had, according to one friend, "clear blue eyes, long lashes, light brown hair with a glint of bronze and a lovely complexion." In an age when slenderness was beginning to be required for beauty, she may have suffered for her weight, in the same way as did her aunt Polly Todd, who once lamented: "I am too fat and my face is too round. Don't you know that fat people are pronounced to be fools." Yet outsiders did not think Mary overweight. One described "her figure as beautiful and no master ever modelled a more perfect arm and hand." Certainly she was proficient in other areas of sociability: She danced well and had plenty to say.[67]

Perhaps she had too much to say or spoke it too sharply and too intelligently for the Lexington blue bloods. Certainly she used her gift for mimicry too often. At least one cousin remembered her "cutting remarks," and friends wondered if they were the targets of her impersonations. In any case, even in her early years Mary Todd was not the oft-recommended suppliant female, at times arguing furiously with Levi and George's tutor over the virtues of Kentucky over Massachusetts. And she behaved this way at a time when every Kentucky girl knew the necessity of suppressing her interests so as not to damage her standing with potential beaux. "Literary topics," said one southern woman, "make them [the boys] run from you as if you had the plague."[68]

In any event, despite Elizabeth's counsel, her status as a Todd, and her own conviviality, Mary Todd was not popular. Or at least—and the difference is crucial—she never considered herself a belle. Years later, in a letter written to her intimate friend Margaret Wickcliffe Preston, she remembered these years as a time of failure—a time "when friends were few."[69]

III

Mary Todd's Lexington

*E*VEN after a half century Lexington, the place that Mary
Todd's grandfathers had founded and in which she grew
up, remained a town set in the wilderness. Just beyond
its periphery, where the most adventurous pioneers had
built their homes, an impenetrable forest enclosed the
community. For one resident Lexington was always
"woods, woods, and more woods and an unpleasant
climate." Where the forest receded, as it did to the
north along the Maysville Pike, Lexington's unpaved
connection to the outside world, a thick underbrush of
canebrake, peavine, and pawpaw obscured the horizon.
On the plateau to the east, large sycamores, maples,
and wild cherries framed the grassy meadows for which
Fayette County would soon become famous. "A dark
and bloody land" the Cherokees had named the region,
and so it stayed. Anything, Lexington's children supposed, could hide in these woods—from wild animals
like buffalo, wolves, and the giant mammoths the bones
of which had been discovered in nearby caverns to dangerous humans like runaway slaves, savage Indians, and
the eerie phantoms of Kentucky folklore. With a dis-

quieting mixture of the grotesque and the ornate, the landscape alternated seasonal lushness with the bleak irregularities of limestone cliffs,
bare hills, and everywhere the dark, melodramatic forests.[1]

With the wilderness at their backs, Lexington's residents had turned
inward, attempting to make their community what Mary Todd's
grandfathers, Levi Todd and Robert Parker, and her great-uncles Robert and John Todd had intended, the most important inland city in
the United States. But after the War of 1812 everyone knew that no
matter how productive the hemp and bagging factories were, the town's
future depended on getting beyond the forests. And by the 1830s
doubt about Lexington's prospects had deepened. In the coffeehouses
along Limestone and Mill streets, where men of affairs met to trade
hemp, land, and slaves, the talk had turned pessimistic. Some of the
citizenry believed that Lexington's golden age had ended in 1815,
when the steamboat *Enterprise* made the journey upstream from New
Orleans to Louisville in twenty-four days. With the Ohio River link-
ing its competitor to New Orleans and with ships capable of paddling
up as well as downstream, Lexington seemed to have lost its commercial logic.

Others calculated the city's decline from the depression of 1819,
when all but one of the hemp factories closed because their products
could no longer compete with cheaper British imports. Five years after
the depression, slow growth and the resulting lack of construction
made hard times seem a permanent condition. Louisville, the town
that Levi Todd once disparaged as having "no residents" and that in
fact had only 359 in 1800, surpassed Lexington in population by 1830,
while Cincinnati, one-quarter Lexington's size in 1800, was four times
bigger that same year. A visitor who had known the place in its best
days saw a town in decay: "Lexington has degenerated beyond measure. The homes and tenants seem to me to have suffered an equal or
similar dilapidation. Where once was the dwelling of gaiety and
friendship with every good and noble sentiment is now a rusty and
moss-grown mansion of ill-nature and repulsive indifference."[2]

Not everyone was ready to give up. Civic boosters like Robert Smith
Todd organized successful subscription campaigns for a turnpike to
Louisville and, in 1830, for a railroad connection through Frankfort
to an undesignated town on the Ohio River. Even so, transportation
remained erratic. In 1829 Henry Clay spent four days traveling "though
mud and mire" the sixty-four miles from Maysville to Lexington, and
four years later, in the best of conditions, it took the English aboli-

tionist Edward Abdy thirteen hours to cover the same distance. Just outside Lexington, road builders had begun laying trees across swamps—what that generation called Dutch turnpikes—to ease the way into a city whose future depended on transportation.[3]

In time, though lagging years after the national economy had mended, some hemp factories reopened or were turned to different uses. Robert Smith Todd and his partner, Edward Oldham, bought one such establishment for a bargain price, using it as a retail outlet for their cotton yarn. Land prices gradually picked up. Commerce revived, the construction of private homes increased, and the population edged upwards from 5,279 in 1820 to 6,026 in 1830 and 6,997 in 1840, with slaves a constant third of the city's residents. Portions of the road to Frankfort were macadamized, and by the 1840s trains had ended the community's seasonal isolation. But by that time Lexington's chance for greatness had vanished.

Many of Lexington's earlier hopes had centered on Transylvania University and the city's unique academic atmosphere. "The university," wrote one resident, "has given tone to the manners of the place and everyone must affect to be more pleased with literature than anything." But, she continued, the city that called itself the "Athens of the West" had yet to produce a Socrates.[4]

Even without a Socrates, the city profited from its scholarly reputation, especially among parents in the South and West who wanted a substantial education for their daughters and sons. In 1821, when there were 150 students at Princeton and 222 at Dartmouth, Transylvania enrolled more than 300. Especially among wealthy southerners, it became common practice to send daughters to the city's female schools chaperoned by sons bound for Transylvania or one of the city's three preparatory academies. "I cannot educate my children in the country," Mary's uncle Samuel Todd, who lived in tiny Gallatin, Kentucky, discovered. Uncle Sam eventually moved back to town so that his children could enjoy the Todd tradition of a first-rate education.[5]

Some of Lexington's schools were merely transitory arrangements run by itinerant, barely literate Ichabod Cranes. But others like Locust Grove for the boys and Ward's for the girls were known for their superior teachers. With annual salaries under $500, the Transylvania faculty furnished an eager pool of instructors. Even the university's president, James Blythe, supplemented his meager income by offering a special instruction in mathematics and natural science to the young ladies of Lexington. At a time when northern schools like Emma Willard's Troy Seminary and Catharine Beecher's Hartford Seminary taught chemistry from manuals only vaguely understood by their instructors, Blythe offered an intensive science course based on his own experience.

The result was a well-educated community where one northern-born professor found, to his surprise, "some females better educated than those in Boston. The system of education pursued here is much better than in New England." In turn, students and their families supported a commercial network of boardinghouses, taverns, inns, and stores. In early Lexington, as nowhere else in the United States, education paid, and city officials, who underwrote the insurance policy for Transylvania's fire-prone buildings, appreciated this.

But when Transylvania faltered, so did the city, and by the late 1820s the university was in trouble. After a controversy among the faculty, city, and state government, the cream of the medical school abandoned Lexington for despised Louisville, where the department reorganized in 1837. More serious were the questions concerning the reputation of Transylvania's liberal president, New Englander Horace Holley. Old School Presbyterians accused Holley of being "a warm advocate of theater, ballroom and card table," and they considered heretical his Unitarian commitment to Christ's humanity. Holley had always held these religious views, and something of a ladies' man, he had never disguised his delight in dancing. In the 1820s Kentuckians began to object. Eventually Holley resigned amid gossip of "several little matters of gallantry unbecoming his vocation." The gentry who had once raised $14,000 to purchase books for Transylvania now sent their sons to the more orthodox Center College in nearby Mercer County. Transylvania's enrollments dropped, and in 1829, when fire destroyed the university's main building, some saw the hand of a vengeful God. Those of more secular inclination were relieved that the city had insured the buildings.[6]

Gradually both university and town lost an essential ingredient of civic success: confidence in the future. No group of Lexingtonians was more affected by this loss of faith than the sons of the founding Todds, who remembered their fathers' invocations to lead Lexington to greatness. Like those of many residents, Robert Smith Todd's fortunes gyrated with those of the community, although his financial position consistently improved—from assessed property of a few thousand dollars in 1818 to assets of more than $14,000 by the 1840s. But his best chance for what this generation deemed a comfortable estate rested with the cotton manufactory. In turn, the prospects for the partnership of Old-ham-Todd depended on improved transportation. And failing that, the company remained a small operation in a northern Kentucky county with eight employees, a good credit rating from the Mercantile Agency, and a retail outlet on Lexington's Main Street.

Like other male Todds of his generation, Robert lived with the unpleasant prospect of slippage. The size of his family limited his advantage, but so did the opportunities of his time and place. While he lived in greater luxury than his father and uncles, he never attained their preeminence. Years later his daughter Elodie remembered the troubles he brought home. "I know," she wrote her husband, "my father's life was made by his friends for him and he accepted it and after all the sacrifices he made for them to acquire fame, he died. . . . Life lost its charms [for him]. . . ."[7]

It was of men like Robert Smith Todd that the Whig party would be made. Todd supported with enthusiasm his friend Henry Clay's plan for higher tariffs, which would protect his cotton yarn from cheaper imports, and for internal improvements, which would get his products to the markets in Indiana, Illinois, and Ohio. Clay had businessmen like Todd in mind when he labeled his program an "American sys-tem." The Kentucky senator believed the entire nation would benefit from a national policy of protectionism linked to government-spon-sored roads and canals, though, of course, entrepreneurs like Todd would reap the greatest returns. Certainly it was in Todd's interest to subscribe to local turnpike companies, to pledge financial support to the Lexington and Ohio Railroad company, and to serve in the City Council and state legislature.

Yet even as he struggled to achieve security and prestige, other Todds were failing to do so. These were the years in which three of Robert's brothers—Sam, Roger, and David—abandoned Lexington for better prospects in Missouri. Eventually Robert became the only one of Levi's five sons to remain in the city his father had expected would advance with, and because of, the Todds. In turn, when the time came for Robert's five sons to make a living, only one stayed in the city. Like many other Lexingtonians, third-generation Todds found better opportunities elsewhere.[8]

NO matter what its economic future, the Lexington of Mary Todd's youth offered titillating amusements to an adolescent girl. In her day, there were three dancing schools, along with the confectionery of Monsieur Giron, where everyone danced at the assemblies held upstairs during the season. Downstairs a Swiss-trained pastry cook turned out meringues, macaroons, and, on the occasion of General Lafayette's visit in 1825, a splendid castellated cake decorated with the French and American flags. There were community celebrations such as balloon ascensions and Fourth of July picnics, in one of which sixty drummers led the way to Trotter's Grove outside the city where the mayor read the Declaration of Independence to an audience that congratulated itself on its patriotism. Though horse racing was prohibited, thoroughbreds still raced down Main Street and along Upper Broadway, to the delight of audiences that had more than sympathy invested in the winner. There were militia drills in the Courthouse Square, where Mary's young brothers and cousins performed martial exercises to the roll of a drum. There was a subscription library complete with a special section for juveniles, and even a young ladies' library to cater to feminine literary tastes in this gender-divided society. And every traveling show that ventured beyond the Alleghenies— from menageries to ventriloquists, from children's theater companies to minstrel shows—played in Lexington. For more ambitious entertainment, there was a theater where traveling companies played Shakespeare and a music hall where the American premiere of a Beethoven string quartet was performed.

Despite its tribulations in the 1820s, Transylvania consistently provided a full calendar of public enlightenment through courses, debates, language instruction, and even a lecture series on the delicate but popular topic of the "Ladies' Physiology." When nervous students underwent their final recitations, they did so publicly before a tight-laced, high-hatted crowd of elegantly dressed females, although the lectures by senior medical students on syphilis and uterine hemorrhage were off-limits. According to one undergraduate, by the 1830s Transylvania had become the "best place to show off new bonnets and dresses." One Lexington girl wrote her aunt: "Everyone has gone to the college, the fashionable place of resort, to hear the young gentlemen declaim. This is the case every Saturday morning."[9] On one of these Transylvania Saturdays, an undergraduate chose as his departing salute to Lexington Philip Freneau's epic poem "On the Emigration to America and Peopling the Western Country." It was not just the student's passionate delivery that brought an applauding audience to

its feet. Freneau's poem could have been the civic insignia of Mary
Todd's Lexington:

> To western woods and lovely plains,
> Palemon from the crowd departs,
> Where Nature's wildest genius reigns,
> To tame the soil, and plant the arts—
> What wonders there shall freedom show,
> What mighty states successive grow![10]

By the 1830s Lexington had become a consumer's paradise; even in
the worst of times thirty shops competed for Fayette County's carriage
trade. Newspaper advertisements assured the fashion-conscious that
neither French royalty nor Philadelphia notables were better dressed
than they. Stitched by the city's eight seamstresses, three mantua makers,
four milliners, as well as uncounted amateurs, the final products were
elaborate. Sophonisba Breckinridge proudly described a new costume
as consisting "of a white turban with feather, a white satin petticoat
and a black satin dress over it with a full suite of pearls."[11]

During the summers, when the annual fevers invaded Lexington,
the special season ended and only the poor and middling classes remained
in town. Like other members of the gentry, the Todds traveled to Blue
Licks Springs, where the new hotel called itself the "Saratoga of the
South." Here the Todd children took the baths, drank the sulfuric
mineral water guaranteed to cure most ailments, and picnicked on the
battlefield where Great-uncle John had been killed by the Indians.
During Mary Todd's youth a family friend described such holidays.
"We are getting the full benefit of Blue Licks. We rise a little after 4
and walk two miles drinking the water going and coming." While
Robert Todd's family vacationed, he inspected his bagging establishment in nearby Sandersville. After his remarriage there were trips to
Crab Orchard, a smaller resort favored by the Humphreys family, as
well as long residences at Buena Vista, Betsey Todd's country estate
on the Leestown Pike, near Frankfort.[12]

For entertainment in every season there was politics. By the early
1820s the county seat of Lexington served as an arena for the incessant
parades, speeches, pole raisings, and election eve celebrations that
accompanied a new era of American party competition. Three Presidents visited Lexington during Mary Todd's youth, and Henry Clay's

persistent presidential aspirations engrossed his neighbors, who, Whig and Democrat, believed a Lexingtonian in the White House would return their city to greatness. Even when Clay lost the presidency in 1824, 1832, and 1844, his hometown honored its famous son with celebrations in which liquor helped dampen disappointment and partisan division. After the Whig Convention in 1848 had chosen Zachary Taylor as its presidential candidate, it was Robert Smith Todd who, at a dinner he had organized, consoled his failed hero with a gracious toast made in the name of all Lexington and Fayette County.[13]

Young Mary Todd was unduly interested in such affairs. As a child she had joined her father's party, and it had been as a confirmed Whig that nine-year-old Mary disavowed Andrew Jackson when he visited Lexington before his election in 1828, refusing to attend a public demonstration in his honor and arguing about his suitability for President with a pro-Jackson neighbor. Four years later Mary had interrupted Henry Clay's dinner to assure him, during his presidential campaign against Jackson, of her support and of her expectation that someday she, too, would live in Washington. Finding public affairs an endeavor worthy of her attention, Mary apprised her friend Margaret Wickcliffe of her views in a letter that Margaret's father considered extraordinary in its political acumen, worthy of a man's, or at least a boy's, intelligence. Even Betsey Todd recognized politics as a safe topic for discussion with her stepdaughter.[14]

Not many American girls of her generation were similarly inclined. Especially in the South, the code of domesticity barred women from public activities or politics. Proper females, it was thought, should be politically aware—good listeners, apt questioners, and, if need be, generous consolers—but never should they mingle in discussion or offer independent judgments about what most men believed they could not understand. Mary's stepmother and older sisters were not exceptions to this rule.

But Mary was. Buried in anonymity by a feminine multitude of eight sisters and a stepmother, Mary used politics to catch a busy father's attention. More than any Todd, she hotly protested Democratic charges that Robert Smith Todd, now a candidate for the state legislature, was "a caterer of slander"—a corrupt candidate who had used his position as a banker to give loans to potential supporters and who, unforgivably to his opponents, had supported the U.S. Bank. The question of whether the national bank should be rechartered had emerged as a divisive issue between Democrats and Whigs. Like most of his party, Todd believed that such a national institution would stabilize the currency and drive out the inflationary paper money printed by local banks. His daughter evidently agreed. Certainly Mary Todd was not the first American girl to enjoy the ferocity of nineteenth-century campaigns, but in her day and her town this interest, along with her advanced schooling, set her apart from the more conventional daughters of Lexington's upper-class families.[15]

Rather than politics, these proper ladies concentrated, as had Mary's mother a generation before, on the genteel sociability that in Lexington came with a French flavor. By the 1820s the city's females had gained national recognition for their high fashion, and they were rumored, among those who followed such matters, to use more eye shadow and rouge than any group outside Paris. Perhaps this was how Lexington supported three perfumeries. The upper crust also created an Americanized version of that noble Gallic institution the ladies' salon. While Lexington produced no Madame de Stäel, it did have Mrs. Lyle, whose death created a crisis among her would-be successors in society. Soon a vigorous competition ensued among four matrons "to come to me on Thursdays."[16]

Mary Holley, the New England-born wife of Transylvania's president, Horace Holley, was repelled by such pretensions: "The ladies of Lexington pay their respects properly and promptly according to the town's social custom of forenoon. . . . [I] was astonished to see callers arrive in satin and silk as if they were going to an evening function. No Boston lady would ever be so conspicuous. 'How is Dr. Holley,' they would ask and would adjust their flounces, scarcely touching their backs to the parlor chair lest they form a wrinkle or disturb a hair."[17]

A Tennessee woman was just as critical. Susan Yandell did not deny that she had met "a few females of polished manners and highly cultivated minds." But, she complained, "there are other places in the world where women may be found who are not always kneeling at the shrine of fashion and its administration"[18] or, she might have added, engaging in the incongruous ritual of muddying expensive red morocco slippers and satin skirts in unpaved streets.

Such a life diverted Lexington's upper-class females from those volunteer activities that increasingly absorbed the time of northern women of the period. Still, the demands of high society even when combined with their maternal burdens of bearing, nursing, and rearing the young, could not hide the fact that the ladies of the town (unlike many planter's wives and daughters) had little to do, save, according to one, "marry young, have many children, read a few romances, and devote what free time they have to dress in which they display a great deal of taste."[19]

There were few domestic tasks for many of Lexington's white females because one-half of the city's families depended on slave labor. By 1830 Robert Todd Smith kept one slave for every white family member of his household. Ten slaves cleaned the house and stables; washed, laundered, and sewed the clothes; cooked the meals; tended the children and horses; and bought the food for ten Todds. Yet no Todd joined Lexington's sole womanly endeavor—the Female Benevolent Society, which administered to local orphans after the cholera epidemic. Such indifference hardly made the Todds unusual. In all Lexington fewer than two dozen women were actively engaged in raising money and gathering clothes for the city's foundlings.[20]

To be sure, one day of the week was always busy for the ladies of the Todd household. Like most Lexington women they spent much of Sunday and one weeknight in the McChord's Presbyterian Church. During Mary Todd's youth the church had not yet spawned the ladies' fund-raisers, lunches, and charitable activities that after the Civil War became a prominent focus for its congregation. Some women did teach Sunday school, but the Todds were not among them, although the children, Mary included, attended the early Sunday morning instruction for the young. An Englishwoman who taught the Bible to the community's free blacks expressed shock at the sluggishness of Lexington's women but thought she knew the explanation. "The Lexington men," Marian Penney wrote her sister in 1836, "treat their wives and females generally as if they were large babies and as if they had no right to possess mind or understanding. They will please them by giving them sweet candy and other sweets, supplying them also with dress."[21]

Like the university, local churches became showplaces for displays of fine dress and *grande toilette*. Nowhere was this more the case than in the McChord Church, where the pulpit, with its back to the adjacent front door, faced pews that were arranged in ascending rows facing the entrance. Latecomers who entered under the pulpit received careful scrutiny from the congregation (for there was no slipping in the back), and it was here that Mary Todd had hoped to display her controversial hoop skirt.[22]

For most Todds, whether male or female, young or old, religion was never a life-directing commitment, any more than Lexington itself was a rigorously observant Protestant community. No one fussed about hymn singing or dancing, and it took the near denial of Christ's divinity by the president of Transylvania to create a theological stir in worldly Lexington. Without ado Robert Smith Todd defected from his brother-in-law's congregation, and when his new rector, James McChord, died, busy Robert lost interest in parish affairs and delegated the religious education of his children to his wives. Faithfully Betsey superintended their attendance, though as an Episcopalian minister's granddaughter she had reservations about the Presbyterian service. Three years before her marriage she and Mary Breckinridge had "as merry a time as we ever had laughing at the preacher. The man seemed to be run mad. His discourse had not one subject but twenty. His text was Canaanite is in the land. He worked himself into a passion and denounced the Baptists, then denounced the members of the church. Said we were lukewarm."[23]

The lack of any purposeful female activity distressed Cassius Clay, Fayette County's most radical critic and a onetime boarder at the Todd house. He urged the Lexington ladies "to free your slaves, make up your own beds, wash your own clothes, throw away your corsets, and nature will form your bustles." But this was bold advice from an abolitionist considered a crackpot by most. Few followed it. Lexington women preferred the gentler directives of the traditional Fourth of July salute that usually came near the end of that celebration, well after the reading of the Declaration of Independence and patriotic address, but before the toast to the artisans. "To the Ladies" it went:

> All are lovely,
> All blossoms of heart and mind,
> All true to their natures, as nature designated.
> To cheer and to solace,
> To strengthen and caress,
> And with love that can die not and body to bless.

Whatever young Mary Todd learned from this environment, it did not include an appreciation of good works.[24]

NEVER far removed from Lexington's genteel churches and parlors lay the city's dark underworld of slavery, dueling, and Indian fighting.

Kentucky's early white settlers had so faithfully observed their state's entitlement as a bloody ground that what was elsewhere considered disorder became acceptable, even honorable, behavior. Visitors to Lexington often characterized the city's males as hot-tempered and angry. Reared with a capacious sense of pride, Lexington's gentlemen held revenge the most satisfying part of its protection and demanded atonement for even imagined slights. Thus Joseph Daviess, scion of a prominent Kentucky family, went to the dueling grounds over remarks he only suspected that his enemy had made during a drinking party at James Taylor's tavern. Later, after he had killed his opponent during the duel, he wrote Taylor to find out what in fact had been said. "Stern looks," warned a Baptist minister, "bring challenges and death" in Lexington.

In time, this penchant for fighting influenced even dress styles among young men who, with bristling sensitivity, raised unfriendly looks at dancing parties to fatal affairs of honor. In Mary Todd's day Lexington's blue bloods required both special pantaloons in which to carry their pistols and ruffled dress shirts in which to conceal the knives that most also carried. With their frequent enactments of legalized brutality, the young dandies of the Bluegrass were as self-indulgent as its daughters.[25]

In this bloody atmosphere, most Kentucky males rarely left their homes without arms. The Lexington of Mary Todd's youth was an armory. In the same shops where she shopped for ribbons and sashes, pistols, dirks, and bowie knives were offered for sale, often in the same display cases as pearls and rubies. In Cheapside's stores, merchants casually hawked an immense variety of firearms, many imported from Europe. The extent of Lexington's weaponry amazed one visitor who considered a local weapon worthy of description: "The dirk has a pointed blade four or five inches long with a small handle. It is worn within the vest, by which it is completely concealed. The advocates for private arms openly declare they are for defense, but the dissipated, the passionate, and the free-booter urge a similar pretext for carrying the stiletto."[26]

For Kentuckians who could not afford expensive weapons, arms, legs, and heads sufficed. Most residents had at some point observed the savage physical beatings that erupted not only outside taverns but anywhere a hot-tempered male might launch an attack. By the 1820s gouging had become the poor man's sword, and socketless casualties who had lost their eyeballs to an antagonist's thumb were by no means an unusual sight in Lexington. Gentlemen did not bite, pull hair, scratch, or gouge, but in Mary Todd's youth both rich and poor used violence as a means of enhancing status and reputation.[27]

Rich and poor shared as well a taste for alcohol, for Mary Todd's Lexington was a hard-drinking society. When Governor Joseph Desha's son murdered a stranger, thereby setting off a series of duels among several families, no one doubted that young Desha had been drunk. By the 1820s alcohol was an essential feature of Lexington's masculine culture. While the ladies drank nothing more than sweet wine (at least in public), rarely did they organize an entertainment in their homes without alcohol. In such a society it was natural that the hallmarks of Todd hospitality were the quantity of liquor the family purchased by barrel and case, not bottle, and their slave's way with mint juleps.

MARY TODD first encountered this violent world in her family's Indian legends. Proud Todds and Parkers told and retold the stories of Great-uncle John's death at Blue Licks, Grandfather Levi's rescue of besieged Kentuckians at Bryan Station, Great-uncle Robert's threatened scalping, Uncle John's survival of a Shawnee gauntlet, and Uncle Sam's imprisonment during the War of 1812.

Perhaps all the young Todds were frightened by such tales. It is certain that Mary was. Once when a band of friendly Cherokees passed through Walnut Hills, her aunt's estate outside Lexington, she hid, along with her cousins, expecting to be captured and scalped. Somehow Mary never found a sufficient hiding place. Unlike the others, she stood in the center of the room, crying in terror, as the friendly Indians went by, the words she had learned from Mammy Sally, "Hide me, oh my Savior, hide me."[28]

Mary learned other things from the family slaves. Mammy Sally, the most constant adult presence in her early years, told menacing stories of spirits, the devil, and that archetypal phantom of West African myth, the jay bird. Mammy's tales of the jay bird terrified Mary. In the traditional splitting of the maternal role into the good and bad, the jay bird was Mammy's evil eye, reporting on the children's misdoings and helping the slave control her numerous charges. Of course, Mammy was supposed to be a Christian, and at least in front of Mary's parents, she probably behaved as one. Although Lexington's free black community supported two of its own churches (for a time a slave preached in one), every Sunday Mammy Sally attended McChord's Presbyterian

Church with the Todds, sitting in the slave gallery upstairs. But in her kitchen she mixed Christian theology with Afro-American belief, and it was Mammy who reinforced an idea Mary later cherished: the notion that the dead, perhaps even the mother who had abandoned her, return to the living in spiritual visitations that are not ill-intentioned.[29]

Mammy also acquainted Mary with the jarring uncertainties of slave life that existed even in a benign household like that of Robert and Betsey Todd. No one in the household of Mary's youth physically abused slaves, although there is evidence that her brother Levi did so later. (According to a formal deposition taken from Betsey Todd after her husband's death, Levi had whipped and burned two family slaves.) For a time in the 1820s Robert Todd Smith had supported the Kentucky Colonization Society's efforts to send freed slaves to Liberia, and as a legislator in the 1840s he revealed his distaste for slave selling (but not slaveholding) when he opposed efforts to open Kentucky's slave markets to out-of-state imports. Believing slavery wrong in the abstract, he was neither abolitionist nor problack but took the reluctant slaveowner's convenient ground that slavery was a regressive institution tying up capital and inhibiting Lexington's commercial growth.[30]

During Todd's last campaign for the State Senate in 1849 proslavery Democrats attacked him as an "Emancipation Candidate," but this was a partisan exaggeration based on his business association with that increasing rarity in Kentucky, an abolitionist. His partner, Edward Oldham, had earlier declared that "domestic slavery is incompatible with the natural rights of mankind, opposed to fundamental principles of self-government and hostile to the prospects of the Commonwealth." But Todd never went so far. Instead, he explained to voters that "slavery preexisted both Kentucky constitutions. It was believed then to have become too much identified with the interests of the state to be successfully assailed and that [identification] is now thrice as great." Denying that he would interfere with a domestic institution, Todd wished only to control the slave trade in Kentucky. Even in this he would be bound not by his own views but by those of his district. And when pressed by his opponents, he wrapped himself tightly in his slaveowning status: "Were I an abolitionist or an emancipator in principle, I would not hold a slave."[31]

Like many Lexingtonians, Todd lived a contradiction, for he was a slaveholding member of a mostly antislavery family in a slave state. Both of Todd's mothers-in-law had set a different standard, emancipating their slaves in their wills. Widow Parker, who once paid Mary's brother Levi $5 to track down and return a runaway from Ohio, nevertheless left bank stock as an annuity to support the elderly Prudence. Mary Brown Humphreys, Todd's second mother-in-law, was from a vigorously antislavery family whose members had sought to outlaw the institution in Kentucky's first constitution. In her will Mary Humphreys directed that all her slaves, including Jane and Judy, who lived with the Robert Smith Todds, be freed at her death, and perhaps these actions along with those of Widow Parker encouraged the antislavery ideals of Eliza's four daughters. Mary's brothers were not so liberal. When their father died of cholera in 1849, Levi and George tried to get the best value for their inheritance, and the family slaves were eventually auctioned to the highest bidder—Harvey for $700, Pendleton for $550, and Chaney together with her six-year-old daughter, Mary Ann, and her infant son, a bargain at $905. Meanwhile, Betsey's five daughters were proslavery (by their adulthood antislaveryism in Kentucky was heresy), and in time all but one became Confederate sympathizers.[32]

But even in indulgent households like the Todds', no Lexington slave, including Mammy, was safe from being sold down the river, and all slaves knew this. According to one, "the trader was all around us and the slave pens close at hand. We did not know what time any of us might be in them. Then there were the rice-swamps, and the sugar and cotton plantations; we had seen them before us as terrors by our masters and mistresses, all our lives. We knew all about them and when a friend was carried off, it was the same as death." A marriage or death in the master's family, a decline in hemp prices, even a fit of temper among men of frequent choler produced catastrophic effects in the back rooms of Lexington's finest houses. Harriet Beecher Stowe properly chose Kentucky to display the agonizing vicissitudes of lives that began in family service with soft owners like the fictional Shelbys (or real-life Todds) and ended in the cotton fields with brutal overseers like Simon Legree.[33]

Apprehensiveness and anxiety accompanied such an existence, and Mammy's nervous moods were one result. At some risk to herself, she helped slaves escape to the Ohio River and freedom. By no means was the Todd house an Underground Railroad station, and it is unlikely that either Mary's father or stepmother heard the mysterious late-night rapping on the back door. But the children did, and they thereby learned Mammy's secret. She had marked the Todd fence with a sign that designated the house as a place for slaves to rest before continuing the journey northward. According to Emilie, the young Todds, Mary included, "trembled" with excitement at this discovery. Later, in her own anguished life, Mary Todd adopted the slave prayers "Hide me, O my Savior" and "O Pray, O Pray" for her own supplications.[34]

She heard these pleas often. On her way back and forth to Ward's school Mary Todd passed through the square where in the southwest corner the black locust whipping post—one foot in diameter and ten feet high—was frequently used by slavemasters. Hearing the screams of the slaves and watching the approving crowd that gathered on such occasions, an observer knew such scenes meant the "death knell of Kentucky liberty." Every Monday, when court was in session, the Lexington slave auctions took place, and even after the 1833 legislature had forbidden the importation of slaves into the state for sale, slave traders gathered in the city.

Some came to meet with Lewis Robards, the notorious broker who did his business from the front room of the Phoenix Hotel; others, to find private bargains among the city's residents. Invariably, a few days after the sales, a long coffle of groaning blacks, manacled together, trudged down Main Street past Mary's home, toward Louisville and the flatboats that were to take them downriver to the markets in New Orleans. Three blocks from Mary Todd's home—at the corner of Short and Mulberry—stood the slave jail, where in unspeakable conditions William Pullum kept slaves in cages for punishment, sale, and sickness. There in 1831 four slaves accused of arson were hanged before a crowd larger than the city's population, and there they stayed for four days until, its being August, the smell overruled the desire to set an example.[35]

Not far from the Todds lived the notorious Turners. The Boston-born mistress of the house beat six slaves to death, burned others, and in 1837 permanently crippled a young slave by throwing him out the window. Such behavior violated even Kentucky standards, and a jury that included Robert Smith Todd inquired into Caroline Turner's state of mind but concluded there was no evidence of insanity. Later Caroline Turner received her due when yet another intended victim of her abuse strangled her.[36]

In light of their family's antislavery heritage, the Todd children saw as brutality what might have passed unnoticed in slavery's more celebrant households. In the manner of the young, the children concentrated on the lurid. In 1834 Mary "shivered with horror" over the story of a Louisiana master whose slaves, having been chained in the attic, had burned up during a house fire. Fascinated by such barbarity, Mary saved the newspaper account from the *New Orleans Bee*. She read and reread the story of "the New Orleans populace repairing to the scene of this cruelty and destroying everything upon which they could lay their hands. . . . [N]early the whole remains but the walls which the popular vengeance have ornamented with inscriptions far from complimentary to its late occupants."[37]

Within her own family Mary observed another brutal aspect of Kentucky race relations in the sexual control exerted by white males over black females. Everyone in town knew that her cousin John Todd Russell, the grandson of Lexington's legendary General John Todd, had fathered a son, Alfred, by a family slave. When young Russell died, his grandmother—Mary Todd Russell Wickcliffe—freed Alfred and his mother, Milly, and in 1827 the last known descendant of General John Todd sailed for Liberia. The price for freedom had been high, though. According to Mary's father in a suit filed in 1848, it had been extortionate. As the administrator of Mary Todd Russell's large estate before her second marriage to Robert ("Duke") Wickcliffe (the nickname recognized his aristocratic pretensions), Robert Smith Todd accused Duke Wickcliffe of refusing to emancipate Alfred and Milly, whom Wickcliffe owned under the doctrine of couverture,* unless his wife conveyed her extensive property to him. This land was Todd land, insisted Mary's father, for his cousin's use during her lifetime and then, if she had no heirs, according to a never-found but oft-quoted will of her father, John, to revert to lineal relations.

Duke Wickcliffe, one of the best haters in a community of many good ones, denied any coercion of his wife, arguing that his own wealth (which amounted to nearly $400,000 and included 100,000 acres in Kentucky alone) removed him from any need to blackmail his wife for such a paltry inheritance. In his affidavit Wickcliffe countered that the Todds were greedy, that some of these "remote collaterals" of his wife were impecunious, and that the Todds sued not on the basis of any just claim but because they needed his wife's money. The fact that Wickcliffe had bought Ellerslie, the Todds' ancestral home, and that he was a proslavery Democrat made compromise impossible. But even after a lower court had dismissed the case and Robert Smith Todd was

---

*This doctrine provided that women became civilly dead at their marriages and could neither own property nor sign contracts.

dead, his sons Levi and George tried to reinstitute the legal action against Wickcliffe.[38]

For Mary, the case meant a certain conspicuousness (and she now had some publicly acknowledged black cousins) as well as a separation from her best friend, Margaret Wickcliffe, Duke's daughter by his first wife. For the rest of Lexington, *Todd's Heirs* v. *Robert Wickcliffe* required taking sides in a nasty battle between two of the city's most prominent families. By initiating the suit, Robert Smith Todd had broken the customary silence (though never ignorance) of midnight doings in the slave quarters, and of this Wickcliffe declared, in the ferocious language favored by Kentuckians, "black and unmanly is the heart who to reach the husband basely involves the innocent wife." But the heart of this matter, at least to the Todds, was money and clan, tangibles well worth the ridicule of neighbors and the notoriety brought to the Todd children. Family possessions should stay in the family, and Robert's battle to make it so displayed the passionate litigiousness of a wronged Todd.[39]

The case also revealed the tangled bonds between Lexington's blacks and whites. Even antislavery families like the Todds feared slave insurrections in their community and the private retributions exacted by slaves on their children and wives. Twice during Mary Todd's youth a sufficiently large number of slaves escaped to require the mustering of Fayette County's militia. During Robert Todd's tenure as sheriff he was called upon to protect Lexington from supposed bands of black liberationists intent on rebellion. Usually such episodes were the creation of guilty imaginations. But within each slaveowning household fears extended beyond these public episodes, for there were enough cases of individual slave reprisals to concern any slaveowner. In the 1840s Mary's friend Cassius Clay accused a slave of fatally poisoning his son, and the whimpering and cowed behavior of Mary's youngest half brother, Alexander, convinced Betsey Todd that one of her household slaves was abusing her infant son.[40]

Other acts of violence grew out of the sexual encounters between white men and women, for only the authors of sentimental romances believed that the ornamental role assigned to upper-class white women in a slave society produced peaceful relationships between the sexes. In fact, as one historian has written, the interchanges were "intense, competitive and almost antagonistic." Nowhere did the anger of men against women appear more blatantly than in the newspapers. Hardly a month went by without the publication of some antifemale humiliation. "Women," noted the *Kentucky Gazette* in 1834, "are magpies at the door, syrens in the window, saints in the church, and devils in the house." Earlier the same newspaper had quoted, for three weeks in succession, the familiar misogynical aphorisms: "I change and so do women too / But I reflect and that women never do"; "Nothing so true as what you once let fall / That women have no character at all." And most Lexingtonians had read the *Gazette*'s favorite demotion of female logic: "Because I did, Because I will, Because I should like."[41]

In 1825 the Lexington papers gave front-page coverage to one murderous exchange among Kentucky gentlemen over their other human possessions: the women of their families. That year in Frankfort Jereboam Beauchamp shot his wife's lover, Kentucky's Attorney General Solomon Sharp. The wife admitted Sharp had fathered her child and, now a pariah, joined her convicted husband in a suicide pact in the Frankfort jail. "We have a vial of laudanum," wrote Beauchamp in a dramatic on-the-scene account later published in a pamphlet along with his wife's lugubrious poetry. "Now my beloved wife and myself have drunk the poison which will shortly launch us into eternity." With his wife's arms "encircling" him, Beauchamp survived both the laudanum and some self-inflicted knife wounds. He was eventually dispatched by hanging.

In the interval the convicted murderer explained the principles of masculine possessiveness that justified his behavior and that informed the proprietary attitudes of Kentucky's white males. "It is in vain to say," wrote the cuckolded husband, "that the laws of society provide adequate redress for all injuries of one citizen towards another. Where is the father [or male protector] of any sensibility or honorable feelings who would not infinitely rather a villain would silently put his daughter [or wife] out of the world, than to seduce and leave her to drag out a wretched degraded existence more painful to the father [or husband] than her death?"[42]

Mary Todd was nine when she read the last details of the Beauchamp case; she was eleven when another savage incident entangled family friends. After the editor of the *Kentucky Gazette* had ridiculed Duke Wickcliffe for his proslavery views and called him a coward (the latter insult certain to touch off some form of retaliation), Wickcliffe's son Charles, the brother of Mary's friend Margaret and a Todd dancing partner, shot the offending newspaperman in the latter's office near Courthouse Square. There had been no challenge because the dueling codes extended only to gentlemen who inhabited a mutually defined circle of aristocrats. Outsiders were dealt with by other means, and young Wickcliffe's gunning down of his father's antagonist was justified because he could not protect Wickcliffe's honor on the dueling grounds.

In the past Duke Wickcliffe had chastised his son for "neglecting matters of good breeding." But now he held Charles's actions to be chivalrous, and he engaged Lexington's best lawyer, Henry Clay, to defend him. In a letter to Clay the senior Wickcliffe described his son's deed as "imprudent" but taken only after "the poor fellow tried to use a cane against him." While this did not explain why the editor was shot in the back, a jury acquitted Wickcliffe in seven minutes. Later a friend of Robert Smith Todd's complained that the sheriff had rounded up "a jury of idlers, loungers and tipplers—in this case the pro-slavery contingent."

The baroque drama was not finished. George Trotter, another hotheaded Lexingtonian, was so enraged by the miscarriage of justice that he challenged Charles Wickcliffe to a duel at the lethal distance of eight paces, rather than the usual twenty. On October 9, 1829, after both men had somehow missed and Wickcliffe insisted on a second fire, Trotter shot Wickcliffe through the heart. In these circumstances, Trotter would not be tried for murder because local custom accepted and even encouraged such behavior. But to protect himself from ambush by the Wickcliffe faction, he now had to arm himself with knives and pistols and avoid entrapment by his enemies. In this episode's final chapter Trotter entered the Lexington Lunatic Asylum, the victim (so his family and friends said) of the Wickcliffes' harassment.[43]

Privately Robert Smith Todd considered dueling barbaric, but as a politician he did not publicly oppose it. In fact, in 1838 Todd presided over a public meeting called to defend dueling, a meeting his daughter Mary probably attended. The occasion had been an instance of political violence. Outside Washington in faraway Maryland, a Kentucky congressman, whose challenge had been written by Senator Henry Clay and whose seconds included most of the Kentucky Congressional delegation, had killed a colleague from Maine in a duel of rifles at eighty paces. Stung by northern criticism, Robert Smith Todd led the community in resolving that Lexington's citizens "irrespective of party do applaud in the face of the whole world the stand of our Representatives in rendering of services to a dauntless fellow Kentuckian when confronted by a hostile Yankee rifle."[44]

FOR twenty-two years Mary Todd inhabited this melodramatic world of dazzling entertainment, uncertain prospects, solid intellectualism, high fashion, and crude brutality. The town's contradictions matched the private losses she suffered in her domestic world. Victims were everywhere—from mistreated slaves to the maimed casualties of duels and fights to children unloved by stepmothers and Todds unable to make a living in stagnant Lexington. Herself a special unfortunate, Mary had suffered a staggering blow when her mother died, and thereafter would be strongly sensitive to other calamities. Surrounded by public episodes of fury in a community in which indulgence went uncorrected, Mary Todd nowhere observed the self-restraint and discipline that might have encouraged flexibility. Instead, everything— the disquieting landscape, the legends of the Todd family, the endless cruelty of a town with a taste for violence, and her own personal troubles—was amplified and exaggerated. The Lexington of her childhood played its part in fostering the weakness that had this daughter of the "dark and bloody land" crying for supernatural intervention: "Hide me, Hide me, O my Savior."

IV
Springfield
Courtship

BY THE summer of 1836 seventeen-year-old Mary Todd
had finished four years at boarding school, but the lan-
guid existence of a Bluegrass lady was not for her. She
made plans to visit her two elder sisters in Springfield,
Illinois. Elizabeth had settled there after her husband,
Ninian Edwards, had resigned his low-paying position
as the Illinois state's attorney general for better prospects as a merchant in Springfield. Then Frances Todd
had taken up permanent residence in the Edwardses'
new and very grand—at least by Springfield standards—house on Second Street. Now Mary wanted to
follow.[1]

The departure of his third daughter embarrassed
Robert Smith Todd, who, after his remarriage, had
wanted no more than a quiet domestic circle where,
"worn down by the cares and perplexities of the world,"
he could enjoy "repose and happiness." Instead his home
was filled with tumultuous quarrels between his second wife and her stepchildren. In 1836 the arrival of
Emilie, the fifth of his second set of children, increased
the number of young Todds living at home to nine,

and soon Betsey was "delicate" again. But no matter how large the family circle and how small the space, the first set of Todds left principally because, as Elizabeth Edwards bluntly put it, "of the circumstances that rendered life unpleasant in our father's home. Mary left home to avoid living under the same roof with her stepmother." George Todd, the youngest of the first Todds, agreed, later testifying under oath that Betsey had tried "to poison" his father's mind against the first Todds and that his stepmother's "relentless persecution" had forced the first children "to abandon" their father's house.[2]

It was the spring of 1837 before Mary Todd left. In winter only the foolhardy traveled the Illinois prairies, where more than twenty people had frozen to death during the great blizzard of 1831. In the summer the roads were dusty, and the riverbeds muddy and impassable. Spring was the best time, and it was an early morning in May when Mary Todd boarded the train to Frankfort with connections by the Accommodation Stagecoach to Louisville. Her father probably traveled the first leg of the trip with her on the railroad that he had sponsored and used often in summer to get to Buena Vista, Betsey Todd's country place. Some male friend or relative accompanied Mary the rest of the way, for ladies were never without a male protector on such journeys. Considering the number of Kentucky cousins already settled in Springfield, possibly her companion was her uncle Dr. John Todd, whose two-story frame house in Springfield was among the town's largest, or her first cousin John Todd Stuart, who this very year had taken on a new law partner, Abraham Lincoln.

From Louisville the steamboats left twice a week for St. Louis, first running downstream to the junction of the Ohio and Mississippi at Cairo and then churning upstream to St. Louis and, after a stop, on to Alton on the Mississippi River. Usually travelers went the final 100 miles east to Springfield in the uncomfortable stagecoaches that nineteenth-century Americans accused of "giving them the jolts." There were overnight stops along the way, and even seasoned travelers complained of the "swarms of gnats that besiege the stagecoach and stagnant waters lying across the road that make it necessary to proceed by foot through horrid places." If the proper connections were made, if the rain did not turn dirt roads into molasses, if an axle did not fall off the wheel or the stage run off the road, the trip from Lexington to Springfield took two weeks. Otherwise the blowing of the stagecoach horn that signaled the arrival of the Missouri coaches might come as much as three weeks later.[3]

The Springfield to which Mary Todd came in the summer of 1837 was raw, unsettled, and with no more than 2,000 residents more like the Lexington of her father's youth than the sophisticated city in which she had grown up. To the Kentuckians who made up a sizable proportion of its population, it seemed as if most of Lexington had relocated to what a few years before had been a cluster of log cabins on the prairie. Now, according to one transplanted Kentuckian, "the flood gates of Kentucky have broken loose, and her population set free naturally turned their course to Illinois and Missouri."

Just a few months before Mary Todd's arrival, Springfield had become what Lexington had briefly been: the state capital. Simeon Francis, the editor of the *Sangamon Journal,* believed the possibilities were endless: "The owner of real estate sees his property rapidly enhancing in value; the merchant anticipates a large accession to our population and a corresponding additional sale for his goods; the mechanic already has more contracts offered him for building and improvement than he can execute; the farmer anticipates, in the growth of a large and important town, a market for the varied products of his farm; indeed every class of our citizens look to the future with confidence that we trust, will not be disappointed."[4]

At least one new resident was already disappointed. As a delegate in the state legislature Abraham Lincoln had supported Springfield's claims to become the capital of Illinois over those of rival Alton, Vandalia, Peoria, Jacksonville, and the legislative fiction Geographical Center. Then, in late April 1837, he moved from New Salem, a village sixteen miles from Springfield, to begin his law practice with Mary's cousin John Todd Stuart. But unlike the rest of town, Lincoln found no more than "a busy wilderness—this thing of living in Springfield is rather a dull business after all, at least it is so to me. I am quite as lonesome here as I ever was anywhere in my life," he assured Mary Owens, whom he had courted in New Salem and with whom, for a time, he maintained a tepid romance. "I have been spoken to by but one woman since I've been here and should not have been by her, if she could have avoided it." With the wistfulness of an outsider in springtime, Lincoln acknowledged Mary Todd's world. There was, he wrote, "a great deal of flourishing about in carriages," and on Sunday there was church, which he had not attended. "I stay away because I should not know how to behave myself."[5]

Lincoln did not exaggerate, for he was neither churchgoer nor socialite. Nearly thirty years old, he remained an awkward, unschooled farmer's son, sharing with the Todds little besides a Kentucky birthplace. Abraham's parents, Nancy and Thomas Lincoln, had been living in Hardin County, Kentucky (the county was linked to the Todds through a Hardin-Todd marriage), when in 1809 their second child had been born in a log cabin with a dirt floor and tiny clay-daubed chimney, exactly the setting so many American politicians fictitiously claimed for their birthplaces. The Lincolns were not dirt-poor, mud-sill farmers; they owned unimproved land, once as much as 300 acres. But like their Hardin County neighbors, they were not prosperous either. As did many other ordinary farmers, they moved often, once to a farm with fresher water in Hardin County and then, when Thomas lost his land because of a defective title, to southwestern Indiana and finally into Illinois. Years later Abraham Lincoln explained this migration to a free state as "on account of slavery and land title."

In Spencer County, Indiana, young Abraham's mother and sister died (an infant brother had died in Kentucky), but his new stepmother, Sarah, proved as congenial an addition to the family as Mary's stepmother was antagonistic. By the time Mary Todd had finished eight years of schooling and was in boarding school, Abraham, 160 miles away in Indiana, had worked as a day laborer, farmhand, carpenter, and ferryman. He had also traveled to New Orleans on a flatboat, and when he returned, he settled on his own in New Salem, Illinois.

In the summer of 1831 two-year-old New Salem was a tiny village of ninety citizens with a magnificent view from the bluffs across the Sangamon River and, unlike its newest resident, great expectations but no future. There Lincoln lived for six years, working on his reading and writing with the local schoolmaster, studying law, surveying, and running the local store. Soon he found himself an elected militia captain during a war against the Black Hawk Indians in which his bloodiest encounter, he later said jokingly, was against the mosquitoes. In 1837 his horizons broadened, and the man who had first introduced himself to voters as "humble Abraham Lincoln" won election on his second try to the Ninth Illinois Assembly. It was time for him to move to the center of things, and that meant the capital of Springfield.[6]

On the hill where the Edwards house overlooked Springfield, Mary Todd spent the summer of 1837 observing the great events of Springfield's beginnings: the festive laying of the cornerstone for the Capitol building; the impassioned dedication speech on July 4 by one of the town's leaders, Edward Dickinson Baker; and the parlor discussions among the Whigs about whether her brother-in-law Ninian Edwards or her first cousin John Todd Stuart should stand for Congress next year. She observed, too, the noisy wagons that continually creaked by the Edwards house, some laden with settlers, others with local stone destined for the Capitol. If her future husband was lonely, she was not. Next door lived Mercy Levering, the daughter of a Baltimore merchant who was on an extended visit to her brother. Down the hill was Julia Jayne, whose father qualified as a true pioneer, having arrived in the 1820s, when the frontier town had no hotels and settlers like the Jaynes took in travelers.

But as Mary Todd had promised her father, this was only a visit to Springfield. No matter how exhilarating Mary's new independence, taking in a second permanent refugee from Lexington was too much for Elizabeth, who had lost a child in 1836 and who had just delivered another the month before Mary came.[7] Unlike Lexington, Springfield offered busy mothers few amenities in the way of either domestic servants or finished goods. Certainly Edwards was not much help. He was too immersed in his business and political ventures to be often at home. There was the matter of expense as well. Robert Todd had given Frances Todd $150 for her board, but at least for the summer Mary paid no rent to the Edwardses.

Sometime in the fall Mary regretfully retraced her way—across the prairie, down the river, and through the Kentucky woods. On her return to Lexington she did not join her contemporaries as they ran their slave-staffed households, made calls, went to parties, and, in increasing numbers, married. Instead, she returned to her first school, John Ward's, not as a pupil but as an apprentice teacher, helping Sarah Ward with the younger children. There is no direct evidence, but Mary may have decided to become a schoolteacher, then to return to Springfield.

These were hard times everywhere. The depression of 1837 had brought unemployment, suspensions of bank payments, and commercial closings to the United States. In Springfield Ninian Edwards, whose cycles of boom and bust came with more frequency than the American economy's, was listed as delinquent on his land taxes; clearly he was in no position to offer free board to Mary Todd.[8] If neither her hard-pressed brother-in-law nor her reluctant father would pay her expenses, she may have intended to pay her own way in Springfield as a schoolteacher. It was the only respectable way for a woman of her class to earn a living, and the two women whom she most admired—Charlotte Mentelle and Sarah Ward—had done so. If she could pay for her own board in her sister's home, no one could keep her in her stepmother's house.

Twenty-two-year-old Frances Todd solved her younger sister's dilemma. On May 21, 1839, the second of Robert and Eliza Parker Todd's daughters married William Wallace, a genial thirty-seven-year-old pharmacist and doctor from Pennsylvania. Wallace had settled in Springfield in 1836, the same year that Frances Todd came to the Edwardses. Although he expected to make money as a land speculator, for the rest of his life he tended the town's sick with his drugs, potions, and good-humored doctoring. But he was never much of a businessman. The early Mercantile Agency records dismissed him as "with not much capacity, can hardly make a living," and his family inhabited the precarious borderland between genteel impoverishment and true poverty.[9]

But with Frances and her husband now boarding at the Globe Tavern, Mary Todd could return to the Edwardses. With haste to be gone from Lexington, she packed a single trunk and carried her possessions to a new home. Probably she arrived in time for Frances's wedding in the Edwards parlor; in any case, by early June 1839 she had returned to the town that was to be home for the next twenty-two years.

MARY TODD left her own record of these first years in Springfield in three letters written before her marriage. Remembered by her contemporaries as an engaging conversationalist (Ninian Edwards once said, "Mary could make a bishop forget his prayers"), she was as adept and lively with pen as with tongue. She also lived at a time when the exchange of letters was a ceremonial practice. For many women—and Mary Todd was one—the ritual became a prominent feature of their emotional life; in letters they could vent intimate sentiments too embarrassing for plain speech. Throughout her life Mary spent many mornings on her correspondence, often measuring her health by her ability to write a letter, until rather than an exchange of news and sentiment, her letter writing became an outlet for her perpetual self-scrutiny.

As with most customs, there were conventions to be observed in letter exchanges. First came the sentimental allusions to the passage of time, specifically to the period since the correspondents had written

or seen each other, followed, if necessary, by a comment about who
had caused any gap in their communication. Mary Todd was especially
demanding of her friends. "Many, many weary days have passed since
mine has been the pleasure of hearing from you" went one complaint,
and in a letter from the summer of 1841, "—I reflect—that your
letters during that time have been far, very far more infrequent than I
could have desired." Next appeared girlish apologies for some deficiency of form or syntax, which Mary Todd little needed, though she
conveyed her sense of inadequacy with the repeated expression "pass
my imperfections lightly by." Finally came the catalog of doings and
feelings, the code words, puns, nicknames, and specialized gossip that
drew the correspondents together in an exclusive, mutually shared
world. "Speed's gray suit, Harrison blues, Lincoln's lincoln green have
gone to dust" went one of these esoterica.[10]

By the summer of her second year in Springfield Mary Todd had a
beloved companion with whom she shared her affection as well as the
gossip of the town, and it was to that friend she wrote in July 1840:
"You know the deep interest I feel for you. Time can never banish
your remembrance. How desolate I shall feel on returning to Springfield without you. Soon [find] our spirits wafted [to the] land of dreams—
Then will I think of thee—still [it does] not require so mighty of effort,
to bring you to mind, for the brightest associations of the past years
are connected with thee." And to the same correspondent in 1841: "I
would my Dearest you now were with us, be assured your name is
most frequently mentioned in our circle. Words of mine are not necessary to assure you of the loss I have sustained in your society."[11]

It was the language of love, but it was not addressed to Abraham
Lincoln or, in fact, to any male suitor. Instead, the object of Mary
Todd's attachment was her female friend Mercy Levering—"My dearest Merce, the sunlight of my heart." Whenever "Merce" returned to
her Baltimore home or Mary visited her Missouri cousins, these young
women were separated by "so many long and weary miles." Mary
Todd wrote in 1840: "Your mate misses you too much from her nest."
But there was hope, for if Mercy Levering married a Springfield man,
"our homes may be near, that as in times past so may it ever be, our
hearts will acknowledge the same kindred ties."[12]

Like many American women of her time, Mary Todd had formed a
strong bond of intimacy and romantic, though not necessarily sexual
or erotic, affection with her female friend. The intensity and the open-
ness with which she avowed her feelings for "Dearest" Merce were not

unusual, or latently homosexual, or prohibitory of male relationships. Nor should these feelings be dismissed as the mawkish sentimentality of Victorians. Rather, Merce and Mary inhabited a female world of intimacy and love[13] which ran parallel to that of courtship and marriage. Both these women expected to marry—it was their compulsory status—and they constantly discussed their marital prospects. Thus Mary warned Merce that her Todd cousins were unworthy of her friend, recommending instead a Parker relative, at the same time that she discussed several of her own suitors. A new Presbyterian church bell reminded Mary Todd not of religion but rather that the "trysting hour is near." Even after marriage Merce and Mary hoped to remain "bound by kindred ties" or, as Mary signed herself, "your ever attached friend."[14]

In a society as sexually segregated as this, save for her relatives Mary did not know well the young men she wrote about. On the other hand, no conventions kept her from spending her idle hours with Merce. While lonely young Abraham Lincoln talked politics with an all-male audience in Joshua Speed's store and managed only one conversation in three weeks with a woman, Mary inhabited an equally one-gender society. An incident from this period suggests her isolation.

Sometime in the spring of 1840, after a long siege of rainy weather had turned the town's unplanked streets into mud (sidewalks in Springfield awaited the reform administrations of the 1850s), the restless, sequestered Mary convinced prim Merce to walk to the courthouse square. It was only a five-block distance, but long dresses, satin slippers, and propriety made it a long way. Mary had an idea. They would jump to town, subduing Springfield's mud by throwing wooden shingles before them. And they did, managing to keep their skirts clean.

But as Merce had predicted, it was impossible to get back, at least not the way they had come, and Mary, but not Merce, ended up in the back of Hart's cart. One of her dancing partners celebrated the adventure in a poem that made Mary famous:

RIDING ON A DRAY

As I walked out on Monday last
A wet and muddy day
'Twas there I saw a pretty lass
A riding on a dray, a riding on a dray.
Quoth I sweet lass, what do you do there
Said she good lack a day

I had no coach to take me home
So I'm riding on a dray.

Up flew windows, out popped heads,
To see this Lady gay
In a silken cloak and feathers white
  A riding on a dray.
At length arrived at Edwards' gate
Hart back the usual way.
And taking out the iron pin
  He rolled her off the dray.
When safely landed on her feet
Said she what is to pay
Quoth Hart I cannot charge you aught
  For riding on my dray.[15]

Unlike such spontaneous adventures with Merce, Mary's encounters with eligible bachelors and widowers took place at organized social affairs, such as weddings, where what she called the "crime of matrimony" was committed, and at dances, picnics, and an occasional "pleasant jaunt to Jacksonville in the cars [with] my humble self, Webb, Lincoln, and two or three others you know not." In early Springfield a lit candle in the window of a female acquaintance had convened a party, but by Mary Todd's time unmarried men called only on the invitation of a male in the household. Ladies who did the inviting suffered barbs for their gauche forwardness or spinsterly desperation. No matter what their form, social affairs became critical episodes for women in their twenties, who soon must marry or be old maids. The men on these mixed outings necessarily remained shadowy acquaintances encountered intermittently and under the most exigent circumstances. Not knowing them well, Mary Todd often relied on Merce Levering for a second opinion.[16]

Perhaps Mary Todd resented the presumptive male authority over her future; perhaps she was simply rehearsing her judgments. In any case, while she found the young women in her life "amiable," "amusing," "pleasant," and "interesting," the men were "hypocritical," "frivolous in their affection," and "uninteresting." All her beaux, she complained in 1839, were "hard bargains." The persistent Mr. Webb (and she certainly called him that, for he was twenty years older than she) was a widower of "modest merit" with "two sweet little objections." Young John Todd had not shown off "to advantage" on a recent visit to Missouri, while Lincoln's roommate Joshua Speed had an "ever-changing heart which he was about to offer to another shrine." Even Merce's future husband, the "gone-case" James Conkling, was indicted for neglect. Only Abraham Lincoln remained above criticism.[17]

Sometime in 1839 Mary Todd had become aware of Lincoln, although she first heard of him two years before from her cousin John Todd. She may even have remembered his name from her Kentucky days, for he was listed in the *Lexington Reporter* as a candidate for the Illinois legislature in the summer of 1832, and she was a thorough newspaper reader. She must have heard talk of a lawsuit Lincoln initiated on behalf of a widow whose inheritance he believed had been stolen by the administrator of her husband's estate, a prominent Springfield attorney. Or she may have gone to the courthouse square on a blustery November day in 1839 to hear Lincoln speak "On the Politics of the Time and the Condition of the Country." It was a measure of Lincoln's prominence that he had been chosen for such an oration, and he filled his hour and a half with talk of local politics, state banks, and the ideals of the founding fathers. Still, the speech disappointed him, and with Mary's high standards she may have held Stephen Douglas's and Edward Baker's speeches in higher regard. Surely Mary was one of the ladies whom Merce's beau James Conkling complimented for their "martyr-like patience" as they listened to "long, tedious speeches."[18]

In any case, her romance with Lincoln was not love at first sight, a condition which outside of poetry was a rare phenomenon in the nineteenth century. Clearly Mary Todd and Abraham Lincoln were an oddly matched couple. She was a self-acknowledged short, "ruddy pine knot" with "periodic exuberances of flesh." On this score she may have reminded him of Mary Owens, whom with uncharacteristic venom he described as having "skin too full of fat to permit its contracting into wrinkles, a want of teeth, and a weather-beaten appearance in general . . . she is a fair match for Falstaff." On the other hand, Lincoln himself often surprised acquaintances with an ugliness that disappeared for most when he smiled or spoke. Tall and gawky, he was ill at ease in the parlors where Mary talked of books, people, and politics. He preferred telling stories delivered in the kind of homespun English that marked him, even if his clothes had not, as a farmer's son. Once Lincoln complimented a friend as the first man he had ever known who wore Sunday clothes during the week. Mary's sister Frances considered Abraham "the plainest man" in Springfield, and his clothes did not help. His swallowtail coats were too short, his patched trousers shabby, and his socks rarely matched.[19]

Poorly matched in background, social standing, as well as size, they were ill suited on the dance floor, where courting often began. James Conkling wrote Merce Levering that when Lincoln danced, he looked like "old Father Jupiter bending down from the clouds to see what's going on." Meanwhile, Mary Todd, in an awkward effort at congeniality, must have appeared as a plump baby crane with neck pronated upward. Under such conditions their first dance was not a success. In the Todd version, which highlighted the class differences between the blue-blooded Bluegrass daughter of Eliza Parker and Robert Smith Todd and the bottomland son of Nancy Hanks and Thomas Lincoln, Abraham wanted to dance with Mary in the worst way possible, after which she punned that he indeed danced "in the worst way."[20]

She had other suitors. The Edwards house offered more possibilities for meeting marriageable gentlemen than any household in town. No matter what her domestic burdens or her financial strains, Elizabeth Todd Edwards remained an energetic hostess to the end of her days and was remembered in her obituary, a half century later, for her hospitality. "We expect a very gay winter," wrote Mary Todd to Merce Levering in 1840, "evening before last my sister gave a most agreeable party, upwards of a hundred graced the festive scene."[21] As a former governor's son and a legislator Ninian Edwards knew all the rising stars in town, and at this stage of his career his was an important acquaintance.

Among the Edwardses' guests was Stephen Douglas, a transplanted New Englander who had settled in Springfield after he was appointed register of the Land Office. Douglas's energy made him seem larger than his ninety-pound, five-foot-four-inch body, and he was something of a ladies' man. Stephen Douglas and Mary Todd nearly reached the stage of a proposal, although her Whig convictions would have made it difficult for her to marry a Democrat. In any case, had Douglas proposed, she would never have admitted it—at least not for a while. Nice girls of her generation were taught never to kiss and tell. It was firmly prescribed in the advice manuals, such as *The Daughter's Own Book,* that "when declining a suitor's proposal, inform him in a manner which will least wound his sensibility, and let the secret of his having addressed you never pass your lips." Yet in the way that small towns do, Springfield remembered Mary Todd and Stephen Douglas as a special pair, and years later, as Mrs. President Lincoln, Mary revealed to one confidante that she had turned Douglas down with the prophetic words "I can't consent to be your wife. I shall become Mrs. President, or I am the victim of false prophets, but it will not be as Mrs. Douglas."[22]

There were others: a grandson of Patrick Henry's, whom she met on a visit to Missouri, and always the widower "of modest merit," Edwin Webb, who was a lawyer and state legislator. Webb served as her insurance policy against spinsterhood. He was, she wrote Merce Levering, her "principal lion" in 1840, although his two children and his age made him an inappropriate husband. (She said he was eighteen or twenty summers older, though actually he was only fifteen, and in this miscalculation Mary Todd began a lifelong practice of underestimating her age.) Despite these suitors, despite the general recognition that she was the "very creature of excitement," and despite her honorific status as a bridesmaid for friends, she was not popular—at least not in her own crabbed self-esteem. When, on a visit to her Missouri cousin Ann Todd, the beaux danced in attendance and "the little throng were hosts within themselves," she wished her Springfield friends could observe her popularity.[23]

This was a time in American history when romantic passion, common interests, and emotional congeniality, rather than the considerations of land, cows, and family that had spurred her mother's marriage, ruled the choice of a spouse. Mary Todd acknowledged as much in a letter to Merce. "I love him not," she wrote of the persistent Webb, "and my hand will never be given where my heart is not." Whom then would she love? To her sister she offered a forecast that reflected the expectations of a woman raised a Lexington Todd: "a good man, with a head for position, fame and power, a man of mind with a hope and bright prospects rather than all the houses and gold in the world." With these criteria, it is no surprise that the beaux of her Springfield days—Douglas, Webb, and Lincoln—were all ambitious politicians.[24]

Sometime in 1840 she and Lincoln moved from friendship, the necessary first stage of male-female affection for their generation, to courting and wooing (what Mary Todd described as having "lovers' eyes'), and finally to the understanding that they might marry. Their romance flourished against the background of the most absorbing presidential campaign in American history, when 80 percent of the electorate turned out to vote for either the Whig William Henry Harrison or the Democrat Martin Van Buren. During the election season Mary became, as she wrote Merce, "quite a politician, rather an unladylike profession, yet at such a crisis whose heart could remain untouched." She was among those women who crowded into the offices of the *Sangamon Journal* to hear about Harrison's chances, and she also watched parades, listened to speeches, and talked issues. No doubt, as she had in Lexington, she made known her opposition to Van Buren, though on what ground save his party affiliation is not known. Lincoln, who shared her interest, may have traveled to Missouri for a campaign speech while she was visiting there, and he may have sat in church with her Todd cousins. At least family legend made it so.[25]

Lincoln was winning her heart, but she was not engaged, at least not in any modern understanding of a limited period preliminary to a marriage ceremony. He gave her no ring, nor did he announce their intentions. Both principals were more likely to consider this a time prior to (as Robert Todd had told Betsey Humphreys) coming to contract. Usually couples moved beyond the stage of courting amid gossip but without public proclamation, although in this exchange of male proprietors it was customary for the future groom to ask the father of the bride for his daughter's hand, and Lincoln may have done so by letter. Elizabeth Edwards, who entertained for lesser cause, organized no celebration. Probably no one knew their intentions, although years later, when their courtship was put under the microscope, Elizabeth Edwards said she had guessed: "I have happened in the room where they were sitting often and Mary led the conversation. Lincoln would listen and gaze on her as if drawn by some superior power, irresistibly so."[26]

Like most middle-class couples, Mary Todd and Abraham Lincoln hesitated because of the many uncertainties that lay ahead. Young men like Lincoln who had prospects, but neither wealthy parents nor other resources, worried about their ability to support families. One modern historian who studied nearly 100 romances in nineteenth-century America found many young men who, after calculating the cost of food and housing, promptly fell out of love. A young theological student of Mary Todd's generation wrote his girlfriend that he had not "the means of making such provisions for your ease as you ought to receive . . . as much as I love you I cannot think of your giving yourself to me unless you can rationally promise yourself that you shall by such a step increase your own felicity." Young men were exhorted, in the press, in behavior manuals, and by their parents and friends, not to embark on marriage unless they had a modest income or prospects of becoming a dependable breadwinner. "Love will not pay your rent bill, nor your board bill," warned the author of *The Family Monitor*.[27]

By average standards Abraham Lincoln could afford a wife in 1840, and at thirty-one he was old to be without one. He made somewhere between $1,500 and $2,000 a year from his law practice and an additional $100 to $300 as a legislator. But his annual income fluctuated. If he lost an election or clients, his money would disappear as quickly as that of the debtors he sometimes defended in court. And no one was more aware of these economic hazards than the conscientious Lincoln, who had already suffered the humiliating attachment of his horse, compass, and surveyor's instruments to pay off a disastrous mercantile venture in New Salem. In the 1840s he continued to repay what he not so jokingly called the "National Debt."[28]

Cautious about finances, Lincoln was also diligently respectful of women, intending, as he informed Mary Owens, that "whatever woman may cast her lot with mine, should any ever do so, it is my intention to do all in my power to make her happy and contented, and there is nothing I can imagine that would make me more unhappy than to fail in this effort." The most indulgent of suitors, he had surrendered any directing influence in this earlier relationship in New Salem. "What I do wish is, that our further acquaintance shall depend upon yourself. If such further acquaintance would contribute nothing to your happiness, I am sure it would not to mine. If you feel yourself in any degree bound to me, I am now willing to release you, provided you wish it; while, on the other hand, I am willing, and even anxious to bind you faster, if I can be convinced that it will, in any considerable degree, add to your happiness."[29] A man who understood courtship in such reciprocal terms in 1837 was unlikely to have changed four years later. But as this nervous bachelor no doubt recognized, the contentment and happiness of a pampered Todd came at a high price.

If there was any temptation to announce marriage plans quickly, the scrupulous Lincoln was too much a lawyer to overlook the consequences of even a verbal infidelity. In nineteenth-century America a matrimonial pledge was as legally binding a contract as any commercial agreement, and the right of the rejected to seek damages was a familiar litigation. Usually it was the female, seduced or not, who brought a breach of promise suit and sought damages. Lincoln himself had successfully represented one such plaintiff. Not that the proud Mary Todd would have used this means of compensation for alienated affections; still, Lincoln's abnormal sensitivity to legal actions (he described a suit against him by Robert Smith Todd's partner as "harassing my feelings a good deal") made him hesitate to avoid welshing on even a tenuous verbal agreement.[30]

Lincoln may have procrastinated for another reason. For nearly a decade he had inhabited the all-male environment of William Berry's general store in New Salem and Joshua Speed's in Springfield, where unmarried men in their twenties exchanged jokes and crude deceptions about sex. Later his law partner and biographer William Herndon incorrectly charged that Lincoln had contracted venereal disease in Beardstown in the 1830s. More likely Lincoln feared the intimacy and sexual union of marriage, not because he suffered from syphilis but because like many Victorian males, he thought he might have the disease. His fear originated in the no less real apprehension of syphilophobia. Not knowing the critical difference between gonococci and spirochetes, nineteenth-century men (more than 50 percent of whom contracted some form of venereal disease) dreaded infecting their wives and in turn fathering the defective children that manuals assured would be the result.[31]

Meanwhile, young women had their own reasons to hesitate about marriage. For them courting was a rare time of power, an appealing circumstance for Mary Todd, who craved the audience she was attracting in Springfield and who therefore delayed the necessary exchange of the parlor's amusement for the kitchen's drudgery. Despite the recognition that marriage was an obligatory status, many vacillated before surrendering a father's control for the uncertain reins of a husband's. This was especially the case for Mary Todd, who, far removed from either Robert's discipline or Betsey's disapproval, was having a good time. Of course, Ninian Edwards considered himself her guardian, but the authority of a sister and brother-in-law was muted. And fun-loving Mary had already discovered the change that overtook newlyweds. "Why is it," she asked Merce Levering in 1840, "that married folks always become so serious?" In early 1839 the *Sangamon Journal* offered one explanation in a sentimental series on a young bride who "with downcast eye, and great reluctance bid adieu to her home—with what struggling emotions she pronounced the Farewell."[32]

In pre-Civil War America, love might not be eternal, but marriage, with divorce not yet an established civil procedure, was. A woman lost her civil and legal rights when she became one with her husband—and he was the one. The choice of a bad mate was an irrevocable error. In Mary Todd's Springfield there were plenty of wives whose lives had been blighted by syphilitic, drunken, nonproviding husbands. On one occasion Abraham Lincoln and his friends had taken just such an abusive husband, strung him up, and invited his wife to thrash him.[33]

At home Mary Todd heard other reasons that made her hesitate before marrying Abraham Lincoln. Her sister Elizabeth, who bore the name of their mother, took seriously her surrogate parenthood and challenged any courting by the rustic, socially primitive Lincoln. "I warned Mary that she and Mr. Lincoln were not suitable. Mr. Edwards and myself believed they were different in nature, and education and raising. They had no feelings alike. They were so different that they could not live happily as man and wife." And Elizabeth's son remembered that his mother tried to break up the match for two years with the kinds of warnings that wellborn mothers employed when their daughters favored men from different social backgrounds.

For while Abraham Lincoln may have joined Springfield society (in 1839 he was listed as one of nine managers of a cotillion), he sometimes wore rough Conestoga boots to evening parties and once burst into a parlor with the comment "Oh boys, how clean these girls look." Once, when asked to tea by the mayor of Urbana, he became, according to a male friend, "demoralized and ill at ease, put his arms behind him, and brought them together as if trying to hide them. Yet no one was present but Mrs. Boyden, my wife, and her mother." Elizabeth Edwards, who greeted her guests in French, was dismayed by such gaucherie and, like Mary Owens, held Lincoln to be "defective in those little links that make up the chain of a woman's happiness." Among them, in Elizabeth Edwards's view, was his inability to do what Mary Todd did so well: "Lincoln was unable to talk to women and was not sufficiently educated in the female line to do so."[34]

Amid such obstacles, the courtship of Mary Todd and Abraham Lincoln floundered. Abruptly, on January 1, 1841, they argued and parted. During Christmas week Springfield's matrons had organized a larger than usual number of dancing parties. Mary Todd called the season "a continual round of company, [and] gayety." The Leverings, the Mathers, and the Bunns had entertained, and so, of course, had the Edwardses. Of special interest to the town's single women, January would end a leap year, and during the season of turnabout in 1840 women had chosen their dancing partners. The ladies of Springfield took the occasion seriously, and even the most timid made known their favorites among the town's abundance of unmarried eligibles.

According to tradition, before the year changed, male suitors had to make their intentions known in the topsy-turvy arrangements of leap year. Despite her understanding with Abraham Lincoln, Mary Todd was having a gay time, perhaps for the last time as a single woman. "Miss Todd," wrote an observer, "is flourishing largely. She has a great many beaux."[35]

In late December, perhaps on New Year's Eve, Lincoln had promised to escort Mary Todd to a party. He was late, and she left without him, no doubt irritated, for she was never a woman to hide her feelings. When he finally arrived, perhaps by way of punishment, perhaps to catch his oft-wandering attention (he had nine cases before the Illinois Supreme Court in December 1840), she was flirting with the faithful Edwin Webb. Rumor had already made Lincoln uncertain of her commitment. James Conkling believed Mary had broken off the romance, and he wrote Merce Levering: "Poor L! how are the mighty fallen! . . . I doubt not but that he can declare that loving is a painful thrill, and not to love more painful still, but would not like to intimate that he has experienced 'that surely 'tis the worst of pain, to love and not be loved at all.' "

Other friends thought that Mary Todd had ended the romance. Wrote Y. A. Ellis: "I had it from good authority that after Mr. Lincoln was engaged to be married to his wife Mary that she a short time before they were to be married backed out from her engagement with him." Yet when Merce queried Mary about her suspected affair with Webb, Mary replied, "The knowing world have coupled our names [hers and Webb's] together for months past merely through the folly and belief of another who strangely imagined we were attached to each other." In her own mind she was a victim of small-town gossip and Lincoln's jealousy.[36]

Furious at her dalliance, Abraham appeared "grim and determined" (according to Mary's sister) at the Edwards home. Fuming, he had to wait until, finally, late in the afternoon the last of the New Year's callers had left. The resulting quarrel over Edwin Webb (whom Lincoln saw every day in the legislature and whom he would recommend for district attorney five weeks later) ended their courtship. In the family accounts Mary Todd was angry, too. "Go," she cried with a stamp of her little foot, "and never, never come back."[37]

Lincoln was devastated. Calling this the "Fatal First," he sank into one of those melancholic episodes that plagued his life. Although he had rarely been absent from the legislature, he now missed six consecutive days of the January session. When he reappeared, Conkling described him to Merce as "reduced, and emaciated in appearance and seems scarcely to possess strength enough to speak above a whisper." In contrast with his earlier activity as a Whig leader, now he could do little save answer roll calls. Lincoln went "crazy as a loon," pronounced Herndon, and one acquaintance described him "as having two catfits and a Duck fit." Wrote another: "Lincoln is in rather a bad way . . . the doctors say he came within an inch of being a perfect lunatic for life." His friend Speed removed his razor, and Lincoln himself acknowledged his "discreditable hypochondriaism" in a letter to John Todd Stuart, Mary's cousin and his law partner: "I am now the most miserable man living. If what I feel were equally distributed to the whole human family, there would not be one cheerful face on earth. Whether I shall ever be better I can not tell; I awfully forbode I shall not. To remain as I am is impossible; I must die or be better, it appears to me."[38]

Mary Todd was suffering as well, although her reaction to this interruption of her love affair was neither morbid depression nor bitter antagonism. Six months after the "Fatal First," in a letter to Merce Levering, she wistfully recalled her former suitor: "[Lincoln] deems me unworthy of notice, as I have not met him in the gay world for months, with the usual comfort of misery, imagine that others were as seldom gladdened by his presence as my humble self, yet I would the case were different, that 'Richard' should be himself again, much happiness would it afford me."[39]

She placed quotation marks around "Richard" because she was referring to Shakespeare's tortured Richard II, the monarch who talked "of graves, of worms, and epitaphs" and whose queen, like Mary, wondered if her Richard had been "both in shape and mind transformed and weakened"? Not many of Lincoln's contemporaries would have found similarities between a deposed English king and a small-town lawyer. With characteristic grandiosity Mary Todd did. If she was unusual for knowing Shakespeare, she was also uncommon for appreciating Lincoln's qualities as early as 1841, and not, as many did, only after 1860. To her he was not a storytelling jokester, a crazy loon, or an awkward country bumpkin. Through this allusion to English royalty she expressed her private worries over Lincoln's mental turmoil as well as her recognition that like Richard, her Abraham was "a sacred King hiding his head."[40]

LINCOLN left Springfield that summer to recuperate with his friend Joshua Speed in Louisville. Mary Todd stayed in town and behaved, in rehearsal for the future, like a quiet matron. At some point she was sick with an undisclosed illness that may have been a migraine headache. In June of that especially hot and dry summer she wrote Merce Levering that she was much alone of late and found her days "too flat, still and unprofitable" to discuss. Earlier she had discovered in the most mundane events a subject for spirited comment, but now little was of interest. Wistfully she described the yellow, vermilion-flecked prairie but could think of little more to say than that it was "as beautiful as it was in olden times." With newfound introspection, she confessed "to lingering regrets over the past," a comment which suggests she bore a principal's part in her quarrel with Lincoln. Much later, when she acknowledged her trespasses on her husband's "great amiability of character," she no doubt included this rift.[41]

Visitors to the Edwards house during the summer of 1841 also found it dull. Sarah Edwards, a niece of Ninian's from Alton, believed this was because the Edwardses had found religion, "joined the church, and given up parties entirely." (In fact, they had only suspended their entertainments for the summer and would begin again in the fall.) Certainly Mary Todd contributed to the household's sobriety, and as a result of her ill-concealed loneliness, she received an invitation to visit Alton, which she uncharacteristically declined. Nor did she undertake her usual trip to visit the Todd cousins in Columbus, Missouri. Instead, contemplating the slow pace of a life that up to this time had been so eventful, Mary Todd read, sewed, and acknowledged the change: "The last two or three months have been of interminable length after my gay companions of last winter departed. I was left much to the solitude of my own thoughts."[42]

It was a critical period in her life. If Lincoln faced the classic male conflict of intimacy and isolation, Mary Todd was caught in a female dilemma between girlish sociability and wifely withdrawal, between a personal need for independence and the required submergence of her autonomy in the collective entity of a husband's household. Just a few years before Mary Todd's summer of contemplation, Alexis de Tocqueville, who acutely observed more than a system of government in his journeys through the United States, had noted the contrast between the nation's active unmarried women and its submissive, sequestered matrons. "The amusements of a girl cannot become the recreations of a wife and the sources of a married woman's happiness are in the home of her husband."[43] What Tocqueville called "a cold and stern reasoning power" had to descend on this fun-loving, attention-seeking girl, who, once wed, would give up "the spirit of levity so annoying" in married women. Mary Todd now had to make her mark through her husband, and she found the renunciation of her independence difficult. Even at twenty-three it was hard to surrender the specialness of being a Todd, of living apart from parents, of being educated, and, mostly, of needing to be different. Flirting with Douglas and Webb and quarreling with Lincoln were means of postponing the necessary change and of getting attention, for all Springfield now gossiped about the lovers' separation.

Still, Conestoga boots and all, Lincoln continued to appeal to her because he was a man of potential majesty—her Richard—and because she sensed that his instincts of justice and equality extended even to married women. He believed, as he once wrote, in "doing right and most particularly so in all cases with women." Few men of his (or any) time accepted his personal charter for a single standard of sexual behavior. According to Herndon, Lincoln held "that a woman had as much right to violate the marriage vow as the man—no more, no less." Marriage to such a man promised fewer alterations in the single state and more room than usual for a wife's self-government.[44]

While Mary Todd reflected, Lincoln, full of uncertainty, was interrogating his friend Joshua Speed about how this recent bridegroom was faring. His admittedly intrusive inquiries ("Are you now, in feeling as well as in judgement, glad you are married as you are?") soon became "so impudent" that Lincoln found it necessary to enclose two letters in one envelope—one for Speed alone and the other to show his bride. Mary may have engaged in the same kind of questioning with her friend Merce, who had married the "long-gone" Conkling in September 1841 and had moved back to Springfield.[45]

Other friends acted as matchmakers, for not everyone in Springfield agreed with Elizabeth Edwards that this was a bad match. Eliza Francis, the wife of Simeon Francis and one of the town's few women to speak out on politics, brought Mary Todd and Abraham Lincoln together in her parlor sometime in 1842 with the entreaty that they be friends. Many other love affairs had begun in friendship, and soon the couple were meeting secretly at the Francises and at Dr. Anson Henry's, where a year earlier Lincoln had taken his case of "discreditable hypochondriaism." Although Mary Todd still lived at the Edwards house on the hill, where Ninian Edwards had become Lincoln's advocate, their forty-foot parlor had become an uncongenial setting for her romance.[46]

In view of the personalities of the principals, the romance would never have revived unless both had shared in its destruction. A unilateral wound to such sensitive psyches would have been beyond healing, whereas a misunderstanding over a phantom lover could be resolved. And though similar separations occurred in many other nineteenth-century courtships, the terms of Mary and Abraham's disbanding revealed some patterns in their relationship that would recur: his precipitating abstraction and forgetfulness, her histrionic claims on his attention by flirting with other men; his melancholy, her choler; his listening, her talking; his infuriating self-containment (several friends, including Edwards, thought him "cold" and "not warm-hearted"), her clamorous need for affection, probably physical, undoubtedly emotional.[47]

Politics helped restore their romance as well, for this was a couple who transformed a mutual interest in public events into a love affair. They had always shared an admiration for Henry Clay and Whig politics. In 1840, when their courtship had first flourished, Mary Todd had seen Lincoln in the offices of the Whig newspaper, where, according to James Conkling, "some fifteen or twenty ladies were collected to listen to the Tippecanoe Singing Club. The journal office had become quite a place of resort, particularly when it is expected there will be any speeches." In 1842 Springfield vibrated with the biennial activities associated with nominating and electing a legislature and governor. Sometime during that fall, though he was never much of a gift giver, Lincoln presented Mary (who had now become the more intimate "Molly") with something few other American women would have received so gratefully: It was a list of election returns in the last three legislative races, and she tied it in a pink ribbon.[48]

Abraham Lincoln had good reason to study these returns. A three-time Whig legislator from Sangamon County, he had emerged as a party leader, and he needed a vote-getting issue to set the Whigs apart from the Democrats. By the fall he had found it. The year before, James Shields, the state's Democratic auditor and a dandy ridiculed for his pretensions by the clique on Springfield's Aristocrat's Hill, had announced that the state of Illinois would no longer accept paper currency as payment for debts—not even the bank notes of its own Bank of Illinois. Only hard-to-get gold and silver would be accepted for tax payments.

The Whigs put this provocative issue to use, and in August 1842 the first of the anonymous Rebecca letters from Lost Townships to Mr. Printer appeared in the *Sangamon Journal*. It was followed, at various intervals during the campaign, by three others. Lincoln wrote the second letter in which the widow Rebecca and her country neighbor Jeff lamented the economic hardships imposed on the people by the "rascally" Democrats. Rebecca and Jeff also complained about the Democratic officeholders (like Shields) who must still be paid in specie. "If some change for the better is not made, it's not long that neither Peggy nor any of us will have a cow left to milk, or a calf's tail to wring," sighed the hard-pressed Rebecca.[49]

It was low satire, good politics, and great fun. But Lincoln also included an uncharacteristic personal attack on Shields ("he is a fool as well as a liar") along with a politically superfluous episode in which Shields "in the ecstatic agony of his soul" rejects the "galls" about town. "Dear girls, it is distressing," Lincoln has Shields say, "but I cannot marry you all. Too well I know how much you suffer; but do, do remember, it is not my fault that I am so handsome and so interesting."[50]

With reason the maligned Shields was furious, but in the Edwards household there was amusement. By the end of the next week Mary Todd and her friend Julia Jayne (the married Merce now presumably gone serious and unable to join in such revelry) had written and published another Rebecca letter. By this time all Springfield knew of Shields's humiliation, and in Mary and Julia's contribution, the widow Rebecca is trying to placate him. "Let him come here and he may squeeze my hand as hard as I squeeze the butter, and if that ain't personal satisfaction, I can only say that he is the first man that was not satisfied with squeezing my hand." But Rebecca was prepared to go farther, even to the point (while blushing) of offering herself to the "rather good lookin' than otherwise" bachelor Shields.

> I know he's a fighting man and would rather fight than eat, but isn't marrying better than fighting, although it tends to run into it. And I don't think I'd be such a bad match either. I'm not over sixty and am just four foot three in my bare feet, and not much more round the girth, and for color I wouldn't put my back to any girl in lost townships. But after all I'm counting my chickens before they're hatched and dreaming matrimonial bliss when the only alternative, reserved for me may be a lickin— P.S. if he consents to marry there is one condition, if he ever happens to gallant any young girls home of nights from our house, he must not squeeze their hands.

A week later, in the last of the Rebecca series, Shields and the widow have married in the Mary Todd-Julia Jayne-authored wedding poem published in the *Journal:*

> Ye Jew's harps awake! The auditor's won,
> Rebecca, the widow has gained Erin's son
> The pride of the north from the emerald isle,
> Has been woo'd and won by a woman's smile.[51]

Whatever their political effect (the Democrats as usual carried Springfield), the Rebecca letters of Abraham Lincoln and Mary Todd served as a public means of reconciling their private affairs. In their future together their disagreements were often public spectacles resolved in private, but for the moment politics mirrored romance. This was why Lincoln placed his opponent Shields in the courting world with a literary convention so unnecessary to the political context of his satire as to suggest some other motivation. With marriage again on his mind, Lincoln's pen had strayed from the partisan stump to the dance floor, where "the married women, finickin' about trying to act like galls, tied as tight in the middle and puffed out at both ends like bundles of fodder that hadn't been stacked yet, but wanted stackin' pretty bad." The private message was heard, and Mary responded, in kind, to advise Lincoln, through Rebecca, that she was interested and in fact not such a bad bargain. Finally it was Mary who predicted the future:

> —O'bright be his lot!
> In the smiles of the conquest so lately achieved.
> Happy groom! In sadness far distant from thee,
> The fair girls dream only of past times and glee.

In terms of personal politics, the Rebecca letters provided a comic theater where, with laughter, Abraham Lincoln and Mary Todd ended their estrangement.[52]

Not privy to the joke, Shields believed his honor had been assailed (certainly his pride had been) and demanded a retraction, which, considering the context of the Rebecca letters, Lincoln could hardly satisfy. Soon the affair escalated to a challenge and plans for a duel. Some historians have held Mary Todd's "amateurish letter" responsible for Shields's challenge, although it was no more amateurish than the others and certainly not by itself the cause of the challenge. In fact, Shields was already enraged by Lincoln's earlier insults, and it is Mary's Rebecca who recommends as weapons "if they have to fight broomsticks, hot water, and a shovel full of hot coals." When the time came, the long-armed Lincoln instead chose cavalry broad swords—and practiced. Still, Illinois was not Mary's murderous Lexington, and when Lincoln and Shields met on the dueling grounds at Bloody Island, Missouri, a reconciliation was reached by their seconds before the fighting began.[53]

There is no record of Mary Todd's reaction to this incident. She had grown up with the practice of dueling and no doubt enjoyed the romantic intrigue of Lincoln as her champion, ready to die defending her name. But for the rest of his life Lincoln was ashamed of the episode of the broadswords. Considering it foolish and illegal, he sought to exorcise it from his memory. Once during the Civil War, when a Union officer asked Lincoln at a White House reception if he had fought a duel— "and all for the sake of the lady by your side"—a red-faced Lincoln snapped: "I do not deny it but if you desire my friendship, never mention it again." Mary Lincoln wrote later of the event that "we mutually agreed never to mention it—except in an occasional light manner between us."[54]

SIX weeks after the duel and three days after the election, Mary Todd married Abraham Lincoln. On that rainy night in November 1842 she wore her sister Frances's white satin dress and a pearl necklace, had two bridesmaids, and gave her answers to an Episcopalian minister. Still, like most events in Mary Todd's life, this wedding was not traditional. She had not engaged in those familiar female rituals of stitching bed linen, stoning raisins, and preparing the customary thirty-six-egg wedding cake. Nor did either set of parents attend. While this was common enough on the groom's side, most brides were married at home.

Many nineteenth-century parents had no more than a week's notice before a wedding. In early Springfield they needed no more, having no caterer to hire or hall for which to compete. Instead, the wedding ceremony usually took place at home before a small audience in the evening. Only two outsiders were necessary: a minister or magistrate to say the words and, for the rich people on the hill, Watson's, the Springfield confectioner who provided the much admired pyramid of macaroons. But Mary Todd's guests received less than the week's notice recommended by the etiquette books.[55]

In light of their mutual predicaments—the recent duel, their still-remembered separation, and Elizabeth Edwards's opposition—the couple intended a private ceremony "without any parade" in Reverend Dresser's home. Often, especially outside eastern cities, the marriage ceremony was, as one traveler wrote, "loosely-performed and lightly considered." But somehow, in the time it took to get the license from the Sangamon County Court and have the lesson of their courtship—"Love is Eternal"—engraved on the bride's gold wedding ring, the word spread. In some accounts (and there are many) Lincoln waited until the wedding day to inform Ninian Edwards, who as Mary Todd's guardian insisted that she be married from his parlor. In other stories Mary Todd told her cousin John Todd Stuart a day before, and after a last family controversy over the suitability of the groom Elizabeth Edwards reluctantly organized the wedding supper. Years later both Todd sisters conveyed the sense that the wedding was not quite proper through their cherished memory that Mary's wedding cakes were still warm. They preferred to forget another incident. After the groom had declared his willingness to endow the bride with all his goods and chattels, lands, and tenements, one old-timer, accustomed to more informal civil ceremonies, blurted out: "the statute fixes that, Lord Jesus Christ, God Almighty, Lincoln."[56]

V

Domestic Portrait: The Springfield Years

To each other they were Molly and Mr. Lincoln, and they spent the first year of their marriage boarding at the Globe Tavern on the corner of Adams and Third. Mary's sister Frances and her husband, William Wallace, had stayed three years in the same eight-dollar-a-week room (double occupancy), meals and some washing included. So Mary's experience was not unique. Still, even by Springfield standards the Globe was second-rate, compared to its principal competitor, the American House. One visitor to town considered the latter "of Turkish splendor—the carpeting, the papering and the furniture weary the eye with magnificence." No one claimed Turkish splendor for the Globe. Despite recent repairs and the "prudent management of Mrs. Beck, eight pleasant and comfortable rooms for boarders as well as convenient resting places for the weary," the former Spottswood Rural Hotel remained a noisy, two-story frame house. It had begun as the office of a stage line, and the bell clapper was still pulled any hour, day or night, that a coach arrived. Next door was the blacksmith's shop, with its incessant clanking and hammering. During the legislative session lobbyists and officials entertained in its parlors, where talk was loud and the brawls (including a murder in 1838) were frequent.[1]

Nor did the Globe offer much privacy to its overwhelmingly male clientele, most of whom did not expect a private table for eating or even beds to themselves. More serious for the new Mrs. Lincoln was the disappearance of those housekeeping chores that filled the hours and defined the identities of America's married women. Lincoln returned to work the Monday after his wedding, and with nine cases in the Christian County courts that week, he was probably gone overnight. By no means was the groom nonchalant about his new status, informing a friend of his "profound wonder" about his "marrying." Yet in April 1843 Lincoln was on the circuit again, and his wife was alone for the entire month. Living in an eight-by-fourteen-foot room, without a parlor for visiting, and taking meals at the Globe's common table represented a drastic change from the elegance of the Edwards household. More critically, it left Mary Lincoln without a domestic thing to do.

Hers was the kind of existence deplored by the ladies' magazines and advice manuals of the day, which encouraged immediate housekeeping for brides. Ignoring the economic necessity for boarding, keepers of decorum inveighed against the lassitude of young wives in boardinghouses who should be learning the duties of running a household when, instead, they were being taught idleness. Wrote one: "Women so situated have nothing to do. Public opinion will not allow her to assist her husband in his business and she cannot interfere in politics." Similarly, England's nosy Mrs. Trollope found uniform dullness and a cold, heartless atmosphere for the married ladies at boardinghouses. In the short stories of *Godey's Lady's Book* the female denizens of boardinghouses were often seduced by male guests and ended their days as fallen women and deserted wives.[2]

To be sure, the Globe was close to the center of things, and Springfield offered many amusements in the 1840s. The circus, minstrel shows, ventriloquists, and theater companies visited the city, and there were special events as well. While Mary Lincoln lived at the Globe, Joseph Smith, the controversial Mormon leader, was arrested in nearby Nauvoo, Illinois, and held for extradition to Missouri on the charge of attempted murder. Shortly after a hearing in the Springfield courthouse, Judge Thomas Browne was impeached for feeblemindedness.

On this occasion the courthouse galleries were full of what the papers called "Springfield's fairest."[3]

As yet the city had none of the organized ladies' aid and philanthropic associations that occupied the time of middle-class reformers in larger cities. By the 1850s the public activities of Springfield women centered on the churches, where they organized suppers and raised money for special projects. Mary's friend Merce Conkling, who was much given to church activities wrote, "[w]e ladies have a sewing society. We have an old farm waggon and pick each other up so that we can raise money for the church." But in the early 1840s there were no such diversions for a lonely wife, who may not have been interested anyway.[4]

No matter what Mary Lincoln did to occupy her time, she may not have had her usual energy. She was pregnant and would not have ventured out often. American ladies of her time and class hid their "delicacy." With swollen bodies an immodest display of a sexual encounter, carrying women stayed out of sight, and the term confinement prescribed a long period of isolation that extended from visible pregnancy through birth into nursing. In all, a women might disappear for as long as two years. Aided by the abundant gored skirts of the day, some were so secretive and seclusive that no one knew they were in the "family way." This was the case with Mrs. DuBois, a neighbor whom Mary Lincoln saw every day. "One of the seven wonders of the world has taken place," wrote Mary. "Mrs. DuBois has a daughter born two or three days since. Until the last hour no one suspected her, as she looked smaller, than she ever had done." There is no record of how Mary Lincoln reacted to her own changed circumstances, but years later she indicated the critical importance of domesticity in her life. "I believe," she wrote her daughter-in-law, "a nice home, a loving husband and precious child are the happiest stages of life."[5]

Yet Mary Lincoln had more reason than most nineteenth-century women to fear childbirth. Both her mother and her husband's only sister had died of puerperal fever, and at an impressionable age she had observed her mother's and stepmother's pregnancy-related illnesses. In Springfield there were no midwives (listed in the public records, at least) to offer reassurance to a first-time mother. Instead, at a time when 1 physician was sufficient for every 700 Americans, there were too many male doctors in Springfield, 12 for a population of 5,100. Several advertised as specialists in obstetrics and women's diseases. Perhaps her uncle Dr. John Todd or her friend Dr. Anson Henry, who charged five dollars for an "accouchement," attended her. Perhaps her brother-in-law Dr. William Wallace supervised the delivery in the tiny room at the Globe, although because of his age and relationship to the patient, this would have been embarrassing. In Springfield, as elsewhere in America, male doctors were still unwelcome in most birthing rooms because their presence violated feminine modesty, though they were sought in difficult labors because of their supposed skill with forceps and their ability to deliver breech-presenting babies who had to be rotated.[6]

No matter who was in attendance, only the catchpenny wisdom that the childless died young in frustrated barrenness consoled women in labor. The standard advice was still Thomas Jefferson's admonition to his pregnant daughter Maria: "Take care of yourself, and have good spirits and know that courage is as essential in your case as that of a soldier." Indeed, Mary Lincoln remembered childbirth as "a suffering time," and she also recalled "my darling husband bending over me."[7]

On August 1, 1843, nine months less three days from the day of her marriage, Mary Lincoln achieved the second of her domestic priorities and delivered the first of her four "precious" sons. It was typical of the times (for this was a period in which women were assigned increasing authority in family matters, and Mary Lincoln had more power than most) that she named the infant. In fact, she named all the children because as her husband later explained to a group of supporters who wanted no more than a name for their small cannon, "Oh, I could never name anything. Mary had to name all the children." She called this son with the slightly turned-in left eye Robert Todd, after her father.[8]

There is a tradition—and it is no more than that—that she refused family help with the baby. Probably little was offered, not from indifference but because Elizabeth Todd Edwards had herself delivered a daughter a few weeks before Robert Todd Lincoln was born and because Frances Todd Wallace had two children under three and a chronically ill husband. Still-unmarried Ann Todd, the last of the four Todd exiles from Lexington, now lived with the Wallaces, but she was never an intimate of Mary Lincoln's. Instead, the bride who had moved so quickly from the gay sociability of a young lady on Aristocrat's Hill to the isolating travail of motherhood in a boardinghouse made her own way.

The Bluegrass ladies of her memory had stayed in bed for months, attended by their slaves. Mary Lincoln had only the assistance of a neighbor at the Globe (there were some compensations for boarding), but this was help, not service. One of her neighbors later recalled that "Mrs. Lincoln had no nurse for herself or for the baby. Whether this was due to poverty or to the great difficulty of securing domestic help, I do not know." While Mary Lincoln is remembered as without servants, Robert, in his three months at the Globe, was recalled for his expansive lungs.[9]

In the fall the three Lincolns left the Globe for a four-room frame cottage on South Fourth Street. The cottage has not survived, but in the pre-Civil war period it was standard housing for the families of Springfield's clerks, artisans, and mechanics who could afford, like the Lincoln's, a rent of $100 a year.

Sometime before Christmas Mary Lincoln's father visited. Leaving Betsey to tend his just completed family (his fifteenth child had been born in 1841), Robert Smith Todd traveled to Springfield, where by 1843 four daughters, three sons-in-law, and six grandchildren lived. Only Mary had used his name. Already two Robert Smith Todds had died, and he was probably closest to the daughter who since her mother's death had clamored for his attention by challenging her stepmother, talking politics, staying in school too long, and now using his name for her firstborn. Either in recognition of a unique relationship formed by gratitude on the father's part and the need for acknowledgment on the daughter's, or in surprise at her genteel poverty, "without remark he dropped a $25 gold piece in her hand." He gave no such help to his other daughters. Todd also deeded eighty acres of land in Illinois to the Lincolns, promised a yearly sum that amounted to $1,100 before his death six years later, turned over to his son-in-law a case against a business creditor, and authorized Lincoln to keep what he collected from some unpaid debts. For a man with thirteen living children, this was generous support.[10]

Todd's assistance helped the Lincolns complete the final stage in their progression from boarding and renting to owning. Later Mary's father noted approvingly, in a letter to his more affluent son-in-law Ninian Edwards, that the Lincolns "are taking up housekeeping." In May 1844 they had moved into their permanent home: a one-story five-room cottage with a loft, some outbuildings, and an eighth of an acre of land, at the corner of Eighth and Jackson. For this Lincoln paid Reverend Charles Dresser, the Episcopalian minister who had married them, $1,200 and a city lot worth $300. They were still on the wrong side of Springfield's tracks, but now Mary Lincoln had the final necessity in her domestic triumvirate: "a nice home."[11]

For her husband, Eighth and Jackson had advantages because it was not on the politically suspect Aristocrat's Hill. Ever since his marriage to a Todd, Lincoln had been accused of joining the rich. Unwilling to give up his log cabin advantage in politics, he protested that "I, twelve years ago . . . a friendless, uneducated, penniless boy, working on a flat boat at ten dollars per month—have been put down here as the candidate of pride, wealth, and aristocratic family distinction. There was too the strangest combination of church influence against me. . . . My wife had some relatives in the Presbyterian church and some in the Episcopal churches."[12]

In addition to demonstrating his populism, his new home was only four blocks from the courthouse square and the second-story office where he and a new partner, William Herndon, practiced law. There during the spring of 1844 Abraham Lincoln was quietly campaigning for the Whig nomination to Congress as well as attending to his clients. After four terms in the state legislature he had not held an elective office since his marriage, and no doubt his wife encouraged his aspirations. But it was Edward Dickinson Baker who won the nomination and election. Lincoln, with domesticity uppermost in his mind, compared himself to "a fellow who is made groomsman to the man who had cut him out, and is marrying his own dear gal." He would have to wait until next time and be content with his selection as a Whig presidential elector.[13]

Their private affairs were more fruitful. Within weeks of Robert's unusually late weaning, Mary Lincoln was pregnant again, and in March 1846 a second son was born. She named him after the man who had defeated her husband for Congress. It was not uncommon to fasten a special star's name onto a son; Abraham Lincoln's name would soon be bestowed on hundreds of American boys. The Lincolns knew Baker and his wife well and, like all Springfield or at least the Whig half of it, admired the golden-voiced orator.

Clearly the English-born Baker had the type of heroic grandeur that impressed Mary Lincoln. To those of his Springfield neighbors who, unlike Mary, failed to sense his greatness, Baker retold the story of his despair when as a young emigrant to the United States he had read the Constitution and discovered there his disqualification as a naturalized citizen from the office he had expected to fill—the presidency of the United States. Nonetheless, Baker intended to serve his adopted country, and in 1846, after war had been declared against Mexico, he cut short his congressional term, returned to Springfield, and was raising a troop of Illinois volunteers when his namesake was born. By the spring of 1847, Edward Dickinson Baker was the local hero of the Battle of Cerro Gordo, while in Springfield Eddie Lincoln was turning out to be a sickly baby.[14]

AFTER the move to her own home at Eighth and Jackson and the birth of her second son, Mary Lincoln disappeared—at least from historical view. Her world narrowed, and behind the wooden doors with the now-famous gold plate marker engraved "A. Lincoln," life became a seamless experience, filled with the recurring domestic tasks that a neighbor described as "the little world of housekeeping cares and runabout children." Neither awe-inspiring nor exciting, such matters are not usually the stuff of which biographical drama is created. Even today, when domesticity has emerged as a respectable historical topic, its allure is only collectively established, and a deep suspicion of homemaking as trivial and mundane remains. It is, after all, women's work. Still to exorcise its performance from the life of a family-centered woman like Mary Todd Lincoln is like omitting politics from a chronicle of her husband. What is significant is not so much what she did, but rather how she accomplished these affairs of the home and what they meant to her.

For example, many middle-class women of her time followed Lydia Sigourney's snobbery that they were little "more than galley slaves without a domestic." Certainly the ladies of Springfield, especially those on the Hill like her sister Elizabeth, felt so, for they searched endlessly for servants, even importing Irish girls from New York through the Women's Protective Emigration Society. By 1850 nearly one out of every four of the town's households included a live-in female, usually under twenty-one and often German- or Irish-born. To their employers these maids delivered respectability as well as leisure.[15]

Throughout her life (and her years in the White House were no exception), Mary Lincoln did more of her own work than her economic position warranted or her husband recommended. "By the way," wrote Lincoln in 1848, "you do not intend to do without a girl, because the one you had left you. Get another as soon as you can to take charge of the codgers." At a time when Elizabeth Edwards depended on two Irish-born servants, a laborer, and two Kentucky slaves (Illinois was a free state, but evidently Edwards believed slavery a permanent condition and so described their black household members to the census taker) and even indigent Frances Wallace could not get along without her German girl, their sister Mary had only occasional assistance.[16]

Mary Lincoln's critics have held that her bad temper drove off her domestic workers, but such judgments remove her from her time and place. Everyone had difficulty keeping hired girls. In fact, the entire problem of finding and retaining good domestic help was a chronic concern for middle-class women. In Catharine Beecher's authoritative *Treatise on Domestic Economy* the issue merited two chapters, one encouraging servants to stay where they were and the other exhorting in employers the good temper that Mary Lincoln never achieved if the potatoes were undercooked or the knickknacks in the parlor broken. Because she frequently depended on young local women who traded domestic work for board and a dollar a week, rather than on dependent, live-in, immigrant women, she had a higher turnover than some, though by no means all, employers.

Unlike the well-trained slaves of her childhood recollection, the independent daughters of Sangamon County's farmers required constant supervision in specific tasks such as the seasonal exigencies of housecleaning. Hired girls did not consider themselves servants, and they did not expect to be in service long, as immigrant women did. Foreign visitors were not alone in their dismay at the insolence of American servants who expected to eat with the family. "They are," confessed one observer, "too thoroughly American to live with." Consequently nineteenth-century domestic life resonated with angry encounters between proud native-born single women temporarily in service and imperious matrons intent on training ladies' maids.[17]

Among Mary Lincoln's hired girls was Lincoln's cousin Harriet Hanks, who sometime in the early 1840s arrived from the country to go to school at the Springfield Female Seminary and to help out in the house. Later as Harriet Chapman, the wife of a Charleston, Illinois, dentist, she provided William Herndon with a devastating portrait of Mary Lincoln. She would freely give information about Lincoln, she said, but "would rather say nothing of his wife as I could say but little in her favor." Twenty years later Herndon promoted this statement into evidence that Mary Lincoln had attempted to make a slave of Lincoln's cousin.[18]

But Mary Lincoln's treatment of Harriet Hanks was common enough. "She always talked to us," complained a similarly aggrieved hired girl of her employer, "as if we had no feelings and I was never so unhappy in my life as while living with her." Wrote another: "I have been a servant with many Christians; I have seen many things; I cannot turn to Christianity after this."[19] It is more a comment on the structure of American domestic work than a defense of Mary Lincoln to suggest that the tribulations of young Harriet Hanks with her mistress were typical.

Once when Mary Lincoln was pregnant, she did employ a live-in servant. The 1850 census listed eighteen-year-old Irish-born Catherine Gordon as a member of the household at Eighth and Jackson, and the state census of 1855 indicates that a female between ten and twenty slept at the Lincolns'. Most likely it was the feckless Catherine who inspired Mary Lincoln's comment to her half sister Emilie: "If some of you Kentuckians, had to deal with 'the wild Irish,' as we housekeepers are sometimes called upon to do, the south would certainly elect Mr. Fillmore [the anti-Catholic, anti-immigrant Know-Nothing presidential candidate] next time."[20] And it was probably Catherine who left her window open at night in order to entertain her boyfriends.

Sometimes these girls stayed for two seasons, and Mary Lincoln reported that one "very faithful servant" had become as "submissive as possible." At other times she depended on Springfield's other minorities. In 1849 a group of religious exiles from Portugal had settled in the community, and its wives and daughters were soon at work in low-paying domestic jobs. Mary Lincoln had a long relationship with one of these women, to whom she entrusted the dreaded Monday chore of washing and ironing. Later this woman described Mary Lincoln as "taking no sassy talk but if you are good to her, she is good to you and a friend to you." And from Springfield's black community she employed Mariah Vance twice a week for many years, but after two weeks of undercooked potatoes and watery gravy, she fired another black woman in the shrew's voice that resounded across Jackson and up Eighth Streets. Frequently she had no one because there was no one to have, the demand for domestics having outrun the supply. By the 1850s the daughters of Sangamon County's farmers could get better jobs running sewing machines in the new clothing factory.[21]

Mary Lincoln on occasion did not have help because she refused to pay the market price, and it is her parsimony more than her bad temper that her employment record reveals. She had grown up in a household where no money changed hands for service far superior to that rendered by the Catherine Gordons or Harriet Hankses about whom

Springfield's matrons complained. In fact, Mary Lincoln's Kentucky background compounded her frugality, for she was one of those house-keepers who believed that what they did for nothing should not command a high price when done less well by others. Occasionally, when the Lincoln budget was strained, she economized by not having anyone. As laid-off servants quickly realized, mistresses like Mary Lincoln found self-help an easy way to save money.

Yet Mary Lincoln would have benefited from a permanent house-keeper because she had no daughter to keep her company in the kitchen. The manualist and schoolteacher Catharine Beecher recommended domestic training beginning at six so that by eight a young daughter was a "true" aid to her mother. And of course, it was blasphemous to instruct sons in the mysteries of domestic economy. More than most women, Mary Lincoln needed help, not so much with the housework, although this surely, too, as for the companionship, for she had married a domestic absentee.

Lincoln was gone from home not just overnight but for long stretches of time. In 1846, the year Eddie Lincoln was born, he was on the circuit trying cases all of April, most of May, a week of June, a week of July, three weeks of October, and a week each of November and December. In 1850 he was in Springfield 190 days and away, either on the circuit or in Lexington, Chicago, or traveling, 175 days. In 1852 he was in Springfield 210 days, away 155. And so it went until his nomination for President in 1860 kept him at home longer than he ever had been in eighteen years of marriage.[22]

His wife, who had grown up in a crowded household, now found herself alone save for the children and whatever transient help she commanded. The length and frequency of Lincoln's circuit riding became a perennial aggravation, especially to a woman disposed through former desertions to receive absence as personal injury. "Mr. L. is not at home, this makes the fourth week he has been in Chicago," she wrote her half sister Emilie Todd in 1857, and exasperation surfaced in the phrasing. "I am again at home and Mr. L. in Wisconsin," she complained in 1859. Mary Lincoln was also quoted, though nowhere did she write such a thought, that "if her husband had stayed at home as he ought to, she could love him better." It was a suggestive comment (for *better* may have implied *more often*) from a sexually interested woman. Later her enemies claimed he stayed away because of her, but in fact, he was kept from home by the location of Springfield on the lower axis of the 830 miles separating the courts in the eighth Illinois circuit, the lack of cross-country railroad lines, and the political uses of circuit riding. Indeed, most of his intimates understood how homesick he was for his wife and his sons.[23]

During these long absences Mary Lincoln's fear of robbers, thunderstorms, and the men who paid nocturnal visits to her hired girls increased. Sometimes young single men like Lincoln's law apprentice Gibson Harris (Mr. Mister, she nicknamed him) or her sister's relative Stephen Smith agreed to sleep in the house. Other times she paid a neighbor's child a dime to sleep in the back room or the loft. On occasion she solicited male neighbors, inviting James Gourley into the bed she was sharing with her son Robert. Or so he later said, though to nineteenth-century Americans sharing beds had no necessary sexual connotations. Still, it bordered on impropriety and revealed Mary Lincoln's urgent need for companionship. Later Gourley made Mary Lincoln into the flirt she was with his remembrance that she dared him to kiss her. But she was not the only circuit court widow to suffer neglect. When Sarah Davis of neighboring Bloomington became depressed after the death of a child, Lincoln's friend Judge David Davis took her and their surviving child with him on the circuit. Lincoln ended up with eight-year-old George Davis in his buggy. But two babies were an impossible burden on the road, so Mary Lincoln stayed home.[24]

At home Mary Lincoln was perpetually engaged in the activities that formed the boundaries of wifely experience: feeding the family (and sometimes friends), cleaning the house, supervising the clothes, and bearing and caring for the children. These things she did energetically, for she was never one of those matrons accused by a Springfield newspaper of being "listless, idle and derelict" in their duties.[25] Laziness was impossible because her marriage had caused her to suffer a significant decline in domestic status. What her mother and stepmother had never done in households staffed by well-trained slaves, she did daily, while benefiting from some laborsaving advantages.

By the 1840s improved methods of salting and icing allowed Mary Lincoln to keep food longer than her mother could. Imported oysters, a delicacy on local menus, could be preserved for weeks by bountiful washings in salted water and some help from the weather. A few heretics (Mary Lincoln was not usually one of them) no longer even baked bread, depending, instead, on a wagon that delivered bread, crackers, and cakes three times a week. The Springfield stores were beginning to sell prepared butter, and in season local farmers brought vegetables and fruits down Jackson Street for the unfixed prices that proper ladies were not supposed to contest. Penny-pinching Mary Lincoln was among those who violated the prescription that ladies don't beat down prices, and she had several public battles with the fruit peddler over the price of his less than perfect strawberries.[26]

Her workday began early in the tiny kitchen at the back of the cottage at Eighth and Jackson. There on the cast-iron Thompson range—the type with a flat top permitting kettles to sit on the surface—she started the soup. Some days the coals were out, and it was her husband's job to start them again, though when he was away she did this herself. She used a dry sink for cleaning dishes and preparing fresh produce. In the yard close to the back porch the well pump provided fresh water for drinking and cooking.[27]

Lincoln was never a fussy eater, and was satisfied most mornings with an apple for his breakfast. Still, he would be home for dinner in the middle of the day, and only delinquent housekeepers kept men waiting. But in Mary Lincoln's home it was the husband whose casual sense of time and lack of appetite made regular hours an impossibility. Once, to Mary Lincoln's rising anger, Lincoln arrived two hours late, by which time the chicken was burned. To prevent such disasters and keep her temper, the children frequently were dispatched to bring their absentminded father home.[28]

Sometimes Abraham helped out by shopping, filling his wicker basket with the things his wife had ordered. His office was close to Irwin's and Smith's, where the family bought its dry goods, and because he was more likely than she to be out of the house, there was nothing unusual about his doing the marketing. Unlike so much else, buying food was a shared enterprise between males and females, undertaken, as Mrs. Trollope noted about Cincinnati, "by the smartest men in the place and those of highest standing [who] do not scruple to leave their beds with the sun to sally forth in search of meat, butter, eggs, and vegetables."[29]

Even with improved technology and help with the marketing, cooking took up the largest part of Mary Lincoln's day. Some Springfield women relished their culinary labors and earned awards at the county fair for their pickles, preserves, cakes, and pies. At one time or another all three of Mary's sisters won recognition for their flower arrangements, sewing, and cooking. Mary Lincoln never entered these competitions, or at least she never won a prize. The one household product for which she was remembered—what the family circulated as Mary's recipe for white cake—was a simplified gloss on the more complicated version of a standard cake. Mary Lincoln never sought her particularity through domesticity, which is not to say that she did not manage her home energetically and efficiently, nor that she did not take pleasure in the acknowledgment of her domestic skills.[30]

Having grown up without practical experience in cooking, Mary Lincoln relied on Kentucky staples. Years later, amid the haute cuisine of France, she fondly remembered the "waffles, batter cakes, and egg cornbread—not to mention buckwheat cakes" of Lexington. The Lincoln menu was also full of what Mrs. Trollope disparaged as America's "sempiternal ham," and Mary Lincoln's frugality encouraged the appearance of cheap local game, such as woodchucks, pheasants, and prairie chickens. In any case, she learned to do what the slaves had done in Lexington: roast coffee, make calf's-foot jelly, preserve fruit, and prepare cheese. In the summer the kitchen ran her, and it was both the repetitiveness and the lack of control that led disaffected matrons to compare themselves to slaves. "I am sick of the smell of sour milk and sour everything," complained one weary housewife who had not made her puddings promptly enough.[31]

By 1851, after nearly ten years of housekeeping, Mary Lincoln had progressed to an advanced version of *Miss Leslie's Cookery,* purchasing this, along with *Miss Leslie's House Book or Manual of Domestic Economy for Town and Country,* for eighty-seven cents at Irwin's store. In the more difficult version there were recipes for everything from family soup to the invalid cookery of beef tea and blackberry preserve, the latter recommended for summer dysenteries. Miss Leslie also included directions for the home-concocted cosmetics that Mary Lincoln used for her rouge and face powder. The latter was a boiled mixture of castile soap, French chalk, and Indian meal, which too generously applied gave a fixed, ghostly look to the face. Family purchases of bear's oil, ox marrow, and Lubin's extract for the otherwise all-male household on Eighth and Jackson reveal that under Miss Leslie's direction, Mary Lincoln was also experimenting with perfumes.[32]

Because she had not learned the vices of sugar and, like everyone in Springfield, innocently believed it the "most nourishing substance in nature," she spent hours making puddings, cakes, candies, and cookies. By modern standards, the Lincoln household consumed a vast amount of sugar. Within a week in 1849 Mary Lincoln had purchased thirteen pounds of sugar, and the family's account at Clark Smith's, the all-purpose store run by Mary's brother-in-law, was charged in

1859 for thirty-two pounds of regular sugar, six pounds of crushed sugar, as well as two gallons of syrup.[33]

Some of these sweets were eaten by others, for if Mary Lincoln was a novice cook, she was a practiced hostess with an easy charm that obscured any shortcomings in her menus. Her contemporary Julia Jayne Trumbull acknowledged her as the "prettiest talker in Springfield," and even in her first years as Mrs. Lincoln she belonged in the parlor and front hall, not the kitchen. Her husband's law partner William Herndon may never have been invited to dinner—partly because she was busy and tired and he lived in the city—but many others, especially out-of-towners, were welcome. From Chicago came Isaac Arnold, who praised her hospitality: "Mrs. Lincoln often entertained small numbers of friends at dinner and somewhat larger numbers at evening parties. Her table was famed for the excellence of its rare Kentucky dishes and in season was loaded with venison, wild turkeys, prairie chickens and quail and other game." Later the ungrateful Arnold remained silent at a critical moment in her life, but in the 1850s he had nothing but compliments for her "western welcome, wit and kind manner."[34]

Even Mary Lincoln's considerable hospitality may not have measured up to the rising standards of gentility demanded of America's middle-class wives. No one with young children and untrained help could manage the complex menu Catharine Beecher so unhelpfully recommended for a bride's first dinner party: "Soup, fish, boiled ham, a boiled turkey with oyster sauce, three roasted ducks and a dish of scalloped oysters, potatoes, celery, parsnips, turnips, pudding, pastry, fruit and coffee."[35] With a few days' notice Mary Lincoln's sister Elizabeth Edwards and the other well-staffed kitchens on Aristocrat's Hill could produce such meals, and as a result, elaborate entertaining had come to separate Springfield's rich from its merely prosperous families like the Lincolns.

In her kitchen at Eighth and Jackson Mary Lincoln relied on simple fare, offering her guests not four courses but tea and cakes and strawberries in season. "This last week, we gave a strawberry company of about seventy," she wrote in 1859. "If your health will admit of venturing out, in such damp weather," went one Mary Lincoln invitation, "we would be much pleased to have you, Mr. B, and the young ladies come round, this eve about seven and pass a social evening." By seven Mason and Mary Brayman would have eaten their middle-of-the-day dinner as well as their supper, leaving the hostess responsible only for dessert.[36]

Unlike some of her friends and family, Mary Lincoln did not use her cooking for charitable purposes. In 1852 she had joined the First Presbyterian Church, which her uncle John Todd had helped establish in the 1830s. When the church needed to replace a cracked bell, the women of the congregation rallied to the cause by organizing suppers and money-raising events. But Mary Lincoln never engaged in such philanthropy, though she often invited friends from the church for tea and cakes.[37]

Grown independent during her husband's absences, she sometimes entertained without him. To one of Springfield's most eligible bachelors, Ozias Hatch, Mary Lincoln carefully explained her invitation. "I would be pleased to have you wander up our way to see us this evening altho' I have not the inducements of meeting company to offer you, or Mr. Lincoln to welcome you, yet if you are disengaged I should like to see you."[38] At the time Hatch was the Illinois secretary of state and a prominent Republican. The subject of their conversation would be politics, slanted less to issues than to her husband's chances for public office.

By the mid-1850s Lincoln's prominence required substantial entertainments, and with money available from his successful law practice, Mary Lincoln hosted large receptions—what in the East passed as *levées*. On the prairies, as elsewhere, French was the language of sociability, used by Mary and her friends to distinguish their grandest affairs from the even more elegant *soirées* or *"grand fêtes,"* where there was, according to her, "dancing as well as eating by beautifully dressed beaux and belles."

Instead, she simply put food on the table, and the crowds poured into the house to eat it. "I may perhaps surprise you," went one description to her half sister Emilie, "when I mention that I am recovering from the slight fatigue of a very large and I really believe a very handsome and agreeable entertainment, at least our friends flatter us by saying so. About 500 were invited, yet owing to an *unlucky* rain, 300 only favored us by their presence, and the same evening in Jacksonville Col. Warren, gave a bridal party to his son . . . which occasion, robbed us of some of our friends." (No doubt Mary Lincoln would remember exactly which ones had preferred Colonel Warren's party to hers.) Even with the rain and the competition, this crowd overflowed up the stairs and into the second-floor bedrooms, where the Lincolns had probably dismantled their beds to accommodate the throng.[39]

By 1860, when the Republican National Committee traveled to Springfield to notify Abraham Lincoln of his nomination for President, his wife was an experienced hostess. For these national figures she provided what nineteenth-century women called a fashionable table. Gustave Koerner found a "long table with glasses, a decanter or two of brandy, and a champagne bottle under the table, cakes and sandwiches." For an added touch of elegance, she had stationed William Johnson (who later went to Washington as Lincoln's valet) at the front door to announce the party eminences as they entered first the hallway and then her parlor. But Mary Lincoln had violated custom by including alcohol. Several committeemen from the East favored temperance, and though she argued against a dry party in what Koerner described as a "lively manner," the candidate's wife was informed that it was bad politics to serve any spirits. After her husband's intervention in a controversy that suggested this First Lady would have her own plans for the White House, the brandy and champagne disappeared. Still, the committee found her, as did most of the press, "amiable and accomplished, gracious, and a sparkling talker."[40]

WHILE cooking was an unremitting drudgery, and entertaining an episodic pleasure, for Mary Lincoln cleaning was a daily labor, with biannual climaxes during the spring and fall occasionally delaying even the noon meal. What had been for her mother's generation a private matter had become for her a public concern connected to the female supervision of family health. Doctors established the link by assigning responsibility for infant deaths to maternal neglect. A widely used pediatric manual promised the mothers of Mary Lincoln's day that "the health of children was assured if they were fruitful in the performances of those duties of mothers." Another influential authority calculated that more than one-half of the country's infants died because of their mothers' mismanagement. To hold women liable for medicine's failure was a pitiless, inaccurate, and guilt-raising charge; yet the effect of the awful responsibility of motherhood was to make a clean home a duty. During the cholera watches and typhoid fever vigils in Springfield the first victims were always located in dirty houses neglected by irresponsible women.[41]

Most filth lay beyond the control of even responsible women. Outside the Lincoln home and beyond the brick and picket fence, rooting pigs, roaming ducks and geese, homeless dogs, and escaped horses ate refuse and left their wastes. Like everyone in town, the Lincolns had an outhouse behind their cistern pump which required periodic liming. Sometimes heavy rains threatened the city's surface sanitation system, but inside her house Mary Lincoln aspired to cleanliness, though the means of its accomplishment lagged behind the intention. Springfield's windows had no screens, and like everyone else, she had to choose in summer between insects and ventilation. According to one observer, several broken windowpanes in the Lincoln house offered additional points of entry to the endemic insect population that ranged from chintzes (bedbugs in the East) to cockroaches, flies, moths, and mosquitoes. Without insecticides, eradication depended on hot water (first pumped outside into buckets and then boiled on the stove) and scrubbing. "Boil the roots of a pokeberry plant, till quite dissolved," went one anticockroach remedy, "then mix it with molasses and set it about in old saucers."

The seasonal necessity of cleaning the rugs was equally laborious. (Lincoln may have helped with this chore, although other than keeping the fire and occasionally churning the butter, husbands were not expected to do any domestic labor. Indeed, it was Mary and her sister Frances who usually took care of whatever greenery adorned the outside of Eighth and Jackson.) To clean the rugs, Mary Lincoln first separated the twenty-seven-inch carpet strips and hauled them outside to beat; then she carried them back into the house, less dusty but probably not much cleaner, to be restitched. On this point municipal standards clashed with middle-class elegance. For like every Springfield housewife, she knew it was a hopeless task to have unsoiled rugs in a town with unplanked sidewalks and dirt roads. The solution was to buy new carpets, and by 1856 the Lincolns' nine floor coverings included some Belgium carpets in the parlor, bought at Lauderman's in St. Louis when Springfield's selections proved too plain.[42]

While the new Thompson cooking and heating stoves had advantages (the Lincolns switched from fireplaces to iron stoves in 1849), they were dirty affairs that periodically had to be cleaned, and they left rims of dust through the house. Constantly Mary Lincoln had to refit the astral lamps, however elegant, with wicks and refill them with oil. And the variety of household bric-a-brac the Lincolns were accumulating tested her energy: the oval pictures on the wall; the vases on the mantel; the candleholders, the books, and the Victorian what-not that sold for ten dollars when the family moved to Washington. Nothing was especially valuable or handsome, and the furnishings at Eighth and Jackson remained more practical than decorous. As was true of her grandfather Levi (though not of her father, Robert), Mary's mattresses were the most valuable item in the house. When the Lincolns sold what they did not store before their move to Washington, it was the beds that brought the top price of twenty-six dollars followed by the wardrobe at twenty dollars and six chairs at two dollars apiece.[43]

By the summer of 1856 Mary Lincoln also had a larger house to clean. With money from the sale of the eighty acres given her by her father in 1844, she finished off the upstairs. The improvements, a considerable construction job in the 1850s, took two months and cost $1,300. But on completion, an artisan's cottage had become a proper upper-class house in the popular Greek Revival style, with four new bedrooms upstairs (there had always been a room in the attic, where Robert probably slept) and a back stairway, which took some kitchen space and made eating in the dining room a genteel necessity. The result, according to a New York reporter in 1860, was "a handsome but not pretentious double, two story frame house, having a wide hall running through the center, with parlors on both sides but not ostentatiously furnished. It was just such a dwelling as a majority of the well-to-do residents of these free Western towns occupy." Downstairs there was more public space in the new double parlor, which had been the Lincolns' bedroom. Now husband and wife had adjoining bedrooms upstairs.[44]

Much has been made of the expansion, and in several versions a grander house displayed Mary Lincoln's lifelong extravagance. Actually it was more a consolation, following, as it did, Lincoln's first defeat for the Senate. Supposedly during one of her husband's absences she conspired to spend his money, and on his return from the circuit he is quoted as not believing he lived in such a palace. "Stranger," said Lincoln to his neighbor the cobbler James Gourley as he walked up Jackson Street, "do you know where Lincoln lives?" The joke has been misunderstood. In fact, Lincoln had been at home when the work was planned, though his wife directed and paid for the renovation. Astonishment was the very best way to indicate approval.[45]

Just as time has turned the meaning of Lincoln's compliment, so the couple's move into separate bedrooms has been mistakenly used as evidence that the Lincolns' sexual relationship ended in 1856. In fact, many Springfield couples, including Ninian and Elizabeth Edwards, had their own rooms. Like the double parlor that displayed Betsey Todd's affluence in Lexington, in the 1850s separate sleeping quarters served as a tangible token of the nineteenth century's emphasis on the divided spheres of men and women. Considering the cost of building, it also displayed prosperity in a society in which entire families still inhabited cabins of two or three rooms.

In Mary Lincoln's case there were special reasons for separate bedrooms that had nothing to do with sexuality. Lincoln often entertained visitors in his bedroom, the children wandered at night, and she had migraine headaches that were relieved by quiet and rest. Occasionally both Lincolns read late into the night, she because she had no time during the day, he because he was a confirmed autodidact. "My wife," Lincoln once wrote a friend, "got hold of the volume, read it half through last night," and this was more easily done in a room of one's own. The volume, it turned out, was *Early Engagements,* a romance by Mary Frazear—typical Mary Lincoln fare during these years.[46]

ALONG with the daily cooking and cleaning, housewives like Mary Lincoln also dressed their families. Jane Todd, her paternal grandmother, had woven a wedding dress from Kentucky weeds and throughout her married life had produced her family's clothes from whatever raw textiles were available. Two generations later Mary Lincoln lived in a transitional period between the domestic production of clothing and the purchase of ready-made clothes in stores. In midcentury Springfield hardly a season passed without advertisements "To the Ladies" to buy finished goods from the merchants along courthouse square. Most of these clothes were for children and for men, and as a result, Mary Lincoln bought socks, shirts, coats, and pants for her household. She was, in this as in other domestic matters, precise and exacting. If something was not available in Springfield, she sought it elsewhere. To the wife of the owner of a St. Louis store went a request for "a white fur hat for a boy of six months—with white trimmings and white feather—of the prettiest quality." But at the same time that she bought ready-made goods, she also produced her family's pillows, sheets, and curtains, mending and patching when necessary. During one visit to Kentucky she engineered a plan for her sister Frances to send children's clothes in order to "save me a few stitches." For the same reason, when Lincoln was in Washington, she asked him to buy a pair of plaid socks for Eddie.[47]

Her own dresses were different, and she intended to have outstanding ones. At the time women's clothing remained a cottage industry shared among professional seamstresses, mantua makers, milliners, and their middle-class customers. Like most of these last, Mary Lincoln first chose material, usually at her brother-in-law Clark Smith's or, less frequently, at John Williams's store. Then she took extraordinary care, often returning goods if they were not exactly what she wanted. Sometimes, if the color was not just right, she sent the material to Philadelphia or St. Louis to be dyed. Months later, after it had been returned, she hired a seamstress to make the dress. Finally, after several fittings, she added flounces, tucks, bows, and especially (for they were her trademark) the ribbons that transformed it into an individual creation.

Two decades before, in Mary Lincoln's youth, four yards of material had sufficed, but by the 1850s sweeping crinolines and starched petticoats required ten yards for a best dress. In 1854 Mary Lincoln made plans for a new gown, buying from John Williams several yards of silk, black velvet, and cambric as well as cord, buttons, trimming, and the inevitable ribbons. It would be months before the bell-shaped circular skirt was finished to her satisfaction, although this particular creation had only a few of the theatrical details of her later gowns. Still, she wore pretty clothes. In those days dress decorations were the extent of her luxury buying, and she bought them often—especially when Lincoln was out of town. But she was not as skilled in sewing as her younger sister Ann, who won prizes for her silk embroidery and needlepoint.[48]

The only surviving photograph of Mary Lincoln's Springfield years, taken in 1846 at Shepherd's newly opened Daguerreotype Miniature Gallery near the square, reveals her stylishness. (See the section of photographs, following page 168.) Her face has a pale, tired look, no doubt the result of too heavy an application of cosmetic paste. The dress she has chosen for this special occasion is a rich silk with the ubiquitous ribbons attached as stripes across the bodice. The dress is surely sufficient unto itself, but she has added to the vertical and horizontal stripes a large cameo pin, rosettes on the skirt, white ruffles at the wrists, and a lace shawl. The effect is a cluttered softness and sensuality that later became her trademark. Other matrons posed in solid-colored dresses with a minimum of decoration. Fanny Speed, wife of Lincoln's friend Joshua Speed, added only a tiny collar to her somber outfit, and Mary's older sisters wore prim, plain day dresses for their portraits. But Mary Lincoln's dress is full of reinforcements, with its accoutrements serving, perhaps, as armor.

There was also the matter of headdress. She was bareheaded in the photograph, but her hats were nonetheless important. "Show us a ladies bonnet," the *Illinois Journal* bantered, "and we will tell you what sort of institution she is. Those with red ribbons are full of love; those with simple colors, sweet, sunny and mild; those with ostrich feathers and juniper berries will never see their fortieth birthdays."[49] What Mary Lincoln's bonnets revealed was a lady of high fashion, for she favored the French creations with huge sashes that made women resemble schooners under full sail. By the 1840s American milliners had aped French fashions to the extent that these complex creations could not be homemade. The dainty lace caps of a previous generation—such as that worn by Mary Humphreys, Mary's Kentucky step-grandmother, in her Matthew Jouett portrait—had disappeared, replaced by the monumental headgear of the Victorian lady.

For her bonnets Mary Lincoln searched the stores for the proper colors and materials necessary for such costly additions to her wardrobe. Again, what Springfield lacked she sought elsewhere. Another note to the wife of a St. Louis storekeeper revealed her fastidiousness. "Would you be kind enough," she wrote in 1853, when pregnancy made it impossible to consider anything but a hat, "to have me a drawn satin bonnet made of this brown [which she enclosed], lined with white. I have some small brown feathers for the outside, also outside trimming, which I suppose is not necessary to send down, please have it made to *your* taste, if fine black lace, will be used this fall, perhaps that would be pretty with it, for the outside. I can put the feathers and flowers inside my self."[50]

BESIDES cooking, cleaning, and sewing, Mary Lincoln spent her time raising children. Unlike her mother and stepmother, she received abundant advice from periodicals and behavior manuals on how to do this. Newly self-conscious about family roles, middle-class Americans of her generation had specific notions about proper parenting, in which mothers supervised their children's health, education, and morals, while the power of the father was shifted, though by no means converted, into male companionship, especially with sons. Struck by the decline in male authority, Tocqueville concluded that American fathers of Mary Lincoln's generation "exercised no powers save those granted to affection and the experience of age." Lincoln perfectly displayed this new species. He pulled his boys in carts, took them to the office, baby-sat when their mother went to church, and used reason, not switching, to shape their character.[51]

But as noted, Lincoln was often out of town, and even when in Springfield he was away from home for most of the day and many evenings. His absence left his wife, whose household ran without a nurse, husband, or grandparent, to raise their boys as a single parent. If she did well as a mother, she could expect approval from neighbors and husband. For according to Miss Leslie:

> Best pleased to be admired at home
> And hear reflected from her husband's praise
> That her house was ordered well.
> Her children taught the way of life.[52]

By every account Mary Lincoln excelled as a mother although the state fair awarded no prizes for this until the twentieth century. Even her critics praised her involvement with her sons, although some carped that both Lincolns were too easy on what Herndon called their "brats." There was, for example, the time when the Lincolns were on a train in Kentucky with a relative of Betsey Todd's. He described Bobby and Eddie as "keeping the whole train in a turmoil and their long-legged father instead of spanking the brats looked pleased as punch and abetted the older one in mischief." When the family came to Washington in 1861, parental tactics had not changed. To the disgust of cabinet members, generals, and official Washington, the boys turned the President's official residence into their playroom.[53]

Certainly neither Abraham Lincoln nor Mary Todd intended a family of congenial equals, although her style of mothering repudiated the shaming techniques employed by her stepmother. Usually she was more lenient than even her permissive husband, once berating Lincoln for what must have been his own feeble effort to discipline the "codgers." "We never controlled our children much," Lincoln acknowledged in a statement of pride to Dr. Anson Henry, who had observed as much. Still, Mary Lincoln did not always spare the rod and was likely to use physical punishment to correct moral failings (when the children stole, they were whipped) and on matters of safety. "Since I began this letter," wrote Lincoln when Robert was three, "a messenger came to tell me, Bob was lost and by the time I reached the house, his mother had found him, and had him whip[p]ed. . . ."[54]

There is a suggestion in Lincoln's language that someone else did the whipping, although it was entirely in keeping with his wife's personality that she would lose her temper, spank, and then forgive. Later the selective memories of motherhood erased any need for punishing her sons. Accused in 1865 of whipping her children, Mary Lincoln responded in a letter to the boys' White House tutor: "I am surprised. It is a new story—that in my life I ever whipped a child— In the first place *they,* never required it, a gentle, loving word, was all sufficient with them—and if *I* have erred, it has been, in being too indulgent." In this same letter she laid claim to her motherhood. "My Beloved Husband's great tenderness and gentleness of character, is well established and in his great love for his children, it is well-known, that I bore an equal part."[55]

Mary Lincoln consistently displayed this indulgent maternal disposition, and she was one of those mothers who tolerated no outsiders' complaints about their sons. When the Lincoln children were young, their worst failing was that they were noisy. While her husband realistically assessed their chances (once Lincoln worried that Robert was a "rare-ripe, smarter at about five, than ever after"), Mary Lincoln's view was filtered through the romantic sentiments of Victorian motherhood and her own personality. Her children were "precious," "dear boys," "darlings," and "angel boys." But she did more than lavish endearments. She also permitted, as few other women did, an outstanding menagerie, and in the White House the Lincoln zoo expanded to include turkeys, goats, ponies, and cats. On a trip to Lexington Mary Lincoln was disgusted at her stepmother's rejection of Eddie's kitten. Clearly she would have him keep it, and it became another of her stepmother's failings that Betsey ordered a servant to get rid of the animal. Typically Mary found in Betsey's indifference to her son's crying another display of the maternal cruelty that she had replaced with leniency in her home.[56]

Instinctively Mary Lincoln entered into the spirit of her children's play. When Robert and a friend organized a morning's entertainment based on Sir Walter Scott's stories, she responded with some moral instruction: "Gramercy, brave knights. Pray be more merciful than you are brawny." On a son's birthday she organized what she described as a "children's gala for fifty or sixty boys and girls," addressing the invitations herself and acknowledging afterward that the birthday party had been "a nonsensical occasion." It was rare in the 1850s to celebrate such events, and in this and much else she was ahead of her time. A few years later, when Emilie Todd Helm was soon to be a first-time mother, Mary Lincoln offered as her half sister's future her own self-portrait as "a happy, loving, laughing Mama."[57]

It was an unusual image in an age when behavior manuals commanded mothers to be stern guardians of their children's morality and education. "Are you not only a housekeeper, but a mother?" enthused childless Catharine Beecher in 1848. "Oh sacred and beautiful name! How many cares and responsibilities [you have]. You are training young minds whose plastic texture will receive and retain every impression you make. . . . A whole nation will have received its character and destiny from your hands." Mary Lincoln understood motherhood in less grandiose terms, once remarking that a married niece had won a prize for a silk quilt. "But [Julia] has nothing but her dear husband and silk quilts, to occupy her time. How different the daily routine of some of our lives are."[58]

Intent on making American women the dedicated mother that Mary Lincoln instinctively was, Beecher omitted the dark side of bearing and raising children. Rarely in the celebration of romanticized motherhood did either fiction or prescriptive literature convey the sense of isolation, boredom, and frustration that many women felt. Mary Lincoln's cousin Mary Nash Stuart, expressed this feeling in a letter to her daughter. "There are," she wrote from Springfield in 1858, "a good many strawberry gatherings which are very pleasant, but I am prevented from participation. When my children are grown up, I hope to have great comfort in them, for I have certainly been a slave for their interest the best part of my life."[59]

Many women felt this way, but in Mary Lincoln's publicly observed transactions with her children or her private comments about them during their youth, no hostility is apparent. Her anger had other targets. Some women berated their children in unseen outbursts of temper inside their homes, but Mary Lincoln's fury appeared in unladylike public displays against hired girls and greengrocers. Nor did she affirm what other mothers recognized as the choke on their maternal power: their future dependence as widows on their children. Only years later, with three sons and a husband dead, did she explain that in old age she had hoped that her sons would take care of her. In fact, it was always the other way around.[60]

Certainly Mary Lincoln played a principal part in the children's education. Schooling was a natural extension of the mother's role, although a decision about a son's future fell within a father's jurisdiction. But the self-taught Lincoln acted on his own experience and was nonchalant. "Let them run," he once said of his youngest son, who did not learn to read until he was thirteen. "He has time enough to get pokey." As the daughter and granddaughter of Transylvania University trustees and the veteran of twelve years in school (Lincoln had spent less than a year), Mary Lincoln felt differently. She understood the intangible social benefits of friendship and manners that schools delivered to their students. True to her Todd background, she wanted the best intellectual and social training for her sons.

In 1853, when Mary Lincoln described her son Robert to an old friend, she expressed her pride in academic terms: "Our eldest at ten is studying Latin and Greek." The emphasis, of course, was on the words *at ten*. At the time Robert was learning classics at Springfield's best academy—the misnamed Illinois State University. By comparison to Transylvania and even Madame Mentelle's, it was third-rate. At some point the Lincolns decided that Robert must go not only to college but to the best institution in the country.

Rarely did the sons of even Springfield's wealthiest families venture across the prairies to eastern universities. Among Robert's contemporaries only a handful did so. Ninian Edwards sent his oldest son to Yale, where Clinton Conkling, Merce's son, and Vergie Hicks went as well. (Later, when Vergie ended up in the state insane asylum, Springfield blamed college life at Yale.) John Hay, Lincoln's secretary in the White House and a future secretary of state, went to Brown, and two other sons of Springfield attended, though did not graduate from, Union College in Schenectady, New York. So it was highly unusual when in the summer of 1859 sixteen-year-old Robert left for Harvard, where he failed fifteen of his sixteen entrance exams and needed a postgraduate year at Phillips Exeter Academy before his admission in 1860.

There is no evidence on how the family made this decision, though Mary Lincoln probably encouraged it. Both parents had reasons to keep their eldest son at home—she because she dreaded the separation; he because he disliked the expense and was vaguely suspicious of anything tarnished with snobbery, as a Harvard education certainly was. Robert later explained that Harvard was his idea, though this is unlikely in view of his age and experience. At the very least, in her role as preceptor of the young, Mary Lincoln had instilled expectations of educational excellence in her eldest son. At most her desire for her son's prominence had routed even her desire to have him at home.[61]

Still, she needed her children. It should not be taken as a chilling comment on maternal attachments (which recently have been promoted to an instinct, albeit not a historically observable one) to suggest that like all human relationships, nineteenth-century mothering had its private agendas. In Mary Lincoln's case her passionate maternity transformed her objects of affection into shields for her own vulnerability. Her sensitivity to her children flourished amid her own emptiness. "I hope you may never feel lonely as I sometimes do," she wrote a friend in 1859 on a day when Lincoln was in Springfield and she had two sons living at home. Then she acknowledged that she felt this way even "when surrounded by much that renders life desirable." When Robert went to school in the East, she missed him "so much that I do not feel settled down." After he had been gone a year, she still described herself as "wild to see him." Throughout these years in Springfield the children filled a void, and she went to great lengths to possess their love. Her Lincoln family was so different from the defective one of her Todd childhood that it served as rehabilitation. Removed from any grandparents, Mary Lincoln created a nineteenth-century version of the intense, mother-led, child-preoccupied modern family.[62]

Not only were the children her nighttime protectors (at various times all the children slept in her bed), but she showed the young Lincolns off—a routine mode of proud parenting in the child-centered twentieth century but an unusual one in the 1840s. In Herndon's description, the boys were always dressed up and trotted out before guests "to monkey around, talk, dance, speak, quote poetry, etc." When Mary Lincoln criticized her sister Elizabeth Edwards for "too often dwelling on the merits of fair daughters and a talented son-in-law," it was self-criticism. She overdid the same thing.[63]

Anxiously attached to the children, she hated separations. At a time when most manuals recommended ten months as the time to start weaning infants, she nursed for as long as two years. One of the Lincoln sons was eighteen months old when, according to David Davis, he got "sore mouth from nursing. I guess she ought to have quit nursing sooner."[64] When Robert ate poisonous lime from the Lincoln privy, his mother did not first call for help, but instead screamed, "Bobby will die, Bobby will die, Bobby will die." Today's psychologists might discover here an unconscious projection of angry motherhood, but Mary Lincoln's cry was one of self-preservation. The objects of her affection had been absorbed as part of herself.

BOBBY survived, but in the summer of 1849 his grandfather Robert Smith Todd died suddenly of cholera during his campaign for the Kentucky Senate. Six months later old Grandmother Parker passed away in Lexington. A month later Mary Lincoln was deserted again.

Sometime in December 1849 Eddie Lincoln, age three and a half, had taken sick of what at first appeared to be diptheria. But he survived too long for that rapidly climactic infection of the lungs. In fact, there is some evidence that Eddie had been chronically ill all his life; certainly there was a long sickness in 1848. By mid-January 1850 Eddie was still, in his father's words, "dangerously ill" from what was in fact pulmonary tuberculosis. Consumption (as it was called in accurate description of its wasting course) was the most lethal disease in the United States, and in 1850 more Americans died of it than of anything else, including cholera. Eddie was in a high-risk population: one-half of all the deaths in the United States came in 1850 among children five and under. In the sentimental fiction of the day these young victims never suffered but, like Little Eva of Harriet Beecher Stowe's *Uncle Tom's Cabin,* consoled their parents from their deathbeds just before they were carried off to what Little Eva foresaw as "the love, joy, and peace of a future in Heaven."[65]

Unlike Little Eva, consumption's real-life victims alternated between the hectic glow of high fevers and coughing and lifeless intervals of exhaustion and anorexia that raised and lowered maternal hopes in a pitiless sequence. If Eddie's disease followed the usual course, he coughed, rested, recovered his breath, and then was racked again by coughing. There was no treatment. In the 1840s Springfield's doctors did no more than recommend bloodletting to lessen the excitability of the blood vessels that they believed caused the fever. When the temperature subsided, as it intermittently did in tuberculosis, the experts followed with heroic doses of emetics and purgatives. Corneau and Diller's, the Springfield pharmacists, carried Wistor's Balsam of Wildcherry, a popular anticonsumptive patent medicine full of cough-suppressing opium. No doubt Mary Lincoln added her own therapies, for nursing was a mother's responsibility. She rubbed Eddie's chest with balsam and on his better days probably fed him the recommended thin diet of invalid cooking—panada, oatmeal gruel, and rice jelly.[66]

On February 1, 1850, after fifty-two days of acute illness, Eddie died. The next day the Springfield papers carried the announcement that "the funeral will take place this morning at eleven o'clock from the residence of Mr. Lincoln." Reverend Charles Dresser, the minister at the Episcopalian church, was out of town, so James Smith, the new rector at the First Presbyterian Church and a native of Scotland, said some words in the Lincoln home. No doubt emphasizing God's will, the resurrection of the dead, and the gift of heaven, Reverend Smith, who described himself as an Old Light Presbyterian and whose emotionalism provided comfort for some mourners, so impressed Mary Lincoln that she later left the Episcopal Church to join Smith's congregation.[67]

After the service the body was buried in Hutchinson's Cemetery a few blocks west of the Lincoln house. Most likely Mary Lincoln did not go to the graveyard, for customarily women did not. When her nephew died from typhoid fever in 1860 (of his death she wrote, "I trust never to witness such suffering ever again"), the Todd sisters consoled Ann Todd Smith in her home. Indeed, the entire convention of mourning—the heavy black crepe material and the obscuring veils—encouraged women to hide their grief from public view, for who would console the consolers? Graveside appearances, where women might break down, violated this expectation, so mothers grieved privately. Many years after Eddie's death, when Mary Lincoln's difficult mournings were well known, her neighbors recalled her prostration, weeping, and melancholy. Such memories may have been retroactive creations, but one friend remembered Lincoln's saying to his distraught wife, "Eat, Mary, for we must live." If her grief was such in 1850, then a pattern was already established.[68]

A week after her son's death Mary Lincoln wrote a poem that appeared in the *Springfield Journal*—printed "by request." A mother's production, "Little Eddie," was one of the last times she referred to her son by name. Lincoln may have helped, although his necrology ran to less mawkish poetry, such as Thomas Gray's "Elegy" and William Knox's "Oh, Why Should the Spirit of Mortal Be Proud?" The sentimentality (and spelling, for Lincoln spelled his son's name with a Y) of "To Little Eddie" suggested Mary's authorship. Not only did she employ her special diminutives of maternal endearment, including "sweet Eddie," "angel child," and "angel boy" (and it was an angel that eventually decorated the tombstone), but she described what she had seen: the tubercular "affliction" that fluctuated between "crimson tinge" and

"pallid lips and pearly cheek." In the last stanza the parents said farewell to Eddie, and in this sense the poem represented an effort to do
what Mary Lincoln found so difficult: move beyond the devastating
first stage of mourning to resignation and acceptance.

> Angel boy—fare thee well, farewell
> Sweet Eddie, We bid thee adieu!
> Affection's wail cannot reach thee now
> Deep though it be, and true.
> Bright is the home to him now given
> For of such is the Kingdom of Heaven.[69]

Grieving Christian mothers were encouraged to find comfort in resurrection, and the kingdom of heaven served as a solid defense for
those who had to watch their children die. What Christianity extended
was the possibility of a future reunion, and mothers like Mary Lincoln
were supposed to be mollified by the expectation that heaven was a
better place than earth in which to rejoin their dead children. As
Christian doctrine, resurrection was not new, but it did receive added
emphasis in nineteenth-century America. The Lincolns were not the
only parents to engrave "Of Such Is the Kingdom of Heaven" on a
child's tombstone.

Along with its spiritual directives, proper mourning, like raising
children and running a home, required great fortitude from mothers.
There was in fact a *Mourner's Book* that explained how to submit to the
dictates of God through resignation and acceptance. A typical bit of
fiction in the popular *Mother's Assistant* established the proper response
by comparing two bereaved mothers. After her child had died as the
result of her "mismanagement," the bad mother cried, "I cannot lose
my child, I cannot. She is so bright and promising." Of higher resolve
was the good mother who in her grief "leaned on the Almighty and
meekly bowed her head to earthly things."[70]

Mary Lincoln never achieved this recommended compliance, although
she did believe in predestination, which she interpreted as set against
her. Moreover, her religious ideas were controverted by some distinctly secular views concerning humankind's earthly powers. Mary
Lincoln prayed, according to Emilie Helm, but never accomplished
the recommended "passive acceptance of fate, if she could divert predestination into more pleasant channels. She said to me one day, "What
is to be is to be and nothing we can say, or do, or be can divert an

inexorable fate, but in spite of knowing this, one feels better even after losing, if one has had a brave, whole-hearted fight to get the better of destiny.' " But she never could be consoled by an appreciation of fate, and so spent her life believing herself a marked character.[71]

Mary Lincoln's was a distinctly unfeminine, unchristian position. Because of the multiple occasions for her mourning, a firm adherence to predestination might have provided better shelter. Dedicated instead to fighting destiny, Mary Lincoln raged against Eddie's desertion. Three years after his death she wrote to an old friend that "our second boy, a promising bright creature of four years we were called upon to part with several years ago and I grieve to say that even at this day I do not feel sufficiently submissive to our loss."[72]

THREE weeks after Eddie's death Mary Lincoln was pregnant for the third time. Having lost a son, she would now challenge fate and replace him. Before 1850 she had carefully controlled her childbearing, as did other responsive women of her time who preferred sexual activity to the depleting cycles of conception, pregnancy, birth, and nursing. In the first eight years of her marriage—a period in which both her mother and her stepmother had borne four children—she had delivered two. There was nothing unusual in this conscious fertility. American women, especially native-born whites, had begun to rationalize the process of reproduction that their mothers and grandmothers had accepted as the woman's lot. In Mary Lincoln's generation she and her eight sisters produced, when their families were complete, thirty children, or an average of 3.3 each, while Eliza Todd had seven and Betsey Todd eight. Prudent procreators of the new age used various means to limit their families: extended nursing; withdrawal, which was called "truncated practice" by that generation; abstinence; and sometimes abortifacient patent medicines ironically advertised in the Springfield papers as not to be taken by those in the family way.[73]

Years before the emergence of any organized birth control movement in the United States, thousands of American couples like the Lincolns were not fooled by the obscure title of Charles Knowlton's 1832 handbook of contraceptive information, *Fruits of Philosophy: The Private Companion of Young Married People*. While this volume had only a small underground circulation, its methods circulated by word of mouth. In Springfield married women sent away for similar pamphlets about reproduction, the contents of which, disguised in brown wrappers, remained a mystery even to nosy mailmen. Newly marrieds did not have to go to such trouble. According to one Springfield doctor, couples received free circulars "offering information and instrumentalities and all needed facilities by which the laws of heaven in regard to the increase of the human family may be thwarted." And an increasing number of bold female lecturers discussed female physiology in the Masonic Hall, using mannequins to illustrate their points.[74]

In December 1850 Mary Lincoln bore her third son. She named him not after a public figure but after the kind brother-in-law who had helped during Eddie's illness. As was her custom, Mary Lincoln nursed William Wallace Lincoln longer than the recommended year, but finally, in June 1852 eighteen-month-old Willie was weaned. A few weeks later, because little Willie must have a playmate, she was pregnant again, and in April 1853 the last of her children—Thomas Lincoln, named for Lincoln's father—was born.

The largest of her babies, Tadpole, promptly shortened to Tad, earned his nickname from his huge head, which injured his mother during his delivery. Two doctors attended her, and she remembered Tad's birth as so difficult that "instruments were on hand if they should be required." Like his brothers, Tad nursed longer than most Springfield infants, and during this period Mary Lincoln doubled as a wet nurse for a neighbor's child whose mother was ill. Unbeknownst to her—for even Mrs. Palmer's popular physiology lectures did not teach this—her husband had inadvertently played a fateful trick. "A son," Cousin Elizabeth Todd once wrote, "is a son until he gets a wife but a daughter is always a daughter." And Mary Lincoln, a woman who especially needed one, had no daughters.[75]

VI

The Politics of
Marriage

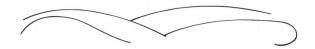

In 1860 a reluctant Abraham Lincoln provided his supporters with an autobiography as lean and spare as his body. He covered his ancestry, birth, and childhood in four pages, spent another four on his political career, and covered his family in three impersonal sentences: "In Nov. 1842 he was married to Mary, daughter of Robert S. Todd of Lexington, Kentucky. They have three living children, all sons—one born in 1843, one in 1850 and one in 1853. They lost one, who was born in 1846." Once Lincoln joked about having had enough sense to marry a Kentuckian, and to Grace Bedell, a young admirer who urged whiskers as a way to gain votes, he wrote: "I have no daughters. I have three sons—one seventeen, one nine, and one seven, years of age. They, with their mother, constitute my whole family." Such references were among the few Lincoln ever made to his marriage, although secondhand recollections of what he is supposed to have said and thought abound. These should be viewed with suspicion, for Abraham Lincoln was the most reticent of men, and his domestic affairs remained veiled by propriety and by his own detachment.[1]

Nor did Mary Lincoln ever write about their marriage—at least not until Lincoln's assassination had transformed a human relationship into a spiritual event. Then she forgot the fight that had temporarily ended their engagement and remembered only that "It was always, music in my ears, both before and after our marriage when my husband told me, that I was the only one he ever thought of, or cared for."

But even before her widowhood the nature of her parallel life with Abraham Lincoln was critical to her existence in a way that was never the case for him. Nineteenth-century wives worked out their destinies within relationships that became the sum of their experiences, and Mary Lincoln accurately portrayed the meaning of marriage when she referred to her husband as her "All." Wives had nothing besides the frameworks of a domesticity imposed by their husbands, and marriage became for them a comprehensive arrangement involving sex, companionship, affection, childbearing and raising, economic support, and work, with spouses providing the only arena in which they might display their talents. In Mary Lincoln's time and place, the accepted rules for a wife's behavior required submissiveness, purity, and piety. Mary's friend Kentucky Senator John Crittenden advised his newly wed daughter: "I have never seen a wife who made her husband happy that was not happy herself. Remember this. Kindness and gentleness are the natural and proper means of the wife. There are wives who seek to rule, to make points with their husbands and complain—ay, scold. To love such a woman long is more than a mortal can do."[2]

Within this male-imposed structure, Mary Lincoln's union with Abraham Lincoln nonetheless involved individual expressions of power and mutual expectations about its exercise. This is always the case. Like the setting of a ring, the social and cultural customs of pre-Civil War Springfield framed the Lincolns' marriage, while like the special stones that ornament a setting, Abraham Lincoln and Mary Todd established their own variations on the themes of nineteenth-century marital politics. Love, ever the opiate of female mentalities, had nothing to do with this. As a modern observer has written, marriage must be seen as "the balance and management of sovereign spheres between man and wife. . . . Marriages go bad not when love fades—love can modulate into affection without driving two people apart—but when this understanding about the balance of power breaks down."[3]

On the surface Abraham and Mary Lincoln balanced well. They complemented each other as if nature and circumstances had carefully divided their spheres of influence so as to make the symbol of their marriage the recommended two halves of an intertwined circle. He was tall and thin; she, short and always tending to, if not, fat. (Once he joked that he was the long and she the short of it, though she hated the jest and refused to be photographed beside him.) On his bad days he was depressed and melancholic; on hers she became excited and hot-tempered. He was sometimes fatherly in his behavior toward a woman he called a girl and more proprietarily his "child-wife"; she was ardent and seductive. He was scruffy in dress, she fashionable; he was plebeian and unschooled, she aristocratic and snobbish. He was humble in the manner of the self-confident; she was egotistical in the way of self-doubters. He was on good terms with everyone; she, on bad terms with many.

Mary Lincoln recognized their reciprocal natures, once commenting that "notwithstanding our opposite natures our lives have been eminently peaceful." Her sister agreed. "They knew each other perfectly," Frances Wallace wrote. "They did not lead an unhappy life at all. She was devoted to him and his children and he was certainly all to her a husband could have been." To say that Mary Lincoln had no counterpart for his complexity of thought, brilliance of prose, and powers of logic is to say nothing that would not have been true of most Americans. In general terms what he lacked she provided (and vice versa), and their courtship had flourished in the excitement of this contrariety.[4]

Once married, Mary Lincoln reigned within the domestic sphere at a time when husbands were turning over to their wives control of the home. Certainly Lincoln exceeded most in his delegation of authority. "Lincoln never interfered in the management of the children nor with her domestic arrangements," Emilie Helm observed. Even Herndon acknowledged that Lincoln exercised "no government at home."[5]

Accorded an unchallenged sovereignty, Mary Lincoln turned energetically to the task of gentrifying her husband. It was common enough for wives to feel themselves the guardians of home and family morality and to serve as exemplars of Christian virtue. It was unusual, even in cross-class unions, for them to supervise so closely their husbands' manners, clothes, and social behavior. But Mary Lincoln had been brought up in aristocratic Lexington and had fixed notions of how the head of the household should look and act. For Lincoln, she provided a marriage-long course in middle-class etiquette.

Some members of her family believed she was too stern a taskmistress, and one told her so: "If I had a husband with a mind such as yours has, I would not care what he did." Still, she persisted, attending to his suits as well as his manners, and it is not surprising that the largest purchase the Lincolns made during their first year of marriage was his new suit of "superior black cloth." Ever after she battled to make his pants longer, his socks match, and his waistband conform to his natural contours. But she was not always successful. After seven years of marriage he appeared once in public with a bobtail frock coat and jean pants that ended sixteen inches above his ankles.[6]

Mary Lincoln did more than dress him. When they were first married, he answered the door in his shirtsleeves—a double breach of etiquette. In Miss Leslie's and Catharine Beecher's manuals, servants and children intercepted callers, and the master of the house never appeared in disarray. Under his wife-mother's direction, Abraham Lincoln learned to stay away from the door. There were other lessons to be learned, including not rubbing his hands down the front of his trousers. "Why don't you dress up and look like somebody?" she said often enough to be remembered as saying it. "She played," wrote Herndon, "merry war when he persisted in using his knife in the butter rather instead of the special silver-handled one." On another occasion she explained to her sister that she was training her husband to see color. "I do not think he knew pink from blue when I married him." And after he was dead, she claimed success, noting that his manners had "got quite polished."[7]

WHILE taking charge of home, raising her sons, and reconstructing her husband, Mary Lincoln trespassed into the male sphere of politics, and this intrusion became the most notable feature of her marriage. Her husband's law practice, the source of the family income, rarely concerned her, though Lincoln had important cases that he typically disparaged as "a great variety of little things." In time these "little things" came to include murder, corporate infractions, fraud, divorce, and the defense of nine Clinton, Illinois, women charged with riot for the destruction of a saloonkeeper's liquor. Envious of the legal matters that kept him away from home, Mary Lincoln thoroughly detested the roughneck Herndon, whom he had taken on as a partner in 1844. But mostly she was indifferent to his profession because unlike politics, the law with its learned canon available only to insiders excluded amateurs.[8]

After 1853 Mary Lincoln had an additional reason to dislike the law. That year her brother Levi masterminded a frivolous suit in which her husband was named as a defendant, and she, with him, became subject to an attachment of $750. In a legal claim that was soon dropped because there was no basis for it, her father's firm (renamed Oldham and Hemingway after Robert Smith Todd's death) alleged that Abraham Lincoln had converted to his own use money collected for them from their Illinois customers. Lincoln was on the circuit when this disturbing news came, and he described himself as indignant at the suit. Alone in Springfield, where she was recovering from Tad's delivery a month before, Mary Lincoln was furious at Levi Todd and no doubt contemptuous of the system that allowed such claims.[9]

Politics was different, and toward the advancement of her husband's public career she turned her considerable energies. Having discerned that the road to a shared prominence ran toward Washington, not the dusty courtrooms of the eighth Illinois circuit, Mary Lincoln fought to make herself her husband's chief adviser on patronage and appointments. Never was she much concerned with issues, however. Like many Americans, she delivered judgments on parties and personnel, but nowhere among her 600 surviving letters is there a reasoned exposition of her political views. By no means was her marriage the American counterpart to that of Harriet Taylor and John Stuart Mill: Mary Todd did not instruct Abraham Lincoln in antislaveryism, although she knew a good speech when she heard it and was quick to criticize her husband's inferior productions. Instead, at times to Lincoln's liking and on occasion to his exasperation, she used her peculiar enthusiasm for politics to get a distracted man's attention. Such a strategy had worked with her father, and with her husband it yielded more lasting results than, as she also did, throwing books and once a log at him.

Mary Lincoln's attraction to politics emerged from certain personal deficits, for there was no better way to fill an empty self than to be involved in a partisan campaign that provided notoriety, adulation, competition, and, if things did not go well, enemies. What she meant to contribute to her husband's endeavors was the special intuition with which females—and none more than she—were endowed. In return she expected to gain recognition, and thus her interest in public affairs displayed a quirky feminism located not in principle but in the psychological necessity to be somebody.

Lincoln's male advisers resented her unseemly usurpation of their authority. Behind Mary Lincoln's back (and after Lincoln's death, publicly) they called her ambitious, the insulting antithesis, when applied to females, of the modest deference sought in wives. Disfranchised and discounted, the wives of Lincoln's advisers and most public men of this period either remained indifferent to public affairs or actively opposed their husbands' participation in such an unrespectable calling. Judge David Davis's wife, Sarah, encouraged her son not to be a politician. "Life seems too valuable to be wasted in the turmoil of politics." Sarah Davis continually threw what she called "cold water" on her husband's political career until the judge finally acknowledged that he no longer listened to her. "I love her too much to thwart her views." Julia Trumbull was preoccupied with her son's failures at school and cared not at all for public events, while Eliza Browning, though she had no children of her own to take up her time, hardly knew a Republican from a Know-Nothing.[10]

By comparison to these conventional women, Mary Lincoln suffered. A woman interested in politics would pass unnoticed today. But in her day a woman absorbed in public matters—no matter what the reason—was a meddling deviant. The supporters of women's rights who ventured to Springfield in the 1850s earned only ridicule for their activism, and for the sake of respectability Mary Lincoln's family always insisted she was, in Frances Wallace's words, "a domestic woman who loved her family above all." In many ways she was domestic, but she was also political. When callers came to Eighth and Jackson, she sometimes leaned out the second-floor window to inquire if they wanted Lincoln for "business or politics." Some said her door opened only to those who answered "Politics."[11]

No doubt her Todd heritage sparked some of this interest. Yet with the same background none of the other Todd daughters in Robert's first and second families was the least concerned with public affairs. Neither Frances Wallace nor Ann Smith had a political husband, nor did either seek one, as Mary Lincoln had in her courting days. Elizabeth Edwards never participated in Ninian's partisan adventures, save to give parties, and even when he was the state superintendent of public instruction, his wife paid little attention.[12]

By the 1850s Mary Lincoln did not need to travel with her itinerant husband to enjoy the public recognition that he, and she through him, were attaining. In her imaginative projection of their life together she had become his collaborator—a full-fledged, home-based counselor available for insightful judgments about the human motivations that were the core of politics. The story of her parallel life with an American hero can be understood only through her involvement in public affairs. Politics had brought them together; politics must remain, from her point of view, a joint enterprise.

IN the late spring of 1846 Abraham Lincoln received the Whig nomination for Congress, and in August (nonpresidential elections were held in the summer) he became one of Illinois's seven congressmen. Neither his nomination nor his election was a surprise. Lincoln and the Whig triumvirate that included Mary's first cousin John Todd Stuart, her third cousin John Hardin, and her son's namesake Edward Dickinson Baker had agreed to rotate what was, at the time, a safe seat for the Whigs, who took their name from the English party that had opposed the tyranny of seventeenth-century Stuart kings. All three men supported the Whig doctrines of an active government, a national bank, and the chartering of corporations. Lincoln, however, did not take office for a year, and in the meantime he discovered, in the way this melancholy man often did about his public honors, "being elected to Congress—has not pleased me as much as I expected."[13]

If Lincoln's pleasure in his congressional status did not match his anticipation, his wife's delight exceeded hers. When she first met Lincoln, he had seemed a rising star, but he had not held public office since 1841. Now his wife intended to share his success by going to Washington. "Mrs. L., I am told," David Davis wrote his wife, "accompanies her husband to Washington city next winter. She wishes to loom largely." In the fall of 1847, when Congressman Lincoln left Springfield, he took with him his twenty-eight-year-old wife, their four-year old son Robert, and Eddie, their one-and-a-half-year-old son, who already showed signs of the tuberculosis that killed him in less than three years.[14]

It was unusual even for childless wives to accompany their husbands to the national capital. It was exceptional for mothers of young infants to travel the 1,626 miles that the freshman congressman calculated as their travel distance for reimbursement at forty cents a mile. As a result, Washington's boardinghouses were crowded with married men whose families had stayed home. In the previous Congress, only 72 of 221 representatives had brought their wives, and in Lincoln's Congress—the Thirtieth—the proportion was lower, 73 of 239. Most of these women were either from nearby states or were rich enough to pay the rents charged by landlords for comfortable houses on Capitol Hill or off Pennsylvania Avenue. Mary Lincoln was neither.[15]

On the way the Lincolns stopped to visit Mary's father and step-mother in Lexington. Betsey had never met either Mary's husband or children, so the Lincolns followed the cumbersome route to Mary's birthplace: by stage to Alton, then the river steamer to St. Louis, next a change to another steamer, downriver to Cairo, up the Ohio to Carrollton, down the Kentucky River to Frankfort, and finally the jerky three-car train into Lexington. It took ten days, and they spent the next three weeks in Kentucky before continuing to Washington—this time by stage, by steamer, and finally by railroad from Winchester, Virginia, through the Harpers Ferry gorge and along the Potomac into Washington. They arrived in December 1847, spent their first night at Brown's Hotel, and then took up boarding at Mrs. Sprigg's on Carroll Row—just across from the Capitol where the Library of Congress stands today.[16]

Lincoln's predecessors—Edward Baker and Mary's cousin John Stuart—had recommended Mrs. Sprigg's. As the Whig exception in his state's all-Democratic delegation, the new congressman preferred to board with fellow party members than to live with Democrats even from his home state. By this time in national history congressmen who voted together lived together in boardinghouse "messes" that carried party labels. The "war mess" had been the name of Henry Clay's boardinghouse in 1810, and names such as Tallmadge's or Clayton's or Barbour's in honor of these respective congressmen were often attached to a house. Certainly the location of Mrs. Sprigg's house was convenient for a man impatient to get, as Lincoln wrote Herndon, "the hang of the House."[17]

The abolitionist leader Theodore Weld had stayed at Mrs. Sprigg's a few years before the Lincolns. "I will tell you," he wrote his wife, Angelina, in 1842, "how I am situated. Mrs. Sprigg's is directly in front of the Capitol. The iron railing around the Capitol comes to within fifty feet of our door. Our dining room overlooks the whole Capitol Park which is one-mile around and filled with shade trees. I have a pleasant room on the second floor with a good bed, plenty of covering, a bureau table, chairs, closets—a good fireplace." When Angelina worried about the food, the vegetarian, dyspeptic Weld reassured her: The "pitcher of milk [is] always at my place—graham bread and corn bread—mush once or twice a day—apples once a day and at dinner potatoes, turnips, parsnips, spinach with eggs, almonds, raisins, figs and bread puddings. Pies, cakes, I have of course nothing to do with."[18]

In Weld's day there had been twenty boarders, only one of whom, the Ohio abolitionist Joshua Giddings, had brought his wife. In Lincoln's time there were ten other boarders, most of whom were Whig congressmen. None had brought his wife. Only when the neighboring Duff Green family came for meals was there a break in the male atmosphere and partisan commentary. Amid the tobacco spitting and scabrous jokes, Mary Lincoln (for one of the few times in her life) was remembered as "very retiring." Samuel Busey, a physician boarding at Mrs. Sprigg's, also recalled Robert as "getting his own way" and entirely forgot Eddie, then a nursing infant kept in the Lincolns' tiny room.[19]

Typically Mary Lincoln did not get along with all the boarders. Her husband would later send her the "love of those in the house with whom you were on decided good terms . . . the others say nothing." These others had probably irritated her by criticizing her children, who were the only ones there. No doubt she responded angrily, but there was little she could do about the complaints. The foul Washington weather kept mother and children inside and gave rise to noisy play. Tubercular Eddie was sick and must have cried a good deal. Even Capitol Park, where Weld walked, ran, and jumped for an hour every day, could not be enjoyed by a mother with a sick baby. Still, Mrs. Sprigg did have domestic help, and the slaves who were buying freedom with their wages watched the children when Mary Lincoln went out.[20]

The Washington that Mary Lincoln relished the winter of 1847–1848 ("you know I enjoy city life," she later wrote) became the standard for her metropolitan preferences. Certainly the city was the biggest, most cosmopolitan community either she or her husband had ever seen, though snobby Europeans disparaged the American capital as parochial. After his visit in 1842 Charles Dickens had dismissed it as "a city of magnificent intentions with spacious avenues that begin in nothing and lead nowhere." A disgruntled French diplomat who believed himself in a hardship post complained that "the so-called city of Washington is neither a city nor a village—it has a desolate look." Certainly the fields that separated every two or three houses gave the place a rustic air. This especially struck Europeans who were accustomed to dense, urban centers like London and Paris, where culture, commerce, and politics were assembled in one location. Women found the federal city especially trying. Harriet Martineau held it the least agreeable place of her American travels, and an anonymous English lady of fashion considered a winter in Washington "a season in purgatory."[21]

With neither London nor Paris as her benchmark, Mary Lincoln thought differently. Washington was smaller and less elegant than New York, Philadelphia, and Baltimore, but it was still the nation's ninth-largest city with 38,000 citizens, some impressive public buildings, an established society, and a lengthening heritage as the center of the Republic. During the 1840s the town nearly doubled in population, and by the end of the decade Washington was on its way to becoming a sophisticated city. More important, the capital embodied the legendary aspirations of a new political experiment. An idea planted in the emptiness of the Potomac flats, Washington, D.C., was the first city in the world to be created exclusively as a center of government. For an ambitious woman it was the place where powerful men made history.

Of course, some features of its small-town origins lingered. Capitol Hill no longer resembled a small New England town, as it had in the 1830s, but as in Springfield and Lexington, the pigs wandered along the unplanked streets, and garbage, dead animals, and human waste littered every neighborhood. Only the lower part of Pennsylvania Avenue was cobblestoned, and until 1847 there were no streetlamps in the city. The sewers from Capitol Hill drained into the mall, but what is today the elegant Ellipse was, in Mary Lincoln's time, a fetid marsh. There were cow sheds next to the Capitol grounds, and when Congressman Lincoln bowled in the alley behind Mrs. Sprigg's or in the bowling saloon opposite the south gate to the Capitol grounds (ten rolls or thirty balls for six and a half cents), the chickens, ducks, and geese took noisy flight. The front of Mrs. Sprigg's boardinghouse afforded a splendid view of the imposing Capitol building, but out back—only three blocks away—Samuel Busey discovered "a loathesome [sic] community of the debauched, debased and drunken." Busey did not mention another neighborhood disgrace: the crowded slavepens where southern representatives sometimes shopped for humans.[22]

But for a woman who once told a childhood friend that she had to marry a man who would take her to the theater, Washington offered splendid opportunities. In 1848 the fabulous Mrs. George Jones starred at the Olympian Theater, while Mrs. Arthurson sang Verdi at Carusi's. Both would have been special events in Springfield, but in Washington they were merely part of the winter-long season that also included minstrel shows. Twice Mary and Abraham Lincoln went to Carusi's saloon, where the black-faced Ethiopian Serenaders performed songs, dances, and jokes. For young Robert there were puppet shows at Christmas and band music in the park when the weather wasn't too miserable. The shops on lower Pennsylvania had fancier goods than Mary Lincoln had ever seen in Springfield, and the hostesses gave more elegant parties than even Betsy Todd could have imagined. The Lincolns also attended some official functions. They went to the New Year's reception at the President's House, though this occasion was a required performance about which guests privately complained. On March 1 they attended a delayed Washington's National Birth Night Ball, for which Abraham Lincoln was an unlikely manager.[23]

For Mary Lincoln the best entertainment was always politics, with her husband playing a leading role. And these were dramatic times. In 1845 the United States had annexed the independent republic of Texas, inflaming Mexican-American relations. The following year President Polk had ordered General Zachary Taylor to take up a position in disputed territory across the Rio Grande, which led to skirmishes between the two armies and some casualties. Lincoln's party opposed the apparent drift toward war with Mexico. Despite his freshman status and uninteresting (though not unimportant) committee assignments, the Whig congressman from Illinois determined to make his mark on the Thirtieth Congress.

Just before Christmas Lincoln was recognized by House Speaker Robert Winthrop, and the next day he offered his spot resolutions, which, if voted, would require the "President of the United States to inform the House whether the spot of soil on which the blood of our citizens was shed was or was not Mexican." Most Whigs believed that the disputed territory where Americans had been killed was in fact Mexican. If they were right, then President Polk's reasons for going to war against Mexico were invalid. As a Whig Lincoln intended to embarrass the Democratic administration during a conflict his party opposed. But like most politicians, the young congressman insisted he had a higher intention than partisan advantage. "Allow the President to invade a neighboring nation, whenever he shall deem it necessary to repel an invasion, and you allow him to . . . make war at pleasure," he wrote Herndon.[24]

The galleries in the ornate red and gold House of Representatives were full that December 1847, and again on January 12, 1848, when

Lincoln expanded on his antiwar, anti-Polk themes. No doubt Mary Lincoln was in the audience that heard Lincoln criticize the President in his longest speech of the session. In a remarkable personal attack for a man who usually discussed principles, not people, Lincoln said of Polk, "He is a bewildered, confounded and miserably perplexed man. . . . God grant he may be able to show that there is not something about his conscience more painful than all his mental perplexity." In April Lincoln spoke again, this time on less sensitive matters relating to his assignments on the post office and military expenditure committees.[25]

His wife did not hear his April speeches. Sometime in the spring Mary Lincoln had retreated to Lexington, a casualty of boardinghouse confinement. While she knew several senators' wives, including those of Crittenden and Douglas as well as Mrs. Congressmen John McClernand and Robert Smith, she had nowhere to entertain—save what even her boardinghouse-habituated husband called "this old room." She was also alone a good deal. Rarely did the conscientious Lincoln miss a session, and he faithfully attended the Whig evening caucuses. His attention to duty impressed his fellow boarder Samuel Busey, who described him "as attending to business, going promptly to the House and remaining until the session adjourned." But Lincoln's industry left his wife with two small children in a city where, no matter what its allures, she could not attend parties without her husband, as she had in Springfield.[26]

Clearly Lincoln encouraged her departure, although when she was gone, he missed her. "In this troublesome world," he wrote in the spring of 1848, "we are never quite satisfied. When you were here, I thought you hindered me some in attending to business; but now, having nothing but business—no variety—it has grown exceedingly tasteless to me." Soon he wanted her back, and in modern ears there is a patriarchal ring to his bargain: "Will you be a good girl in all things, if I consent? Then come along, and that as soon as possible . . . I shall be impatient till I see you. . . . Come on just as soon as you can." But she did not come promptly. By July the lonely congressman had capitulated. "Father expected to see you all sooner; but let it pass, stay as long as you please and come when you please."[27]

In Lexington Mary Lincoln missed her husband, too, and she wrote often, although only one letter has survived. It was a wife's production full of family news and complaints about her stepmother who, "if she thought any of us were on her hands again, . . . would be *worse* than ever." Yet behind the lines ran a strain of sexuality. Mary Lincoln was a reticent Victorian woman who never made explicit references to sex or even anatomy. Like most females of her time and class, she took pains to keep her private concerns private, discussing sex only in connection with reproduction and then mainly when talking to women and doctors. Even in a letter she wrote some years later to a close female friend she referred to an injury she had sustained during Tad's birth as "a disease of womanly nature." But then she crossed out this obscure reference as if the mere mention of such matters were indecent. In this light her letter to Lincoln suggested that this nineteenth-century wife had not become so absorbed in her children as to deny her husband or herself sexual warmth. From Lexington in May 1848 she wrote: "How much I wish instead of writing, we were together this evening. I feel very sad away from you. With love I must bid you good night." Then she scratched through "With love," knowing that this night she would not physically love her husband.[28]

This letter also revealed the subtle balance of power between husband and wife. She had been banished to Kentucky (though no doubt with her concurrence); still, she held the means of influencing her return. Her uncle James Parker was traveling north. "I believe it would be a good chance for me to pack up and accompany them—you know I am fond of sightseeing. . . . But perhaps dear husband like the *irresistible* Col McClernand [a Springfield congressman] cannot do without his wife next winter, and must needs take her with him again—I expect you would cry aloud against it—How much, I wish instead of writing, *we* were together this evening, I feel very sad away from you." Then Mary encouraged her husband to come to Lexington and Crab Orchard when the session ended. But if he didn't come, "I must go down about the time [Mr. Webb was at the springs] and carry on quite a flirtation, you know *we,* always had a *penchant* that way." Of course, Lincoln knew, for her dalliance had disrupted their romance in 1841, and as she no doubt intended, hers was not the slightest of threats.[29]

Such bantering was one way Mary Lincoln limited her husband's power. In the face of his paternalism (she had to ask him for money, which he sent in care of her father), Mary Lincoln imagined other husbands. No doubt such fantasies grew out of Lincoln's obsession with death and the fact that he was a widow-producing nine years older than she. But they also emerged from her coquetry and flirtatiousness. So Mary Lincoln teased her husband about future mates, who, she once wrote Emilie Helm, would be rich and able to take her to Europe. Apparently the discussion of her matrimonial possibilities was a recurrent theme in their marital politics, and Lincoln responded by agreeing that she might get "so well and fat and young as to be wanting to marry again. Get weighed and write how much you weigh." This was Lincoln's way of getting back at his plump wife, who used tight-laced corsets to look slender in a society that decreed thinness essential to beauty.[30]

In the summer of 1848 the Lincolns were reunited and, with the two boys, traveled across New York State, saw Niagara Falls (Lincoln wondered where "all that water came from"), and took the steamer from Buffalo across the Great Lakes. After nine days they arrived in Chicago and returned by train to Springfield. They had been gone for nearly a year, and for Mary Lincoln this was the first of many long odysseys. Some women, she once wrote, "cannot feel comfortable away from home"; she was never one of them.[31]

But she did not return to Washington for the second session of the Thirtieth Congress, though the house at Eighth and Jackson was still rented. Eddie was now sick; the trip was expensive, and the lame-duck session was expected to end before General Zachary Taylor's inauguration as President in early March. But with a case before the Supreme Court it was April before Lincoln returned to Springfield. In the meantime, Mary Lincoln made a sentimental choice and boarded at the Globe with her two sons.

When her husband returned, he was gloomy about his political prospects. Ridiculed as "Spotty" Lincoln, he had become notorious for his unpatriotic objections to President Polk's war. The signing of the peace treaty with Mexico in February 1848 brought the United States a vast western territory, and those who had opposed the war became easy targets for the Democrats. Although the Whig nomination for Congress from Illinois's Seventh District now rotated to another eager partisan (in this case Mary's cousin Stephen Logan), Whigs held Lincoln responsible for the loss to a Democrat of what had been a safe seat. Everywhere Abraham Lincoln was condemned as having inflicted "a deep and mischievous wound on the whole Whig party."[32]

These bleak moments (and there were several in Lincoln's political career) stimulated Mary Lincoln's behind-the-scenes participation. She consoled, encouraged, and, extending conventional female deportment, advised. An unchecked ascent from Vandalia to the White House would have chilled Mary Lincoln's serious involvement in her husband's career, for there would have been no point at which to intrude. But amid his reverses Lincoln listened to his wife. As a result, theirs was a more companionate marriage than the separated halves of his public life and her private one. To be sure, Mary Lincoln's essential contribution to her husband's eventual success lay in her faith in his ability, a traditional spouse's donation. But in keeping with her need to make a mark, she transformed the usually wifely applause into an inspirational prophecy of his greatness, which cause she intended to advance. The record is full of those who remembered Lincoln's saying that his wife expected him to be President, to which idea he responded with bemused astonishment, at least until November 6, 1860.

After his catastrophic congressional term Lincoln nonetheless determined to have a patronage post. He had been a loyal, if controversial, congressman, and these were Whig times with Zachary Taylor in the White House. Others with less service to the party had been rewarded, and the commissioner of the Land Office, which paid $3,000 a year for little work, was traditionally held by an Illinoisian. In fact, Lincoln's former antagonist, the Democrat James Shields of the Broadswords affair, had just resigned it. There were other contenders, including Lincoln's friend Edward Dickinson Baker and Ninian Edwards's cousin Cyrus Edwards. Lincoln hesitated, but by the late spring of 1849, with only one other contestant still in the field, he determined to have it.

The competition took him back to Washington, and in his absence his wife undertook a letter-writing campaign to gain President Taylor's attention. During the hot days of June 1849 she played her supporting role, writing in her careful slanting hand to important Whigs in the Midwest: "It is now certain that either Mr. Butterfield or I will be Commissioner of the General Land Office. If you are willing to give me the preference, please write to President Taylor." And to at least forty others: "Would you as soon I should have the General Land Office as any other Illinoisian? If you would, write me to that effect." At the bottom she signed "A. Lincoln."[33]

In the end Lincoln lost, partly because he was still remembered for his opposition to the war. Later the Whig administration in Washington offered him two lesser plums—first, the secretaryship of the Oregon Territory, which he had no trouble refusing, and then, though he was not Taylor's first choice, the more acceptable $3,000-a-year governorship of Oregon. He hesitated over the latter, though Mary Lincoln was opposed. Certainly it was a political promotion for a

one-time congressman to become a territorial governor. To the surprise of many, Lincoln declined, and there was never any doubt in
Springfield that his wife's opposition had been a critical factor. Both
the newspapers and his friend Anson Henry described his reasons as
"private" ones.[34]

Mary Lincoln had solid grounds for her objections, ranging from
the difficulty of the trip (two children of the incumbent governor had
died of yellow fever rounding Cape Horn), her reluctance to live in a
frontier community the primitiveness of which had been vividly
described by friends, Eddie's frailness, and the poor prospects this
Democratic territory held for a Whig. Left to himself or with a more
compliant wife, Lincoln might have chosen political exile. Herndon
once quoted him as saying it was "a good thing I am not a woman,
for I cannot refuse anything." But after his wife's veto he told friends
that his political and economic prospects in Oregon were not as good
as those in Illinois. All things considered, that stood as an accurate
prediction.[35]

During the next six years Lincoln's political career stalled. Mary
Lincoln was busy with two new babies, and while her husband continued to be an active Whig, his party was disappearing. A political shift
had begun in the early 1850s as voters gave up their established allegiances and as parties gradually identified with sectional interests. In
1849 Mary Lincoln's friend the seventy-year-old Senator Henry Clay
had emerged from retirement to seek reconciliation over the stubborn
issues related to slavery and national expansion that increasingly divided
Americans into northerners and southerners. When Clay failed, her
former suitor Senator Douglas presented a compromise bill designed
to resolve differences arising between northerners and southerners over
such nagging concerns as fugitive slaves and the balance in the nation
(and Congress) between slave and free states. Because Douglas was a
more effective negotiator than Clay, the Compromise of 1850 finally
passed.

It did not, however, end the shift of party allegiances. The free-soil
movement, the organizers of which believed that slavery blighted the
economy and that free labor and slave labor could not coexist, was on
the rise in the North. Partisans everywhere sensed changes during this
period of political realignment. Even the persevering Lincoln described
himself as "unwhigged." In Springfield the anti-immigrant, anti-
Catholic Know-Nothings gained in strength and for a time seemed to
hold the future. Lincoln attended a meeting, but later he dismissed

them. "I am not a Know-Nothing. How could I be? . . . When the Know-Nothings get control, [the Declaration of Independence] will read that all men are created equal, except negroes, and foreigners, and Catholics."[36]

In the summer of 1854, amid these shifting party allegiances, Cassius Clay, Mary Lincoln's childhood friend from Lexington, arrived in Springfield. The issue of slavery in the territories would soon dominate national politics, but in the wake of the 1850 Compromise it was still one among several public concerns. But not to Clay, whose abolitionist newspaper the *True American* had already been destroyed by a Lexington mob and who had never been a tepid, milk-and-water antislavery man. So radical was he that Springfield's town fathers denied him the statehouse rotunda for his speech. Instead, in Mather's Grove on the west side of town, he delivered the sharpest attack on slavery that local audiences had ever heard: "Slavery must be kept a sectional, and liberty, a national institution. It is not the part of American freemen to act as bloodhounds for the slave hunter." The *Springfield Journal* deemed it a "Heroic Speech." But Democratic papers described Clay as a "foul traitor meditating the destruction of the country." During his two and a half hours of oratory Clay observed Abraham Lincoln, "the husband of my old friend of earlier days," lying on the grass whittling, while Mary Lincoln sat on a nearby wagon.[37]

Earlier that year Senator Douglas had set the stage for Clay's comments. As the chairman of the Committee on Territories the Illinois senator had shepherded the Kansas-Nebraska Act through Congress. By voiding the time-honored prohibition on slavery in territories north of 36° 30′ (a latitude that ran through southern Missouri), this new legislation disrupted the political balance between free and slave states. Douglas held to the theory that Americans should choose for themselves whether they wanted slavery or not; in practice the Illinois senator believed laws of climate, production, and geography would exclude the institution from most of Kansas and Nebraska.

Still, many Americans now saw that under Douglas's scheme the West would be available for the "peculiar institution," and it was this terrible possibility that propelled Cassius Clay to charge that slavery, not freedom, was being nationalized. Many northern and western Democrats were similarly offended by Douglas's bill, and the resulting political disruption surfaced in Illinois. When Springfield's Democrats blew off cannons of celebration—one volley each for the 133 congressmen who had voted for Douglas's policy of remanding to local communities the decision over slavery—Whigs, Free-Soilers, Know-Nothings, and defecting Democrats denounced their senator as a puppet of the southern slaveocracy. Later Douglas wryly noted that he could travel from Washington to Springfield by the light of the bonfires burning his effigy.[38]

Six weeks after Clay's speech Douglas appeared at the Illinois State Fair to campaign for the Democratic legislative ticket. Through his efforts the senator hoped that Illinois would elect state legislators who, in turn, would send a member of his party to join him in the Senate. Held on the grounds of the Farmers and Mechanics Association west of Springfield, the fair was only a year old, but amid consideration of hogs, cattle, and jellies, politics quickly intruded. Mary's sister Ann Todd Smith had just won an award for her embroidery when Douglas delivered a speech that, in a downpour, was moved to the statehouse. There, under cover, Illinois's senior senator ranged through the themes that he and Abraham Lincoln were to dispute for the next six years. At the end of Douglas's speech Lincoln, who had been sitting in the front of the hall, rose to announce that either he or another opponent of the Kansas-Nebraska Act would reply.

At two o'clock the next day it was Lincoln who challenged Douglas's views on popular sovereignty, advancing his propositions with the interrogatories that soon became a hallmark of a political style learned in the law. "What natural right requires Kansas and Nebraska to be opened to slavery? Is not slavery universally granted to be a gross outrage on the law of nature?" For three hours Lincoln talked with a range and power grounded in the conviction that slavery must not enter the Northwest. And as Lincoln had done in Douglas's audience, so afterward and then again in Peoria two weeks later, the Little Giant rose to dispute Lincoln's argument that the original intention of the framers was to keep slavery out of the Northwest.[39]

Among anti-Democratic, anti-Douglas partisans, Lincoln's performance was such a success that he was soon running for the state legislature, at the same time that he surveyed the larger prize of the United States Senate. At home he received encouragement from Mary for ambitions that were mutual. A newspaper reporter who shared a train ride with Lincoln quoted him as saying, "Mary insists that I am going to be Senator and President of the United States too," at which Lincoln shook with laughter at the thought of "such a sucker as me President." Henry Whitney, a lawyer who traveled the circuit with Lincoln, recounted a similar incident in which Lincoln used the words of *Macbeth,* his favorite Shakespeare play, to acknowledge "my dearest partner of greatness."

What David Davis distastefully described as Mary Lincoln's desire "to loom largely" was a wife's service to her husband's self-confidence, though in Mary Lincoln's case the expectations were grand. To live with a woman who expected the White House (but who might settle for Mrs. Senator Lincoln) was a perpetual tonic for a man whose fluctuating career and episodic depressions encouraged surrender. He was, after all, a successful lawyer and could have so remained. Without her he might have been a U.S. senator and President, but with her he was guaranteed a public career. On the other hand, without him her need for distinction would have floundered; with him a precarious self found fortification in fame.[40]

In November 1854 Lincoln won a seat as a state assemblyman, but belatedly discovering that the Illinois Constitution made newly elected legislators ineligible for election to the United States Senate, he resigned. To his embarrassment, a Democrat won the special election for his replacement. The papers described his gaffe "as a family decision," by which they meant that his wife had played a part, and Mary Lincoln may have demanded that he move beyond the position of legislator, which he had already filled four times. To others Lincoln explained his resignation with the farfetched justification that he had supposed he was helping the state ticket, especially his friend Richard Yates, by running for the legislature.[41]

Done forever with local office, Lincoln now campaigned for the United States Senate, calling in political debts amassed during seventeen years of circuit riding. "Some friends," he wrote to other friends, "are really for me for U.S. Senator." To another: "I have really got it in my head to be U.S. Senator." And to a third: "You used to express a good deal of partiality for me, and if you are still so, now is the time." Lincoln expected these supporters to lobby the state legislators who could elect him senator. Before the legislature met, Lincoln calculated the preferences of each member. New affiliations and party names made this a more difficult enterprise than it had been in the two-party days of Whigs and Democrats. By 1855 an unpredictable array of Know-Nothings, Anti-Nebraska Democrats, Free-Soilers, temperance advocates, as well as Whigs and Democrats, sat in the legislature.[42]

During January 1855, in the week before the state legislature was first to nominate and then to elect a senator, a great blizzard cut Springfield off from the rest of the world. The meeting of the legislature was postponed, the courts were closed, and Abraham Lincoln had nothing to do but think about politics. So he and Mary measured his chances, filling several tiny notebooks with the name and partisan disposition of each legislator. By their count, his chances were good, for there were forty-one Democrats, thirty-seven Whigs, and nineteen anti-Nebraska Democrats. If these last supported him, as there was every reason to expect, he would win easily.

Three weeks later, with high expectations, Mary Lincoln, Elizabeth Edwards, and their visiting half sister from Lexington, doe-eyed Emilie Todd, climbed the stairs to the gallery that overlooked the semicircular legislative chamber. Most likely the three women arrived early, for only those in the front rows of the balcony could see the entire room, and only then by craning their necks over the railing. On the first ballot of the joint session Mary Lincoln's champion led with forty-four votes; the ubiquitous Shields of the Broadswords affair had forty-one, and seventeen other votes were scattered among several candidates. Lyman Trumbull, Lincoln's friend and the husband of Mary Lincoln's bridesmaid Julia Jayne, had five. Throughout the afternoon roll calls, to Mary's chagrin, her husband's total went no higher. Like many another front-runner, he had received his maximum support, and his opponents now searched for a compromise candidate. Finally the legislature adjourned for supper.

In the evening balloting a Democrat was gaining when Lincoln released his supporters and threw his votes to Trumbull, who was promptly elected. Later Lincoln explained that "it was hard for the forty-four to surrender to the five and a less good humored man than I, perhaps would not have consented to it—I could not, however, let the whole political result go to ruin on a point merely personal to myself." In other words, Lincoln had elected Trumbull rather than see a Democrat win, although he was "splendidly consoled" by the thought that the Democrats were "worse whipped than I." He wrote his friend Elihu Washburne, "I regret my defeat, but I am not nervous about it," by which he meant he was not depressed.[43]

By several accounts his wife was. She could never take rebukes lightly. Nor did she carry the sort of ideological protections that made the cause more important than the person. Always her one-dimensional view of politics focused on who won, not on who else lost. From her perspective, an aspiring politician with nearly a majority should not deliver his support to a competitor with only a handful of votes. She would never have done so. Besides, that evening her sister Elizabeth

Edwards, the inveterate hostess, had planned a reception to honor the Lincolns, and though Elizabeth suavely replaced Mary and Abraham Lincoln with Julia and Lyman Trumbull, Mary was humiliated. At the party Lincoln extended his hand to Trumbull, but Mary Lincoln withdrew hers permanently. Thereafter Julia and Mary were enemies, and Mary dismissed her intimate friend as "ungainly," "cold," "unsympathizing," and "unpopular," even a "whited Sepulchre," by which she conveyed the idea that Mrs. Trumbull was dead to her. A year later, when these two met outside church, as Julia Trumbull described it, "I took pains to meet Mary but she turned her head the other way and pretended not to see me." Even the negotiating talents of their mutual friend Anson Henry failed to put back together what politics had sundered.[44]

The friendship ended because Mary Lincoln believed that Julia Trumbull could—and should—have influenced her husband's politics. Extrapolating from her own marriage, she thought a true friend would have encouraged her husband to deliver his few votes to Lincoln's greater number. With them Lincoln would have required only two more and could have gotten these from the anti-Nebraska Democrats. Incorrectly Mary assumed that other women had as much influence over their husbands' political careers as she had, so she held Julia accountable for Lyman Trumbull's behavior. (When, in another instance, Ninian Edwards became a Democrat, she was outraged at Elizabeth as well as Ninian for this duplicity.) In the case of Trumbull, Mary Lincoln was not alone in believing the new senator had followed a deceitful course. Both David Davis and Isaac Arnold never forgave what Davis called his "cold selfish treachery." The only difference was that they did not extend their judgments to his wife, as Mrs. Lincoln did.[45]

In the 1850s Mary Lincoln's circle of friends dwindled as she continued to graft partisanship onto her private affairs. Relationships became extensions of politics, and her party was ever the Lincoln one of her marriage. To be sure, Lincoln was often despondent after defeat, but he was never angry because as a politician he anticipated a bittersweet alternation of defeats and victories. Lacking this professional perspective, Mary Lincoln created enemies out of rivals. Sometimes her fury helped prod Lincoln from his dejection. Not many nineteenth-century women employed the language of vilification that she adopted from politics. Antagonists were "dirty dogs," "connivers," and "dirty abolitionists." (Mary Lincoln, like her husband, was against the extension of slavery but not, like the abolitionists, for its immediate eradication.) Nor was she above the kind of mud-slinging accusations that abounded during campaigns. Of her husband's friend Norman Judd, who had voted consistently for Trumbull, she later claimed, with only light gossip as her guide, that "if Wall Street testifies correctly, his business transactions, have not always borne inspection."[46]

To some Springfield neighbors, Mary Lincoln was so incurably hostile as to do permanent damage to any friendship. By her own calculations she did not initiate disagreements; she merely responded, though of course she was incapable of brushing off even a minor provocation. (In Washington this sensitivity made the gossipmongers' job easy.) What she could not admit was that the mildest criticism stoked the fires of vulnerability that had burned since her childhood losses and that now escalated skirmishes into wars. Rather than forget, she harbored grudges, collected injustices, and rehearsed her anger. Once when an acquaintance gossiped about her payment of a seamstress's bill, Mary Lincoln condemned the woman to hell: "In another world she may discover when too late, what the fate of a liar and hypocrite is."[47]

Her best-known, longest-lasting, and most annoying antagonist was William Herndon. He precipitated their quarrel when as her dancing partner he likened her waltzing to the gliding of a snake, after which comment she left him alone on the dance floor and never, for she controlled the social invitations at Eighth and Jackson, asked him to her house. By the early 1850s, when she and Herndon were competing, in his phrase, "To educate Lincoln up to action," their rivalry fueled an already profound dislike.[48]

If foes like Herndon were villains, friends were allies, and like any good precinct captain, Mary Lincoln demanded loyal service from her friends. "I want you to spend the month of May with us," went a typically exigent note. Like her clothes, her demands on her friends were conspicuous claims for attention. "Remember that I shall expect you—I shall claim the month." And to a friend who had changed her mind about a visit: "You must keep your word. . . . I feel I must have you with me. I have set my heart on having you with me. If you love me give a favorable answer." The context was personal, but the importunity was as much derived from her favorite vocation of politics as from her personal sense of entitlement.[49]

AFTER her husband's defeat in 1855 Mary Lincoln's emerging sense of herself as a political counselor appeared in her explanations of his policies. Not only did she review editorial opinions for her busy husband, but when a Kentucky friend of the Todds proclaimed him "a nigger lover," she took on the role of interpreter. Lincoln might be a member of the newly formed Republican party (he was at its organizing convention in 1856, though he had not been among its national founders in 1854), but she meant everyone to know that he was not an antislavery fanatic. To Emilie Todd Helm, who had married into a politically prominent Kentucky family, Mary Lincoln explained that "although Mr. L is, or was a Frémont man you must not include him with so many of those who belong to that party, an Abolitionist. In principle he is far from it—All he desires, is that slavery shall not be extended, let it remain where it is."[50]

Perceptively she recognized that the days of Democratic hegemony in Illinois were ending. William Bissell had defeated a Democrat for the Illinois governorship in 1857, and the same year another Republican, Richard Yates, had replaced a Democrat in Lincoln's congressional seat. According to Mary Lincoln's analysis, "the Democrats in our state have been defeated in their Governor, so there is a crumb of comfort for each and all. What day is so dark that there is no ray of sunshine to penetrate the gloom." The political weather improved further when her husband received 110 votes for vice president at the Republican nominating convention of 1856, after which he joked: "There is a great man named Lincoln in Massachusetts and he must be the one for whom votes were cast." Meanwhile, at home Mary Lincoln was, according to Herndon, "like a toothache, keeping her husband awake to politics day and night."[51] Said Abraham in one reported conversation: "Nobody knows me." Said Mary: "They soon will."

By 1858 there was another opportunity for her Lincoln party. The Republicans hoped to carry the legislature and then elect a member of their party to replace the incumbent Democrat in the U.S. Senate. With his wife's encouragement Lincoln won the Republican nomination. In the four years between his senatorial campaigns he had become such an active party leader that one client complained that "he had more politics than law on his mind." Save for his momentary lapse in 1854, Lincoln had avoided the lesser offices of state legislator, state senator, and even congressman, and in this selectivity he was influenced by his wife's undaunted vision of the White House. Amid his uncertainties he still needed someone who dressed him with importance—as well as matching socks.[52]

In 1858 Lincoln's senatorial opponent was his wife's former suitor Stephen Douglas. By early summer the two candidates—one with a national reputation and intent on the presidency; the other with a self-described "poor, lean, lank face with no cabbages [of patronage] sprouting forth"—agreed to debate seven times across the length and breadth of Illinois. From Freeport in the north to Jonesboro in the south, from Quincy in the west to Charleston in the east, they argued about the extension of slavery, the Dred Scott decision (in 1857 the Supreme Court had ruled that slaves were property and as such could not become American citizens), and whether American slavery would grow or wither away. With more campaign money than Lincoln, Senator Douglas traveled in a private railroad car bedecked with flags and accompanied by a secretary, a reporter, a band, and his beautiful wife, labeled the Belle of Washington by the Democratic newspapers. Lincoln went differently—sometimes by ox-drawn wagon, sometimes by railroad, more often by stagecoach. His wife stayed home.[53]

Mary Lincoln rarely saw her husband that summer. When not debating Douglas he was speaking at crossroads, witnessing balloon ascensions, debating in picnic groves, and trying to, as his wife explained, put "a little life" into the Republican campaign for legislators who, if elected, could vote him to Washington. In all Abraham Lincoln gave sixty-three speeches between August 12 and October 30, and he traveled 4,200 miles, missing even the fall session of the courts. Once he managed a political rarity when he delivered a sixty-second speech at Petersburg. But for the most part Lincoln needed more than an hour to explain, and sometimes defend from misrepresentation, his theme that "A house divided against itself cannot stand. I believe this government cannot endure permanently half slave and half free."

Lincoln was home, however, for a July 4 celebration at which he toasted the Pioneer Fire Company of Springfield: "May they extinguish all the bad flames, but keep that flame of patriotism ever burning brightly in the hearts of the ladies." During this holiday the Lincolns may have collaborated on what had become a fixture of his campaigns: an eight-page tabulation of the probable voting behavior of each legislative district in Illinois.[54]

Mary Lincoln did her own campaigning, though it was restricted to Springfield. Anyone who would listen heard that Douglas was "a very little giant" beside "my tall Kentuckian." She may also have pasted the newspaper accounts of her husband's speeches into the scrapbook that he later edited and that became the standard text for the Lincoln-Douglas debates. But as his prominence grew and what he had earlier called the "cabbages" of influence sprouted, she was relegated to the traditional female role of helpmate rather than partner. As such she was ready with coffee whenever her husband returned home with the retinue that increasingly attached itself to him.[55]

In mid-October Mary Lincoln did travel to Alton to hear the last of the debates. Obligingly the Sangamon–Alton Railroad ran a special half-price excursion train from Springfield, and the Lincolns, along with son Robert, were aboard. Fifteen-year-old Robert, who was to leave for Harvard the next year, was a member of the Springfield Cadets, and grandly attired in a dark blue gold-trimmed coat and white pants, he took part in the ceremonies that his father had once dismissed as the "fizzle-gig and fireworks" of campaigning. Thousands of others came by horseback, carriage, wagon, and steamer.

It was a cloudy, threatening day, and when the train arrived, only the Democrats seemed to be celebrating. Somehow (or so it seemed to Mary Lincoln's sensitive ears) the cheers for the "Little Giant," "No Black Republican," and "Popular Sovereignty" drowned those for "Old Abe" and "Free Territories and Free Men." Although Alton was Democratic territory and the Republican candidate was not expected to win there, both Lincolns, especially Mary, were depressed. So when Lincoln saw the Republican state legislator Gustave Koerner, he encouraged him "to go up and see Mary. Now tell Mary what you think of our chances. She is rather dispirited." Koerner, who had known Miss Todd from his student days at Transylvania, went up to the hotel room and assured the candidate's wife that "we will carry the state and we are tolerably certain of carrying the Legislature."[56]

The debate must have reassured her, too, for Alton witnessed one of Lincoln's best performances. And he had the advantage of Douglas's hoarseness, which made it possible for the audience to hear the Little Giant's voice but not his words. According to their prearranged schedule, Douglas started and closed. During his hour, as he had throughout the summer, the senator accused Lincoln of extending the Declaration of Independence to blacks. He cast as radical abolitionism Lincoln's prediction that a house divided against itself cannot stand and offered, as his solution to the national troubles over slavery in the territories, popular sovereignty based on local decision.

When Douglas finished, Lincoln responded for an hour and a half. There were those who said that with or without the five-foot-four

Douglas as his opponent, Lincoln always seemed seven feet tall on a platform. No doubt he appeared so to Mary. Certainly he spoke more quickly than Douglas (the published transcript reveals the extent of the difference), and sometimes his high-pitched voice, according to one observer, "stopped for repairs before finishing a sentence." What was memorable about Lincoln's speech at Alton was not his delivery but the clarity, the logic, and the chaste expression of complex ideas.[57]

In rebuttal Lincoln accused his opponent of "garbling" his stand on equality, and then, switching to the attack, he challenged Douglas on slavery. "The real issue in this controversy is the sentiment on the part of one class that looks upon the institution of slavery as a wrong and another class that does not look upon it as a wrong—that is the real issue. It is the eternal struggle between these two principles that have stood face to face from the beginning of time. . . . Douglas looks to no end of the institution of slavery."

On this point Lincoln, who himself looked to no sudden end to the institution, took the moral high ground, leaving for Douglas the shoddy inconsistency of community control over slavery. In fact, Douglas had earlier said that he didn't care whether "slavery was voted up or down," and though taken out of context, the comment does not distort his position that abstract propositions should be sidestepped because they lead to uniformity. The senator favored diversity, but as Lincoln pointed out, Douglas had once supported the Missouri Compromise, which had established the regularity of no slavery in the new western territories. When Lincoln finished, the crowd cheered, and his supporters threw dahlias and roses onto the platform. Probably he had changed few votes, for party prejudices were firmly fixed. But in the way that audiences sense a transcendent moment, those at Alton knew themselves to be part of history.

Two weeks after the Alton debate the Democrats won the legislature, though the Republican vote increased. In January Douglas was elected to a third term in the United States Senate by a vote of fifty-four to Lincoln's forty-six, and what Lincoln called the "emotions of defeat" again settled into the household at Eighth and Jackson. By November 15, 1858, just two weeks after the election, the defeated candidate pronounced himself "convalescent." A week later a philosophical Lincoln was typically pessimistic about his political future. "The losing campaign," he assured Anson Henry, had given him a "hearing on the great and durable question of the age,—and though I now sink out of view, and shall be forgotten, I believe I have made some marks that will tell for the cause of liberty long after I am gone." The local newspapers were less highblown and simply complimented him for taking his defeat in "a good-natured way as any sensible man would."[58]

Meanwhile, he was broke—or at least he thought he was. Every time Lincoln turned his undivided attention to politics he sacrificed income from his law practice. "I shall go to the wall for bread and meat if I neglect my business this year as well as last," he said in exaggeration to one of his wealthy friends. Earlier he had described himself "as on expenses so long without earning anything I am absolutely without money now for household purposes." Still, he did not give up politics but in 1859 combined his legal duties with political appearances in Illinois as well as—for his national reputation was growing—Kansas, Iowa, Ohio, Indiana, and Wisconsin. Despite his comment about his recovery, some friends found him intermittently depressed about his defeat.[59]

Mary Lincoln convalesced, too, for Douglas had defeated not just Lincoln and the Republican party but a political partnership. Her consolations were womanly in nature and, like her husband's, characteristic. In April she began another dress and went seven times during that month to her brother-in-law Clark Smith's store, where she spent forty dollars on six yards of plaid silk, ten and a half yards of cambric and cashmere, and assorted ruches, chenilles, buttons, and stockings. She underestimated the amount of material she needed and in May had to return for more of the expensive silk. By July the dress was finished, and her husband paid thirty-eight dollars to Mrs. LaBarthe, Springfield's Irish-born dressmaker, who used her French surname to advantage in the local competition for customers.[60]

Although it is impossible to separate family from personal items, Mary Lincoln shopped often in 1859. After Lincoln had collected a contested fee of $4,800 from the Illinois Central Railroad, she certainly had more money to spend. But only a few women went as frequently as she to John Williams's general store or to Clark Smith's, where everything from turkeys to cashmere material was for sale. Some women avoided shopping entirely by sending husband or children; she sent her sons and Lincoln but went herself as well. That year she spent $196.55 for her clothes, and the cost of just one of her dresses represented two months' pay for a typical Springfield family. One thrifty father reported that his family of five lived comfortably in Springfield on $404 a year—$120 for rent, $284 for food and fuel—with nothing spent on clothes because of his wife's dexterity with a needle. On the prairies a careful wife was considered worth a year's rent. But Mary Lincoln no doubt compared herself to the fine ladies of New York and Washington, who spent ten times as much on their wardrobes.[61]

Unlike her thrifty neighbors, Mary Lincoln bought things she did not need and sometimes returned purchases that did not suit. Her cousin Mary Stuart decided that "Mary seldom uses what she has," though utility was no longer the point of shopping in a society that measured middle-class status by the gap between the essential and the superfluous. Cousin Mary had been raised when the dry goods store was the only shopping place, and her generation resisted the flood of goods that loosened purse strings. Still, Mary Lincoln's purchases were different from those of other women of her generation because they established a pattern of buying undertaken, as with the extension of her home in 1856, to make restitution for personal and political defeats. With shopping a necessitous private compensation, she could have lived at no worse time. The casual credit arrangements of Springfield's stores (some accounts were collected once a year) placed the moderation of Mary Lincoln's buying with an inattentive husband.[62]

IN 1860 Mary's Lincoln party was again enmeshed in politics, and this time the prize was the presidency. Early in the year Abraham Lincoln's name began to appear on the mastheads of the Republican papers in Illinois, and soon he was spoken of as a presidential possibility outside the state. He did not have much of a public record, but he had given several important speeches that had impressed party leaders. More important, he had few enemies. His friends found him, amid the clamor, as unassuming (and uncertain) as ever. In his correspondence Lincoln seemed not to covet the presidency, and with characteristic self-deprecation he wrote a friend that he did not think himself "in candor" fit for it.[63]

His actions suggested otherwise. For $400 Lincoln purchased a German-language newspaper—the *Illinois Staats-Anzeiger*—and leased it back to its editor with the stipulation that it support the Republican party. He also traveled to New York City during the winter to give a political speech at Cooper Institute. If he was not famous before, he was after this powerful repetition of his position on the Dred Scott decision and the meaning of the Constitution. Warily he refused to support any other Republican candidate, saying of Salmon Chase what he said of himself: "He is not suitable." When pressed for a choice, Abraham Lincoln picked the weakest prospect in the field: Edward Bates of Missouri. To his nemesis Senator Lyman Trumbull he sent a warning: "[y]ou better write no letters which can possibly be distorted into opposition or quasi-opposition to me. There are men on the constant watch for such things, out of which to prejudice my peculiar friends against you.[64]

Still, as his wife knew, Lincoln was a long shot. He had held no public office since his disastrous congressional term twelve years before, and there were better-known contenders when the spring of 1860 arrived. Salmon Chase was the favorite of antislavery Republicans, and unlike Lincoln, the aggressive Ohioan held no reservations about his suitability. Then there was the sleazy Pennsylvania senator Simon Cameron, whose support of high tariffs attracted those who wanted to sidestep slavery for less disruptive issues. The colorless Bates of Missouri appealed as a compromise candidate if the Republican National Convention deadlocked. Looming above all these possibilities was the front-runner, New York's Governor William Henry Seward. In such company Lincoln seemed an outsider, despite his growing prominence. Ironically, his losing senatorial campaign and the debates with Douglas remained his best advertisement. For like a Siamese twin, Stephen Douglas, the Democracy's strongest candidate for the presidential nomination in 1860, carried Abraham Lincoln everywhere.

Moreover, Lincoln's cadre of "peculiar friends" was working hard for his nomination. Somehow they had persuaded party leaders to hold the Republican convention in Chicago. Even before nearly 500 delegates, assorted newspapermen, and party followers arrived in the city, Lincoln headquarters had been established in the Fremont Hotel, five blocks from the Republican convention site, that architectural oddity at Lake and Market streets known as the Wig-Wam. From their rooms Norman Judd, David Davis, Isaac Arnold, and Orville Browning sallied forth to cajole and promise in the name of their man in Springfield. Of course, every contender had lobbyists. But Lincoln had the fewest enemies, and he became a popular second choice, though many Republicans were betting on a first-ballot victory for Seward.[65]

When the voting began on May 18, 1860, Seward was still the favorite. The large Republican delegations from New York, Wisconsin, Michigan, and California supported the New York governor, who led on the first and second ballots. But Lincoln was second and gaining. On the third ballot those who would not have Seward took Lincoln, and he won. Later the convention agreed to a platform that supported the Declaration of Independence, denied that the Constitution carried slavery into the territories, and approved the right of each state to "order" its own domestic institutions. Many Americans were more familiar with these ideas than with the Republican candidate. In some parts of the country editorial writers wondered who Abraham Lincoln was. Both the author of an early campaign biography and the chairman of the Republican National Committee spelled his name "Abram," requiring a correction by the candidate.[66]

Neither Abraham nor Mary Lincoln was in Chicago for the convention, though Mary would have enjoyed this recognition of her clairvoyance as much as any event in her life. Now she was somebody, and friends who flooded the house acknowledged as much. But in the custom of the day candidates did not seek public office, which was a gift of the people. Such a view kept candidates and their wives from the convention and, if they won the nomination, from campaigning.

Lincoln did not violate tradition. He had been playing handball when the news came, turned pale, and went to tell his wife immediately. Then he stayed home for more days than he ever had before, describing himself to a friend as "shut up in Springfield." He wrote letters, corrected misapprehensions about his position on slavery, and hosted the party's great and greedy when they traveled to Springfield to assess the candidate and their cabinet chances. First came Seward, then Chase and Cameron, followed by Horace Greeley, and the Mexican chargé d'affaires Matías Romero. In between, newspapermen, photographers, and fellow citizens arrived. Some found Lincoln in the office set aside for him in the state Capitol; others (and by September there were as many as 100 a day) went to his home, where they met his wife. Most believed, along with a reporter of the Springfield (Massachusetts) Daily Republican, that "it is not often in good taste for visitors to bring ladies in any way before the public but I shall be proud as an American citizen when the day brings Mary Lincoln to grace the White House."[67]

Overnight Mary Lincoln had become public property, a role for which she was ill prepared despite her interest in politics. Henceforth she was of two minds about this awful but wonderful prominence. On the one hand, she remembered that the ladies of her generation were never mentioned in the press, save—and only a few then—after death. Female abolitionists and suffragists gained no respect from her; she believed them unwomanly creatures. She had no interest in obtaining the vote, intending instead to influence her husband. On the other hand, she delighted in favorable press reports that she was, according to the *New York Tribune,* "amiable and accomplished . . . vivacious and graceful . . . a sparkling talker." What Mary Lincoln was unprepared for was the inevitable rebuke, which as every politician including her husband knew, lurked in glory's shadows.[68]

Certainly most reporters were not prepared for her. In the past political wives (with a few exceptions that included Mary Lincoln's distant relation by marriage Dolley Todd Madison) were so retiring as they stood mutely behind their husbands that the press forgot them. Newspaper gossip about females was limited to young single women like Senator Chase's beautiful, auburn-haired daughter Kate and President Buchanan's niece Harriet Lane. From the beginning Mary Lincoln was different. Her knowledge of politics made good copy, and those newspapermen and favor seekers who failed to find Lincoln found in her a talkative, intelligent informant at Eighth and Jackson. To one visitor Mary Lincoln told of the election bet she had made with her neighbor Mrs. Bradford, the bookseller's wife. At stake was a pair of new shoes. (When Lincoln won, Mrs. Bradford, a good Baptist who believed gambling a sin, paid off with a new Bible, not the shoes). With other visitors, Mary Lincoln discussed patronage until she became known as the new administration's kitchen cabinet.[69]

To all comers that summer of 1860, Mary Lincoln acknowledged her anxiety over the outcome, though she was too well versed in politics not to appreciate the opportunity presented her husband by a split in the Democratic party between Douglas as a northern candidate and John Breckinridge as a southern one, along with a third-party candidate—the Constitutional Unionist John Bell. After the October state elections in Indiana and Pennsylvania gave what she called "fair promise," she concluded that the chances in November were good. Still, Mary Lincoln was nervous, unusually so for a candidate's wife, many of whom hoped for defeat, not victory. As she wrote Hannah Shearer, an old friend who had moved to Pennsylvania, "You used to be worried that I took politics so coolly you would not do so, were you to see me now. Whenever I *have time,* to think, my mind is sufficiently exercised for my comfort. Fortunately the time is rapidly drawing to a close, a little more than two weeks will decide the contest. I scarcely know how I would bear up under defeat. . . . If Mr. L. *is elected,* I hope that time will come, I trust that we may all meet at Phillipi [*sic*]," an obscure reference to the 42 B.C. battle at which Mark Antony and Octavian had defeated Brutus and Cassius or, in her comparison, the Democrats Douglas and Breckinridge.[70]

Meanwhile, Mary Lincoln campaigned, using up all the ink she had purchased the day after her husband's nomination. Many of her letters have been lost, but those that remain reveal that she intended to clarify Lincoln's positions. "Mr. Lincoln," went one such letter to an influential minister in Ohio, "has never been a Mason or belonged to any secret order." By this time Lincoln had hired young John Nicolay as his secretary, but his wife still handled some correspondence and entertained as never before.[71]

In August of that long, hot, expectant summer the Republicans of Illinois held a grand rally and ratification meeting. Two days before, from all over the state, the faithful started arriving in Springfield, some wearing their party uniforms, others with broadsides celebrating "Old Abe—The Railsplitter." A few had prepared floats. By the day of the parade Springfield's 10,000 had become the Republican party's 50,000. Sometime in midmorning the first line of paraders reached Eighth and Jackson, singing as they passed "Ain't you glad you joined the Republicans / Ain't you glad you did?" and to the tune of "The Old Gray Mare": "Old Abe Lincoln / Came out of the Wilderness." A professional photographer from Chicago climbed to the second floor of Harriet Dean's house across Eighth Street to take a daguerreotype of the scene.[72] (See the section of photographs, following page 167.)

In it the Lincolns' door is open, seemingly off its hinges as a cascade of neighbors, friends, and partisans fills the front stairs and lawn. Lincoln is outside, no doubt able to see above the crowd as a float passes by. Tad is leaning—somewhat precariously—out the upstairs window, while Willie surveys the scene, more sedately, from his father's bedroom. There are five women in the picture. One is a domestic helper; the others are relatives and neighbors. Mary Lincoln, elegantly dressed (though it is hot August) in dark silk with an elaborate yoke collar, looks on from her husband's bedroom. In symbolic representation of her new status, she has become a spectator.[73]

Three months later Abraham Lincoln was elected President of the United States. There were conflicting accounts of what he and his wife did that November 6, 1860, but all agreed on one point. When he heard in the Springfield telegraph office that the Republican electors had carried Pennsylvania, he immediately went home, saying, "I guess there's a little lady at home who would like to hear this news." As he hurried down Eighth Street, he called out, "Mary, Mary, *we* are elected."[74]

Despite the triumph, Mary Lincoln had lost something. Gone beyond local politics, where she knew the contestants and could contribute her intuitive assessments, Lincoln had destroyed the equilibrium of their marriage. Still, she believed that she knew more than the trusting President-elect about people. He might understand the issues, but she knew character. Mary did not relinquish her portfolio easily, and as her husband moved into another world, she sought to follow. In January 1861, before the Lincolns left for Washington, she wrote an extraordinary letter to David Davis, who had been one of her husband's campaign managers. In it—and she marked it "Confidential"—she condemned Norman Judd, an old enemy from the senatorial campaign of 1854, who now wanted a cabinet post. She asked Davis to intervene with her husband against Judd. "Mr. Lincoln's great attachment for you," she wrote, "is the reason for writing. I know, a word from you will have much effect, for the good of the country, and Mr. Lincoln's future reputation, I believe you will speak to him on this subject and urge him not to give [Judd] so responsible a place." In the old days she would never have needed an outsider to reinforce her judgments.[75]

VII
First Lady

L*ONG* before the train was due, the residents of Poughkeepsie had lined the railroad tracks. They came, this
windy February day of 1861, expecting to see their
new President, who, if his voice held up and there was
time, might say a few words. Across Indiana, Ohio,
Pennsylvania, and into New York, Lincoln had greeted
similar groups with those unrevealing short speeches
of which he was a master. In one Indiana town he joked
that the train had started up before his story got to the
place "where the laugh came in." Reporters who wanted
to know his reaction to the secession of seven southern
states were already complaining about his banter, but
with the Union in danger Lincoln used anecdotes to
divert attention from the controversies that awaited him
in Washington. It was enough to present himself for
observation, to praise the Union, to declare himself
"an accidental instrument of the People," and to leave
his listeners contemplating the question that would
become the critical issue of his administration: "Shall
the Union and the liberties of this country be preserved
to the latest generation?"[1]

Many of those along the tracks came not for politics but for a look at Old Abe's family. Sometimes they were treated to public displays of the couple's affection when the President-elect bent over for his wife to smooth down his unruly hair or wrap his throat in a muffler. Then, as he straightened up, in that sensual way of hers Mary Lincoln kissed him and linked her arm through his. When Lincoln was not available, loud calls brought mother and children to the station platform or train window. But in Ashtabula, Ohio, when she did not appear, her husband laughed and in an accurate assessment of his marriage acknowledged that he had always found it "difficult to make [my] wife do what she did not want to."[2]

At first Mary Lincoln had not expected to be on the train, though of course, she wanted to be. At forty-two she was ready to exchange the anonymity of a small-town housewife for prominence as the President's partner; considering her education and upbringing as a Lexington Todd, she believed herself well equipped for this role. But for safety's sake her husband had discouraged her from accompanying him. Husband and wife had argued about when and how she, Tad, and Willie would get to Washington, though seventeen-year-old Robert, who had returned from Harvard to accompany his father, was assured a place on the train.[3]

Even before the secession of South Carolina, in December 1860, there had been threats on Abraham Lincoln's life. Several anonymous letters decorated with skulls and crossbones had come addressed to Mrs. Lincoln, warning that if her husband attempted to take office, he would be assassinated. Just before Christmas she had received a sketch of Lincoln with a noose around his neck, his feet chained, and his body tarred and feathered. Even little Tad had gotten a grim reminder of the hatred felt for his father in the South when a grotesque black-faced doll had arrived at the Springfield Post Office addressed to Master Lincoln. Later Mary Lincoln's mail included so many uncertainties that she turned it over to a White House secretary. But in 1861 this woman who was terrified of storms, robbers, and loud noises was less fearful of political violence, especially if it interfered with her resolve to be part of the presidential progress to the White House. In the end considerations of security worked to her advantage when General Winfield Scott decided that the presence of Lincoln's family might deter an assassin. So Mary Lincoln joined the President-elect in Indianapolis the day after he left Springfield.[4]

They had been on the special four-car train for more than a week when, late in the afternoon, it pulled into the Poughkeepsie station. Lincoln's greeting was hurried. When he disappeared to meet with local notables, the cry went up among those who had waited so long: "Where's the Missus? Where's Mrs. Abe? Give us the Old Lady and the Boys." At first Mary Lincoln had been surprised at such familiarity, but in time she grew accustomed to the irreverence. No one knew her first name anyway. To the public, she was Mrs. Abraham Lincoln, and those bold enough to yell never used her proper title, Mrs. President Lincoln. When she came to the train window this particular afternoon, the crowd insisted, "Show us the children. Where are the children?" With his customary graciousness, ten-year-old Willie bowed and waved amid the applause. But unpredictable eight-year-old Tad scrambled under his mother's skirts and could not be raised for an appearance. In any case, according to one reporter, everyone laughed, including Mrs. Lincoln.[5]

Indeed, these were good times for Mary Lincoln. She was full of the smiles and lively conversation that were her hallmark. Ever since Lincoln's election she had been in fine spirits, though detractors like David Davis and the journalist Henry Kreisman added that this was to be expected from an ostentatious female who had gotten what she wanted and took too much credit for her husband's success. But her friends deemed Mary Lincoln "just as agreeable as ever. Mrs. L. does not put on any airs but is as pleasant and talkative and entertaining as she can be." A neighbor pleased her—and she needed such reinforcements— by naming a daughter Mary Lincoln Melvin. From Harvard Robert had written after the election to inquire if she wasn't tired of the constant uproar. Her answer is unrecorded. Most likely it was a resounding no, although she worried about her husband's safety. Having had a childhood prediction and adult preoccupation come true, she now faced the unsettling prospect that the ominous premonitions that occasionally made her too nervous for sleep might also come to pass.[6]

But there was not time to contemplate such possibilities. Determined to make her mark, Mary Lincoln had prepared for her move to Washington by traveling to New York in the bitter cold of January 1861. No matter how complete her brother-in-law's stock (Clark Smith advertised "The Best Ladies Goods in Illinois"), his fashions were not up to big-city standards. Unlike most of her neighbors, Mary knew it. Already she had read patronizing newspaper comments about her supposed western vulgarity, though she meant to surpass the elegance of the Washington ladies. Some of her friends—Mercy Levering Conkleny was one—disapproved of such frivolous rivalry in light of the present state of political affairs.

Mary Lincoln disagreed and left the President-elect alone in Springfield for nearly two weeks while she bought materials, stood for seamstresses' tape measures, located a milliner on Broadway and Tenth, and entertained at tea in the ladies' parlor of the Astor. Already there was grumbling about her violation of female decorum. One reporter believed it "shocking" that a future President's wife was "kiting about the country and holding levées in which she indulges in a multitude of silly speeches," though to call her informal greetings speeches was an exaggeration. No matter where she was, the special treatment accorded by strangers bolstered her morale. It did not take long for Mary Lincoln to expect favors, which if omitted, were demanded. When the State Line Railroad charged her for a ticket on her return trip to Springfield, Robert informed the agents, "The Old Lady is raising hell about her passes." Generally such complaints were not necessary, and Mary had such a good time that her husband met the Chicago train for three nights before she finally returned to Springfield in late January.[7]

The results of her New York expedition appeared during the February journey from Springfield to Washington. As she had planned, when the train stopped long enough and the town was big enough, she gave a reception in the largest hotel. Usually the next day an approving notice appeared about Mrs. Lincoln's "ease, grace and fashionability." The *Home Journal* had already dubbed her the "Illinois Queen."[8]

After Poughkeepsie the train headed south, but in Pennsylvania Lincoln's protectors heard reliable reports of an assassination plot. With the Confederate government now in place, the President-elect had become a symbol to secessionists of the detested Union government and a natural target for assassins. Heeding the warnings of Detective Allan Pinkerton and telling only his wife, Lincoln took a special night train from Harrisburg through Baltimore, where local Republicans had been attacked during the presidential campaign of 1860. But at least one man was not fooled by the ploy when the President-elect arrived a day early at the Baltimore and Ohio Station in Washington. "Abe"—his old Illinois friend Elihu Washburne, who had been lurking behind a post, laughed—"you can't play that with me."[9]

Robert led a chorus of "The Star-Spangled Banner" when the train, without the President, crossed the Mason-Dixon Line. As promised, Lincoln telegraphed his wife of his safe arrival, but like everyone else on board, Mary Lincoln was frightened when she encountered a mob of Baltimoreans, some of whom searched the railroad cars for the man they called the "Black Ape." Now, instead of friendly calls for Tad, Willie, and the "Missus," these grim-faced men wanted her husband—"that bloody Republican." But by this time Abraham Lincoln was safely in the capital. And so it happened on a damp day in late February 1861 that Mary Lincoln arrived in Washington as she would leave it a little more than four years later—without her husband.

THE city had changed in the thirteen years since the Lincolns had boarded at Mrs. Sprigg's on Capitol Hill. Henry Adams, whose father served as Lincoln's minister to England, dismissed Washington as "the same unfinished Greek temples for workrooms and sloughs for roads; the same rude colony—camped in the same forest as in 1800 and 1850 and so in 1860." Mary Lincoln, who had spent her adult years in a western city of fewer than 10,000 residents, disagreed. In the single decade of the 1850s the Washington she had known had grown by more than three times the entire population of Springfield. For all its country airs, it was no drowsy, grass-grown backwater. But despite its gains in sophistication and size, the capital had lost something. No longer did it represent, as it had during Mary's first stay, national aspirations for a bold new experiment in government. Now, according to the flippant advertisements of local merchants, "The Union is in danger but by buying your presents at our store, you may save it."

In 1861 the immense, though domeless, United States Capitol dominated the city. A decade before, Mary Lincoln had observed it from ground level through the heavily wooded park in front of Mrs. Sprigg's boardinghouse. Then the building had a wooden dome. Now its shining marble Senate and House wings towered above the White House, a physical arrangement that some Americans believed conveyed the proper relationship between the legislative and executive branches of their government. Covered with scaffolding as it awaited a cast-iron dome and the bronze figure of Liberty, the Capitol remained a luminous symbol of American majesty only for northerners. For southerners it increasingly stood for a government opposed to their proslavery and states rights' convictions.[10]

Several other government buildings—the Post Office at Seventh and

ABOVE. *The elegant, fourteen-room Todd house on Main Street, Lexington, Kentucky. The Todds moved to this house in 1832, but Mary, estranged from her stepmother, never considered it her home. (University of Kentucky Photographic Archives)*

Main Street, Lexington, Kentucky, around 1860. (University of Kentucky Photographic Archives)

These earliest photographs of Mary and Abraham Lincoln were taken in 1846, after Lincoln's election to Congress from Springfield, Illinois. (Lloyd Ostendorf Collection)

OPPOSITE ABOVE. *The west side of Courthouse Square, Springfield, Illinois, in 1860. (Illinois State Historical Library)*

ABOVE. *The Lincoln home at the corner of Eighth and Jackson, Springfield, Illinois, during the Republican parade of August 1860. (Lloyd Ostendorf Collection)*

OPPOSITE BELOW. *The Lincolns—Willie, Mary, and Tad—after Abraham Lincoln's election to the presidency in 1860. (Lloyd Ostendorf Collection)*

ABOVE. *Pennsylvania Avenue,
looking west toward the Capitol,
1861. A new cast-iron dome,
with the bronze figure of Liberty,
was being installed. (National
Archives)*

*Abraham Lincoln, President of
the United States. (National
Archives)*

*Mary Todd Lincoln, in a
photograph by Mathew Brady,
November, 1861. (National
Archives)*

ABOVE. *Tad Lincoln, in the uniform of a Union officer, around 1864. (National Archives)*

OPPOSITE. *Mary Lincoln, dressed in her widow's weeds, around 1867. (Lloyd Ostendorf Collection)*

RIGHT. *Robert Lincoln in 1868. This photograph was taken just before his marriage. (National Archives)*

*The "spirit" of Abraham Lincoln hovers protectively
over Mary Todd Lincoln in this 1872 photograph by
Mumler, a spiritualist photographer. (Lloyd Ostendorf
Collection)*

F, the huge, bricked Patent Office across the street, and the turreted Smithsonian—had recently been completed. Even in 1861 only ten buildings, a few dubious statues, and a truncated shaft honoring George Washington constituted the physical presence of the federal government. Privately Europeans continued to joke about the American capital's rustic quality: "To make a Washington street," wrote an Englishman, "take one marble temple, or public office, a dozen good houses of brick and a dozen of wood and fill in with sheds and fields." But the city's connecting roads were vastly improved from the muddy morasses of Mary Lincoln's first years in Washington, and the shops on Pennsylvania Avenue rivaled, if not those in New York, Philadelphia, and Boston, at least those in Baltimore, Chicago, and Springfield.[11]

As for the President's House, overseas visitors familiar with Paris's Tuileries, Madrid's Palacio Real, and London's Buckingham Palace dismissed it as more like the country home of a merchant than the residence of a national leader. But Americans had never glimpsed those enormous edifices. Believing the White House their own property, the sovereign people enjoyed roving about its downstairs reception rooms, inspecting and sometimes snipping off material from the presidential curtains for souvenirs. In 1861 the mansion remained the center of twenty-two wooded acres, separated from Pennsylvania Avenue by the most casual of iron fences. It was garnished by a statue of Thomas Jefferson, and across Pennsylvania Avenue in Lafayette Square a bronze representation of Andrew Jackson. The presidential grounds included stables, orchards, a woodshed, outhouses, a garden, the new Buchanan conservatory, and several other all-purpose buildings. Some said the place resembled a poorly kept southern plantation.

Few plantations smelled as bad. For the President's House had been built near the Potomac flats and the fetid Washington Canal, which was responsible for the noxious air that supposedly struck down District residents every summer. At the foot of the President's Park, another marsh, once an outlet for sewerage, offered up unpleasant scents. When the breeze came from the southeast, suffocating odors wafted into the presidential quarters, but when the wind shifted, the smell was arguably worse. Ten blocks north was the commons where carts dumped the city's night soil.[12]

Mary Lincoln could not move into her new home immediately, and the family stayed for the ten days before the inauguration at Willard's Hotel, the center of the nation's political life at Fourteenth and Pennsylvania, where the Willard brothers managed to feed as many as 1,500 guests a day. In the new order of things to which she was growing accustomed, both brothers greeted her on her arrival. She had chosen their hotel over its competitors because her husband's predecessor, James Buchanan, had been taken dangerously ill (some said poisoned) during his preinaugural stay at the National Hotel.

The presidential family had hired two bedrooms and two parlors, hoping to escape some of the hotel's communal life. Immediately Lincoln disappeared into one, surrounded by a stream of callers, most of whom either offered solutions to the worsening crisis between North and South or sought patronage jobs in his administration. Mary Lincoln meanwhile held teas for the local ladies, though many declined to attend. Even before the election southerners like Mrs. Senator Clement Clay of Alabama had refused to allow Republicans to escort them to dinner. By the secession winter of 1861 those members of Washington society who had not gone south had no intention of admiring Mrs. Lincoln. Instead, they gossiped among themselves about how common she was, though most had never met her.

Finally it was Monday, March 4—a raw, windy, but occasionally sunny day. There had been several threats that Lincoln should leave his wife at home because he would be shot or kidnapped, but Mary Lincoln had no intention of missing her Lincoln party's installation. Besides, General Winfield Scott had stationed his troops along Pennsylvania Avenue and around the Capitol. For the first time in American history a wooden barricade shielded those on the inaugural platform from the crowd, which numbered 30,000. After Senator Edward Dickinson Baker (now a senator from Oregon) had introduced her husband, Mary Lincoln watched Lincoln take the oath of office from the doddering Chief Justice Roger B. Taney. Then she listened to his conciliatory inaugural address, which concluded, "We are not enemies, but friends. We must not be enemies. Though passion may have strained, it must not break our bonds of affection." That night, surrounded by a retinue of sisters, cousins, and nieces ("a dozen Todds of the Edwards breed are in the house," complained Lincoln's secretary), Mary Lincoln put on a watered blue silk gown and sallied forth with her habitual pearls, some gold bracelets, and a few new diamonds.[13]

Her first inaugural ball as the president's wife took place in a disappointing temporary structure behind City Hall, and to Mary Lincoln's chagrin, etiquette required that she promenade not with her husband but with another partner. Stephen Douglas extended his arm, and she danced a quadrille with him. Later the Democratic senator from Illinois explained that this was his response to those who would ostracize the President's wife from their southern-sympathizing society. Mary Lincoln may have seen it differently. For her the occasion demonstrated her prescience in choosing a President, years ago, between two insistent suitors.

Exhausted and constantly fidgeting with his new white kid gloves, the President retired at midnight. Earlier in the day he had received the disturbing news that Major Robert Anderson's troops at Fort Sumter in Charleston, South Carolina, were running out of food and must either be resupplied or abandon another United States fort to rebel forces. So Lincoln left behind his wife and her relatives, who stayed until early morning, talking, dancing, and enjoying the buffet provided by Gautier's, the city's best caterer. Mary Lincoln received rave reviews for her first official performance in the city. "She is more self-possessed than Lincoln," commented the *New York Herald,* "and has accommodated more readily than her taller half to the exalted station to which she has been so strangely advanced from the simple social life of the little inland capital of Illinois."[14]

Mary Lincoln proved more at home in this "exalted station" than her predecessors, who had remained shadowy private persons during their tenure in the White House. Anna Harrison had opposed the political career of her husband, William Henry, and even after the general's election in 1840, had hoped to remain in North Bend, Ohio. Likewise, Margaret Taylor had sought to avoid Washington. When she finally arrived in 1849 and was seen smoking a corncob pipe, the ensuing ridicule kept her in the private quarters for the year and a half her husband, Zachary, was in office.

To be sure, Abigail Fillmore had organized the upstairs library at 1600 Pennsylvania Avenue, collecting books for the large south-side room where the Lincoln family spent so much time. But her endeavors were restricted to the second-floor private quarters. Both she and Sarah Polk so despised the ceremonial entertainments that took place on the first floor that guests sensed their displeasure and complained of the inhospitable atmosphere. On her arrival in Washington in 1853, Jane Pierce proclaimed herself an invalid, though she seemed to have no more than a sore ankle and in fact outlived her husband, Franklin. Their son had just been killed when her husband took office, and she could be expected to stay in seclusion for a time. But Mrs. Pierce went beyond the conditions of even deepest mourning by remaining sequestered for four years.[15]

Unlike these women, Mary Lincoln intended to become the "First Lady" that the correspondent for the *Times* of London promptly dubbed her. Certainly she was the first presidential wife who could have been so considered. Enjoying the masculine world of politics, she sought to exert authority within the female domain of the household. In this she was not exceptional. What made her noteworthy was the public nature of her home and the lust for notoriety that was a psychological necessity for a woman who, amid her bravado, had been rendered insecure by her family abandonments. Overnight Mary Lincoln made herself a celebrity, closely watched by underemployed Washington-based newspaper correspondents who found the President's wife good copy during the pauses between military campaigns.

Like twentieth-century celebrities, Mary Lincoln soon learned that there was no better way to certify her importance than to find herself discussed in the newspapers, even if she did not always like what she read. Not only did reporters get things wrong (they exaggerated the severity of the boys' measles and the cost of her gowns), but some, thought to be supporters, proved fickle. Even defenders such as the *Chicago Tribune,* which once described her as "a plain common sense American wife and mother," diminished the domesticity she claimed with unacceptable comments concerning her ambitiousness. Nor did the papers universally acknowledge her handsomeness. According to the *New York Times,* she had "a large and well developed head [and] a nose that was not Grecian" and was bestowed "with firmness and a form inclined to stoutness."

Acutely vulnerable to criticism but resolutely committed to standing beside her husband in the spotlight, she complained: "My own nature is very sensitive and I have always tried to secure the best wishes of all with whom through life I have been associated. No one is as little desirous of newspaper notoriety as my own inoffensive self." Of course, criticism of her "inoffensive self" came from men who preferred females of incontestable docility and who were shocked at this one's interest in the public world. Detesting public women herself, Mary Lincoln could not discount these criticisms of her worldliness as merely the narrow-minded attitudes of her male-directed society. Instead, she denied her strong need for public attention, thereby creating an internal conflict between her conventional ideas about female reticence and her psychological need for acknowledgment.

Throughout her four years in Washington, Mary Lincoln inhabited both the male sphere of public affairs and the female's secluded habitat. Through her marriage she had become public property, though she had only to retire upstairs to prevent herself from being so. In any case, she had not selected her public status for a principle, in the same way that female leaders of the abolition and women's rights movements had. Instead, it came because she had chosen to marry a man for his potential greatness. No matter what her contribution to Lincoln's political career, no matter what her participation in her own not-so-innocent conspicuousness, Mary Lincoln denied seeking celebrity status at the same time that for personal reasons she craved the recognition that during a civil war came with mixed reviews. "My character is wholly domestic," she insisted when she thanked James Gordon Bennett, the editor of the *New York Herald,* for his newspaper's perceptive recognition of her "female amiability and reticence." But her actions continually belied this insistence.

Reports of her ambitiousness, such as the *New York Times'* comment that "Mrs. Lincoln is making and unmaking the political fortunes of men and is similar to Queen Elizabeth in her statesmanlike tastes," irritated her. Never doubting the prevailing ideas about the separate spheres of men and women, she preferred femininity for every woman, including herself, and so suffered a wrenching opposition between what she had to do as Mary Todd Lincoln and what she believed nineteenth-century ladies should do. Again, as in her school days in Lexington, she accomplished the wrong thing with distinction. Thus Mary Lincoln mirrored the civil war raging around her, and her frequent flashes of anger emerged, like those of the ruptured Union, from a profound ambivalence about herself. [16]

Later the semipublic status of American wives permitted females an off-camera "little woman behind the great man" authority. But that was not the case in Mary Lincoln's day. As a result, she suffered because nowhere could she observe the necessity for female independence and autonomy, undertaken not for a cause but for self-respect. An unlucky victim of personal tragedy, Mary Lincoln was also punished because she lived too soon. [17]

IMMEDIATELY after her husband's inauguration, Mary Lincoln took measure of her new home. The executive business of the nation took place in a huge room with a southern exposure on the second floor. Farther down the hall were the family quarters, the President's bedroom in the southwest quarter, his wife's adjoining, and Tad and Willie's across the hall. In the eastern end of the house were the tiny bedrooms assigned to John Hay and John Nicolay, Lincoln's secretaries. Most observers found the White House disappointing. "Seedy and dilapidated," reported Mary's outspoken cousin Elizabeth ("Lizzie") Todd Grimsley, who discovered in its thirty-one rooms broken furniture, peeling wallpaper, and tawdry decorations unacceptable in a simple Springfield cottage. The place reminded William Stoddard, a White House secretary, "of an old and unsuccessful hotel." In fact, the mansion's only elegance appeared in the East and Blue rooms, and there the threadbare rugs and curtains looked, in Grimsley's words, as if "they were unchanged from George Washington's day." In the west wing the state dining room could not serve more than ten with matched china. [18]

Yet, as Mary Lincoln soon learned, every President since William Henry Harrison had received a $20,000 allowance for refurbishing and redecorating the White House, along with a stipend for its annual repairs. Few used the allocation to advantage, and for years there had been rumors about whose pockets were being lined by appropriations designated for the White House. In recent years the private quarters had been neglected because Harriet Lane, Buchanan's niece and hostess, gave her attention to parties rather than to redecorating. Her contribution was no more than the purchase of some expensive crystal and gold spoons for her tea parties, after her uncle's glass-domed plant conservatory had used up most of the Buchanan appropriation. [19]

Mary Lincoln seized her opportunity. Royalty, she understood from Agnes Strickland's *Lives of the Queens of England,* enhanced its authority by reigning from grand settings that displayed its power. Just as the domeless Capitol conveyed the sense of an unfinished republic, so a shabby President's House would express the powerlessness of a chief executive who managed and administered but rarely initiated policy. Armed with the experience of running the Lincoln family and house in Springfield, Mary Lincoln set out to parallel in the domestic sphere her husband's extension of political power. While the President raised armies and searched for a fighting general, she transformed the President's House into an appropriate setting for the leader of a great nation and, of course, his wife.

With characteristic energy, Mary Lincoln turned to the job of transforming the dismal interior of the President's House into a demon-stration of her Lincoln party's position. But she was delayed in her search for the best wallpaper, rugs, china, and crystal. On April 12, 1861, the Confederates began their bombardment of Fort Sumter, and within the week four other southern states had joined the rebellion. After Virginia's secession the nation's capital shared the easily breached boundary of the Potomac River with its enemy.

Momentarily a Confederate attack on Washington was expected. Each day brought more reports of treason: first the resignation of dis-loyal army and navy officers, including Commodore Franklin Buch-anan, who had earlier welcomed the Lincolns to the navy yard; next the speeches of Confederate sympathizers in Washington; then the disappearance of members of the White House staff who strolled across the Long Bridge to join Jefferson Davis's army on the other side of the Potomac. Lincoln called up 75,000 militiamen, but when the first units en route to protect the capital reached Maryland, they were attacked by a mob. On April 16, 1861, the first casualties of the Civil War came in Baltimore, leaving the President to wonder if there was a solid North.

Most women would not have considered a journey through Mary-land at a time when the Lincolns had only to climb to the roof of the White House to see the Confederate flag waving atop Marshall's Tav-ern in Alexandria and the flickering lights from General Beauregard's campfires. Just outside Baltimore, armed secessionists continued to sabotage railroad lines and bridges, and the army was soon to arrest a Baltimore County farmer, John Merryman, for destroying railroad tracks along the route to Philadelphia. Amid rumors of a Confederate inva-sion of Washington, Mary Lincoln had become a possible target. Sen-sible women were evacuating Washington as the city became a deserted village awaiting what some hoped would be its liberation by the South. Some said Washington would soon be the new capital of a great slave-holding Confederacy. In early May Charles Stone, the commander of the District volunteers, heard reports that a Confederate regiment planned to occupy the President's House and kidnap the presidential family along with the cabinet. General Scott again urged Mary Lincoln to return with Tad and Willie to Springfield.

She refused. Instead of abandoning Washington for Springfield's obscurity, Mary Lincoln grew accustomed to living with the Frontier Guards and the Zouaves (a troop of New Yorkers who took their name from and dressed like Algerian soldiers) camped in the East Room.

When the Pennsylvania and Massachusetts regiments finally reached Washington in late April and paraded past the White House, Mary Lincoln was there, waving from a second-floor window. The next day she was on hand for a review of the Seventh New York Regiment. "Thousands of soldiers are guarding us," she advised a Springfield friend. "If there is safety in numbers, we have every reason to feel secure. We can only hope for peace." During her wait she had made Tad a Zouave doll, replete with the unit's spectacular scarlet and blue uniform, though Jack, the doll, was prone, as real-life Zouaves were not, to neglect his duties and was once tried for desertion.[20]

Despite General Scott's warnings, by the middle of May Mary Lincoln would wait no longer and left for Philadelphia and New York, accompanied by the acting commissioner of public buildings and her cousin Lizzie Todd Grimsley. By law the commissioner supervised White House purchases and submitted vouchers for payment to the Treasury Department. In the past the selection of this official had been a routine matter. The ladies of the house deferred to whatever patronage considerations dictated the choice of a loyal partisan to arrange receptions and supervise the repair of the White House. In 1861 several Republicans were competing for a sinecure that paid $2,000 a year and might lead to better things. Among the front-runners was a Pennsylvania Republican who, according to a newspaperman, "lives with a kept woman and is nothing but a pimp and procures strumpets for members of Congress."[21]

Mary Lincoln had her own ideas and insisted on the appointment of William S. Wood, though neither of the Lincolns had known the New Yorker before 1861. A friend of Secretary of State William Seward's, Wood had impressed the President's wife with his supervision of the Lincolns' travel arrangements from Springfield to Washington. At some point Mary Lincoln and William Wood had become friends and possibly more. In June an anonymous correspondent warned the President about "the scandal of your wife and Wood. If he continues as commissioner, he will stab you in your most vital part." Though their relationship was probably a flirtation raised to scandal by their trips to New York, the White House secretaries remembered the Lincolns' fight over Wood. "Do you remember," John Nicolay later wrote Schuyler Colfax, "the war [Mary Lincoln] had with Mr. Lincoln about the Commissioner? They scarcely spoke together for several days. It impressed me painfully but I suppose such scenes were rare."[22]

Typically the President's wife prevailed. With Wood as the acting commissioner and her male companion, she invaded the best stores in Philadelphia and New York. From the beginning she reversed the usual arrangement between the commissioner and the lady of the White House. It was she, not he, who led the way into the stores, chose the furnishings for the White House, and, in a style-setting behavior that shocked New Yorkers, impatiently carried whatever she could back to her hotel rather than wait for its delivery. Reporters followed everywhere. "Mrs. Lincoln," wrote one, "who has been engaged since her arrival in making large purchases at some of the leading merchants was out yesterday enjoying herself in the usual way." From Philadelphia she dispatched a merchant to buy wallpaper in Paris, and after Alexander Stewart, New York's greatest merchant, had given a dinner party in her honor, the President's wife ordered $2,000 of rugs and curtains from him in a single day. His block-size marble emporium at Broadway and Chambers Street was a place, according to Henry James, "fatal to feminine nerves" and in this instance national budgets. Twice more in 1861 Mary Lincoln undertook buying expeditions to New York, and during her tenure as First Lady she made eleven such trips, though Wood soon became too controversial a companion.[23]

Returned to the capital after nearly two weeks, Mary Lincoln found Washington a military camp and her husband exhausted by the patronage seekers who clustered in the upstairs hall outside his office. Of this the President made a joke, saying he felt like an innkeeper besieged for rooms in one wing of his hotel while he tried to put out a fire in the other. And it was the fire that most concerned him, though all was quiet on the Potomac. Then, the day after Mary's return, she and her husband wept over the news that their young friend Colonel Elmer Ellsworth, the commander of the Zouaves, had been shot by a Virginian while removing the Confederate flag waving atop Marshall's Tavern in Alexandria. In the first of her White House funerals Mary Lincoln placed a wreath on the dead soldier's casket, and in the weeks that followed she took her turn reviewing the troops.

In late July the skirmishes ended and the battles started, the first at Bull Run in northern Virginia. What began as a gay outing for Washington officials who went to northern Virginia with picnic baskets to see a Union victory ended in defeat with the weary survivors of Irwin McDowell's army straggling back into Washington. Again there was talk of a rebel invasion, and Lincoln was up for several nights, patiently listening to eyewitness accounts of what had gone wrong on the battlefield. For his wife, trips to the Washington hospitals now replaced her more preferred activity of reviewing the troops. Soon she had visited enough of the makeshift accommodations to earn a public commendation. "Among the many ladies who visit the hospitals none is more indefatigable than Mrs. Lincoln," the newspapers stated. Sometimes she went with the President; sometimes, with her sons, though she was reluctant to expose the boys to the putrid atmosphere of these battle-spawned death traps. Sometimes she was accompanied by a friend, though it seemed to one White House secretary that she should invite newspapermen on these missions instead of just to her parties.[24]

Like the other matrons who descended on the pavilions crowded with Union casualties, the President's wife did not tend the wounded. This was the job of Clara Barton's nurses, who dressed wounds, attended surgery, and dispensed medicines. Instead, Mary Lincoln provided companionship and special food to Union soldiers. Arriving once at Campbell's Hospital just after several legs had been amputated, she stayed, though many ladies were unable to stand the stench and the sound of groaning soldiers. On another occasion she and Lincoln asked one soldier why he was laughing and were told that a previous visitor had solicited this double amputee's pledge to an antidancing campaign.

Usually Mary Lincoln brought flowers, read books, organized special holiday meals, served as a waitress, and wrote letters. "I am sitting by the side of your soldier boy," went one letter. "He has been quite sick and is getting well. He tells me to say that he is all right." No doubt with her civilian son Robert in mind, she signed the letter "With respect [for] the mother of a young soldier." Energetically she raised $1,000 for the Christmas dinner at Douglas Hospital, and when there was a danger of scurvy, she provided, through a personal donation of $1,000, lemons and oranges. And she made certain that unsolicited gifts of liquor to the White House went to the soldiers.[25]

In the fall, accompanied by the White House gardener, Mary Lincoln returned to New York, this time to fill the empty White House cupboards with china and glassware from E. V. Haughwout's on Broadway. The last White House china had been purchased almost ten years before, during the Pierce administration; few pieces of the plain red-bordered porcelain survived. After much deliberation Mary Lincoln chose her set: a 190-piece "fine porcelain dining service decorated with royal purple and double gilt," according to the invoice, "with the arms of the United States on each piece." In testament to her politics, the gold border was entwined with two lines signifying the union of North and South. Unable to resist a bargain, she then ordered a duplicate Limoges set for herself at a savings of $2,000 (though a cost of more than $1,000), replacing the United States seal with the initials ML. (No doubt she abandoned the Todd initial because her three half brothers had joined the Confederate army and because a two-letter monogram that featured a President's initial was more regal.)[26]

By the fall of 1861 Mary Lincoln had succeeded in her self-appointed task of improving the White House. Critics like Mrs. Donn Piatt, who before had found the mansion "miserable," complimented the First Lady on her taste. "We now occupy the state guest room," went Mary's progress report to Lizzie Grimsley in October 1861.[27] The Lincolns did so because an array of painters, curtain hangers, floor waxers, and molders had taken over their connecting bedrooms. Of course, Mary had included the private living quarters in her renovations, though former commissioners of public buildings had omitted them to concentrate on the public rooms downstairs.

The exact cost of her refurbishing remains uncertain, though it was soon embarrassingly clear that Mrs. President Lincoln had overspent the $20,000 four-year allowance in less than a year. Or, more accurately, William Wood had, for he was in charge of the accounts. The $6,000 annual budget available for invisible necessaries such as repairs to the pipes and the leaky north side roof was gone, too.[28]

In fact, just two items on Mary Lincoln's shopping list—the china set from Haughwout's for $3,195 and the French wallpaper for $6,800 (scraping, mortaring, and hanging included)—accounted for more than one-half the appropriation. And this just headed the list of improvements, which included heavy gold-fringed draperies with loops and tassels in the Green Room, an ornate mahogany bed with rosewood carvings and a Victorian canopy of queenly proportions upstairs, and new damask curtains complemented by a $2,500 carpet in the East Room. The carpet replaced a threadbare predecessor damaged by the Frontier Guards who had practiced presenting and sometimes discharging arms into the plaster walls while they protected the White House. In the Red Room old-timers recognized the Gilbert Stuart portrait of Washington, but not much else amid the refinished furniture, damask drapes, and French wallpaper.

Soon Mary Lincoln read about her extravagance and, although probably stung by the criticism, remained undaunted in her mission. Other Presidents had overspent their budgets, in part because notions of republican frugality clashed with the realities of keeping a thirty-one-room mansion. In the previous administration, deficiency allowances had been buried in civic appropriation bills, and no one had held the President's wife responsible. But Mary Lincoln was a visible culprit. She and the commissioner had not so much spent carelessly and need-lessly (for the White House was dreary) as hastily, expensively, and tastefully. Unlucky Mary Lincoln had arrived in Washington at pre-cisely the moment when Americans demanded strict economy from their officials. Even in 1861 military spending emerged as a critical issue, and the cost of the war increased each year until four years later the total reached $20 billion. "We must place every last dollar in the war chest," insisted Congressman Roscoe Conkling of New York, a sentiment with which Mary Lincoln's husband agreed.[29]

As her husband did in the selection of generals, Mary Lincoln had miscalculated. In the past Washington's merchants—especially those along fashionable Pennsylvania Avenue and Tenth Street—had prof-ited when the commissioners patronized their shops. In return—for the White House account was no small matter—retailers discounted their goods for the commissioner's private purchases without the knowledge of the President's wife. Such practices explained why a position that paid a clerk's salary of $2,000 was sought by so many. In fact, William Wood was quoted as saying that he would not stay in Washington for this salary if he could not make something on the "outside." But overnight Mary Lincoln had replaced the District's merchants with their New York and Philadelphia competitors, thereby interrupting a mutually profitable arrangement. As word of this treachery spread, in Lafayette Square, just across Pennsylvania Avenue from the White House, where the southern colony had lived before the war and a somnolent men's club still offered quiet rooms for gossip, Mary Lin-coln became the talk of the town.[30]

Lincoln, accustomed in Springfield to letting his wife run things, was slow to learn the truth. At the time he was more concerned with military matters in the West and General George McClellan's lassi-tude than the growing elegance of his residence. Moreover, he knew best that other side of his wife, who as a parsimonious Springfield housekeeper had underpaid domestic help and bargained with street vendors for a few pennies. Still, he had to sign the vouchers, and eventually he learned of her overexpenditures. Pronouncing the White House the best house in which they had ever lived, the President complained that her shopping would "stink" in the land and that she

must take responsibility for her "flub-a-dubs." But when he threatened to pay the White House bills from his salary, Mary Lincoln protested "we can not afford that."

Impulsively she implored others to intercede, and both the commissioner of public buildings and the secretary of the interior soon
appeared in the President's office to discuss the matter of the White
House bills. Meanwhile, Mary Lincoln denied any culpability, though
she did plead for forgiveness from her husband. "In truth," she later
wrote, "I have had to be as economical as possible, more so than I ever
have been before in my life." At a time when Washington's married
women had neither the means for earning money nor the power of the
purse, Mrs. President Lincoln was nevertheless held liable for what
neither law nor custom gave her control of. In any case, criticisms that
might have tainted her husband instead stuck to her and the hapless
commissioner.[31]

By fall the President was furious. The Senate would not confirm the
commissioner; Wood was out of a job, and Mary Lincoln was searching
for a replacement and trying to make up with her husband. Her choice
for commissioner, Benjamin French, had served in that post during
Franklin Pierce's administration and, changing parties in the nick of
time, had become one of the District's Republican leaders. With Lincoln's election he expected at least an appointment in the Post Office.
Instead, he was now appointed commissioner of public buildings, and
during the struggle to pay off the White House bills he wrote Mrs.
Lincoln, whom he saw almost daily, what she already knew. "A
gentleman papering several rooms in the White House has purchased
wallpaper in Paris by your order and desires to have the old paper
taken off. . . . It is my duty to state that there is no money for this
papering. The $6,000 in annual repairs for the president's house is
nearly exhausted by unusual painter's and other bills and there is no
other fund out of which the payment for papering can be made."

Even with unpaid bills mounting and creditors hounding him, French
admired Mary Lincoln. "She is a smart intelligent woman who likes
to have her way pretty much. I was delighted with her independence
and her ladylike reception of me. . . . She bears herself in every particular like a lady," this praise indeed from the snobbish commissioner. In turn, Mary Lincoln may have hoped that French's qualities
included a willingness to follow her orders.[32]

In time French found a way to pay the White House bills, and Mary
Lincoln received her first instruction in the legerdemain of the budget

transfer. Along with the budget for the White House, the commissioner's office controlled appropriations of nearly a half million dollars for the Capitol and other federal buildings. It was easy to reassign money to the White House account from other projects. So the unused appropriations for a culvert on Pennsylvania Avenue, a promenade for senators in the Capitol, and gas lamps on Capitol Hill were diverted to pay for wallpaper in the Green Room. With an insider's knowledge of how these matters were arranged, Commissioner French advised his superior, Secretary of Interior Caleb Smith, a newcomer to Washington, that such transfers were routine and had been made legal by a statute passed during Van Buren's presidency. Then during the next session of Congress French encouraged a sympathetic congressman to introduce a deficiency appropriation of $4,500 for the White House which passed with little comment, buried as it was in a long list of civil and military appropriations.[33]

Meanwhile, Mary Lincoln was looking for her own ways to pay off the overexpenditure and to prevent her husband from using any of his salary. First she initiated a sale of secondhand White House furniture, though the broken rosewood and walnut antiques brought little cash. Typically she had overestimated the value of used presidential goods. Then she ordered the gardener to sell manure from the stables at ten cents a wagonload, though this inflated price led to more jokes than sales.

Next she reevaluated the White House staff for possible savings. Traditionally Congress paid for the President's steward, doorkeepers, watchmen, gardener, and laborers. The President hired his own cooks and domestic servants and also paid, there being no expense account, for his official entertaining. About this arrangement Mary Lincoln complained: "It would have been a great delight to me to have had the means to entertain." Such demands on the executive purse led her to advise her dressmaker that despite the President's $25,000-a-year salary (worth, she correctly calculated, not more than $10,000 in gold, less $900 in taxes), "we are from the west and are poor."

To reduce their poverty, Mary Lincoln discharged the steward and ran the house with a small crew of free blacks: Peter Brown, a butler and waiter; Cornelia Mitchell, the cook; and several maids. The nurse who had accompanied the Lincolns from Springfield was sent home with a reference; finally Mary Lincoln had admitted that eight-year-old Tad and eleven-year-old Willie "have grown too large to require a nurse," though Tad still did not dress himself. Later she saved money on the boys' tutor, who received most of his salary from the Treasury Department. Soon the former White House employees gossiped that the President's wife was pocketing the steward's yearly wage and using it to pay White House bills. Lincoln's secretary nicknamed Mary Hell-Cat and told his friends that she came to him to collect the money usually paid the steward, whose work she was in fact doing.[34]

Meanwhile, John Watt, the Scottish-born gardener who controlled the payroll of the outside staff, padded his expense accounts and kicked back funds to the lady of the house, who used the money for her bills. Never one to miss his opportunities (and such there were in wartime Washington), Watt bought the provisions for the White House. It was easy enough to sign vouchers for nonexistent purchases, especially after he and Mary Lincoln had ordered more than $1,000 worth of seeds, fruit trees, and bushes from a Philadelphia nursery. Throughout the summer Watt collected for more camellias, roses, lettuce, and strawberry bushes than ever were planted at Pennsylvania Avenue.[35]

Later there were rumors that Watt tried to blackmail the President with three letters Mary Lincoln had supposedly written, though the daily contact of mistress and gardener rendered letters superfluous and potentially embarrassing. With her husband less accessible than ever, Mary Lincoln had probably confided indiscreetly in Watt about her money problems, or her relationship with William Wood, or even her knowledge of military affairs. In any case, Watt, who was under fire for his southern sympathies, soon found himself out of the White House and in the Union army. (His staff aroused suspicion, too; one of Watt's workers sported the blue cockade of the Confederacy while he tended Abraham Lincoln's vegetables.) For whatever reason, Mary Lincoln remained loyal to Watt, advising officials in the War and Interior departments that the groundskeeper "was rigidly exact in his payrolls with us," that he was not a secessionist, and that he should be released "from his present troubles," by which she meant the accusations of his disloyalty and dishonesty.

Whatever their relationship, John Watt had met his match in Mary Lincoln. Thirty years later he asked Simon Cameron, who had been secretary of war during his tenure on the presidential grounds, for a letter of recommendation, explaining that he had once paid for Mary Lincoln's trip to Boston—an outlay for which he had never been reimbursed.[36]

The final measure of Mary Lincoln's success in underwriting her redecorating campaign emerged only later. Most Presidents retired from Washington poorer men than when they had arrived, having used their salaries to pay for official entertainments and house expenses. In contrast, the Lincolns lived on $6,600 a year, not much more than they had spent during their last years in Springfield. Under Mary's direction (for her husband was negligent about money matters) they saved $70,000 of his $100,000 salary, less $3,600 for taxes. One journalist had predicted as much: "Mrs. Lincoln will manage the affairs of the White House (I do not mean State affairs) with ability and will see to it that the old man does not return to Springfield penniless."[37]

INCLUDED in Mary Lincoln's expenses were clothes, which cost a great deal more in Washington than they had in Springfield. Brought up among the overdressed ladies of Lexington, she chose to make her mark through the remembered elegance of her stepmother's parlor rather than the Todd tradition of wedding gowns spun during the Revolution from Kentucky weeds. Still, as the President's wife she dutifully joined an association to boycott international goods, which floundered when the government needed the return from its import taxes more than the sacrifice of its matrons. But even without European materials Mary Lincoln intended to stand out for her clothes. Behind her back Mercy Levering Conkling was calling her "Our Royal Highness," and sister Ann Smith joked of the overdressed "Queen Victoria's court" in Washington. When Mary Lincoln heard this, she retaliated with a sovereign's lèse-majesté by "removing" her sister farther from the White House. But even strangers compared her to European royalty. "The Illinois Reine" she was called, in part because of her lavish costumes.[38]

Like England's Queen Victoria and France's Empress Eugénie (the latter a red-haired Spanish beauty who had married Napoleon III in 1853 and who tended to what the papers delicately called "embonpoint"), Mary Lincoln considered a costly dress as essential an emblem of station as any general's outfit. Winfield Scott's army uniform, with its gold filigrees and silk lapels and sash, in fact cost more than her most expensive gowns, though she had many, and he only the one. But high Victorian fashion with its extravagant materials and design was expensive, especially after Eugénie had created the "look" by enlarging the rings of hoopskirts into spherical circles of steel that doubled the amount of material required for a dress.

For the first time in American history bare arms and necks were available to display costly jewelry. So was the head. With the long hair of the boudoir put up, parted in the middle, and drawn smoothly over the ears, a concealer or cache-peigne made of jewels or exotic flowers covered the lady's coils of hair. Mary Lincoln favored pearls and fresh jasmine, and her particular adornments sometimes made her look not so much like Eugénie, as she would have liked, as like a garden in motion.[39]

Mary Lincoln generally followed Eugénie's tastes, and in this sense her clothes were derivative. Certainly she outdid the disappointing performance of dowdy Queen Victoria, who, after Prince Albert's death in December 1861, dressed only in black and half mourning's purple and white. Along with Mary Lincoln, a fascinated American press deserted the British queen to follow Eugénie's clothes and parties. In *Godey's Lady's Book,* the *Vogue* of its day and one of Mary Lincoln's favorite magazines, the Eugénie look appeared in line drawings and detailed discussions of materials and styles.

No matter what the war news and no matter what the financial concerns of the Union government, there was always room alongside the casualty lists for detailed descriptions of Eugénie. "She arrived," gushed the correspondent for the *Washington Daily Chronicle,* "in a pale tulle dress completely covered with violets. At the heart of each violet sparkled a diamond—800 in all." Sometimes Mary Lincoln clipped from *Godey's Lady's Book* accounts of the empress as she appeared in the Bois de Boulogne, wearing, for example, "a violet taffeta dress trimmed with rouches of the same and bias bands of black velvet edged with white at the bottom of the skirt." Soon seamstress Elizabeth Keckley was put to work on an American version that took twenty-five yards of material, and by early 1862 Mary Lincoln had sixteen new dresses. Meanwhile, the gossips wondered whether the American First Lady did not rival the French empress in the number of her bonnets.

Like Eugénie, Madame President's clothes were, if not front-page news, guaranteed inside coverage in national newspapers. Mary Lincoln doted on the compliments, intending, as she instructed her seamstress, photographer, and milliner, to be "elegant and genteel" and, though she may not have said so, to look younger than her forty-three years. The publicity infuriated some and mesmerized others. She wore, according to the approving correspondent of the *Washington Chronicle,* "a rich-watered silk deeply bordered, with camellias in her hair and pearl ornaments."[40]

Unlike the two queens, Mary Lincoln intended to find donors for her dresses. With money a reassurance and expensive clothes a badge of importance, she looked to outsiders to pay the bills so that the Lincoln purse strings could remain closed. In fact, only when her clothes were gifts did she win the painful personal battle between saving and spending. So in the fall of 1861, during her fourth visit to the North, when the New York merchant Alexander Stewart proposed an imported shawl as necessary to keep the First Lady's naked shoulders warm from the White House drafts, Mrs. Lincoln accepted the merchandise. Immersed in the prerogatives of her station, she must have recognized that Stewart wanted influence with her husband. But four months later she was surprised when Stewart sent a bill. It was the first of a flood. Henceforth Mary Lincoln was never sure what separated a donation from a purchase. Some bills she renegotiated; others were withdrawn after she had accomplished a favor. Still more remained unpaid, and these, according to Keckley, amounted to an astonishing $70,000 by 1865. Actually the figure was closer to $10,000, though still an enormous debt.[41]

Soon Mary Lincoln was holding off her creditors. "I write to thank you for your patience," went a penitential note to Stewart in which humiliation overrode grammar, "and soliciting as an especial favor to me, (having been a punctual customer and always hoping to be so, a delay of the Settlement of my account with you. . . ." While proposing an extension, Mary Lincoln assured Stewart of her continuing patronage so that he might find it worthwhile to extend her credit, rather than write her off as a bad risk or, even worse, tell Lincoln about her bills. So in this same letter she ordered a new black camel's hair shawl for $1,000. The more Mary Lincoln owed, the more she had to buy in order (or so she believed) to prevent her informal loans from being called.[42]

Mary Lincoln was more careful when she dealt with artisans who, in light of their circumstances, demanded quick payment. Here frugality reigned. "I do not wish any lace," she wrote Ruth Harris, her New York milliner. "Therefore the bonnet must cost but $25 which is more than I expected to pay for a bonnet furnishing the velvet myself." The penny-pinching over this particular creation ended with an admonition: "very especially [because] black velvet is so expensive do not fail to turn in the sides."[43]

Nor was the First Lady above barter and requisition. Armed with a natural importunity raised to arrogance as a President's wife, she demanded what she wanted, sometimes from other wardrobes and once off a friend's head. When Willian's of Pennsylvania Avenue, Washington's best-known milliner, could not match a lavender ribbon for her bonnet strings and she spied the unusual shade on an acquaintance's hat, with a queen's mandate she insisted Mrs. Taft surrender her strings in return for others (though of a slightly darker color) freely installed by Willian himself. According to her daughter, Mrs. Taft was "amazed and provoked" but eventually surrendered.[44]

In 1861 Mary Lincoln posed for Mathew Brady, choosing for the occasion her most flattering dress—an off-the-shoulders, heavy white silk onto which Elizabeth Keckley had sewn sixty velvet bows and countless black dots. (See photograph 9, page 173.) Tight-laced in futile pursuit of a bell-shaped silhouette (Mary Lincoln was always more sphere than hourglass), she had flowers on her bodice and in her hair. Just as in a photograph previously taken in Springfield, the dress overwhelmed her, partly because she was short and hoops made her look squatter, partly because she used clothes as armor and overdressed. Like a peacock protecting itself through distracting decoration, she was all body and tail, and in the photograph her face is slightly out of focus. The dress has the spotlight; Mary Lincoln seems insignificant compared to what Lincoln once called "her cat tails."[45]

Typically she was disappointed with the results. After measuring expectation against actuality, self-image against daguerreotype, she instructed Brady to destroy all the portraits save one—"the only one at all passable, is the one standing with the large figured dress—back almost turned—showing only side face, you will readily remark the one."[46] It was a realistic estimate, for this pose diminished her heavy-jowled stubbiness. To make certain her commands were followed, she not only advised Brady's Washington studio of her decision but also insisted on confirmation from New York that the less flattering photographs had been destroyed. But she was a celebrity, and Brady kept the others in his archives.

Like any leader of fashion, Mary Lincoln was criticized. Some complained that it was wartime and expected her to set an example of republican frugality from which a French empress, but not a wartime First Lady, could be excepted. Especially northerners misunderstood Mary Lincoln's background and believed she was putting on pretentious airs as she social-climbed. Few Americans seemed to respect, or for that matter even apprehend, this First Lady's purpose of representing her country through high standards of elegance and fashion. Westerners, accustomed to simple high-necked muslins on their matrons, disapproved of her bare shoulders. When the senior senator from Oregon met Madame President at an East Room reception (which room he advised his wife was "about as big as our barn"), James Nesmith found "the weak-minded Mrs. Lincoln and her sorry show of skin and bones. She had her bosom on exhibition, a flower pot on her head— There was a train of silk dragging on the floor behind her of several yards in length." Mary Lincoln, continued Nesmith, who used "to cook Old Abe's dinner and milk the cows," now seemed ambitious "to exhibit her milking apparatus to public gaze."[47]

Even her harshest critics were too discreet to complain publicly that the forty-three-year-old Mrs. Lincoln preferred the styles and colors of the young—especially white (the traditional insignia of youth and purity) but also bold blues, magenta, canary yellow, and royal purple. While Elizabeth Edwards and Lizzie Grimsley (the latter eight years younger than Mary) stuck to somber grays, dark browns, and unmemorable shades of blue, Mary Lincoln was as likely to appear in the same attention-getting primary colors as twenty-one-year-old Kate Chase, the dazzling red-haired daughter of the secretary of the treasury.

No matter what her critics said, Mary Lincoln pleased her husband, who after years of training praised her clothes, hair, and eyes and noticed when things matched. He noticed, too, when her neckline plunged to a stylish, though perhaps inappropriate, décolletage. "Whew," he is quoted as saying, "our cat has a long tail tonight—if some of that tail was nearer the head, it would be in better style." Always moved by her looks in the way of long-married couples who pass imperfections lightly by (and Mary Lincoln did not age well), he praised his wife's appearance to bystanders. Once he remarked at a White House reception that "my wife is as handsome as when she was a girl and I a poor nobody then, fell in love with her and once more, have never fallen out."[48]

FINELY outfitted and elegantly housed, the President's wife also intended to make her mark as the first hostess of the land. In Lexington and Springfield she had acquired the necessary mix of poise, empathy, and coquetry, although some men believed she talked too much and was not sufficiently deferential. But even the uninvited William Herndon acknowledged the success with which she "got up her own parties."[49]

Many married women of her generation loathed entertaining and had little to say to men who were not relatives. Cautioned by parents and advice manuals to beware of strange men unless properly introduced (with the emphasis on *properly*), wives were generally undereducated, poorly read, and completely ignorant of the public affairs that sustained conversation in wartime Washington. In fact, many had so long inhabited a domestic culture that the language of sociability had become as foreign to them as any European tongue.

The wives of Lincoln's administration were typical. Frances Seward's neurasthenia kept her either in bed or in New York. When she did come to parties, she was pale and withdrawn. Mrs. Secretary Usher's headaches made it impossible for her to come to Washington, and Ellen Stanton smiled so rarely that when she did, it seemed to pain her. Adeline Judd, wife of the senior American official in Berlin, "wasn't in society" and by her husband's account welcomed the chest colds that excused her from party giving and going. Even bold Mary Logan, the wife of an Illinois congressman, worried about "having enough ideas to carry me through a long state dinner."[50]

Mary Lincoln was different. With relish she organized the White House receptions and attended them even when she was sick with migraine headaches, gynecological problems, or fevers. Benjamin French found many reasons to stay home on the "handshake days," and the commissioner came to admire the First Lady's endurance. Even Lincoln's young male secretaries took more time off than she from their duties. Instead, with a natural taste for the spotlight that entertaining brings and a sense of duty that matched her husband's, Mary Lincoln charmed her guests. Some, like journalist Jane Swisshelm, admired her "simple and motherly manners"; others, usually male, were impressed by her animation and intelligence. Among the latter was the Massachusetts historian George Bancroft, who wrote:

> Mrs. Lincoln was just dismissing a visitor or two so I was left to a tête-a-tête. . . . She tells me she is a conservative, repudiates the idea that her secessionist brothers can have any influence on her, spoke of the *Herald* as a paper friendly to Mr. Lincoln, . . . discussed eloquently the review the other day. . . . She told what orders she had given for renewing the White House and her elegant fitting up of Mr. Lincoln's room—, her conservatory and love of flowers . . . and ended with giving me a gracious invitation to repeat my visit and saying she would send me a bouquet. I came home entranced.[51]

Mary Lincoln communicated this information in the viscous Kentucky drawl that led some northerners to insist she was a Confederate sympathizer, perhaps even a spy. William Russell, the correspondent for the *Times* of London, complained that she waved her fan and said "sir" too much, though these were common afflictions among well-born southern women. In the end only Kate Chase Sprague was so admired as a conversationalist, though the younger woman could not speak French as Mary Lincoln had done with the Chilean ambassador.[52]

Most of Mary Lincoln's public appearances took place during the traditional twice-a-week winter and spring receptions when as many as 4,000 citizens crowded into the East Room. Levees were arranged for New Year's Day and holidays, with special entertainments for the diplomatic corps, judiciary, Congress, and the armed forces. In previous administrations eggnog and a punch bowl had leavened these affairs, but the temperance movement had ended any possibility of serving alcohol. Moreover, the size of the crowd made food or punch an expensive proposition for which Lincoln had to pay from his private purse.

Still, it would have been scandalous to end the receptions. They had become entrenched in the republican tradition that gave every American the right to pay his respects to his President. This proved especially important during the Civil War, and Mary Lincoln demonstrated through these social affairs the political point that the Union government, no matter what the Confederates threatened, would remain in Washington. In a display of republican camaraderie and good manners, she intended at one reception to shake every guest's hand. She failed, but even Lincoln could not manage this in the throng of guests.

Sometimes the not-so-genteel citizenry came, too: souvenir hunters who snipped material from the new damask curtains, pickpockets who found easy targets in the crush, and even the homeless, who welcomed a temporary shelter in winter. Occasionally Mary Lincoln added music, but always she was there, beautifully attired, gracious, and captivating. Sometimes after a few hours she glanced at the wristwatch that she, and few other women of her generation, wore. But for the most part she was as engaged with her guests as they were with her. Years later a White House employee who served five Presidents acknowledged that the mansion was "more entirely given over to the public in Lincoln's administration than in any other.[53]

Soon Mary Lincoln was contesting more strategic territory. Traditionally the secretary of state gave the administration's first dinner for the diplomatic corps in the state dining room at the White House. Mesdames Polk, Harrison, Pierce, and Harriet Lane had not cared, but Mary Lincoln, who still considered Secretary Seward her husband's rival, insisted that the dinner be given by the President. Unable to challenge the secretary in the cabinet room, she intended to deny him her dining room. Elizabeth Edwards quoted her sister as saying that she would show Seward that Mr. Lincoln was President and that Mary Lincoln, not some minion at the State Department, was in charge of this administration's social events. But accustomed to strawberry parties rather than seated dinners, Mary Lincoln had no idea how expensive her ambitions were. In this case they cost over $900. Everyone in Washington knew what she did not: The social leaders of Washington's past had spent more than $75,000 a season.

For a few days the diplomatic dinner hung in the balance. Finally Mrs. Lincoln prevailed and hired a New York caterer for what was now, no matter what it had been before, her affair. "Our dinner," she wrote to a Springfield friend, "comes off this evening, a party of twenty-eight will dine with us." She did not add that she and Lizzie Grimsley were the only women. Later the bills went to the State Department, and ever after Seward's friends gossiped that Mrs. Lincoln padded her bill and that the secretary could have put on a cheaper, better dinner than the Hell-Cat.[54]

In August Mary Lincoln gave another dinner party—this time for Prince Napoleon, Lucien Bonaparte's son and the nephew of Napoleon III and Eugénie. Like many Europeans, the prince had crossed the Atlantic for the amusement of observing the Americans at war. Leaving his wife on board his yacht in New York Harbor (Washington in August was deemed too hot and unhealthy for Princess Clothilde, although Lincoln's catty secretaries in a possible reference to Mrs. Lincoln believed she wanted to avoid "the profanation of vulgar eyes"), the prince traveled to Washington for a visit. When he arrived at the President's House to pay a call, through some inadvertence not even the doorkeeper, Edward McManus, was at the front door. Instead, it was the imperturbable Willie Lincoln who did the honors, bowing low to French royalty with the majesty of which the third Lincoln son was capable. Later the prince confided to his diary that "one goes right in [the White House] as if entering a café." The office seekers in the upstairs hall would have agreed, though to them it was more employment office than café. Secretary of State Seward, according to the prince, looked like "a rural farmer with his yellow-striped coat." The President resembled a "bootmaker."[55]

The next night Mary Lincoln entertained her first prince. The week before she had described her preparations to a Springfield friend. "The Prince and suite are expected in Washington and on Saturday, we dine them at *8 o'clock P.M.*" (The time itself was sufficiently impressive for two Springfield women accustomed to supper at 5:00 P.M. that she underlined it.) "Very different from home. We only have to give our orders for the dinner and dress in proper season."[56]

Of course, she had done more than that because the White House was operating with fewer servants than in the days of Buchanan and Pierce. Mary Lincoln had chosen the menu, surveyed the prospects for vegetables from the garden, supervised the cooking, and arranged the fresh flowers that became her trademark. Still, there were lapses. Instead of the imperial anthem, the Marine Band unaccountably struck up the "Marseillaise," (one of Lincoln's favorites). In the awkward silence that followed, the prince saved the evening with his gallantry that in the United States he, too, was a republican. Later someone foolishly asked him to compare Paris and Washington. Again good manners prevailed, and he replied that Paris was not the world, though he obviously considered Washington a much lesser part of it.[57]

Mary Lincoln used her French that night, and though her private reaction to Prince Napoleon went unrecorded, he described her as "dressed in the French style without any taste." As for his meal, it, too, was "a bad dinner in the French style." (In fact, this French-style cooking was special, for Mary Lincoln explained to a friend who thought Mary's headaches came from fancy food, "we dine in plainest manner."[58]) Ignorant of the French style, the American press was more complimentary and compared the President's lady to Queen Victoria and Empress Eugénie. By the time the bills came, Mary Lincoln had left for Long Branch, New Jersey.

DURING her parties Mary Lincoln attended to the business of patronage. She had grown accustomed to receiving presents and knew politics well enough to understand that she was exchanging a whisper in her husband's ear (or sometimes an angry tantrum in his presence) in return for expensive gifts, which included a handsome sewing machine "worthy of a duchess." Even before Lincoln's inauguration Isaac Henderson, who was in pursuit of a customs office in Boston, gave Mary

Lincoln some diamonds, and his gift led to a fight between the Lincolns in which Mary implored her husband to give Henderson, at least, a naval agency, and he did.[59]

Her best present, a stylish black barouche with four black carriage horses (the horses to be exchanged "if Mrs. Lincoln preferred another color"), had arrived in Washington before the inauguration, the donation of some New York merchants who hoped to gain her business and his favors with their investment. The President had no scruples about riding in this handsome coach during the late-afternoon rides that became a private recreation enjoyed by a couple with little opportunity to be alone. Accepting the barouche was hardly a conflict of interest, at least not as understood by freewheeling nineteenth-century politicians. But once in the White House, Lincoln refused large gifts that trespassed his rigorous standards of propriety, though he did not interfere with his wife's acquisitions. As the President explained to the king of Siam, who sent diamonds, swords, and the elephants for which Tad must have clamored, "Our laws forbid the President from receiving these rich presents as personal treasures. They are therefore accepted in accordance with your Majesty's desire as tokens of goodwill and friendship in the name of the American People."[60]

But the First Lady felt differently. Not only did Mary Lincoln consider her views more typical of prevailing standards, but she believed her husband a fanatic—"almost a monomaniac on the subject of honesty." Unlike the easygoing Pierce, the unaware Buchanan, and the improbious Grant, President Lincoln closed off the flow of favor buying, forcing it into alternate avenues. "I hear," wrote one patronage seeker, "the ladies of the house may have some influence." George Ashmun, the chairman of the Republican National Committee, agreed, explaining that "Mrs. Lincoln keeps me informed of everything." Other White House visitors received promises from the First Lady. "Your wife told me the last time you would remember Mr. Moody," wrote one suppliant to the President.[61]

Soon Mary Lincoln became the tainted alter ego of Honest Abe. In the overcrowded upstairs hall through which she had to walk on her way to her room or in the downstairs cubbyhole where the doorkeeper tried to sequester patronage seekers, the President's wife was available. Favor seekers recognized in her an experienced influence peddler and made known their claims. The President tolerated this, just as he did the unsavory insider buying of Salmon P. Chase, his secretary of treasury, and for a short time the more obvious corruptions of Secretary of

War Simon Cameron. Nor did Lincoln stop the long-established system that permitted Commissioner French to serve as a congressional lobbyist for fifty-dollar fees collected from private citizens.[62]

Mary Lincoln was assiduous in honoring her promises, and the task kept her at her desk writing as many as three letters a day. As her debts increased, she may have initiated the exchange of her influence on Lincoln for a bill paid or new material for a dress. Not all her interventions were self-serving, though; some involved friends, relatives, and worthy causes. "Dear Mr. Seward," went a request to the secretary of state, "Our friend Colonel Mygatt, comes to us very highly recommended as a gentleman and as an earnest Republican." The secretary of war received her recommendation that the department buy "some young Kentucky horses owned by an especial friend of mine—a strong Union man."[63]

Besides patronage, Mary Lincoln took a special interest in her husband's cabinet, where she would have liked to sit. After all, she had advised Lincoln about politics for more than twenty years, and she intended to continue as his counselor in Washington. But now the President was so distant that she had to enlist outsiders in her campaigns. When, in 1863, conservative Republicans pressed for General Nathaniel Banks's appointment to the cabinet, Mary Lincoln encouraged several friends, including Senator Charles Sumner, to write her husband of their opposition. Banks's appointment turned out to be far from Lincoln's mind, though it was no doubt farther after his wife's intervention. Triumphantly she informed Sumner: "Mr. Lincoln now says he has no idea of [appointing Banks] himself and that General Banks is to return to his command in New Orleans immediately." Sometimes the President teased that if she had her way, she would remove his entire cabinet. Indeed after she had fathomed the treachery of Salmon Chase, who intended to replace her husband as President, she referred to Lincoln's cabinet as "that happy family" and wished that she might have at least a say in its composition.[64]

Mary Lincoln also intervened for selected members of her family, although her husband, much to the irritation of his Republican cronies in Springfield, needed little urging from her to give federal appointments to his two Democratic brothers-in-law. Near bankruptcy in 1860, Ninian Edwards was appointed to the Commissary Department of the U.S. Army, while the always impecunious Dr. Wallace ("he is needy," wrote Lincoln, "and I personally owe him much") became a local paymaster of the volunteers. For this appointment Mary Lincoln took credit, informing Lizzie Grimsley: "Frances [Wallace] often spoke of Mr. L's kindness—in giving him his place. She little knows what a hard battle, I had for it—and how near, he came to getting nothing."[65]

In the scramble for jobs presidential relatives did well, but not well enough to deserve the *New York World*'s complaint that Lincoln "in an unparalleled display of nepotism has appointed his whole family to government posts." His wife responded with technical accuracy that these are "villainous aspersions. . . . Mr. L. has neither brother nor sister, aunt or uncle and only a few third cousins. That clears him entirely as to any connection."

She did not mention her side of his family, though she had worked hard to get Lizzie Grimsley the Springfield Post Office. In her judgment Grimsley had served a First Lady. Having come to Washington for the inauguration in March, her loyal cousin had remained, not entirely voluntarily, through the summer. "I have overstayed my time so long," Grimsley explained to Cousin John Stuart, "because Mary urged and urged and seemed to feel hurt at the idea of my leaving her." Discovering that "Mary hates to be alone," she was no nearer in May "to getting away than I was six weeks ago." It was August before she finally returned to Springfield, full of promises from her hostess about the post office. Both Lincolns encouraged the Republicans to nominate Grimsley; but the local party preferred a man, and Mary's cousin lost the three-way election.[66]

When Mary Lincoln failed to get her way, she intercepted cabinet officers and pressed state officials at her receptions. By the end of her first spring in the White House there was hardly an important official in Washington who had not received a request made in the name of the presidential "we." And many were appalled at the intrusions. When a Parker relative turned up in Secretary of War Edwin Stanton's office, fortified by a verbal reference from Mary Lincoln for a sutlership, Stanton paid no attention. The next day the man was back—this time with a "small smile of triumph" and Mrs. Lincoln's personal card on which she had written, "If you can grant his petition, you will bestow a personal favor upon me." Undaunted, Stanton tore up the endorsement and marched to the White House to lecture the First Lady, according to his secretary, "on her duties to the nation and her husband." She promised not to bother him again, but within the week a messenger had delivered newspaper clippings criticizing the army and its heartless officials. These came anonymously, but Stanton had no doubt they were the donation of Mary Lincoln. Thereafter avoiding

Stanton, Mary Lincoln instead sent her cousin to General James Hardie, and eventually Robert Parker got his sutlership.[67]

For all her intrusiveness, Mary Lincoln was self-conscious about her trespasses onto male territory, though they were irresistible encroachments. Like a tomboy disgraced for dirtying a party dress, she displayed her embarrassment in apologetic appeals that begged the male pardon. "Excuse my intrusion"; "May I hope as this is the only request I have asked of you, or will ever again, that you will grant it"; "It is unbecoming of me to write thus," went her disclaimers. "I have a terror of strong-minded ladies," said this one, "but if a word fitly spoken and in due season can be urged at a time like this, we should not withhold it." Intellectually conventional, she behaved boldly in demanding masculine indulgences and suffered for her internal contradiction.[68]

By no means was Mary Lincoln the only American woman during the Civil War to cross the barrier dividing the public activities of men from the private world of women. With masculine protectors gone to battle, wives, sisters, mothers, and daughters sought licenses to sell cotton, claimed patronage for relatives, begged clemency for deserters (this last usually reserved for mothers trying to save sons from firing squads), and encouraged promotions for family members. Some women addressed their requests to Mrs. President Lincoln, expecting sympathy from a female, and in so doing, they inadvertently encouraged Mary Lincoln's understanding of herself as a public person.[69]

Rarely did these women request favors for themselves, although occasionally a single woman sought a clerical job in the government or a pass through the Union lines. Instead, they interceded for others. Prim, respectable Eliza Browning (whose husband once became "too distressingly loving" in a carriage ride with Mary Lincoln) was unusual only in that she wanted her husband appointed to the Supreme Court. She had known Lincoln as a young man in New Salem and wrote the President: "I do not ask this because I am thirsty for distinction. I ask it because I know my husband to be the wisest, best man in the nation." Clearly the war had suspended the prejudice against women's muddling in public affairs, but the waiver was only for appeals made, as in Eliza Browning's case, for male relatives. Mary Lincoln's transgressions were thus twofold. She promoted the claims of men who were not relatives (how indeed could a proper nineteenth-century wife know a man well enough for such a reference?), and she did so for the same reason that men did: to gain an advantage for herself.[70]

BY January 1862 Mary Lincoln could take pride in several achieve-
ments. The busiest First Lady in history, she had redecorated the White
House, modified the forms of presidential entertaining, outfitted herself like a queen, participated in patronage decisions, reviewed the
troops, and visited the hospitals. "If you were aware how much *every
moment* is occupied, you would excuse me" became a standard excuse
to friends whose letters went unanswered for months. Frequently
exhausted, Mary Lincoln was often ill with Washington's seasonal chills
and fevers, and once she was incapacitated by a concussion sustained
in a carriage accident. Several times migraine headaches sent her to
bed. No matter what the problem, she did not stay out of action long.
Still, amid her energetic endeavors she sometimes yearned for "more
leisure, *that blessed* assurance [that] frequently quiets my nerves."[71]

But like most periods in her ill-starred life, this first year in the
White House brought failure as well as achievement. Not only was
there public ridicule of Mrs. Lincoln in the papers (which the requirements of fame made it impossible for her to resist reading), but she
had several fights with her usually understanding husband, who had
erupted in anger over Commissioner Wood and her expenditures.
Because of her temper and her interest in patronage, she had also made
enemies. Worst of all, with Lincoln often depressed and preoccupied
with the war news, she was lonely, especially after Lizzie Grimsley
had returned to Springfield.

Nor had nine months of war brought any indication that the Union
armies would soon defeat the Confederates. Like everyone else in the
North, Mary Lincoln had expected the war to end in three months,
but it had dragged on. Ever since the Battle of Bull Run the Union
army had retreated in one humiliating disaster after another. In the
fall the Confederates had managed to trap a Union force between Virginia's cliffs and the Potomac River and there had killed her friend
Colonel Edward Dickinson Baker. Ball's Bluff symbolized the inept-
ness of the Union forces, for it was an easily avoidable disaster. Thereafter morale had sagged despite General McClellan's efforts to train an
army. Even optimistic Unionists felt what Walt Whitman described
as "awful consternation, uncertainty, rage, shame, helplessness and
stupefying disappointment."[72] Lincoln had been especially depressed
at Christmas, the gray, damp Washington weather matching his mood.

With nothing to celebrate after Christmas, Mary Lincoln believed
this the best moment for a party that would simultaneously lighten
spirits and convey through its magnificence the power of the govern-

ment. She had in mind an evening affair, a replacement for the expensive state dinners for which the Lincolns had to pay. "La Reine," wrote John Hay, "has determined to abrogate dinners." Unlike the public receptions, this party would be by invitation only. If her project succeeded, she would serve her conflicting mistresses of frugality, lavishness, notoriety, and gentility and would enhance the Lincoln party's prestige as well as create a diversion for her husband.

By the end of January 1862 nearly 500 invitations had been extended, and there were not-so-subtle hints from those left off the list. Such pleading pleased the hostess, for when Mary Lincoln had come to Washington only a year before, the city's elite had boycotted her supposedly vulgar affairs. "Half the city is jubilant in being invited," wrote Nicolay, "while the uninvited half are furious at being left out." A few Republicans like Senator Benjamin Wade of Ohio declined. "Are the President and Mrs. Lincoln aware there is a Civil War? If they are not, Mr. and Mrs. Wade are and for that reason decline to participate in feasting and dancing." Despite such reminders, Mary Lincoln went ahead and hired Maillard's, possibly the most expensive caterer in the country; she ordered champagne and wine from another New York firm, Clement Heerdt's on Water Street, and she even placed a new coatrack in the dressing rooms. (In the past the coat issue had been a problem, and once her archrival Kate Chase had angrily refused to surrender her cloak for fear of having it lost or stolen at a Mary Lincoln reception.)[73]

A little before nine on February 5, 1862, the carriages started arrivin. Doorkeeper McManus had strict orders to admit only those with invitations. The generals (few under that rank had been invited) arrived first in dress uniform, and they included the handsome, mustachioed George B. McClellan, who, for the last several months, had been dashing about Washington intent on his mission of transforming raw farm boys into well-drilled soldiers. Present as well in full court dress, though they arrived later, were the cock-hatted, besworded, overdecorated diplomatic corps. Finally there was the government—the cabinet, the Supreme Court, and selected stars from the House of Representatives and the Senate. In their black coats they were as colorful as crows among peacocks, especially since Mary Lincoln had dressed her staff in new mulberry-colored uniforms, the color complementing her new solferino-edged china set. Of course, she had also included some personal friends from Washington and New York. The President wore his black swallowtail coat, and she chose a loamy white silk, decorated with hundreds of black flounces, the latter in sympathetic remembrance of Queen Victoria's Prince Albert, who had died two months before.[74]

The gossips expected dancing, but instead Mary and Abraham Lincoln received in the East Room, with the Marine Band playing in the hall. The music included the "Marseillaise" and a sprightly new piece, "The Mary Lincoln Polka," written specially for the party. Finally, after an embarrassing delay at midnight, when no one could find the key (the dining room was locked to assure a collective entrance of 150 at a time), the doors swung open to reveal a magnificent buffet. Maillard had been in Washington for five days, concocting sugary molds based on war themes such as Fort Pickens and the Ship of State. As a centerpiece Mary Lincoln used the Japanese punch bowl brought by Matthew Perry from the Orient, and there was barely room on the table for the immense buffet of turkey, duck, ham, terrapin, and pheasant. Dinner was served until three, and even duty-bound generals did not leave until daybreak. The soiree was "the most superb affair of its kind ever seen here," concluded the *Washington Star,* and it established Mary Lincoln's ascendancy over her rival, Kate Chase. No expense having been spared, it cost the Lincolns more than $1,000.[75]

The party should have been a highpoint in her career as First Lady, but like so much else in Mary Lincoln's calamitous life, she could not enjoy her triumph. Upstairs Willie Lincoln was running a high fever, and both parents spent much of the evening sitting by his bed.

VIII

A Vanishing Circle

Two weeks and a day after the party eleven-year-old Willie Lincoln was dead. Some said he died from bilious fever or a malarial infection; others (and they were more likely correct, considering the time of year and his symptoms) believed the third Lincoln son succumbed to typhoid fever, the invisible bacterial scourge transmitted by fecally contaminated water. For the past five years the President's household had drawn its water from the Potomac River—a supposed improvement over the local springs. But during the war, when Washington's normal population of 60,000 swelled with military personnel, profiteers, and patronage seekers to 200,000, the District's few sewage mains broke and drained into the river. When the army set up camps without latrine trenches along the banks of the Potomac, the contamination increased. Soon the Potomac had become a vast septic tank the lethal contents of which were piped back into the White House.

No one thought much about sanitation at the time. Public health and proper sewage disposal would not be connected until the late nineteenth century, though

Mary Lincoln had complained about both the swamp and the malodorous stench. Within easy range of Tad and Willie's explorations was a marsh that had remained a refuse heap for dead animals and for the night soil dumped from overloaded carts. There had been several typhoid epidemics that winter in the army hospital nearby, and in the White House both Tad and Willie Lincoln were sick. [1]

During that third week of February 1862 some gave up hope for both boys. But it was the older one who died and, like his brother Eddie twelve years before, died hard, from either internal hemorrhaging or ulceration of the intestine. An earlier case of scarlet fever, which his mother saw as "a warning to us that one so pure would not remain long here," had probably damaged Willie's kidneys and heart, making him an easy target for a fatal bacterial infection. As he became more emaciated, the symptoms of his typhoid fever—the cramps, diarrhea, and intestinal spasms—were difficult for any parent to watch.

Later Mary Lincoln wrote that "all that human skill could do was done for our sainted boy." She referred here to the ministrations of Dr. Robert Stone, the dean of the Washington medical community, who assiduously dosed Willie with useless and countervailing therapies: Peruvian bark, calomel, and jalap given at half-hour intervals when he was conscious. Like most nineteenth-century illnesses, his was also treated by home remedies of beef tea, blackberry cordial, and Miss Leslie's bland puddings. But neither medicine nor folklore prevailed, and like many typhoid victims, Willie became listless, dehydrated, and wasted. Two days before he died, when he lapsed into a coma, the newspapers reported that the President's son was not expected to live. [2]

Willie's unconsciousness robbed his mother of a consolation that nineteenth-century mothers anxiously sought during their bedside vigils. Mary Lincoln's friend Mercy Conkling once described the visions of the dying as the signals that a dying child "was going on to a better world and was resigned to his fate." In the sentimental fiction of the age, children saw heaven and reassured their mothers that the family would be reunited in a better place. The imagination of this generation's "scribbling women" transformed Christian resurrection into a heavenly paradise. In Ellen Price Wood's popular *East Lynne*, which Mary Lincoln read shortly after Willie's death, the long-suffering hero—a boy exactly Willie's age—announced to those at his bedside that "Jesus is coming for me—I see heaven, a beautiful city, precious stones, pearly gates, beautiful fruits and flowers." Mrs. Wood assured her readers that "those whom God loves he takes first."[3]

A century before, the church had consoled; in worldly mid-nin-teenth-century America dead children returned from the spirit world to comfort their grieving mothers. Such sentimentality stood as a valuable defense against the hard fact of a child's death, and so the deathbed became a critical moment for survivors. Eddie Lincoln had been too young for such visible signs. Now the course of Willie's illness made it unlikely he could offer such a consolation to his mother.

In Willie's death Mary Lincoln lost her favorite son, the one who called himself (though surely his mother must have whispered it in his ear) "Mama's boy." She acknowledged in a letter written a few months after his death: "I always found my hopes concentrating on so good a boy as he." Others also found him the most interesting of the Lincoln boys, and the President's admirers found reflected in the third Lincoln son his father's humor, intelligence, and generosity of spirit. Mary's friend Nathaniel Willis published a touching remembrance of Willie's virtues in the *Home Journal,* which she wanted reprinted in the Spring-field newspapers. Much later Lincoln's barber in Springfield recalled Willie "as a smart boy for his age, so considerate, so manly, his knowledge and good since [*sic*] far exceeding most boys more evi-denced in years."[4]

In the inexplicable calculus of her mothering, Mary Lincoln's other sons were flawed. Tad would always be "dear little Taddie" with his speech defect, overactivity, slow learning, and dependence, while she and Robert were never kindred spirits. After Willie's death she tried to promote her eldest son and wrote a Springfield neighbor: "Robert will be home from Cambridge in about six weeks and will spend his vacation with us. He has grown and improved more than anyone ever saw."[5] But unlike the perfect Willie, Robert would always have room to reform his coldness and reserve.

The day after his death Willie was laid out in the Green Room. After his mother had placed a sprig of laurel on his chest (these were open coffin days and Willie had been embalmed), she never again entered either this room or the second-floor guest room where he had died. This exclusionary process of mourning became a characteristic behavior for a woman who felt the death of her kin as a personal abandonment, not as an opportunity for their salvation. This view had developed early through her loss of a mother, brother, and son in death and a father to a wretched stepmother. Orphaned herself, Mary Lin-coln was never able to incorporate memories of her dead into the comforting recollections that today's psychologists consider a vital part of a normal recovery from bereavement. In time—for she was an energetic, resourceful woman—she was to seek and find some unconventional consolations.[6]

Part of her problem was cultural, for she lived in an age in which attention had shifted from the dead to the response of the living to the dead. How to mourn, now as closely monitored in the behavior manuals as the ritual of calling, had replaced the private self-examinations of conscience that death had evoked in earlier generations. Now nineteenth-century Americans practiced a sentimentalized cult prescribing how to dress and how to display sadness. In a romantic age of exaggerated postures, bereavement became the occasion on which to show the deepest emotions of earthly experience. Good mourners must reveal a proper mix of pious emotion and sorrowful restraint, however difficult this might be.

To violate these standards was to risk nasty gossip. It was the talk of Washington that Secretary of War Stanton had exhumed his daughter's body for cremation more than a year after she had been buried. After his first wife had died, Stanton dressed her in her wedding dress, moaning that "this is my bride and she shall be dressed and buried like a bride." Thereafter (or at least until his second marriage) her lace cap lay on his pillow. In 1861, when Victoria's beloved Prince Albert succumbed to typhoid fever, the British queen was reported in the American press as practicing mummification by placing wreaths on his bed, setting a place for him at the table, and organizing séances at which he supposedly appeared.[7]

Like Queen Victoria when Albert died, Mary Lincoln did not attend Willie's funeral in the White House or what turned out to be his temporary interment in a Georgetown cemetery. This was not unusual. Women, especially the mothers and wives of the deceased, often stayed home during public ceremonies. Secluded in daily life, they mourned privately, especially if they did not have control over their tears. "Tears are not for the gaze," advised one manual, and those who cried in solitude were said to be more sincere in their sorrow for not having "blazoned it upon the housetops." Good Christian women knew better than to mourn excessively; visible emotion only displayed their lack of faith in the doctrine that the dead passed from this world into God's better one. According to one mourning manual, only "Jews and heathens howl in impious anguish and they do so because they don't know any better."[8]

On February 24, 1862, during a tornado that uprooted trees and ripped roofs from Washington buildings, Mary Lincoln's eldest son and husband shared a coach to the Georgetown cemetery with Secretary of War Stanton. Mary Lincoln stayed in the White House, her emotions as stormy as the weather. She had always connected sadness and ill health. Now she took to bed with spasms of sorrow—what Elizabeth Keckley described as "paroxysms of grief." In time her weeping produced its own bodily afflictions: a sore throat, impaired eyesight, shaking, and weakness. Through this childlike replay of anguish (what she may have done at six when her mother died), she mimicked Willie's last illness and Tad's current one. In fact, Mary Lincoln was in bed for three weeks before anyone could persuade her even to get up and put on her mourning clothes.[9]

With Tad critically ill and his mother as incapacitated as any invalid, the Lincolns needed help. They got it first from a sympathetic friend, Mary Jane Welles, who herself had lost five children and who stayed for a period of time in the White House, and from Elizabeth Keckley, the seamstress who had become as much confidante and intimate as the creator of fashionable gowns. Then, on the recommendation of Dorothea Dix, who had been appointed superintendent of women nurses in 1861, an experienced army nurse arrived in the White House. Rebecca Pomroy fascinated both Lincolns because she had come to terms with the deaths of her husband and three sons. In Lincoln's description, Pomroy "cheerfully" and "exclusively devotes herself to our sick and wounded soldiers." A telegram brought Elizabeth Edwards to Washington, though Mary's eldest sister was soon chafing to return to her family in Springfield. Before, Elizabeth Edwards had been her sister's best healer, but having presided over her own child's deathbed with fewer histrionics than Mary Lincoln, she was impatient with her younger sister. "Aunt Mary," she commented to her daughter Julia, "is nervous and dependent upon the companionship of someone." And later, to encourage her niece, Frances Wallace's daughter, to take her place, Elizabeth Edwards explained that "Aunt Mary is so constituted as to present a long indulgence of such gloom."[10]

Six years later in a ghostwritten exposé that Mary Lincoln considered a breach of their intimacy, Elizabeth Keckley remembered that during this tormented period Lincoln led his wife to the window, pointed to a lunatic asylum, and said, "Mother, do you see that large white building on the hill yonder. Try and control your grief or it will drive you mad and we may have to send you there."[11] The testimony is suspicious, for the Lincolns were in the White House until June and could not see the new million-dollar Government Hospital for the Insane, though it was easily visible from their summer residence, the Soldiers' Home, where Keckley rarely went. If Lincoln did caution his wife, he was responding to a body of opinion that linked excessive female weeping to hysteria and the nineteenth century's catchall mental impairment, "mania."

In turn Mary Lincoln worried about her husband, for she was never so self-absorbed as to lose sight of him. Lincoln might console the grieving relatives of the war dead with platitudes about the universality of sorrow and the need for time "to alleviate distress," but his wife knew that he could not sleep and was again having those bizarre nightmares that lurked in his subconscious. She also knew that in striking contrast with her own behavior—for she could not go near the place—the President locked himself in Willie's room every Thursday, there to sit alone commemorating the day his son had died. Gradually Lincoln came to see Willie's death as his personal version of the country's sorrows, and in view of the contamination of the Potomac by the army, Willie's illness may have been an indirect result of the war. Moreover, his son had died just after the important Union victory at Fort Donelson in Tennessee, and through his private tragedy Lincoln believed he participated in the nation's collective grief over its wartime casualties. Thereby he found solace.[12]

Few nineteenth-century women—certainly not Mary Lincoln—could have gained consolation from such an abstract identification. Instead, the First Lady continued to destroy the physical signs of her dead son. Though she had diligently nursed her children in the past, now Tad evoked memories of Willie. Consequently she spent little time with him in the spring of 1862. In fact, Willie's playmates the Taft boys elicited such punishing recollections that Mary Lincoln exorcised them from the White House. "Please keep the boys home the day of the funeral. It makes me worse to see them," she wrote to their mother, who waited in vain for Bud and Halsey Taft to be invited back to the White House to play with Tad. Soon Willie's clothes and toys—even the two cars without the engine—had been sent off to Springfield relatives. Only his pony and Nanko and Nannie, the fraternally owned goats, remained, though two years later, almost to the day of Willie's death, the pony was burned to death in a stable fire that Mary Lincoln considered a certain sign of an impending catastrophe. Throughout her hibernation in the spring of 1862 she avoided "all communication with those who would most forcibly recall my sorrows to my mind."[13]

Slowly Mary Lincoln recovered. She was out of bed by April and, along with Tad, recuperated in the family quarters from what she continued to call "this stroke." During this period both Lincolns read the consolatory sermons of the Washington clergyman Francis Vinton. In late April Mary Lincoln went to her church, the New York Avenue Presbyterian, "in such an immense black veil—and very deep black flounces—that one could scarcely tell she was there."[14]

In a way she wasn't. For Mary Lincoln never gained comfort from Reverend Phineas Gurley's sermons—even those on the redemption of sin and the resurrection of the body. Presbyterian women were supposed to respond to their sorrows by "fleeing to God with melted hearts" and accepting, even rejoicing in the dismal providential finality that "the Lord giveth and the Lord taketh away." The well-known Presbyterian minister Lyman Beecher taught that the death of some of his thirteen children inspired the others to conversion experiences, so that according to this cost-benefit analysis, death served as a spiritually productive force among the living. Encouraged by such attitudes, churchgoing women often reported that after "drinking the cup of bereavement," they discovered God.

Never could Mary Lincoln come to terms with Willie's death as a God-delivered affliction to which she must acquiesce. She knew what she was supposed to believe—"If we could only realise how far happier they now are than here on earth," she wrote Mary Jane Welles—but she couldn't, and so sought instruction in how to submit from Rebecca Pomroy. As the nurse described these conversations, Mary Lincoln "said she was tired of being a slave to the world and would live on bread and water if she could feel as happy as I do." But Mary Lincoln never reached such equanimity and instead raged against God's injustice to her. Five months after Willie's death she wondered "if our Heavenly Father has forsaken us in removing so lovely a boy from us." She was too much a Christian not to be frightened by such blasphemy. "Yet I know a great sin, is committed when we feel thus."[15]

In the consolation literature that she avidly read during this period, most women felt no such conflict. Those who were afflicted came to love God—and be loved by Him—more than those who had no such trials. Like Job, the best were selected for the greatest trials. "Brambles do not get pruned," counseled Nehemiah Adams in his lachrymose study of the parental acceptance of a child's death, *Agnes and the Little Key, Or, Bereaved Parents Instructed and Comforted.* Flowers and vines are "cut and thinned out." But to Mary Lincoln's thinking, if Willie was such a special child, then that was all the more reason why he should stay on earth with her.[16]

Eventually she resolved the ancient problem of theodicy in a personal way that made God share responsibility with her. In the past every instance of what Mary Lincoln called "our own political advancement" had been so closely attended by misfortune as to indicate a causative relationship. Eddie's tuberculosis had worsened during his father's term in Congress. Lincoln's nomination for President in May 1860 had been followed a month later by Tad's and Willie's near-fatal scarlet fever. Both boys had gotten measles after the inauguration. Now Willie's death had come just after her glamorous party; in fact, his fever had worsened that very night. The symbolic connection between a now-forbidden white party dress and the dull necessity of black mourning was so inescapable that Mary Lincoln believed her son's death a judgment for her party. In the title of her husband's favorite poem her mortal spirit was too proud, so she had been horribly penalized. "Our home is very beautiful," she wrote a former neighbor in Springfield. "The grounds are very enchanting, the world still smiles and pays homage and we are left desolate—the world has lost its charm."

Life, she reasoned, was a cruel seesaw of triumphs and tragedies in which she had never been an accidental victim. Instead, like the highest tree of a forest that lightning strikes first, she stood out as a target. Mercy Levering Conkling understood the juxtaposition. "How soon is Mary's gaiety turned into sadness," she wrote, a sadness for which, after Willie's death, Mary Lincoln held herself responsible.[17]

The public knew little of these private agonies. In the way that victims are often blamed for the evil that befalls them, the gossips judged her guilty of neglecting her children for extravagant parties and selfish frivolity. On this point public condemnation accorded with private guilt. Like Job's friends who believed he must have committed some mischief (we reap what we sow, said Eliphaz the Temanite), many thought Mary Lincoln deserved her fate. A Washington merchant expressed the widely held view: "I suppose Mrs. Lincoln will be providentially deterred from giving any more parties which scandalized so many good persons who did not get invitations—Providence seems to have interfered to put a stop to any more parties at the White House this winter." In such an accounting the death of little Willie had become God's scourge on an evil woman.[18]

No matter what the gossips said, Mary Lincoln did not stay out of the public eye for long, as she began to stand out, if not in submission to God, at least for her mourning. In place of the French empress Eugénie, Queen Victoria, the high priestess of grief, became the First Lady's model. In May, three months after Willie's death, Mary Lincoln wrote her New York milliner: "I am in need of a mourning bonnet—which must be exceedingly plain and genteel. I want one made of crape with folds, a bonnet of black crape . . . to be the *finest, jet black* English crape. . . . The black one must be exceedingly, plain, rich, very best material and genteel." But the bonnet did not suit. "I wished," went a subsequent letter, "a much finer black straw bonnet for mourning—without the gloss. I want you to select for me the *very finest* and blackest and lightest long crape veil." She used the words *genteel* and *fine* repeatedly in these short notes, once raising *genteel* to a superlative by which she meant to convey the sooty, lusterless look of fashionable grieving clothes. Men escaped such conventions with simple black bands on their sleeves or sprigs of myrtle around their hats. Lincoln added nothing to the lapels of his black swallowtail coat. But for women, night's color, the opposite of life, served as an external badge of their withdrawal from the world.[19]

For more than a year, though the manuals called for only six months, Mary Lincoln wore first-degree mourning, thereby reminding herself and everyone else of her special case. Like Mrs. Pipchin in Charles Dickens's *Dombey and Son,* "she was so dark that even gas lights could not lighten her appearance." Her headgear—that black crepe bonnet and veil Milliner Harris had finally fashioned to her liking—made it impossible for her to turn her head. Always she must look forward; nothing must distract her from her misery. In time Mary Lincoln bought jet black jewelry to accompany her costumes, and she used writing paper with the thickest margins of black, all of which purchases added to her unpaid accounts. Finally, in 1863, she exchanged all black for the next stage of her grief and another new expensive wardrobe, the half mourning of lavender, gray, and somber purples with a little touch of white at the wrist.[20]

During her mourning Mary Lincoln expected the world to suffer with her. Irritated by the gay music of the Marine Band that customarily played Saturday afternoons on the presidential grounds, she canceled the summer concerts. "When we are in sorrow"—she gave as her dictate—"quiet is necessary." But her fellow citizens were outraged by this interference with their pleasures, and a government crisis ensued involving the secretary of the navy, Gideon Welles, who argued for the concerts, and the commissioner of public buildings, Benjamin French, who took Mary's side. Finally, when the season was nearly over, the concerts were resumed across Pennsylvania Avenue in Lafayette Park.[21]

BY July 1862 Mary Lincoln had sufficiently recovered to move to the Soldiers' Home, the presidential retreat on a wooded hill three miles from the White House in the northern part of the city. Since Willie's death she had paid no attention to the war, not wanting to merge her special loss in that of others. Her husband, however, had been optimistic about victory in May, when the Union forces had penetrated to within fourteen miles of the Confederate capital at Richmond. Then, before General Lee's defenders, McClellan's offensive stalled in the swamps near the Chickahominy River. When word of the bloody June battles at Beaver Dam Creek, Gaines's Mill, Savage's Station, and Malvern Hill filtered back to Washington, Lincoln spent his days and nights in the War Department, watching the telegraph operators decode the story of a failed campaign. In early July the President visited the Army of the Potomac in Virginia and shortly thereafter he replaced McClellan with Henry Halleck in his continuing search for a successful general.

In the meantime, his lonely wife went North. Dressed in her widow's weeds, she visited New York, ostensibly to raise money for the army hospitals and to get Tad out of a city ridden with smallpox and malaria. In November she repeated her trip, this time spending more than a week in Boston. Robert was now a sophomore at Harvard and a heroic figure to nine-year-old Tad, who often sought his older brother's company.

But New York and Boston had other attractions. During the 1850s both cities had become centers of the spiritualist movement. In darkened private parlors, on curtained public stages, through opaque crystal balls, and with misshapen wizzening rods, Americans were raising their dead during a war that killed disproportionate numbers of the young. According to the novelist William Dean Howells, every other house in Boston held a medium ready to console parents and wives, while Mary Lincoln's friend Nathaniel Willis had somehow counted 300 circles and 40,000 spiritualists in a city of 177,000. Four spiritualist newspapers and the Society for the Diffusion of Spiritual Knowledge had turned the Massachusetts capital into a meeting ground for those who believed that after the dead had shed their bodies like a snake's skin, their spirits remained available to those who knew how to contact them. Meanwhile, in New York hundreds of mediums placed the living in touch with the identifiable spirits of the dead.[22]

Spiritualists dated their secular resurgence (the seeds of the movement had always existed in certain evangelical denominations) from the Rochester rappings in the tiny village of Hydesville, New York, where an old clapboard house belonging to Jack Fox had come alive with the sound of a spirit's knocking. By the early 1850s Kate and Margaret Fox, the daughters of the household (guileless young women established the best rapport with the other world), were traveling about the country, bringing messages from the dead to grieving relatives. By 1854 there were more spiritualists than abolitionists and enough of the former to petition Congress for an investigation of the authenticity of "certain physical and mental phenomena from departed souls." Unimaginative lawmakers of the Thirty-third Congress never could decide, amid their hilarity, whether the Committee of Foreign Relations or that of the Post Office should look into these matters. And it was Senator James Shields, Abraham Lincoln's old antagonist, who announced that the investigation of sounds and occult forces from the departed demonstrated that the "gullibility of dupes is as inexhaustible as the prevention of knaves is impossible." But millions of Americans, including Mary Lincoln, believed otherwise.[23]

Her introduction to spiritualism had probably taken place first in Lexington from the household slaves and then in Springfield from the white prophets who appeared in the Midwest during the early 1850s. Thereafter rarely a season passed without a spirit conveyer standing on the stage of the Masonic Hall and answering, with suitable melodrama, immensely difficult and intimate questions about the local persona being exhibited. As early as 1842, when the Lincolns boarded at the Globe, a mesmerist using some sort of apparatus had drawn electrical power from the heavens and cured the spasms of a fellow boarder's facial tic. Sometime in the 1850s a clairvoyant had set up permanent headquarters three blocks south of courthouse square on Fifth Street.[24]

No matter when Mary Lincoln became a believer, by 1862 she had so many spiritualist friends that she lacked only a medium for a séance— and had that sometimes. Nathaniel Willis had a cousin who had been expelled from Harvard for his spiritualism, and his sister Sarah Willis Parton was a confirmed believer in raising the dead. Mary Lincoln's confidant Henry Wikoff had been hypnotized by a seer in Romania and had written an account of the experience which he retold to his intimates. Hoary old Isaac Newton, the commissioner of agriculture, boasted of knowing every clairvoyant in Washington, while Congressman Daniel Sickles of New York, addressed in séances as Crooked Knife, had been attracted to the movement after he shot his wife's lover, with whom presumably he wanted to correspond. Mary Jane and Gideon Welles both had consulted clairvoyants when their children died, as had New York Senator Ira Harris. Despite her husband's opposition, Mrs. James Gordon Bennett held weekly séances, and within a mile of the White House lived Thomas Gales Foster, a lecturer on spiritualism whose cousin Charles Foster was the world-renowned "Seer of Salem."

Meanwhile, from Europe came further confirmation when Mary Lincoln learned that both Empress Eugénie and Queen Victoria were practitioners. The latter was said to be in close communication with her beloved Prince Albert, and there was talk that the queen's groundskeeper John Brown knew little about ivy and hedges but a great deal about materializing the dead. Across the English Channel in Paris Eugénie's favorite sorcerer was reported to be the senna-haired Madame Blavatsky, who was able to produce letters from the dead that, on command, floated down from the ceiling.[25]

But it was Lizzie Keckley who may have been most responsible for Mary Lincoln's conversion. Keckley had sought out spiritualists after her only son had been killed in the Civil War. Denied the consolation of a deathbed interview, the seamstress joined the movement and now held conversations with her son's disembodied spirit. When Willie died, Keckley offered the same prescription to Mary Lincoln, and in time séances proved more comforting than the visits of Presbyterian clergymen. In the spring of 1862 Mary Lincoln's black barouche was often outside the home of the Lauries, the well-known mediums who lived in Georgetown. Here their friend Nettie Colburn darkened the parlor and arranged her patrons in a circle with their hands on the table, so that they could communicate with those invisible beings that "surround us like a great cloud." Sometimes Colburn was herself; sometimes she was appropriated by a spirit control called Pinkie who reached the dead "across the river."

Whenever the clairvoyants were unable to put Mary Lincoln in touch with her sons, they offered predictions about Confederate battle plans and information about the treachery of members of the government so important that she rushed them to the White House to advise her husband. Sometimes when Willie was not available, Mary tried to hear the posthumous messages of army officers. Once she took a letter from the spirit of General Edward Baker to see if that would put her in touch with her old friend from Springfield. But mostly she searched for her children. "Mrs. Lincoln," wrote Senator Orville Browning in January 1863, "has been out to see a spiritualist who has made wonderful revelations to her about her son Willie. Among other things [the medium] revealed that the cabinet were all enemies of the President."

Impressed on another occasion with a supposed member of English royalty, Mary Lincoln brought Lord Colchester to counsel her husband. The self-designated English lord had spent a season in New York doing good business as a "celebrated medium who can be consulted on any affairs of life, past, present, or future." But his White House séance was more than one friend of Mary Lincoln's could stand. The journalist Noah Brooks "rose and grasping in the direction of the drumbeat grabbed not a disembodied spirit, but rather the very solid and fleshy hand of the Lord Colchester himself who was beating a drum in the darkened Red Room."[26]

Colchester was encouraged to leave the United States, but Nettie Colburn remained, with her principal patron determined to find her a position in the Interior Department so that this most successful of the Willie raisers could stay in Washington. Colburn had come to the capital as a visitor, and business, with many rivals and payment at a dollar a séance, was insufficient. But with Mary Lincoln's aid, she stayed and helped her client accept spiritualism's essential doctrine that as Mary Lincoln advised Charles Sumner, "a very slight veil separates us from the loved and lost and to me there is comfort in the thought that though unseen by us they are very near."[27]

Through spiritualism Mary Lincoln lifted that veil. Able to hear and see her sons, she triumphantly announced to her astonished half sister that "Willie lives. He comes to me every night and stands at the foot of the bed with the same sweet adorable smile he always has had. He does not always come alone. Little Eddie is sometimes with him." Such independent conjuring was unusual. Most mediums protected their livelihoods by permitting the dead to emerge only under paid supervision. Unorthodox as always, Mary Lincoln knew the spiritualist fiction of the English novelist Edward Bulwer-Lytton in which the dead frequently visited believers without the intervention of a medium. By the fall of 1862 Mary Lincoln could accomplish what one

expert described in the *Spiritualist Magazine* as "the unconscious celebration of somnambulistic visitations" through self-induced trances or
dreams.[28]

At first glance Mary Lincoln seemed an unlikely candidate for the
suspension of reason that serious spiritualism required. Finding a son
through hocus-pocus psychics and self-induced apparitions violated an
exclusionary mourning style that depended on the forgetting, not the
recalling, of Willie. But spiritualism served a more compelling purpose. When she or Nettie Colburn was successful in reaching Willie
(and sometimes he was reported as happy, though not communicating), Mary Lincoln reconstituted the family that was her first priority.
At Colburn's she did so within a circle of friends who acted like kin
as they sat in darkness, holding hands around a table. The Mary Todd
of Lexington and Madame Mentelle's boarding school easily adopted a
therapy that flattered her intuition and histrionic talents and depended
on magic; she may also have been attracted to the sensual atmosphere
of the séance room where spirit forms brushed against audiences in
darkened rooms.[29]

Despite the séances held in the White House (and possibly there
were as many as eight), the spiritualists claimed too much when they
made Abraham Lincoln a believer. Certainly the President accepted
presents and even read letters and books from mediums, but he was
just a curious man with a persuaded wife. The spiritualists were correct, though, when they included Mary Lincoln in their ranks.[30]

Still, no matter how popular and therapeutic, spiritualism was neither a respectable nor a safe enterprise. In Illinois a Presbyterian minister declared his wife, Elizabeth Packard, a lunatic on the ground of
her spiritualism. Kidnapping this entirely sane woman, Reverend
Phineas G. Packard kept her in the Jacksonville Asylum for three years
and was able to do so because superintendents of aslyums needed no
more diagnosis than spiritualism to find a female mentally ill.

In fact, doctors reserved for nineteenth-century psychics the vocabulary they usually applied to lunatics. Thus spiritualists, in the lexicon
of medicine, had trances and deliriums and became hysterical—the
last term appropriate for the predominantly female audiences at séances.
Believers in spirit rapping were, wrote one physician, "feverish in
their delusions"; as "confused as any maniac," concluded another. In
most states of the Union mediums were subject to fines, and everywhere séances were considered tawdry affairs, cause for ridicule, contempt, and even prosecution. For every novel that celebrated raising

the dead, there was another, such as Bayard Taylor's *Hannah Thurston,* that made mediums into frauds. And newspapers were full of jokes about gullible adults who believed in ghosts.[31]

The orthodox ministry—Mary Lincoln's Reverend Phineas Gurley included—castigated mediums as dishonest sinners more in touch with Satan than God. Fully aware of the ways in which mediums challenged their special link to the world of immateriality and eternal life, ministers condemned their competitors as pagan sorcerers; "diabolical agents of apostasy," complained one. In response, spiritualists defended themselves as progressive Christians intent on expanding the doctrine of resurrection. The voices they heard in séances were available to every Christian through an enlightened understanding of the doctrine of the Holy Ghost. Indeed, to believe in God at all, according to the *Spiritualist Magazine,* was to suspend reason and accept the immanence of a nonmaterial being.

The opposition to spiritualism forced Mary Lincoln, in her acute grief, to make a painful choice between the respectability of orthodox Christianity and an unsavory, though more comforting, association with mediums. For a time she depended on both, but eventually séances helped her come to terms with Willie's death, though she never fully accepted it. Gradually she called him less often, but for the rest of her life Mary Lincoln remained in touch with the spirit world, sometimes actively pursuing its counsels, at other times using the circle in the dark as a replacement for the intimacy of her vanishing family.

TWO months after Willie's death Mary Lincoln suffered another blow when her half brother Sam was killed. She had told everyone that her three half brothers, Sam, David, and Aleck, had abandoned her when they joined the Confederate army, but she could never completely end her emotional membership in the now-divided Todd clan. (Of Robert Smith Todd's fourteen living children, eight supported the Confederacy, six the Union.) Actually the boys had made their choice years before, when, after their father's death in 1849, they moved to New Orleans, where a maternal uncle owned a prosperous sugar plantation. Still, the preference mortified their half sister and became the source of accusations that the President's wife sympathized with the Confederacy. Levi, her full brother, might have restored the balance, but too old and unfit for military service in the Union army, he died in 1864, shortly after dunning the Lincolns for a loan. Her other full brother,

George Rogers Clark Todd, went South in 1861 to serve as a surgeon in a Confederate hospital in Camden, South Carolina.[32]

With the battle glory required of his family, Sam Todd, according to the Richmond papers, died leading a charge at the Battle of Shiloh in Tennessee, a sharpshooter's bullet through his temple. More infamous was David Todd, who for a time was in charge of a Confederate prisoner of war camp in Richmond, where, according to some reports, he tortured Yankee prisoners. Mary Lincoln did not know David well. The second of Betsey's sons, he had run away from home as a boy and was notorious in family annals for the Chilean flag tattooed on his arm. Posted to the West, David was mortally wounded at Vicksburg in 1863. Then, in the fall of 1863, everybody's favorite, ebullient red-headed Aleck, died during a skirmish near Baton Rouge, Louisiana. On hearing this, Mary Lincoln cried, "Oh little Aleck, why had you to die?" Though she wept, she would not grieve for traitors, even if they were relatives.

As she explained to Elizabeth Keckley, "it is but natural that I should feel for one so nearly related to me, but not to the extent that you suppose. He [Aleck] made his choice long ago. He decided against my husband, through him against me. He has been fighting against us and since he chose to be our deadly enemy, I see no special reason why I should bitterly mourn his death," though of course, she did. To another friend she explained of these heretical Todds that "they would kill my husband if they could and destroy our government." Still, amid this personalized view of politics there was remembrance. Some nights when Willie and Eddie returned from the spirit world, they brought Aleck with them. Then on a semiannual pilgrimage to New York, Mary Lincoln received a telegram from her husband with the news that General Benjamin Hardin Helm, Emilie's husband, had been killed at Chattanooga.[33]

Three weeks later Mary Lincoln greeted her younger half sister. On her way back to her childhood home in Lexington after her husband's funeral, Emilie Todd Helm had to cross Union lines. Lincoln had sent a pass protecting her person and property except for slaves, but Emilie stubbornly refused to swear her allegiance to the government of the United States and therefore could not enter Union territory. "Bring her to me" was the President's terse solution, and so Emilie Helm came to the White House early in December 1863. The two sisters had not seen each other since the war had begun and Lincoln had offered her now-dead husband high rank in the Union army.[34]

Both saw their own misery reflected in the other. Appalled at her half sister's adventures with the spiritualists, Emilie Helm found Mary Lincoln nervous, upset, and excitable. "She seems to fear other sorrows," wrote Helm, who knew that Mary was having premonitions of future tragedies. In her diary Helm also recorded an incident that revealed Mary Lincoln's clamorous grandiosity. One morning after reading some criticism of herself in the newspapers, Mary Lincoln dropped the paper and "held out her arms to me. Kiss me, Emilie, and tell me that you love me. I seem to be the scape-goat for both North and South." In a sense she was, though it took a heightened sensitivity to see things in such a light.[35]

Throughout her half sister's visit, Mary Lincoln kept silent about the Confederate Todds and about the promising war news. Though 1863 had begun inauspiciously with defeats for the Union at Chancellorsville and Fredericksburg, by midyear the military tide had turned. In July George Meade had turned back Lee's invading army at Gettysburg, although the President had been disappointed that the Confederate army had retreated largely intact across the Potomac. Lincoln believed that had he been on the field, he would have "licked" the Confederates. That same week in July 1863 General Grant's daring campaign in the West had ended in the surrender of the Confederate garrison at Vicksburg, Mississippi. But Mary Lincoln could not discuss these victories with her half sister.[36]

If Emilie Helm found Mary changed, Mary Lincoln was saddened by her favorite half sister, who overnight had been transformed from a gay almond-eyed belle, around whom beaux had clustered, into a bitter, grief-sotted widow. For a time the sisters consoled each other, expunging public affairs from their conversation. But with outsiders this was impossible, and one night they entertained two Union generals in the Blue Room. Dan Sickles had lost his leg at the battle of Gettysburg and was scandalized that a Confederate was living in the White House. For a time Lincoln had tried to keep Emilie Helm's visit quiet, but like most Todds, she would not keep still. "If I had twenty sons," she angrily told General Sickles and Senator Ira Harris, "they would all be fighting yours."

Sometime during this same evening Senator Harris asked Mary Lincoln why Robert Lincoln was not in the army. It was a sensitive subject for a woman who could not bear the thought of being abandoned again. For a time she had prevailed over her son and her husband, though the latter had reminded her of the courageous Widow Bixby who sent five sons off to die in the Union army. As Mary Lincoln explained to Senator Harris, "Robert is making his preparations now to enter the Army; he is not a shirker—if fault there be it is mine, I have insisted that he should stay in college a little longer as I think an educated man can serve his country with more intelligent purpose than an ignoramous." In fact, Robert joined Grant's staff more than a year later. But this reply was vintage Mary Lincoln—a quick, intelligent, not entirely accurate retort—though Senator Harris had the last word, reminding the President's wife that he had only one son and that son was in the army.[37]

Not all their evenings were so difficult, and the Lincolns would have given Emilie Helm and her three children a permanent home. She was the female companion Mary needed. But she left for Lexington in mid-December 1863 with an invitation to return and a special pardon contingent upon her taking an oath of allegiance. She came back the next fall, demanding what everyone from shoddy speculators and cabinet officials to impoverished widows wanted: a license to sell 600 bales of cotton. Lincoln had the power to grant such a permit, but he would not surrender his own code of honor while Emilie Helm remained a Confederate. In turn she believed such an oath of allegiance would desecrate her husband's grave. Angrily she left for Kentucky.[38]

Returned to Lexington and the influence of Betsey Todd, Emilie Helm now wrote a stormy letter to "Mr. Lincoln." Hers was, she wrote, "a final appeal in the name of humanity for a poor widow who has used up all her money to go on her long, tedious, unproductive, and sorrowful visit." And then with that quick-rising, bridge-burning temper of which many Todds were capable, she blamed the deaths of her husband and her half brother Levi on the Lincolns. According to Emilie Helm, her mother was "prostrated" by the death of her step-son, though Betsey Todd had in fact consigned Levi, the family failure, to an unmarked grave. In any case, Levi Todd had died, according to Helm, "from utter want and destitution—another sad victim of more favored relatives." And then she ended her letter with the words her half sister never forgave: "I also remind you that your minié bullets have made us what we are."[39]

With this strike Emilie Helm was as dead to Mary as her half brothers were. They had fought against her on the battlefield, but the woman whom Lincoln called "Little Sister" had used scorching words to commit an equally unforgivable breach. During the rest of a life in which she moved as often as Mary Lincoln, Emilie Helm stayed in touch with Elizabeth Edwards and her other Springfield sisters. But Mary never saw or corresponded with her.[40]

It was easier to forget another half sister. Fifteen years younger than Mary Lincoln, Martha Todd had married an Alabamian and moved to Selma. Although she hardly knew her famous sister, this rebel adventurer planned to make the most of the connection. From Selma she wrote to ask the President, carefully underlining the "Todd" in her signature, for a pass through the lines in order to come North to "recruit my health, to replenish my wardrobe, and to take for my own use articles not now obtained in the South." No doubt she had heard from her mother of Emilie Helm's White House welcome and had her own ideas about how to use such hospitality. Pass in hand, Martha White traveled to Washington, amid rumors that her numerous trunks were intended for more than clothes. Lizzie Grimsley believed she carried away her weight in quinine, destined, along with gold, for the Confederacy's black markets. At Willard's Hotel, Martha White talked secesh and behaved so obnoxiously that Mary Lincoln refused to see her. But White had her revenge: She told everyone she was Mary Lincoln's sister.[41]

While her brothers were dying on the battlefield and her sisters were exiling themselves through unforgivable acts, Mary Lincoln was also losing a little of her husband. No one ever had the complete attention of this distracted man; still, that part of him Mary Lincoln possessed was "truly my all—Always-lover-husband-father and all,all to me." Yet ever since the war began, he had slipped away—not so much from design or through conflict as from the exhausting circumstances of running a country during a civil war. "I consider myself fortunate," Mary Lincoln wrote a friend, "if at eleven o'clock, I once more find myself, in my pleasant room and very especially, if my tired and weary Husband is *there,* waiting in the lounge to receive me."

Because the President rarely traveled, the Lincolns were together more than they had ever been, at the same time that they were farther apart. A few overnight visits to the army in Virginia and to the neighboring states of Pennsylvania and Maryland, and once to West Point, were the extent of Lincoln's absences from wartime Washington. He had never heard of vacations and so rarely strayed from a small rectangle—with the White House in the center, flanked by the War Department and Treasury Building. In the summers the household moved to the cooler, less formal Soldiers' Home on Seventh Street near the District line, where Lincoln worked as hard as ever, even holding midnight meetings after a long day in his White House office.[42]

Some things in their domestic life remained unchanged. Mary Lincoln still administered the household, even deciding when and what they would pack in the nineteen wagonloads of clothes, toys, and furniture that accompanied the family to its summer residence. At the same time in 1862 that Lincoln was urging General McClellan into action, establishing provisional courts in Louisiana, and ordering the secretary of war to appoint a quartermaster, he deferred to his wife in a domestic matter. "Mrs. Cuthbert and Aunt Mary want to move to the White House because it has grown so cold at the Soldiers Home. Shall they?" The President telegraphed this message to his wife in Boston, and the response was apparently yes.

Earlier Lincoln had specifically delegated the supervision of the servants to her. "She is," concluded White House insider William Stoddard, "absolute mistress of all that part of the White House inside the vestibule and of all the upper floor east of the folding doors," and, Stoddard did not add, though it was no doubt the case, of all the Soldiers' Home, which she hoped to improve, as she had the White House.[43]

To some extent, though, Lincoln had disappeared as a husband. Once, during his reelection campaign in 1864, his old Illinois cronies urged him to come to Springfield for a change of scene and a political speech. Bleakly the President apologized for the press of affairs that kept him in Washington and that kept him from his wife as well. The wartime Lincoln was chronically depressed, distracted and exhausted. His wife asked everyone who had known him before the war the question she put to Emilie Helm in 1863: "What do you think of Mr. Lincoln? Do you think he is well?" The answers varied but were usually negative. Some found him as gray as her French wallpaper, and she was frightened when he contracted varioloid, a mild form of smallpox. With the patronage in mind Lincoln joked, "Now I have something I can give everybody," and shortly thereafter recovered. One measure of his wife's concern for his health and safety emerged in the uncomfortable trips she made to the front, because as she explained to those who wondered why the President's lady tolerated damp tents and uncertain weather, the "change will benefit him."[44]

Some say an emotional barrier dropped between husband and wife during these years, but of this there is little evidence. They were close enough so that one of her intimates returned to Springfield with the gossip that forty-four-year-old Mary Lincoln was pregnant. This proved unfounded, but it is incorrect to assume, as some have, that the Lincolns' physical intimacy ended on their arrival at the White House. It is equally specious to make Mary Lincoln's childlessness after Tad's birth in 1853 (when she was thirty-five and he forty-four) into a case for sexual abstinence. Indeed, sex was probably one of the bonds that made the marriage of two uneven personalities a success. Mary Lincoln's friend Elizabeth Blair Lee once explained to her husband, Admiral Samuel Lee, "Mary has her husband's deepest love. This is a matter upon which one woman cannot deceive another."[45] Wartime observers of the Lincoln marriage detected the same mutual understanding that Lincoln's sister Frances had noted about their relationship in Springfield. After getting to know Mary Lincoln, the journalist Jane Swisshelm concluded that the President's wife completely merged herself in her husband.[46]

Such absorption did not preclude marital spats which the public nature of the White House made into communal performances. Even before an audience, even with her husband the President of the United States, Mary Lincoln refused to stifle her uxorial aggravations in the self-sacrificing submissiveness expected of proper wives. Abram Wakeman, a New York politician, observed one fight and soon received an explanation from the lady of the house: "I well know, how deeply grieved, the P. feels over any coolness of mine. We have had quite a laugh together, most fortunately for both my Husband and myself who [would] have broken our hearts, had it been otherwise, notwithstanding our opposite natures, our lives have been eminently peaceful."[47] No matter what others thought, this last sentence portrayed Mary Lincoln's own image of her marriage. Their quarrels were, in her understanding, no more than summer showers, and she would have no one think otherwise.

Still, like all marriages, the Lincolns' relationship had altered over the years; there was less passion and more business in their letters. Even before his election as President, Lincoln had exchanged the wistful expression of his desires to see his wife for matter-of-fact descriptions of his travel plans. After her importance to him as a political counselor had diminished, by way of compensation she fixed up the White House, bought new clothes, and traveled. Now, instead of the husband, it was the wife who was an absentee, and in that age a traveling woman needed a chaperone or a good explanation.

Often Mary Lincoln had neither. "The president's wife wanders around among watering places unprotected by any member of her family or by the company of any respectable gentleman and lady or worthy consort of her husband," complained one outraged male. Often she combined one of her three shopping trips a year to Boston, Philadelphia, and New York with a vacation in New Hampshire. In 1863 she undertook the longest trip of her White House years and, joined by Robert, traveled to the White Mountains of New Hampshire, where twice, to the surprise of reporters unaccustomed to such female vigor, she climbed a mountain.[48]

Once, in 1861, she traveled by private railroad car to Long Branch, New Jersey, the premier resort of the Atlantic coast, where red flags on the dunes warned the ladies when underclad male bathers were swimming in the surf. On this occasion Mary Lincoln intended a rest at the seashore, but instead, she encountered a ceremonial program that included a fancy-dress ball and a parade. More and more often she carried her official prestige and, as no other President's wife before or for many years after, represented her husband, reviewing troops and inspecting ships.

Usually the weather determined her return to Washington, though once Lincoln telegraphed, "I really wish to see you." In these arrangements the President served as a health officer, reporting on September 20 1863: "I neither see nor hear of sickness here now. . . . I wish you to stay, or come just as is most agreeable to yourself." The next day he telegraphed, "The air [in Washington] is so clear and cool, and apparantly [sic] healthy, that I would be glad for you to come. Nothing very particular, but I would be glad [to] see you and Tad." Just before the Battle of Gettysburg, when she wanted to get back to Washington, not escape from it, the President knew better than to dictate her decision and telegraphed: "It is a matter of choice with yourself whether you come home. . . . I do not think the raid into Pennsylvania amounts to anything at all."[49]

She was offended by his short, impersonal telegrams, and for this neglect she berated him, hoping once "for one line to say that we are occasionally remembered." During a critical week in the fall of 1862, when the President replaced the procrastinating General McClellan with an even more inept Ambrose Burnside, his wife fiercely contested his attention. "My Dear Husband, I have waited in vain to hear from you, yet as you are not *given* to letter writing, [I] will be charitable enough to impute your silence, to the right cause." In the very next sentence she forgave him. "Strangers come up from [Washington]— and tell me you are well—which satisfies me very much. Your name is on every lip and many prayers and good wishes are hourly sent up, for your welfare." Anxious to play some part in the government, she included the war news as seen by New Yorkers and closed by asking for money and sending Tad's tooth.[50]

In this letter Mary Lincoln also discussed her health in a manner that suggested an established intimacy with her husband. "A day or two since," she wrote, "I had one of my severe attacks. If it had not been for Lizzie Keckley, I do not know what I should have done. Some of *these periods* will launch me away." From her early adulthood she had suffered from migraine headaches, but invariably she described them as her "fearful" or "neuralgic" headaches. Here the reference is to the common female plight of a near-hemorrhagic menstrual period. It was information that nineteenth-century husbands rarely heard, for wives discussed details of their reproductive system seldom with doctors, occasionally with female friends and daughters, and almost never with husbands. Evidently the Lincolns were an exception.[51]

Along with her trips Mary Lincoln used a circle of friends to compensate for her husband's dwindling attention. She had always been a woman with many male acquaintances and only a few female friends. The White House years proved no exception. Impatient with what she considered silly and undereducated females, she could not accept the other extreme: intellectual reformers working for women's rights. For those who would be her intimates she created tests and challenges which, if passed, indicated to this insecure woman that these friends cared. Three academy-educated women—Elizabeth Blair Lee, Elizabeth Dixon, and Mary Jane Welles—passed and became the recipients of Mary Lincoln's generosity and warmth.

So, too, did Elizabeth Keckley, who, despite or perhaps because of the inequality between an ex-slave, mulatto seamstress and a President's wife, became Mary Lincoln's closest friend. Keckley was regal in bearing. Ladylike, she displayed excellent taste and had survived the importunate demands of her employer to become, in the First Lady's view, "although colored, . . . very industrious . . . very unobtrusive and will perform her duties faithfully."[52] To a woman who had grown up with Mammy Sally, it was natural to have close ties to a black woman, and Keckley cemented the friendship by encouraging spiritualism after Willie's death. Then, in 1863, Keckley solicited Mary Lincoln's help in a campaign of her own.

From the beginning of the war thousands of Virginia slaves, mostly field hands, had freed themselves by flooding into Union military camps.

In time these refugees, some with bundles of possessions, others with nothing save their rags, moved into the relative safety of Washington. Mary Lincoln and her sons saw their dismal villages on Carroll's Row where the Lincolns had lived during his congressional term, and on Twelfth Street. No one knew what to do with an indigent black population that increased after the District's 1,800 slaves had been freed in 1862 until it numbered 15,000 by 1863. In fact, the name by which white Americans knew these freed people—the contraband of war—established the policy of neglect practiced toward them. Lincoln's Emancipation Proclamation of January 1863 did nothing to improve their situation.

By 1863 Elizabeth Keckley had convinced Mary Lincoln that something must be done. Full of instincts rather than programs, the President's wife responded, and eventually what set Mary Lincoln apart from other Union ladies was not her attention to good causes but rather her commitment to an unpopular one. "These immense number of Contrabands," she wrote in 1862, "are suffering intensely, many without bed covering and having to use any bits of carpeting to cover themselves—many dying of want." Both she and Keckley raised money for the Contraband Relief Association, though it was easier, the First Lady discovered, to do so for white soldiers. Frustrated, she appealed to her husband. "Out of the $1000 fund deposited with you by General [Michael] Corcoran, I have given [Keckley] the privilege of investing $200 here in bed covering. . . . The cause of humanity requires it."[53]

Some of those to whom she turned for help were male friends, of whom the gossips said Mary Lincoln had too many. While Lincoln stayed upstairs in his office with generals, patronage seekers, abolitionists, and what he ruefully called the sovereign people, his wife gathered around her "My beau monde friends of the Blue Room." Members of the first salon in American history, these friends discussed books, politics, and people under the conversational direction of their hostess. But because some of the regulars were not considered fit company for respectable women, Mary Lincoln received anonymous warnings to which she paid no attention. Admission to her Blue Room Salon was earned by interesting men, no matter what their pasts, who, in a description of one, "could talk of love, law, literature and war, could describe the rulers and thinkers of the time, could gossip of courts and cabinets, of the boudoir and salon, of commerce and the church, of Dickens and Thackeray."[54]

Among them was Henry Wikoff, a notorious womanizer whose kidnaping of his fiancée had landed him in a Neapolitan jail on a charge of seduction. Wikoff had just published an account of this affair along with his adventures as an English spy. Soon after his inclusion in the salon he repaid Mary Lincoln's hospitality by stealing a copy of the President's annual message to Congress and selling it to the *New York Herald,* for which he was briefly imprisoned in Old Capitol Prison. Dan Sickles, another habitué, was a notable philanderer best known for murdering his wife's lover, though he had earlier established himself as a rogue by taking a mistress with him to London and installing her in a nearby boardinghouse while he worked at the U.S. consul's office. Then there was Oliver Halsted, the black sheep of a blue-blooded New Jersey family, and it was to Halsted that Mary Lincoln wrote coquettishly, "I fancy 'the blue room' will look dreary this evening, so if you and the Gov. are disengaged, wander up and see us." From the world of letters came Nathaniel Willis, the editor of the *Home Journal.* Willis intended his posh magazine to "cultivate the memorable, the progressive and the beautiful," and in his chatty column, "Lookings On at the War," he wrote glowingly of Mary Lincoln as the "Republican Queen in her White Palace."

Like most of the salon, Willis was married, but he left his wife at home when he "wandered up" to Mary Lincoln's after-dinner parties. Though their husbands spent many hours in the White House, most wives never met Mary Lincoln. "Some day I hope to have the pleasure of meeting your wife," she wrote to one of her Blue Room regulars. But there were occasional exceptions to the all-male cast, especially when Joanna Newell, the wife of the New Jersey governor, and sprightly Virginia Woodbury Fox, the wife of the assistant secretary of the navy, were in town.[55]

They talked of the world, of European royalty, and of the Civil War; these sophisticated men and this President's wife spoke of the great Union victories at Gettysburg and Vicksburg and of the hero of Chattanooga and Missionary Ridge, General Ulysses Grant. Always they left time to gossip about doings around Washington: Kate Chase's parties, the incompetence of the Union generals in Virginia, the marriage of the Spanish ambassador's daughter, and the shortage of fine wines and champagnes. In time they gave each other nicknames. Among themselves they were "Gov" Newell, "Pet" Halsted, "Chev" Wikoff and "Cap" Sickles, and behind her back, Madame was the "Queen" or "La Reine."[56]

Only the redoubtable Massachusetts senator Charles Sumner escaped such familiarity, and he was above membership in what he no doubt considered a frivolous circle of dandies. But the silver-locked abolitionist frequented the White House as often as the members of Mary Lincoln's Blue Room set. Teased that he could always be found there, Sumner explained it was "the first administration in which I ever felt disposed to visit the house and I consider it a privilege." Meanwhile, his competitive hostess "was pleased knowing he visited no other Lady."[57]

Sumner used his social visits to demonstrate his influence with Lincoln, while the president had a similar intention when the support of abolitionists was needed. ("I suppose," wrote author and teacher Francis Lieber to Sumner, "all this civility to you in the White House is a help in getting right with the antislavery people.") With her infallible detection of great men, Mary Lincoln enjoyed Sumner for "all that is excellent." She would later acknowledge that he was "heavy-handed, though he could make himself very, very agreeable," and that he was a man who "entertains one idea at a time" (during the war it was the freeing of the slaves). Still, like her husband and Stephen Douglas, he was a man of destiny, so she permitted his lectures, though she preferred the mutual banter in which she could participate as a sophisticated lady of the world, not as an ignorant student. She complimented Sumner's "deep studies" of opera, theater, and history and tried to establish her intellectuality by sending him books, including Napoleon III's *Histoire de Jules César*.[58]

Sometimes she extended too many invitations. Once Lincoln intervened, explaining to the senator that "Mrs. Lincoln is embarrassed a little. She would be pleased to have your company again this evening, at the Opera, but she fears she may be taxing you. I have undertaken to clear up the little difficulty." But Mary Lincoln was not too embarrassed to choose Sumner as her escort for the second inaugural ball.[59]

However esteemed, Sumner was not exempt from either Mary Lincoln's patronage campaigns or her temper. Irritated when he failed to appear at a White House reception (later the senator grandly explained he never attended affairs with large crowds), she berated him so sharply that she later apologized for her "inadvertent manner. . . . I pray you accept this little peace offering for your table—a few flowers brought by the gardener." Accustomed to more punishing reproofs by his enemies, Sumner forgave. A week later he received a request that he meet with "two colored persons who came to us very highly recommended from some of our loyal families of Philadelphia—both appear to be very genteel and intelligent persons." Knowing Sumner's inexhaustible capacity for flattery, Mary Lincoln ended her request with a compliment to the man "whom all the oppressed race, have so much cause to honor."[60]

In 1864 Mary Lincoln welcomed a new member to her Blue Room Salon. Abram Wakeman was an ambitious lawyer who, after serving as Lincoln's postmaster in New York City, wanted to move up the patronage ladder to the more prestigious and better paid post of port collector. His campaign included the usual testimonies from notable Republicans establishing his loyalty to the party. To this Wakeman added his intimacy with the President's wife. At a time when many patronage seekers got only one invitation to her evenings (some were too unpleasant; others vulgar and not sufficiently ingratiating to their hostess), Wakeman impressed the First Lady with his intelligence and his spiritualism.[61]

Others were less impressed with the New Yorker. Secretary of the Navy Welles believed Wakeman "affable, insinuating, and pleasant, though not professionally reliable. He believes everything fair and proper in party operations and supposes everyone else is the same." But no matter what Welles thought, after Wakeman had engineered an early endorsement for the President's renomination from New York's Republican Central Committee, he was welcomed both upstairs and downstairs in the White House. But Wakeman was careful, balancing his attentions by asking Lincoln's permission to escort his wife when she was in New York. "I learn Mrs. Lincoln is to be in New York the first of the week. May I present my compliments to her and say if I can serve her in any way I should be most happy." Soon Mary Lincoln was sharing secrets with her other Abraham. "Please say not a word to anyone," went one admonition, "not even [New York politician Thurlow] W[eed] about the 5th Avenue business." No doubt her reference was to a problem with her bills that Wakeman, because he knew all the merchants, had settled.[62]

In 1864 Wakeman did more than renegotiate her bills. Along with several other members of the Blue Room Salon, he served as a listening post in the world of politics from which Mary Lincoln was increasingly excluded. No matter that Wakeman had been closely aligned with her archenemy Seward or that he was still a friend of Thurlow Weed, whom she loathed. Mary Lincoln intended to use him—and the others—to get her husband reelected. As she told Lizzie Keckley, "I have an object in view. In a political canvass it is policy to cultivate every element of strength. These men have influence, and we require influence to re-elect Mr. Lincoln." And as Wakeman exploited her friendship to insinuate himself into the President's favor, so she used him to make sure that her husband stayed in the White House. "I fear that you had not a very encouraging report to make of your conversation with Mr. Lincoln as regards Mr. B. [James Gordon Bennett] and General S. [Sickles]. A little notice of them would strengthen us very much," she advised Wakeman during the campaign. In such directions she took a modern view of politics, intending that state leaders like Wakeman and Sumner deliver blocs of voters to her Lincoln party.[63]

By 1864 Mary Lincoln had become a campaign issue herself. Benjamin French reported "rumors that Democrats are getting up something in which they intend to show up Madame Lincoln." And Republicans from Philadelphia and New York worried that unpaid merchants would embarrass the President by revealing the cost of her clothes. An unrepentant Mary Lincoln defended her spending, explaining to Lizzie Keckley the connection among her clothes, her husband's position, and the people's votes. "The President glances at my rich dresses and is happy to believe that the few hundred dollars that I obtain from him supply all my wants. I must dress in costly materials. The people scrutinize every article that I wear with critical curiosity. If he is elected, I can keep him in ignorance of my affairs, but if he is defeated, then the bills will be sent him." Mary Lincoln was hardly the first wife to hide bills from a husband who controlled the purse, but she was among the few who justified private expenditures as business expenses.[64]

By the summer of 1864 both Lincolns worried about his reelection. Before the Democrats saddled General McClellan with a disastrous peace platform, Lincoln distributed a memo that revealed his doubts. "It seems exceedingly probable that this administration will not be reelected," he wrote.[65] Preoccupied with the campaign, his wife shortened her trip to New England and stayed in Washington.

Mary Lincoln was in the capital when a last Confederate offensive threatened the city. Ever since General Philip Sheridan's springtime raids south of the Rapidan River near Richmond, northerners had believed that the end of the war was imminent. But then General Jubal Early's corps had driven Union forces from Lynchburg, and in early July his troops made a bold raid on Washington after defeating a Union army in western Maryland. From their vantage point at the Soldiers' Home, the Lincolns could watch Washington's civilian refugees streaming down Seventh Street, though it was uncertain where safety lay after the Confederates had ringed the city and burned Postmaster Montgomery Blair's home.

Again Mary Lincoln was asked to leave the city or at least to return to the White House. She refused and instead rode with her husband to Fort Stevens, the thinly manned earth fortification that guarded the northern approaches to the city. The President was nearly killed on the parapets that day when the Confederates began lobbing shells at the improbable target of a presidential top hat. An exasperated aide, who turned out to be Oliver Wendell Holmes, shouted to the President, "Get down you fool." Some said Mary Lincoln was standing beside her husband; others placed her in the presidential carriage. In any case the Lincolns finished their tour of the defenses, reviewing the troops at the perimeter forts of De Russy and Slocum. The next day the First Lady informed Secretary of War Stanton that the forts were inadequate.[66]

Two days later Washington's defenders, a ragtag army of invalids and local volunteers, were reinforced by General Lew Wallace's troops. With a detachment of Grant's troops also en route to Washington, Early gave up hope of capturing or even sacking the city, as Lincoln thought he might. The danger over, Mary Lincoln went north for a short trip, but politics pulled her back to Washington.

Finally—for election seasons always passed too slowly for her—it was Tuesday, November 8. From the second floor of the White House the President, Tad, and Noah Brooks—the latter now officially a secretary—watched the soldiers voting. In Brooks's account, Jack, a turkey saved from the White House table by Tad, was stalking around the polls when the President asked whether Jack would vote. "He is under age," replied his son adroitly. For the rest of the day Lincoln told the story to anyone who would listen. Later the President strolled across the grounds to that little upstairs room in the War Department where a few telegraph lines kept him in touch with the world. On this night his universe was no more distant than the voting booths in the North. Later, without his wife, the President ate an oyster supper in the telegraph office, and he knew by the early morning that he had been reelected.[67]

The next day both Lincolns rejoiced. The President had carried every state but three, although the popular vote was close. But Noah Brooks spoiled the victory for Mary Lincoln when he reminded her of an earlier dream of the President's. Like his wife, Lincoln often had morbid premonitions. After one such "ugly dream" he telegraphed her "to put Tad's pistol away." But the dream Brooks now recalled was more personal. Four years before, on election day 1860, he had lain down on his bed. In Springfield the dresser in the corner had a full-length mirror, and in it he saw reflected two images of his face, one a separate, paler, though entirely distinct version of the other. No matter how he shifted his position, two faces remained.[68]

Mary Lincoln understood immediately. He would be elected to a second term but would not live to complete it. Reminded of this prophetic warning, she turned apprehensive. Since Willie's death she expected every success to be followed by some counterstroke. As if to cheat fate by acknowledging its power, she ordered, a month later, $1,000 worth of mourning clothes. And she wrote a friend two weeks after the election a sad but accurate calculation of her future. "Our Heavenly Father sees fit, often times to visit us, at such times for our worldliness, how small and insignificant all worldly honors are, when we are *thus* so sorely tried."[69]

MARY LINCOLN chose white silk with a bertha of point lace for her second inauguration as First Lady; she wore a lace shawl over her shoulders, had jasmine and purple violets in her hair, and carried an ermine fan with silver spangles. In the White House she prevented Lincoln from promenading with another woman. The established etiquette irritated her, and she had explained to Keckley: "The President at every reception selects a lady to lead the promenade with him. Now it occurs to me that this custom is an absurd one. On such occasions our guests recognize the position of President as first of all; consequently he takes the lead in everything; well now, if they recognize his position, they should also recognize mine. I am his wife." But outside the White House a different protocol prevailed, so she circled the huge 280-foot floor of the Patent Office on the arm of Charles Sumner.[70]

Two weeks later Abraham, Tad, and Mary Lincoln traveled to Virginia for the last days of the Confederacy. This time even the pessimists agreed that the war would soon be over. General Grant had pushed to within a few miles of Petersburg, and now the Union army pressed the thin flanks of Lee's protective circle around Richmond. After his march through Georgia had severed the Confederacy, General William T. Sherman had meanwhile turned northward, and by

March he was in North Carolina. Lincoln, who had always taken seriously his constitutional duties as commander in chief, held strong convictions about the appropriate tactics and strategy his generals should use. He intended to go to the Virginia front and oversee the end of the Confederacy.

Tad went for different reasons. The steamboat journey down the Potomac was only slightly less exciting than the many troop reviews at which the twelve-year-old had galloped his pony on the parade grounds. This time he was promised both. For Mary Lincoln visiting the troops fostered that sense of herself as the "Presidentess," the term that after her husband's reelection the *Herald* had taken to using. And as she explained to Charles Sumner before leaving the White House, "The change of air and rest may have a beneficial effect on my good husband's health."[71]

On March 23, 1865, the Lincolns boarded the *River Queen*, the steam-engined side-wheeler that while neither as safe nor as fast as some steel-hulled navy vessels, nonetheless had more appropriate accommodations for the ladies. The presidential family had used it before, but this time their drinking water from the Potomac was contaminated. All the Lincolns were sick the first night out, as the *River Queen* quietly made its way out of the Potomac, down the Chesapeake Bay, and up the James River to City Point, where the river widened and a Union depot had been established. Sometime during the night Lincoln dreamed that the White House was burning, and ever responsive to portents from the spirit world, the next day Mary Lincoln telegraphed a White House maid: "Send a Telegram, direct to City Point . . . and say if all is right at the house. Every thing is left in your charge—be careful." Sometime after the *River Queen* had docked at City Point, Robert Lincoln, now a volunteer captain on Grant's staff, came aboard for a family reunion.[72]

The next day General Grant had planned a presidential review of General Sheridan's and Edward O. C. Ord's troops, to be accompanied by a navy flotilla on the James. The President left early. He was eager to see firsthand the military events that seemed so abstract when they appeared as official reports. And that day there was much to see, for Lee was trying to break through Grant's hammerlock east of Petersburg. In the afternoon the President planned to meet his wife on the parade grounds near Malvern Hill on the south side of the James.

Later in the morning Mary Lincoln left the *River Queen* and, accompanied by Julia Grant, entered the slow-moving ambulance carriage that had been assigned to her. The grand review was planned for early afternoon, but it seemed that she would never arrive. Passage along corduroyed roads made of lashed-together striplings was nerve-rackingly slow and constantly jarring. Once after a terrific bounce her head slammed against the top of the ambulance and a migraine started. She began to fear that she would miss the parade. Increasingly impatient and angry, Mary Lincoln berated horses, driver, aides, and Julia Grant. At one point she tried to abandon the coach and walk, but the mud of Virginia's springtime proved as impassable as the roads.

When Mary Lincoln finally arrived, the review had begun. From her inconspicuous position on the parade grounds, she immediately spied her husband on horseback, his top hat visible above everything save the flags and battle standards. Alongside him, in an elegant feathered Robin Hood's cap (of the kind popularized by Empress Eugénie), rode the handsome Mrs. General Ord, astride a magnificent bay that she handled, as Mary Lincoln heard once too often, with splendid horsemanship. Too late the general's wife wheeled her horse to take her place unobtrusively beside the First Lady's coach.

Never under strict control, Mary Lincoln's temper was now given a very public display before the entire high command of the Army of the Potomac. After clambering out of the hateful ambulance toward the President, according to one officer, "Mrs. Lincoln repeatedly attacked her husband in the presence of officers because of Mrs. Griffin [who had also been on the reviewing field] and Mrs. Ord. He bore it as Christ might have done with an expression of pain and sadness that cut one to the heart, but with supreme calmness and dignity. He called her mother, with his old-time plainness. He pleaded with eyes and tones, till she turned on him like a tigress and then he walked away hiding that noble ugly face so that we might not catch the full expression of its misery." Though this version was written long after, other accounts testify to Mary Lincoln's high dudgeon that March day of 1865. Later, on the *River Queen,* she continued to vent her anger, as she lashed out at Julia Grant and the President, whom she now insisted must dismiss General Ord to atone for her humiliation.

Mary Lincoln had always been jealous of her position as First Lady. The demands on her impaired self-esteem required the special handling that Lincoln usually gave in exchange for her vivacity and charm. Throughout the war she had reviewed parades in a more dignified manner than her husband. One northerner had complained to the President that "he slouched . . . and leaned and talked, when you should sit erect and talk to nobody," whereas his wife had savoir faire and was charming enough in these ceremonial events to make up "for all your deficiencies." But that day at City Point—at least from her perspective—the President had committed an egregious assault on the established procedures of their marital arrangement. To a woman who still imagined herself his political partner, a public display of anger was justified in return for her just as public embarrassment.[73]

Later, as she always did, Mary Lincoln paid the price for her temper. Mortified and apologetic, she stayed in her cabin on the *River Queen* and was only seen walking along the bank near Point of Rocks with Tad and Robert or sitting on a chair on the ship's stern. Those who inquired were told that she was indisposed, as indeed, she was. No doubt the ride, the migraine-producing bump, the anger at Mrs. Ord's usurpation of her limelight, and the ensuing scene had incapacitated Mary Lincoln with a bad case of self-inflicted shame.[74]

A few days later she decided to leave Tad with his father and return home. (Of Tad, she wrote that "after three days of exposure to rebel shots, my Darling Boy is well and happy.") Both Lincolns wanted to see the fall of Richmond, but it was slow in coming. By the end of the week even the President worried that he, too, should go home, though "I dislike to leave without seeing nearer to the end of General Grant's movement." Lincoln stayed, and Mary Lincoln retraced her way to Washington, traveling part of the way with Republican Congressman Carl Schurz. He had known her in Springfield, and when they docked at the naval yard she offered him a ride in her carriage. Later Schurz wrote to his wife that "the Mother of the Country is extremely kind. She is an astonishing woman—in just a few hours I learned more state secrets than I ever would."[75]

Soon the presidential couple were reconciled, although the exact means of their marital recuperation remains obscure. Probably Mary Lincoln apologized with great passion, and her husband admitted a certain culpability. Once in the White House, she telegraphed how much she missed "Taddie and yourself." In turn the President responded to her self-avowed "deep interest in army matters," telegraphing every two or three hours, she noted with exaggeration to Sumner. Throughout the week the president sent the detailed news of victories that she wanted to hear. "Last night," went one such telegram, "General Grant telegraphed that Sheridan with his Cavalry and the 5th Corps had captured three brigades of infantry. . . . This morning General Grant, having ordered an attack along the whole line, telegraphs as follows:

Both Wright and Parke got through the enemy lines. The battle now rages furiously. . . ."[76]

Mary Lincoln did not intend to miss the final advance into Richmond, and exacted from her husband a promise that he would include her in his plans to enter the Confederate capital. After a complicated set of arrangements she was back at City Point on April 6, just four days after Lee had evacuated Petersburg and Richmond and two days after her husband had entered Richmond. Accompanied by a most "charming party" of Robert's girlfriend Mary Harlan, a French marquis, and Senator Sumner, whom she had invited to dine with her "in Jeff Davis's deserted banqueting hall," Mary Lincoln triumphantly toured the empty capital. None savored the moment more than the former slave Elizabeth Keckley, whom the First Lady had thoughtfully included.[77]

Even amid the jubilation Mary Lincoln was preoccupied and worried about her husband. After a morning in a Virginia army hospital shaking hands with those who could, the President admitted to an exhaustion that made him want to go to bed in midday. More than ever—now that victory was assured—his wife feared the assassination attempt that he dismissed by saying he could not be shut up in a cage. Even when the Lincolns were safely out of hostile Virginia and their black barouche was moving through streets thronged with Washington's celebrating Unionists, Mary Lincoln warned her husband that the city was full of their enemies.

Back in the White House, Lincoln told his wife of another dream in which he was awakened by the sound of weeping and, after wandering through the house, came to the East Room, where there was a catafalque on which rested a coffin with a corpse inside. "Who is dead in the White House?" he had asked of the soldiers attending the coffin, and the answer came: the President. He also recounted a dream of a ship moving toward a dark shore and discussed with others as well as his wife the meaning of these nocturnal revelations. Even his bodyguard, the redoubtable U.S. Marshall Ward Lamon, who sometimes slept in front of his bedroom, was horrified by his premonitions. Mary Lincoln, who believed in the actuality of the spirit world, was chilled.[78]

After their return from the front Abraham and Mary Lincoln had only a few days left together. On Palm Sunday, April 9, 1865, Lee had surrendered the remains of his once-proud Army of Northern Virginia, and Washington was celebrating. Somehow Commissioner French had contrived a huge gaslit transparency that sparkled from the western pediment of the U.S. Capitol with the legend "This is the Lord's doing. It is marvellous in our eyes." Amid the revelry the crowds always seemed to end up at the President's House, where Lincoln's time was filled with the informal ceremonies of victory and with his plans for the impending reconstruction of the Union.

With Mary Lincoln observing from the second-floor window (as she used to do in Springfield during torchlight parades) and with Tad impishly waving a rebel flag, Lincoln talked about reconstruction and, in the last address of his life, "the best way to bring the South into proper relation with the Union." If her husband was all forgiveness, asking the bands to play "Dixie," she was full of vengeance as she remembered "that lights glare from windows from whence rebellious hearts have been wont to gaze." Sometime this week Abraham Lincoln wrote her an affectionate note—"playfully and tenderly worded," though like most of their correspondence, it has disappeared.[79]

April 14 began differently from most days Mary Lincoln had spent in the White House. The war had ended, her family was safe, and the tumultuous celebrations of peace continued. Robert arrived for breakfast after a tiring trip from Virginia, and the President was busy with various officials and cabinet members. Tad planned an excursion with one of the White House doormen, and there was uncertainty about the Lincolns' plans. There had been talk that they would attend Tom Taylor's "Celebrated Eccentric Comedy *Our American Cousin,*" which was playing at Ford's Theatre on Tenth Street. Robert declined, pleading exhaustion. The Grants were invited, but Julia, who disliked Mary Lincoln, left with General Grant for New Jersey and her children.

Later Mary Lincoln would write that on this Good Friday she had a headache and would have stayed home, but the President insisted: "His mind was fixed upon having some relaxation and bent on the theater." Sometime in the late morning the Lincolns made up their minds, and a White House messenger alerted the management at Ford's—the theater was only eight blocks from the White House— that the president and his party would attend that night. Immediately James Ford set about the task of preparing the box with the special presidential rocker, the regimental flags, and red, white, and blue bunting. At the last minute Senator Harris's daughter Clara and her fiancé, Major Henry Rathbone, were included.[80]

Late in the afternoon, as the Lincolns had done so often during the war, the two went for a ride. In her account "he was cheerful—even playful." By his preference Lincoln had wanted to ride alone without the guests who sometimes shared their carriage. Later she remembered they talked of the "miserable time" they had had during the war. Lincoln had said they must be more cheerful. They discussed their future: where they might live and whether they might travel. After their carriage ride and supper they prepared for the theater, she in her pretty bonnet and a small-patterned blue dress, he by brushing his hand through his stubborn hair and picking up his silk hat.[81]

The presidential party arrived late and took their places amid the show-stopping applause of nearly 1,700 theatergoers and the orchestra's "Hail to the Chief." The Lincolns had been in their seats for an hour and a half when Mary Lincoln turned to her husband, slipped her hand in his, and leaned toward him to ask what Clara Harris and the major would think of her hanging on to him like this. Then, in that unearthly moment, John Wilkes Booth showed his pass to the guard stationed at the bottom of the stairs, walked along the back of the row of boxes to the anteroom of the presidential box, looked through the sight he had earlier bored, opened the inner door to the box, and shot Abraham Lincoln in the back of the head. In the pandemonium that followed, everyone remembered Mary Lincoln's moans and screams and her singular cry. "Oh, my God, and have I given my husband to die?"[82]

IX

Mrs. Widow Lincoln: The First Years

*T*HEY carried Lincoln to the Petersen house, a private home across the street from Ford's, careful, though it made no difference, to steady his body and what remained of his brain. Mary Lincoln followed, helped by Clara Harris, who a few minutes before had been laughing along with her hostess at the foolishness of *Our American Cousin*. Both women's dresses were stained with blood that Mary Lincoln insisted was her husband's. In fact, it was from the flesh wound that Major Rathbone sustained when he rose to seize the President's assailant, only to be slashed by Booth's sword. In the darkness outside the theater, the Lincolns had been separated, and Mary Lincoln began screaming, "Where is my husband? Why didn't he kill me? Why was I not the one?" Once in the Petersen house she clambered up the stairs and down the hall to the back bedroom, where she tried to revive him. "How can it be so? Do speak to me," she implored, and then began kissing Lincoln until someone dragged her back to the front parlor.

There, in a prim sitting room furnished with horsehair-covered chairs and an unyielding sofa, a room indistinguishable from thousands of other middle-class parlors, Mary Lincoln spent the next nine hours waiting for her husband to die. Mostly she was alone, though Robert Lincoln and Reverend Gurley occasionally sat with her. Toward midnight her friend Elizabeth Dixon arrived. But the two who meant the most never came. Somehow the carriage sent to bring Lizzie Keckley had gone to the wrong address, and Tad stayed in the White House.

Every hour Mary Lincoln struggled to her feet and, moaning and wringing her hands, made her way to the increasingly crowded bedroom where Lincoln lay across a bed turned catty-corner to accommodate his long frame. Like a fairy godmother endowed with some life-giving potion, she tried to kiss her husband into consciousness, begging him to wake up and trying, as had often been necessary during their marriage, to catch his attention through some extravagant gesture. When her magic failed, she insisted that Tad come. Always in the past, Lincoln had responded to his youngest son.

Such uncontrolled anguish irritated the all-male watch of government officials, generals, and doctors. They were having trouble with their own emotions, and the sight of a frantic woman led someone to growl, "Keep that woman out of here." Whether Mary Lincoln heard or not, the roughness of the command signaled her new status.

When Mary Lincoln saw Abraham Lincoln for the last time, it was morning. In Elizabeth Dixon's description the light that raw, rainy April day "was struggling with dim candles." During the night Lincoln's pillow had become soaked with blood, and the President's face, especially around his right eye, behind which the bullet from Booth's derringer had lodged, was bloated and discolored. Hours before, Lincoln had begun breathing with the clacking noise that his doctors recognized as a death rattle. Perhaps Mary Lincoln did, too. In any case she raised again the plaintive cry of her vulnerability. "Oh, have I given my husband to die?" Then she collapsed, and Robert Lincoln and Elizabeth Dixon dragged her away.[1]

When Mary Lincoln recovered, her husband was dead. Again she had been denied what she craved—some deathbed acknowledgment that her family would be together again and that her faithful husband, through what the spiritualists called "hovering," would always watch over her. Even Americans who ridiculed the idea of special visitations gathered around the beds of dying relatives, hoping for some inspirational message.[2]

The circumstances of Lincoln's death robbed his widow of this. "In my hours of deep affliction," she later explained to a friend, "I often think it would have been some solace to me and *perhaps* have lessened the grief, which is now breaking my heart—if my idolized had passed away, after an illness, and I had been permitted to watch over him and tend him to the last." Comparing herself to a friend who had nursed her husband during a long illness, she lamented to Charles Sumner that she had not "with trembling anxiety . . . been permitted to watch over and minister to my idolized husband, through an illness and receiving his loving farewell word in return, I could have thanked him for his lifelong—almost—devotion to me and I could have asked forgiveness, for any inadvertent moment of pain, I may have caused him."[3]

Reversing the usual flow of consolation from the living to the dying, Mary Lincoln held herself responsible for the President's death, and this made her bereavement uniquely painful. "My own life," she advised a friend after the assassination, "has been so chequered; naturally so gay and hopeful—my prominent desires, all granted me—my noble husband, who was my 'light and life,' and my highest ambition gratified—and that was, the great weakness of my life. My husband—became distinguished above all. And yet owing to that fact, I firmly believe he lost his life and I am bowed to the earth with Sorrow."[4]

Guilt is ever the close companion of bereavement, but to the normal instincts of the grieving, Mary Lincoln brought a special liability. At the moment of triumph when she expected to relish victory in a peacetime White House, she was again rendered a victim and not, in her reckoning, by chance. Throughout her life she had been instructed in her worthlessness by family disappearances. Now her ambitions had cost her the President, her "all," and indeed, Lincoln had been more than a husband. While he called her his child-wife, along with his services as a paternal figure he included the role of a successful son championed by an enterprising mother-wife.

For the next forty days Mary Lincoln remained in bed enveloped by emotions so intense and overwhelming that they matched Queen Victoria's farewell to Prince Albert. Like Victoria, who secluded herself for months until even staunch royalists complained of her dereliction of duties, Mary Lincoln made mourning a permanent condition. In the nineteenth century some form of withdrawal or retirement was encouraged, but after a time Americans expected their widows to show heroic firmness, not hysterical emotion. But only once in the next seventeen years of her life did Mary Lincoln wear anything but the most severe widow's weeds—what the behavior manuals called first-stage mourning—and then only when Tad persuaded her on his birthday to wear something (it turned out to be a black silk dress) other than her lugubrious uniform. Nor did she ever write a letter on anything but mourning paper decorated with the widest of black bands. Once when she used regular paper, she apologized to a friend for a breach of the etiquette that had become her badge of particularity. For she was not just any widow; she was Abraham Lincoln's survivor.[5]

John Wilkes Booth had ended forever her days in diamonds, paisley shawls, elegant dresses, and furs; even the new Russian sable boa that had just arrived from Adolph Hosch's New York fur shop had to be renounced for her competitive mourning. No matter that the keepers of Victorian customs decreed two years of special clothing after which women were to return to conventional dress. Mary Lincoln affirmed her specialness by never surrendering the badges of widowhood—the heavy black crepe clothes crowned by an awkward stiff bonnet wrapped with an immense tulle veil—that made her an anonymous somebody. Years later, when she was returning from France to the United States, she met Sarah Bernhardt, and the latter, no doubt recognizing another histrionic talent, commented on the overwhelming blackness of Mary Lincoln's outfit.[6]

WHEN Mary Lincoln returned to the White House that terrible Saturday morning after the assassination (before leaving the Petersen house, she had cursed "this awful place, this awful place"), she could not find a bedroom. "Oh, no, not there," she cried as her friends led her along the upstairs hallway. "Oh, I couldn't go in there," she said, trying to deny—or at least avoid—her tragedy in the same way she had when Willie died. But all the White House rooms were repugnant with memory. Finally Elizabeth Dixon and Mary Jane Welles put her to bed in a tiny spare room that she had fixed up for Lincoln's use during the summer. Now began the paroxysms of grief—what Lizzie Keckley described as "the wails of a broken heart, the unearthly shrieks, the terrible convulsions."[7]

On Easter Sunday 1865, work began on the wooden platform that was to hold Lincoln's coffin in the East Room. The hammering reminded his widow of Booth's shot. "Will you please allow things in the East Room to remain in status quo for a few days," wrote Edgar Welles,

Mary Jane Welles's son, "and let the arrangements made yesterday remain as they are? Mrs. Lincoln is very much disturbed by noise. The other night when putting them up every plank that dropped gave her a spasm and every nail driven reminded her of a pistol shot." More softly the hammering continued, and though Mary Lincoln did not attend Lincoln's funeral, she heard the muffled sounds of those who gathered for the services on Wednesday. Had she been in the room, she would have listened to the Presbyterian minister Phineas Gurley claim Lincoln for God and then encourage the President's survivors to accomplish what she could not. "Yield to the behest of God and drink this cup of submission—God of the Just," intoned Gurley, "Thou givest us the cup / We yield to thy behest and drink it up."[8]

Instead, Mary Lincoln stayed in bed. Eventually her mental anguish—childlike in its manifestation, epic in its duration—produced the physical ills of headaches, weak limbs, swollen eyes, lung congestion, and back pain. This time no one sent for Elizabeth Edwards or any of the Springfield relatives. For at least a year before the assassination the sisters had been feuding. Anson Henry took Mary Lincoln's side in this quarrel, explaining to his wife that he believed the Springfield relatives had behaved poorly in a disagreement that centered on Lincoln's removal of his possibly corrupt, but certainly anti-Republican, brother-in-law Ninian Edwards. And there was a female dimension to the fight after the First Lady had read, in a letter of an Edwards daughter, some unkind remarks about herself.[9]

So it was Anson Henry, Elizabeth Keckley, Mary Jane Welles, Elizabeth Blair Lee, Elizabeth Dixon, and several spiritualists who, as best they could, consoled the widow. To Elizabeth Blair Lee, Mary Lincoln gave her most vivid description of the assassination. Her husband, she said, had never quivered, but "his head drooped upon his chest and his eyes closed . . . his spirit fled then for he was never once moved by my anguish." According to Henry, "Mrs. Lincoln almost refuses to be comforted. I am the best comforter she finds and I spend several hours a day with her—you know, I am a half-way spiritualist. That is I believe our departed friends hover around and are fully cognizant of all that transverses while we are not sensible of their presence. I have made Mrs. L. a convert to this doctrine."

Official Washington paid sympathy calls and was offended when word came that Lincoln's widow would see no one, though Senator Sumner and Secretary Stanton were exceptions. Those who did gain admittance to her room were dismayed by her condition. One visitor found her "more dead than alive—broken by the horrors of that dreadful night as well as worn down by bodily sickness." Even Anson Henry, who was accustomed to the range of her emotions, thought "Mrs. Lincoln more composed than I anticipated but the moment I came within reach she threw her arms around my neck and wept most hysterically for several minutes. Then she talked most composedly about what had happened, though by the time I left she was again weeping."[10]

Awaiting the widow's departure from what was now his home, the newly sworn President of the United States attended to the nation's business from a tiny room in the Treasury Department. In late April President Andrew Johnson received a progress report from Robert: "My mother and myself are aware of the great inconvenience to which you are subjected by the transaction of business in your present quarters but my mother is so prostrated that I must beg your indulgence. Mother tells me that she cannot possibly be ready to leave here for 2½ weeks."[11] If she had kept to usual practice, she would have left quickly in order to avoid the memories. (A century later under similar conditions Jacqueline Kennedy was gone in ten days.) But for Mary Lincoln to abandon the White House was to surrender her ambitions, and this took time. Loveless, she was also homeless and so stayed in the place where she had been somebody, a Republican queen, many had said.

Downstairs the servants and a stream of unauthorized visitors were making off with the china and silver she had tastefully collected. By early May several pieces of the Haughwout crystal and the new buff-colored china had been seen in a secondhand shop in Georgetown, while the huge Japanese punch bowl—the one Mary Lincoln had used to such effect for her special parties—was on display at Christopher Shaw's saloon on High Street in Baltimore. How it had gotten there, no one knew or would say. Rumor had it that shifty old Benjamin French had borrowed both silver and vases for parties held at his Capitol Hill home.

Although the commissioner hotly denied this, he was called before a congressional committee on public buildings, at which, through his strategic silences about the contents of Mrs. Lincoln's trunks, he managed to implicate his former patron. Eventually neither the state china with its distinctive seal of the Republic nor the nanny goats "my poor husband loved so well" were safe; something happened to the goats on their way to Francis Blair's country estate in Maryland. By the time an inventory was taken, the White House closets were nearly bare, and the real culprits were a greedy staff and negligent supervision. Mary Lincoln removed only her husband's night table and personal gifts, though henceforth she was widely condemned for having stolen government property.[12]

Still bedridden in May, the widow roused herself several times for the familiar activity of obtaining jobs for her friends. She had despised the new President ever since he had embarrassed her husband's second inauguration with a drunken speech. No doubt she would have disliked any successor to her "Great One," but at some point Mary Lincoln moved Johnson into a special category of enemy. The new President was "wicked." But in May 1865 he held the power of patronage, and temporarily suspending her indignation, she urged on him, "in the memory of my late lamented husband," several appointments, including that of Tad and Willie's tutor—Alexander Williamson—a young Scotsman with a university degree from Edinburgh. Johnson complied, but the new President neither paid the obligatory call on the widow of the man who had raised him to national prominence nor wrote a sympathy note, thereby earning her damnation "for behaving towards me in a most brutal way."[13]

Johnson had his reasons. Earlier he had felt the sting of Mary Lincoln's contempt when, an uncertain outsider raised to history the night of Lincoln's assassination, he had hurried to the Petersen house, only to be told that the sight of him so disturbed her that he must leave. This was humiliating enough, but in late April she called Secretary of War Stanton to the White House to discuss her accusations that Johnson had conspired with John Wilkes Booth. "Why was that card of Booth's found in his [Johnson's] box—some acquaintance certainly existed," she speculated. "I have been impressed with the harrowing thought that he [Johnson] had an understanding with the conspirators and they knew their man. Did not Booth say there is one thing he would not tell?" Neither the trial of the assassins nor the hanging of four conspirators in July ever shook this conviction. When the President, in an effort to gain support for his Reconstruction policies, came to Illinois on his "swing around the circle" in the summer of 1866, Mary Lincoln accused him of "desecrating" her husband's grave.[14]

In early May 1865 Robert Lincoln returned to the White House with more bad news. The eldest of the Lincoln sons had accompanied his father's body on its mournful pilgrimage home and had been present at the final funeral ceremonies in Springfield. Now he advised his mother that the town fathers intended, without any consultation with her, to bury Lincoln in the old Mather property near the center of town. In fact, Mary Lincoln's old friends—Ozias Hatch, who used to enjoy her strawberry parties, and Mercy Levering's husband, James Conkling, along with most of Illinois's officialdom—were raising money for a suitable monument without any provision for a family vault. Whatever Lincoln had been to his neighbors before his death, he was being resurrected as Springfield's fallen hero. The proper place for his interment was a hill in the middle of the city from which any decent memorial would tower above even the spire of the Presbyterian church.

Mary Lincoln intended otherwise. Startled out of melancholic self-absorption by this news of another, possibly permanent separation, she fought the Springfield patriarchy for her husband's body. Soon every member of the Lincoln Monument Association had been advised of her objections, through Robert, through John Todd Stuart, or first-hand. "My determination is unalterable," she informed Illinois Governor Richard Oglesby after a series of negotiations had failed. "Without I receive by the 15th of this month a formal and written agreement that the monument shall be placed over the remains of my beloved husband in Oak Ridge Cemetery with the written promise that no other bodies, save the President, his wife, his sons and sons' families shall ever be deposited within the enclosure—in the event of my not receiving a written declaration to that effect, I shall have his precious remains placed in a vault of the National Capitol—a Tomb prepared for [George] Washington." Of course, she was only threatening, for even the grandness of Lincoln's burial in Washington meant nothing if there was no room for her.[15]

What Mary Lincoln wanted and eventually got was a family burial place in Springfield's Oak Ridge, the new rural cemetery a few miles north of the city. In this desire she was by no means unique, for many Americans were burying their relatives in pleasant countryside settings, rather than overcrowded church graveyards in cities. Rapidly growing towns made permanent resting places into temporary affairs, available for destruction any time a civic father determined a new building, road, or factory was needed. In the 1850s there had been a scandal about several disinterments in the boomtown of Chicago, and eastern cities had begun chartering rural cemeteries that promised privacy in perpetuity. Boston's Mount Auburn was the best known, and Mary Lincoln had probably seen two others: Philadelphia's Laurel Hill and Baltimore's Greenmount.[16]

The Lincolns had been living in Springfield when Oak Ridge Cem-

etery had opened for business in 1860, and the event had been celebrated by James Conkling's long dedication speech about its "pleasant
hills and dales." Soon the William Wallaces, the John Todds, the
John Stuart Todds, the Ninian Edwardses, and the Clark Smiths, in
fact, all of Mary Lincoln's many Springfield relatives, had bought lots.
In May 1865 she insisted that her husband be buried there as well.
Lincoln might be Springfield's local hero and Illinois's first President,
but he was Mary Todd's husband.[17]

Still, the association and city government balked. Having paid the
inflated price of $5,300 for their mistake, they refused to consider the
dead Lincoln anything but civic property and wanted him displayed
downtown. But the widow insisted, showering Governor Oglesby and
others with letters of vehement opposition. Mary Lincoln was alone in
this unpopular crusade, but she had powerful weapons. First she invoked
the widow's prerogative to decide a husband's burial place, a custom
which the "whole civilized world" accepted. Next she cited Lincoln
himself, who on their last trip to Virginia had informed her of his
preference for a burial place of "quiet repose—You are younger than
I," she quoted him as saying, "and you will survive me. When I am
gone, lay my remains in some quiet place like this," he said, pointing
to the land along the James River near City Point, Virginia. After Tad
had reminded her (though she hardly needed it) that "three of us are
on Earth, three in Heaven," she stiffened her resolve that all six would
eventually be together in Oak Ridge. By the summer—with Lincoln's
body temporarily stored in a vault in Oak Ridge—she had won, though
her concern over an appropriate monument persisted for another decade.
Eventually five Lincolns (Robert preferred Arlington National Cemetery) came to rest on a hill—one of Springfield's few—across from and
slightly above the tombs of relatives and neighbors.[18]

It was a costly victory, though in the short run the campaign provided Mary Lincoln relief from weeks of passive despondency. In the
long run, whatever Springfield's feelings about her before the battle,
henceforth the community despised her. Eventually the association
took a loss on the Mather property. As one neighbor explained, "they
[the association] had already bought the Mather place, a beautiful
grove of native trees. Now the people are in a rage. Mrs. Lincoln has
no friends here."[19]

IN Washington the dreary spring weather was improving. A military commission had begun hearing evidence against John Wilkes Booth's eight coconspirators, and the newspapers were full of Mary Surratt's court appearances in hood and shackles. The last southern army had surrendered in North Carolina, and on May 19, 1865, Jefferson Davis, the president of the former Confederate States of America, was captured, wearing women's clothes, it was rumored. But in the White House nothing had changed. Mrs. Lincoln was still there, promising to leave but then, when the day approached, relapsing into passionate melancholy. "Mrs. Lincoln has nearly recovered. She will leave the White House next Wednesday," predicted the *New York Herald,* but ten days later she was still there.[20]

Uncertain about when to leave, she also did not know where to go. Robert Lincoln and David Davis, the 325-pound Supreme Court justice whom Lincoln had selected as administrator of his father's estate, directed her to Springfield, insisting that she live in the house at Eighth and Jackson. She could afford nothing else, they warned. But Mary Lincoln would not go back to Springfield. "After the many years of happiness there with my idolized husband to place me in the home deprived of *his* presence and the darling boy we lost in Washington, it would not require a day, for me to lose my entire reason—I am distracted enough, as it is, with remembrances, but I will spare myself and my poor sons this additional grief." Besides, her husband had promised that he would "never carry me back to a place which would remind us both of so great a loss." Against the advice of both her male protectors, she chose Chicago instead.[21]

She left on a special day. For weeks official Washington had been planning a victory celebration, and on May 23, at the very hour that Mary Lincoln had chosen for her departure, the blue-uniformed veterans of the Army of the Potomac were swinging up Pennsylvania Avenue, regimental flags snapping in the wind, bands playing in celebration of the army's magnificent triumph in Virginia. On the reviewing stands in front of the White House—where Mary Lincoln might have been—President Johnson and General Grant took the soldiers' salutes.

Inside the official residence that Johnson had yet to occupy, Mary Lincoln was finally packing the twenty trunks and fifty boxes that represented home. The ceremonies were underway when her gloomy troop of Robert, Tad, Lizzie Keckley, and Tad's friends, the White

House guards Thomas Cross and William Crook, boarded the late-afternoon train for the fifty-four-hour trip to Chicago. Twelve hours later they changed cars in Pittsburgh, though the ghoulish crowds gathered to see the widow were disappointed when she somehow eluded them. By this time she had one of her migraines.

Before leaving Washington, Mary Lincoln had explained her feelings: "I go hence brokenhearted with every hope in life almost crushed." Doubting "the goodness of the Almighty," she also doubted her ability "to submit" to His will. When Eddie and Willie had died, "our griefs were one." Together she and Lincoln had read Henry Wadsworth Longfellow's "Resignation," a lachrymose poem written after the poet's daughter had died in 1848. Mary Lincoln believed Longfellow a spiritualist, and his understanding "There is no Death! / What seems so is transition" conformed to her own ideas of eternal life. But now, without Lincoln, "Alas, all is over with me."[22]

THEY settled—she and Tad and Robert—first in an expensive hotel in the city and then in a cheaper version, where the weekly board ran to nearly $40 a week for three. No longer could she afford Lizzie Keckley, and though the two women were to share another unforgettable experience, for a time they were separated. Returned to Washington, Keckley sewed for the ladies of the new regime and eventually received $210 from Congress, calculated at the rate of $35 a week, for six weeks of what government records called "Services to Mrs. Lincoln."[23]

Sometime during the hot, disease-laden summer Mary Lincoln's "broken little band" moved again—this time to a new hotel that had just opened in the Hyde Park area along Lake Michigan, seven miles south of the city. The Hyde Park Hotel was a four-story wooden affair with a country look and a wide wraparound porch for its rocking chairs. From here Robert Lincoln took the streetcar into town, where he was apprenticing in a law firm. In keeping with the prescriptions of early mourning and her own incapacity, his mother did nothing. She spent her days contemplating the waves of Lake Michigan, tending to a correspondence made voluminous by sympathy notes, and walking in the park along the water's edge.

Tad, for the first time, was attending school. He either accompanied Robert on the streetcars or rode the pony that his mother had brought from Washington to a private academy in downtown Chicago. Now twelve years old, the youngest Lincoln was embarrassingly illiterate. Asked to read the word *ape* in a primer, Tad could do no better, even after his mother's hints, than *monkey*. In Washington his tutor Alexander Williamson had tried to teach him reading and writing in the state dining room, where a blackboard had been briefly installed. But Willie's death and a father who didn't want his son to become "pokey" had made schooling a difficult task. Overactive and slow to learn, Tad may have been slightly retarded; even his mother referred to him as a "marked character." Still, by June Mary Lincoln informed Williamson that Tad "was saying two or three lessons a day and at length is seized with the desire to be as diligent at studies as play." But by August Tad had relapsed. In the next maternal report he was not "applying himself as much as he ought."[24]

In any case, the education of her youngest son diverted Mary Lincoln from gloomy self-contemplation, as did Tad's speech problems. At first she took him to a dentist, who inserted a brutal steel frame to force his recalcitrant pronated teeth into a better position. In this apparatus Tad, who did not speak well to begin with, could hardly speak at all. Eventually this barbarbic device was replaced by a sympathetic elocution teacher.[25]

With her sons in the city during the day, Mary Lincoln returned to the inactivity that she had known first as the petted daughter of the Lexington aristocracy and then briefly as a bride boarding at the Globe Tavern. Meals arrived from the hotel kitchen, and maid service for three rooms was included in the rent. She saw almost no one, thereby irritating several Chicagoans who called. Their visits were painful reminders of what she sometimes tried to forget rather than expressions of support. With characteristic attention to the exceptionalism of her circumstances, she explained: "I have not been able to summon sufficient courage, to receive but very few, of my friends who, with all the world, surely sympathize in my unutterable distress of mind."[26]

The few who were admitted found a widow completely absorbed by the assassination. Isaac Arnold, the steely-eyed lawyer who had dined often at her table at Eighth and Jackson and who in the summer of 1865 was completing a hasty biography of Lincoln, found her obsessed with the details of the shooting, which she "told and retold. It was as if she had lost all power of choice in the topics of her conversation." At times during this endless summer Mary Lincoln wished, though only her female friends heard this, that she would go "under the wild waves of Lake Michigan."[27]

But these were not serious suicide threats. Mary Lincoln had, as she put it, "sufficient grace to await God's time." Her complaints that life on *this* earth was insupportable were attention-getting tactics that emerged from her spiritualism. And so while she blustered about not wanting to remain on earth and about living only for her sons, her persistent foe was not self-destruction but rather the widow's lot: poverty, loneliness, abandonment, and nervous uncertainty about the future. Occasionally she prayed for death "to end my misery," though such expressions were commonplace hyperbole for widows. However much she threatened, she never intervened.[28]

In fact, sometime during the late summer of 1865, she began transforming her grief over a human experience into Mrs. President Lincoln's mourning. Thereafter she would never disconnect herself from her husband but instead would maintain an attachment to him through alternate swings of avoiding and cherishing her private Lincolnalia. Both extremes displayed a case of unresolved mourning, as she came to prize her bereavement for the very reason that it made her special. While Lincoln was alive, she had often heard him defiled; now she intended to preside over the installation of her husband as an American hero and of her adjunct status as a deprived widow. Thus Mary Lincoln exchanged the human she had chided, quarreled with, and dressed for a Christ-like figure—"My Sainted Idol, . . . the one who cast his bread upon the waters. . . . A sainted man who had a holy smile" she called him, with relentless religiosity. She even remembered his promise of a trip to Palestine after his second administration. And according to her recollection, a few days after this conversation, "the crown of immortality was his—He was in the midst of the Heavenly Jerusalem."[29]

Even a lukewarm Christian might have discovered a spiritual significance in the assassination of a husband on Good Friday, and his consignment to heaven just after Easter. In fact, though some clergy had been outraged by Lincoln's presence in a theater on a religious holiday, most eulogized the President as an American Christ who died for his countrymen's sin of slavery. In one preacher's view, "Jesus Christ died for the world, Abraham Lincoln died for the country." So it was not by chance that Mary Lincoln left the White House forty days after Lincoln's assassination.

Later, when friends began offering the traditional consolations about time's healing powers, she summarily rejected such routine therapy. Her bereavement was different. "No *such sorrow*," she maintained, "was ever visited upon a people or family, as when we were bereaved of my darling husband, every day, causes me to feel more crushed and bro-kenhearted. . . . Time, does not soften [my grief] nor can I ever be reconciled to my loss until the grave closes over the remembrance and I am reunited to him."

Four years after Lincoln's death she still felt that "time brings to me, no healing on its wing." Even Lucy Little, a blind girl from Wisconsin who had written a sympathy note, was better off than she. "Our Heavenly Father, has afflicted you, in the deprivation of your sight, yet you are surrounded by loving friends, whose lives are passed in contributing to your comfort. My dearly beloved husband, was the *light* of our eyes, we never felt, notwithstanding our *great* love for him, so *good* and great as he was, that we could love him sufficiently. . . . To *me,* as you may well believe, life is all *darkness,* the sun is a mockery to me, in my great sorrow," she wrote, the excessive commas and dashes underscoring her distress.[30]

In time this personal bathos took on a spiritual significance, and what she called "my heavy cross, . . . my daily crucifixion, . . . my Gethsemane" produced an anthology of biblical stigmata that ren-dered her nearly blind, bowed her down, crushed her body, and pro-duced bleeding, if metaphorical, wounds. She had been "baptised with Sorrow." Four years later Mary Lincoln still thought of her bereave-ment in religious terms. "I feel that I am a *very* Martha," she wrote in a reference to the sisters of Bethany who tended Christ. In the Book of Luke Mary had sat docilely at Jesus' feet while Martha had cleaned and cooked. But it was the efficient Martha who, after asking Jesus if He did not care that she worked alone, was rebuked for being anxious and bothered. "I hope you will pray for me that I may personnate instead the 'Mary of the Bible,'—sitting at the feet of Jesus—resign-ing myself to his will," wrote Mary Lincoln.[31]

IN the fall, when cooler weather dispelled the summer's germs, Mary Lincoln and her two sons returned to the city, this time renting rooms in the Clifton House. Off and on for the next three years this estab-lishment on the corner of Wabash Avenue and Madison Street in downtown Chicago was home for Tad and his mother. Robert made other plans as quickly as possible. "I would," he declared of the hotel, "almost as soon be dead as remain three months in this dreary house." By January 1866 he had used the $1,500 Judge Davis dispensed as his annual share of his father's unprobated estate to find something more comfortable in a pair of rooms above Crosby's Opera House on Washington Street.[32]

For Tad and his mother, Clifton House was not only dreary but noisy and public. Popular with transients and newcomers to the boom city of Chicago, it lacked what women like Mary Lincoln considered refinement. It was also an inconvenient distance from the parks and promenades where, enshrined in her restrictive widow's weeds, Mary Lincoln liked to walk. Still, she had little choice: "We are left with only $1,500 each [annually] to live upon—the interest of our money and as a matter of course must board plainly and genteely as possible."[33]

Soon even genteel boarding had become "revolting and offensive," and Mary Lincoln began a capital campaign. "I must arouse myself for a little action," she alerted her friend Sally Orne, the wealthy wife of a Philadelphia carpetmaker. Mary sought the kind of permanent residence that every gentlewoman required and to which she, as the widow of the "Great One", was entitled. As with the fight over Lincoln's burial place, the deploying of her resources temporarily dispelled her melancholy, though it embarrassed Robert and infuriated Davis, the executor of Lincoln's still-unsettled estate.[34]

Before Mary Lincoln could afford a house, she had to pay off debts that probably ran to $10,000. Already she had discovered (though it was an oft-forgotten lesson) that her husband's reputation was not transferable and that as Widow Lincoln she was treated with none of the indulgence she had received as Mrs. President Lincoln. Like cockroaches come out at dark, the merchants and jewelers who had so casually extended credit in the past now emerged, demanding payment for finery she had purchased on an income of $25,000. Though she had no means to do so with Lincoln's estate in Judge Davis's hands, her creditors threatened that if she did not pay, they would describe her sable boas and $1,500 shawls to the newspapers. Worst of all, they might sue, as the New York retailer Alexander T. Stewart was threatening. Such publicity would destroy the impression of a destitute, albeit worthy, widow available for donations. Somehow the bills must be paid.[35]

Typically Mary Lincoln fought her own battle, and in the summer of 1865 she enlisted Sally Orne to sell a dress "presented by a friend of my husband's and myself—a *very* elegant lace dress, very fine and beautiful—lace flounce about six inches, in width, for the bottom of the skirt—same pattern as the dress—a double lace shawl, very fine,

. . . worth $3500." This she would sacrifice at the bargain price of $2,500, along with sixteen yards of white moiré antique material. At $125 a yard the latter was the most magnificent, and expensive, Alexander Stewart had ever imported into the United States.[36]

Next she negotiated the return of jewelry valued at $2,612. Back to Washington's best-known jeweler Matthew Galt, in her estimation the only gentleman among her creditors, went two $550 diamond and pearl bracelets, a $440 diamond and pearl ring—"all never worn—scarcely looked at and never shown to anyone," along with two gilt clocks and a dozen and a half gilt spoons. She had bought the last out of pocket for the White House when the "old rascal" French (in her words) had been too slow authorizing purchases. Even with this credit it was a year and a half before her Galt bill was cleared, and sometime during 1866 Mary Lincoln had to refinance her debts through a high-interest loan from Jay Cooke, the wealthy financier.[37]

Among her overdue accounts were bills for the multiple purchases of identical items. During her years in the White House Washington had gossiped about the eighty-four pairs of gloves Mary Lincoln had bought before the inauguration. After Lincoln's reelection she had selected a new set of state china from John Kerr, whose Philadelphia store specialized in English and French imports. Kerr had simultaneously offered her an irresistible price for a personal replica of the buff-colored, gilt-trimmed 508-piece official china that she chose as a replacement for the official set of solferino Limoges she had purchased in 1861. The staff had been hard on the first set, and few pieces remained, though some said it was bad-luck china, appropriate for the family that used it. Again she replaced the seal of the United States with the initials ML on her personal set. Even after Lincoln's death her acquisitive self overpowered her miserliness, and she refused to cancel the order, scolding Kerr for his delay in sending the china: "I cannot be satisfied, without I have, of the same kind—two dozen tea cups, 2 sugar bowls, 2 slop bowls, some small meal dishes . . . it will never do not to have the set complete . . . it will be a great disappointment if you do not soon forward it to me."[38]

At some point in 1866 Mary Lincoln also tried to sell the silver mining stocks that Simon Cameron and others had urged on her during the war. While First Lady, she had registered them in Frances Wallace's name to avoid impropriety. Now someone told her that these claims might be worth thousands, and she set to work searching for the certificates in the White House, where she had left them.

Eventually located, they were returned with curt notes, and with great expectations Mary Lincoln sent them off to Noah Brooks to sell. But like so much else on which she had counted, the stocks proved worthless. Brooks could not find buyers at any price for her stock in either the Nevada or Mexican silver mines that had gone bust.[39]

Next Mary Lincoln encouraged the subscription funds gotten up to support what her unexpected ally, the New York editor Horace Greeley, was describing in the *New York Tribune* as "the late President's grieving widow and fatherless sons." In an age with neither life insurance nor pensions, such solicitations were a respectable means of providing for the destitute survivors of prominent men. By the end of 1865 Mary Lincoln collections had been discreetly begun in Boston, Chicago, Philadelphia, and even Baltimore, where neither she nor her husband had been popular. With proper handling, she expected them to raise thousands, as similar efforts had done for other widows.

She also gave her attention to wealthy potential donors such as Marshall Roberts, the New York shipping magnate; Norman Bentley, a merchant and importer on lower Broadway; Oliver Halsted; and the veterans of her Blue Room Salon. Even Alexander Stewart, the best-known philanthropist in America, was not forgotten, though it was hard to make a claim on his generosity when she still owed him money. Off to possible benefactors—some personal friends, others rich strangers—went what Robert Lincoln despised as "Mother's begging letters." Soon wealthy Republicans everywhere understood that with a stroke of the pen, they could prevent "my future spent without a home, forever a wanderer on the face of the earth."[40]

By way of encouragement Mary Lincoln bestowed a seemingly endless number of Lincoln's canes as "a slight momento {*sic*}—[a] little relic of my Beloved Husband." Marshall Roberts got Henry Clay's snuff box, given to Lincoln by John Clay in 1862. A few prospects received a piece of the "Great One's" hair, though as Mary Lincoln complained to Sally Orne, there was not much of the latter to give. "Only a bunch as large as one of our fingers was saved me." She also informed special contributors of a particular way in which to honor the President: They could purchase "the handsome home in Chicago the President intended to buy [so that] instead of going North we might this summer come here [to Chicago] at our pleasure."[41]

At some point during her first winter of widowhood Mary Lincoln hired an agent. She chose Alexander Williamson, the boys' tutor, who now held a part-time position that she had arranged in the Treasury

Department. Employed for a contingency fee of $35 for every $1,000 he collected, Williamson was to settle her accounts, fend off creditors, and stop the gossip about her extravagance. But mostly he was to do what she could not: personally solicit rich Republicans for contributions to the Mary Lincoln Fund. This enterprise soon became a nationwide effort, as under her orders Williamson sought out Bullitts in Kentucky, Andersons in Cincinnati, Garretts and Gilmors in Baltimore, and "that very rich Mr. Harrison in Philadelphia—an elderly gentleman living in great style." Despite strict orders that he keep away from "old Davis," the duplicitous agent made certain that Judge Davis was apprized of Mrs. Lincoln's campaigns as well as her "nervous and agitated style, urging me to use every endeavor to relieve her of pressing importunities for payment of debts."

Under strict orders about how to proceed ("do not fail to write the letters word for word"), Williamson copied the appeals Mary Lincoln composed and then, also under her instructions, signed Charles Forsythe, the fictitious prosperous-sounding name she had chosen. With the promotional sophistication of a modern fund-raiser, Mary Lincoln instructed Williamson-Forsythe to appear as an influential donor who "had been a warm friend of the Lincolns' and who had already responded generously to the widow's needs." When some of her best prospects would not put their "hands in their pockets," she ordered Williamson to stay in their offices until they signed their notes and checks in his presence. "Appeal," she directed, "to their kind feelings, in my behalf." There could never be enough of these, although she did raise about $10,000 to pay off her debts and prevent any claims against the President's estate. Mary Lincoln took pride in her accomplishment. ". . . out of every dollar I could command I paid to the uttermost farthing." Still, she had expected more than she received, and in a perverse, self-defeating way her well-known extravagances discouraged some benefactors from contributing, at the same time that they made a large fund necessary.[42]

By taking over her own affairs instead of leaving them to Robert and Judge Davis, not only was Mary Lincoln acting in an unwomanly fashion but she was competing with influential organizations like the Lincoln Monument Association. Since May, 1865 this group had been briskly raising money for a proper monument in Springfield, and many who might have given to a housing fund for Mary Lincoln instead contributed to a monument for her husband. As a result, whenever she compared her subscription funds to those raised for other families, she knew she had failed, and she suffered another blow to her self-confidence. "Roving generals have elegant mansions showered upon them," she quoted a friend, "and the American people leave the family of the Martyred President to struggle as best they can."[43]

Already General Grant's friend and field commander Daniel Butterfield had raised enough money to pay off the $30,000 mortgage on Grant's Washington house, and eventually the Grants were offered two other houses, one in Galena, Illinois, and the other on Philadelphia's posh Chestnut Street, this stocked with the elegant linens and silver that Mary Lincoln coveted. When Grant was elected President in 1868, Mary Lincoln was angry that the man her husband rescued from obscurity did not even return the favor and give Robert Lincoln his just due—a foreign mission.[44]

Then Mary Lincoln discovered that a private subscription drive had raised $100,000 for Secretary of War Stanton's widow, Ellen—a woman who in her estimation had done nothing for the war effort. Even the widows of minor figures fared better than she. When Secretary of War John A. Rawlins, a former neighbor of Grant's, died, the President, according to Mary Lincoln, gave "a royal decree and $43,000 was raised for Mrs. R. besides $20,000 from Cuba." The forgotten wife of the man who had made Rawlins a general had meanwhile become "a living monument to the nation's ingratitude." Such comparisons were always to her disadvantage. Her public explanation for such shabby treatment pointed to an ungrateful nation, not to an unpopular Mary Lincoln, forsaken again.[45]

Among Williamson's tasks was lobbying Congress for a pension and the remainder of Lincoln's salary. Well schooled in the art of legislative persuasion, Mary Lincoln timed her letters to congressmen on the Pension Committee to coincide with Williamson's visits. Lincoln's friend Elihu Washburne received such an appeal in mid-December 1865, just as the Thirty-ninth Congress was organizing for its first session. At issue was the final solution to her poverty. If Congress would grant the remainder of Lincoln's salary, she would receive nearly $100,000—$25,000 for each of the four years of his term minus a month's salary for the six weeks he had served of his second term. She wrote Washburne: "May I urge you in view of the necessities of our case to insist upon the four years salary—for a home, furniture, and interest to live on. Otherwise"—and this was the perdition she feared—"our portion is a boarding house forever—a fitting place," she added with her famous sarcasm, "for the wife and sons of the man who served his country so well and lost his life in consequence."[46]

Both Alexander Williamson and Robert Lincoln advised Mary that she must expect no more than the remaining months of her husband's 1865 salary. It was the Harrison precedent, and two other presidential wives, Anna Harrison and Margaret Taylor, had received this settlement silently and gratefully. Mary Lincoln was unpersuaded; her circumstances were different. Not only had Lincoln been killed in wartime in his country's service, but "perhaps never in history, will such a case again occur as ours—therefore there is no parallel to our case." Congress did not appreciate Mary's argument, however, and refused to reward it in 1865. Though bills for the four-year salary were introduced, both Senate and House voted her the one-year salary along with a lifetime franking privilege that was useful during her solicitation campaign. There had been one embarrassing moment when John Wentworth, the Illinois congressman who had introduced the four-year salary bill, mysteriously withdrew it, explaining that the House "knew all the circumstances" and he would say no more. Had he, Wentworth might have explained that he believed public money should not go to pay for Mary Lincoln's expensive gowns and jewelry.[47]

Early in 1866 Mary Lincoln received this congressional donation of $22,025. From Lincoln's annual salary of $25,000, the comptroller had deducted six weeks' pay along with the quarterly federal tax, the latter sent to David Davis. Well aware that the same congressmen who voted her the paltry year's salary had recently appropriated more than $100,000 for White House repairs and furnishings, Mary Lincoln protested to Davis. "Be pleased to write me on what authority he [the treasurer of the United States] can deduct the half month of April—from the pay—Also why $847.83 is paid to you—now. It is a pitiful offering at best and most ungraciously bestowed."[48]

It was another humiliating moment in a full season of them, especially since the exact amount of her inheritance was locked away with tight-lipped Robert and disapproving David Davis. They knew what Mary Lincoln did not: that the President's estate amounted to $85,000, nearly all of it from the White House salary that his wife had helped preserve by getting others to pay her bills. Only months after her husband's assassination had she learned the size of the estate, and then only from the newspapers when Davis had entered the public affidavits required for probate. By law she would receive only the widow's portion of a third, another irritant. For if Lincoln had written a will, she had no doubt he would have left her everything. As it was, Judge

Davis often neglected to send the semiannual interest of $4,500 she shared with her two sons. Both she and Robert had to remind him. "Please draw and send me the interest now due" went an urgent request in 1866. That same month Robert advised Davis he was "running out of funds" and, like his mother, needed the interest from his father's estate.[49]

In the days when the fat judge and her lean husband had shared carriages, lice-ridden beds, greasy meals, and foolish juries on the Illinois circuit, Mary Lincoln and David Davis had not gotten along. Though Davis was often at her parties, behind her back he described her as "not agreeable."[50] In fact, he confessed to his wife, he didn't "fancy the whole family of Todds." Nothing in the intervening decade had changed his mind or hers. Mary Lincoln begrudged him the wealth that matched his corpulence, for he grew fat on his real estate speculations while Lincoln stayed lean and comparatively poor.

But her husband liked Davis and in 1864 appointed him an associate justice of the United States Supreme Court. Robert Lincoln considered the judge a second father, and after the assassination he had telegraphed Davis "to come at once to Washington and take charge of my father's affairs." Mary Lincoln was too agonized to object, though she was soon complaining that this garguantuan figure of patriarchal authority who now controlled her money was "complacent, . . . without any warmth in his nature," and "intensely selfish." Davis further irritated her by offering the unacceptable advice that she could not afford a house. "He would like to force us back to Springfield," she wrote Anson Henry, "but I would eat the bread of poverty first here [in Chicago]. Admittedly "perfectly honorable" in her estimation, "he loves to rule" and "cannot understand how others unblessed by his hundred thousands feel deprived of their All."[51]

There was justice in her complaints, for Davis was a busy man who gave only desultory attention to the Lincoln estate. During his tenure as administrator he was still suffering from a painful carbuncle that kept him in bed for months, and judicial affairs (several important Reconstruction cases were pending) diverted him from the minor matter of Mrs. Lincoln's inheritance. Still, Judge Davis was slow. Though it had nothing to do with the estate, a check that happened to be on the President's desk in April 1865 was not returned to its owner until 1867. Possibly Davis intended to keep the principal away from a woman he believed a prodigal for as long as possible. In any case, most managers of nineteenth-century estates of similar complexity and size distributed assets within a year, and an energetic administrator could have moved the estate with more dispatch through the process of collecting assets, establishing and paying claims, selling property, publishing notices, and, there being no estate tax, distributing funds to Mary Lincoln and her two surviving sons.

While she fumed, Davis eventually discovered that there was only one outstanding debt. In 1857 the Chicago lawyer Norman Judd had borrowed $3,000 from Lincoln. Now Judd, who told his friends that he did not intend that Mrs. Lincoln could say of him what he was saying of her (and he was saying she could not pay her bills), announced he was ready to repay interest and principal. There had been some threatened claims against the estate, especially by the jeweler Galt, but they were withdrawn when Mary Lincoln raised the money to pay them. By 1866 nothing stood in the way of distribution save the administrator's procrastination, which would continue through 1868.[52]

More damaging than Davis's leisurely stewardship was his gossip. Everyone who inquired about the widow's circumstances heard from him that Mary Lincoln would inherit enough money to keep her in the style she deserved. Initially, among even her friends, there was uncertainty on this point, and several potential donors asked Davis further about "the painful controversy . . . the *Tribune* says that you had notified Mrs. Lincoln the finances of the estate would not admit of her keeping house, while others say that the estate is sufficient to place the family beyond want." Davis had said both things, and his loose talk behind the widow's back compromised his fiduciary relationship to the Lincoln heirs as well as Mary Lincoln's ability to raise money.

When a Springfield friend revealed Davis's chilling effect on her business, Mary Lincoln confronted him. "A lady friend, whom I respect very much, visited me, on yesterday and remarked, that a gentleman told her, that you had told a friend of his, that our means were very ample, and no assistance was required to enable us to live *very* comfortably—I replied to her, that there *must* be, some mistake, that it was impossible, that you could have said this, or overrated an income, which enabled us to board in the plainest manner *only*." Davis, a judge unaccustomed to challenge from anyone, much less a woman whose money he was handling, was furious.[53]

IN the spring of 1866, after boarding a year, Mary Lincoln would wait no longer for a permanent home. Both Robert and David Davis disapproved of her decision, and she knew from experience how expensive Chicago was. Still, she had a new patron, or thought she had, though Simon Cameron was an unlikely benefactor. The former Pennsylvania governor had lasted less than a year as Lincoln's indolent, corrupt secretary of war. Then, after serving as the American ambassador in St. Petersburg, the wily Pennsylvanian began making a comeback. Sullied by his wartime performance in the cabinet (not only had Lincoln dismissed him, but the House of Representatives had censured him in 1862), the ex-Democrat needed to cleanse his Republican slate. Helping Mary Lincoln was an opportunity, so he tendered his services for a new drive to raise $20,000 from large donors. With this, Lincoln's widow would have what she most desired: "a quiet home, where I can freely indulge my sorrows" and where "as a family we shall be more pleasantly and becomingly situated." Cameron, she now expected, would relieve her anxiety "about this pecuniary business."[54]

Buoyed by Cameron's promises and her expectation that Robert would return to a home (as reluctantly he did), though never to a boardinghouse, Mary Lincoln bought a house on Chicago's West Washington Street. The first anniversary of Lincoln's death was approaching, and she often bolstered her meager self by buying things. This purchase would serve the additional purpose of putting her family together again. Still, it was mid-June 1866 before mother and sons were settled in the substantial stone house situated in one of the city's new middle-class neighborhoods. West Washington Street was hardly the best address in town. That distinction belonged to the North Shore mansions along Lake Michigan where Robert settled in the 1890s. Yet it was close to Union Park (the so-called Bois de Boulogne of West Side Chicago); Tad could walk to school, and Mary Lincoln was keeping house again.

No sooner had she moved than Simon Cameron won his senatorial nomination and lost interest in her affairs. Though she chased him him with tart reminders ("my home is plain, yet elegant, very much like the one *you* occupied in Washington"), her future as a homemaker was in jeopardy. "If I am not assisted," she acknowledged only a month after she moved, "I shall have to dispose of [the house]." Not ready to give up even after Cameron's desertion, she sent off another round of solicitations to Leonard Sweet, a friend of Lincoln's in the circuit-riding days, Elihu Washburne, and her husband's associates who had not yet contributed to her funds. When no one responded, she used the congressional donation of Lincoln's 1865 salary to pay for her house and the splendid set of solid rosewood furniture that graced its two downstairs parlors. But with Lincoln's estate still undistributed, she could not keep house on a "clerk's salary."[55]

By the spring of 1867 the struggle was over; Mary Lincoln had lost again. "It is," she wrote David Davis, "so painful to me now without sufficient to live upon, and in such a nervous afflicted state to be compelled to give up a home." Robert, who had consistently opposed the purchase of a house that he would necessarily have to live in, was vindicated; he let his mother know as much in the abrasive tone that he adopted with her: "I hope you will come out of this better than I think you will—I am surprised that you have allowed [the contractor] Cole to blind you again, but I am done with wasting time in urging you to beware the advice of those who must possess such a deep interest in your welfare." Although she did not sell the West Washington Street house for seven years, using the rent to live on, this was Mary Lincoln's last try at the domesticity that came from owning and inhabiting a residence surrounded by family. Henceforth she was a permanent exile, a self-proclaimed vagabond, living in other people's places— hotels, boardinghouses, a sanatorium, and finally the upstairs bedroom of her sister Elizabeth's Springfield house. "No place is home for me," she lamented.[56]

IN the midst of financial troubles came another humiliation. On the night of November 16, 1866, her husband's former law partner—the Billy Herndon whom she had never asked to dinner—strode to the podium to address the full house gathered in Springfield's Old Courthouse. Cranky, alcoholic Herndon was often wrong about things and was again this evening. Still, he had correctly gauged the interest in what he was going to say, though to make sure he had posted broadsides around the courthouse square previewing his remarks on "A. Lincoln—Miss Ann Rutledge, New Salem, Pioneering, the Poem." Everybody in Springfield knew that Herndon had been rummaging around in Lincoln's past. Earlier even Mary Lincoln had broken her vow to stay away from Springfield in order to have a long conversation with him at the St. Nicholas Hotel.[57]

What Herndon thought he had discovered and had hinted at in the letter that brought Mary Lincoln to Springfield was Lincoln's true love. In the thwarted Gothic romance of Herndon's imagination, Ann Rutledge had given her heart to two men in New Salem. One of them was Abraham Lincoln. In Herndon's flowery prose, this "beautiful, amiable, and lovely girl of nineteen" suffered a Victorian "conflict of duties, love's promises and womanly engagements," which made her "think, grow sad, become restless and nervous. She suffered, pined, ate not, and slept not." Soon the only woman Lincoln ever adored died of love. Lincoln was disconsolate. "His mind," according to Herndon, "wandered from its throne, and when he finally recovered, he had lost the woman he should have married." As for his marriage to Mary Todd seven years later, that was a disaster, "a domestic hell. . . . For the last twenty-three years of his life, Mr. Lincoln had no joy." As evidence of the couple's misery, Herndon charged that Honest Abe could never bring himself to use the words *love* or *yours affectionately* to Mary Lincoln. Instead, he signed his letters to his wife, as to his political acquaintances and clients, "your friend."[58]

In late November Mary Lincoln read Herndon's speech. The *Chicago Tribune* had printed nearly every word of it, and like brushfire, the Ann Rutledge story spread. From Scotland James Smith, the former minister of Mary Lincoln's Springfield church and a Lincoln-appointed consul at Dundee, promptly defended her claim to her husband's affection. Later the other man in Herndon's triangle—John McNamar—also denied Lincoln's romantic attachment to Rutledge. Still, the gossip burned on, and the widow who was in danger of losing her domestic status as a homemaker lost another linchpin of domesticity—her husband's love.[59]

Publicly Mary Lincoln said nothing, but privately, like a star-crossed Lady Macbeth, she damned Herndon, who in a world crowded with antagonists had become a principal enemy. First she swore out an oath against him:

> [It] will not be *well with* [*Herndon*]—if he makes the *least* disagreeable or false allusion in the future. He will be closely watched. W. H. may consider himself a ruined man, in attempting to disgrace others, the vials of wrath, will be poured upon his own head. . . . If W. H. utters another word—and is not silent with his infamous falsehoods in the future, his *life* is not worth living for— I *have* friends, if his *low* soul thought that my great affliction—had left me without them. In the future, he may well say, *his prayers*—"Revenge is sweet" especially to womankind but there are some of mankind left, who will wreak it upon him. . . . He is a dirty dog.[60]

No doubt Mary Lincoln remembered how the men of Lexington had defended their lady loves with their swords and pistols and how in Springfield Abraham Lincoln had taken up her cause during the Shields affair. Now things were different, though Robert dutifully went to Springfield to try to dissuade Herndon from a national lecture tour. David Davis, to whom Mary Lincoln also appealed for support against this "malignity," proved unhelpful. He wrote back that each and everyone have a little romance in their early days. And so the matter rested, with most of the world (in Mary Lincoln's imagination all the world must have a position) believing her husband had loved someone else and that she was Lincoln's misfortune. She was dead when the Springfield poet Edgar Lee Masters immortalized Ann Rutledge:

> I am Anne Rutledge who sleep behind these weeds,
> Beloved in life of Abraham Lincoln,
> Wedded to him, not through union,
> But through separation.[61]

IN the summer of 1867 Mary Lincoln tried to sell her rosewood furniture (she finally did so in November) and, packing her other belongings into what she called "poor boxes," went traveling for her health. Tad and Robert had gone to Washington to testify at the trial of John Surratt, who had fled the United States after the assassination and was accused of conspiring to murder Abraham Lincoln. Mary Lincoln had been asked to appear as well because government prosecutors believed that she could identify Mary Surratt's son from an encounter at City Point, Virginia, in 1864.

But she pleaded ill health and was indeed sick with the kind of nervous affliction that led thousands of upper-class women to take to their beds under physician's orders. Philadelphia's Dr. S. Weir Mitchell was notorious for condemning his nervously prostrated female patients to months of bed rest, and in some circles it had become acceptable, even fashionable, for ladies of leisure to break down. Some women led full lives of chronic invalidism, though they had no ascertainable physical complaints, while others—Alice James was one—languished intermittently. With the nerves reigning supreme in America's health, scientific papers in the new *Journal of Nervous Exhaustion* alerted doctors to the specialized meanings of various nervous afflictions.

Mary Lincoln was too energetic for the rest cures that sent other

Victorian women to bed, there to act out their culturally imposed femininity in illnesses that made them ethereal and interesting through inertia. She had always contested, in action, if not word, the fraility and submission symbolized by the lady's breakdown. Yet many of her complaints—especially her back trouble, eye problems, and head-aches—did fall into the vague symptomatology of neurasthenia,—at least as it was being defined in the 1860s by a new camp of specialists like New York's Dr. George Beard and Boston's Dr. James Putnam. These doctors of medicine called themselves nerve specialists or neu-rologists, and their gender-specific diagnoses posited overwrought nerves, especially those in the female reproductive organs, as the cause of female ill health. By 1867 Mary Lincoln had seen enough of them to connect her nervousness with her physical ailments. "I have," she complained, "a chill brought on by excitement and suffering of mind."[62]

But it was more than functional complaints that she described to Dr. William Clark, a sympathetic Chicago practitioner who served as her family doctor. Besides migraines, she suffered from cystitis, and her fevers and chills were most likely the result of chronic urinary tract infections. But at the time neurologists held nervous disorders to be the source of bladder trouble, rather than the reverse. One local expert had just delivered to the Chicago Society of Physicians and Surgeons a paper on reflex bladder problems and their origin in nerve troubles. In Mary Lincoln's case, it was the opposite. During Tad's difficult deliv-ery his large head had damaged her urethra, making her a continuing target for the bacterial infections that in turn led to her fevers and micturia—"my running waters," she once called it. Nineteenth-cen-tury medicine had no treatment, and Dr. Clark became the first of many doctors to recommend traveling and the baths, "an entire change of air, scene for me."[63]

Mary Lincoln did not go far the summer of 1867, partly because of money, partly because she was not yet accustomed to traveling by herself without a male protector. Still, she was independent enough to venture to the new spas at Racine, Wisconsin. On the steamship that churned its way up the Lake Michigan coast from Chicago to Milwaukee, her mind was still on William Herndon's insults. Accord-ing to a fellow passenger, "It happened this summer that I met Mrs. Lincoln on a Lake Superior steamer. I was introduced to her and inquired regarding Herndon and other matters. Mrs. L. assured me that Hern-don was a person wholly untolerable, that his habits were bad, that Mrs. Lincoln never admitted him to her house, that he followed the

Pres. to Washington, that Mr. Lincoln tried to do something for him, that he was too intemperate. As for Anne Rutledge, Mrs. L. said it was an untrue fabrication, never was any substantiation."[64]

Once she was in Racine, Mary Lincoln's health improved. With Wisconsin's Senator and Mrs. James Doolittle (it was Doolittle who once said that after God he believed in Abraham Lincoln), Mary Lincoln took two-mile walks daily and gazed at the lake, where the merging of sea and sky into an endless horizon suited her spiritualist views on the continuity of life in death. She considered a boarding school for Tad, though she was offended by the Racine Academy's "air of restraint and almost high church te deums." Of course, she could not surrender Tad to those "little white cots of the boys . . . reposing so far away from the loving Mothers, who would at any moment, give almost their life to see them. . . . How could I, who have been deprived of so much and am left so little to love—how can I be separated from my precious child." So incontestable was this point that she did not bother with a question mark. "It's my intention in the future not to be separated from Taddie for even a day." And only rarely were they, this mother and son who sometimes shared a room—at least for a few more years.[65]

Sometime during that summer Mary Lincoln decided to hold a clothing sale. She had already advised Lizzie Keckley of her need "to make my circumstances easier." For two years, while Judge Davis trifled, she had known only the "servitude of having to count every cent I spend" and the humiliation of second-class boarding.[66] With poverty as much an emotional as a material condition, a full purse would make her feel, as well as live, better.

Like most widows, Mary Lincoln had only one asset, though it was not easily negotiable. Having undertaken permanent widowhood, she could sell what she referred to as her wardrobe. The term accurately described the satin, furs, and jewelry that were costumes from a leading role that others now played. To be sure, Mary Lincoln might have gone to work, though only a few employments such as teaching, domestic service as a governess, and running a boardinghouse were respectable. She never considered them. "You men," she lectured Alexander Williamson, "have the advantage of us women, in being able to go out, in the world and earn a living."[67] Nor did she think of writing a discreet memoir of her life with the "Great One," though she got many requests for information from Lincoln's friends who intended to make money from their associations with her husband.

Still, Mary Lincoln did not intend to live on $2,000 a year, the interest on her share of her husband's unprobated estate plus the rent from West Washington Street. "I must extricate myself as best I can," she said, and this meant selling the wardrobe.[68] Admittedly such a venture was indelicate, though everyone in Springfield knew at least one needy widow who survived on periodic sales of clothes and heirlooms. In New York the secondhand stores on Seventh Avenue flourished by discounting the used finery of the gentry, while impoverished members of European royalty routinely sold their clothes. However, such an enterprise, especially when undertaken by the widow of a national hero, held possibilities for self-abasement.

But Mary Lincoln was accustomed to setting traps for herself in order to get attention. On the one hand, a sale would be a daring adventure in self-reliance, a solvent for the gloomy inactivity and virtual anonymity of the last two years, as well as a solution to her poverty. On the other hand, if mishandled, it could inflict the sort of public disgrace that in her White House years had mortified her. But she would take the chance, and so, for the first time since the graveyard fight, she had a cause.

As a woman of fashion Mary Lincoln knew her sale must coincide with the fall season in New York when merchants like Alexander Stewart offered the latest from Paris. Then the elegant women promenaded along that stretch of Broadway known as the "Ladies' Mile," gathering at the fountain between Eighteenth and Nineteenth streets to gossip and admire one another's gowns. Since her days of shopping, styles had not changed. In fact, the voluptuous, sensual appearance that Mary Lincoln had featured before its time in wartime Washington had become high fashion, and the expensive shawls and rich materials of her best dresses remained in vogue. Still, timing was critical, and so was a companion.

SOMETIME in the early evening of September 16, 1867, a heavily veiled woman dressed in black descended from the Chicago train, waited for several trunks to be unloaded, and went by carriage to the St. Denis Hotel on lower Broadway in New York City. Mrs. President Lincoln would never have stayed at such a second-rate house, but Mary Lincoln was traveling incognito as Mrs. Clarke of Chicago. Even in her widow's habit she feared recognition (and its rival, obscurity) in the parlors of the fashionable Astor and Metropolitan hotels. She seldom went anywhere without a printed announcement in the newspapers about her whereabouts, and at various times both she and Robert had been erroneously placed in Paris and California, with the correction never quite catching up with the mistake. By remaining anonymous in New York, she would retain, perhaps, her refinement.

Impatiently she awaited Lizzie Keckley. "Come by the next train, without fail. Come, come, come," she demanded after discovering that Keckley was still in Washington. Finally, her former seamstress arrived, but both women had underestimated the severity of New York's color bar and found themselves assigned to the only integrated chamber in the hotel—a miserable three-corner attic room on the fourth floor.[69]

The next day an odd couple—the stylish, tall mulatto woman with regal carriage and the stubby widow rendered squarer by her black bombazine outfit and slightly stooped shoulders—sallied forth to make a fortune. Their plan was simple. They must find an agreeable commission merchant, settle on terms, and then consign to him the treasure of Mrs. Lincoln's wardrobe, though she reserved for special handling her best jewelry. Soon they were in the hands of the ingratiating William Brady and his partner, Samuel Keyes, at 609 Broadway.

Perhaps through inadvertence, perhaps through her never dormant instincts for notoriety, Mary Lincoln handed over for appraisal a diamond ring inscribed with her name. Under questioning, Mrs. Clarke suddenly became Mrs. Lincoln. The mask of oblivion had lasted only a day. Now the brokers confirmed what she wanted to believe: Her fame enhanced the value of her goods. Having earlier observed the uses of conspicuousness by Empress Eugénie, Mary Lincoln had already been demanding outrageous prices for the few single items sold before this lot. "The Princess," she informed Keckley, "disposed of her expensive clothing without any unkind remarks about the propriety of doing so." Indeed, the empress added a surcharge for those who would buy a celebrity's clothes.[70]

Assured of $100,000 by the commission agents, the two women moved to a better hotel. There, supported by Brady and Keyes, Mary Lincoln wrote letters soliciting a select group of New Yorkers who would rather not have heard from her. It seemed more decorous for the widow to be removed from this business, and so datelined Chicago, though actually written in New York, her pleas referred to an "urgent necessity and painful embarrassment." In a letter coached by (and written to) Keyes and Brady, Mary Lincoln singled out Republican officeholders, such as her companion from the Blue Room Salon Abram Wakeman, who "should be indebted for the many favors my husband and myself always showered on him" and who must be "only too happy to relieve me by purchasing one or more articles you will place before him".[71]

But the sunshine friends of yesteryear had forgotten a dead President's wife. Like Henry Wikoff, some were already following the current star and assuring Andrew Johnson of his Napoleonic abilities. Others like Wakeman had renounced the spiritualism they had shared with Mrs. Lincoln. No longer beholden, they bought nothing. When they refused, Mary Lincoln's high-class pawnbrokers forwarded her letters to the press, with the widow permitting the shakedown. "Anything to raise the wind," she warned Keckley. "One might as well be killed for a sheep as a lamb," though in this episode she got neither.[72]

While Mary Lincoln wrote letters in her hotel, Lizzie Keckley was successfully canvassing her friends among the black community. They remembered Mary Lincoln's husband for the Emancipation Proclamation and recalled as well her efforts to raise money for the Contraband Relief Association. And as Mrs. Lincoln reminded them, ". . . tell Mr. [Frederick] Douglass and everyone, how deeply my feelings were enlisted in the cause of freedom." Indeed, they were, though to Mary Lincoln's disgust the newspapers seemed to notice only her Confederate relatives. "Why harp upon these half-brothers whom, I never knew since they were infants?" she despaired.

Eventually both Frederick Douglass and the black clergyman and editor Henry Highland Garnet offered their services as lecturers, with the proceeds going to the widow. "If the thing is done," explained Douglass to Keckley, "it should be done on a grand scale. The best speakers in the country should be secured for the purpose. You should not place me at the head nor at the foot of the list, but sandwich me between, for thus out of the way, it would not give *color* to the idea." But selling clothes and organizing a lecture fund with blacks as the principal speakers were two different things. Like many Americans, Mary Lincoln's antislaveryism was tinged with a racism that made such a project insupportable. "I want neither Mr. Douglass nor Garnet to lecture in my behalf" went her orders to Keckley.[73]

With mounting expenses and lagging sales, Mary Lincoln agreed to a public showing of her clothes. In early October the Russian furs, English shawls, and French silks (along with a pair of bracelets and the diamond ring she valued at more than $1,000) went on display at

609 Broadway. Now New York—and the world—were shocked. MRS. LINCOLN'S WARDROBE. THE CROWDS AT MR. BRADY'S, U.S. SENATORS AMONG THE VISITORS read the headline in the *New York World*. Soon *Frank Leslie's Illustrated Weekly* was carrying an illustration of what was derisively titled "Mrs. Lincoln's Second-hand Clothing Sale." As much spectacle as sale, the display became the season's curiosity, though Mary Lincoln believed that more money would have been raised had not the "do nothing" Brady and Keyes delayed the sending of advertising circulars. In any case, no one bought, and what might have been a legitimate business enterprise to improve the widow's portion became an unseemly sideshow with its principal everywhere lampooned.[74]

A special humiliation rested in the pages of a small book lying on a table near the showroom's entrance. In it prospective viewers were encouraged to pledge at least a dollar to help out Mrs. Lincoln. Instead, those who signed promised niggling amounts—a penny, a dime, and the not-quite-real offer of seventy-five dollars from the Committee to Save Us from National Disgrace. Now Mary Lincoln suffered a double mortification. In her ledger of personal estimation, clothes were as much self as accessory. Not only had she surrendered her cherished respectability (sharp-eyed reporters were describing her shawls as soiled and her gowns as perspiration-stained), but having been promised a great deal of money by her agents, she discovered that no one valued her things and consequently her.[75]

By late October an affair that began as a private adventure had degenerated, in the weeks before a hotly contested state election, into a political scandal, with Democrats charging New York's Republican establishment with bribing Mrs. Lincoln to get jobs during the Civil War. With the evidence supposedly on display, many Americans were asking the same question as the former Confederate general Jubal Early, whose troops had nearly shot the President in 1864. "By the way," wrote Early to a friend, "have you seen the exposé of Mrs. Lincoln in regard to her wardrobe and do you think it possible that the wife of a president of the United States could have received $30,000 worth of shawls, laces and fine dresses for her services in procuring contracts and appointments for the donors without his [Lincoln's] knowledge or connivance?"[76]

Those Democrats who did not use the old clothes sale as an example of Republican corruption took another tack, charging their opponents with stinginess to a poor widow. "The men who besought her influence," preached the *New York World,* "and were profuse with promises if she would gratify their wishes now give her the cold shoulder." Frederick Douglass agreed. "Shame on the man or woman," he said, "who would grudge a few dollars to smooth the pathway of such a widow." Gradually the principal figure in this affair learned that "they are making a political business of my clothes and not for my benefit either."[77]

With furious indiscretion a wounded Mary Lincoln began naming names, and the *World* was delighted: "She is particularly severe against such persons of that party [the Republicans] as Henry Raymond, Thurlow Weed, and William Seward, and claims it was through their influence that the plan to raise a fund for her was thwarted." Still, Mary Lincoln was loyal to the Republicans and insisted that she would never relinquish her "attachment to that party to which [my] husband belonged and in whose cause his life was given."[78] Rather, according to this woman, who had become a partisan liability, the problem was the party's current leadership, though her husband had known about their treachery before his death. She did not say so, but she had learned of their disloyalty from her mediums.

This was too much for Thurlow Weed, the crusty old newspaper editor and respected eminence of the Republicans. Ever since Mary Lincoln had discharged Edward McManus, the White House door-keeper, who had promptly told tales to Weed, there had been hostility between the two. Now Weed, who had worked against the Mary Lincoln subscriptions, used the pages of his *Commercial Advertiser* to attack the widow "[p]ainful," he noted patronizingly, "as it might be to reprove and assail a woman . . . [h]ad Mrs. Lincoln, while in power borne herself becomingly, the suggestion of a Lincoln Subscription Fund would have succeeded." Instead—and now Weed listed the gravamen of the gossip against Mary Lincoln as First Lady—she had diverted funds to pay for her parties, sold Lincoln's speeches (and after his death his linen shirts), and taken bribes. Moreover, her husband had left her better off than she deserved.[79]

By this time Mary Lincoln had retreated to Chicago. On the train ride from New York she overheard a discussion of the sale by two strangers and was pleased when one took her side. Unexpectedly she also found herself seated next to Charles Sumner in the dining car, though the latter, for once in his life, was rendered nearly speechless when he realized that it was Mary Lincoln behind the double veil of black crepe.

But wherever she went the scandal followed. For weeks every newspaper in the nation had something to say. Some even collected editorial opinions as if to run an opinion poll on Mrs. Lincoln. "Was there ever such cruel newspaper abuse lavished upon an unoffending woman as has been showered on my head?" she asked Keckley, who had remained in New York to do what she could. Even the mildest of her critics adjudged her "gaudy," "impudent," "greedy," and "vulgar," accusations that added up to the charge that a woman who in fact treasured the idea of femininity, if not its practice, and who disliked the suffragists was unwomanly.

Behind newspaper commentary about "this termagant with arms akimbo" rested conventional expectations about female behavior that Mary Lincoln, in one way or another, had been violating for years. For private reasons she needed the spotlight, although to get it entailed the public notoriety that rendered her suspicious. Unlike the Gilded Age reformers of her sex who worked for the vote, or for the property rights of married women, or for temperance, her cause was personal. Instead of being "attractively suppliant," according to the *Columbus* (Georgia) *Sun,* "this mercenary prostitute was repugnantly individual. . . . If Mrs. Lincoln had studied her true mission as a mother and wife she could not have discredited her sex and injured the name and fame of her country and husband."[80]

It was the penultimate charge, with worse still to come when several midwestern papers supposed her insane. Four days after her return the *Chicago Journal* printed its exposé: "The most charitable construction that Mary Lincoln's friends can put on her strange course is that she is insane." Though no one said so publicly, behind this gossip rested the presumption that only an insane woman would try to sell her clothes and then blackmail those who failed to buy them. And only an insane woman would undertake such a scheme when she had enough money for moderate living. In the rigid Victorian codes of female respectability, eccentricity was easily transformed into lunacy.

Neither Robert Lincoln nor David Davis stanched the rumors of her insanity. Both men were now irrevocably committed to the view that, as Robert wrote his future wife, Mary Harlan, "My mother is on one subject not mentally responsible—it is very hard to deal with someone who is sane on all subjects but one." He meant, of course, that his mother could not handle money and that she was a spiritualist. To others he was more direct. The *Boston Daily Evening Transcript* reported that "the intelligent, quiet, industrious, unassuming courteous Robert Lincoln . . . resembled his father, not his mother. . . . The conduct of his mother is as deep a mystery to him as to all of her friends, and the only theory he can suggest in her defense is that she is insane."[81] It was a peculiar and damaging defense, calculated more for the protection of his own respectability than his mother's well-being.

Still, Mary Lincoln was strong enough to repeat these accusations to Lizzie Keckley, who knew they were not true. "The *Springfield Journal*," she wrote, "had an editorial a few days since with the important information that Mrs. Lincoln has been known to be deranged for years and should be pitied for all her strange acts." Four days earlier Mary Lincoln had spied a similar piece in the morning *Tribune:* "B. pretending to be a lady"—she believed B. to be Jacob Bunn, the Springfield banker and editor—"says there is no doubt Mrs. L. is deranged and has been for years past and will end her life in an lunatic asylum. They would doubtless like me to begin now." As protection from the public diagnosis of her condition, Mary Lincoln armed herself with ferocity, extending her providential explanation of her own tragedies to others. First she saw God's retribution in the robbing of Bunn's house in Springfield. Then, when the child of another enemy was blinded, she wrote Keckley that "justice was being rendered for evil words—who will say that the cry of the widow and fatherless is disregarded in His sight."[82]

By no means insane, Mary Lincoln was, for all her consoling anger, soaked with the humiliation and the sense of abandonment that often accompanied her efforts at autonomy. She lacked the understanding that part of her misery had been inflicted by a male-ordered society that offered her few possibilities for the economic independence she so avidly sought. "I am friendless," she confessed to Keckley, as she continued to denounce a host of enemies. Self-pity alternated with anger. "What a world of anguish this is and how I have been made to suffer. The glass shows me a pale, wretched, haggard face and my dresses are like bags on me."[83]

Robert Lincoln, who had been out of town during his mother's misadventure in New York, now returned to Chicago, enraged by this maternally inflicted embarrassment. In her description to Keckley, "Robert came up last evening like a maniac, and almost threatening his life, looking like death, because the letters of the *World* were published in yesterday's Chicago paper."[84] Ever the mother, Mary Lincoln cried not for herself this time, but instead at Robert's misery.

Meanwhile, Keckley suggested a European sale (the clothes were currently in Providence), but Mary Lincoln scotched this, warning that "Robert would go *raving distracted* if such a thing was done and would blast us if this was done." But she was still trying to get what she could in New York. "What has been the cause of the delay of these circulars [of Brady's]?" she wondered.[85] Even two months after the sale, she hoped that her agents would send out 150,000 advertisements.

Then, with suspicious suddenness in early November 1867, Lincoln's estate was ready for distribution—or so Mary Lincoln read in the papers. Neither Robert nor David Davis had bothered to tell her, so she inquired of the executor; "The papers are abounding with notices of settlement of the estate, and the amount left each of us. As I have not heard a word from Robert on the subject, I consider it necessary that *I* should be quite as well-informed as the Press—regarding our own business." She also learned from the *Illinois Journal* that while she had been living on $130 a month since her husband's death, Davis had given her son nearly twice that much during the thirty-one months of his administration. Such outlays were to be subtracted from the final settlement, but the discrimination was obvious. While her requests for more money were refused when she hoped to stay in her home, Robert's had been granted. Without his mother's knowledge he had asked Davis for $3,000 to invest and had received extra money to fix up his bachelor quarters.[86]

In any case, Mary Lincoln was now a wealthy woman, having inherited $36,000 from Lincoln's estate. Davis had invested Lincoln's savings in twenty- and thirty-year federal bonds at 7 percent interest, a routine procedure for executors, and their value, with some of the interest reinvested, had increased in the bullish bond market of the postwar years. Now Davis was preparing, so the newspapers said, to divide assets of $110,000 among the three heirs, with Robert, as Tad's temporary guardian, controlling his younger brother's share. Consistently negligent, Davis forgot the final interest on part of the bonds, and it was July 1868 before Mary Lincoln received all her inheritance. Still, she was grateful, though she could manage—and probably at Robert's urging—only the most peremptory acknowledgment of the judge's kindness.[87]

By the time her husband's estate was in her hands, Mary Lincoln had reached a conclusion that she shared with Lizzie Keckley—and probably no one else. Her son had hastened the division of the estate "to cross my purposes." It could not be coincidence that an estate so long dormant was suddenly ready for the heirs at exactly the same time as her clothing sale. Just when she needed her poverty to sell her clothes as a widow's mite, she had been robbed. News of her inheritance destroyed any opportunity to beg for funds from patriotic philanthropists, Republican patronage holders, or even charitable Americans, many of whom were not as well-off as she was. While Robert believed his mother obsessed by money and spiritualism, Mary Lincoln came to see her eldest son as disloyal. She saw as another victim of disloyalty her friend Mrs. Brown of Chicago, who had "toiled and economised" for her husband throughout their marriage and had been left, Mary Lincoln wrote sarcastically, "a noble pension—$3000 a year. This will be a lesson for ladies who have rich husbands," she concluded, though what they could do about it she left unsaid.[88]

In New York Lizzie Keckley also read the news of Mrs. Lincoln's inheritance and expected that she might be paid something more than promises and old dresses. According to the contingency agreement between the two women, the widow owed Keckley nothing. The secondhand clothes sale had cost, not raised, money. In the spring Lizzie Keckley had turned over to Brady and Keyes Mary Lincoln's check for $824. But instead of cash from Chicago, Keckley received only descriptions of Mary Lincoln's hard times. Even with $36,000 in bonds and the West Washington Street house, the widow considered herself "in a very narrow place" and described at length an episode in which she had lost money in a streetcar. In the end Keckley got no more than an invitation: "I leave this place early in the spring; had you better not go with me and share my fortunes, for a year or more?"[89]

Sometime during Keckley's six months in New York the seamstress undertook her own means of repayment, and in the spring of 1868 *Behind the Scenes; Thirty Years a Slave and Four Years in the White House* appeared. The book was subtitled a novel, but few readers considered it fiction. Though Keckley had disavowed any intention at muckraking, her retaliation included intimate tales of Mrs. Lincoln as wife and widow, along with her employer's letters about the secondhand clothes sale. The book's principal target read it in early May and thereafter renounced the "colored historian" as friend and confidante. At the same time that Mary Lincoln expelled her best friend, she made plans to leave "this ungrateful Republic" for exile in Europe. Ashamed and humiliated, she preferred seclusion and anonymity among strangers to notoriety among her own people.[90]

X

Exile And
Return

FINALLY the steamer was ready for departure. The tugs
that like imperious sheepdogs were to nudge the *City
of Baltimore* out of its slip, down the harbor, around
Locust Point, and into the open waters of the Chesapeake Bay were in place. The cabin boys had finished
stowing the huge Saratoga trunks required by every
international traveler. Belowdecks sweaty workers—
for it was unseasonably warm—had loaded the tobacco,
resin, and cotton that made up the *City of Baltimore*'s
freight. On top deck the ship's human cargo—$100
poorer for the passage to Germany—were waving and
shouting farewell to family and friends.

Among the forty passengers this sunny first day of
October 1868 were a wealthy Baltimore family
embarking on a grand tour of Europe; a honeymooning
couple who, according to one observer, were soon spat-
ting; two female invalids en route to the European spas
with their husbands; three Catholic priests bound for
Rome with a young novitiate; the sculptor Leonard
Volk, who had done a life mask of Abraham Lincoln;
a scholar off to study the classics in Italy; four young

doctors; and an odd couple, as yet unnamed in the list of travelers bound for Bremen. One of the mysterious pair was a stubby woman whose thick widow's weeds seemed as uncomfortably warm for Baltimore's Indian summer weather as they were indecently somber for a gay transatlantic voyage. The other, no doubt her son, was somewhere between boy and man, with heavy-lidded brown eyes and a full face that hinted of his mother's well-developed jowls.[1]

There were rumors that this was the famous Mrs. Lincoln and her youngest son, Tad. Everyone in Baltimore knew that she had been staying at Barnum's—arguably the city's best hotel—and that she had attended her eldest son's wedding in Washington D.C., on September 24. This much, along with an account of the marriage of Robert Todd Lincoln to Mary Eunice Harlan, the only daughter of Iowa Senator James Harlan and Mrs. Harlan, had appeared in the *Baltimore Sun.* Omitted from the press accounts had been Mrs. Lincoln's dread of returning to the city where her husband had been murdered three and a half years before. Somehow her delight in Robert's choice ("I consider this marriage a great gain") never overcame her terror of having "to proceed to Washington to witness it." Nonetheless, dressed in her perpetual black, she had survived the small evening wedding ceremony and reception at the Harlans' house on H Street in downtown Washington.[2]

Returned to Barnum's late that evening, she fainted in the dining room the next day—either from the heat or, as she explained to a friend, "the after effects on my mind." Thereafter Mary Lincoln disappeared from the hotel's public rooms, some said to avoid the obnoxious curiosity that trailed her wherever she went. Once during her stay in Baltimore, she had taken friends into the dining room only to encounter, as she often did, the sibilant buzz: "There's Mrs. Lincoln; there's Mrs. Lincoln; there's Mrs. Lincoln."[3]

Just as there had never been much uncertainty in Barnum's public rooms that the hooded figure in black was Mrs. Lincoln, so now on board the *City of Baltimore* there was little doubt that the President's widow and son were en route to Germany, without relative or friend to say good-bye.

Mary Lincoln had not wanted it this way. She had implored several friends to join her in Baltimore before she went into an exile undertaken to place "the waters between myself and unkindness."[4] No matter how intense her shame over the old clothes scandal or how familiar the anguish of leave-taking, she needed a witness to her boldness. The

Civil War had compelled even proper ladies to travel unchaperoned. But in the years after the war going alone still ran counter to expectations of female dependency and immobility, and it would be sometime before the behavior manuals grudgingly acknowledged the respectability of female journeys made without male surveillance.

In these postwar years more wealthy Americans were embarking on the grand European tour in order, as Henry James's American explained, "to get the best out of it I can. I want to see all the great things; and do what the clever people do." But tourists were mostly males or females traveling with what Mary Lincoln called a male protector, for which role fifteen-year-old Tad was too young and inexperienced. In any case, widows of uncertain age who intended to settle in a non-English-speaking country were rare and suspicious. Once again Mary Lincoln was running against the tides of convention and family opinion. In fact, Robert Lincoln, David Davis, and Tad all had objected, and even in her own mind she vacillated between anger at the ungrateful Republic that had driven her abroad and attachment to the "Blessed land" that her husband had saved.[5]

With Robert and her new "daughter" on their wedding trip, Mary Lincoln had claimed Eliza Slataper for her audience. The two women had spent the summer of 1868 in the Pennsylvania Alleghenies, sharing the mineral waters and baths of Cresson and nearby Bedford Springs. Not only had their sons become friends (Danny Slataper was a year younger than Tad), but both women shared an attachment to spiritualism. On occasion Eliza Slataper acted as an amateur clairvoyant whose predictions so often came true as to earn Mary Lincoln's belief in her divining powers. "I wish those dear eyes of yours could become clairvoyant and visit Italy," Mary Lincoln once wrote Slataper.[6]

Sometime toward the end of the summer Eliza Slataper had promised to witness Mary and Tad's departure. Yet when the time came, Slataper was ill and resisted Mary Lincoln's importunate telegrams and letters—four of the latter in eight days. All were variations on the same plea: "I feel I shall be lonely beyond expression without you—*come to me*. . . . Do come if you love me." Three days before sailing Mary Lincoln complained, "You have not arrived and I have been awaiting you."[7] But Slataper was sick, and Mary and Tad Lincoln left uncelebrated.

Their voyage was not an easy one. The journey down the Chesapeake Bay was smooth enough, but once they were in the ocean, calm seas gave way to what Charles Tilghman described "as long swells—I never had an idea before what sea sickness was." Even the captain acknowledged the waves ran higher than at any previous time in his fifty years of crossing the Atlantic. According to Tilghman, "there was no sleeping the first night of the gale . . . everyone tumbled about first on top then under the table, among the trunks with broken china, women frightened crying and praying, children hollering, and thus we spent sixteen hours. Since which time it has been very rough. . . ."[8]

Twelve days later the *City of Baltimore* was winding its way up the Weser River to Bremen. By this time Mary Lincoln had made some enemies. Tilghman, a Maryland doctor whose jaundiced view may have been influenced by his pro-southern politics, described her as "first certainly on vulgarity. She is fit only for a fishmarket being like [that] class in all particulars—figure, face, cleanliness and conversation. I have not the honor of her acquaintance, that is, I have not spoken to her, which does not require an introduction on ship, for this she did me the honor of saying to the passengers I was not a gentleman."[9]

Mary Lincoln had made some friends as well, and with them, once the storm had passed, she marveled at the vastness of the ocean, complained, along with Tilghman, of the terrible Dutch food, which was covered with sugar and almonds, and, finally, searched for landfall. Sometime during the trip F. W. Bogen had become her male protector, and the former Union army chaplain helped on the transfer of her many trunks from Bremen to Frankfurt.

Once in the ancient city on the Main River, Mary Lincoln planned to put Tad in school, for she had been impressed by the reputation of a German education, and then to go on to the spas. Wiesbaden, Marienbad, and Baden-Baden—the last a special sanctuary for neurasthenics—had been recommended by Dr. Clark for her nerves and arthritis. With no intention of staying, Mary Lincoln rented a room in Frankfurt's best hotel, the "aristocratic" (in her words) Angleterre in the center of the city. Near her hotel, the street broadened into a square, and from one corner angled the renowned shopping promenade the Zeil. Planning to stay a week, Mary Lincoln lived in Frankfurt for the next two years.

From the beginning the city claimed her in a way that American cities no longer did. She had heard about Frankfurt during the Civil War, when its businessmen, unlike the English and French bankers, had purchased Union bonds in patriotic abundance. Few had been as generous in their support as the Seligmans, a family of eight brothers who ran an international banking house. Two brothers lived in Frankfurt, two in the United States, and in Mary Lincoln's thinking, these American Rothschilds were still serving the cause. For it was Joseph Seligman who had paid, in gold, for her ticket on the *City of Baltimore*.[10]

Like other innocents abroad, Mary Lincoln immediately measured the vulgarity of America against the quiet refinement of the Old World. "I am beginning to realize why it is," she informed Slataper, "that Europe spoils so many men and especially women. There is an independence here and a reverence which we do not dream of in America."[11] Not only did European men have manners—the kind of formal etiquette she had always tried to implant in her husband—but more worldly than their republican cousins, they tolerated eccentricity with neither stare nor comment. Finally she had found the privacy and solitude the craving for which still alternated with her occasional quest for fame. The Germans mostly ignored her because on the Continent eyes and tongues attended European royalty, leaving the Republican queen from America an infrequent target for gossip. Still there were lapses as when rumors spread in 1869 of Mary Lincoln's impending remarriage.

Once she was settled, the anonymity of her new life encouraged her to subtract yet another year from her age. In Springfield, when the census taker had come to the door and asked how old every member in the Abraham Lincoln household was, Mary Lincoln had subtracted four years. Now fifty-one, she became forty-six, adding in a letter to Sally Orne, who was still in her forties, "I feel 86." She also refused to surrender her Americanized spellings, the legacy of a youthful acquaintance with Frankfort, Kentucky. Even after a year she often added an *e* to what she called "Frankfort am Maine."[12]

Inside the Hotel Angleterre—the name of which accurately described the national origin of its guests—Mary Lincoln found a new family amid the community of English-speaking expatriates who gathered in the parlors to complain of high prices, to worry about the city's political status, and to talk, as expatriates invariably do, of affairs back home. A month after Mary Lincoln arrived, the American consul sent his annual report to the secretary of state, informing William Seward that Frankfurt's permanent American colony numbered 201 males and 177 females. These, along with the British, made an English-speaking community of more than 700. The reserve that kept these strangers apart at home—and that especially isolated women—disappeared amid the mutual camaraderie of a strange place.

Soon Mary Lincoln had friends among visiting entrepreneurs like the "Organ Masons," as she called the Henry Masons, whose family business was the manufacture of organs. She had tea with bankers and writers and past acquaintances who arrived at the Angleterre. During her second month in the hotel the Robert Allens from Springfield came to town. A delighted Mary Lincoln informed Eliza Slataper "we have a little colony here at the hotel."[13]

Among her friends were several female invalids who stopped in Frankfurt on their way to Baden-Baden or the more remote Bohemian spa of Marienbad. Like many widows, Mary Lincoln depended on women to be her intimates. With them, as with no man save a doctor, she could discourse about her ailments. "A very pleasant little Penn. lady from West Chester lives near me—she is a very sweet person, and is acquainted with many of my friends—only a few doors separate us." Yet, for this was a letter to her *best* friend Sally Orne, Mary Lincoln added: "[N]o one approaches you in my regard." To Eliza Slataper, another special friend, she avowed her attachment to Mrs. Organ Mason—"a very superior woman, we are much together—yet the attraction is so different—from what I feel towards you."[14]

Ever the flirt, Mary Lincoln was not without male friends. One of these was only doing his job, for the American consul kept close watch over his flock. While William Murphy's attendance to Mary Lincoln was perfunctory, other men also called. Once, to her delight, the duke of Nassau sent flowers, and enough men placed their cards on her table in the dining room as to call to mind her own Blue Room salon. "On yesterday," she wrote in December 1868, "two American gentlemen friends called to see me, they asked me if I was homesick. I told them I pined for a glass of American ice water. The latter here is impossible and dangerous."[15]

Then there was Count Schneiderbutzen, grand chamberlain to the duke of Baden and the fictional creation of a libelous story in an American newspaper. Both the *Portland Eastern Argus* and the *New York World* carried straight-faced accounts of Mary Lincoln's engagement to "the short-of-funds count now in ecstasies at securing a heiress—the Court tailor, Count Katzenbratzen, is cutting down Abe Lincoln's clothes to fit the tiny bridegroom. Poor little S," concluded the *World* malevolently, "we don't begrudge him a stitch of the sacred wardrobe. He will have earned it before he is done with Mary Lincoln."[16]

Of course, she saw the story. Mary Lincoln could never shut eye or ear to her own publicity, so when Tad brought the London papers report of her impending marriage to the count, she was furious at this "malign invention." In the United States the joke was timed to embarrass a pension bill drawn in her favor. But in Europe the English community relished the account, and she was briefly mortified. When she counted her New Year's Day callers as ten—"The U.S. consul and his son, two Doctors, three of the womankind, and three other miscellaneous individuals"—she added that "the Count, be assured, did not present himself."[17]

Gentleman and lady callers did not fill the empty days, so Mary Lincoln had time for the therapeutic indulgence of shopping along the Zeil, Frankfurt's broad avenue that, according to the American consul, offered "as many attractions as any street of the same length in any other city of Europe." Buyers from all over the Continent crowded the city's book and jewelry fairs as well as its special exhibitions of birds and animals. In every season the moneymen of Europe and America visited the city. Here, wrote the American consul glowingly, "all the great national loans are negotiated; here in Frankfurt all the coupons of these loans are paid by European governments." For the ladies there were different pleasures, including good buys in gloves, porcelain ware, Bohemian glass, lace, and linens.[18]

On many expeditions Mary Lincoln simply reconnoitered without the least intention of buying. She called this "looking with my eye but not my mind," though in American cities the new female recreation was already celebrated as window-shopping. As yet Frankfurt lacked the centralized sanctuaries of consumption called department stores, in which an abundance of commodities was offered for sale in a setting of sensuous pleasure, full of color, glass, and light. In Frankfurt the fashionable ladies still promenaded along the Zeil, taking their time to look in the tiny store windows. Such surroundings convinced Mary Lincoln that "the shops are beautiful and full of bargains."[19]

Mostly Mary Lincoln shopped for the Robert Lincolns, and at this point her relationship with "my first love of daughter in laws" was more that of a worldly mother counseling a naïve daughter than that of a bossy mother-in-law trespassing onto a young wife's preserve. Before the end of the year the first of many gift boxes full of pillowcases, evening dresses, needle-worked vests (such "a bargain" in Frankfurt), and even a bonnet made by a Parisian milliner was on its way to Chicago. No longer able to adorn herself, Mary Lincoln substituted her daughter-in-law and sent the Continent's high styles along with a stream of advice. Plaids, she informed her son's wife, were extremely fashionable; the "falling-leaf color" was the rage of the Continent; needle-worked vests were smart this season. After purchasing a wrapper for Mary Harlan Lincoln, the senior Mrs. Lincoln described it with the detail only a fashion-conscious woman could muster: "The dress is a silver gray, plush white, trimmed with Marie Louise blue, just as distinguished, and as pretty as can be." She recalled with the accuracy of an accountant the clothes she had left in Chicago and now urged on her daughter-in-law "the double India shawl with a red center" that had not sold in New York.[20]

With the news that her daughter-in-law was pregnant Mary Lincoln had another object for her interminable expeditions along the Zeil. She was disappointed that she could not "superintend the accouchement," but "I have great pleasure, and remembering happier days, to inspect the little articles—the dainty dresses, little sashes and shawls not to mention, not to speak of, the precious little shoes for the dear little feet." Soon bunting, a coral set, and "other choice little things" were included in boxes for America.

When the time of the baby's arrival neared in the fall of 1869 and the mother-to-be confessed anxiety, she was exhorted "not to allow yourself such gloomy thoughts regarding your safety. With your good constitution and the doctors," the older woman felt certain all would go well. Once the baby came, there was more advice. First "do not allow the baby to walk too soon or she will become bowlegged." Then to the mother: "Don't mope around the house. Attend operas and concerts." And if Robert would not hire another nurse, Mary Lincoln offered to pay for one. "If I was in Chicago, I would take young Miss Lincoln out for afternoon carriage rides, so her young mother can be as gay as a lark." And then Mary Todd Lincoln offered her life's lesson: Have fun; be happy. "Trouble comes soon enough, my dear child."[21]

That winter, after Robert complained, the elder Mary had to defend her choice of a baby's outfit considered unsuitably grand by the parents. "The baby is not supposed to be able to walk out in the street this winter and certainly a simple embroidered cloak is not too much for people in our station of life. The very middle classes in Europe dress their children quite as much and as I do not consider ourselves in that category I would not care what the mean and envious say."[22]

She also searched, during her first days in Frankfurt, for every lady's necessity, a reputable, talented dressmaker, and she found one to suit what she considered her station in the obliging Popp, whom she described as "the most charming of all dressmakers who sewed for royalty." Unlike the fallen Lizzie Keckley, Popp did not boast of his connections, though as Mary Lincoln informed her friends in America, he made dresses for Queen Victoria's daughter the crown princess of Prussia. That alone was a sufficient recommendation for her, and soon Popp was working on some new mourning dresses.[23]

To satisfy prodigality's constant attendant—her miserliness—Mary Lincoln consoled herself with the notion that she had got a bargain. "The heaviest black crape here is only in our money $1.50 per yard," she informed Eliza Slataper. "Think of it when in war times I once gave, ten dollars per yard, for the heaviest." By no means did new mourning clothes, even by Popp, signal her entrance into society. "I have, of course, accepted no dinner invitations and have kept very quiet," she informed her friends in America.[24]

Still, even in her exile from the gay world, there were entertainments, especially reading and sight-seeing. "I visited a building 1000 years old to see the portraits of about fifty German Emperors, some of them older than the building," she gushed in a long letter to Eliza Slataper. "The chairs on which these men sat, the stone floors on which they trod, everything, of course, possesses a charm for me." So did the Church of St. Paul, where the Frankfurt Assembly of 1848 had held its sessions, and Goethe's house, where the poet had been born in 1749. Mary Lincoln, who never lived in a city without a river, also savored her walks along the Main. And because she took her European education seriously, "as I advance in my travels, the interest will surely increase."[25]

Sometimes Tad joined her on these expeditions, though he was boarding at Dr. Hohagen's Institute on nearby Kettenhofstrasse and had only one free afternoon a week. Charging a tuition of 600 florins ($360) a year, Dr. Hohagen catered to the wealthy sons of the English-speaking community. The colony at the hotel and the Seligmans had recommended the institute, though it offered commercial rather than classical training. Like many another solicitous mother, Mary Lincoln did not approve of its food. "It does not agree with him," she complained, and Tad soon had special permission to join his mother for dinner at the Angleterre whenever she pleased. But more than bad food brought him to the hotel. "My precious child Taddie" survived as her uncompleted domestic mission—the only one remaining to her now that Robert was married. "[Tad's] presence has become so necessary, even to my life," she advised her daughter-in-law in 1869.[26]

As for Tad, he was "greatly improving," according to his mother, though this youngest of the Lincoln boys was one of those unfortunate scholars who earned praise for their progress, never for their accomplishments. In his first months in the institute his mother reported him homesick, and even after he had recovered, Tad may have shared another expatriate's gloom at Teutonic schooling. A decade earlier Henry Adams had suffered the "closed windows and minds" of a Berlin high school, and the Bostonian had despaired, as no doubt Tad did, of Germany's system of "arbitrary training given to the memory."[27]

With Tad in school, Mary Lincoln had time to write the long letters of a widow's solitude. Now a necessary form of companionship, her correspondence replaced the congenial social occasions of married life. Those correspondents who did not understand the critical importance of this epistolary intimacy were rebuked, as if like rude teatime callers, they had committed a breach of Miss Leslie's rules of courtesy. "I have been anxiously hoping to receive an answer to my last for a long time," went one complaint to Eliza Slataper, who was later reprimanded for her "painful silence." Even the loyal Sally Orne was criticized for being an "exceedingly naughty woman to neglect me so long."[28]

Her daughter-in-law was also urged to "more frequently address me. . . . Do write, my dear girl, more frequently," though it was hard work to match letters with a woman who sometimes wrote fifteen pages a week. "I have so little to comfort me." Through her daughter-in-law Mary Lincoln kept alive the image of a domesticity that had survived even the disappearance of family and home. So Mary Harlan Lincoln received advice on how to keep out moths ("wrap everything in the horrid Chicago papers and use camphor. I have such a terror of moths"); on how to curtain her home (not with worsted but with silk brocatelle or imitation brocade), and especially on motherhood.[29]

Mary Lincoln also filled the empty days by reading. She had always been better informed than most women and in Washington had chosen her female friends from those, like Elizabeth Blair Lee and Mary Jane Welles, who kept up with political and literary affairs. Even as a young student at Madame Mentelle's Mary Todd had defied the gentlemen's ban on the weaker sex's reading fiction, which supposedly distracted the female mind from its domestic tasks and encouraged its tendencies toward emotionality.

After Willie's death Mary Lincoln had replaced best-sellers and classics with the chilling melodramatic fiction of spiritualism. Full of eerie effects and victims to be rescued, otherworldly novels dwelt on tragic bereavements, spectral appearances, prophetic dreams, and, necessarily for the resolution of their improbable plots, magical coincidences. A master of this supernatural fiction, England's Edward Bulwer-Lytton placed his characters in melancholy settings that accorded with Mary Lincoln's sense of tragedy: ". . . it was a dark and stormy night; the rain fell in torrents—except at occasional intervals when it was checked by a violent gust of wind which swept the streets" goes the opening of *Paul Clifford*.[30] Among the characters in another of Bulwer-Lytton novels was an attractive heroine who communicated with the dead. In this novel and those of two other favorite authors, Charles Reade and Wilkie Collins, victims were rescued through interventions by spirits or humans, the line between the two often blurring in romantic exaggeration. Then in 1868, just after her arrival in Frankfurt, Mary Lincoln discovered the spirit literature of an American woman, Elizabeth Stuart Phelps.

She was not alone. By 1869 Phelps's *The Gates Ajar* had become a best-seller in Europe and the United States, despite the book's many deficiencies. Its appeal lay in its reassuring tale of a grief-stricken victim's journey from morbid bereavement to satisfied mysticism. Phelps's fiction was Mary Lincoln's fact, from the central character's oppressive sense of abandonment after a family death ("The house feels like a prison. There has been hell in my heart. I wish I could go away and creep into the ground and die") to her agonized rejection of resurrection and of the orthodox ministry. According to Phelps, the Christian heaven is a dull circle of disembodied souls cut off from the living. But after coaching by a clairvoyant, the bereft mourner finds the key that successful mediums always extend to their clients. With it she unlocks the "gates of heaven," communicating at will with her departed through trances.[31]

Like Phelps's heroine, Mary Lincoln had been trying to end the division between the dead and living so that her husband and sons could be constant presences, "with us always, whilst life lasts and afterwards"—not just on recall through intermediaries. In *The Gates Ajar* death promised a family reunion, to be anticipated while still undergoing what Mary Lincoln called "my terrible probation on earth." The heroine concludes: "How pleasant it will be to go to heaven and see faces never seen in this world such as President Lincoln or Mrs.

Browning." No wonder Mary Lincoln enthusiastically recommended the book to Eliza Slataper, noting that it reminded her of her psychic friend in Pittsburgh.[32]

In Germany Mary Lincoln also attended to her health, especially the arthritis that was, as she wrote Sally Orne, "turning me into an old veteran of 70—with limbs painful and unbending and a burning pain in my spine." During her first winter in Frankfurt the warm weather lingered through the Christmas season, but in January it turned cold and damp—a sure sign that the neuralgia the medical fraternity associated with climate and nervousness would worsen. Then Mary Lincoln learned the painful lesson taught so many American expatriates. No matter what the refinements of life abroad, European heating systems were no match for those at home.[33]

Still, it was early February 1869 before she took the invalid's route, traveling south. She stopped first in Baden-Baden for the sulfurous baths that were becoming a fixture in her search for better health. In late February, after a long train ride, she was in Nice, "growing stronger and stronger day by day, for I had been sick in Frankfurt." Some health pilgrims pressed on to another shrine—Naples, where the renowned Dr. Rubini treated neurasthenics with his popular water cure. Only a depleted pocketbook kept Mary Lincoln in Nice, where she complained about overdressed Americans who "wore velvet costumes at ten or eleven in the morning." Still, she appreciated the weather. "Was there ever such a climate, such a sunshine, such air— flowers growing in the gardens, oranges on the trees, my windows open all day, looking out upon the calm, blue Mediterranean."[34]

Habitually enthralled by royalty, she discovered some in Nice. One day, while she was shopping for Turkish linens for Robert and Mary Lincoln, she came "face to face" with the Prussian princess, who was selecting "some gorgeous table covers. . . . Our eyes met," Mary wrote Eliza Slataper, who understood such extrasensory encounters, "we looked earnestly at each other. Yet until I left the store, I did not know *who* she was." And then because Mary Lincoln despised anonymity before the mighty, with whom she intended equality, she lamented that the princess "will always remain in ignorance, regarding *me.* Such is life."[35]

Back in Frankfurt by early spring, Mary Lincoln was soon planning another trip—this time to Scotland as the guest of the Reverend James Smith. Like few others, the former pastor of her Springfield church had remained loyal, publicly defending her during the Ann Rutledge controversy. Most of Mary's acquaintances either loved or hated her (she permitted no middle ground), and Smith was among the former, even to the point of remembering her birthday. Now came an invitation from the heavyset Scotsman with the thundering preacher's voice. He was no doubt repaying both Lincolns for the appointment of his son Hugh Smith as the American consul at Dundee. When the son resigned, Lincoln had appointed the elder Smith, despite Secretary of State Seward's objections, partly because Mary Lincoln remembered her pastor's kindness after Eddie's death. Both Lincolns had also been moved by Smith's pitiful circumstances. "I am," he had written in 1863, "poor in the world's goods and needing just enough for the old lady and myself to support ourselves." So Lincoln had appointed him to the $1,500-a-year consulship at Dundee that he had held ever since.[36]

Now sixty-eight and suffering from heart trouble, Smith believed this summer of 1869 would be his last, and he insisted Mary and Tad Lincoln come as soon as possible. So an odd threesome—the widow in black, the minister in starched collar, and the youth—explored Scotland with the energetic thoroughness that only a native guide can provide. Mary Lincoln was breathless. "We visited—Abbotsford, Dryburgh Abbey—passed six days in charming Edinburgh—seeing *oh so much:* Glascow, journey on the Clyde, all through the west of dear old Scotia, Burn's [sic] birthplace—went to Greenoch, heaved a sigh over poor Highland Mary's grave—went out into the ocean—entered Fingal's cave—Visited Glencoe—*Castles* unnumerable—Balmoral." The British queen was not in residence, though her spiritualist adviser John Brown probably was. Had Victoria been at Balmoral, "I have every assurance that as sisters in grief a warm welcome would be given me."[37]

Strangely—for in her travels Mary Lincoln preferred cities and health spas to rustic villages and scenery—"dear old Scotia" was a delight; in fact, it "spoilt" her for "seeing any other place in Europe." She was visiting the Todds' ancestral homeland, but her affection arose from more than that. Like many well-read Americans, she was already familiar with the land of Sir Walter Scott and Robert Burns. Macbeth's Highlands she knew from her husband's lugubrious recitations of Shakespeare, so when she visited Glamis Castle and "saw the room and bed on which poor King Duncan was murdered," Mary Lincoln experienced the exhilarating connection of the actual and the imagined that stands at the heart of successful touring.[38]

Scotland may also have aroused in Mary feelings first excited by the wild landscape of her childhood Kentucky. Unlike the sophisticated settings of her water cures, the country was dramatic, mysterious, and, during its chronic bad weather, ghastly in a way that Frankfurt and Nice could never be. She found the spectral summer lights of the north country eerie. She could imagine in Rob Roy's land that famous marauder roving about the glens, much as the family legends had her Todd ancestors protecting Kentuckians from the Indians. She also braved Fingal's Cave, though the boat ride from Oban through the inner Hebrides to the rock of Staffa terrified many. There she heard the Old Hundred sung by 200 voices. Repeatedly Scotland's desolate terrain matched her own wasteland; Mary Lincoln had found a proper setting for herself. In the face of such natural wonders she did what she was supposed to do but rarely achieved: She submitted to the "greatness and power of the Creator."[39]

BY mid-August Tad and his mother were back in Frankfurt. She found now that at $30 a week the Angleterre strained her annual budget of less than $2,500, the interest at 6 percent on her $36,000 in bonds. (She had turned over the rent from the West Washington Street house to Robert.) So she gave up its fancy parlors and camaraderie for the dingy second-rate Hotel Holland and its uncarpeted floors. There was a rumor that Mrs. Lincoln had been evicted from the Angleterre for not paying her bill, but she had enough money to spend the rest of Frankfurt's hot summer in the Taunus Mountains overlooking the city. To Kronberg, the mountainside resort community where wealthy Frankfurt merchants went for the fresh air, Mary Lincoln came that August and again the following year. Lacking money for its fashionable hotel, she boarded and spent her days inspecting the architectural remains of the houses of German grandees. "Three ruined castles are in sight and one, a *very near* neighbor [Kronberg Castle]—all of them dating back to the 12th and 13th centuries—when the robber knights inhabited them."[40]

One night Mary Lincoln received a surprise visitor. Sally Orne, a friend from her White House days, was traveling in moneyed style with two daughters, her brother, a maid, and a valet. It was to this "sweet, affectionate ally in both sorrow and joy" that Mary Lincoln had consigned some clothes immediately after Lincoln's assassination. Orne had both consoled and purchased, earning Mary Lincoln's praise that unlike other acquaintances, "she was unaffected and overflowing with love for her friends as if she were penniless." Even before coming to Europe, Orne had encouraged her husband and brother, the latter a congressman from Philadelphia, to work for Mary Lincoln's pension.[41]

Now in Frankfurt, Mary Lincoln claimed her friend with a smothering embrace that revealed her loneliness. Her otherworldliness in full season, she was pleased that Orne had located her through a premonition. "Mrs. Orne and myself," she wrote an American friend, "have been together for many days and nights." Like noisy schoolgirls, the friends talked so much that *"a gentleman* next door, knocked several times, during the night, saying ladies I should like to sleep some. We amused ourselves very much, over his discomfiture, last night—another sufferer rang the bell for the waiter and *quiet* at 2 ½ o'clock THIS A.M."[42]

Shocked at Mary Lincoln's circumstances, Orne joined the campaign for her pension. Possibly under coaching, for the appeal is framed in Mary Lincoln's style of flattery, Orne implored Charles Sumner to use your "great and powerful influence" for the pension bill that, since 1868, had languished in the Senate Committee on Pensions. Not only, wrote Orne to Sumner, had she found "the wife, the petted, indulged wife of a noble-hearted, just, good, murdered President," on the fourth floor of a second-rate hotel, but the "cheerless desolate" room had "but one window, two chairs, a wooden table with a solitary candle." The meager external surroundings, according to Orne, reinforced Mary Lincoln's sense of abandonment. "I never knew what the word alone meant—Mary Lincoln was completely overwhelmed with grief, her sobs and tears wrung my heart and I thought if her tormenters and slanderers could see her they might surely be satisfied."[43]

Like everyone else, Orne had heard Robert Lincoln's gossip about his mother's losing her mind. On the basis of close observation, she rejected it, separating "a wounded heart" from a diseased mind. She wrote Sumner: "As it has been suggested by some that Mrs. Lincoln is partially deranged, having seen her so recently it may be proper for me to say to you that I have watched her closely by day and night for weeks and fail to discover any evidence of aberration of mind in her, and I believe her mind to be as clear now as it was in the days of her greatest prosperity and I do believe it is unusually prolonged grief that has given rise to such a report." While she was writing this, the newly formed Association of Superintendents of Mental Asylums was gathering statistics on the growing number of women whose supposed insanity had been caused by excessive grief.[44]

Knowing her friend, Sally Orne understood that the best treatment for Mary Lincoln's grief—better, in fact, than any spa—was the passage of a government pension bill that would give her a yearly stipend like that given other widows of Union veterans. Once it was approved and signed by President Grant, Mary Lincoln could keep house again— "if that house in Chicago could only be fitted up for her and Thomas {Tad] and income sufficient to keep it—to be given on Lincoln's birthday," Orne added.[45]

Enveloped by Sally Orne's enthusiasm, Mary Lincoln now recovered a natural vitality sometimes mislaid during her bouts of ill health, nerves, and depression—"when my heart fills with dreariness." Contests always revived her, and now, with Orne as her lieutenant (she was soon complimenting Orne's "executive ability"), an invigorated Mary Lincoln meant to fight. Recognizing how differently she behaved from the worldly English ladies of Victorian fiction who only commented on public affairs or at most manipulated from their parlors, Mary Lincoln confessed to Orne that they both were "a little inclined to be politicians." To further the cause, she temporarily suspended her spiritualism, reassuring Orne, who disapproved of séances, that "I am not either a spiritualist, but sincerely believe—our loved ones, who have only *gone before* are permitted to watch over those who were dearer to them than life."[46]

Like any successful politician, Mary Lincoln tried to make hers a compelling cause. In letters sent to Vice President Schuyler Colfax and the United States Senate, she argued that Lincoln's assassination— "that sad calamity"—had "greatly impaired my health." Here a tactful statesman might have stopped, but she continued: "On the advice of a physician I have come over to Germany to try the mineral waters and during the winters to go to Italy. But my financial means do not permit me to take advantage of the advice given me, nor can I live in a style becoming to the widow of the chief magistrate of a great nation, although I live as economically as I can."[47]

This debatable assessment, along with the implicit censure of Congress and the frank admission of her European travels, hardly impressed men who believed Mary Lincoln an extravagant nuisance. Nor did the rumors that the style to which she was accustomed required $5,000 annually, the exact salary of hardworking congressmen and an amount several thousand dollars above the income of most American households with four or five members.

Soon the American press was again ridiculing Mrs. Widow Lincoln, with the Atlantic Ocean no protection from the humiliation that in fact, she pursued. "Though my face begins in advance to burn but may perhaps grow ghastly pale," she was drawn to the English-language reading rooms of Frankfurt and Nice, there anxiously to scan the American newspapers. In case she missed anything about herself, Mary Lincoln implored the faithful Orne to send "any little notices pleasant or otherwise." Most were unpleasant, and soon Mary Lincoln was complaining that "the American newspapers are tomahawking me now to slay me afterwards." So preoccupied with the pension battle did she become that images of money colored her language. Throughout, as she informed Orne, she remained "Micawber-like,'" though the reference to Dickens's amiable indigent inaccurately described her frenzied activity.[48]

Remembering campaigns when her husband had sought public office, Mary Lincoln kept careful count of her supporters. Among them she numbered Orne's brother Charles O'Neill as well as the other members of the House from Pennsylvania, who must "agitate and make it [the bill] effectual before Congress gets immersed in other business." She was certain of the support of Senators Reuben Fenton, Carl Schurz, Zachariah Chandler, Ira Harris, and perhaps William Sprague. The last was now feuding with his wife, Mary Lincoln's former rival, Kate Chase Sprague, and might, on the principle that the enemy of an enemy is a friend, support a cause his wife no doubt opposed. Others, like Michigan's Chandler, were uncommitted. Politics was a matter of timing; Mary Lincoln knew that. It also required persistence and confidence, and she had those. *"I will be remembered,"* she informed David Davis, who was repelled by her audacity. In any case, those who helped would be "installed in the memory of all good people" and would be performing, like Sally Orne, "the work of love to be recorded on High."[49]

Mary Lincoln especially counted on Charles Sumner and rallied her friends to write him, instructing them in what to say and how to say it. Reverend Smith, her host in Scotland, was to "render my language more elegant especially as I am a woman placed on so high an eminence that the free American low-minded press would like to get hold of." Obediah Wheelock, a spiritualist acquaintance from Boston, needed twenty-nine pages for his arguments. Not only had Lincoln, and through him the entire Union, benefited from her private advice to the President, but if Lincoln were "telegraphed" (something which was possible in Wheelock's world), the dead President would be "embarrassed" by his wife's "impoverished circumstances." To give the wife a pension was to honor a dead President and his living counselor. Another petition came from her traveling companion on the *City of Baltimore*. No doubt under her orders, F. W. Bogen reported to Sumner that Mrs. Lincoln led "a dignified and quiet life" in Frankfurt, though "the severe pain in her spine had led her doctors to insist that she travel to both the German and Italian spas." But, concluded Bogen grimly, "her financial condition precluded it."[50]

Throughout the pension battle Mary Lincoln recognized Sumner as a principal ally, though as she warned Sally Orne, "I know him to be all that is excellent, yet by this time my claims may have passed out of his mind and his thoughts may be absorbed in Cuba and something else." She was right; Sumner was preoccupied with foreign affairs as well as such pressing domestic matters as the readmission of Virginia to the Union. He also believed Mrs. Lincoln had, as he put it, "many failings." Still, he had undertaken her cause for charity and to honor her husband, not for friendship's sake. Dutifully that spring of 1870 he found time for her pension bill. Almost alone, the Massachusetts senator badgered his fellow Republican George Edmunds, the ranking member of the Pensions Committee. "Why is Mrs. Lincoln's pension bill slumbering in the committee when it had been introduced so early in the session and when other private bills had passed?"[51]

In the previous session Senator Edmunds had stalled. Few members enthusiastically supported Mary Lincoln's precedent-shattering claims. On the other hand, no one wanted to insult the memory of a fallen hero. The best solution was to do nothing and hope that Mrs. Lincoln would go away. Usually some legislative matter could be found to take priority over the widow's affairs, and Edmunds had delayed by using them. But in the face of Sumner's insistence on a $5,000 annual pension for a fifty-two-year-old woman who might live thirty more years, Edmunds needed another excuse. The committee, he now explained, was writing a special report that would be ready any day. Then in May without debate, the House of Representatives approved, by a partisan vote, a $3,000 annual pension for Mary Lincoln.[52]

In Frankfurt an exultant Mary Lincoln responded to Congressman O'Neill's news "with most profound gratitude." Characteristically she magnified her consequence by informing her benefactor that "after your powerful efforts in my behalf it must be a great relief to your mind to have had such a success." Now within a single roll call of victory, Mary Lincoln looked to the "noble-minded and patriotic men of the Senate."[53]

The day after the House vote, Senator Lyman Trumbull, whom Mary had never forgiven when he, not Abraham Lincoln, had become the United States senator from Illinois, rose to ask his fellow senators' silent and unanimous acquiescence in Mrs. Lincoln's pension. But by 1870 everything about Mary Lincoln was debatable. After the old clothes sale she had become one of the most unpopular women in America. Only the advocates of free love, actresses, and Madame Restell, the Manhattan abortionist who dispensed French pills from her brownstone, were so notorious.[54]

In June the Senate, again under Sumner's prodding, finally debated her pension bill. In the meantime, Edmund's committee had released an unfavorable report. In faraway Frankfurt, Mary Lincoln read the bad news in the English reading room, nearly fainted, and under doctor's orders was soon on her way to Marienbad's soothing baths. While she was there, a Catholic priest dunned her for money for his church, though she was no easy mark. His contemptuous response to her contribution of three florins led her to believe that like everyone in the world, the Catholic clergy knew about the battle over her pension.[55]

Meanwhile, in Washington her supporters said little; her detractors, much. Some senators objected to the pension bill by citing the worthy others who had not, like Mary Lincoln, inherited $58,000. According to the Edmunds report, 200,000 Americans now received pensions that cost a reluctant government $27 million a year, or nearly 10 percent of the nation's annual budget. More than half were widows of soldiers who had died in battle or from service-connected wounds. With no other source of income they were dependent on the government's niggardly $12.65 a month. Survivors of officers fared a little better. Their widows, including Mary Lincoln's friend Mrs. General Edward Baker, received $600 a year.

But foolish, extravagant Mary Lincoln, who was already a rich woman, wanted ten times that amount.[56] Senator Edmunds wondered about "the poor needy widows who do not have fifty or sixty thousand dollars." They had only the government "to put a little bread in their mouths . . . and after their cases have been decided, then when we come to Mrs. Lincoln's bill, we can attend to her case." Accordingly Edmunds wanted this vote delayed until the next session—or even the one after that.[57]

Waving the bloody shirt of post-Civil War politics, Nebraska's Senator Thomas Tipton reminded the Senate that there were veterans such as Jerry Gordon—"a man of color who lost both his feet at Bull Run—who comes here day after day on his stumps imploring a pension which has already passed the House of Representatives." Flinty Justin Morrill of Vermont objected on the ground that Abraham Lincoln had died in Ford's Theatre, not on the battlefield at Antietam. More to the point, a pension for his widow would initiate the kind of civil list perhaps appropriate in European countries where undeserving royal favorites often lived off the state, but not in republican America, where only soldiers' families should receive doles. For Mary Lincoln, the congressional donation of Lincoln's 1865 salary should be sufficient. Indeed, with talk of an increase in the presidential salary to $100,000 a year (four times that of Lincoln's), such an arrangement would be sufficient in the future. (Later, when Congress increased the presidential salary to $50,000, Mary Lincoln complained that her husband "did the great work of the war, but Grant had all the pecuniary compensation.")[58]

In July, with the end of the session approaching, Mary Lincoln's opponents shifted their attacks to her. In polite preface to their vilification, they found it necessary to establish their credentials as gentlemen, as Edmunds put it, with "feelings in support of women" and "impulses of gallantry." It was, they insisted, only her outrageous behavior—her ill-gotten wealth, her indiscretion, her disloyalty during the war, and her marital infidelity—that required them, for duty's sake, to criticize a woman in public. Cloaked in the guise of chivalry, several senators launched one of the harshest assaults ever made against anyone—male or female—in a nineteenth-century Congress. The stakes were high, for if passed, Mary Lincoln's pension would be the largest individual annuity ever granted to an American citizen.[59]

At the heart of the senators' complaints rested traditional notions of how women should behave. First, according to Senator Morrill, they stayed home. "Why should she be an absentee from America? Did not Mrs. Madison win fame by staying here at home?" Certainly they did not take the sons of American Presidents abroad. "In my judgment," continued Morrill, "her brilliant boy had much better be educated here at home under American institutions than to be educated abroad, where he will not grow up in the principles of his father." Nor should American widows wander about Europe's watering places. If the Senate wanted to exercise "liberality, magnanimity and charity," concluded one aggrieved senator, "select a Martha Washington, select a proper object"—not unrepublican, un-American, unfeminine Mary Lincoln.[60]

Above all, good women were faithful to their husbands, and according to Senator Richard Yates's hints, Mary Lincoln had not been: "There are recollections and memories sad and silent and deep that I will not recall publicly which induce me to vote against this [pension] bill. Amid all the perils of life and its devastation, amid good and evil report, a woman should be true to her husband. Mr. President, the occasion does not require, and I shall not, so far as I am concerned, go into details. Mr. Lincoln's memory is sweet to me. God almighty bless the name and fame of Abraham Lincoln."[61]

Why, then, if his tongue was sealed, had the senator introduced this treacherous innuendo, and what did he mean by it? Yates, who lived in Springfield and who knew the Confederate Todds, had been in Washington when Emilie Helm was hidden away in the White House. Did Yates have evidence that Mary Lincoln had opposed her husband's Unionist principles? Or was he speaking of some other kind of disloyalty? For most nineteenth-century Americans being true to a husband involved the bedroom, not the political stump. Was Yates referring to the White House gardener's suspicions that Mary Lincoln had done more than flirt with William Wood, her first commissioner of public buildings? Or—for Yates was a notable inebriate—was the senator in the same kind of drunken stupor that had turned his inauguration as Illinois governor in 1862 into such a farce?[62]

In any case the Senate floor was no place for gossip, and a sanctimonious Democrat was soon on his feet protesting the body's lack of decorum. Tut-tutted Delaware's Willard Saulsbury: "Don't invade the sanctuary of home and the character of a widow clothed in weeds. Throw that out. Let it be gone. It is unbecoming the American Senate." Certainly the argument was ineffective, for in the end Yates changed few votes.[63]

On the day before adjournment the Senate finally passed Mary Lincoln's pension bill, nearly three years after it had first been introduced. The next day, July 15, 1870, President Grant signed the bill allowing her an annual pension of $3,000, thereby doubling Mary Lincoln's income and moving her (for her bonds were income-producing capital) from the margins of genteel poverty to middle-class affluence. Of course, she had hoped for $6,000, though she acknowledged, in a letter to Sally Orne, that "the sum that was voted me, will greatly assist me and not a murmuring word, shall be heard from me as to the amount. I feel assured that if a larger sum had been insisted upon, it would have fallen through, all together." What Mary Lincoln did not mention was the partisan nature of her victory. Twenty-eight senators, Republicans all, had voted for her pension bill, with eight Democrats and twelve Republicans (including her old friend Roscoe Conkling) opposed. Nearly a third of the body had abstained. Most saw the pension as a grudgingly bestowed partisan memorial to her dead husband, though its living recipient was now more unpopular than ever. After Yates's outburst Mary Lincoln could be suspected of anything.[64]

IN the summer of 1870 the Prussians and the French went to war and disrupted Mary Lincoln's exile. At the time she and Tad were in Austria, celebrating a school holiday along with her new prosperity. Returning to Frankfurt amid rumors of a French invasion, she discovered that the French army, with Napoleon III as its field commander, was advancing on Saarbrücken, the city less than seventy miles from Frankfurt. (Eugénie, who had reportedly cried *'C'est ma guerre, c'est ma petite guerre,"* now replaced her husband on the powerful Council of Regency in Paris.) Urgently the consul warned Americans to evacuate. Everyone in the city expected a great battle—what the French newspapers were calling *le grand choc,*—if not for, at least near, Frankfurt. Certainly it did not take a great strategist to recognize that in a war the French were expected to win, Frankfurt was the key to the railroad lines into Prussia.[65]

Unlike many expatriates, Mary Lincoln held her ground—at least for a time. War had not frightened her from Washington in 1861, and the Prussian mobilization did not do so now. In fact, she was more concerned about her trunks than her safety and wrote Sally Orne that she must "secure her baggage." Soon, however, Frankfurt was no place for an American widow and her teenage son. The graceful commercial city had become a military staging ground, short of food and services, but full of soldiers in need of quarters and overseas observers come to assess the Prussian army. Among the observers was brash young Phil Sheridan, the hero of the Shenandoah Valley campaign and one of Lincoln's most successful generals. Both France and Prussia had invited Sheridan to watch their armies, but with the proper military instincts Sheridan chose the victors.[66]

Sometime in August the general called on Mary Lincoln, who was still in Frankfurt, and then in September he accompanied General Helmuth von Moltke's army to the Meuse River valley. There he watched the Prussian and Saxon artillery decimate the French infantry in a battle that ended any threat to Frankfurt. Shortly thereafter Sheridan offered his advice to the German high command. "The proper strategy," he declared after the Battle of Sedan, "consists in inflicting as telling blows as possible on the enemy's army and then in causing the inhabitants so much suffering that they must long for peace." The general had learned that lesson in the American Civil War, but the Prussians were not fighting a war of attrition. Within a few weeks of the Battle of Sedan, they were besieging Paris, Napoleon's Second Empire was dissolving, and Eugénie, the high-fashion queen of ruche, tight-lacing, and décolletage, was hurrying out the side door of the Tuileries to make her escape to England.[67]

At the same time that Eugénie began her permanent exile, Mary Lincoln decided to go home. She had come to Europe to avoid her bad press, though once there, she suffered it almost as much as she had at home. With her pension now secure there would no longer be any need for the public denunciations of what she still called "my poor self."[68] But the price of public abuse had not been too high, considering her $3,000 per annum success.

THERE were other reasons to go home. After her two years in Germany, a people she had at first admired for their sophisticated reserve were now adjudged guilty of neglecting her. They were "cold and unsympathizing strangers who never dreamed of my anguish." Then there was the matter of her health. Invariably her German doctors advised a drier, warmer climate, and hot weather and sulfurous mineral baths were available in the United States. By the 1870s even Springfield offered electric baths at A. H. Lamphears. And the sight-seeing that had earlier thrilled her had paled as a diversion. Meanwhile, Tad had become impatient—"wild, to come home"—she wrote the other Mary Lincoln. As a final incentive there was the new Lincoln whom neither expatriate had seen—the granddaughter Mary, Robert's firstborn, named in honor of mother and perhaps grandmother, too. Still, she lingered, moving first to England.[69]

When the Lincolns arrived in England in the fall of 1870, they settled in Leamington, a town 100 miles northwest of London. It was an obvious choice, for not only did Leamington boast famous mediums, but since Roman times invalids had flocked to its baths. After Princess Victoria's visit to the town in 1830 the honorific appellation *royal* had been added to its advertisements, and thousands of health pilgrims proclaimed the virtues of its dry air and warm salty springs. During his years as an American consul in the 1850s Nathaniel Hawthorne found the town "a little quiet pool, and few or none of the inhabitants seem to be troubled with any business or outside activities," though by noon the baths were crowded with "the great people alighting from their carriages—the elderly ladies and infirm Indian officers, drawn along in bath-chairs, the comely rather than pretty English girls, the mustachioed gentlemen with frogged surtouts and a military air."[70]

Like most spas, Leamington offered, along with its gardens and promenades, special treatments for the sufferers. Some took the shower douches, or sprays; others used the vapor and steam baths that were labeled "Turkish" to distinguish them from the Russian baths. Everyone sat, sweated, plunged, and dunked. The Germans had developed the elaborate vocabulary of this new science of balneology, distinguishing among treatments such as Touchbad, Wannenbad, Hopfbad, Sitzbad, Douchebad, and Schwitzen. All were available in Leamington, where a huge pump forced water from the nearby springs into an elaborate bathhouse of classical design. And in order to restore the equilibrium of the body and mind essential to their health, everyone drank large amounts of Leamington's chalybeate mineral water at intervals prescribed by symptom. Sufferers from headaches, like Mary Lincoln, were encouraged to interrupt a night's sleep for a nocturnal draft of the tonic water that tasted like rotten eggs.

Like Marienbad and Baden-Baden, this English temple of health came with its resident physicians, on whom Mary Lincoln depended for advice about her cough, her headaches, her biliousness, and her "faithful companion—the neuralgia that makes my head and limbs ache." Often in bed, she was pleased when a doctor complimented her bravery and "wondered to find me sitting up." Nor was she fooled by these professionals who promoted bed rest, recognizing their financial investment in her bad health. "As a general rule," she wrote Mary Harlan Lincoln, "I think the doctors would especially like to keep one in bed. The love of money, is the root of all evil."

Despite the expense, the Leamington water cure accomplished some of its promises. It lifted her spirits, no matter how effective it was in combating her diseases, and it cleansed, purified, and redeemed in the way water does. Surrounded by the solicitous keepers of the baths, she was no longer an unloved outcast but an indulged victim attended by several doctors. Mary Lincoln agreed with one of her favorite authors, Edward Bulwer-Lytton, that hydrotherapy was a "wonderful excitement" where "cares and griefs are forgotten and a sense of the present absorbs the past and future."[71]

After nine weeks in Leamington the Lincolns moved to London, where they first stayed at the fashionable Langham Hotel recommended by Sally Orne and then boarded on Woburn Street in the St. Pancras section of the city. There, across from the immense garden in Russell Square, within blocks of the British Museum and several spiritualist circles in Southampton Row, mother and son spent their third Christmas abroad. Nearby lived friends and acquaintances such as Bishop Matthew Simpson, who had delivered Lincoln's eulogy in Springfield; Governor and Mrs. John Evans of Colorado (the latter, to Mary Lincoln's horror, had hired a wet nurse for her month-old baby and gone off to the Continent); and the Paul Shipmans of Kentucky. Once she went to tea and was admired by Benjamin Moran, the chargé d'affaires at the American Embassy, who wrote that he had met Mrs. Lincoln— "dressed in deep black and widow's cap—an unpretending woman of excellent manners, such intelligence and very lady-like appearance." In February 1871 Mary Lincoln joined the winter swallows, this time traveling south to Milan, Lake Como, and Florence, "the beauties of which," she informed her daughter-in-law, "were simply indescribable." Thanks to the United States government, she could now afford a companion who sometimes doubled as a nurse.[72]

During this trip Tad stayed in London with his tutor. Again his mother was optimistic about her son's academic progress, assuring her daughter-in-law that Tad "realizes the great necessity of an education." Now nearly eighteen, Tad had come late to this appreciation. Still, he was "studying hard—so hard that study more than he does now he could not do." As always, there was room for improvement, and his mother indicated as much in her exasperation. "If he only had the information of his tutor, I told him I would be willing to live on a crust of bread a day—almost." No doubt Tad did work hard, perhaps hoping to persuade his mother through his good work that they should go home.[73]

There were tentative plans for him to go alone at Christmas. Passage was booked on a Cunard Line steamer, but at the last moment she could not let him go. "To trust my beautiful, darling *good* boy to the elements, at this season of the year, makes my heart faint within me. Each breath I drew would be a prayer for his safety which only those who have been as deeply bereaved as myself could fully understand."[74] Instead, mother and son left Europe as they had come, together and alone.

She chose the *Russia,* the Cunard liner that now held the transatlantic record of eight days and twenty-five minutes for the Liverpool to New York run. They crossed in May 1871, and as on their trip over, the weather was foul, prolonging the voyage by two days. On board was General Sheridan, who had seen all there was of the Franco-Prussian War, though he would be unable to apply its lessons to his next enemy— the Plains Indians.

When the *Russia* finally passed Sandy Hook and turned into New York Harbor, a cutter drew aside the steamer for the general and his special party, so that they might avoid the three-day quarantine imposed on other passengers. Along with his staff and the earl and countess of Ellesmere, Sheridan included the Lincolns, so Mary Lincoln returned to the United States amid cheering and the music of a military band playing "Hail to the Chief," the song that reminded her of her husband. A *New York Times* reporter who sought her out for an interview when the crowd around General Sheridan proved impenetrable found "Mrs. Lincoln delighted to be home in her native land. Tad speaks English with a foreign accent and Mrs. Lincoln is looking well, but yet seems oppressed by her husband's death. She will proceed to Chicago on Monday."[75]

And so she did, but not before spending a few days in New York with Rhoda White, a companion on many of Mary's shopping expeditions. Both women were now widows with married children, and the possibility of settling in New York—perhaps in a cottage near Central Park—temporarily engaged Mary Lincoln. Homeless, she could live anywhere, a nerve-racking prospect since she still expected some rich benefactor to rescue her with a free house. In the meantime, she detested the idea of selling any of the bonds that, because Lincoln had "placed them," now had sentimental value. Besides, she hated divesting herself of capital that would reduce the income she considered "delicate." To Rhoda White went a self-pitying assessment: *"and so* I must go forth in search of *lodgings*—My face burns at the *mere* thought. . . . As I now stand, I can BOARD! plainly and *economically* with all I have."[76]

In Chicago the reunion with Robert, Mary, and little Mary was warm and affectionate, and for a few days Mary Lincoln's earthbound family lived under the same roof in Robert's small three-bedroom home on Wabash Avenue. It was not, however, Mary Lincoln's roof, and in time disagreements between mother-in-law and daughter-in-law erupted. Later one of the younger Mary Lincoln's friends acknowledged this break between the mother-in-law and daughter-in-law and took the younger woman's side: "There could be no sweeter daughter-in-law and true friend to her than you dear, if she [Mary Lincoln] would only do half way right." By the end of May 1871 Mary and Tad Lincoln had moved to the Clifton House, and Tad was sick with what his mother was describing as a severe cold.[77]

Tad had probably caught his cold aboard the *Russia*. The weather had been fickle, with chilly winds off England and a severe storm in the mid-Atlantic. Knowing little about germs, his doctors believed the exposure to wet weather was the primary cause of his coughing. No doubt Mary Lincoln wished she had returned later in the season. By the first week of June, in his mother's words, Tad had become "very dangerously ill. May we ever be sufficiently grateful should his precious life be spared." Three Chicago specialists were in attendance, gathered in room 21 of the Clifton House, listening with their stethoscopes to Tad's heart and lungs, tapping his pleural spaces to see if there was liquid, encouraging his mother to use hot poultices on his chest, and, to relieve the painful stitch that occurred when the boy breathed, prescribing opium compounds such as Godfrey's cordial or Dover's powders.[78]

Still, according to his mother, "his lungs are not at all diseased, although water has been formed on part of his left lung." Remembering Eddie, she was relieved to learn that Tad did not have tuberculosis. According to Dr. Nathan Davis, the dean of the Chicago medical fraternity and a lung specialist, the water was gradually decreasing. Later events proved him incorrect. In fact, Tad was suffering from an intractable pleurisy, caused by either pneumonia or a primary infection from tuberculosis bacilli in the lining of his lungs. Gradually the pleural spaces in his chest were filling with serum and pus from an unchecked bacterial infection. In June the doctors still believed that his condition was reversible and that the fluid was being absorbed in a process that should be the final curative phase of pleurisy.[79]

But Tad did not get well. Periodically his fever diminished, his appetite improved, and his mother rejoiced. By late June, however, he was under pleurisy's final sentence and, with his lungs filling with water, was condemned to sleep upright. Devastated by her son's torture, Mary Lincoln bought a new chair with a bar across the front to prevent him, when he nodded off, from falling on the floor.[80]

Sometime in early July the infection, now in the bloodstream, reached the sac surrounding the heart, and the city's best-known pediatrician, Dr. C. G. Smith, was making daily calls—$275 worth in all. By this time Tad was so weak and debilitated that everyone, save perhaps his mother, knew he would die. David Davis visited in early July and advised a friend that "Thomas Lincoln is dangerously ill. If he recovers, it will be a miracle. The disease is dropsy on the chest. He has been compelled to sit upright in a chair for upwards of a month. His mother is in great affliction."[81]

Inexplicably, on July 13, he improved, and his mother hoped for the best. But three days later, with the water on his chest accumulating around his heart, Tad turned blue. His legs became edemous; he took his breath in gasps. At seven-thirty on the morning of July 15, 1871, eighteen-year-old Tad Lincoln slumped forward against the railing of his chair, dead of what the papers called "compression of the heart."[82]

This time Mary Lincoln had not been denied a deathbed vigil as she had with her husband and two other sons. But nursing Tad in an impersonal hotel room, mostly by herself, had proved the most arduous of her watches. The miserable way her son died made it difficult to think of his death as a triumphal entry into heaven, where he would join the other Lincolns. It was easier—in fact, by this time necessary—for Mary Lincoln to forget Tad and to see herself as punished and abandoned once again, a marked character. "Ill luck," she wrote, "presided at my birth and has been a faithful attendant ever since."[83]

She managed, in violation of her customary practice, to attend a brief service for Tad at Robert's house, sitting stunned and exhausted on a sofa during the remarks of a Baptist minister summoned for the occasion. But Mary Lincoln did not travel to Springfield for her youngest son's interment with what was now more than half her family circle. Instead, afflicted with a relentless grief and its physical sign, heart palpitations, she took to her bed. Whatever comfort Robert provided was brief. Ten days after Tad's death he left (on doctor's orders, according to his mortified mother) for the Rocky Mountains, a favorite resting place for nervous gentlemen. He promised a short trip but in fact was gone for more than a month. Years later Robert described himself as "all used up" after Tad's death.[84]

Entirely forsaken—for she refused to go, as Robert wished, to her sister Elizabeth's—she called on her spiritualist friends. "I pray you," went an appeal to Eliza Slataper, "by all that is merciful to come to this place—I feel I must see you. I promised Robert that I would remain in his house. A gentleman friend occupies his only spare room at night—yet each day I am entirely alone, in my fearful sorrow. Come, come to me."[85] Especially she feared the monthly anniversaries, the dreadful fourteenth of Lincoln's assassination, now followed by the terrible fifteenth of Tad's death. So she insisted that Slataper be with her, at least in mid-August.

Sometimes, during the acute phase of her mourning, a depressed Mary Lincoln craved solitude and dispensed with even the spiritualists. Alone, she calculated her lifelong abandonments, figuring Tad's death as the payment for her success in the pension struggle. At these times the attentions of her friends merely reopened what she called "bleeding wounds. . . . I am ordered perfect quiet—as much as can be obtained by a person so broken-hearted as my poor self. I MAY grow calmer, yet I very much doubt it. As grievous as other bereavements have been, not one great sorrow, ever approached the agony of this," she advised Slataper, who had come and gone by October.[86]

Three days after Mary Lincoln wrote these words, the great Chicago fire began. She may not have noticed the weather, but the hot dry summer of 1871 had continued into the fall. There had been earlier fires that season, though this was not unusual for incendiary Chicago. But this one, as she and all Chicago soon learned, was different.

In folklore it began on the South Side in Mrs. O'Leary's barn, where a cow kicked over a lantern. That first night, with the wind as its bridge, the fire leaped the Chicago River and burned uptown, systematically destroying hotels, homes, and stores, in all, a city. Sometime in the early morning the guests of the Clifton House on Wabash Avenue emptied into the streets in a scene of terror many remembered as an earthly version of hell. Soon the 600 block of Wabash Avenue was in danger, and Mary Lincoln evacuated Robert's house, where she was temporarily living; in the confusion she may have left behind a bundle of her husband's personal letters. Like most Chicagoans, she probably spent the night—and perhaps part of the next day—along Lake Michigan, watching what seemed to many the end of the world. For nearly a week the great Chicago fire burned, destroying 2,100 acres and killing more than 200 people.[87]

NOW began Mary Lincoln's fugitive years: the restless encounters with spiritualists, the endless visits to health spas, and the occasional panics when an anniversary brought to mind her losses. Mostly she stayed in the rebuilt Chicago hotels, for it was impossible to remain at Robert Lincoln's after his wife had returned from nursing a sick mother in Iowa. A final curtain of animosity had dropped between the two Mary Lincolns. The younger held the traditional grievance that her mother-in-law interfered with her household, sometimes even dismissing her servants, while Mary Lincoln, Sr. had a reason to intrude: She may have discovered the dark secret of her daughter-in-law's alcoholism. Now lacking any family, Mary Lincoln gave up her domestic dreams and in 1874 sold her son the unaffordable West Washington Street house that she had rented for five years.[88]

For a short time after the fire she lived in St. Charles, a center for spiritualists outside Chicago along the Fox River, where a Universalist congregation had transformed itself into a spiritualist sect. There the clairvoyants gathered to induce trances and serve as spirit guides. Mediums also used the Howard House, the town's hotel, for their meetings, and it was said that the darkened parlor rooms resonated with tappings and spectral appearances. Because Mary Lincoln liked to test mediums by appearing as an anonymous widow, she registered under a fictitious name.[89]

By winter 1872 she was back in Chicago, offering to divide Tad's estate of $35,750 with Robert. She was entitled to two-thirds, and her son praised as generous her gift of $6,000. Fortified by her own increased principal (she was now worth more than $75,000), she did what she had steadfastly refused to do in the past and lent Robert $10,000 for one of his real estate speculations in North Chicago.[90]

That summer Mary Lincoln traveled to Waukesha, Wisconsin, a health spa along Lake Michigan that advertised miraculous cures for everything from dyspepsia and consumption to derangement of the liver, gout, jaundice, epilepsy, hysteria, neuralgia, and rheumatism. Robert Lincoln and his family were in Europe for six months. Again utterly alone, she boarded in a private home on the outskirts of town and had to face reporters who discovered they had a celebrity in their midst. "Poor Mrs. Lincoln," wrote the reporter for the *Waukesha Daily*, "she comes daily to the baths with heavy heart and is often in tears." Later the paper disclosed that she had a "dropsical condition" (probably either heart trouble or phlebitis) and would not see visitors, though old friends like New York's Governor Reuben Fenton "penetrated," as she put it, "her solitude."[91]

During the summer Mary Lincoln showed off a new photograph taken in Boston. Sometime during the previous year she had traveled to Moravia, New York, in the heart of the dark parlor country, where she had seen twenty-two spirit faces, including Tad's. Then she went on to Boston and sought out a well-known medium on Washington Street. At one séance during her two-week stay her dead husband appeared. Though she had called herself Mrs. Tundall to prevent any tricks by the unscrupulous miracle makers who took advantage of the unwary, the President had immediately recognized her and placed his arms on her shoulders. Inspired by this reunion, she sat for William Mumler, the spirit photographer who had just been acquitted of fraud in New York.[92]

At Mumler's Mary Lincoln pretended again she was someone else (as if that were possible), and the result of this sitting was her last picture. (See page 176, photograph 13.) For the only time in her life she may not have objected to the camera's reality, though Mumler's photograph was by no means flattering. In it Mary Lincoln appeared as a pulpy, square-jawed woman, dressed in high mourning with the traditional widow's peak obscuring her hair. Looking more than her fifty-four years, her face sagged as if the weight of her grief had finally sapped her vitality. Her eyes were glassy and clouded, and like a huge catacomb, her black widow's weeds confined her.

What Mary Lincoln liked about this photograph had nothing to do with her. In the background Mumler had superimposed an image of Abraham Lincoln, with his hands on her shoulders and a tender expression directed at her. Such a spirit likeness gave permanent proof that Lincoln was hovering, and it was the spiritualist's ability to reproduce her fantasies that had brought Mary Lincoln to the sleazy studio in the first place. Once there—and in the séances she attended—she responded to something that was lacking in orthodox religion. Unlike the ministers, the spiritualists never encouraged her to submit and behave like a resigned, Job-like victim; instead, they offered a form of power by which she could defy her punishers and undo the terrible things in her life.

Whatever comfort the photograph gave, she now needed. For William Herndon and what Mary Lincoln called the other "barking dogs" were now assailing her husband's legitimacy and his religiosity. The long-awaited biography of Abraham Lincoln—with Ward Lamon's name, Chauncey Black's words, and William Herndon's research—had appeared in 1872. In it the authors revealed (incorrectly) that Nancy Hanks, Lincoln's mother, had not been married to Thomas Lincoln, a charge that sent Robert Lincoln scurrying to Kentucky to find a family Bible. Then, in December 1873, Herndon gave another lecture to his Springfield neighbors. This time he turned Lincoln into a nonbeliever—"an infidel." To document his charge, he used Mary Lincoln's own words during their meeting in 1866.[93]

Mary Lincoln had never tolerated anyone else's criticism of her husband, even when he was alive to hear her own. Since Lincoln's assassination her attachment to spiritualism made his Christianity a personal issue. Believers in the supernatural might rework the orthodox Christian interpretation of resurrection, but this could be done only by those who began with its doctrine. If Lincoln denied himself heaven by being an atheist, then he was not available to hover protectively. To deny Lincoln's Christianity was to threaten Mary Lincoln's supernaturalism.

She wasted no time with her rebuttal. In it Mary Lincoln denied that she had had the conversation with Herndon "as stated by him." Like any good lawyer, Herndon saw his opportunity in this ambiguity, for she had certainly met with him at Springfield's St. Nicholas Hotel in 1866. Soon he was in the field with a broadside which later ran in most newspapers and which he entitled "Mrs. Lincoln's Denial and What She Says."[94]

Herndon's friends and Mary Lincoln's enemies congratulated the author. William Jayne, the brother of Julia Trumbull, believed that Herndon "had been pushed into the argument," though, as all men knew, "it is always unfortunate to get into a controversy with a woman." Still, according to Jayne, Herndon had abided by the canons of masculine chivalry through his omissions. "In this affair with the First Lady of the Land; you do not like a clodhopper call her a d——d old liar and hussy—but like a courtly gentleman and lawyer you say that the good poor woman crushed beneath a mountain of woe . . . is not altogether a competent and trustworthy witness—every one I have heard speak of it pities the woman for again obtruding herself before the public."[95]

Again in the public eye, she was humiliated, for the effect of Herndon's attack was to make her into a liar—and a crazy one at that. In fact, she had denied only Herndon's interpretation of what she had said, not the meeting itself. But after Herndon had finished, no one understood the difference, and she was left with only her angry countercharges that Herndon was a drunk. "The flowing bowl," she wrote her first cousin John Todd Stuart, "must have been entirely exhausted when [Herndon] wrote that intellectual production." But this true bill appeared in a private letter, and no matter how venomous her words against the "wretched drunken madman," her adversary fought on a public stage. Few could forget his stinging assertion that Mary Lincoln was a lying madwoman.[96]

IN the summer of 1873 Mary Lincoln went to a new resort in Canada where she intended to be anonymous. "Quiet is necessary to my life," she advised her friends. It was the first time she had been out of the country since Tad's death, and she chose St. Catharines, a health spa eight miles from Niagara Falls. Twenty-five years earlier she, her husband, and their sons had marveled at the falls, which Lincoln later described as "a world's wonder—with power to excite reflection and emotion." Now she returned, this time to the Canadian side.[97]

St. Catharines, like Leamington, Marienbad, and Baden-Baden, was a self-proclaimed garden city, where the invalids took the baths and promenaded along special walks. In the 1830s the community had become well known among invalids for its salty, magnesium-laden water. Flowing through underground rock beds, these springs surfaced in small brownish pools throughout the area. But before other communities had seen the advantage, the promoters of St. Catharines had exploited their natural resource. As early as 1848 a local doctor had begun bottling and selling the local water, and a few years later the town fathers had drilled wells and bought a pump in order to assure a constant supply of water. By 1853 the final ingredient for a successful health spa was in place when the elegant Stephenson House opened its doors and discreetly advertised the benefits of St. Catharines for neuralgia and falling of the womb. "Finely situated for pleasure or health," wrote a reporter who promised New Yorkers that they could be in St. Catharines after only a day's trip from the city.[98]

Mary Lincoln came in the summer by steamer to Buffalo and by train to the falls. She knew so little about her destination that she inquired about the hotels with characteristic bluntness. Soon she was in the papers: "On her arrival here several weeks ago the widow of President Lincoln inquired [of an omnibus driver] the names of the different hotels. They were given. The prices of board were asked and the driver said he was unable to say. Several other questions were put upon which the driver professed ignorance. Finally the lady asked how long he had lived in St. Catharines. [The answer was] a good many years. 'Did you know much when you came?' 'Not a great deal.' 'Well,' responded Mrs. Lincoln, 'I don't think you have learned much since you came.'"[99]

Eventually she chose the Stephenson House, for fourteen dollars a week, and began taking the baths and drinking the water. The hotel's owner was a wellborn Virginian, Beverley Tucker, and Mary Lincoln's residence in a hotel full of former Confederates led to more rumors of her disloyalty. In fact, she kept to herself. Since Tad's death she spent more time in the shade-drawn, candlelit rooms that were the best settings for communicating with departed relatives.[100]

After enduring Chicago's brutally cold winter of 1874, Mary Lincoln went south in 1875. Florida was the rage, and Chicago's doctors were recommending its mild climate for sickly patients whose diseases defied classification and treatment. Dr. Clark had encouraged several Chicago families to take their invalids there. Among them were the Newberrys, who hoped their neurasthenic daughter Julie would recover her health. David Davis had sent his wife and children to St. Augustine, and along with hundreds of others, Mary Lincoln took the train to Jacksonville by way of Savannah. She was accompanied by her maid, and when the two women arrived, they boarded the steamer for the trip down the St. Johns River, past Magnolia to Green Cove, where the sulfur springs were especially recommended for arthritis sufferers. Most likely she stayed in one of the local boardinghouses surrounded by lush vegetation, a soft climate, and bad memories.[101]

That season Mary Lincoln was confronted by the tenth anniversary of her husband's murder. Under the influence of a sedative she used to induce sleep and the suggestive landscape, she had a premonition. Her vision may have come as a dream (for she often saw Willie and Tad in her sleep), or perhaps it was the result of a self-induced trance similar to the episodes recommended by spiritualists and described in Gothic novels. In any case Mary Lincoln came to believe that Robert was dying. Hurriedly she returned to Jacksonville and sent two telegrams, one to Robert's law partner, Edward Isham, the other to her son. Then she boarded the train for Chicago and another calamity.[102]

XI
Trial and Confinement

AFTER her return from Florida and the discovery that
Robert was neither dead nor sick, only unsympathetic
to her claims on his attention, Mary Lincoln occupied
herself in the stores. During March, April, and now
May 1875 the squat figure in black crepe—made even
bulkier by the addition of a petticoat pocket into which
she had stitched her bonds—had become a recogniz-
able eccentric in downtown Chicago. Some clerks
believed Mary Lincoln peculiar because she talked too
much. In their experience proper ladies engaged in
limited conversation with those who waited on them.
But this woman bargained for lower prices and gave
her life's history to anyone who would listen. Even
more peculiar was her practice of buying multiples of
the same item: a dozen pairs of curtains to decorate a
nonexistent home, ten pairs of gloves to remind her of
presidential inaugurations, and on one occasion five yards
of scarlet ribbon, perhaps to recall her years as a seductive lady of fashion. Once a purchase had been made,
there followed confusing negotiations about credit as
well as instructions about delivery to her hotel room.[1]

Mary Lincoln was living that spring in one of Chicago's postfire miracles—the newly opened and very elegant 500-room Grand Pacific Hotel, which boasted a domed inner court, a conservatory, and several elevators. She had rented a third-floor room without parlor or bath, and she could certainly have afforded more spacious quarters. Even with meals, the luxury of the Grand Pacific came to only $45 a week, a small proportion of her annual income of $8,000. In the past she had spent that and more, but now, permanently incarcerated in widow's weeds, Mary Lincoln no longer bought expensive dresses and jewelry. For a time Robert's wife had served as a surrogate, but the permanent estrangement of mother-in-law and daughter-in-law had ended such benevolences. Then after the consignment of the house on 375 West Washington to her son, Mary Lincoln did not even have a place to indulge. Only Robert and her granddaughter, Mamie, remained as objects for the love that she expressed, as to herself, with presents.[2]

On the morning of May 19 Mary Lincoln had been to Gossage's on State Street and was expecting the delivery of eight pairs of lace curtains. But when she opened the door to a knock, behind the delivery boy were two uniformed men and Leonard Swett, the Chicago lawyer who had nominated Lincoln for President in 1860. Surprised at the intrusion—for proper gentlemen had their cards delivered before calling—Mary Lincoln was nonetheless cordial. She apologized for her disheveled appearance, and then, in the southern accent that still marked her as a Confederate in some ears, she inquired what she could do for this tall, bearded friend who resembled her dead husband.[3]

The answer was terrifying. She must, Swett announced, this very afternoon go to the courthouse, where a jury was waiting to judge her sanity. In the writ of arrest that Swett held in his hand and waved periodically during their hourlong negotiations, Mrs. Abraham Lincoln was charged with lunacy. According to state law, she had to be present at a civil proceeding to hear the charge that she was non compos mentis and defend herself, if that was possible.

Only three states dictated such a public proceeding for involuntary commitments. Most states merely required a certificate from two doctors of recognized responsibility, a formal request from the alleged lunatic's family or guardian, and a court-issued certificate of lunacy. But in Illinois the jury trial represented an improvement over the silent tyranny that had given husbands the right to banish their wives and minor children to institutions without any formal hearing. "Married women and infants," according to an 1851 Illinois law, "who in the judgment of the medical superintendent are evidently insane or distracted may be entered or detained in the hospital at the request of the husband of the woman without the evidence of insanity required in other cases."[4]

The most flagrant use of this statute had occurred in 1860, when Elizabeth Packard's husband, a stern Presbyterian minister of inflexible orthodoxy, demanded that his wife renounce her spiritualism. It was, the Reverend Mr. Packard believed, a heresy that contradicted the penitential submission to God's will. When his wife would neither give up her beliefs nor end the spiritualist meetings in their home, Packard had her kidnapped and imprisoned in the state asylum at Jacksonville, Illinois, where the superintendent needed no persuading that a woman who believed in the spirit world was a lunatic. Dr. Andrew McFarland had already diagnosed and treated many female inmates for the mania of spiritualism.[5]

Illinois law had changed, but it was the humiliation of a forced arrest that Swett wanted to avoid in his confrontation with Mary Lincoln. "Your friends," the Chicago lawyer said smoothly, "with great unanimity have come to the conclusion that the troubles you have been called to pass through have been too much and have produced mental disease." To this Mary Lincoln replied, according to Swett's account, "You mean to say I am crazy—I am much obliged to you but I am abundantly able to take care of myself. Where is my son Robert?"[6]

Such was Robert's duplicity that Mary Lincoln did not know that he had sworn out the warrant for her arrest as a lunatic, "for her benefit and the safety of the community." Now Robert Lincoln chose to avoid his mother until they met in court, where he would be the star witness for the prosecution. Later Mary Lincoln discovered that it had been her son who had hired men to follow her. One had been on the train from Florida, while others—the Pinkerton detectives to whom he was to pay $150 of her money—sat in the lobby of the Grand Pacific Hotel or by the elevators. It was these detectives who had informed Robert of her intention to leave the city and of the supposedly strange-looking people who visited her room. Sometime in early May Robert had determined that she must go to an institution, although he gave her no warning. Instead, he carefully organized his case, rounding up doctors, hotel maids, waiters, and store clerks to testify against her. His father's friend Leonard Swett had taken on the worst task: persuading her to come peacefully to court.[7]

Failing to move Mary Lincoln with soft persuasion about what others thought, Swett next employed an argument from authority. The doctors, he announced, also believed her insane. As none had recently examined her, she objected: "They know nothing about me. What does this mean?" In fact, six doctors had met with Robert and his lawyer the previous Saturday and had signed statements of her unsoundness of mind, for which Robert paid them fifty dollars apiece "for professional services in consultation."[8]

Finally Swett pointed to the officers. "I then explained to her that nothing in her case remained but to go with me or have me turn her over to the officers and let them take her. I told her there were two carriages downstairs, one of them was mine and the other belonged to the officers, and unless she yielded to me I either had to seize her forcibly myself or turn her over to the officers, who might handcuff her if necessary and certainly would take her to court. How much better—if you put on your bonnet and go along with me as you ordinarily would," appealed Swett.[9]

Still, Mary Lincoln protested and talked of changing her muddy dress, though Swett resolutely refused to let her out of his sight. Then she tongue-lashed Swett, telling him that he should go home and take care of his own wife, rather than meddle with her. (For years Laura Swett had been a mysterious homebound invalid.) "I have heard some stories on that subject about [your wife] and you my husband's friend you would take me and lock me up in an asylum." Then, in Swett's account, "Mary Lincoln threw up her hands and the tears streaming down her cheeks prayed to the Lord and called upon her husband to release her and drive me away." In the end she went without coercion, without "unladylike expression," and without any sign of the madness for which, from now on, her uncertain accusers had to search. But she did refuse Swett's chivalry as he tried to help her across the curb and into his carriage. "I ride with you from compulsion but I beg you not to touch me," she said.[10]

Minutes later a veiled Mary Lincoln entered the massive Cook County Courthouse through a side door, under Swett's escort and with the two policemen trailing discreetly. When Swett swung open the huge mahogany door to the courtroom, Mary Lincoln shrank back from the crowd of witnesses, officials, and, because court news travels fast, spectators. (Eventually extra chairs were needed for the audience.) With Robert's help—though now she was casting stony glances at her perfidious son—she was seated in a chair at the end of a table facing the court, her long veil of black crepe thrown over her left shoulder.

The proceedings were then delayed when her lawyer—or at least the counsel chosen by her accusers—had second thoughts. Like Swett, Isaac Arnold was a well-known Chicago lawyer and an old friend of Lincoln's who had early seen the greatness of a man he considered Illinois's strongest jury lawyer in the 1840s. Arnold had already published a laudatory account of Lincoln and, now at work on a full-scale biography of his hero, wanted to use the presidential papers stored in Judge Davis's vault in Bloomington. Recruited by Swett and Robert's lawyer (an arrangement similar to having plaintiff's counsel choose the defense lawyer), Arnold was suffering from a belated attack of conscience. Perhaps he remembered his hero's dictum about the importance of staying out of court if possible. Perhaps he wanted no part in a kangaroo court. Perhaps he remembered Mary Lincoln's recent gift of a set of Shakespeare, which she had inscribed "To Isaac Arnold, from your friend Mrs. A. Lincoln."

In any case Arnold then declined to serve as Mary Lincoln's counsel. Swett was outraged and reminded his friend of the necessity of a speedy trial. "You," said Swett to Arnold, "will put into her head that she can get some mischievous lawyer to make us trouble and defend her. Do your duty." Arnold eventually did, though the duty was to Robert, not Mary, Lincoln.[11]

For the next three hours Mary Lincoln listened to descriptions of her unsoundness of mind calmly and with sufficient dignity as to surprise Swett. In all, seventeen witnesses paraded to the stand. Robert had asked more, though at least two family members—John Todd Stuart and Elizabeth Todd Grimsley Brown—had declined. First came the doctors—five of the best-known specialists in Chicago. Robert had already sent them interrogatories "as to whether my mother is insane." Now they testified publicly to this effect. Admittedly they had only heard about Mary Lincoln's bizarre behavior from Robert and the lawyers, but on the basis of circumstantial evidence, they pronounced her fit for an asylum. To this Arnold offered neither objection nor cross-examination.[12]

The testimony of the fifth doctor was especially damaging. Dr. Willis Danforth, a professor of surgery at Hahneman Hospital, had seen Mary Lincoln on several occasions. According to Danforth, he had first been called to Robert Lincoln's house in 1874 and there had observed Mary Lincoln's "nervous derangement," including "the fever in her head" and her vagaries. Under questioning by Swett, Danforth described her as "possessed with the idea that some Indian spirit was working in her head and taking wires out of her eyes, particularly the left one." In April the accused had a delusion about being poisoned. "She said she drank two cups of coffee and believed by this means she received an overdose and vomited it up." According to Danforth, she believed that she would die on September 6, 1874, and that her son would follow her sometime during the tenth anniversary of his father's assassination. [13]

Next several hotel employees testified to Mary Lincoln's bizarre behavior during her nine-week residence at the Grand Pacific. Mrs. Harrington, the housekeeper, began with the obvious: "Mrs. Lincoln's manner was often nervous and excitable. She was not like ladies in general." Terrified of being alone, according to Mrs. Harrington, Mrs. Lincoln sometimes paid the upstairs maids to spend the night in her room. Once, according to Edward Fitzhenry, a second waiter, she appeared "carelessly dressed and repeated 'I am afraid, I am afraid.' " Some days, according to cleaning woman Mary Gavin, Mrs. Lincoln heard voices through the walls or from a certain place in her room. She also believed someone watched her through the tiny window in her washroom. One day she told the Grand Pacific's manager, Samuel Turner, that the South Side of Chicago was on fire, whereupon she enlisted his help in dispatching her trunks to safety in Milwaukee.

Arnold asked his first question of the manager, though his interrogation was designed to incriminate his client rather than establish her sanity. "Did Mrs. Lincoln look as if she had fever?" If the answer was yes, a physical condition might explain her delusions. On the contrary, answered Turner, "her face was as white as it is today. There was more an expression of fear than anything else about her—a fear of personal violence." [14]

Finally there were the salesclerks with tales of Mary Lincoln's extravagance and multiple purchases. The jewelry merchant from Mayo's remembered that she had bought not one but three watches for her son (who had immediately returned them), while Mr. Dapp of Mattock's recalled a shopping spree that ended with the purchase of several sets of lace curtains, which, according to the earlier testimony, remained unopened in her hotel room. Another clerk, recalling her feckless shopping habits, described her efforts to "beat down" the thirty-dollar price he was charging for gloves and handkerchiefs. She was "crazy," this witness concluded.

As good a criminal lawyer as any in Chicago, Swett saved his star witness until last. This was a case he had to win, and Swett had already told Isaac Arnold and Robert Lincoln that "an unfavorable verdict would be disastrous in the extreme." Acquittal would reveal Robert Lincoln and him as double villains who had tried to take advantage of a widow at the same time that they had dishonored the memory of Abraham Lincoln.[15]

It was late afternoon before Robert Lincoln took the stand. The next day the Chicago papers commented sympathetically on his pallid, tear-flecked face. Still, for all his emotion, he coolly defended himself from the implication that he was after his mother's money. He already managed her affairs, he told the jury, and had in fact telegraphed the money that enabled her to return from Florida. (At this Mary Lincoln shook her head in disbelief.) Certainly, Lincoln briskly announced, he was in good health, and there was no need for his mother's hysteria about him. As a dutiful son he had met the train from Florida and had urged his mother to stay at his home on Wabash Avenue—at least while his wife was away, for admittedly there was ill feeling between the two women. When against his wishes Mary Lincoln had preferred living in a hotel, he had spent the night in the next room. But that night she knocked on his door. "I told her that if she did not stop such proceedings I would leave the hotel." And so he did. Even then he had not abandoned his mother but had hired Pinkertons to watch her. Then he uttered the words that condemned his mother to an asylum: "I have no doubt my mother is insane. She has long been a source of great anxiety to me. She has no home and no reason to make these purchases."[16]

Finally Robert Lincoln's lawyers—Leonard Swett and Benjamin Ayer—summarized the prosecution's case: Mary Lincoln's uncontrollable grief after Lincoln's assassination, her old clothes sales in New York, her mania for buying things she could not use, and her peculiar delusions all demonstrated the charge. Although no specific reference was made to her spiritualism, any one of these other peculiarities should be sufficient for the jury to find her guilty of lunacy.

Arnold did not contest the case. He called no witnesses, not even Mary Lincoln, who, unlike her lawyer, would have denied that she was mad. Those who sat near the accused along the west side of the courtroom had already heard her audible dissent from parts of Dr. Willis Danforth's and Robert Lincoln's testimony. Had Mary Lincoln accepted her son's diagnosis, she would have gone voluntarily to a private asylum as many nervous ladies did, thereby sparing herself the most public of her lifelong humiliations. But she knew herself to be sane, and again a victim, she found herself robbed of any defense by her sex and her consequent unfamiliarity with the legal system, by the suddenness of the trial, and by her duplicitous counsel. An innovation designed to prevent precipitous commitments had not served Mary Lincoln, for she was as much a casualty of legal procedures weighted against unsuspecting females as Elizabeth Packard had been a decade before. Had Mary Lincoln found the "mischievous lawyer" Swett feared (and later she did), what case would the defense have presented?

FIRST Mary Lincoln would have called her friends of the spiritualist persuasion, her counselors in magic, to explain the difference between what the doctors called delusions and what dark-parlor habitués knew as visions. Then she would have described her reliance on mediums who kept her in touch with her dead sons and husband. The children, especially Willie, visited in brief emanations, while Lincoln hovered constantly and protectively. Everyone knew she needed companions. That was her nature, and with her family destroyed, spiritualists and sometimes even hotel maids provided companionship.

In Florida this past winter her husband had cautioned her about Robert's health, just as he had sent her a premonitory message (incorrect, as it turned out, though she may have misunderstood) that her own death would occur on September 6, 1874. The day made sense to any numerologist. In 1874 she would reach the same age Lincoln had been when he was murdered. Perhaps she had exaggerated her fears in those telegrams from Jacksonville, but Robert was all she had left. Anyone who had grieved knew the morbid anxiety that accompanied death's anniversaries. Then, after her return to Chicago, she had discovered that her hotel room resonated with voices. Just that Monday past she had asked a spiritualist who lived down the street from Robert to hold a séance, and on the third floor of the Grand Pacific Hotel they had sat on carpet-covered footstools in order to get in touch with the other world.[17]

Robert, Mary Lincoln would have continued, had always resented her spiritualism, though the loyal friends from her séances remained when everyone else deserted, including this false son, who had abandoned her after Tad's death. Unlike his father, who invited mediums to the White House, Robert was too unimaginative to understand the spirit world. He had always been this way. Once she had even written her daughter-in-law that she wished he would give up his proper lawyer's ways, and she remembered vividly his disapproval of a party she had organized in the White House for Tom Thumb and his wife. "Mother," Robert had said then, "I do not propose to assist in entertaining Tom Thumb. My notions of duty are somewhat different from yours." Robert had always tried to make her into the conventional woman she was not, denying even her interest in politics. She had tried to humor this stiff son of hers, sometimes by hiding her spiritualist connections in order to prevent his displays of bad temper.

Though he bore her father's and husband's name, Robert was neither Todd nor Lincoln. Recently he had displayed his greediness when he complained that the mediums would make off with her registered bonds, though how this could be done without her consent, she had no idea. In fact, the only reason she was on trial now was that her son's spies had observed her friends leaving her hotel room with something she had willingly bestowed on them—the silver service set that he coveted.[18]

As for her fears for her life, the trial proved what she had before only suspected: She was being followed and had been ever since Tad's death. Without her knowledge Robert had hired strange men (and sometimes even hotel maids) to spy on her. Gradually she had become aware of these shadowy presences, though before the trial she had no idea why rough-looking men should trail her. Once she had fooled them by leaving Marshall and Leiter's store through the Clark Street exit and taking another carriage back to the hotel. But that night, when she went into the hall to the lavatory (as she often had to), there was one of the men skulking in the corridor. This man resembled the poisoner on the train whom she had observed putting something in her coffee in the dining car. Another man had joined him at Kankakee, after the train had crossed from Indiana to Illinois.[19]

As for the small-time merchants, how dare they judge her behavior? Hadn't Robert tipped them two weeks' wages to testify against her? She could find as many who found nothing strange about her, and she would have brought them as witnesses had she been warned. Was spending money a mental illness? It was no one's business (and certainly not Robert's) how she spent her money and time. That very summer she expected to buy a fireproof cottage in Wisconsin and there, at last, unpack her trunks.

Why did Robert worry that she would spend the Lincoln inheritance on curtains when since her husband's death he had been her greatest expense? She had already given this son of hers more than

$10,000 in real estate, $6,000 in bonds from her share of Tad's inheritance, $5,000 in cash in 1873 for his law library, as well as furniture and jewelry—in all nearly $25,000. Despite this, he continually asked for interest-free loans for the real estate ventures that his father would have despised and that, especially a recent one with John Forsythe, so often lost money. If he could squander money on real estate, why could she not buy curtains?[20]

She had, Mary Lincoln would have told the jury, no intention of cashing in the registered bonds her beloved husband had left her. In fact, every year she added a little to her principal from unspent income, and she intended to manage her money with as much prudence as Judge Davis had. Even if she could bankrupt herself by buying ribbons, curtains, and gloves, the federal pension would keep her off Robert's hands. If he would be patient, it would not be long before he and his daughter (for she had changed her mind about leaving anything to his wife) would inherit more than $70,000 from the will she had written in 1872.[21]

As for the doctors who so casually pronounced her fit for an asylum, they had never examined her. They were Robert's friends and would say what he directed. She could find others who would declare her as sane as her son. The worst offender was Dr. Danforth, who had mistaken her migraine headaches for hallucinations. Before a bad attack she often saw streaks of light and flashes of yellow. The worst spasms did make her feel as if an Indian (mediums often used Indians as their spirit links to the other world) were pulling strings through her eyes, though only her left eye because the headaches were one-sided. How a reputable doctor could have twisted this suffering into a case of unsound mind was beyond understanding.[22]

Admittedly she was nervous and miserable, but a broken heart was not a ruined mind. It was the tenth anniversary of the death of the "Great One," and in July there would be, for the fourth time, the terrible remembrance of Tad's departure. In Florida the enormity of these abandonments had interrupted her sleep, and a helpful pharmacist in Jacksonville had suggested the new Squibb hypnotic chloral hydrate. Perhaps she had taken too much. Certainly the sedative clouded her mind temporarily, especially when she mixed it with a laudanum compound of opium, saffron, cinnamon, and wine that her son's doctor had earlier recommended. Even by itself the pungent-tasting drug excited her, though it gave others a dreamy sense of ease. Still she was no morphia-crazed opium eater. Finally Mary Lincoln would have closed with the defense she had earlier given Swett: "I have always been very careful about money matters. I am abundantly able to take care of myself and I have done so for over ten years. . . ."[23]

Had she been permitted an advocate instead of a biased friend of Swett's, such a lawyer would have directed the jury, after her testimony, to consider the defendant more disturbing than disturbed. For years this woman had trampled the canons of womanhood. Even when her husband had been alive, she had spent too much money, traveled too far, and interfered too much in political matters at a time when wives and especially widows were expected to be frugal, invisible homebodies. Mary Lincoln had been the opposite: a restless profligate who had defied the chief justice and embarrassed a son embarking on a career. Whatever Mary Lincoln's peculiarities, her lawyer might have continued, there were no indications of madness, at least not in the definition of one expert, Dr. Robert Patterson, who characterized insanity as "a chronic disease of the brain which produces derangement of the intellectual faculties and prolonged changes of feelings, affections and habits."[24]

The jury retired without the benefit of any such defense. During the recess Robert approached his mother, and sharp-eared reporters overheard, as the son tried to take his mother's hand, Mary Lincoln's only outburst of the afternoon: "Oh, Robert, to think that my son would do this to me." Meanwhile, in its chambers the jury was listening to Dr. Samuel Blake, who had been one of Tad's doctors during his fatal illness in 1871. After 1853 any Illinois jury hearing an insanity case included a doctor who guided its decision. Fortunately for Robert (and perhaps not coincidentally) Dr. Blake had been chosen for this duty, and he documented Mary Lincoln's mental illness by describing her overwrought reaction to Tad's death. According to one juror, Dr. Blake described her case as "dementia or degeneration of the brain tissue, which would become progressively worse."[25]

Within ten minutes the all-male jury had reached its decision: "We the undersigned jurors in the case of Mary Lincoln are satisfied that Mary Lincoln is insane and is a fit person to be in a state hospital for the insane—that her age is 56—that the disease is of unknown duration—that the cause is unknown—that she is not subject to epilepsy—that she does not manifest homicidal or suicidal tendencies and that she is not a pauper." Years later one juror recalled that in view of the lack of any other evidence, "there seemed to be no other course than for us but to find the lady guilty as charged."[26]

After the trial the crowd gathered around her carriage, peering into the windows just as rude Washingtonians had during the war when she had given them a regal wave. Now Mary Lincoln, having learned the terms of her sentence, cowered in the corner. She was to hand over her bonds (angrily she tore them out of her petticoat); the court would appoint a conservator to control her money, and she must go the next day to a private asylum forty miles outside Chicago in Batavia, Illinois. In the meantime, Robert had hired several guards whose instructions were, according to Swett, "to in no event let her go out."[27]

But Mary Lincoln did go out sometime the next day, or so the Chicago papers reported. ANOTHER SAD CHAPTER IN THE LIFE OF THE DEMENTED WIDOW, ran the *Inter Ocean* headline. MARY LINCOLN'S ATTEMPTS TO POISON HERSELF. According to these stories, on the morning of her departure for Batavia, she had eluded her guards and had rushed into the hotel pharmacy, where she had ordered a three-ounce bottle of laudanum. When the proprietor recognized her, she headed for another store on Clark Street. Somehow forewarned, this druggist stalled by telling her to return in a half hour. Hurriedly she left for yet another pharmacy. When Mary Lincoln finally obtained two ounces of laudanum (not a lethal dose), she hurried into the street, swallowed the contents of the vial, and returned, still on foot, to her hotel room to die. In fact, Mary Lincoln had received sugar water and camphor, and the newspapers complimented the alert druggists for their vigilance in foiling a suicide attempt.[28]

Like so much else in the Mary Lincoln apocrypha, this story was probably false. Never before or after did she try to take her life, though she had ample opportunity to do so. Indeed, a well-rehearsed jury had just acquitted her of any suicidal tendencies. What makes the newspaper story even more implausible is the suggestion that a fifty-six-year-old woman—stiff in limb and gait from arthritis and gout, readily identifiable in her widow's black, watched by three attendants, a sheriff's deputy, and a maid stationed in her room—could elude her guards, walk three miles, swallow the purgative camphor, and return again on foot to her room, just at the moment of her son's timely arrival and her removal to the asylum. This unlikely tale first appeared in a newspaper owned by Robert Lincoln's former law partner and was more a son's exculpation of filial treachery than a mother's demonstration of suicidal tendencies.

HOURS after her supposed suicide attempt, in the early evening of May 20, 1875, Mary Lincoln arrived in Batavia and for the first time met the bearded patriarch of the Bellevue Place sanatorium, Dr. Robert Patterson. The superintendent knew all about her. His younger brother, Dr. DeWitt Patterson, probably had treated her during the Civil War for her bladder problems, and he may also have informed his brother of her concussion from a carriage accident in 1863. Just that April Dr. Patterson had met with five other doctors in the office of Robert Lincoln's lawyer. After hearing Mary Lincoln's symptoms discussed, he had immediately proposed Bellevue as a solution. But if she would not come voluntarily, Patterson made clear, there must be a legal commitment.

Ever since the Packard case Patterson had been careful to avoid any suspicion of false confinement and so far had avoided the habeas corpus warrants sworn out for the release of inmates in other Illinois institutions. Recently he had advised a husband who had wanted to put his wife in the asylum that he must follow the required legal procedures, and that meant a jury trial. Like most of his colleagues in the Association of Medical Superintendents of American Institutions for the Insane, Patterson detested the new state law, not so much for its humiliation of patients and the shock to domestic privacy of public trials (an affront especially offensive to women) as for his belief that uninformed juries could not distinguish between sane and insane behavior. Along with other alienists (like so much in the field, the term was of French origin), Patterson considered the determination of lunacy—as well as its treatment—an issue for experts like him. Just that fall, at a meeting of the Fox River Medical Association, of which he was president, he had argued that Illinois should replace what he privately called the "infernal law" with a commission of experts.[29]

Usually Patterson had no time for insanity trials, but he had attended Mary Lincoln's, leaving Bellevue in the competent hands of his wife, his son John—a doctor trained in the new specialty of gynecology—and a staff of twelve nurses and attendants. In the 1870s Dr. Patterson was often in Chicago, recruiting patients in his rooms along Doctors Row on Washington Street, where he advertised his services as an expert in cases of insanity: five to fifteen dollars for consultation, two to five dollars for house calls, five to ten dollars for night calls. Because of the competition from other private asylums, such as Dr. Andrew McFarland's Oak Lawn, and the fact that half the insane in Illinois (and throughout the United States) were not in hospitals at all, Bellevue was less than three-quarters full. In the 1870s the American asylum was only partially discovered. Naturally Dr. Patterson advocated institutional treatment and justified the necessity of removing the mad from their families by the therapeutic value of Bellevue. To one uncertain husband he wrote, "Mrs. S's sickness will not yield to treatment at home. For the most part it is not practical properly to treat such diseases in private practice."[30]

Early in his career, after his graduation from the Berkshire Medical College and during his first job as an asylum superintendent, Dr. Patterson had been optimistic about restoring the reason of his patients. Over the years he had become less hopeful until like his colleagues, he deemed only a portion of the mentally ill curable. In his long career in public institutions he had never achieved the inflated cure rates of 80 percent promised by some of his colleagues. Still, in the 1850s, while he was superintendent at Iowa's Mount Pleasant State Hospital, half his charges were usually released each year as cured. So Patterson accepted the probability of cure (or at least improvement) for the deranged, but only if they were in institutions. Without such an advantage, most became irreversibly insane. If their nervousness continued for a long period, permanent destruction of the mind occurred.[31]

No doctor knew why this was so. Some superintendents speculated that the nervous passions and excesses of the deranged vibrated like a jackhammer, eventually blasting the brain of its vital force. According to this theory, if lunatics lived long enough, they died of the brain deterioration that Dr. Blake had described to Mary Lincoln's jury as dementia and the progressive degeneration of brain tissue. Robert Patterson's theory was slightly different. Like the famed New York neurologist Dr. George Beard, Patterson believed the body to be an energy-producing dynamo that could create only a limited amount of power. In nineteenth-century America, cities, noise, and a thousand other energy-demanding distractions—including new standards of punctuality and education for women—drained vitality from what often became an overloaded system in susceptible individuals.

For women, the prisoners of their demanding reproductive systems, the chances of nervous disorders were great, for female nerves were smaller, more delicate, and more likely than those of males to be exhausted. If the resulting deficits, which Patterson's friend Dr. S. Weir Mitchell called the wear and tear of progress, were not corrected, permanent mental impairment resulted. Thus, to Patterson's thinking, nervous maladies such as spinal irritation, insomnia, fear of lightning, and even frequent urination were the price civilized Americans paid for their evolution. As Dr. Beard had asked, who in Africa suffered neurasthenia? And if the turmoil of late-nineteenth-century life caused mental illness, then it followed that the best sedative was rest in the country.[32]

At first Patterson could not make a specific diagnosis of Mary Lincoln's condition because he had received conflicting answers to the critical question of the date of onset and first manifestations of her sickness. Robert Lincoln believed that his mother's insanity had begun ten years ago, after his father's assassination. Others (and they included David Davis and Leonard Swett) considered Mary Lincoln a lifelong lunatic, and if this was correct, certain brain centers had probably already been irreparably damaged. Those who had known her longest agreed about her long-standing peculiarities, though she had never needed confinement. In any case, Patterson was persuaded that her derangement was at least a decade old, and hence her stay in Bellevue might be a long one. On the other hand, she might even be a candidate for the state asylum at Jacksonville, where the superintendent sent his most intractable cases. No matter which, the reward for prompt treatment might be an eventual recovery.[33]

Gradually Dr. Patterson arrived at a diagnosis. From the testimony at the trial he knew Mary Lincoln's was not an hereditary illness, that there was no inherited mental disease in the Todds or Parkers. (Robert had neglected to mention the impairments of his mother's brothers—now-deceased alcoholic Levi and erratic George Rogers Clark Todd.) Mrs. Lincoln was too old for any of the lesions that were thought to occur at the menopausal turn of life. Certainly Dr. Patterson had no reason to believe that she had syphilis or epilepsy, though those were established classifications for insanity, as was melancholy. Neither was she, in the standard diagnostic measures of 1870, intemperate, idiotic, hysterical, or an opium eater. As yet he knew little about the drug dependence that doctors were calling "chloral-eating."[34]

Yet his new patient complained of two physical symptoms commonly associated with an overloaded nervous system. She had the "vesical distress" of frequent urination that Dr. William Goddell called a "hysterical bladder," and she also suffered from a spinal irritation that suggested nervous debility. To Patterson's way of thinking, both resulted from the action of her excessive grief on her brain force. As he summarized in his patient report, "Mrs. Lincoln's case of mental impairment probably dates to the murder of Pres. Lincoln, [it became] more pronounced since the death of her son, but especially aggravated during the last two months."[35]

After the trial Patterson heard testimony to the effect that Mrs. Lincoln also suffered from the religious excitement of spiritualism. Some alienists called this aberration "theomania," and as many as one-quarter of America's female mental patients were so classified. As explained by the neurologist Dr. William Hammond, "the false sensuous impressions [conjured up by mediums] force too much blood to the brain and eventually predispose séance seekers to lunacy." Dr. Patterson had made the same point in his annual report to the trustees of the Indiana State Asylum, where he had explained how spirit rapping led to insanity. "Spiritualists," he had written in 1852, "reject the inspired authority of scripture and regarding the human family as ignorant of their relations to God and their condition in eternity, teach that man by some mysterious unintelligible process may possibly arrive at some definite truth. This error so arouses the passions as to bring on the derangement."[36]

In Patterson's final differential diagnosis, Mary Lincoln was suffering from a classic case of monomania, the partial, though progressive, form of insanity that rendered her irrational in some behaviors but perfectly normal in others. To Dr. Patterson *mania* did not mean an "elevated state of euphoria," but rather described a compulsion that overrode the moral instincts so critical for women. Sufferers often appeared entirely sensible. As Robert Lincoln explained to those who were unconvinced of his mother's derangement: "[A]t the height of my mother's mental troubles she usually appeared to me personally to be perfectly sane." Along with her physical symptoms—the nervous irritation of her bladder and spine and her headaches—Mary Lincoln's monomania appeared in what Patterson described as her "extended rambles, the indulgence of her purchasing mania, and other morbid mental manifestations"—by which he meant spiritualism.[37]

TODAY'S Dr. Pattersons see Mary Lincoln's behavior as annoying, improper, and unnatural but dangerous neither to herself nor to society—and therefore not an instance of medical or legal insanity. She was always more bewildering than bewildered and more sickening (especially to her son) than sick. Rather than a progressive brain-destroying mania that required confinement, Mary Lincoln suffered from the personality disorder of narcissism. In this, as in other aspects of her life, she was ahead of her day, for narcissism is so common a twentieth-century malady that some authorities promote it as the neurotic disposition characteristic of our times. Still, no one needs hospitalization for this impairment. Certainly Mary Lincoln did not.

Her problem had begun with her mother's death and had worsened with each abandonment. A perennial sufferer by the time she left Springfield in 1861, Mary Lincoln then watched her favorite son's death and her husband's murder and thereafter knew herself to be, in the way of chronic victims, unlovable and unloved. She fed this embedded, frequently nourished sense of worthlessness with exhibitions of grandiosity that, like the old clothes sale, were calculated to restore a tattered self. Usually their effect was an additional dose of humiliation, and her efforts at self-promotion made the disease worse in a ratcheting process that she seemed unable to avoid.

Over the years Mary Lincoln's oft-practiced therapy of self-aggrandizement made the friendships for which she clamored more difficult. Acquaintances found her requisitions of their time, money, and sympathy too expensive and gave her up. Death narrowed her family circle at the same time that she ruined other associations through her angry assaults. Like many narcissists, she had found someone to idolize in Abraham Lincoln, and it was an especially cruel fate that ended her affiliation with the man who supplied the grandeur that Mary Lincoln needed more than most human beings.

Thereafter, like self-surveilling narcissists of other places and times, she considered herself entitled to a house, a pension, and the payment of her bills. Such expectations—natural to her but abnormal to others—irritated potential supporters. Shopping in stores, another survival tactic, made her feel important, as she negotiated with salesclerks whom she expected to admire her standing and taste. It was the attention-getting aspects of her shopping—as much as the collecting of unused curtains and bonnets in trunks—that satisfied.[38]

In the spring of 1875, disconnected from family, friends, and even her Chicago circle of spiritualists, Mary Lincoln had suffered a post-traumatic stress syndrome as the tenth anniversary of Lincoln's death approached. At the time she was also taking large doses of chloral hydrate for insomnia. Unconsciously she again made herself into a victim, and exhibited her emotional poverty in a telegram to her son: "My dearly beloved son, Robert T. Lincoln, rouse yourself and live for my sake. All I have is yours from this hour. I am praying every moment for your life to be spared to your mother." In the tragedy that followed she was both an unwilling victim and at times an agent provocateur.[39]

Willie and Tad would have handled their mother's appeal with more sensitivity, but Robert had never understood her. Moreover, he lived in an age when the doctors he turned to for advice knew no middle ground between sanity and insanity, normality and abnormality. Freud's work on narcissism and neuroses lay three decades away, and this generation condemned borderline cases to institutions that, like Patterson's Bellevue, had empty rooms. In counseling Robert, the superintendent could make no demarcation between what he described to another prospective client as "undoubted insanity and doubtful sanity." Both belonged in Bellevue.[40]

During the nineteenth century Americans lost their tolerance for eccentrics like Mary Lincoln. In the eighteenth century James Otis had exploded in mad freaks, but no one challenged his right to sit in the Massachusetts Assembly. Samuel Checkley, a New England minister, gave sermons in gibberish and wandered about Concord. Joseph Moody wore a handkerchief over his face, and another Massachusetts resident named Jack Dawn lifted the wigs off fellow worshipers with a fishing pole. All would have been at risk for involuntary confinement in post Civil War Chicago, where for the first time there was a place to put them. Like Mary Lincoln, they would have become institutional casualties of what alienists, neurologists, and superintendents of asylums were calling a great epidemic of mental illness sweeping the country. In the twenty years from 1860 to 1880, a period in which mental illness became the national concern it had never been before, such prophecies had led to a sixfold increase in the population of Illinois asylums.[41]

BELLEVUE, of course, differed from the public asylums in Jacksonville and Elgin, Illinois. Dr. Patterson took no more than twenty-five "genteel" ladies at an average weekly charge of fifteen to twenty-five dollars. (Mary Lincoln paid closer to forty-five dollars but this included a private attendant and unlimited access to a carriage.) Patterson offered these inmates "the modern management of mental disease by rest, diet, baths, fresh air, occupation, diversion, change of scene, an orderly life, and no more medicine than necessary." He refused syphilitics, the furiously mad, and those of filthy habits, though at least one patient during Mary Lincoln's stay smeared excrement on the walls.

Still, despite the superintendent's selective admissions policy and his emphasis on the family atmosphere of his institution, in 1875 his patients included Mrs. Wheeler, who raved in the mornings and, when not drugged by chloral hydrate, pounded on the floor and walls at night; Mrs. Edouard, who lay in bed all day; Mrs. Munger, who grabbed another inmate's scissors and stabbed herself; Mrs. Johnston, who urinated on the floor with the explanation that "God imposes higher duties than cleanliness"; and long-staying anorexic Minnie Judd, who had to be periodically force-fed.[42]

To treat these inmates, Dr. Patterson relied, for the most part, on the rest and quiet that he believed critical to the restoration of reason. As an institutional counterpart to rural cemeteries like Springfield's Oak Ridge, Bellevue qualified as a country retreat. The twenty-two-acre estate, with its massive four-story limestone mansion set in the center of the grounds, was full of majestic shade trees. Its location, southwest of the picturesque village of Batavia, afforded a pastoral view of the Fox River from the third- and fourth-story windows. Carriages were available for those who were permitted to ride, and the most energetic diversions were croquet on the lawn and piano playing in the parlors.[43]

Soon after he had purchased the place from the owners of a girls' school, Patterson had installed a greenhouse and hired a French gardener. In good weather inmates were encouraged to wander about the back lot, where Mrs. Patterson kept an elaborate flower and vegetable garden. The homegrown food was therapeutically bland (spicy food excited the nervous system), and like any country estate, Bellevue had its pigs, chickens, and cows. So important was this bucolic image to the promotion of the institution that it was common for the daily patient reports to include, along with the inmates' condition, information concerning the harvesting of vegetables and the reorganization of the rose garden.[44]

Like most superintendents, Dr. Patterson did not rely entirely on custodial care, nutritious food, and the soothing benefits of rest in the country. Although his advertisements promised treatment with as little medicine as possible, under his orders the staff dispensed large doses of opium, morphine, cannabis indica, belladonna, ergot, conium, and Bellevue's notorious whiskey-laced eggnog. In the early 1870s he had begun using chloral hydrate, the popular alkaline compound recently synthesized by German chemists. Doctors and patients everywhere were finding this bitter-tasting, foul-smelling substance an excellent hypnotic, though the maximum dosage, the degree of dependency, and the reaction of patients (some became aroused rather than sleepy) had not yet been established. European doctors were already warning that its effects ranged from the desired euphoria and sleep to frenzied hysteria and slurred speech and that it was addictive. But at Bellevue Patterson continued to apportion huge amounts to inmates who either could not sleep or were unruly. According to the patients' records, during Mary Lincoln's stay Mrs. Edouard "awoke last night screaming. Had taken at bedtime forty grains of chloral. I gave her then at three A.M. twenty grains chloral." The next day Mrs. Edouard upset the staff by sleeping most of the day.[45]

By the 1880s Patterson would be treating a new generation of patients for their chloral habits, though such a dependence was never as physically addicting (at least as measured by withdrawal symptoms) as opium. But even in the early 1870s there were warnings in the professional journals about dosages over 100 grains. One superintendent had recently warned, in the *American Journal of Insanity,* that the combination of chloral and laudanum produced dangerous melancholias, and more and more suicides preferred easy-to-get chloral hydrate over laudanum and arsenic. When the United States government began to control narcotics in the twentieth century, chloral hydrate was included in its first list of dangerous substances.[46]

It is certain that Dr. Patterson had delivered a lethal amount to one of his patients a few months before Mary Lincoln's arrival. According to the patients' reports of September 1874, "Mrs. Harcourt raving and walking to and fro—tearing clothing and bedding—sores around the mouth disappearing—gave her 35 grains of Squibbs hydrate of chloral. [She] slept until 2 o'clock and [awoke] screaming—forcibly held down—more chloral—40 grains—no quieting effect—at 3 A.M. gave 35 more grains—2 hours [she] awoke—pounding on the door. Suddenly [she] sank down at 7:30, called physician—pulseless—life was extinct. It is probable that the immediate cause of death was the exhaustion of the mania." In other words, Mrs. Harcourt's nerves had become so demanding that like an electrical short circuit, they had exploded in her brain, destroying her force and shortly thereafter her life. Accepting this view of the brain and its effect on the mind, the attendants at Bellevue were always measuring inmates' force of conversation, energy, and physical activity. In this case a nervous mania—not the 110 grains of chloral hydrate—had caused Mrs. Harcourt's death, at least according to the superintendent.[47]

Along with rest and drugs, Patterson relied on the moral treatment that an earlier generation of alienists had favored and that linked Victorian treatments of mental disease to twentieth-century psychoanalysis. If the therapies were similar, the motivation was not. This school of nineteenth-century alienists believed insanity a matter of lost control and unrestrained impulses without any organic basis. In their view, a lunatic's immoral thoughts and deeds created unhealthy passions that could be cured only by better self-government.

In a reversal of today's rules, doctors like Patterson acted as preachers, instructing their patients in right behavior. Asylums became "reformatories" as alienists talked, judged, exhorted, and castigated inmates for everything from drinking and drug taking to masturbation and séance attending. One nineteenth-century study of 550 mental patients discovered forty-three different moral aberrations, caused by everything from loss of property, political excitement, and the cultivation of mediums to excessive study, irregular eating habits, and, especially in women, extended, uncontrolled mourning.

By the 1870s a new generation of specialists—neurologists like Beard and Hammond—had rejected such old-fashioned notions of mental illness. The idea that nervous derangements had no organic basis and could be cured by counseling patients how to rule their impulses seemed as ridiculous to them as eighteenth-century notions that bad behavior was the devil's work. But Robert Patterson had been trained before the Civil War and had no difficulty fusing the organic interpretation of madness with his acceptance of the modern views about nervousness destroying brain matter. Along with drugs and rest, he continued to use moral therapy on his female inmates at Bellevue.[48]

WHEN Mary Lincoln arrived at Batavia the cool spring evening of May 20, 1875, she walked up the spiral staircase to her tiny second-floor room having no idea how long she must stay. Like other court-certified lunatics, she had been given an indeterminate sentence with confinement necessary until, in the words of the Illinois statute, her "reason was restored"—or at least until Dr. Patterson and Robert Lincoln allowed that it was. Discharge through a writ of habeas corpus was easier than it had been in Elizabeth Packard's day, and superintendents who detained sane persons were subject to fines and jail sentences; this made them at least cautious. But especially for women whose relatives disapproved of their being discharged, obtaining releases was still a difficult matter.

Perhaps this was why Bellevue's inmates stayed so long, although those who were disruptive, filthy, or incurable or who otherwise evinced signs of lost brain force were eventually sent to state hospitals. Nerves, in Dr. Patterson's thinking, took months to respond, especially if the lesions were of long duration, as he believed Mary Lincoln's were. Teaching self-control through moral therapy might require several years. And like most asylums, Bellevue employed a hierarchy of rooms that demarcated the status of each inmate, so that patients had report cards on how they rated with their keepers. After eighteen months Minnie Judd still had not moved from the third-floor east hall reserved for the most deranged, whereas after a year Mrs. Norris had finally moved to the second-floor west wing.

Mary Lincoln had one of the shortest incarcerations in Bellevue's history. She was in the asylum exactly three months and three weeks, during which time, in prudent advertisement of her sanity, she was a model patient who required no chloral hydrate, cannabis indica, hypodermics of morphine, or even the physical restraint exercised by Mrs. Ruggles, Bellevue's uniformed matron, and her staff of attendants. In the daytime Mary Lincoln went where she wanted and never tried to throw herself out the window because of an imagined fire, as the Chicago doctors had predicted. Robert Lincoln who gave himself away with his displeasure at his mother's rationality, explained that "my mother could control her behavior if she had an object," as now she did.[49] Certainly Mary Lincoln fooled her son on his bimonthly visits. "Mother and I are on the best of terms—Mother is happier every way in her freedom from care and excitement than she has been in ten years," he explained to his mother's friend Sally Orne, who had inquired why Mary Lincoln was in an institution at all.[50]

In fact, Mary Lincoln was already plotting her exit from the despised twelve-by-twenty-one-foot room that, with its ragtag bureau and rocking chair (she bought her own mattress), had the furnishings of a third-class European hotel. But locked in at night, she could not walk or ride away. Robert Lincoln, who ever after tried to make a comfortable hotel out of an asylum, had ordered the bars on her window removed, suggesting that no one believed Mary Lincoln a candidate for suicide. But even if she could climb down from her second-story room or escape on a carriage ride, Robert had her money. In the meantime, from an adjacent room her private attendant, who did the laundry and brought the meals, spied on her through the wooden slats that Robert neglected to mention in his descriptions of Bellevue. Any peculiar behavior was quickly reported to the Pattersons.

So Mary Lincoln did what she had been convicted of failing to do: She lived a normal life. She visited with the superintendent's wife, took rides in her carriage, talked to the Pattersons' retarded daughter Blanche, sat on the front stairs, and wrote letters. In all she behaved as if she didn't have to be in Bellevue.

Still, more than good works were required for release. Aware of the incriminating performance of Isaac Arnold at her insanity trial, Mary Lincoln needed the kind of "mischievous" lawyer that Swett had wanted to avoid. But it was no easy matter to hire an independent lawyer, especially since the Pattersons censored her mail. Every correspondent had to be approved or Dr. Patterson forwarded the letters to Robert. Outgoing mail was deposited in the office, where snoopy Mrs. Patterson made sure the recipient was on her list. Once Mary Lincoln sneaked a letter to the postman on a carriage ride but was reported. Then she had a better idea. She would write two letters, enclose both in a letter to an approved correspondent, in this case her Chicago washerwoman, and direct her to post the second letter.[51]

This plan, which had somehow been exposed, exhibited what Patterson considered symptoms of Mary Lincoln's moral insanity. Connecting bad behavior and mental derangement in the manner of the traditional alienists, he admonished her to reform. According to the patients' records of July 30, "Mrs. Lincoln had a long talk with Dr. Patterson. He told her that Mr. Lincoln was her legal conservator and in cases that he [Dr. Patterson] did not know those written to by Mrs. Lincoln, he would send the letters under cover to him." Mary Lincoln had no choice but to agree.[52]

Two weeks later she was again in trouble and received another reprimand from the superintendent: "I told her that I did not think she was treating us fairly." Then, in August, her attempts at freedom of correspondence became evidence of a persistent lunacy: "Mrs. Lincoln is frequently untruthful in her statements. Her lying and deceit should be put down to insanity." Like most institutions, Bellevue demanded a level of cooperation from inmates which, when not obtained, became an illustration of their moral insanity. Those who were progressing made their beds, cleaned their rooms, walked on the grounds, and took carriage rides when told to do so. No matter what the activity, they were habitually polite and cheerful to their attendants. Though Mary Lincoln was "cheerful and pleasant" more often than not, she did not always meet these measures for proper behavior, and her keepers considered her monomania unimproved.[53]

Her conflict with the staff centered on the mail and the carriage. "Mrs. Lincoln sent down word after dinner, that she would like a ride today" went one report. "Then sent word she would ride in the morning." On another day in July: "Mrs. Lincoln makes an appointment to ride in the morning. Then when the time comes puts it off until night. Then delays until next morning and so on." There was also the matter of food, reported in the patients' records on September 6: "Mrs. Lincoln seems more capricious and with a little tendency to irritability. She insists on corn breads every morning and leaves them untouched and calls for rolls. Griddle cakes are ordered for every supper which she doesn't eat but calls for rolls."[54]

Along with an unpredictability that Dr. Patterson considered evidence of insanity, Mary Lincoln was indecisive about packing and sending a trunk to her son. Such behavior revealed a dangerous failure of force and was typical of the unproductive behavior that female neurasthenics often displayed. Then on three afternoons she was reported as melancholy, with the worst episode occurring in mid-July. No one at Bellevue seemed to know the occasion, but she was in fact remembering Tad's death four years before on July 15. As the weeks dragged on, the Pattersons still believed that she needed more rest and moral instruction. Two months after her arrival the superintendent told a reporter that he could give "no encouragement that Mrs. Lincoln would ever be well."[55]

By August, with both Dr. and Mrs. Patterson advising continued confinement, Mary Lincoln intensified her efforts to obtain the outside help she required to get out of Bellevue. Off to influential public figures—Congressmen Henry Blow of Missouri and General John Farnsworth of Illinois, as well as her spiritualist friend Stephen James, the editor of the *Religio-Philosophical Journal*—went smuggled appeals. Some recipients responded out of duty's sake and paid social calls. But one took up her cause, and without Myra Bradwell, Mary Lincoln might have remained in Bellevue indefinitely.[56]

In many ways Myra Bradwell and her husband, Judge James B. Bradwell, were unlikely rescuers. Both husband and wife were lawyers, though after passing the bar she had been denied the right to practice. In *Bradwell* v. *Illinois,* an 1873 decision concurred in by all the justices save David Davis, the Supreme Court held that Mrs. Bradwell was not an independent agent and as such could not sign contracts or serve as legal counsel. "The paramount destiny and mission of women are to fulfill the noble and benign offices of wife and mother" went the majority opinion. Denied the right to have clients because of her sex, Bradwell instead published the influential trade paper the *Chicago Legal News* and crusaded for the rights she had been denied. At first, such activism had not endeared her to Mary Lincoln. In the past Mrs. Lincoln had disliked females who mixed in public affairs as first parties, rather than as behind-the-scenes arrangers.[57]

What Mary Lincoln had initially shared with the statuesque, elaborately coiffed Myra Bradwell was not women's suffrage but spiritualism. Both women had lost three of their four children. Both found consolation in séances, though Bradwell's affiliation was brief. (Robert Lincoln once called Bradwell the "high priestess of a gang of spiritualists.") As neighbors on West Washington Street in 1867, Mary Lincoln and Myra Bradwell had become friends, sharing a mutual failure to conform to the dictates of conventional ladyhood as well as an interest in public affairs. Then, in 1872, Mary Lincoln, who did not intend to make the same mistake as her husband, asked the Bradwells to assist her in drawing up a will.[58]

Two years later she again turned to them in her crusade for freedom. Not only did Myra Bradwell know the Illinois lunacy statutes—she had recently analyzed them in the *Legal News*—but her husband was a county judge and former state legislator who could put the case back in the newspapers and thereby embarrass Robert Lincoln and Dr. Patterson until they agreed to a release.

From Myra Bradwell's perspective, Mary Lincoln was a victim of male injustice and family treachery. Of all the lawyers in Illinois, the "legal lady," as the press called her, was the best equipped to confront the established forces of Robert Lincoln's camp. By no means did Myra Bradwell consider Mary Lincoln a conventional woman, which judgment Dr. Patterson promoted into agreement with his diagnosis of insanity, but this was not Bradwell's meaning. Accustomed to being labeled irrational and even crazy herself, Myra Bradwell knew what Robert Lincoln did not: Mary Lincoln was a peculiar woman, but lunacy, eccentricity, and male-disapproved behavior (such as Dr. Patterson's complaint about "her extended rambles and the indulgence of her purchasing mania") had to be distinguished. Asked by a *Chicago Times* reporter whether Mrs. Lincoln was insane, Myra Bradwell ironically replied, "Mary Lincoln is no more insane than I am."[59]

By the time the Bradwells took up her cause, Mary Lincoln had a plan. She would leave the asylum and live quietly with her sister Elizabeth Edwards in Springfield until Robert Lincoln returned her money. Earlier Robert had advised Dr. Patterson of the two sisters' estrangement, and it was a surprised superintendent who, in mid-July, heard Mary Lincoln propose a permanent visit to the Edwardses'. "It is the most natural thing in the world to live with my sister," Patterson quoted her as saying. "She raised me and I regard her as a sort of mother." No one scrutinized her correspondence with Elizabeth, and Mary Lincoln had already invited herself. After some uncertainty her loyal sister-mother agreed without a word to her nephew.[60]

Robert was furious at "Aunt Lizzie's interference with my painful duty." True madness, he had been told, took years to cure and in his mother's case might be permanent. He hoped it was so. Having endured the public humiliation of what he called the "Inquisition" of a trial, he would be hard pressed to explain such a rapid recovery. And though he still controlled her money as a court-appointed conservator, Mary Lincoln was threatening to embarrass him by exposing his disastrous investment schemes.

So instead of supporting her probation at the Edwardses', Robert exaggerated his mother's illness. "How sorely Aunt Lizzie misjudges on the general subject of my mother's devotion to spiritualism," he informed Judge Davis.[61] To dampen his aunt's hospitality, he now charged that his mother intended to kidnap his daughter, Mamie. Soon Elizabeth Edwards had withdrawn her invitation, and a vindicated Robert informed his mother that "a dreadfully disappointed Aunt Lizzie [is] not well enough to have you visit her. . . . You must trust me that I can and will do everything that is for your good and you must not allow yourself to think otherwise for in that you will retard the recovery that I am looking for." With that, he left for his summer vacation at Rye Beach, New York.[62]

In his absence his mother pressed Myra Bradwell for the means of her release from what she now called a prison. Soon a reporter from the *Chicago Times* interviewed an entirely rational Mrs. Lincoln. Then, in late August, Myra Bradwell traveled to Springfield to persuade Elizabeth Edwards to reissue her invitation. Now Judge Bradwell played his part. On August 18 the Chicago papers received a copy of his letter to Dr. Patterson, in which the judge, acting as "Mrs. Lincoln's friend and legal advisor," threatened a warrant of habeas corpus. "I am satisfied," wrote Bradwell, "that Mrs. Lincoln does not require to be confined in a house for the insane and that it would be greatly for her good to be allowed to visit her relatives and friends. She pines for liberty. Some of the best medical men in America say that it is shameful to lock Mrs. Lincoln up behind grates as she has been. I believe that such confinement is injurious."[63]

It was, as Robert Lincoln later complained, "an extraordinary interference," though from his mother's perspective an effective one. For no matter how much Robert condemned Myra and Judge Bradwell as "pests and nuisances," their public campaign had dampened Superintendent Patterson's desire to keep his notorious inmate. Near bankruptcy (four months later Patterson signed Bellevue over to his son), Patterson could ill afford bad publicity, and before Mary Lincoln left, he protected himself by making her swear that she had never been treated "unkindly or improperly." To defend himself in the newspapers, Patterson created an arcane distinction between patients who needed interdiction and those who needed restraint, announcing that Mary Lincoln was much improved but still of an unsound mind and in need of restraint. Then he denied issuing—and withdrawing—any certificate of restored reason, as some newspapers claimed he had. Still, wrote the vacillating superintendent, "if Mrs. Lincoln should secure a quiet home for herself, I should favor it unless her condition should change for the worse."[64]

Her son disagreed. Having found a convenient way to get rid of his inconvenient mother, he opposed her release and paid $341 of her money for the expert opinion of two outside consultants. One, the same Dr. McFarland who had incarcerated Elizabeth Packard, doubted the safety of Mary Lincoln's removal to Springfield "unless she was all the time under the care of some discreet responsible person." In Dr. McFarland's pessimistic prognosis, the next months and years were a critical time. "Unless the utmost quietude is observed, unless success is soon achieved, she will regress and all reasonable hope of restoration must be abandoned."[65]

Even with McFarland's support, Robert Lincoln had been outmaneuvered. With the Bradwells prepared for a court hearing "to open the prison doors" and Patterson's resolve flagging as bad publicity mounted, Robert acceded. On September 11, 1875, the accuser met his victim in the Chicago railroad terminal. Then son and mother, accompanied by the "competent white person" requested by Elizabeth Edwards, took the train to Springfield.

IT had been thirty-six years since the twenty-one-year-old Mary Todd had come from Lexington, in the spring of 1839, to live in Elizabeth and Ninian Edwards's house on Second Street. Fifteen years had passed since the damp, drizzly day in early February 1861 when she and her husband had left for Washington and the White House. After Lincoln's death she had returned only twice for brief visits. Now, in the fall of 1875, Mary Lincoln came back to Springfield, a convicted lunatic, with no husband, child, or home.

Like everything else in the city, the Edwardses' rambling brick mansion on Second Street had changed. Despite Edwards's financial reverses, there was a new kitchen wing and a new railing around the veranda. Inside the house the heavy rosewood and mahogany furniture was the same, though during times of family prosperity Elizabeth Edwards had managed to replace the black horsehair upholstery on the parlor furniture with elegant embroidered brocatelle.

Mary Lincoln had seen neither her brother-in-law nor sister since the Civil War. Now in his mid-sixties, craggy-faced, goateed Ninian Edwards was still erect, though the glorious black mane of hair so admired by the Lexington girls during his youthful days as a law student had turned white. He remained active in civic affairs and had just authored a plan to save Springfield's public schools. At sixty-two sister Elizabeth still favored the lantern-jawed Parkers and not, as Mary Lincoln and Ann Smith did, the moon-faced Todds. In her prim high-necked silk dresses, hair parted in the middle and tied tightly in a bun, Elizabeth Edwards resembled the sensible grandmother that she aspired to be. (Ten years before, she had written her daughter that the only things she cared about were her home, children, and grandchildren.) These days Elizabeth Edwards was sometimes sick with heart problems and a persistent cough that Dr. Wallace's successor treated with the conventional remedies of chloral hydrate and opium. In fact, like so many nineteenth-century Americans, she had built up a tolerance. "The doctor says I couldn't take enough opium [by mouth] to allay the pain without affecting me unpleasantly."[66]

In the months to come, Mary Lincoln saw that Springfield had changed, too. Now there were gas lamps on most streets, not just on the downtown corners, as had been the case in her day. There were more sidewalks, though a few roads remained as impassably muddy as they had been when she and Mercy Levering had jumped to town on wooden slats and had ridden back on the drayman's cart. No one seemed to call First Street Todd Street anymore, and across town the house at

Eighth and Jackson needed a new coat of paint.

But Springfield's most conspicuous transformation—its physical growth—was everywhere apparent. The Edwards house was now inside a city, not, as it had been in Mary Lincoln's day, on the edge of the flower-flecked prairie she had described to Merce. What was once open field had been surveyed and set off in blocks, sixteen houses to a lot. In fifteen years Springfield had become a small city of 25,000 inhabitants with six banks, twenty-two hotels, two bowling alleys, and an astonishing eighty saloons. During her absence, a new railroad line had been built through the city parallel to the Chicago and Alton line on Third Street. She could hear the steam engines, as well as the noise from the construction on the new State Capitol, scheduled to be completed by the next year's centennial. The structure's onion-shaped dome had not yet been placed on its tower, giving the building an unfinished look that may have reminded Mary Lincoln of the U.S. Capitol in 1861. Set on a slope, the new statehouse was already high enough to ruin the view from the Edwardses'. No longer could the residents on Aristocrat's Hill look down on a country town, as they had in the old days.[67]

Mary Lincoln spent the next year in Springfield, living with her sister and battling her son for the restoration of her property. The law had required that within thirty days of her conviction of lunacy a conservator be granted control of her property for at least a year—as was the case for idiots and drunkards, who were likewise held to be incompetent. (As a convicted lunatic Mary Lincoln could not even be held responsible for a valid debt, as her son acidly informed the Springfield merchants he thought too eager for her business.) For a year the son who had accused his mother had the power of her pocketbook, from which he doled out $4,599.28 for her board and expenses in Springfield. Expectedly the arrangement infuriated his mother, who, though removed from Dr. Patterson's authority, would not be free until she controlled her money. In Robert Lincoln's mind, however, his mother was incorrigibly insane, and though others did, he never gave her back her reason.[68]

Elizabeth and Ninian Edwards came to see this battle as harmful to both mother and son. "To her proud spirit," Elizabeth advised her nephew two months after Mary Lincoln's arrival, "it is very galling awaiting the time when right of person and property will be restored to her."[69] On this ground Mary Lincoln organized a final battle of her lifelong militancy.

At first Robert Lincoln was intransigent. As he informed his intimates Leonard Swett and David Davis, his mother had been released against his wishes, and like them, he regarded her as "unsound in mind and not to be trusted with the power of impoverishing herself." Mary Lincoln was correct that only under pressure would her son surrender the conservatorship and release her bonds, her trunks (she had kept the keys), and her income.[70]

Not that Robert was using the money for himself. In fact, he kept scrupulous accounts and proudly noted that during his stewardship he had saved enough of his mother's money to buy two $1,000 bonds. (Part of the surplus came from his monthly repayments for the West Washington Street house she had sold him at half price.) Still, it rankled him that his mother spent $5,000 during nine months in Springfield; this was less than one-half her annual income but more than his own in these early years of his law practice. Had she remained at Bellevue, he calculated that he could add $4,000 per year to her holdings.

For a time Elizabeth Edwards tried to justify her sister's expenses to her nephew. "I quite agreed with her," she wrote Robert, "that her dust-soiled veil bonnet and shawl were too shabby for her to wear in visiting or churchgoing." Robert responded that she had bought four bonnets in the week before her trial and did not need any more. No one could convince him that his mother's compulsion to shop, which he considered derangement because in his eyes she neither used nor needed her purchases, was, as Elizabeth Edwards recognized, "the only available pleasure" in a miserable existence marred by tragedies beyond human imagining. "I hesitate to presume to oppose what I really think she is entitled to," Elizabeth advised her nephew. But Robert Lincoln, who was still his mother's beneficiary, denied the innocuousness of her addiction.[71]

What did it matter if his mother spent all her money? the Edwardses inquired. Her insurance policy was the government pension. To this Robert Lincoln responded that he had reason to believe that Congress would repeal his mother's pension, though there was never any such official discussion, even when the Democrats became the majority party in the House. Even if the pension ended, according to Elizabeth Edwards, Mary Lincoln could have a permanent home with them. As his aunt and uncle politely pressed the termination of his conservatorship, the nephew remained adamant: "[S]upposing her to be insane, . . . is it not better to give her every opportunity to develop her vagaries . . . than get her discharge and . . . perhaps [she would] ruin herself before I could stop it."[72]

As Mary Lincoln's advocate, Elizabeth Edwards finally shared a family secret, intended as womanly advice for her nephew. Like him, she had a household member who was nervous and difficult. "For six months my daughter was also decidedly flighty as to be closely guarded. . . . [H]er back from irritants to this day is scarred its length. At the birth of each child [of hers], the same symptoms were shown and severely felt, particularly by her husband, and myself. At no time, has she ever been natural in her demeanor." Elizabeth Edwards did not say so (or at least did not in the fragment of this letter Robert Lincoln chose to keep), but the family had never considered putting her daughter in an asylum.

Yet Elizabeth Edwards's purpose was not to endorse home care. Rather, it was to instruct her nephew that from a tribulation that was worse than her husband's financial reverses, the death of her first child, and the estrangement of the Edwardses and Lincolns during the war, she had learned the lesson of life that she now offered him. "The most availing remedy in life's trials is to let them alone when you have done what you could." To this Robert sternly replied that his mother's case was a matter of duty which he couldn't abandon "if I would."[73]

By late fall Mary Lincoln had convinced the Edwardses that if she had ever been a lunatic, she no longer was one. Both her sister and brother-in-law knew she had always been eccentric and might always be so, as they informed their nephew in separate letters. Still, they were satisfied about the cause of her admittedly erratic behavior in the spring of 1875. It was the result of a fever and the overuse of chloral. "She had used chloral very freely for the purpose of inducing sleep," Elizabeth Edwards wrote Robert Lincoln. Hence the evidence of derangement had arisen from "a temporary physical disorder," not an intractable monomania. "I have no hesitation," she concluded, "in pronouncing her sane and far more reasonable and gentle than in her former years."

To her surprise (for she had read frightening stories about her sister's behavior in the newspapers and had also listened to her nephew's descriptions), Mary Lincoln was consistently cheerful, accommodating, and sociable—the last certain proof of normality in Elizabeth Edwards's mind. "She has dined at Mrs. Smith's, taken tea at sister Frances's, received every visitor with a manifestation of cheerfulness and pleasure as surprised me. The reunion with her family, [the] receiving the calls of former acquaintances and returning visits has already had a very beneficial effect upon her spirits." Edwards agreed and informed Robert Lincoln that "save for the subject of her bonds, she gives less trouble than any person I ever saw . . . [and] is cheerful and happy and in good health. She is very entertaining in conversation, enjoys the society of her friends, returns and receives calls."[74]

But Robert Lincoln had his own informants, and they were sending back different reports. In January he heard that his mother was back in the stores, giving IOUs to merchants. In this he detected the "possible freaks" and "catastrophes" the doctors had warned him to anticipate. After his own investigation Edwards agreed that his sister-in-law did spend "one half the day with the dressmakers and in the stores." Then, after Robert had refused permission and funds for her annual winter pilgrimage to the South, Mary Lincoln threatened her son. Ninian wrote Robert: "Your mother is very embittered and has on several occasions said that she has hired two men to take your life. On this morning we learned she has had a pistol in her pocket." The following day he wrote: "Elizabeth thinks she could get [the pistol] from her but she fears in so doing my daughter Clover would know it and be alarmed. We do not think she would use it for the injury of anyone."[75]

No doubt it was Tad's pistol, either the one bestowed on the youngest Lincoln by a member of the friendly Pennsylvania volunteers guarding the White House in 1861 or the one bought from Gus Gumpert's store in Philadelphia to go with Tad's military costume. In 1863 Abraham Lincoln had telegraphed his wife: "I think you better put Tad's pistol away. I had an ugly dream about him." And so Mary Lincoln had, for each Lincoln took seriously the other's premonitions. After Tad's death the pistol had remained in the steamer trunk with the canvas ducking and imprinted teacup design. In December 1875, after numerous requests, Robert Lincoln had sent this trunk along with two others to Springfield, where it was now stored in the Edwardses' spare room, next to Mary Lincoln's bedroom.[76]

She must have seen the pistol when she was rummaging through her trunks, for she often used her clothes and mementos to recall her bittersweet past. At the time she was angry enough to want her son's life, at least metaphorically, in exchange for the mind, reputation, affection, and money she believed he had stolen from her. As weapons serve the weak, the pistol symbolically redressed the uneven scales between female and male, between mother and son, between insane and sane. Mary Lincoln may well have told someone in Springfield that she had a pistol and "could kill" Robert Lincoln.

At some point Elizabeth Edwards searched her sister's handbag. Finding nothing, she convinced her husband that Mary Lincoln's was an empty threat, the kind of a rhetorical excess that so often got her sister in trouble. Thereafter both Edwardses came to believe the story a hoax—another one of her self-inflicted exorbitances compounded by malevolent gossip. As Edwards advised Leonard Swett, "I have reason now to believe that the story in relation to the pistol was not true."[77]

But now Robert Lincoln had evidence that his mother was nearing another catastrophe, and he prepared to return her to Bellevue. His friends, especially those who had been involved in her trial and felt the need for continuing demonstrations of her insanity, agreed. Leonard Swett asked Ninian Edwards, "Shall we friends of the family permit her to go with a pistol, announcing her purpose to shoot [her son] and shall we permit her to break him down and ruin him by harassing or annoying him?"[78]

This time Mary Lincoln could not be taken by surprise. Now there were supporters like the Bradwells and Edwardses who would testify to her sanity, and there were as well several lawyers fighting the young Lincoln on the conservatorship issue. In the spring of 1876, while Robert Lincoln was seeking the Edwardses' agreement to return his mother to Bellevue, she proposed through her sister and brother-in-law (for mother and son did not communicate directly) that Robert place her bonds in the hands of a Springfield banker, where they would remain undisturbed for the rest of her life. As an incentive she disclosed the details of her current will, which specified Robert Lincoln and his daughter as her beneficiaries.[79]

Her offer contained a veiled threat, for at her direction Judge Bradwell could easily disinherit her son and substitute her very appropriate, favorite charity, the Springfield Home for the Friendless. Still, Robert Lincoln declined her request. The county court would not hear any petition for his removal until early June, when his year of guardianship ended. Besides, as he informed the Edwardses, his friends had pledged nearly $70,000 as his bond. Should his mother lose or spend her money during his guardianship, he would be liable.[80]

Advised of this, Mary Lincoln tried again. Robert Lincoln must surrender his position to another conservator, perhaps former Illinois Governor John Palmer, who had agreed to serve, or one of the New York lawyers she had hired through her old friend Marshall Roberts. Even the matter of Robert's control of her trunks no longer posed a problem after her brother-in-law Clark Smith had offered a storage room in the upstairs of his department store.

Finally, as the end of his year as conservator approached, Robert Lincoln surrendered. In answer to a series of letters from Governor Palmer, he conditionally agreed to his removal. "I can duly say that unless my duty to my mother is barred by the strongest evidence to forbid it, I shall gladly aid in procuring her discharge from the disabilities which are so unpleasant to her."[81]

ON June 15, 1876, the earliest date permitted by law and in the same Chicago courthouse where she had been convicted of lunacy, another jury convened to judge Mary Lincoln's condition. But this time it was Mary Lincoln who had petitioned the court that she was a proper person to have the care and management of her own estate. Ninian Edwards had come up from Springfield to testify to her good behavior during her nine months in his household. Robert Lincoln produced an inventory of assets worth $73,000, including $60,000 worth of bonds, as well as a careful accounting of his conservatorship. This jury had as little difficulty declaring Mary Lincoln "restored to reason and capable to manage and control her estate," as, thirteen months before, another had in finding her non compos mentis.[82]

Robert Lincoln was not pleased. In his view, the jury had extended its prerogative and had failed, in its verdict, to add an important qualification: the fact that Mary Lincoln was a fit person to manage her property did not imply that she was sane. He and Leonard Swett blamed Edwards for their embarrassment. Not only had he twice described Mary Lincoln as a fit person without adding the qualification that her rationality extended only to managing registered bonds, but he had also signed a statement for the newspapers that she was sane— that is, restored to reason.[83]

Edwards wanted no trouble with Robert Lincoln and his influential Chicago friends and so apologized: "The reason for the repetitions in my oral testimony in the case of your mother was because the judge asked me to speak louder. After the case was over and the jury rendered their verdict, a statement was read to me in your presence with a request that I should sign it and I remarked that it contained repetitions but supposing it was for your private use I signed it with the expectation it would be returned to me on my furnishing you with a statement in my handwriting. I had no idea it would be published."

Then for the sake of peace Edwards accepted Robert Lincoln's equivocation that a person might be insane and still fit to manage her property.[84]

In Springfield, where she had anxiously awaited the outcome, an elated Mary Lincoln sent the Edwardses' grandson Lewis Baker to the newspaper office with the card Edwards had signed. She hoped to have this proclamation of her sanity printed in every major American newspaper, or at least those that had noticed her insanity. Now to her son's irritation the news of Mary Lincoln's restored reason flashed across the United States: A HAPPY DENOUEMENT, the *Chicago Times* proclaimed, MRS. ABRAHAM LINCOLN RESTORED TO HER REASON AND FREEDOM.[85]

Without any further need to mask her fury, Mary Lincoln now claimed a daunting restitution from her "monster of mankind son." Unable to write even the salutation "dear" before his name, she addressed a letter, perhaps her last, to Robert T. Lincoln and demanded the return of everything she had ever given him.

> Do not fail to send me without *the least* delay, *all* my paintings, Moses in the Bullrushes included also the fruit picture which hung in your dining room—my silver set with large silver waiter presented me by my New York friends . . . also other articles your wife appropriated and which are *well known* to you, must be sent, without a day's delay. Two lawyers and myself, have just been together and their list, coincides with my own and will be published in a few days. Trust not to the belief, that Mrs. Edwards tongue, has not been *rancorous* against you all winter and she has maintained to the very last, that you dared not venture into her house and our presence. Send me my laces, my diamonds, my jewelry—My unmade silks, white lace dress,—double lace shawl and flounce, lace scarf—2 bk lace shawls—one bk lace deep flounce, white lace sets 1/2 yd in width and eleven yards in length. I am now in constant receipt of letters, from my friends denouncing you in the bitterest terms. . . . Two prominent clergymen, have written me, since I saw you, and mention in their letters, that they think it advisable to offer prayers for you in Church, on account of your wickedness against me and High Heaven. . . . Send me all that I have written for, you have tried your game of robbery long enough.

Then in a postscript Mary Lincoln remembered her engravings and favorite books—"Whittier, Pope, Agnes Strickland's *Queens of England,* other books, you have of mine." And she signed herself "Mrs. A. Lincoln."[86]

In friendlier times, when Robert was still her son, Mary Lincoln had given his family the things she now demanded. Repeatedly she had implored her daughter-in-law to take anything the younger Mrs. Lincoln fancied from the West Washington Street house. From Europe had come similar encouragements: "Do not stint yourself"; "There are some engravings I think you would like"; "I give you full liberty to take and keep for ever and aye." Now Robert Lincoln clipped these sentences from his mother's letters for what he named the Insanity File. Uninterested in his mother's correspondence as a whole, he selected for history those written statements in which his mother had donated the possessions that now she wanted returned.[87]

As it turned out, he kept the diamonds, shawls, and silver, though *Moses and the Bullrushes* and a few other things went back to Springfield. It would be impossible, Leonard Swett advised Edwards, "to return so many things from baby clothes to dress materials. Over the years some things had been lost or stolen such as the beautiful engraved watch Mary Lincoln had given her daughter-in-law as a wedding present. It was," concluded Swett, "not an issue of judgment but one of courage for Robert to keep these gifts." Instead, according to Swett, Lincoln would send specific items, and their return was by no means an admission of his impropriety. Meanwhile, as final testament to her filial disownment, Mary Lincoln returned everything she had of Robert's, which was not much, for their gift giving had been as one-sided as their affection. Still, she sent his set of Charles Dickens's works.[88]

Mary Lincoln never forgave Robert Lincoln and so ended her life childless. He had committed an unforgivable breach by bankrupting an already impoverished self. Not time or distance or even the isolation of her remaining years could surmount this rebuke. Henceforth she blamed him for making her a displaced person, for she saw that her son's need to justify his actions would always make him suspicious and ready, at any sign of her instability, to send forth his detectives and doctors. There was also the matter of public opinion. As Mary Lincoln told Elizabeth Edwards, "my former friends will never cease to regard me as a lunatic. I feel it in their soothing manner. If I should say the moon is made of green cheese, they would heartily and smilingly agree with me. I love you but I cannot stay in Springfield. I would be much less unhappy in the midst of strangers."[89]

XII

Last Years

ELIZABETH EDWARDS was surprised. For weeks her sister
had been impatient to go. Then, in September 1876,
when the train to Chicago was leaving the Springfield
depot, at the last moment Mary Lincoln had what
Elizabeth called a gush of anguish. Embracing her sister, she delivered a sobbing farewell: "I go an exile and
alone. Will you not join me in Europe next year?"[1]

Since June Elizabeth Edwards had been trying to
persuade her sister not to go at all—at least not alone
to Europe. No doubt Springfield held memories of a
dead husband and sons, but there were other places in
the United States that carried no such punishing associations. Both Edwardses had argued with Mary about
the need to put an ocean between herself and her son,
especially now that Mary Lincoln had control of her
money. To the threadbare Edwardses, $8,100 a year
(the $3,000 annual government pension, the $3,600
interest on her bonds, and the $1,500 loan repayment
by Robert) seemed more than enough for a single
woman. Granted, Mary Lincoln could not afford a home
of her own; still, her income delivered independence

and, if necessary (though the Edwardses did not think it was), protection from Robert Lincoln.

But Mary Lincoln could not forget. And as she made her plans to emigrate during a summer when Americans were celebrating their nation's centennial, she reminded the Edwardses that Robert Lincoln had sent a sane woman—his own mother—to an institution. Who could guarantee he would not do so again? Through his "cruel persecution," she would carry to her grave the stigma of madness. In the meantime, she refused to live where stares and whispers acknowledged lunacy and where her son and his doctor friends could threaten her freedom whenever they wished. Only among foreigners, who attended other scandals and who would not, as she had learned in Germany, care about Mrs. Lincoln, could she be anonymous. If solitude was the cost of privacy, she was willing to pay that price—at least for the time being.[2]

Impatient to leave before winter closed the Atlantic to an old woman traveling alone, Mary Lincoln enjoined Elizabeth Edwards to secrecy. Her son must not know her plans until she was gone. Then her vengeance demanded that he be held responsible for her banishment. As Mary Lincoln packed her trunks (at least the ones she was not storing in Springfield), she put in her black widow's weeds and exquisite peau de soie nightgowns to be carried overseas along with a well-worn image of herself as an outcast driven from her native land by her son, "a wretched young man but old in sin."[3]

Mary Lincoln left Springfield exactly a year after her return from the Bellevue asylum. In Europe she would be spectacularly alone, but at least for her journey to New York she had a companion in the Edwardses' grandson Lewis Baker, who stayed in Springfield with his grandparents rather than in Argentina, where his father was the newly appointed consul in Buenos Aires. An aspiring journalist, Lewis took a professional interest in Great-aunt Mary's anecdotes of wartime Washington as well as her impersonations of famous generals and politicians.

For Mary Lincoln, young Baker was more than an appreciative audience. Sometime during their year together in the Edwards home he had become Tad incarnate. Nearly the same age as Tad when he died, Baker had her dead son's "intelligence, good looks and sweet sympathy—Love crowned you at your birth," she flattered her 17-year-old nephew, remembering a bottle of water from the Jordan River that she had sent from Washington for his baptism. Rather than the remoteness of a great-aunt, she offered a mother's intrusiveness, insisting that he avoid a career in either politics or journalism, that he go to college, and that he learn more about the world. Mary Lincoln intended to show him some of it on their trip to New York.[4]

They began in Kentucky, traveling south from Chicago to Cincinnati, then across the Ohio River, and by railroad on the Southern line through Williamstown and Georgetown into Lexington. The unfamiliar views of Fayette County previewed the changes that awaited Mary Lincoln in a city she had not visited for twenty-five years. Baker had never seen his grandmother's birthplace or his grandfather's university, and his great-aunt meant to serve as a guide to their family places, though as it turned out, many had disappeared.

Ellerslie, the imperious but now decaying brick mansion of her grandfather Levi Todd, was still standing on the Richmond Pike, and so was Grandma Parker's home on Short Street, though it had been redesigned by the architect living there. A fire had gutted her birthplace next door, and during the Union army's evacuation of the city in 1862, her father's storeroom had also burned. Nearby the Main Street house of Betsey Todd's sovereignty survived, though it was now a boardinghouse soon to be enveloped by Lexington's commercial district. A new mill straddled Elkton Creek, where, years before, the Todd children had played Big Indian and Hurl Ball. And a stranger lived in John Ward's schoolhouse.

Relatives had disappeared, too. In Mary Lincoln's youth every Lexingtonian and most of Fayette County knew of the Parkers and Todds. Now, after the upheaval of Reconstruction, Prather's Directory listed, among the 17,000 residents within the expanded city limits, almost as many blacks as whites. Most had never heard of her ancestors, though they no doubt knew about Mary Lincoln. In fact, there were only eight white Parkers in Lexington, and of the five Todds living there in the fall of 1876, two were white and three black. Second cousin Alex Parker continued to sell dry goods on Main Street, while his invalid brother Robert had retired. Wilford Parker (Mary may have been unsure whether he was Alexander or James Parker's grandson) was a miller, pursuing a traditional family occupation. As for the Todds, Levi turned out to be a black porter at the Williams shop, but first cousin Lyman Beecher Todd still practiced medicine on Upper Street.

One afternoon she and Baker found some of the missing Todds in the Lexington cemetery. Slightly behind and entirely overshadowed by the tall obelisk dedicated to Henry Clay (in death as in life the relationship of Clay to the Todds remained the same), the Todd lot was crowded with new graves. Stepmother Betsey had died in 1874, and following her instructions, her daughters had commissioned a substantial twenty-foot monument inscribed, without birthdate, "Elizabeth H. Todd" on one side and on the other, "In memory of my beloved sons—all Confederate soldiers—Samuel B., David H., and Alexander H." Consistent in her partiality, she had not marked her stepson Levi's grave, though from the cemetery records Mary Lincoln knew he was somewhere in the Todd lot. No doubt the size and politics of Betsey Todd's memorial outraged Mary Lincoln. By comparison her parents' graves were no more than stepping-stones on the path to her stepmother's monument. In Lexington, at least, her stepmother had had the final word.[5]

Mary Lincoln did not leave Kentucky without showing Lewis Baker the state's principal wonder: the Mammoth Cave, south of Lexington in Hart County. Every Kentuckian of her generation knew the story of the pioneer who had discovered the subterranean labyrinths while bear hunting, just as every child had believed the place haunted by the wandering spirits who in young Mary Todd's imagination traveled as far as Lexington. Once the Todds had visited the caverns, for Mammoth Cave was near Crab Orchard Springs, and there was a respectable hotel at Cave City. Now, a half century later, Mary Lincoln and Lewis Baker walked the menacing underground avenues. On the way back to Lexington the road ran close to her husband's birthplace in Hodgenville and his second home at Knob Creek, Kentucky. Perhaps, though there is no evidence, they also stopped there.

In any case great-aunt and nephew were soon on their way to the northeast and Philadelphia's centennial exhibition. There Mary Lincoln toured displays designed to celebrate the greatness of a nation she believed her husband had saved. To her delight, one artist had placed Lincoln atop a tower marked the "U.S. Constitution," which was the focus of a huge oil canvas entitled *An Historical Monument of the American Republic.* There were other reminders of Lincoln, but Lewis Baker probably spent as much time watching the tireless Corliss engine empower thousands of smaller machines. In 1876 machines, not men, were the most popular exhibits in Philadelphia, and they, not the remembrance of dead Presidents, established the national genius of America's first century.

From Philadelphia Mary Lincoln and Lewis Baker went on to New York and there spent a week, she shopping and keeping "aloof" from friends, he sight-seeing. Having renounced the theater after her husband's assassination, she left him to go alone to the season's fare—Mrs. Howard in *Uncle Tom's Cabin,* Barnum's circus, and Madame Puppenheim in *Die Walküre.* Then, on October 1, Lewis Baker completed his mission, helping his aunt board the steamship *Labrador* from the Transatlantic Company's pier at the bottom of Barrow Street. The weather was cool, but amid the excitement of gangplank raising and horn blowing, Mary Lincoln, along with forty-eight other passengers, stayed on deck. This time she had a witness to her departure.[6]

Twelve days later she arrived in Le Havre. In a letter to Lewis Baker, who was now back in Springfield, she described her recovery from her third stormy crossing of the Atlantic. Now she planned to go by steamer south to the French port of Bordeaux and from there by train the five hours to her final destination at Pau, in southwestern France near the Spanish border.

Mary Lincoln had never been to Pau before she decided to live there, but she had heard and read about the place for years. In the 1850s Sarah Ellis, the wife of an English missionary, had popularized its glories in a breathless account of sunny days spent in the city at the foot of the Pyrenees. A few years later an English physician, Dr. Alexander Taylor, had transformed Mrs. Ellis's amateurish enthusiasm into a full-fledged scientific explanation of Pau's medicinal powers. According to Dr. Taylor, the city's climate relieved most symptoms of illness. The air was fresh, the barometric pressure constant, the humidity low, and warm mineral springs were available in the nearby mountains. Nervous patients especially benefited from the calm atmosphere, which kept blood and bile constant and, like a bromide, moderated the nerve-draining organic exchanges of the body. Wind, in Dr. Taylor's estimation, was bad for nerves, and his measurements established Pau as one of the stillest places on earth. An American visitor agreed. The poet and writer William Cullen Bryant pronounced the city a treasure of silence and slumber, a place where the murmur of Pyrenean streams rushing downward to the river at the city's southern boundary could be heard for miles and where, when a gentle breeze came from the south, the smell of balsam and pine perfumed the promenades.[7]

By the 1870s, when Mary and Tad Lincoln were living in Germany, Pau was on the lips of those wealthy invalids who roved about Europe, searching for healthy places in the sun. Young Mary Louisa Newberry of Chicago had died there, although other acquaintances had survived to promote its healing powers. Then a Dresden publishing house circulated Mrs. Griffin's *Vagaries from the Notebook of a Traveller,* in which Pau emerged not only as a health spa but as a tourist's find—the cradle of the Bourbons. (Henry IV had been born in the château that furnished the city's only legitimate historical attraction.) In 1870, when Sally Orne needed a quiet retreat for her sick daughter, Mary Lincoln had recommended Pau.[8]

Of course, Mary Lincoln also chose Pau because she spoke French. With self-preservation foremost, she needed to understand the language, as she had not in Germany, where Tad had helped. There were other French cities, but she knew Nice, Cannes, and Paris as noisy, expensive, and full of overdressed Americans, while Vichy, the best known of French spas, had a reputation for being dirty. On the basis of language and politics ("I could not ever rest in France without it was a Republic"), she dismissed Italy, Spain, and Germany. She found the English climate as impossible as the people. So she went to Pau and within months of her arrival proudly informed her banker that "the French cannot take advantage of me as is frequently done with strangers who do not understand their language. Happily I am not in the latter category."[9]

The city of 30,000 to which Mary Lincoln came in October 1876 had changed since Sarah Ellis's day. Before the Franco-Prussian War, the city fathers had been content with a minor reputation as a health station near the Pyrenean spas and a refuge for the human swallows of winter the French labeled *hivernants.* Then after the war, in the glory days of France's Third Republic, Pau underwent a civic reformation. Hotels were renovated or, if they interfered with views of the Pyrenees, leveled. The grand promenade on the Boulevard des Pyrénées, with its panoramic view of the river valley and distant mountains, was extended and widened. There was talk of a new luxury hotel and a casino. A famous chef was lured from Paris and installed in the newly built and very grand Gassion Hotel, where he presided over the creation of pigeon dishes and complex cassoulets, sometimes served to as many as 1,500 guests. In aggressive pursuit of the Belle Époque tourist, the municipal bureau published an English newspaper in which news of the international community appeared. The *Journal of Strangers,* along with Galignani's *Messenger,* chronicled the royalty that visited Pau, lending it a special cachet: Queen Isabella of Spain, Prince Fernando of Portugal, Princess Amelia of Schleswig-Holstein, and Abdul el Kader of Morocco. The newspaper also noted the arrival of one of Mary Lincoln's favorite authors, Baron Lytton, and in November 1876

Mrs. Lincoln's name appeared, though she was located in the wrong hotel, with the notation that she was traveling "in strictest incognito."[10]

To her surprise, Mary Lincoln discovered that Pau had become a little bit of England, with British doctors, dentists, chemists, Presbyterian and Anglican churches, tea parties (the lack of tea had been one of Sarah Ellis's complaints), toasts to the queen, and, especially in the 1870s, British sports. Perhaps because of its early promotions by English travelers and doctors, perhaps because of its recent inclusion on a Cook's tour, the capital of the French province of Béarn now resounded with the cries of polo players and cricket fans. In Beaumont Park English families promenaded and heard the Eighteenth French Infantry band play a Gallic rendition of "God Save the Queen." Beyond the park, in the countryside, the Cercle Anglaise organized fox hunts, renaming their quarries' lairs with an ethnocentricism that sometimes angered the natives—Leicestershire, Old England, and Home Circuit. When the city fathers took a census of the population in 1878, the results confirmed the obvious: Well over half the 6,000 *hivernants* were English, and among the permanent population of 350 foreign families, 164 were British, with Mary Lincoln included in the 39 American households.

Only the center of town—the streets around the Palais Royale and Nouvelle Halle—resisted Anglicization. There in the Grand Hotel, on the elegant chestnut- and sycamore-lined square, Mary Lincoln first settled. A few months later her hotel was demolished, and she moved to the cheaper Henri Quatre in the noisy market square, across from the English reading rooms.

After hearing from Mary, Elizabeth Edwards predicted that her sister would soon weary of her isolation and come home. She was wrong. Although Mary Lincoln took two long trips—one to Italy in the winter of 1878 and another to Marseilles and Avignon two years later—and though she spent most of the summer in the mountain spas outside town, Pau was headquarters (nowhere was home anymore) for the next four years. "I live, very much alone," she wrote in 1877, "and do not identify myself with the [French]—have a few friends and prefer to remain secluded—My *Gethsemane* is ever with me. . . ."[11] The biblical reference conveyed her sense of betrayal, in her case not by a friend but by a perfidious son.

EXPECTING to be as quiet as windless Pau, Mary Lincoln was soon embroiled in money problems. Not that the city tested her extravagance, for despite its claims as a luxury resort, Pau's best stores opened only during the season. By April Mary Lincoln could not even find suitable lace among the local merchants. What upset her was not the temptation of extravagance but rather the danger of poverty posed by the erratic delivery of her funds. Money had caused her imprisonment in a mental institution; through its conscientious management, she meant to establish her competency, and sometimes this was a nerve-racking challenge.[12]

Before leaving Springfield, she had recruited Jacob Bunn as her financial agent. For a time the two had detested each other. Bunn had publicly condemned Mary Lincoln's old clothes sale, and in return she had privately pronounced him a war profiteer unscrupulously risen from the ranks of small-time grocers to first place among Springfield's wealthy. But time had softened mutual disdain, and after she had deposited $60,000 of United States bonds in Bunn's bank, he agreed to collect, change into francs, and send to Pau her annual interest of $3,600, along with her two other sources of income: Robert Lincoln's loan repayment of $125 a month and her quarterly pension of $750.

But when she arrived in Pau nearly penniless after her transatlantic trip, she found that her money was not there; at least she was unable to find it for several days. Thereafter Mary Lincoln lived with the unsettling prospect of delays and, even worse, lost checks. In 1877 "my lawful allowance," due in March, did not reach her until summer. Sometimes she held the "unprincipled heartless avaricious French" responsible, and in an effort at better security she cautioned Bunn to send two envelopes and omit his name from the outside.[13]

More often it was the cumbersome system, not the covetous French, that accounted for the delays. First Bunn received the pension certificates from the U.S. Pension Bureau in Chicago; then he sent them overseas for Mary Lincoln's signature and their notarization by the British consul. She returned the signed and notarized papers to Bunn, who sent them to the redoubtable Miss Sweet of the Chicago office of the Pension Bureau, who sometimes rejected them. In that case the entire process had to begin again. Once the British consul suggested that her legal name as a widow was Mary Todd Lincoln and that she must so sign her documents, but she refused to be anything other than Mrs. Abraham Lincoln. Finally, if Miss Sweet deemed everything correct, she sent the quarterly payment of $750 to Bunn, who changed it to francs—usually at the rate of four and a half to the dollar—and sent a check for that amount to Mrs. Lincoln.[14]

Punctilious about her financial affairs, Mary Lincoln answered Bunn's letters the day they arrived, informing him well in advance of her bankers' addresses when she traveled. For Bunn, theirs was a business correspondence requiring more than fifty letters a year. For Mary Lincoln, running her affairs was an exercise in self-government that demonstrated Robert Lincoln's persecution. Still, when the money did not come on time, her nervousness surfaced in repetitious directions to Bunn, though redundancy and underlining had always been her style. Sometimes there was desperation, as in a letter to Bunn in June 1877: "There are now two pensions due me, that of March 4th and June 4th. The proceeds I am needing *very greatly,* and as I have sent you 3 pension papers signed within the last four weeks, wanting two days, I can but hope that a *very few days* will elapse, *ere* I receive my money from the Pensions, *one* of them *now* due me, so long." Finally the money came, but five months late.[15]

Gradually "my little business" became an absorbing enterprise. She followed the exchange rates avariciously, understood the influence of gold on national currencies, kept an accurate list of her bonds, and turned dollars to gold and francs with an accountant's dexterity. Conservative fiscal management had finally defeated speculation and deficit financing. Now on her own, Mary Lincoln refused to owe money to anyone. When four bonds matured in 1880, the Edwardses suggested that a better return of 8 percent could be realized from real estate or mortgage investments. "I prefer," she informed Bunn in 1879, "the four bonds reinvested in the safest and most remunerative bonds. I wish nothing to do with property and mortgages." Then she directed her banker to invest in government bonds paying no less than six percent: "I cannot afford to lose a dollar on the interest."[16]

Just as with her previous trespass into male politics, Mary Lincoln was uneasy with her unconventional interference in the man's world of business, apologizing time and time again for pursuing her affairs in a "womanly-like way," for "troubling you too much," and for "managing my money with the dullness of a woman," though she believed the British consul more incompetent than she. True ladies did not mix in money matters, so her success at managing her affairs, like her excellence in schoolwork years before, was more a cause for self-depreciation than pride. Thus, when Bunn's bank failed and she thought his creditors might seize her money, she begged pardon for her ignorance. Once Mary Lincoln knew the bonds to be safe, "if I had *four* times, as much as I now have, most willingly would I place it in your hands for safe-keeping."[17]

In the winter of 1878 Mary Lincoln took her maid, joined an unnamed woman friend in Marseilles, and traveled to Rome, Naples, and Sorrento. On her return nearly three months later, she visited Vichy, where the thermal waters proved no more therapeutic for her arthritis than those available an hour from Pau at Les Eaux-Bonnes and St.-Sauveur-les-Bains, where she went in the summers when the city was too bright and sunny. (In Pau even Englishmen carried parasols at noontime on bright summer days.) Italy, she wrote, was soft and pleasant, but she had been there before and so compared not the sights but her levels of melancholy. "As sorrowful as I then was, my grief has greatly intensified." As a result, Italy neither distracted nor amused. "I take no interest whatever in [these] fresh scenes and objects."[18]

Even new places could not rouse her from self-scrutiny. Not Paris, where she went to arrange for trunks of warm clothing to be sent to the still-impecunious Frances Wallace, or Avignon, where she had never been but fell sick on a visit in 1880, or even the seaside resorts of Biarritz and St.-Jean-de-Luz, where Eugénie (whom she had demoted to ex-empress) had a château and where the shoreline bluffs piqued the imagination of the most jaded travelers. Nothing moved Mary Lincoln. "To the deeply bereaved," she wrote Lewis Baker in 1879, "grand mansions and broad lands, enter but little into thoughts—and yet," she added in testimony to her mental and physical endurance, "whilst we have life, there is a positive necessity for the means of subsistence."[19]

Then Ulysses and Julia Grant came to Pau and snubbed Mary Lincoln. The former President was traveling around the world and, en route from Madrid to Paris in December of 1879, stopped in Pau. No matter how tarnished Grant's reputation at home, the town fathers welcomed their first American President with parades, receptions, and an elegant dinner at the Hôtel de France. Here local society gathered to meet the famous American and to enjoy a six-course meal of Bearnais foie gras, pigeon, Château Margaux burgundy, and for dessert the chef's special creation of egg whites—bombe à la Vicksburg.

While Julia Grant prattled to her French hosts in English (the general's wife had solved the language barrier by offering soliloquies in English to uncomprehending audiences of foreign speakers), Mary Lincoln was being helped to bed by her maid in a back room of a nearby hotel. Later Julia Grant explained her failure to call on a White House predecessor as a mistake, though it was more likely her repayment for past slights. "The night before we left [Pau] we learned that Mrs. Abraham Lincoln was there and I was very very sorry we had not learned this sooner, as it was now too late to make her a visit. We had our tickets and our train and a party was with us. We could not at this late hour change our plans."[20]

Earlier Mary Lincoln would have erupted in anger at such rudeness; now she hardly cared. A minimal existence without family or intimates had reinforced the internal emptiness of "my great desolation." Alone in Pau, what she felt matched how she lived, and the quiet French city became the graveyard of a lifelong struggle for notoriety. By any standard, though especially her own, her life had been a misery, but having experienced the worst, she meant to survive. So amid the grandeur of the city's scenery and elegant sociability, she became an outsider who looked and watched but no longer participated.

Still, Mary Lincoln was no hermit. Reading (she managed to finish five volumes of François Guizot's *L'Histoire de la France*), walking along the Boulevard des Pyrénées, and writing letters sometimes turned loneliness into tolerable solitude. With outsiders she risked little, save a few light friendships with female friends, such as the baronne de Bunnecker. Accustomed to triumphs closely escorted by tragedies, Mary Lincoln was amazed that nothing happened to her in Pau and joked to Lewis Baker that she was incorrectly placed in such an eventless latitude. Unlike the scenery, life had become a flat, barren place, where she awaited the end of her separation from "the noblest and purest, most talented sons and husband."[21]

For the first time in her life Mary Lincoln gave up politics, though there were lapses. She continued to subscribe to American newspapers, including the *Illinois State Journal*. When she read that President Rutherford Hayes had appointed a Tennessee Confederate to his cabinet, she bristled at "this great mistake," though she believed it was to be expected from the inferior men who followed her husband to the White House. Then she opposed Julia Tyler's campaign for a presidential widow's pension on the same ground that some had opposed her own: "A woman who was so bitter against our cause during the War with, much Northern property and money . . . so *fearful* a Secessionist—Our Republican leaders will, I am sure, remember ALL THIS and the Country will not have fallen upon such evil times as to grant her impudent request."[22] Clearly Mary Lincoln's reconstruction policies had no room for the pardons and amnesty of her husband or his successors.

Then, in 1879, she spied a column that described Robert Lincoln and Stephen Douglas as presidential prospects for the 1880 campaign. As she had often done for her husband, Mary Lincoln created an imaginary cabinet of "superior" persons for her son's administration. "In the event of success" she pictured a continuation of the Lincoln dynasty with granddaughter Mamie (but no mention of her daughter-in-law or two other grandchildren) gracing the White House.[23]

Mostly, though, she reserved her passion for sorrow and anger, the first nourished by the remembrance of her own and others' afflictions, the latter kept alive by her feud with her son. When Empress Eugénie's only son was killed in a battle in Zululand, Mary Lincoln understood: "The Ex-Empress is alone and desolate like my own very sorrowful self." When Elizabeth Edwards's grandchild died, Mary Lincoln offered her sister the special sympathy that only a practiced mourner could provide. "I have drank [*sic*] so deeply of the cup of sorrow, in my desolate bereavements, that I am always prepared to sympathize, with all those who suffer, but when it comes *so close* to us, and when I remember that precocious, happy child, with its loving parents—what can I say? In grief, words are a poor consolation—silence and agonizing tears are all, that is left the sufferer."[24]

Grief alternated with anger, and Mary Lincoln stayed alive by hating the bad son. She recalled to Lewis Baker her son's childhood as a "troublemaker, always trying to obtain mastery in the family." Then his father had controlled him, though "it was a great relief to us when he was sent East to school." Now, with Lincoln dead, Robert Lincoln had become "more insolent than ever," eventually forcing her into an institution and out of the United States. After three years in Pau, Mary Lincoln wanted to come home but could not because of him. "How much I long to see you all," she advised Elizabeth Edwards's grandson in 1879, "to have a taste of your Grandma's good food— *waffles, batter cakes,* egg corn bread are *all* unknown here—as to biscuits, light rolls they have never been dreamed of—not to speak of *buckwheat* cakes." Pau might be a sanctuary in a homeless world, but "a long period of absence from America is not agreeable, but to an oppressed heart-broken woman it is simply an *exile*"—the final deprivation of a perpetual victim.[25]

Meanwhile, she prayed—for herself, of course, so that "the ruler of us all will reconcile and soften the pathway I have been called upon to tread," and occasionally for her son, who, in her judgment, needed it. Temporarily religion had replaced spiritualism, though the two had coexisted for many years. "God wills it and we must bow to his irrevocable decrees" became Mary Lincoln's rendition of the Book of Job. But her faith carried more Old Testament vengeance than Christian compassion. "God does not allow sin to go unpunished," she hoped. Certainly Robert Lincoln had "a fearful account yet to render to his Maker."[26]

In Springfield, Elizabeth Edwards continued her efforts to bring about a reconciliation between mother and son, so that Mary Lincoln could come home. "Of one thing be certain," wrote the ever-loyal sister to the widow, "I love you dearly and sympathize with you deeply, nothing that I can do shall be spared to make you as comfortable as in my power." She meanwhile demanded the first concession of her nephew. The son must write his mother, for he had been the aggressor. Stiffly he refused: "I am afraid a letter from me would not be well received." He disclaimed any future intentions to interfere in his mother's life. "I therefore hope that no fear of me will prevent my mother from returning to America. Under no possible circumstances would I control her in any way—not only have I no reason to think that such interference is now or will hereafter be proper but whatever I might think afterward, I would under no circumstance do anything." And then, in the self-referencing style he had learned at his mother's knee, he announced that he had suffered enough because of Mary Lincoln. "The ordinary troubles and distresses of life are enough without such as that."[27]

Later Robert Lincoln omitted his mother's four-year exile in Europe from his self-protective recollections of her life. With an astonishing lapse of memory, he informed a publisher in 1914 that "my father's death had deranged my mother so much that she had become dangerous to herself. She was placed in a private asylum and after a prolonged stay there she went to my aunt's. Her health seemed to improve so much there that my aunt undertook to care for her in her house. This she did until my mother's death in 1882."[28]

IN 1880, at the age of sixty-two, Mary Lincoln had to come home. Her health had deteriorated until she could no longer live alone. A cataract had formed on her right eye, she had lost what she called "her great bloat" in the enfeebling process of aging until she weighed only

100 pounds, and her arthritis forced her to the thermal baths frequently. Then, while hanging a picture in her room in December 1879, she fell from a ladder, injuring an already arthritic spine on the corner of a table. Now she added a broken back to the broken heart of her figurative complaints. Four months later she fell again when her left side gave way on a flight of stairs. Plasters and bed rest helped, but in October 1880 she wrote Lewis Baker to meet her in New York at the end of the month. "I cannot trust myself any longer away from you all. I am too ill and feeble in health."[29]

Alone save for her trunks, Mary Lincoln left Pau as she had come—on a steamer from Le Havre. This time it was the *Amérique,* and she shared a rough passage with the actress Sarah Bernhardt. As famous now as Mary Lincoln had been fifteen years before, the Divine Sarah was on her way to the United States for her first American tour. Bernhardt had worried about the *Amérique,* for it was well known in France as a bad-luck ship, but this time only the weather interfered with the crossing.

One early morning the two women met on deck when, in Bernhardt's account, "a wild billow dashed so violently against our boat that we were both thrown down." Bernhardt clung to a bench. On the wet deck Mary Lincoln slid dangerously close to a staircase until at the last moment the actress grabbed the widow's skirts. "You might have been killed down that horrible staircase," said Bernhardt, no doubt in the throaty voice her audiences adored. Mary Lincoln replied, with a sigh of regret, "it was not God's will." Then Mary Lincoln stepped back, and drawing herself up, her face very pale and her brows knitted, she said in a scarcely audible voice, "I am the widow of President Lincoln." With an actress's appreciation of tragedy, Bernhardt wrote that she had done Mrs. Lincoln the only service that she ought not to have done: "I had saved her from death."[30]

The two women met again on the New York docks, and this time a reporter, come with twenty others to interview the actress, observed their encounter. In this account a white-haired, frowning Mary Lincoln, barely able to walk as she leaned on her grandnephew's arm, was trying to cross the street just as Bernhardt's carriage arrived. Curtly a policeman ordered Mrs. Lincoln to stand aside until the Divine Sarah had driven off.[31]

MARY LINCOLN returned to Springfield that autumn of 1880 and spent her first Christmas in five years with what was left of her family. Elizabeth Edwards had kept her promise of four rooms, so Mary Lincoln slept in the long front room along Second Street, sat in an adjacent parlor, and stored sixty-four trunks weighing nearly four tons in two back rooms, where they threatened the floorboards. Again a boarder, she paid her sister rent plus three dollars a month for the trunk room. It was worth it. Temporarily a shut-in, she spent hours reexploring her possessions.[32]

There was talk in Springfield that the sisters argued and that Mary Lincoln would not leave her room. Certainly both were near invalids, with hearing, sight, and heart problems, and possibly, in Mary Lincoln's case, diabetes. It was Ninian Edwards, though, who nearly died that winter. His wife cheerfully accepted what she described to Emilie Helm as "shadows before nightfall." But Mary Lincoln bored visitors with her medical history and predictions of imminent death. When the local children passed by the Edwards house, they snickered at the shade-drawn windows where the crazy woman lived, while their parents gossiped that Mary Lincoln sat in darkness. She did but not because of the insanity they suspected.[33]

In fact, she was nearly blind. Later in the year a Philadelphia ophthalmologist diagnosed cataracts and reflex paralysis of one iris, with reduction of sight to one-tenth normal standard. Mary Lincoln added another reason for her poor eyesight: She had been blinded by tears, the physical stigmata of her sorrows. And she had been, at least to the extent that her weeping had caused the surface of her corneas to become swollen and edemous. Like rubbing a blister, blinking hurt. So she closed her eyes and sat in the dark while the neighbors called her mad, and at least one wrote the *New York Times* of her "hysterical condition."[34]

Robert Lincoln, who had wanted his mother sick in 1875, now proclaimed her reasonably healthy—in body, if not mind. Perhaps the son did not know better, for he saw his mother only once after her return from Pau, perhaps he could not bear to give up the burden she inflicted on him, or perhaps he wanted to forestall any embarrassing money campaigns undertaken in the name of paying the doctor's bills. In any case, he transformed his mother into a malingerer, another sign for him of her insanity. Granted, she was in far from perfect health, he informed Sarah Orne; still, "some part of her trouble is imaginary."

And his friends in Springfield advised the newspapers that no one who ate so heartily and slept so well without opiates could be "really sick."[35]

Accepting Robert Lincoln's view—for he was now prominent as President James Garfield's secretary of war—the Chicago and New York papers reported on Mrs. Lincoln's whims and eccentricities. In 1875 no one had called her a hysteric, the catchall condition for female lunatics; now they did. According to the *New York Times,* "Mrs. Lincoln is not really sick. . . . She does complain of severe pains—she does suffer from a slight trouble causing this hysterical condition. Her sufferings are wholly imaginary. She could live for many years."[36]

IN the fall of 1881 Mary Lincoln left Springfield and traveled to the mineral baths at St. Catharines and then to New York. Dr. Lewis Sayre, a noted expert on bones and a childhood acquaintance from Lexington, had recommended for her ailments electrical currents applied to the back followed by hot baths and massages. When a New York reporter interviewed the doctor on the unforgettable subject of Mrs. Lincoln's mental illness, Dr. Sayre testily replied, "She is no more insane than you or I are and if you come with me to talk with her you would understand that."[37]

Dr. Sayre diagnosed his patient as physically ill with kidney, eye, and back problems—the last a "spinal sclerosis and hardening of the spinal cord." So she spent this winter in New York City in a halfway house—the medical hotel of Dr. Miller's Home of Health, on Twenty-sixth Street between Broadway and Sixth Avenue, where Turkish vapors, Russian sitz baths, electrical therapy, and nursing care were available at sixty dollars a week. But even the water cure did not improve her aching spine. In February 1882 Mary Lincoln described her condition to a friend: "I am very feeble with my spine and limbs and without the least eye sight." Attendants carried her up and down the stairs on a litter. But her tongue was still sharp. With that vividness of language that had gotten her in trouble in 1875 when she described Indians pulling wires from her eyes, Mary Lincoln now told everyone who would listen, "I feel like I am being hacked to pieces."[38]

This last winter of her life, half-paralyzed and nearly blind, alone in Dr. Miller's hotel, Mary Lincoln roused herself for a final crusade. In her own shriveled self-esteem she was always impoverished, a condition that shopping and attention getting had relieved in the past. Now unable to shop, she had also lost her reputation as a President's wife and, after her conviction for insanity, her notability as a worthy sufferer. Only money consoled, and she needed more of it to pay her medical bills.

The murder of another American President provided Mary Lincoln with the occasion for her last campaign. In July 1881 a disappointed patronage seeker had shot President Garfield in Washington's train station. Rushing to Garfield's bedside, Robert Todd Lincoln spent his second night in a presidential deathwatch and was heard murmuring, "How many hours of sorrow I have passed in this town." But Garfield survived that night, and many more, until his death in September created another presidential widow. In 1881 neither the casual philanthropy of rich friends nor a $3,000-a-year pension sufficed for Lucretia Garfield. Her supporters insisted on and eventually won a federal pension of $5,000 a year. And what Mrs. Garfield got Mrs. Lincoln intended to have.[39]

With a frenzy reminiscent of the past, sixty-four-year-old Mary Lincoln enlisted old friends. Especially sympathetic was a former Springfield neighbor, the Baptist minister Noyes Miner. Now living in New Jersey, Reverend Miner had come to New York on Mary Lincoln's invitation and had found her alone, without maid or nurse, in a dingy back room of Dr. Miller's second-rate establishment. Easily recruited, the minister received specific orders for the campaign. He must leave immediately to lobby Congress, and for every $1,000 raised, his employer would pay $20. (She had offered Lizzie Keckley and Alexander Williamson better terms.) As in the past, Mary Lincoln directed her advocate to sympathetic congressmen, such as Samuel Cox of New York, an acquaintance from Pau, and Cyrus Field, a friend from Illinois. But Miner must stay away from the "old villain" David Davis, now an Illinois senator, and that younger villain Secretary of War Robert Lincoln. As for Illinois Congressman William Springer, Ninian Edwards would approach him. Finally, her conspiratorial instincts undiminished, Mary Lincoln referred "dear Miner" to a mysterious patron identified only by his address as "575 Broadway."[40]

Proper timing had long been the hallmark of Mary Lincoln's politics, and so she instructed Miner: "It is a positive necessity that you are there at the opening of Congress. We all consider it an absolute necessity." The "we" was mostly editorial, though Rhoda Mack and the Edwardses were helping. "Get before the committees of the Senate and House. Do not read a written statement—your noble lip eloquence is very far the best."[41]

To strengthen her case for $10,000 a year and back payment with interest (she had long ago learned to inflate a first claim), Mary Lincoln summoned four doctors to her hotel. On New Year's Day 1882 an ophthalmologist from Philadelphia, a neurologist, a specialist on kidney diseases, and Dr. Sayre examined Mary Lincoln. On her instructions they promptly dispatched their findings to the Pensions Committee of the House, and in time Mrs. Lincoln's physical condition was entered into the public record. "Mrs. Lincoln," the doctors had written," is suffering from chronic inflammation of the spinal cord, chronic diseases of the kidney, commencing cataract, disorder of the spinal cord and reflex paralysis of the iris."[42]

By this time Mrs. Lincoln was familiar business in Washington. Without a murmur, save the populist complaints of one Indiana congressman who opposed all pensions as unrepublican, elitist favors, the Senate and House increased Mary Lincoln's pension to $5,000 and awarded her $15,000 in back payments. Unlike 1870, the Pensions Committee had given its colleagues plenty of reasons to be generous. First, there was the country's self-respect and responsibility to widows in general and presidential ones in particular. Then there was the importance of the presidency and the matter of equity, for Lucretia Garfield must not be the only presidential widow receiving $5,000. And no matter what Robert Lincoln had said about his mother's health, the doctors' report persuaded even the stingy that Mrs. Lincoln would not collect $5,000 for long. But she was first among presidential widows, for her pension bill passed two months before Julia Tyler's, Sarah Polk's, and even Lucretia Garfield's.[43]

Mary Lincoln never collected a cent. Six months later, on the afternoon of July 15, 1882, the dreaded anniversary of Tad's death, she collapsed in her bedroom at the Edwardses, and that night lapsed into a coma. In the early morning of July 16 she died of a stroke.

Three days later, if she had hovered at her funeral, she must have been pleased. Again Mary Todd Lincoln was somebody. The mayor had declared a holiday, Springfield's stores were closed, and thousands lined the streets. Even the newspapers that had insulted her in the past appeared with black bands around their columns, and in their obituaries they returned her to female respectability as a loyal wife. In the crowded First Presbyterian Church, where four clergymen officiated, the elaborate decorations that filled the apse and transept included a floral representation, in carnations, roses, and daisies, of the spiritualist convention—"the Pearly Gates Ajar." The citizens of Springfield had sent a floral cross as tall as she, with her name emblazoned in forget-me-nots. The choir, which included Lizzie Grimsley's son Will, sang "Nearer My God to Thee," and though there was no eulogy, one pastor spoke of two pines that had grown so close that their roots were intertwined. When one was struck by lightning, the other wasted away.

Then with Robert Lincoln, whose wife did not attend, and the Edwardses leading the long line of carriages, the procession moved slowly off to Oak Ridge Cemetery and a final prayer before Mary Lincoln's casket was placed in the burial chamber, underneath the 120-foot obelisk commemorating her husband. Abandoned in life, in death she was again surrounded by her family.

TWO years later Robert Lincoln inherited his mother's money. Like her husband, she left no will, having destroyed several earlier ones. Unable to accept her son as her beneficiary, she apparently did not disinherit him. In any case, by Illinois law her son was her natural heir and so was enriched by $84,035. A year later her daughter-in-law began sorting through the sixty-four trunks on whose contents Mary Todd Lincoln had so often relied to replace the people who had forsaken her.[44]

Notes

CHAPTER I
FIRST FAMILY: PARKERS AND TODDS

1. *Lexington Journal,* February 14, June 5, 1818.

2. Miscellaneous Records, 1818–1828, Transylvania Archives, Lexington, Kentucky; *Kentucky Gazette,* December 27, 1818; William Moody Pratt Diary, p. 271, University of Kentucky; Judith Walzer Leavitt, "Science Enters the Birthing Room, Obstetrics in America Since the Eighteenth Century," *Journal of American History,* vol. 70 (September 1983), pp. 281–83; Richard W. Wertz and Dorothy C. Wertz, *Lying-In: A History of Childbirth in America* (New York: Free Press, 1977).

3. "André Michaux's Travels," in Reuben Gold Thwaites, ed., *Early Western Travels* (Cleveland: Arthur H. Clark, 1901), vol. 3, p. 199; John Palmer, *Journal of Travels in the United States of North America and in Lower Canada* (London: Paternoster Row, 1818), p. 105. See also J. Winston Coleman, "Lexington as Seen by Travellers, 1810–1835," *Filson Club History Quarterly,* vol. 29 (July 1955), pp. 267–80.

4. There is uncertainty about Levi O. Todd's exact birthdate. He certainly was not born on the date given in the genealogy written by his half sister. Frances Todd was born in March 1817, according to her gravestone, and thus it was impossible for any other child to have been born in 1817. In view of Mary's birth the following year, it is likely that Levi was born after Mary and before Robert Parker Todd. Both U.S. Census records and the family Bible owned by his descendants in the Keyes and Stoess family corroborate this. See also W. A. Evans, *Mrs. Abraham Lincoln* (New York: Alfred A. Knopf, 1932), p. 65n.; Sarah Breckinridge to Sophinisba Breckinridge, November 21, 1820, Breckinridge Family Papers, Library of Congress.

5. "Todd Family," *Kittochtinny Magazine* (January 1905), pp. 69–94, 104–6, 172–87, 253–78, 357–83; manuscript notes, Helm Papers, Kentucky Historical Society, Frankfort, Kentucky.

6. Levi Todd to John McCulloch, February 15, 1784, August 12, 1788, McCulloch Papers, Maryland Historical Society.

7. Ibid., September 24, 1790.

8. Alexis de Tocqueville, *Journey to America* (New York: Doubleday, 1971), p. 281.

9. Lee Weissbach, "The Peopling of Lexington, Kentucky: Growth and Mobility in a Frontier Town," *Register of Kentucky Historical Society,* vol. 81 (Spring 1983), pp. 115, 126.

10. Levi Todd to John McCulloch, September 24, 1790, McCulloch Papers, Maryland Historical Society.

11. Ibid., February 15, 1784.

12. Sarah Hughes, *Surveyors and Statesmen: Land Measuring in Colonial Virginia* (Richmond: Virginia Surveyors Foundation, 1979); J. Moore to Reverend Samuel Keene, April 1, 1800, Episcopalian Diocese Records, Maryland Historical Society.

13. For the description of his duties, see Beverly West Hathaway, *Inventory of Kentucky County Records* (Bountiful, Utah: n.p., 1974), p. 14.

14. Clay Lancaster, *Ante-Bellum Houses of the Bluegrass* (Lexington: University of Kentucky Press, 1961), p. 22; James Allen, *The Blue Grass Region* (New York: Harper's, 1892), p. 214.

15. C. W. Hackensmith, "Family Background and Education of Mary Todd Lincoln," *Register of Kentucky Historical Society,* vol. 69 (July 1971), p. 189; Harry Toulmin, "Comments on America and Kentucky," *Register of Kentucky Historical Society,* vol. 47 (April 1949), p. 250; James F. Hopkins, ed., *The Papers of Henry Clay* (Lexington: University of Kentucky Press, 1959), vol. 1, p. 315.

16. Fayette County Tax Lists, 1790, 1800, Kentucky Historical Society. Inventory of Levi Todd's Estate, Fayette County Courthouse, Lexington, Kentucky.

17. "Memoirs of Micah Taul," *Register of Kentucky Historical Society,* vol. 27 (January 1929), p. 356.

18. William Leavy, "A Memoir of Lexington and Its Vicinity," *Register of Kentucky Historical Society,* vol. 40 (July 1942), p. 257; Robert Parker to John Clifford, September 11, 1789, March 9, 1790, Historical Society of Pennsylvania, Philadelphia, Pennsylvania; Deposition of Elizabeth Parker, June 17, 1817, *Robert Todd's Heirs* v. *Robert Parker's Heirs,* Wickcliffe-Preston Papers, University of Kentucky Library.

19. Fayette County Tax Lists, 1851, Kentucky Historical Society.

20. Last Will of Robert Parker, March 1800, Will Book A, p. 711, Fayette County Courthouse, Lexington, Kentucky.

21. *Kentucky Gazette,* July 19, 1806; Robert Peters, *History of Fayette County* (Chicago: O. L. Bakin, 1882), p. 312. See also Edna Talbott Whitley, "Mary Beck and the Female Mind," *Register of Kentucky Historical Society,* vol. 77 (Winter 1979), pp. 15–25; Gladys V. Parrish, "The History of Female Education in Lexington and Fayette County" (master's thesis, University of Kentucky, 1932).

22. Quoted in Bernard Mayo, *Henry Clay, Spokesman of the New West* (Boston: Houghton Mifflin, 1937), p. 215. See also Charles R. Staples, "The Amusements and Diversions of Early Lexington" (master's thesis, University of Kentucky, 1925).

23. Barb Simon, "Waste Not Your Pity" (seminar paper, Bryn Mawr College, 1981).

24. As on this and other matters of southern behavior, Bertram Wyatt-Brown is perceptive. See Bertram Wyatt-Brown, *Southern Honor* (New York: Oxford University Press, 1982). Quote is from James Flint in Thwaites, *Early Western Travels* (Cleveland: Arthur Clark, 1904), vol. 9, p. 137.

25. Records of Transylvania Library, 1805–1810, Transylvania Archives, Lexington, Kentucky.

26. William Little Brown, "A Law Student at Transylvania University," *Filson Club History Quarterly*, vol. 31 (July 1957), p. 268.

27. William Townsend, *Lincoln and the Bluegrass* (Lexington: University of Kentucky Press, 1955), p. 362; Mayo, *Henry Clay, Spokesman of the New West*, p. 215.

28. "List of Lawyers in State of Kentucky and Their Places of Residence, 1822," Breckinridge Family Papers; Joan Wells Coward, *Kentucky in the New Republic* (Lexington: University of Kentucky Press, 1979), pp. 174n., 177.

29. Julius Pratt, *Expansionists of 1812* (Gloucester, Mass.: Peter Smith, 1957), pp. 54–58; *Lexington Reporter*, December 20, 1811; *Annals of Congress*, 12th Congress, 1st Session, p. 1639; James Wallace Hammack, *Kentucky and the Second American Revolution—the War of 1812* (Lexington: University of Kentucky Press, 1976), pp. 16–22.

30. Anderson Quisenberry, *Kentucky in the War of 1812* (Frankfort: Kentucky Historical Society, 1915); *Papers of Henry Clay*, vol. I, pp. 598–99.

31. Emilie Helm, "Todd Family," *Kittochtinny Magazine* (January 1905), pp. 69–73.

32. David Todd to Robert Todd, January 6, 1848, Filson Club Historical Society, Louisville, Kentucky.

33. John Todd Stuart to Emilie Helm, May 14, 1880, April 1, 30, 1880; Elizabeth Edwards to Emilie Helm, May 14, May 24, 1880, Helm Papers, Kentucky Historical Society.

34. On this point, see George Forgie, *Patricide in the House Divided: A Psychological Interpretation of Lincoln and His Age* (New York: W. W. Norton, 1979); Quisenberry, *Kentucky in the War of 1812*, p. 86.

35. Tocqueville, *Journey to America*, p. 282; Elizabeth Edwards to Emilie Helm, April 30, 1880, Helm Papers, Kentucky Historical Society; Helm, "Todd Family," p. 264; Palmer, *Travels*, p. 131.

36. Helm, "Todd Family," p. 172; William Porter, "A Sketch of the Life of Andrew Porter," *Pennsylvania Magazine of History and Biography*, vol. 4 (1880), pp. 287–93.

37. Michael Grossberg, "Law and Family in Nineteenth-Century America" (Ph.D. dissertation, Brandeis University, 1979), pp. 101–15.

38. James S. Brown, "Social Class, Intermarriage and Church Membership in a Kentucky Community," *American Journal of Sociology*, vol. 57 (November 1951), pp. 232–42.

39. *Todd's Heirs* v. *Parker's Heirs*, Fayette County Circuit Court Records, File 1389, p. 589, Fayette County Courthouse; Third U.S. Census, Fayette County, p. 18, Fayette County Courthouse.

40. Eliza Todd to "my dear Grandpapa," June 20, 1813, Huntington Library, San Marino, California.

41. *Lexington Journal*, June 11, 1818, December 6, 1817.

42. Eliza Carrington to "my dear Sister," July 2, 1824; J. R. Witherspoon to Robert Breckinridge, October 15, 1824; Robert Breckinridge to A. Harrison, November 27, 1824, Breckinridge Family Papers; Mary Breckinridge to Joseph Breckinridge, April 20–21, 1823, Breckinridge Family Papers; Flint, "Letters from America," in Thwaite, *Early Western Travels*, vol. 9, p. 143.

43. Mary Breckinridge to Joseph Breckinridge, April 20, 1823, Breckinridge Papers.

44. The more frequent the nursing, the higher the rate of hormone-stimulating serum production, and the more certain infertility resulting from the failure to ovulate. Alberto Angeli, *The Endocrinology of Cystic Breast Disease* (New York: Raven Press, 1983), p. 31; P. Delroye et al., "Serum Prolactin . . . ," *American Journal of Obstetrics and Gynecology*, vol. 130, pp. 635–39.

45. Bayless Hardin, "Dr. Samuel Brown, His Family and Descendants, 1769–1830," *Filson Club History Quarterly*, vol. 26 (January 1952), p. 9; C. S. Hodge to Robert J. Breckinridge, July 31, 1833, Breckinridge Family Papers.

46. Mary Todd Lincoln to Elizabeth Todd Grimsley, in Justin and Linda Turner, *Mary Lincoln—Her Life and Letters* (New York: Alfred A. Knopf, 1972), p. 105; hereafter cited as Turner, *Letters*.

47. Quoted in Leavitt, "Science Enters the Birthing Room," p. 289.

48. Mary Breckinridge to "my dear husband," May 8, 1823, Breckinridge Papers.

49. Charlotte Mentelle to her mother, Lexington, December, 1803, April 26, 1804, University of Kentucky Library.

50. Mary H. Breckinridge to Joseph Breckinridge, September 3, 1813; Fran Preston to Isaac, February 15, 1821, Breckinridge Family Papers.

51. Townsend, *Lincoln and the Bluegrass,* p. 48; William Leavy, "A Memoir of Lexington and Its Vicinity," *Register of Kentucky Historical Society,* vol. 41 (April 1943), p. 118.

52. Professor Richards, "Notes on Obstetrics and Diseases of Women and Children," Transylvania University Library; William Richardson, "A Case of Preternatural Membrane in the Vagina Requiring an Operation During Labor," *Transylvania Journal of Medicine,* vol. 2 (February 1829), pp. 45–46; David Holt to Dr. Todd and Warfield, June 16, 1810, Todd Family Papers, Kentucky State Archives; William P. Dewees, *A Compendious System of Midwifery* (Philadelphia, 1843), pp. 354, 356–57; Dr. Pindel to R. J. Breckinridge, circa 1824, Breckinridge Family Papers.

53. Almira Phelps, *Fireside Friend or Female Student Being Advice to Young Ladies on the Important Subject of Education* (Boston: Capon, Lyon and Webb, 1840), p. 35. Mary Breckinridge to "my dear husband," May 8, 1832, Breckinridge Papers; *Kentucky Gazette,* March 20, 1841. Obituaries in *Kentucky Gazette,* 1820–1830. See, for example, *Kentucky Gazette,* May 13, 1828.

54. Eliza Parker Todd to "my dear Grandpapa," June 20, 1813, Huntington Library, San Marino, California.

55. Linda Ashley and Elizabeth Wills, "Funeral Notices" (Lexington, Kentucky, 1800–1887)," Lexington Public Library; Louisiana Hart to ?, April 6, 1823, Breckinridge Family Papers.

56. "Samuel McCullough's Reminiscences of Lexington," *Register of Kentucky Historical Society,* vol. 27 (January 1929), p. 419; Records of the First Presbyterian Church, Lexington, Kentucky; Kentucky Historical Society.

57. Emma Furman, *A Child's Parent Dies: Studies in Childhood Bereavement* (New Haven: Yale University Press, 1974); John Bowlby, "Loss, Sadness and Depression," in *Attachment and Loss,* vol. 3 (New York: Basic Books, 1980); James McDowell to Robert Breckinridge, November 17, 1832, Breckinridge Family Papers. For a Baptist funeral, see William Moody Diary, University of Kentucky, pp. 143, 148. For McChord's sermon, see Reverend James McChord, *A Last Appeal to the Market Street Presbyterian Church and Congregation* (Lexington: 1818).

58. John Bayliss, *Black Slave Narratives* (New York: Macmillan, 1970), pp. 147–52; B. A. Botkin, *Lay My Burden Down* (Chicago: University of Chicago Press, 1945), pp. 29–41; Thomas Webber, *Deep Like the Rivers: Education in the Slave Quarter Community* (New York: W. W. Norton, 1978); Ivan McDougle, *Slavery in Kentucky* (Westport: Negro Universities Press, 1970).

59. Bowlby, "Loss, Sadness and Depression," pp. 265–344.

CHAPTER II   A SECOND FAMILY

1. Quotes on the following pages are from Robert Smith Todd to Elizabeth Humphreys, January 13, February 15, October 23, October 25, 1826, in the Illinois State Historical

Society, Springfield, Illinois; and Robert S. Todd to Elizabeth Humphreys, July 11, 1826, Filson Club Historical Society.

2. Brown Family Papers, Filson Club Historical Society.

3. Ellen K. Rothman, "Courtship and Transition to Marriage, 1770–1900" (Ph.D. dissertation, Brandeis University, 1981), passim. Elizabeth offered various ages to the census taker (as Mary Lincoln did later), and before 1840 ages were given by decades, making it impossible to know her specific age. For information on the age of her brothers, see their tombstones in the Humphreys lot in the Frankfort Cemetery and *The Humphreys Family in America* (New York: Humphreys Print, 1883).

4. Katherine Helm, *The True Story of Mary, Wife of Lincoln* (New York: Harper, 1928), p. 35; *Kentucky Commonwealth,* January 30, 1836.

5. Mary Todd Lincoln to Abraham Lincoln, Lexington, May, n.d., n.y., Turner, *Letters,* p. 37.

6. Answer of Elizabeth P. Edwards, Frances Wallace, and Mary Lincoln, April 1852, Wickcliffe-Preston Papers.

7. Geraldine Clifford, "Home and School in Nineteenth Century America: Some Personal History Reports from the United States," *History of Education Quarterly,* 18 (Spring 1978), p. 7; Susan McDowell to "Sophie," April 1, 1825, Breckinridge Papers.

8. *Kentucky State Journal,* May 29, 1836.

9. Helm, *Mary, Wife of Lincoln,* p. 35; Last Will of Elizabeth Todd Humphreys, Helm Family Papers, Kentucky State Archives; Portrait of Elizabeth Humphreys, Helm Place, Lexington, Kentucky; Carl Sandburg, *Mary Lincoln, Wife and Widow* (New York: Harcourt, Brace, 1932), p. 16.

10. Helm, *Mary, Wife of Lincoln,* pp. 26–29; Elizabeth Norris to Emilie Helm, September 28, 1895, Ruth Randall Papers, Library of Congress.

11. Helm, *Mary, Wife of Lincoln,* pp. 29, 4, 47.

12. Wyatt-Brown, *Southern Honor,* pp. 154–56; Helen B. Lewis, *Shame and Guilt in Neurosis* (New York: International University Press, 1971); Helen Lynd, *On Shame and the Search for Identity* (New York: Harcourt, Brace, 1958), pp. 13–71.

13. Wyatt-Brown, *Southern Honor,* p. 199.

14. *Kentucky Gazette,* September 14, 1833; January 5, 1837.

15. Sarah Preston to Sophinisba Breckinridge, January 27, 1824, Breckinridge Papers.

16. Helm, *Mary, Wife of Lincoln,* pp. 4, 22, 53; Elizabeth Norris to Emilie Helm, n.d., Randall Papers.

17. Wyatt-Brown, *Southern Honor,* pp. 134, 139, 224, 276–77; Robert Smith Todd to Betsey Todd, February 15, 1826, Illinois State Historical Society.

18. Robert Wickcliffe, "To the Freemen" (n.p., n.d.); *Kentucky Gazette,* July 7, 1845; *Louisville Weekly Courier,* July 4, 1849.

19. R. S. Todd to J. B. Breckinridge, March 24, 1821, Breckinridge Papers; Robert Todd to Elizabeth Humphreys, February 15, 1826, Illinois State Historical Society; Leavy, "Memoir," p. 110.

20. Robert Todd to Walter Reid, October 31, 1813, Todd Papers, Wisconsin Historical Society, Madison, Wisconsin; Robert S. Todd to Richard Anderson, February 7, 1819, Huntington Library, San Marino, California; General Basil W. Duke, *History of the Bank of Kentucky 1792–1895* (Louisville: John Morton, 1896), p. 37.

21. Robert Smith Todd to Betsey, February 23, 1826, Illinois State Historical Society.

22. *Kentucky Gazette,* August 1, 1835; Robert Smith Todd to Elizabeth Humphreys, July 11, 1826, Filson Club Historical Society; J. Winston Coleman, *Slavery Times in Kentucky* (Chapel Hill: University of North Carolina Press, 1940), p. 37.

23. Reverend Robert Sanders, *History of the Second Presbyterian Church* (Lexington: United Presbyterian Church, 1965); Robert Bishop, *A Discourse Occasioned by the Death of James McChord* (n.p., 1821); Thomas Marshall Green, *Historic Families of Kentucky* (Cincinnati: R. Clarke, 1889).

24. *Kentucky Gazette,* September 7, 10, 1827.

25. Susan Yandell to Dr. Wilson Yandell, November 25, 1825, Yandell Papers, Filson Club Historical Society; *Kentucky Gazette,* September 7, 1827.

26. Phelps, *Fireside Friend,* p. 224. See also Ann Firor Scott, "Almira Lincoln Phelps, the Self-Made Woman in the Nineteenth Century," *Maryland Historical Magazine,* vol. 75 (September 1980), pp. 203–15.

27. Levi Todd to Mary O. Russell, December 4, 1812, Filson Club Historical Society.

28. *Kentucky Gazette,* August 31, 1827, May 1, 1818; Parrish, "Female Education," p. 9; Inventory of Estate of Levi Todd, October 22, 1807, Fayette County Courthouse.

29. Mary Wollstonecraft, *A Vindication of the Rights of Women* (New York: W. W. Norton, 1967), pp. 49, 212–13.

30. Parrish, "Female Education"; Jo Della Alband, *History of Education of Women in Kentucky* (M.A. thesis, University of Kentucky, 1934); Meg Wickcliffe to "My dear Ma" Wickcliffe, July 27, n.d., Wickcliffe-Preston Papers; Dr. Wilson Yandell to "my dear child," November 20, 1825; Langford Yandell to David Wendell, December 9, Yandell Papers.

31. Dr. Wilson Yandell to Susan, December 9, 1825, Yandell Papers.

32. Carl Kaestle and Maris Vinovskis, *Education and Social Change in Nineteenth-Century Massachusetts* (New York: Cambridge University Press, 1980), pp. 252, 18, 28–33; Barbara Finkelstein, "Governing the Young: Teacher Behavior in American Primary Schools: A Documentary History" (Ph.D. dissertation, Columbia University, 1970); Barbara Finkelstein, "Pedagogy as Intrusion: Teaching Values in Popular Primary Schools in Nineteenth-Century America," *History of Childhood Quarterly,* vol. 2 (Winter 1975), pp. 361–66.

33. Helm, *Mary, Wife of Lincoln,* p. 21.

34. Reverend Jackson to Bishop Kemp, November 27, 1817; William Worsely to Bishop Kemp, June 1, 1820, Episcopalian Archives, Maryland Historical Society; Frances K. Swinford and Rebecca Smith Lee, *The Great Elm Tree: Heritage of the Episcopal Diocese in Lexington* (Lexington: Faith House Press, 1969), p. 25.

35. *Kentucky Gazette,* August 31, 1827; Parrish, "Female Education," p. 46; Henry Dupre, "Transylvania University and Rafinesque," *Filson Club History Quarterly,* vol. 35 (1961), pp. 110–21.

36. *Kentucky Gazette,* August 27, August 29, 1827; Lansford Yandell to David Wendell, November 17, 1825, Yandell Papers; Susan Yandell to Mr. and Mrs. Wendell, November 30, 1825, Yandell Papers.

37. *Kentucky Gazette,* May 8, 1829.

38. Helm, *Mary, Wife of Lincoln,* p. 21; Susan Yandell to Father, November 22, 1825, Yandell Papers; Jean Baker, *Affairs of Party* (Ithaca: Cornell University Press, 1982), pp. 79, 86.

39. Lewis Collins, *History of Kentucky* (Covington, Ky.: Collins and Company, 1874), vol. 2, p. 244. The examples are taken from the copybook of Harriet Stone, Harriet Stone Papers, University of Kentucky Library.

40. Elizabeth K. Smith and Mary Didlake, *Historical Sketch of Christ Church Cathedral* (Lexington: Transylvania, 1898), p. 28; Townsend, *Lincoln and the Bluegrass,* p. 51; Elizabeth Humphreys Norris to Emilie Todd Helm, September 28, 1895 (copy), Randall Papers.

41. Inventory of Robert S. Todd, Fayette County Courthouse.

42. *Kentucky Gazette,* October 19, 1828.

43. Ibid., June 22, 1833.

44. There has been a local controversy about the exact location of the school and whether

it still is standing. See William Townsend, *The Boarding School of Mary Todd Lincoln* (privately printed, 1941). In any case, the general location of Mentelle's was across from Ashland in what is presently Mentelle Park, Lexington. *Lexington Intelligencer,* March 6, 1838.

45. Kathryn Kish Sklar, *Catharine Beecher: A Study in American Domesticity* (New York: W. W. Norton, 1973), pp. 91–94; James McLachlan, *American Boarding Schools* (New York: Scribner's, 1970).

46. Charlotte Mentelle to her parents, April 6, 1804, University of Kentucky Library.

47. *Kentucky Gazette,* July 25, 1798; *Lexington Intelligencer,* March 6, 1838; *Lexington Kentucky Statesman,* September 14, 1860; *Kentucky Gazette,* June 10, 1816; *Papers of Henry Clay,* vol. 2, pp. 243, 350, 353, 576, 913; vol. 1, pp. 121 n, 708–711; Harriet Martineau to "dear friends," June 2, 182?, University of Kentucky Library.

48. Gustave Koerner, *Memoirs of Gustave Koerner,* Thomas J. McCormack, ed. (Cedar Rapids: Torch Press, 1909), vol. I, pp. 360, 361; *Lexington Statesman,* September 14, 1860.

49. Charlotte Mentelle to C. C. Moore, December 23, 1836, University of Kentucky Library.

50. Henrietta Clay, "Bits of Family History," Helm Papers; Townsend, *The Boarding School of Mary Todd Lincoln; Kentucky Gazette,* July 19, 1834; *Lexington Statesman,* September 14, 1860; *Lexington Sunday Herald Leader,* April 6, 1941.

51. For an example of Madame Mentelle's own writing style, see Mrs. C. Mentelle, *A Short History of the Late Mrs. Mary O. T. Wickcliffe;* Helms, *Mary, Wife of Lincoln,* p. 45.

52. Interview with Mrs. Joe Murphy, July 25, 1983, Helm Place, Lexington; Inventory of Levi Todd, 1807; Inventory of Robert S. Todd, Fayette County Courthouse. A small piece of this damask still exists and is owned by Mrs. Joe Murphy of Helm Place. See *George R. C. Todd, complainant* v. *Elizabeth H. Todd, Abraham Lincoln, et al., defendants,* File 1389, Fayette Circuit Court, Fayette County Courthouse.

53. Turner, *Letters,* pp. 447, 588.

54. Leavy, "A Memoir," *Register of Kentucky Historical Society,* vol. 41 (April 1943), pp. 107–37; ibid., vol. 42 (January 1944), pp. 26–31; "Sketch of Michael Shuck," ibid., vol. 44 (1946), p. 110; C. Keiser to Robert Breckinridge, June 6, 1833, Breckinridge Papers.

55. Leavy, "A Memoir," *Register of Kentucky Historical Society,* vol. 42 (January 1944), p. 26; *Kentucky Observer,* June 28, 1832; Mary Breckinridge to Sophonisba Breckinridge, July 8, 1833, Breckinridge Papers; Charles Rosenberg, *The Cholera Years* (Chicago: University of Chicago Press, 1967), pp. 42–45.

56. Leavy, "A Memoir," *Register of Kentucky Historical Society,* vol. 42 (January 1944), p. 27; *Lexington Observer and Register,* August 22, 1833; *National Gazette and Literary Register* (Philadelphia), June 27, 1833.

57. Rosenberg, *The Cholera Years,* p. 3.

58. Lunsford Yandell, *An Account of Spasmodic Cholera as it Appeared in Lexington in June 1833* (n.p., n.d.); Nancy Baird, "Asiatic Cholera's First Visit to Kentucky," *Filson Club History Quarterly,* vol. 48 (July 1974), pp. 228–40; Helm, *Mary, Wife of Lincoln,* pp. 49, 50.

59. Ninian Edwards, *History of Illinois from 1778–1833 and the Life and Times of Ninian Edwards* (Springfield, Ill.: State Journal Company, 1870), p. 22; *Lexington Observer and Register,* August 7, 1829; Frances Preston to Sophie Preston, September 17, 1822, Breckinridge Papers. On the general issue of parental choice on mate choice, Ellen Rothman, *Hands and Hearts: A Social History of Courtship* (New York: Basic Books, 1982).

60. Bernhard, duke of Saxe-Weimar Eisenach, *Travels Through North American During the Years 1825 and 1826* (Philadelphia: Carey, Lee, 1828), pp. 129–30.

61. Carroll Smith-Rosenberg, "The Female World of Love and Ritual: Relationships Between Women in Nineteenth-Century America," *Signs,* vol. 1 (Autumn 1975), pp. 1–29.

62. Bernard Mayo, "Lexington: Frontier Metropolis," in Eric Goldman, ed., *Historiogra-*

phy and Urbanization: Essays in American History in Honor of W. Stull Holt (N.Y. Kennikatt Press, 1968), p. 27.

63. Frances M. Trollope, *Domestic Manners of the Americans*, vol. 2 (New York: Dodd, Mead, 1894), p. 132. For a description of a dinner party where the ladies retired, Charles Augustus Murray, *Travels in North America During the Years 1834, 1835 and 1836* (London: Richard Bentley, 1839), p. 229; Ellen Rothman, *Hands and Hearts*, passim.

64. Cassius M. Clay, *The Life of Cassius Marcellus Clay* (New York: Negro University Press, 1969), pp. 47, 67.

65. John Carl Parish, *George Wallace Jones* (Iowa City: Historical Society of Iowa, 1912), p. 260.

66. Koerner, *Memoirs*, p. 355.

67. Helm, *Mary, Wife of Lincoln*, p. 52; Emily Norris to Emilie Helm, Randall Papers; Mentelle, *A Short History of the Late Mrs. Mary O. T. Wickcliffe*, p. 10.

68. Helm, *Mary, Wife of Lincoln*, p. 52; Wyatt-Brown, *Southern Honor*, p. 201.

69. Mary T. Lincoln to Margaret W. Preston, July 23, 1853, University of Kentucky Library.

CHAPTER III   MARY TODD'S LEXINGTON

1. William Montell, *Ghosts Along the Cumberland: Deathlore in the Kentucky Foothills* (Knoxville: University of Tennessee Press, 1975); Palmer, *Travels*, pp. 19, 108; Charlotte Mentelle to "Dear Parents," August 24, 1804, University of Kentucky Library.

2. Richard Wade, *The Rise of Western Cities, 1790–1830* (Cambridge: Cambridge University Press, 1959); Mayo, "Lexington: Frontier Metropolis," pp. 21–42; J. Winston Coleman, "Kentucky River Steam Boats," *Register of the Kentucky Historical Society*, vol. 63 (October 1965), p. 299; *Louisville Public Advertiser*, November 28, 1829.

3. Mayo, "Lexington: Frontier Metropolis," p. 38; Palmer, *Travels*, p. 3; Edward Abdy, *Journal of a Residence and Tour in the United States of America* (New York: Negro Universities Press, 1969), vol. 2, p. 340.

4. Susan Yandell to her father, November 22, 1825, Yandell Papers.

5. Samuel Todd to Robert Breckinridge, December 2, 1820, Breckinridge Papers; *Kentucky Gazette*, March 13, 1828; James Atherton to Charles Atherton, January 1, 1832, University of Kentucky Library.

6. Wade, *Western Cities*, p. 70; F. Gavin Davenport, *Antebellum Kentucky, 1800–1861* (Oxford: Mississippi Valley Press, 1943), pp. 1–50; Dupre, "Transylvania University and Rafinesque," "Samuel McCullough's Reminiscences of Lexington," *Register of the Kentucky Historical Society*, vol. 2 (January 1929), pp. 411–25; *Kentucky Gazette*, April, May 1824.

7. Fayette County Tax List 1818–1849, Kentucky Historical Society, p. 4; Elodie Todd to N. H. P. Dawson, June 12, 1861, Dawson Papers, microfilm edition, North Carolina Historical Society.

8. Mercantile Agency, vol. 2, Kentucky, Fayette County, 1848–1880, Baker Library, Harvard University, Cambridge, Massachusetts; *Kentucky Gazette*, February 12, 1830; *Kentucky Observer*, May 7, 1832; *Kentucky Gazette*, January 16, 1836.

9. Koerner, *Memoirs*, p. 353; Jane Short Wilkins to Peyton Short, June 18, 1818, in "Letters of Jane Short Wilkins," *Register of the Kentucky Historical Society*, vol. 51 (January 1953), p. 62.

10. Fred Lewis Patlee, ed., *The Poems of Philip Freneau* (Princeton, N.J.: University Library, 1903), vol. 2, p. 280; Coward, *Kentucky in the New Republic*, p. 1.

11. Sophonisba Breckinridge to Robert Breckinridge, November 29, 1828, Breckinridge Papers.

12. Sally Wollsey to Margaret Wickcliffe, n.d., Wickcliffe-Preston Papers; J. Winston Coleman, "Old Kentucky Watering Places," *Filson Club History Quarterly*, vol. 16 (January 1942).

13. *Kentucky Gazette*, May 16, 1829; *Lexington Observer and Reporter*, November 17, 1847; *Kentucky Gazette*, May 21, 1848.

14. Helm, *Mary, Wife of Lincoln*, pp. 1–4; Townsend, *Lincoln and the Bluegrass*, p. 98; Glyndon G. Van Deusen, *The Life of Henry Clay* (Boston: Little, Brown, 1937), p. 376.

15. *Lexington State Journal*, July 19, 1882; Wyatt-Brown, *Southern Honor*, p. 50.

16. Davenport, *Antebellum Kentucky*, p. 25; Susan Yandell to mother, November 19, 1825, Yandell Papers.

17. Rebecca Smith Lee, *Mary Austin Holley, a Biography* (Austin: University of Texas Press, 1962), p. 120.

18. Susan Yandell to father, November 22, 1825, Yandell Papers.

19. E. S. M., *Memoir of Eliza Quincy* (Boston: 1861), p. 62.

20. Records of the Managers of the Lexington Orphan Asylum, 1825–1835, University of Kentucky Library.

21. Marian Penney to Hester Penney, October 3, 1838, Penney Family Papers, University of Kentucky Library.

22. Koerner, *Memoirs*, p. 355.

23. Robert Davidson, *History of the Presbyterian Church of the State of Kentucky* (New York: Robert Carter, 1817), pp. 277–85; J. H. McChord, *The McChords of Kentucky and Some Related Families* (Louisville: Westerfield Co., n.d.); Sanders, *History of 2nd Presbyterian Church*, p. 7; James Peter, *A History of Fayette County* (Chicago: O. L. Baskin, 1887); Mary C. Breckinridge to Joseph Breckinridge, February 2, 1823, Breckinridge Papers.

24. *True American*, June 17, 1845, quoted in Coleman, *Slavery Times in Kentucky*, p. 39; *Kentucky Gazette*, July 12, 1838.

25. For another reference to gouging, see Frances Dyer and Jacqueline Dyer, eds., *Bluegrass Craftsman Being the Reminiscences of Hiram Stedman Papermaker 1808–1885* (Lawrence: University of Kansas Press, 1969), p. 25; also see Elliott J. Gorn, "Gouge and Bite, Pull Hair and Scratch: The Social Significance of Fighting in the Southern Back Country," *American Historical Review*, vol. 90 (February 1985), pp. 18–43.

26. Flint, "Letters from America," in Thwaites, *Early Western Travels*, vol. 9, p. 138.

27. Susan Yandell to father, September 6, 1825; Lansford Yandell to father, November 1825, Yandell Papers; Tocqueville, *Journey to America* (New York: Anchor Books, 1971), p. 284; Abdy, *Journal of a Residence*, vol. 2, p. 354. See also Robert Ireland, "Homicide in Nineteenth-Century Kentucky," *Register of the Kentucky Historical Society*, vol. 81 (Spring 1983), pp. 134–50; Wyatt-Brown, *Southern Honor*, pp. 366–71.

28. Helm, *Mary, Wife of Lincoln*, p. 33.

29. Ibid., pp. 24–27. On African survivals and the blue jay, see Eugene Genovese, *Roll Jordan Roll* (New York: Vintage Books, 1974), p. 217.

30. Affidavits of William McChesney, Mrs. E. H. Todd, George R. C. Todd and Thomas C. Redd, George R. C. Todd v. Elizabeth Todd, October 1852, Fayette County Court, File 1389; Order Book 36, Fayette County Court; Townsend, *Lincoln and the Bluegrass*, p. 205.

31. Kentucky House of Delegates, *Journal of the House of Representatives*, 1841, 1842, 1844, 1845 (Frankfort, Ky.: A. G. Hodges); *Lexington Observer and Reporter*, June 12, 13, 1845, June 12, 27, 1849.

32. Coleman, *Slavery Times in Kentucky*, p. 118; Deposition of William McChesney et al., *Todd's Heirs* v. *Todd's Administrators*, Fayette Circuit Court, Fayette County Courthouse; Townshend, *Lincoln and the Bluegrass*, p. 205.

33. Coleman, *Slavery Times*, p. 186.

34. Will of Elizabeth Parker, December 24, 1849, Will Books, p. 576, Fayette County

Courthouse; Inventory of the Estate of Elizabeth Parker, Fayette County Courthouse; Helm, *Mary, Wife of Lincoln,* pp. 35–37; Townsend, *Lincoln and the Bluegrass,* p. 205.

35. Helm, *Mary, Wife of Lincoln,* pp. 22–25, 40; Townsend, *Lincoln and the Bluegrass,* pp. 73–75; Coleman, *Slavery Times,* pp. 142–72; William Strother, "Negro Culture in Lexington, Kentucky" (M.A. thesis, University of Kentucky, 1939); William Townsend, *Lincoln and His Wife's Home Town* (Indianapolis: Bobbs-Merrill, 1929), p. 81; Samuel Brown, *Immigrants Directory* (n.p.), p. 91.

36. One of the most gruesome episodes in Lexington's history, the Turner case is covered in Townsend, *Lincoln and the Bluegrass,* p. 93; *Commonwealth of Kentucky* v. *Caroline Turner,* Fayette Circuit Court, File 899, April 17, 1837, Fayette County Courthouse.

37. Helm, *Mary, Wife of Lincoln,* p. 38; *New Orleans Bee,* April 11, 1834.

38. *Todd's Heirs* v. *Robert Wickcliffe,* in Wickcliffe-Preston Papers; Townsend, *Lincoln and the Bluegrass,* pp. 178–90; Mentelle, *A Short History of the Late Mrs. Mary O. T. Wickcliffe; Speech of Robert Wickcliffe in Reply to Rev. R. J. Breckinridge* (Lexington: Observer Reporter Print, 1840).

39. Mary Todd to Margaret Wickcliffe Preston, July 23, 1853, University of Kentucky Library; *Speech of Robert Wickcliffe in Reply to Rev. R. J. Breckinridge Delivered in the Courthouse in Lexington; The Second Defense of Robert Breckinridge Against the Calumnies of Robert Wickcliffe* (Baltimore: Matchet, 1841), p. 33.

40. Townsend, *Lincoln and the Bluegrass,* p. 127; *Commonwealth of Kentucky* v. *Emily, a Slave,* Fayette Circuit Court, File 1103, April 15, 1845, Fayette County Courthouse. See also Clay, *Memoirs,* pp. 559–60; and Robert Breckinridge to Sophonisba, January 15, 1835, Breckinridge Papers.

41. *Kentucky Gazette,* March 3, 1826; May 10, 1834, September 30, 1830, February 10, 1826, September 3, 1842; Wyatt-Brown, *Southern Honor,* p. 226.

42. Loren Kallsen, ed., *The Kentucky Tragedy: A Problem in Romantic Attitudes* (Indianapolis: Bobbs-Merrill, 1963), p. 22; *The Confession of Jereboam Beauchamp* (Bloomfield, Ky. n.p., 1826); *Kentucky Gazette,* June 9, July 14, 1826.

43. J. Winston Coleman, *The Trotter-Wickcliffe Duel: An Affair of Honor in Fayette County, October 9, 1829* (Frankfort, Ky.: Roberts Printing Co., 1950); James Cowen to Robert Breckinridge, June 20, 1829, Breckinridge Papers; Robert Wickcliffe to Henry Clay, March 15, 1829, University of Kentucky Library; Robert Wickcliffe to Charles Wickcliffe, April 14, 1825, Wickcliffe-Preston Papers; *Kentucky Gazette,* March 13, 1829.

44 *Kentucky House of Delegates, Journal,* p. 5; Townsend, *Lincoln and His Wife's Home Town;* Kenneth Greenberg, *Masters and Statesmen, The Political Culture of Slavery* (Baltimore: Johns Hopkins Press, 1985), pp. 28–33.

CHAPTER IV   SPRINGFIELD COURTSHIP

1. Helm, *Mary, Wife of Lincoln,* p. 72.

2. Robert Smith Todd to Betsey Humphreys, Lexington, January 13, 1826, Illinois State Historical Library; "The answer of Elizabeth Edwards et al.," April 1852, University of Kentucky Library; Elizabeth Edwards to William Herndon, August 3, 1887, Herndon-Weik Papers, Microfilm Edition; "The Separate Answer of George R. C. Todd, *Todd's Heirs* v. *Todd's Admin.,"* Fayette Circuit Court, File 1389, Fayette County Courthouse.

3. J. Winston Coleman, *Stage Coach Days in the Bluegrass* (Louisville: Standard Press, 1935), pp. 131, 143, 144. See also "Historical Notes: From St. Louis to Springfield in 1836," *Journal of Illinois State Historical Society,* vol. 26 (1933), pp. 308–09.

4. Paul Angle, *"Here I Have Lived": A History of Lincoln's Springfield 1821–1865* (New Brunswick, N.J.: Rutgers University Press, 1935), p. 57; John Hardin to Robert W. Scott,

September 24, 1830, Hardin Papers; *Sangamon Journal,* March 2, 1837.

5. Abraham Lincoln to Mary Owens, Springfield, May 7, 1837, in Roy Basler, *The Collected Works of Abraham Lincoln* (New Brunswick, N.J.: Rutgers University Press, 1953), vol. 1, p. 78.

6. Ida Tarbell, *In the Footsteps of the Lincolns* (New York: Harper's, 1929); Louis Warren, *Lincoln's Parentage and Childhood,* (New York: Century Company, 1929).

7. Linda Ashley and Elizabeth Tapp Wills, "Scrapbook of Funeral Notices," Lexington Public Library, Lexington, Kentucky; Statement of Frances Wallace, April 1852, University of Kentucky Library.

8. Ninian Edwards, Illinois Mercantile Agency Records, vol. 1, p. 56, Baker Library, Harvard Business School, Cambridge, Massachusetts.

9. Ibid., p. 104; *Lincoln Herald* (Summer 1961), p. 55.

10. Helm, *Mary, Wife of Lincoln,* p. 81; Turner, *Letters,* pp. 19, 22, 25, 21. Lincoln green was a popular color during the Victorian period, although the idea of the less than sartorially splendid Abraham Lincoln having a Lincoln green coat is astonishing. Duncan Crow, *The Victorian Women* (London: George Allen, 1971), p. 127.

11. Turner, *Letters,* pp. 17, 20.

12. Ibid., pp. 22, 20.

13. Smith-Rosenberg, "The Female World" pp. 1–29.

14. Turner, *Letters,* pp. 22, 28.

15. "A Story of the Early Days in Springfield and a Poem," *Journal of the Illinois State Historical Society,* vol. 16 (April 1923), p. 146. In a letter to his friend Joshua Speed in June 1841, Lincoln referred to "Hart, the little drayman that hauled Molly home once." Basler, *Complete Works,* vol. 1, p. 258.

16. Turner, *Letters,* p. 22; John Stuart, *History of Sangamon County,* p. 335.

17. Turner, *Letters,* pp. 18, 26, 27, 20.

18. Helm, *Mary, Wife of Lincoln,* p. 64; *Lexington Reporter,* August 18, 1832; James Conkling to Mercy Levering, November 18, 1840, Conkling Papers, Illinois State Historical Society; William Baringer, *Lincoln Day by Day* (Washington: Lincoln Sesquicentennial Commission), p. 121.

19. Rothman, "Courtship and Transition to Marriage," p. 64; Turner, *Letters,* p. 22; Lincoln to Mrs. Orville H. Browning, April 1, 1838, in Basler, *Collected Works,* vol. 1, p. 117; Helm, *Mary, Wife of Lincoln,* pp. 119, 120; Ruth Painter Randall, *Mary Lincoln: Biography of a Marriage* (Boston: Little, Brown, 1953), p. 19; Henry Whitney, *Life on the Circuit with Lincoln* (Boston: Estes and Laurent, 1892), p. 24.

20. James Conkling to Mercy Levering, March 7, 1841, Conkling Papers; Helm, *Mary, Wife of Lincoln,* p. 74.

21. Turner, *Letters,* p. 20.

22. Rothman, "Courtship and Transition to Marriage," p. 61; *The Daughter's Own Book* (Boston: Lilly Wail, Colman and Holden), p. 10; Elizabeth Keckley, *Behind the Scenes* (New York: G. W. Carleton, 1868), p. 230; F. P. Webb to B. P. Hinch, November 5, 1852, B. P. Hinch Papers, Illinois State Historical Society.

23. Turner, *Letters,* pp. 16, 20; U.S. Census Records, 1850, Carmi, Illinois; James Conkling to "Merce," September 21, 1840, Conkling Papers.

24. Turner, *Letters,* p. 18; Statement of Mrs. N. W. Edwards, n.d., Herndon-Weik Papers.

25. Turner, *Letters,* p. 21; Helm, *Mary, Wife of Lincoln,* p. 78.

26. Elizabeth Edwards to William Herndon, n.d., Herndon-Weik Papers; Walter Stevens, *A Reporter's Lincoln* (St. Louis: Missouri Historical Society, 1916), pp. 73–80; Robert Todd to Betsey Humphreys, February 15, 1826; George Howard, *A History of Matrimonial Institutions* (Chicago: University of Chicago Press, 1904), vol. 2, p. 401.

27. Rothman, "Courtship and Transition to Marriage," pp. 9–10, 51; John James, *The Family Monitor or a Help to Domestic Happiness* (Boston: Crocker and Brewster, 1833), p. 63.

28. Harry Pratt, *The Personal Finances of Abraham Lincoln* (Springfield: Abraham Lincoln Association, 1943), pp. 25–27; J. G. Nicolay and John Hay, *Abraham Lincoln* (New York: Century Co., 1890), vol. 1, p. 112. It is impossible to estimate Lincoln's exact income from his practice during this period. Certainly it was no more than $4,000 and no less than $2,000 per year in the early 1840s.

29. Basler, *Collected Works,* vol. 1, p. 94.

30. Grossberg, "Law and the Family in Nineteenth-Century America," pp. 32–36. While the number of breach-of-promise suits decreased after the Civil War, one on the most extraordinary took place at the end of the century. It involved Mary's friend William Breckinridge and a Lexington, Kentucky, schoolgirl. See *The Celebrated Trial of Madeline Pollard versus Breckinridge: The Most Noted Breach of Promise Suit in the History of Court Records* (New York: American Print, 1894); Basler, *Collected Works,* vol. 2, p. 204.

31. Charles Stozier, *Lincoln's Quest for Union: Public and Private Meanings* (New York: Basic Books, 1982), pp. 39–40; Milton Shutes, *Lincoln's Emotional Life* (Philadelphia: Dorrance, 1957); Edward Dixon, *A Treatise on Woman and Her Diseases* (New York: Dewitt and Davenport, 1849); William Herndon to Jesse Weik, January 1891, Herndon-Weik Papers; Charles Stozier, "The Search for Identity and Love in Young Lincoln," in *The Public and Private Lincoln: Contemporary Perspectives,* ed. Cullum Davis et al. (Carbondale and Edwardsville, Ill.: Southern Illinois University Press, 1979), p. 12.

32. Turner, *Letters,* p. 21; *Sangamon Journal,* January 27, 1839.

33. William Herndon, *Life of Lincoln* (New York: Albert and Charles Boni, 1930), pp. 151–52.

34. Randall, *Mary Lincoln,* p. 15; Mary Owens Vineyard to William Herndon, May 23, 1866, Herndon-Weik Papers; Statement of Elizabeth Edwards, July 27, 1887, Herndon-Weik Papers; Henry Whitney, *Life on the Circuit with Lincoln* (Boston: Estes Lauriat, 1892), p. 36.

35. Turner, *Letters,* p. 26; Rothman, "Courtship and Transition to Marriage," pp. 51, 54; U.S. Census figures for 1860; *Lincoln Herald,* 1949, p. 47.

36. James Conkling to Mercy Levering, January 24, 1841, Conkling Papers; G. W. Miles to William Herndon, March 23, 1866 (postscript by A. W. Ellis), Herndon-Weik Papers; Turner, *Letters,* p. 26.

37. Helm, *Mary, Wife of Lincoln,* p. 89; Basler, *Collected Works,* vol. 1, p. 233.

38. James Conkling to Mercy Levering, January 24, 1841, Conkling Papers. Martin McKee to John Hardin, January 22, Hardin Papers; Jane Bell to Ann Bell, January 22, 1841, in *Lincoln Herald,* 1949, p. 47; Basler, *Collected Works,* vol. 1, pp. 228, 229; Herndon to Isaac Arnold, November 20, 1866, Herndon-Weik Papers.

39. Turner, *Letters,* p. 27.

40. William Shakespeare, *The Tragedy of King Richard II,* Cambridge Edition Text (New York: Garden City Books, 1936), pp. 370, 376, 377.

41. Randall, *Mary Lincoln,* p. 59; Turner, *Letters,* p. 26, 293.

42. Randall, *Mary Lincoln,* p. 59; Turner, *Letters,* p. 25. There have been many explanations for the ending of the courtship with the sex of the observer determining the point of view. Male historians including Roy Basler and Charles Strozier argue that Lincoln ended the engagement and that his subsequent depression resulted from his guilty recognition that he had hurt Mary Todd. William Herndon even fabricated a story about Lincoln's not showing up at his wedding, while Ruth Randall, the most sympathetic of Mary's biographers, believed Elizabeth Edwards finally prevailed on her headstrong sister to break off her relationship.

43. Alexis de Tocqueville, *Democracy in America* (New York: Vintage Books, 1960), vol. 2, pp. 212, 213.

44. William Herndon to General James H. Wilson, September 23, 1889, Herndon-Weik Papers; Basler, *Collected Works*, vol. 1, p. 94.

45. Basler, *Collected Works*, vol. 1, pp. 78, 94, 280, 303.

46. Randall, *Mary Lincoln*, p. 64; Mary Raymond, "Some Incidents in the Life of Mrs. Benjamin Edwards," p. 13, Illinois State Historical Library, Springfield, Ill.; Ninian Edwards to Abraham Lincoln, June 18, 1863, Robert Todd Lincoln Papers.

47. Statement of N. W. Edwards to William Herndon, September 22, 1865, Herndon-Weik Papers, microfilm edition.

48. James Conkling to "Merce," September 21, 1840, Conkling Papers; Basler, *Collected Works*, vol. 1, p. 299.

49. Common throughout the United States, the device of satiric letters appears earlier in Springfield and was used in 1837 by Abraham Lincoln in his Sampson's ghost letters. *Sangamon Journal*, September 6, 7, 1837; May 7, 1838; August 27, 1842. See also Basler, *Collected Works*, vol. 1, pp. 100, 297.

50. Basler, *Collected Works*, Vol. 1, pp. 100, 297. See also Roy Basler, "The Authorship of the Rebecca Letters," *Abraham Lincoln Quarterly*, vol. 2 (June 1942), pp. 80–90.

51. *Sangamon Journal*, September 8, 1842. The reference to squeezing grew out of an incident in which Shields squeezed a girl too ardently and she rewarded him by sticking a pin into him. *Lincoln Lore*, September 19, 1955.

52. *Sangamon Journal*, September 15, August 27, 1842; Basler, "The Authorship of the Rebecca Letters," pp. 80–90.

53. *Sangamon Journal*, September 8, 1842. Now part of East St. Louis, Bloody Island was under no state jurisdiction and as neutral territory hosted many illegal duels.

54. Turner, *Letters*, pp. 293, 295, 296. Lincoln's embarrassment was increased by the publication in Springfield's newspapers of a full account of what had happened.

55. Rothman, "Courtship and Transition to Marriage," pp. 297–300; Elizabeth Wallace, "My Personal Recollections," Herndon-Weik Papers; *Abraham Lincoln Quarterly*, vol. 3 (March 1945), pp. 236–38; Wayne Temple, ed., *Mrs. Mary Edwards Brown Tells the Story of Lincoln's Wedding* (Harrogate, Tenn.: Lincoln Memorial University Press, 1960).

56. Helm, *Mary, Wife of Lincoln*, pp. 94–95; James Matheny to Weik, August 21, 1888, Herndon-Weik Papers.

CHAPTER V
DOMESTIC PORTRAIT: THE SPRINGFIELD YEARS

1. Angle, *"Here I Have Lived,"* p. 88; *Sangamon Journal*, April 30, 1842. See also James Hickey, "The Lincoln's Globe Tavern: A Study in Tracing the History of a Nineteenth-Century Building," *Journal of the Illinois State Historical Society*, vol. 56 (Winter 1963), pp. 629–653. For the size of the room, see *Lincoln Herald*, April 21, 1947.

2. Marianne Finch, *An Englishwoman's Experience in America* (New York: New York University Press, 1969); Mrs. Trollope, *Domestic Manners of the Americans* (New York: Alfred A. Knopf, 1949), pp. 282–85; *Ladies Book*, vol. 17 (July 1838), p. 38; Basler, *Collected Works*, vol. 1, p. 305.

3. Angle, *"Here I Have Lived,"* pp. 126–27; *Sangamon Journal*, July 8, 1842.

4. Merce and James Conkling to "mother" (Mrs. Levering), January 13, 18, 1843, Conkling Papers.

5. Turner, *Letters*, pp. 60, 506.

6. Dr. Anson Henry's Notebook, A. G. Henry Papers, Illinois State Historical Society.

7. M. L. Holbrook, *Parturition Without Pain: A Code of Directions for Escaping from the Primal Curse* (New York: Holbrook, 1871) passim; *Sangamon Journal*, December 15, 1838;

Vivian Fox and Martin Quitt, *Loving, Parenting and Dying, the Family Cycle in England and America* (New York: Psychohistory Press, 1980), p. 248; Turner, *Letters,* pp. 520, 539.

8. William Smith, "Old Time Campaigning," *Journal of the Illinois State Historical Society,* vol. 13 (April 1920), p. 27; Rufus Rockwell Wilson, *Intimate Memories of Lincoln* (Elmira, N.Y.: Primavera Press, 1945), p. 61.

9. Pratt, *Personal Finances,* p. 84.

10. Deposition of Mary Todd Lincoln, October 1852, University of Kentucky Library.

11. James Hickey, "Robert S. Todd Seeks a Job for His Son-in-Law," *Journal of the Illinois State Historical Society,* vol. 72 (November 1979), p. 52; Wayne Temple, *By Square and Compasses: The Building of Lincoln's Home and Its Saga* (Bloomington, Ill.: Ashlar Press, 1984).

12. Basler, *Collected Works,* vol. 1, pp. 319, 320.

13. Joseph Wallace, *Sketch of the Life and Public Service of Edward D. Baker* (Springfield, Ill.: Journal Co., 1870), p. 18; Basler, *Collected Works,* vol. 1, p. 319.

14. Wallace, *Sketch,* passim. Others thought differently. Justin Butterfield, Lincoln's opponent for the commissioner of the Land Office, described Baker as a "vain supercilious Englishman." Donald Riddle, *Congressman Abraham Lincoln* (Urbana: University of Illinois Press, 1951), p. 349 n.

15. Ellen Hatch to O. M. Hatch, February 6, 1860, Hatch Papers, Illinois State Historical Society; Mrs. L. H. Sigourney, *Advice to Mothers* (New York: Harper's and Brothers, 1839), p. 4; U.S. Census, 1850, Seventh Census, Springfield (the 1850 census does not list female occupations). See also *Illinois Journal,* January 6, 1858.

16. Basler, *Collected Works,* vol. 1, p. 496; U.S. Census, 1850, Springfield, "Ninian W. Edwards."

17. Catharine Beecher, *A Treatise on Domestic Economy* (New York: Harper's, 1848), pp. 204–8; Faye Dudden, "From Help to Domestics, American Servants, 1800–1880" (Ph.D. dissertation, University of Rochester, 1981), p. 119; Hasia Diner, *Erin's Daughters in America* (Baltimore: Johns Hopkins University Press, 1983); Eliza Leslie, *The House Book* (Philadelphia: Carey and Hart, 1848), p. 3.

18. Harriet H. Chapman to William Herndon, November 21, 1866; William Herndon to Jesse Weik, December 1, 1885, Herndon-Weik Papers; William Herndon and Jesse Weik, *Herndon's Life of Lincoln* (Cleveland: World Publishing Co., 1930), p. 345.

19. Beecher, *Treatise,* p. 208; Dudden, "From Help to Domestics," p. 2.

20. Turner, *Letters,* p. 46.

21. Ibid., p. 59; Octavia Roberts, *Lincoln in Illinois* (Boston: Houghton Mifflin, 1918), p. 71; *Sangamon Journal,* February 17, 1852; Lloyd Ostendorf, "A Monument for One of Lincoln's Maids," *Lincoln Herald,* vol. 66 (Winter 1964), pp. 184–86; Jordan Fiore, "Lincoln's Portuguese Neighbors," *Lincoln Herald,* vol. 73 (Fall 1972), pp. 150–52; Thomas Dyba, *Seventeen Years at Eighth and Jackson: The Story of Life in the Lincoln Home* (Lisle, Ill.: IBC Publications, 1982).

22. Beecher, *Treatise,* p. 49; Richard Lufkin, "Mr. Lincoln's Light from Under a Bushel," *Lincoln Herald,* vol. 52 (December 1950), pp. 2–21; ibid., vol. 54 (Winter 1952), pp. 2–26.

23. Turner, *Letters,* pp. 49, 59; James Gourley to William Herndon, n.d., #3055, Reel 11, Herndon-Weik Papers; Willard King, *David Davis, Lincoln's Manager* (Cambridge: Harvard University Press, 1960), p. 85; James Conkling to Mercy Conkling, April 18, 1843, Conkling Papers.

24. James Gourley, #3050, Herndon-Weik; King, *David Davis, Lincoln's Manager,* pp. 69, 85.

25. *Sangamon Journal,* November 8, 1851.

26. Ibid., November 6, 12, 20, 1851; *Miss Leslie's Behavior Book* (Philadelphia: T. B. Peter and Bros., 1859), p. 74; *Lincoln Chronicle,* vol. 3 (September 25, 1983).

27. *Miss Leslie's Directions for Cookery,* 10th ed. (Philadelphia: Carey and Hart, 1840), p. 57; Dyba, *Seventeen Years at Eighth and Jackson.*

28. Helm, *Mary, Wife of Lincoln,* p. 112.

29. Trollope, *Domestic Manners of the Americans,* p. 85; Frances Brown, *The Everyday Life of Lincoln* (New York: Putnam's, 1913) p. 114.

30. James Aiken to Abraham Lincoln, August 16, 1858; "A Husband's Confession," Robert Todd Lincoln Papers; Brown, *Everyday Life of Lincoln;* Frances Wallace, n.d., #3191, Herndon-Weik Papers; *Sangamon Journal,* June 7, 1851, June 14, 1852, September 22, 1857, October 8, 1858; *Quincy Whig,* February 1, 1840; "Mary's Recipe for White Cake," Helm Papers.

31. Turner, *Letters,* p. 690; Trollope, *Domestic Manners,* p. 297; Anne Fields, *Life and Letters of Harriet Beecher Stowe* (Boston: Houghton Mifflin, 1897), p. 110.

32. James Hickey, "Lincolniana: The Lincoln Account at the Corneau and Diller Drug Store, 1849–1861," *Journal of the Illinois State Historical Society,* vol. 77 (Spring 1984), pp. 60–66.

33. *Godey's Lady's Book,* vol. 18 (May 1839), p. 207; *Miss Leslie's Cookery,* pp. 15, 80; C. M. Smith Account Books, Illinois State Historical Society. See also Pratt, *Personal Finances,* p. 154; Baringer, *Lincoln Day by Day,* vol. 2, p. 14.

34. Isaac Arnold, *The Life of Abraham Lincoln* (Chicago: Jansen, McClurg, 1885), pp. 82–83.

35. Beecher, *Treatise,* p. 234.

36. Turner, *Letters,* pp. 56, 51.

37. "Took Tea at Mrs. Lincoln's: The Diary of Mrs. William M. Black," *Journal of the Illinois State Historical Society,* vol. 48 (Spring 1955), pp. 59–64; First Presbyterian Church Records, 1852–1860, Illinois State Historical Association; Roger Chapin, *Ten Ministers: A History of the First Presbyterian Church of Springfield, Illinois 1828–1953* (n.p., n.d.); *Sangamon Journal,* February 18, 1853.

38. Turner, *Letters,* p. 60.

39. The exact income of the Lincolns during these years is impossible to ascertain, but it probably was under $5,000. The best-paid lawyers in the state, such as Isaac Arnold, made about $20,000. In 1857 Lincoln received the largest single fee of his career—$4,000. No matter what the figure, the Lincolns did not spend all their income, and Lincoln was a moneylender by the 1850s. One of his loans was to his brother-in-law Ninian Edwards. See Pratt, *Personal Finances,* p. 75; Turner, *Letters,* pp. 48, 49.

40. Koerner, *Memoirs,* vol. 2, pp. 93–95; *New York Tribune,* May 25, 1860; *Illinois Journal,* February 9, 1861.

41. Beecher, *Treatise,* p. 215; Richard Meckel, "The Awful Responsibility of Motherhood: American Health Reform and the Prevention of Infant and Child Mortality" (Ph.D. dissertation, University of Michigan, 1980), p. 133; *Sangamon Journal,* July 1, 1856; *The Lady's Medical Pocketbook* (Philadelphia: Kay, 1833); Eliza Farnham, *Life in Prairie Land* (New York: Harper's, 1846), pp. 126, 183; Helm, *Mary, Wife of Lincoln,* p. 112.

42. J. L. McCouson, "Mr. Lincoln's Broken Blind," *Lincoln Herald,* vol. 50 (June 1948), pp. 43–46; Dudden, "From Help to Service," passim; *Miss Leslie's House Book,* p. 110; Dyba, *Seventeen Years at Eighth and Jackson,* pp. 6, 7, 10, 11.

43. Basler, *Collected Works,* vol. 4, p. 189.

44. Interview with Tom Dyba, Lisle, Illinois, June 1983. See Dyba, *Seventeen Years at Eighth and Jackson;* Kenneth Scorr, "Lincoln's Home in 1860," *Journal of the Illinois State Historical Society,* vol. 44 (Spring 1953), pp. 7–12, quote pp. 7–8; Temple, *By Square and Compasses,* pp. 41–54.

45. Whitney, *Life on the Circuit with Lincoln,* p. 20; Temple, *By Square and Compasses,* pp. 41–54.

46. Basler, *Collected Works*, vol. 2, p. 211; Strozier, *Lincoln's Quest for Union*, p. 88; Paul Angle, *Lincoln: 1854–1861* (Springfield, Ill.: Abraham Lincoln Association, 1933), p. 6.

47. Turner, *Letters*, pp. 42, 37; Basler, *Collected Works*, vol. 1, p. 465.

48. Allison Lurie, "Sex and Fashion," *New York Review of Books* (October 22, 1981), pp. 37–43; *Illinois Journal*, September 19, 1854; Baringer, *Lincoln Day by Day*, vol. 2, p. 18; Pratt, *Personal Finances*, pp. 146–47; Turner, *Letters*, p. 50; Lloyd Ostendorf, *The Photographs of Mary Todd Lincoln* (Springfield: Illinois State Historical Society, 1969), pp. 6–7.

49. *Illinois Journal*, March 9, 1854.

50. Turner, *Letters*, p. 42.

51. For example, *Godey's Lady's Book*, vol. 26 (April 1843, November 1847); Jacob Abbott, *Gentle Measures in the Management and Training of the Young* (New York: Harper Brothers, 1871); Beecher, *A Treatise*, preface; *The Mother's Assistant*, vol. 3 (July 1843); William Alcott, *Young Mother or Management of Children in Regard to Health* (Boston: Little, 1836); Tocqueville, *Democracy in America*, vol. 2, p. 205.

52. *The Mother's Assistant*, vol. 6 (January 1845), preface.

53. Helm, *Mary, Wife of Lincoln*, pp. 101–02.

54. Harriet Chapman to William Herndon, November 21, 1866, Herndon-Weik Papers; Basler, *Collected Works*, vol. 4, p. 82, and vol. 1, p. 391; Rufus Rockwell Wilson, ed., *Intimate Memories of Lincoln* (Elmira, N.Y.: Primavera Press, 1945), p. 135.

55. Turner, *Letters*, p. 251; *Washington National Republic*, June 13, 1865; *Chicago Journal*, June 14, 1865.

56. Basler, *Collected Works*, vol. 1, p. 391; Turner, *Letters*, p. 37.

57. Helm, *Mary, Wife of Lincoln*, p. 108; Turner, *Letters*, pp. 61 and 50; Fox and Quitt, *Loving, Parenting and Dying*, pp. 319, 320.

58. Beecher, *Treatise*, p. 279; Turner, *Letters*, p. 50.

59. Mary Nash Stuart to Bettie Stuart (1858), Stuart-Hays Papers, Illinois Historical Society.

60. Mary Ryan, *Cradle of the Middle Class* (New York: Cambridge, 1981), pp. 27–31, 223–24.

61. Mary Lincoln to Margaret W. Preston, July 23, 1853, University of Kentucky Library; Ruth Painter Randall, *Lincoln's Sons* (Boston: Little, Brown, 1955), pp. 64–66.

62. Turner, *Letters*, pp. 57, 59, 64; Heinz Kohut, *The Restoration of the Self* (New York: New International Universities Press, 1977). Kohut's explanation of narcissism as enfeebled self-esteem and his separation of defensive structures and compensatory structures is helpful in understanding Mary Lincoln's mode of childraising.

63. Emanuel Hertz, *The Hidden Lincoln* (New York: Viking Press, 1938), p. 128; Turner, *Letters*, p. 104; William Herndon to Jesse Weik, January 6, 1866, Herndon-Weik Papers.

64. David Davis to Sarah Davis, May 17, 1852, David Davis Papers, Illinois State Historical Society.

65. U.S. Census, Seventh Census, Mortality Schedule, Springfield, Illinois, "Causes of Death, 1850"; Basler, *Collected Works*, vol. 2, p. 77; Turner, *Letters*, p. 463; Harriet Beecher Stowe, *Uncle Tom's Cabin* (New York: Washington Square Press, 1962), pp. 301–02.

66. *Miss Leslie's Cookery*, pp. 411–423; Milton Shutes, "Mortality of the Five Lincoln Boys," *Lincoln Herald*, vol. 57 (Spring 1955), p. 4.

67. *Illinois Journal*, February 2, 1850.

68. Turner, *Letters*, p. 64; Harry Pratt, "Little Eddie Lincoln—We Miss Him Very Much," *Journal of the Illinois State Historical Society*, vol. 4 (Autumn 1954), pp. 300–5; Octavia Roberts, *Lincoln in Illinois* (Boston: Houghton Mifflin, 1918), p. 65.

69. *Illinois Journal*, February 7, 1850.

70. *The Mother's Assistant*, vol. 8 (February 1846), p. 56; Sigourney, *Advice to Mothers*, pp. 261–74; *The Mourner's Book* (Boston: Benjamin Mussy, 1849).

71. Helm, *Mary, Wife of Lincoln*, p. 111.

72. Mary Lincoln to Margaret Preston, July 23, 1853, Wickcliffe-Preston Papers.

73. Ryan, *Cradle of the Middle Class*, pp. 157–58; *Illinois Journal*, June 7, 1852, March 29, 1854, January 9, 1854.

74. Randall, *Mary Lincoln*, pp. 219–20; Strozier, *Lincoln's Quest for Union*, p. 88; David Kennedy, *Birth Control in America* (New Haven: Yale University Press, 1970), p. 45; Charles Knowlton, *Fruits of Philosophy* (Boston: A. Kneeland, 1833); *Illinois Journal*, January 15, February 3, 1852.

75. King, *David Davis*, p. 84; William Chenery, "Mary Lincoln Should Be Remembered for Many Kind Acts," *Illinois State Register*, February 27, 1938; Elizabeth Todd to Mary Todd, n.d., Todd Papers, Kentucky State Archives; Leavitt, "Science Enters the Birthing Room"; Mary Todd Lincoln to Mary Harlan Lincoln, October 16, 1869, Insanity File, Fort Wayne Lincoln Library, Fort Wayne, Indiana; Frederick Falls, "Early Obstetric Practice in Illinois," *Illinois Medical Journal*, vol. 133 (February 1968), pp. 149–55.

CHAPTER VI   THE POLITICS OF MARRIAGE

1. Basler, *Collected Works*, vol. 4, pp. 60–68, 129, 325; Turner, *Letters*, pp. 296, 299, 302.

2. Frances Wallace, "Lincoln's Marriage," published in *Journal of the Illinois State Historical Society*, September 2, 1895; Turner, *Letters*, pp. 296, 236; Mrs. Chapman Coleman, *The Life of John Crittenden* (Philadelphia: Lippincott, 1871), vol. 1, p. 80.

3. Phyllis Rose, *Parallel Lives: Five Victorian Marriages* (New York: Knopf, 1983), p. 7.

4. Turner, *Letters*, p. 200; Strozier, *Lincoln's Quest for Union*, pp. 119–23; Wallace, "Lincoln's Marriage."

5. Helm, *Mary, Wife of Lincoln*, p. 115; William Herndon and Jesse Weik, *Herndon's Life of Lincoln* (Cleveland: World Publishing Co., 1930), pp. 344, 345.

6. Henry Rankin, *Personal Recollections of Abraham Lincoln* (New York: Putnams, 1916); King, *David Davis*, p. 74; Whitney, *Life on the Circuit*, p. 27; Pratt, *Personal Finances*, pp. 145–61; Harry Pratt, "The Lincolns Go Shopping," *Journal of the Illinois State Historical Society*, vol. 48 (Spring 1955), p. 66.

7. Helm, *Mary, Wife of Lincoln*, p. 109; Herndon, *Life of Lincoln*, pp. 344–45; Mem., October 15, 1914, #1212, Herndon-Weik Papers; Temple, *By Square and Compasses*, p. 134; Mary Todd Lincoln Statement to William Herndon, November 14, 1871, Herndon-Weik Papers.

8. Angle, *Lincoln, 1854–1861*, pp. 12, 16.

9. Answer of Abraham Lincoln, *Oldham, Hemingway* v. *Abraham Lincoln*, File 1268, Fayette County Courthouse; Abraham Lincoln to George Kinkaid, May 27, 1853, in Basler, *Collected Works*, vol. 2, pp. 194–97.

10. King, *David Davis*, p. 142; David Davis to Julius Rockwell, February 10, 1841, Davis Papers; Theodore Calvin Pease, ed., *The Diary of Orville Hickman Browning* (Springfield, Ill.: Blakely Printing Co., 1925).

11. Wallace, "Lincoln's Marriage."

12. Robert Henry Parkinson, "The Patent Case That Lifted Lincoln into a Presidential Candidate," *Abraham Lincoln Quarterly*, vol. 4 (September 1946), p. 113.

13. Basler, *Collected Works*, vol. 1, p. 391.

14. Ibid., p. 319; David Davis to Sarah Davis, August 15, 1847, Davis Papers.

15. As the crow flies, the distance from Springfield to Washington was about 700 miles and there were some objections to Lincoln's accounting, especially from Horace Greeley. See

Riddle, *Congressman Lincoln*, p. 13; Turner, *Letters*, p. 61; Constance McLaughlin Green, *Washington Village and Capital 1800–1878* (Princeton: Princeton University Press, 1962), p. 155; *Official Congressional Directory*, Thirtieth Congress (Washington, D.C.: 1849).

16. Baringer, *Lincoln Day by Day*, pp. 295–96.

17. Basler, *Collected Works*, vol. 1, p. 430; James Young, *The Washington Community, 1800–1828* (New York: Columbia University Press, 1966), pp. 89–109.

18. *Letters of Theodore Dwight Weld, Angelina Grimké Weld and Sarah Grimké, 1822–1844* (New York: Appleton-Century 1934), vol. 2, pp. 883, 884, 887.

19. Samuel Busey, *Personal Reminiscences* (Washington: 1895), p. 25.

20. Basler, *Collected Works*, vol. 1, p. 465; Weld, *Letters*, p. 887.

21. Green, *Washington*, pp. 147–49, 173; Charles Dickens, *American Notes to General Circulation* (London: Chapman Hall, 1842), pp. 163, 168–69; Turner, *Letters*, p. 56.

22. Busey, *Reminiscences*, p. 65; *National Intelligencer* (Washington, D.C.), February 7–11, 1848.

23. Helm, *Mary, Wife of Lincoln*, p. 119; *National Intelligencer*, January 6, 17, 1848; *Lincoln Chronicle*, June 20, 1985.

24. *Congressional Globe*, Thirtieth Congress, First Session, p. 64; Basler, *Collected Works*, vol. 1, pp. 451–452.

25. Basler, *Collected Works*, vol. 1, pp. 441–42.

26. Ibid., p. 465; Busey, *Reminiscences*, p. 26.

27. Basler, *Collected Works*, vol. 1, pp. 465, 477, 496.

28. Turner, *Letters*, pp. 475, 37. For a new interpretation of supposedly sexless Victorian women, see Peter Gay, *The Bourgeois Experience* (New York: Oxford University Press, 1984). There is an anecdote about Lincoln's being asked why he looked "so powerful weak" and his wife's cousin so fit. He responded: "Nothing out of common, Ma'am, but did you ever see Stuart's wife or did you see mine? I just tell you whoever married into the Todd family gets the worst of it." The context here, I believe, is sexual. *Journal of the Illinois State Historical Society*, vol. 19 (October 1926), p. 64.

29. Turner, *Letters*, p. 38.

30. Basler, *Collected Works*, vol. 1, p. 473; Turner, *Letters*, p. 50.

31. Herndon, *Life of Lincoln*, pp. 238–39; Baringer, *Lincoln Day by Day*, vol. 1, pp. 319–321; Turner, *Letters*, p. 61.

32. Riddle, *Congressman Lincoln*, p. 122.

33. Baringer, *Lincoln Day by Day*, vol. 2, pp. 11–17; Riddle, *Congressman Lincoln*, pp. 208–10, 214; A. Lincoln to ———, June 18, 23, 1849, Robert Todd Lincoln Papers.

34. Riddle, *Congressman Lincoln*, p. 222; Anson Henry to Thomas Ewing, August 21, 1849, Thomas Ewing Papers, Library of Congress; John Todd Stuart to William Herndon, July 21, 1865, Herndon-Weik Papers.

35. Herndon, *Life of Lincoln*, p. 301.

36. Blunderer to *Baltimore County* (Maryland) *Advocate*, July 3, 1852; Basler, *Collected Works*, vol. 2, p. 323.

37. *Illinois Journal*, July 11, 14, 1854; Townshend, *Lincoln and the Bluegrass*, p. 213.

38. *Springfield Journal*, May 24, 1858; Robert Johannsen, *Stephen A. Douglas* (New York: Oxford University Press, 1973), pp. 252–53.

39. Basler, *Collected Works*, vol. 2, p. 245; Angle, *"Here I Have Lived,"* pp. 185–87.

40. Henry Villard, *Memoirs of Henry Villard* (Boston: Houghton Mifflin, 1904), pp. 1, 96; Whitney, *Life on the Circuit*, p. 93; Davis to Sarah Davis, August 15, 1847, Davis Papers.

41. Riddle, *Congressman Lincoln*, pp. 249–50; A. J. Beveridge, *Abraham Lincoln* (Boston: Houghton Mifflin, 1928), vol. 2, p. 143; Basler, *Collected Works*, vol. 2, pp. 306–7.

42. Basler, *Collected Works*, vol. 2, pp. 304, 306, 290, 286–90.

43. Walter B. Stevens, *A Reporter's Lincoln* (St. Louis: Missouri Historical Society, 1916), p. 48; Basler, *Collected Works,* vol. 2, p. 307.

44. Basler, *Collected Works,* vol. 2, pp. 304–06; Turner, *Letters,* pp. 56, 57, 258, 264; Julia Trumbull to Lyman Trumbull, April 14, 1856, Trumbull Papers, Library of Congress; Anson Henry to his wife, February 18, 1863, Illinois State Historical Society; W. Jayne, n.d. #3016, Herndon-Weik Papers; Caroline Owsley Brown, "Springfield Society Before the Civil War," *Journal of the Illinois State Historical Society,* vol. 15 (April 1922), p. 488.

45. Mark Krug, *Lyman Trumbull* (New York: Barnes, 1965), pp. 216–22; King, *David Davis,* pp. 107–8.

46. Turner, *Letters,* p. 71; Sandburg, *Mary Lincoln,* p. 81.

47. Turner, *Letters,* pp. 54–55.

48. Herndon and Weik, *Herndon's Life of Lincoln,* vol. 2, p. 201; David Donald, *Lincoln's Herndon* (New York: Alfred Knopf, 1948), pp. 131, 188–91.

49. Turner, *Letters,* pp. 94, 96.

50. Ibid., p. 46; Helm, *Mary, Wife of Lincoln,* p. 108.

51. Turner, *Letters,* p. 46; William Herndon to Jesse Weik, January 12, 1886, Herndon-Weik Papers; Baringer, *Lincoln Day by Day,* p. 172.

52. Helm, *Mary, Wife of Lincoln,* pp. 140–44; Dwight Anderson, *Abraham Lincoln: The Quest for Immortality* (New York: Knopf, 1982), p. 16.

53. Basler, *Collected Works,* vol. 2, pp. 506, 284.

54. Pratt, *Personal Finances,* p. 105; Basler, *Collected Works,* vol. 2, p. 461, 483.

55. Helm, *Mary, Wife of Lincoln,* p. 140; Pratt, *Personal Finances,* p. 149; Koerner, *Memoirs,* vol. 2, p. 61.

56. *Springfield Journal,* June 29, 1858; Basler, *Collected Works,* vol. 3, pp. 283–325; *Alton Courier,* October 14, 15, 17, 1858; Koerner, *Memoirs,* vol. 2, pp. 66–67.

57. Stevens, *A Reporter's Lincoln,* p. 46.

58. Basler, *Collected Works,* vol. 3, pp. 283–324, 336, 339; Baker, *Affairs of Party,* pp. 183–187; *Illinois Journal,* November 20, 1858.

59. Whitney, *Life on the Circuit,* pp. 139, 462, 376, 494.

60. Pratt, *Personal Finances,* pp. 149–50, 154–61, 169; C. M. Smith *Account Book, 1859,* Illinois State Historical Society.

61. C. M. Smith *Account Book, 1859,* John Williams *Account Book, 1859,* Illinois State Historical Society; *Illinois Journal,* March 7, 1858.

62. Mary Stuart to Bettie Stuart, April 3, 1856, Stuart-Hays Papers.

63. Basler, *Collected Works,* vol. 3, pp. 377, 395.

64. Pratt, *Personal Finances,* p. 112; Pease, *Diary of Orville Hickman Browning,* February 8, 1860; Basler, *Collected Works,* vol. 4, p. 46.

65. Harry Carman and Reinhard Luthin, *The First Lincoln Campaign* (Cambridge: Harvard University Press, 1944), p. 139.

66. Ibid., p. 168; Basler, *Collected Works,* vol. 4, p. 68.

67. Clipping from *Springfield Daily Republican,* May 23, 1860, Robert Todd Lincoln Papers.

68. *New York Tribune,* May 25, 1860.

69. William Dickson to Abraham Lincoln, May 21, 1860, Robert Todd Lincoln Papers (postscript by Annie Dickson); Stevens, *A Reporter's Lincoln,* p. 49.

70. Turner, *Letters,* p. 66.

71. Ibid., p. 67.

72. *Springfield Journal,* August 9, 10, 1860; Temple, *By Square and Compasses,* p. 57.

73. Photograph from the Collection of the Illinois State Historical Society.

74. Stevens, *A Reporter's Lincoln,* p. 46.

75. Turner, *Letters,* p. 71.

CHAPTER VII   FIRST LADY

1. *New York Times,* February 11–21, 1861; Basler, *Collected Works,* vol. 4, p. 194.

2. Basler, *Collected Works,* vol. 4, p. 218; J. G. Randall, *Lincoln the President* (New York: Dodd, Mead, 1945), vol. 1, p. 109; Baringer, *Lincoln Day by Day,* p. 16; *New York Times,* February 20, 1861.

3. Henry Villard, *Lincoln on the Eve of '61* (New York: Alfred A. Knopf, 1941), pp. 52, 53.

4. Almira Lincoln Phelps to Mary Todd Lincoln, January 23, 1861, Robert Todd Lincoln Papers; W. O. Stoddard, *Inside the White House in War Times* (New York: Webster, 1890), p. 34; *New York Times,* February 11, 20, 1861; Elihu Washburne to Abraham Lincoln, January 30, 31, February 3, 1861, Robert Todd Lincoln Papers; Mercy Conkling to Clinton Conkling, February 12, 1861, Conkling Papers.

5. Villard, *Lincoln,* pp. 19–20; *New York Times,* February 20, 1861; *Poughkeepsie Daily Eagle,* February 19–21, 1861; *New York Herald,* February 18, 1861; "Lincolniana Notes," *Journal of the Illinois State Historical Society,* vol. 47 (Summer 1954), p. 186.

6. Ada Bailhache to Mary Brayman, November 20, 1860; Mercy Conkling to Clinton Conkling, November 7, 1860, Conkling Papers; Harry Pratt, *Concerning Mr. Lincoln* (Springfield, Ill.: Abraham Lincoln Association, 1944), pp. 30, 32; David Davis to Sarah Davis, October 15, 1860, Davis Papers; Robert Lincoln to "Dear Mother," December 2, 1860 (copy), Randall Papers; Turner, *Letters,* pp. 85–86.

7. Henry Kreisman to Charles Ray, n.d., 1861, Huntington Library; Mercy Conkling to Clinton Conkling, January 19, 1861, Conkling Papers; *Baltimore Sun,* February 7, 22, 1861; Baringer, *Lincoln Day by Day,* p. 7.

8. *New York Herald,* February 21, 1861; *New York Times,* January 28, 1861; Jeannie James and Wayne Temple, "Mrs. Lincoln's Clothing," *Lincoln Herald,* vol. 62 (Summer 1960), pp. 54–65; *Home Journal,* March 16, June 29, 1861.

9. Norma Cuthbert, *Lincoln and the Baltimore Plot of 1861* (San Marino, Calif.: Huntington Library, 1949), pp. xiv, 149; Margaret Williams, "A Brief Reminiscence of the First Inauguration of Abraham Lincoln as President," Manuscript Division, Library of Congress.

10. Green, *Washington,* p. 21; Henry Adams, *The Education of Henry Adams* (Boston: Houghton Mifflin, 1927), p. 99; Margaret Leech, *Reveille in Washington, 1860–1865* (New York: Harper's, 1941), p. 41.

11. Green, *Washington,* p. 238.

12. Dickens, *American Notes,* vol. 1, p. 281; Leech, *Reveille,* pp. 6–7.

13. Basler, *Collected Works,* vol. 4, p. 217; Dr. Robert King Stone to Professor Campbell Morfit, May 7, 1857, New York Historical Society; Allan Clark, "Abraham Lincoln in the National Capital," *Records of Columbia Historical Society,* vol. 27 (1925), pp. 1–175; Mrs. Virginia Clapton Clay, *Memoirs* (New York: Doubleday, 1904), p. 140; Tyler Dennett, ed., *Lincoln and the Civil War in the Diaries and Letters of John Hay* (New York: Dodd Mead, 1939), p. 39.

14. Leech, *Reveille,* pp. 37–45; Adams, *The Education of Henry Adams,* p. 107; Clark, "Abraham Lincoln in the National Capital," p. 6; *New York Herald,* March 6, 1861.

15. William Howard Russell, *My Diary North and South* (London: Breadbury, 1863), pp. 132, 269; Edna Colman, *Seventy-Five Years of White House Gossip* (New York: Doubleday, 1926); Lorna Logan, *Ladies of the White House* (New York: Vantage Press, 1962); Ben Perley Poore, *Perley's Reminiscences of Sixty Years in the National Metropolis* (Philadelphia: Hubbard Brothers, 1886), pp, 1, 221, 298, 313, 356, 468; Turner, *Letters,* pp. 111, 138.

16. *New York Times,* February 23, 1861; Turner, *Letters,* p. 111; *New York Herald,* Octo-

ber 21, 1861; *Springfield* (Massachusetts) *Republic,* June 7, 1875; *Chicago Tribune,* August 31, 1861. For an understanding of the public-private separation, see Jean Strouse, "Semi-Private Lives," *Studies in Biography,* ed. Daniel Aaron (Cambridge: Harvard University Press, 1978), pp. 113–29.

17. Leech, *Reveille,* pp. 49, 292–93; Stoddard, *Inside the White House,* p. 12; Elizabeth Todd Grimsley, "Six Months in the White House," *Journal of the Illinois State Historical Society,* vol. 19 (October 1926–January 1927), pp. 66–67, 50–51.

18. Grimsley, "Six Months in the White House," pp. 47–48; Stoddard, *Inside the White House,* p. 49.

19. *Congressional Globe,* Twenty-sixth Congress, First Session, pp. 326, 327, 331–41; Register of First Auditor, 1858, 1859, 1860, Treasury Department, RG 217, National Archives.

20. Charles P. Stone to William Henry Seward, April 5, 1861, Seward Papers, Library of Congress; Turner, *Letters,* p. 86; *New York Times,* May 1, 1861.

21. Henry Kreisman to Charles Ray, January 16, 1861, Huntington Library.

22. "Union" to Lincoln, June 26, 1861, Robert Todd Lincoln Collection; John Nicolay to Schuyler Colfax, July 17, 1875, Nicolay Papers, Library of Congress.

23. *New York Herald,* May 23, 1861.

24. *Washington Daily Chronicle,* August 29, 1862; March 11, 1863; *Washington Star,* August 29, 1868; "An Eyewitness Account of a Visit by President and Mrs. Lincoln to Campbell's Hospital Washington D.C.," *Lincoln Herald,* vol. 77 (Spring 1975), p. 68; *New York Tribune,* December 25, 1862; *New York Herald,* December 6, 1862; *Washington Evening Sun,* August 29, October 4, 1862; *Boston Journal,* December 2, 1863; Wayne Temple, "Mrs. Lincoln's Jewelry," *Lincoln Herald,* vol. 64 (Spring 1962), p. 85; Stoddard, *Inside the White House,* pp. 87–88; Julia Taft Bayne, *Tad Lincoln's Father* (Boston: Little, Brown, 1931), p. 172; Clark, "Abraham Lincoln in the National Capital," pp. 73–83.

25. Hannah Ropes, *Diary of a Civil War Nurse* (Knoxville: University of Tennessee Press, 1980), pp. 49–119; Bayne, *Tad Lincoln's Father,* pp. 172–74; Turner, *Letters,* p. 179; Kenneth Bernard, "Will the Leader of the Band see Mrs. Lincoln?" *Lincoln Herald,* vol. 64 (Spring 1962), pp. 3–8; Basler, *Collected Works,* vol. 5, p. 377; "An Eyewitness Account of a Visit to Campbell's Hospital, Washington, D.C.," p. 68; Noah Brooks, *Washington in Lincoln's Time* (Chicago: Quadrangle Books, 1971), p. 19.

26. Harry Pratt and Ernest East, "Mrs. Lincoln Refurbishes the White House," *Lincoln Herald,* vol. 47 (February 1945), pp. 12–22; Bill of Alexander Stewart Company, Department of Interior, Commissioner of Public Buildings Account, RG 42, National Archives; Grimsley, "Six Months in the White House," p. 54; Margaret Klapthor, "White House China of the Lincoln Administration," Smithsonian Institution, *United States National Museum Bulletin,* vol. 250 (1969), pp. 111–20.

27. Turner, *Letters,* p. 106.

28. Ledgers of the Commissioner of Public Buildings, 1859–1865, Commissioner of Public Buildings, RG 42, National Archives.

29. Mercy L. Conkling to Clinton Conkling, January 9, 1861, Conkling Papers; *Congressional Globe,* Thirty-seventh Congress, Third Session, app. pp. 214–15; Second Session, pp. 215, 705, 706.

30. Benjamin French to Henry French, October 13, 1861, French Papers, microfilm edition, Library of Congress; Ledger Appropriations for Commissioner's Office, Commissioner of Public Buildings, RG 42; *U.S. Congress Select Committee,* Extract, August 30, 1861, Robert Todd Lincoln Papers. For an example of how the New York merchants tried to move in on White House business, see Leonard Wheeler to Lyman Trumbull, January 11, 1861, Trumbull Papers.

31. Benjamin French to Pamela French, December 24, 1861, French Papers; Benjamin

French Journals, December 16, 1861; Turner, *Letters,* p. 181; A. Henry to Caleb Smith, 1861 (copy), Randall Papers; Benjamin French to Abraham Lincoln, May 9, 1861, Robert Todd Lincoln Papers.

32. Benjamin French to Mary Todd Lincoln, September 28, 1861, Records of Commissioner of Public Buildings; Basler, *Collected Works,* vol. 5, p. 71; Entry, September 8, 1861, Benjamin French Journals, French Papers.

33. Benjamin French to Caleb Smith, October 10, 1861, Records of Commissioner of Public Buildings, RG 42. Caleb Smith to French, October 17, 1861, Letters Received, Commissioner of Public Buildings; Elijah Whitley to George Harr, March 6, 1862, Letters Received, Commissioner of Public Buildings; *Congressional Globe,* Thirty-seventh Congress, Second Session, pp. 706, 783.

34. Keckley, *Behind the Scenes,* p. 85; Turner, *Letters,* p. 180, 181, 90; Caleb Smith to W. H. Seward, October 27, 1861, Seward Papers; "Bill Rendered to Abraham Lincoln for Nine Months Salary," Ward Hill Lamon Papers, Huntington Library; *Lincoln Lore,* May 4, 1942.

35. Vouchers, First Auditor, Treasury Record, 1861, Miscellaneous Papers, Huntington Library; John Washington, *They Knew Lincoln* (New York: E. P. Dutton, 1942), pp. 120, 225, 228; John Watt, "Bill Rendered to Abraham Lincoln Commissary Stores for Use of the President's House," First Auditor's Records, 1861, Treasury Department Records; John Blake to Caleb Smith, April 4, 1861, Records of Commissioner of Public Buildings; Dennett, *Hay Diaries,* p. 40.

36. Dennett, *Hay Diaries,* p. 273; Turner, *Letters,* pp. 102, 103 (and n. 5), 104, 112; Alex Williamson to John Watt, August 11, 1863, Huntington Library.

37. *Springfield Republican,* October 19, 1861; *New York Herald,* October 21, 1861.

38. Turner, *Letters,* pp. 105, 106; *Springfield Republican,* October 19, 1861; Howard Glyndon (Mrs. Laura Redden Searing), "The Truth About Mrs. Lincoln," *Independent,* August 10, 1882; Mercy Levering to Clinty, March 9, 1863, Conkling Papers.

39. Karen Halttunnen, *Confidence Men and Painted Women: A Study of Middle Class Culture in America 1830–1870* (New Haven: Yale University Press, 1982), pp. 70–81; Lois Banner, *American Beauty* (New York: Alfred A. Knopf, 1983).

40. *Washington Daily Chronicle,* March 4, May 10, May 33, 1863, November 17, December 15, 1862; *Godey's Lady's Book,* enclosure, June 23, 1863, Robert Todd Lincoln Papers; Keckley, *Behind the Scenes,* p. 90.

41. Keckley, *Behind the Scenes,* p. 204.

42. Turner, *Letters,* p. 174; *Washington Daily Chronicle,* January 1, 1863; January 5, 1864.

43. Turner, *Letters,* p. 194.

44. Bayne, *Tad Lincoln's Father,* pp. 43–46.

45. Turner, *Letters,* p. 109; James and Temple, "Mrs. Lincoln's Clothing," *Lincoln Herald,* Summer 1960, pp. 54–58; Keckley, *Behind the Scenes,* p. 101.

46. Turner, *Letters,* p. 116.

47. Senator Nesmith to "wife," February 5, 1862 (copy), Randall Papers; Eunice Tripler, *Some Notes of Personal Recollections* (New York: Grafton Press, 1910), pp. 133, 137.

48. Basler, *Collected Works,* vol. 1, p. 466; Keckley, *Behind the Scenes,* p. 101; *Journal of the Illinois State Historical Society,* vol. 19 (April 1926), p. 125; "A Kindly Word for Abraham Lincoln's Widow," *Christian Register,* September 7, 1872; Randall, *Lincoln the President,* vol. 1, p. 70.

49. William Herndon to Isaac Arnold, October 24, 1883, Herndon-Weik Papers.

50. Leech, *Reveille,* p. 160; Norman Judd to Lyman Trumbull, March 5, 1865, Trumbull Papers; Mrs. John Logan, *Reminiscences* (New York: Scribner's, 1913), p. 83.

51. Benjamin French Journals, March 5, 1865, French Papers; Jane Swisshelm, *Half a Century* (Chicago: Jansen, McClurg, 1880), pp. 236–37; M.A. De Wolfe Howe, ed., *The*

Life and Letters of George Bancroft (New York: Scribner's, 1908), vol. 2, p. 143.

52. Russell, *My Diary,* p. 269; *Washington Daily Chronicle,* January 2, 1863; Grimsley, "Six Months in the White House," p. 62.

53. William Crook, *Through Five Administrations* (New York: Harper's, 1905), p. 52; John Niven, *Gideon Welles, Lincoln's Secretary of Navy* (New York: Oxford University Press, 1978), p. 466; Russell, *My Diary,* p. 269; Zachariah Chandler to wife, January 21, 1865, Zachariah Chandler Papers, Library of Congress; Benjamin French Journals, December 18, 1861, French Papers.

54. Leech, *Reveille,* p. 15; Grimsley, "Six Months in the White House," pp. 49, 69; First Statement of Elizabeth Edwards, n.d., Herndon-Weik Papers; Clay, *Memoirs,* p. 87; Turner, *Letters,* p. 81.

55. John Nicolay to Theresa Bates, August 2, 1861, Nicolay Papers; Daniel Carroll, "Abraham Lincoln and the Minister of France," *Lincoln Herald,* Fall 1968, pp. 146–47; Frederick Seward, *Reminiscences of a Wartime Statesman and Diplomat, 1830–1915* (New York: Putnam's, 1915), pp. 182–84.

56. Turner, *Letters,* p. 96.

57. *Springfield Republican,* October 21, 1863; *New York Herald,* August 5, 1861; *Lincoln Herald,* 1968; Virginia Fox to "ma," March 10, 1864, Gustavus Fox Papers, New York Historical Society.

58. *Lincoln Herald,* Fall 1968, pp. 146–47.

59. Basler, *Collected Works,* vol. 5, p. 125; *New York Times,* February 24, March 7, 1861; *Providence Journal,* February 26, 1861.

60. *Chicago Tribune,* January 24, 1861; Villard, *Lincoln on the Eve of '61,* pp. 70–71; Horace White to Herndon, New York, January 26, 1891, Herndon-Weik Papers. For evidence that Kreisman's description was a fabrication and typical of the inaccurate gossip about Mary Lincoln, see Randall, *Mary Lincoln,* pp. 195–97. Also Charles Francis Adams, *An Autobiography* (Boston: Houghton Mifflin, 1916), pp. 102–3.

61. Turner, *Letters,* p. 180; "JBL" to Lockwood Todd, June 10, 1861; Mrs. S. B. Moody to Abraham Lincoln, July 19, 1861, Robert Todd Lincoln Papers; George Ashmun to N. P. Banks, February 6, 1864, Banks Papers, Library of Congress.

62. Benjamin French to Henry French, January 22, 1861, French Papers.

63. Turner, *Letters,* pp. 81, 86, 108.

64. Keckley, *Behind the Scenes,* p. 131; Turner, *Letters,* pp. 190, 191, 193; W. A. Swanberg, *Sickles the Incredible* (New York: Scribner's, 1956), p. 270; Harold Holzer et.al., *Images of Lincoln* (New York: Scribner's, 1984), p. 121.

65. Turner, *Letters,* p. 105; Basler, *Collected Works,* vol. 4, p. 412; C. Smith to Abraham Lincoln, February 7, 1864; O. M. Hatch, Wm. Butler, et al., to Lincoln, July 22, October 21, 1861, Robert Todd Lincoln Papers.

66. Turner, *Letters,* p. 180; *New York World,* September 22, 1864.

67. Abraham Lincoln to Edwin Stanton, October 21, 1862; Basler, *Collected Works,* vol. 5, p. 472; Harry Carman and Reinhard Luthin, *Lincoln and the Patronage* (New York: Columbia University Press, 1943), p. 113; Turner, *Letters,* p. 193; Benjamin Thomas and Harold Hyman, *Stanton: The Life and Times of Lincoln's Secretary of War* (New York: Alfred Knopf, 1962), p. 165; *Boston Daily Evening Transcript,* January 7, 1870; Frank Flower, *Edwin McMasters Stanton* (Akron: Saalfred Publishing Company, 1905), p. 255.

68. Turner, *Letters,* pp. 146, 140, 193, 174, 101, 103, 138; *The Etiquette of Washington* (Baltimore: Murphy, 1857); Pratt, *Concerning Mr. Lincoln,* pp. 80, 82, 83; Abraham Lincoln to John T. Stuart, March 20, 1861, in Basler, *Collected Works,* vol. 4, p. 296; John Nicolay to O. M. Hatch, March 31, 1861, Nicolay Papers. John Stuart to Abraham Lincoln, April 3, 1861; John Nicolay to O. M. Hatch, March 31, 1861, Hatch Papers.

69. Edgar Harnott to Mrs. Lincoln, February 17, 1863; William Richmond to Mary

Todd Lincoln, August 25, August 8, September 21, 1861, Robert Todd Lincoln Papers; Mrs. W. A. Burnett to Mrs. President Lincoln, April 13, 1861, Huntington Library; John Reynolds to Mrs. President Lincoln, October 21, 1861, Robert Todd Lincoln Papers.

70. Eliza Browning to Abraham Lincoln, June 8, 1861; Mrs. W. H. Planck to Abraham Lincoln, February 1, 1864, Robert Todd Lincoln Papers; Leonard Swett to Laura Swett, August 19, 1862, Davis Papers, cited in King, *David Davis*, p. 195.

71. Turner, *Letters*, p. 81.

72. Malcolm Cowley, ed., *The Complete Poetry of Walt Whitman* (New York: Penguin, 1976), vol. 2, pp. 17–18.

73. John Nicolay to Theresa, February 2, 1862, Nicolay Papers, Huntington Library; Leech, *Reveille*, p. 295.

74. *New York Herald*, February 6, 1862; *Washington Star*, February 4, 5, 6, and 7, 1862; *Washington Daily Chronicle*, February 5–8, 1862; Nicolay to Theresa, February 7, 1862, Nicolay Papers; *Home Journal*, August 17, 1861.

75. *Washington Chronicle*, February 9, 1862; *Washington Star*, February 6, 1862; Ben Perley Poore, *Perley's Reminiscences of Sixty Years in the National Metropolis* (Philadelphia: Hubbard Bros., 1886), vol. 2, pp. 116–20; Pratt, "Mrs. Lincoln Refurbishes the White House," p. 22. For gripes about dancing, see "A Citizen" to Abraham Lincoln, #7385, Robert Todd Lincoln Papers; Virginia Fox to uncle, January 30, 1862, Fox Papers; Samuel Heintzleman Papers, February 1862, Library of Congress; John Nicolay to Edward Bates, February 6, 1862, Bates Papers; "The Grand Presidential Party," *Lincoln Lore*, April 1967; Kenneth Bernard, "The Music of the Civil War," *Lincoln Herald*, vol. 63 (Fall 1961), pp. 121–33. "Lincoln's First Levee," *Journal of the Illinois State Historical Society*, vol. 11 (October 1918), p. 386; Madeleine Vinton Dahlgren, *Memoir of John Dahlgren* (Boston: James Osgood, 1882).

CHAPTER VIII   A VANISHING CIRCLE

1. The most convincing evidence regarding Willie's disease comes from Rebecca Pomroy, the army nurse who nursed him. The Washington papers sometimes reported him better, though typhoid fever is usually not accompanied by remissions. *Washington Star*, February 10, February 14, February 19, 1862; Anna Boyden, *Echoes from Hospital and White House* (Boston: D. Lathrop, 1884), pp. 47–54.

2. Leech, *Reveille*, p. 7; Green, *Washington*, pp. 350–54; Turner, *Letters*, pp. 127, 128; *Washington Star*, February 19, 1862; *Washington Daily Chronicle*, February 18, 19, 20, 1862.

3. Mercy Conkling to Clinton Conkling, February 24, March 23, 1862, Conkling Papers; Mrs. Ellen Price Wood, *East Lynne* (New York: n.p., n.d.), pp. 152, 183; *Receipt Book and Lending Record*, 1862, Library of Congress.

4. Turner, *Letters*, p. 128; Elizabeth Edwards to Julia Baker Edwards, n.d., 1862 (copy), Randall Papers; Wm. Florville to Abraham Lincoln, December 27, 1863, Robert Todd Lincoln Papers.

5. Turner, *Letters*, p. 128.

6. Bowlby, *Loss, Sadness and Depression* vol. 3, pp. 96–100; Halttunnen, *Confidence Men*, pp. 124–53; B. B. French to Robert Stone, May 21, 1862; letters sent by Office of Commissioner of Public Buildings, Record Group 42, National Archives.

7. Thomas and Hyman, *Stanton*, pp. 27, 35; *The Mourner's Book;* Frances Parkman, *An Offering of Sympathy to the Afflicted, Especially to Parents Bereaved of Their Children* (Boston: Lilly, Wait, Colman and Holden, 1833); Mrs. M. A. Patrick, *The Mourner's Gift* (New York: Charles S. Francis, 1837); J. B. Syme, *The Mourners Friend: or Sighs of Sympathy for Those Who Sorrow* (Worcester, Mass.: William Allen, 1852); John Morley, *Death, Heaven and the Victo-*

rians (Pittsburgh: University of Pittsburgh Press, 1971), p. 14.

8. Halttunnen, *Confidence Men,* p. 132; Morley, *Death, Heaven and the Victorians,* pp. 29, 32; Frederick Anspach, *The Sepulchres of our Departed* (Philadelphia: Lindsay and Blakisten, 1854), p. 52.

9. Turner, *Letters,* p. 127; Keckley, *Behind the Scenes,* p. 104; Elizabeth Edwards to Julia Edwards, March 2, March 12, April 26, 1862 (copy), Randall Papers; Benjamin French Journals, March 2, 1862, French Papers.

10. Basler, *Collected Works,* vol. 5, p. 326; Boyden, *Echoes;* Elizabeth Edwards to Julia Edwards, April 26, 1862 (copy), Randall Papers.

11. Keckley, *Behind the Scenes,* pp. 104–05.

12. Basler, *Collected Works,* vol. 6, pp. 16, 17; Milton Shutes, *Lincoln and the Doctors: A Medical Narrative of the Life of Abraham Lincoln* (New York: Pioneer Press, 1933), pp. 36–37; Baringer, *Lincoln Day by Day,* vol. 3, p. 126.

13. Bayne, *Tad Lincoln's Father,* p. 200; Keckley, *Behind the Scenes,* p. 181; Turner, *Letters,* p. 189.

14. Turner, *Letters,* p. 128; Pratt, *Concerning Mr. Lincoln,* p. 94.

15. Boyden, *Echoes,* p. 58; Halttunnen, *Confidence Men,* p. 128; Morley, *Death, Heaven and the Victorians,* p. 32; George Morgan to Secretary Welles, August 27, 1853, Welles Papers, New York Public Library; Turner, *Letters,* p. 131.

16. Nehemiah Adams, *Agnes and the Little Key* (Boston: Gould and Lincoln, 1841), p. 41; "Lincoln's Executive Mansion Library," *Lincoln Lore,* December 12, 1949; Ledger of the Library of Congress, 1862, Library of Congress.

17. Turner, *Letters,* pp. 189, 128, 189, 147; Mercy Conkling to Clinton Conkling, February 24, 1862, Conkling Papers; David Todd to John Todd, June 11, 1862 (copy), Randall Papers.

18. George Haviland to "Mother," February 23, 1862, Walter Rowland Papers, Duke University.

19. Turner, *Letters,* pp. 125, 127; E. P. Tisdale, *Queen Victoria's Private Life* (New York: Jarrold's, 1961), pp. 53–54, 64.

20. Charles Dickens, *Dombey and Son* (London: Oxford University Press, 1953), p. 99. See Whitman's description of Mary Todd Lincoln in mourning, Walt Whitman, *Complete Writings* (New York: Putnam's, 1902), vol. 1, p. 72.

21. Turner, *Letters,* p. 128; John Morse, ed., *Diary of Gideon Welles* (Boston: Houghton Mifflin, 1909), vol. 1, pp. 325, 326.

22. Robert Lawrence Moore, *In Search of White Crows: Spiritualism Parapsychology and American Culture* (New York: Oxford University Press, 1977); Howard Kerr, *Mediums and Spirit Rapping and Roaring Radicals: Spiritualism in American Literature, 1850–1900* (Urbana: University of Illinois Press, 1972), p. 80. On Boston as a center, see E. C. Rogers, *Philosophy of Mysterious Agents* (Boston: Herbert and Robbins, 1852), p. 258; Uriah Clark, *Plain Guide to Spiritualism Handbook* (Boston: William White, 1863).

23. Warren Chase, *The Gift of Spiritualism* (Boston: William White, 1865); Harrison Barrett, ed., *Cora V. L. Richmond* (Chicago: Hack and Anderson, 1895); E. W. Capron, *Modern Spiritualism: Its Facts and Fanaticisms* (Boston: Bela Marsh, 1855), pp. 359–69; *Congressional Record,* 33d Congress, 1st Session, pp. 923–24.

24. "The Lincolns and Spiritualism," *Lincoln Lore,* April 15, 1946; "Lincoln's Attendance at Spiritualist Séances," *Lincoln Lore,* January, February 1963.

25. Tisdale, *Queen Victoria; Lincoln Lore,* April 1946; Nettie Colburn Maynard, *Was Abraham Lincoln a Spiritualist?* (Philadelphia: n.p., 1891), p. 42; Geoffrey Nelson, *Spiritualism and Society* (London: Routledge and Kegan Paul, 1969); Charles Foster, *The Salem Seer* (New York: Lovell, 1891); "The Spirit of E. Baker," December 28, 1861, Robert Todd Lincoln Papers; Brooks, *Washington, D.C., in Lincoln's Time,* p. 66; *Washington Chronicle,* May 10,

1863; Janet Oppenheim, *The Other World* (Cambridge: Cambridge University Press, 1985).

26. Maynard, *Was Abraham Lincoln a Spiritualist?*, pp. 42, 153; *Spiritual Magazine*, vol. 8 (1872), p. 7; *New York Herald*, April 18, 1865; Theodore Pease, ed., *The Diary of Orville Browning* (Springfield: Illinois State Historical Library, 1925), vol. 20, pp. 1, 608; J. S. Hastings to Abraham Lincoln, August 9, 1861, Robert Todd Lincoln Papers; Brooks, *Washington, D.C., in Lincoln's Time*, pp. 66–68.

27. Turner, *Letters*, p. 256; Maynard, *Was Abraham Lincoln a Spiritualist?*, p. 99; *Washington Chronicle*, April 7, 1863.

28. Helm, *Mary, Wife of Lincoln*, p. 227; Lydia Smith to Abraham Lincoln, October 4, 1862, Robert Todd Lincoln Papers; *Spiritualist Magazine*, vol. 8 (1872), p. 7. For a modern interpretation, see Vieda Skultans, *Intimacy and Ritual: A Study of Spiritualism, Mediums and Groups* (Boston: Routledge and Kegan Paul, 1974).

29. Emma Harding Britten, *A Twenty Year Record of the Communion Between Earth and the World of Spirits* (New York: n.p., 1870), p. 306.

30. J. W. Edmonds to Abraham Lincoln, June 1, 1863, Robert Todd Lincoln Papers; Maynard, *Was Abraham Lincoln a Spiritualist?*, p. 184; Barrett, *The Life Work of Cora Richmond*, pp. 312–20; Abraham Lincoln to Edwin Morgan, January 16, 1864, in Basler, *Collected Works*, vol. 7, p. 133; "Lincoln's Attendance at Spiritualist Séances," *Lincoln Lore*, January 1963; Cornelia Fonda to Abraham Lincoln, January 28, 1864, Robert Todd Lincoln Papers.

31. Nelson, *Spiritualism and Society;* J. S. Hastings to Abraham Lincoln, September 7, 1861, Robert Todd Lincoln Papers; Elizabeth Packard et. al., *The Prisoner's Hidden Life or Insane Asylums Unveiled* (Chicago: A. B. Case, 1868); *Mrs. Packard's Reproof to Dr. McFarland for His Abuse of Patients* (Chicago: n.p., 1860).

32. Helm, *Mary, Wife of Lincoln*, p. 213.

33. Ibid., pp. 220, 225, 227; Keckley, *Behind the Scenes*, p. 135; Reverend N. W. Miner, "Mrs. Abraham Lincoln: A Recollection," Illinois State Historical Society; *Boston Transcript*, October 2, 1861, *House Reports*, Fortieth Congress, Third Session, 1869, vol. 45, p. 802.

34. Helm, *Mary, Wife of Lincoln*, p. 220–23.

35. Ibid., p. 225.

36. Baringer, *Lincoln Day by Day*, p. 197.

37. Helm, *Mary, Wife of Lincoln*, p. 229.

38. "To Whom it May Concern," December 3, 14, 1863, Robert Todd Lincoln Papers; Nicolay and Hay, *Works*, vol. 9, pp. 255–56; Browning, *Diary*, vol. 2, p. 215; Basler, *Collected Works*, vol. 7, pp. 219, 484.

39. Even today Levi Todd's grave is unmarked, though the Lexington cemetery record indicates he is buried somewhere in the Todd plot. Emilie Helm to Abraham Lincoln, October 31, 1864, Robert Todd Lincoln Papers.

40. Basler, *Collected Works*, vol. 6, pp. 517, 553; Townshend, *Lincoln and the Bluegrass*, p. 333; Ninian Edwards to Elodie Todd Dawson, June 11, 1869, N. H. R. Dawson Papers.

41. Martha Todd White to Abraham Lincoln, December 19, 1863, Robert Todd Lincoln Papers; *National Intelligencer*, March 29, 1864; *New York Herald*, April 2, 1864; Welles, *Diary*, vol. 2, p. 21; Grimsley, "Six Months in the White House," p. 57.

42. Turner, *Letters*, pp. 534, 187; Charles Gwinn to Abraham Lincoln, August, 1864, Robert Todd Lincoln Papers.

43. Benjamin French to Pamela French, April 10, 1864, French Papers; Basler, *Collected Works*, vol. 5, pp. 472, 477, 492, 143; Stoddard, *Inside the White House*, p. 62.

44. Helm, *Mary, Wife of Lincoln*, p. 226; Turner, *Letters*, p. 206; Baringer, *Lincoln Day by Day*, p. 222.

45. Elbert B. Smith, *Francis Preston Blair* (New York: The Free Press, 1980), p. 313.

46. O. M. Hatch to George, November 2, 1861; John Nicolay to Theresa, November 21, 1861, Nicolay Papers; Jane Swisshelm to *Chicago Tribune*, July 20, 1882; Frank Klement,

"Jane Grey Swisshelm and Lincoln," *Lincoln Quarterly,* vol. 16 (December 1950), pp. 227–38; *Frank Leslie's Illustrated Weekly Newspaper,* October, November 1863.

47. Turner, *Letters,* p. 200.

48. *The Old Guard,* September 1861, p. 199; *New York Herald,* October 19, 1861; *Boston Daily Courier,* November 12, 1862.

49. Basler, *Collected Works,* vol. 6, pp. 283, 471, 469.

50. Turner, *Letters,* pp. 139, 140.

51. Ibid., p. 140. According to one authority, migraine headaches are closely associated with menarche and menstrual cycles, though the hormonal relationship has not been demonstrated (Dr. William Speed to Jean Baker, August 1, 1984).

52. Turner, *Letters,* p. 149.

53. Turner, *Letters,* p. 141; Elaine and English Showalter, "Victorian Women and Menstruation," in Martha Vicinus, ed., *Suffer and Be Still: Women in the Victorian Age* (Bloomington, Ind.: Indiana University Press, 1972), pp. 38–44; Gay, *Bourgeois Experience: Education of the Senses,* vol. 1, pp. 214–15, 286–87.

54. John Forney, *Anecdotes of a Public Man* (New York: Harper's, 1873) pp. 366–67; David Davis to Sarah Davis, December 15, 1861, Davis Papers.

55. Swanberg, *Sickles,* pp. 20–24, 135–36; Henry Wikoff, *My Courtship and Its Consequences* (New York: Clarke and Breta, 1855); *New York Herald,* February 10, 1862; Henry Wikoff, *The Adventures of a Roving Diplomatist* (New York: W. P. Fetridge, 1857); Turner, *Letters,* p. 102; Leech, *Reveille,* p. 298.

56. Turner, *Letters,* p. 181; *Home Journal,* May 23, June 29, July 20, August 10, 1861; Mary Lincoln to Virginia W. Fox, June 11, n.d. (1862), Fox Papers; Grimsley, "Six Months in the White House," p. 61.

57. Turner, *Letters,* pp. 533–34.

58. Ibid., p. 521; Francis Lieber to Charles Sumner, February 4, 1864, Henry Huntington Library.

59. Turner, *Letters,* pp. 521, 534, 205; Basler, *Collected Works,* vol. 6, p. 185, vol. 8, p. 334; *Boston Daily Advertiser,* January 7, 1871.

60. Turner, *Letters,* pp. 172, 174.

61. Ibid., p. 212.

62. Welles, *Diary,* vol. 2, p. 122; Carman and Luthin, *Lincoln and the Patronage,* pp. 245, 278; Abram Wakeman to "my dear Judge [Blow]," March 25, 1864; Henry Raymond to Abraham Lincoln, March 10, 1864; Arbel Corbin to Usher, June 27, 1864; Abram Wakeman to Abraham Lincoln, August 12, 1864, Robert Todd Lincoln Papers; Turner, *Letters,* p. 180.

63. Keckley, *Behind the Scenes,* p. 145; Turner, *Letters,* p. 180; Benjamin French to Pamela French, September 4, 1864, French Papers.

64. Keckley, *Behind the Scenes,* p. 148; *Columbus,* (Ohio) *Crisis,* May 15, 1861.

65. Basler, *Collected Works,* vol. 7, p. 514.

66. John H. Cramer, *Lincoln Under Enemy Fire* (Baton Rouge: Louisiana State University Press, 1948), p. 4; *Washington Daily Chronicle,* July 13, 1864; Leech, *Reveille,* pp. 342–46; Pratt, *Stanton,* p. 375.

67. Brooks, *Washington, D.C., in Lincoln's Time,* pp. 196–99.

68. Dwight Anderson, *Abraham Lincoln: The Quest for Immortality* (New York: Knopf, 1982), pp. 196–99; Basler, *Collected Works,* vol. 6, p. 256.

69. Basler, *Collected Works,* vol. 6, p. 250; Brooks, *Washington, D.C., in Lincoln's Time,* pp. 194, 199–299; Benjamin French to "my dear Pamela," May 21, 1865, French Papers; Turner, *Letters,* p. 189. For a slightly different version of Lincoln's dream, see Francis Carpenter, *Six Months at the White House* (New York: Hurd and Houghton, 1867), pp. 163–64.

70. Keckley, *Behind the Scenes,* p. 144; *Madame Demorest's Illustrated Monthly,* vol. 8 (April 1865), p. 4.

71. *New York Herald,* March 8, 1865; Turner, *Letters,* p. 209; Baringer, *Lincoln Day by Day,* pp. 321–27.

72. Turner, *Letters,* p. 210. The following account is based on Adam Badeau, *Grant in Peace* (Hartford: n.p. 1887), pp. 356–65; Horace Porter, *Campaigning with Grant* (New York: Century, 1897), pp. 414–23; Julia Grant, *Personal Memoirs of Julia Dent Grant,* ed. John Simon (New York: Putnam's 1975), pp. 142, 146–47, 150; John Barnes, "With Lincoln from Washington to Richmond in 1865," *Appleton's,* vol. 9 (May 1907), pp. 516–24. Head injuries often precipitate and intensify migraine headaches (Dr. William Speed to Jean Baker, August 11, 1984).

73. Badeau, *Grant in Peace,* pp. 356–365; Cramer, *Lincoln Under Enemy Fire,* pp. 4–208; Robert Colby to Abraham Lincoln, May 18, 1861, Robert Todd Lincoln Papers.

74. Baringer, *Lincoln Day by Day,* vol. 3, p. 323–24; Basler, *Collected Works,* vol. 8, p. 377.

75. Turner, *Letters,* p. 211, 213; Mary Lincoln to Charles Sumner, April 2, 1865, Charles Sumner Papers, Houghton Library, Harvard University; Abraham Lincoln to Mrs. A. Lincoln, April 2, 1865, in Basler, *Collected Works,* vol. 8, p. 381; Carl Schurz to Margarethe (Schurz), April 2, 1865 (copy), Randall Papers.

76. Mary Lincoln to Charles Sumner, April 2, 1865, Sumner Papers; Turner, *Letters,* pp. 213, 216; Keckley, *Behind the Scenes,* p. 178; Basler, *Collected Works,* vol. 8, p. 381.

77. Keckley, *Behind the Scenes,* p. 171; Marquis Adolphe de Chambrun, *Impressions of Lincoln and the Civil War* (New York: Random House, 1952), pp. 815–92; Brooks, *Washington, D.C., in Lincoln's Time,* p. 74; "Assassination Relic," *Lincoln Herald,* vol. 48 (June 1941), p. 26. Dwight Anderson, *Abraham Lincoln: The Quest for Immortality* (New York: Alfred Knopf, 1982), pp. 199–200.

78. Ward Hill Lamon, *Recollections of Abraham Lincoln 1847–1865* (Washington, D.C.: Dorothy Teillard, 1911), pp. 112–21, 271–83.

79. Leech, *Reveille,* p. 379; Basler, *Collected Works,* vol. 8, p. 404; Turner, *Letters,* p. 213.

80. Turner, *Letters,* p. 285; William S. McFeely, *Grant: A Biography* (New York: W. W. Norton, 1981), p. 224.

81. Turner, *Letters,* p. 257, 285; Anson Henry to Elizabeth Henry, April 19, 1865, Henry Papers; Jim Bishop, *The Day Lincoln Was Shot* (New York: Harper's, 1965), pp. 190–95.

82. Howard Peckham, "James Tanner's Account of Lincoln's Death," *Abraham Lincoln Quarterly,* vol. 2 (December 1942), p. 179; Dorothy Meserve Kunhardt and Philip Kunhardt, "The Assassination," *American Heritage,* April 1965, p. 34.

CHAPTER IX
MRS. WIDOW LINCOLN: THE FIRST YEARS

1. *New York Times,* April 15, 20, 1861; February 12, 1950; George Frances to Josephine, May 5, 1865, Chicago Historical Society; Keckley, *Behind the Scenes,* pp. 188–89; Howard Peckham, "James Tanner's Account of Lincoln's Death," *Abraham Lincoln Quarterly,* vol. 2 (December 1942), p. 129; Elizabeth Dixon to Laura Wood, John Usher to wife, April 10, 1865 (copy), Randall Papers; Clara Harris to Mary ———, April 25, 1865, New York Historical Society; Dorothy Meserve Kunhardt and Philip Kunhardt, *Twenty Days* (New York: Harper's, 1965); "Tragic White House Days," *Lincoln Lore,* February 26, 1940; Welles, *Diary,* pp. 280–90.

2. Anson Henry to wife, May 1, 1865, Henry Papers.

3. Turner, *Letters,* pp. 347, 355.

4. Ibid., p. 302.

5. Elizabeth Longford, *Queen Victoria Born to Succeed* (New York: Harper & Row, 1964), pp. 305–38; J. W. Hubbard to Mrs. Lincoln, May 18, 1865, Quartermasters Records, National Archives; Helm, *Mary, Wife of Lincoln*, p. 272.

6. Sarah Bernhardt, *Memories of My Life* (New York: Appleton, 1907), p. 370.

7. Elizabeth Dixon to Louisa Wood (copy), Randall Papers; Keckley, *Behind the Scenes*, p. 191.

8. Edgar Welles to George Harrington, April 20, 1865, Bixby Papers; *New York Times*, April 20, 1865.

9. Today's studies of the bereaved describe the physical symptoms of mourning as "a feeling of tightness in the throat, choking with a shortness of breath, a need for sighing, an empty feeling in the abdomen, a lack of muscular power and an intense subjective distress." Geoffrey Gorer, *Death, Grief and Mourning in Contemporary Britain* (London: Cresset Press, 1965), p. 123.

10. Randall, *Mary Lincoln*, p. 384; Benjamin French Journals, April 15, 1865, French Papers; Anson Henry to Eliza Henry, April 19, 1865, Henry Papers; Crook, *Through Five Administrations*, p. 69; Elizabeth Blair Lee to Samuel P. Lee, April 19, 1865, Blair-Lee Papers, Princeton University Library, New Jersey.

11. Robert Todd Lincoln to Andrew Johnson, April 25, 1865, Andrew Johnson Papers, Library of Congress.

12. Benjamin French to Pamela French, January 24, 1866; Benjamin French to Thomas Stackpole, March 1866, French Papers; Benjamin French to Andrew Johnson, October 19, 1865, Johnson Papers. The inventory of the White House taken in January 1866 showed no furniture was missing. Turner, *Letters*, p. 268.

13. Turner, *Letters*, p. 345; *New York Herald*, June 4, 1903.

14. Keckley, *Behind the Scenes*, p. 192; Robert Todd Lincoln to Edwin Stanton, April 28, 1865, Stanton Papers; Turner, *Letters*, pp. 345, 379.

15. Turner, *Letters*, p. 244.

16. R. Kent Lancaster, "Government and Introduction of the Rural Cemetery into Baltimore," *Maryland Historical Society Magazine*, vol. 74 (Spring 1979), pp. 62–79.

17. *Oak Ridge Cemetery: Its History and Improvement* (Springfield, Ill.: H. W. Rolker, 1879), p. 5.

18. Turner, *Letters*, p. 245; Arnold, *The Life of Abraham Lincoln*, p. 435; Turner, *Letters*, p. 302.

19. H. P. Bromwell to father and mother, April 30, 1865, Illinois State Historical Society.

20. *New York Herald*, May 12, 1865.

21. Turner, *Letters*, p. 351; Browning, *Diary*, vol. 2, p. 24.

22. Turner, *Letters*, pp. 228, 256, 236, 261, 496; Keckley, *Behind the Scenes*, p. 200; Benjamin French Journals, May 22, May 24, 1865, French Papers.

23. *Lincoln Lore*, February 26, 1940; "List of Expenses Attending Lincoln Funeral," National Archives.

24. Keckley, *Behind the Scenes*, p. 217; Turner, *Letters*, pp. 229, 250, 264.

25. Robert T. Lincoln to David Davis, January 17, 1868, Davis Papers.

26. Turner, *Letters*, pp. 256, 258; Benjamin French Journals, June 26, 1865, French Papers.

27. Arnold, *The Life of Abraham Lincoln*, p. 459; Turner, *Letters*, pp. 258, 255, 272.

28. Turner, *Letters*, pp. 272, 363.

29. Ibid., pp. 389, 526, 400.

30. Ibid., pp. 260, 268, 502, 354; Stephen Oates, *The Man Behind the Myths* (New York: Harper & Row, 1984), p. 4.

31. Turner, *Letters,* pp. 256, 275, 268, 525, 553, 237, 271, 304.

32. Keckley, *Behind the Scenes,* p. 212; Robert Todd Lincoln to David Davis, January 2, 1866, Davis Papers; Randall, *Mary Lincoln,* p. 231; Pratt, *Personal Finances,* p. 139.

33. Turner, *Letters,* p. 270.

34. Ibid., p. 353.

35. Ibid., p. 326.

36. Ibid., p. 270.

37. Ibid., pp. 321, 376; Robert Todd Lincoln to Mr. Harris, December 21, 1915, Robert Lincoln Letter Books; Joseph May, "Bill," March 5, 1866, Davis Papers; Henry Cooke to ——, January 1, 1866, Cooke Papers, Historical Society of Pennsylvania.

38. Turner, *Letters,* pp. 262, 276; Margaret Klapthor, "White House China of the Lincoln Administration," Smithsonian Institution, *United States National Museum Bulletin,* vol. 250 (1969), pp. 111–17.

39. Turner, *Letters,* pp. 362–63; Luis Stein to Mrs. Lincoln; R. Morrow to Mrs. Lincoln, June 20, 1866, Johnson Papers.

40. Robert T. Lincoln to Mr. Yard, April 11, 1914, Century Collection, New York Historical Society; *New York Herald,* May 13, June 23, 1865; *Illinois Journal,* April 22, May 8, 19, 1865.

41. Turner, *Letters,* pp. 338, 236, 312, 368.

42. Ibid., pp. 337, 338, 343; Williamson to Davis, November 24, 1865 (copy), Davis Papers.

43. Turner, *Letters,* pp. 339–40, 562, 242, 314; Pratt, *Personal Finances,* pp. 135–40; Alexander Williamson to J. A. Speed, November 24, 1865, Davis Papers. Several stores, including Galt's, did send bills to Davis as the executor of the estate, but Mary Lincoln paid them before they became claims against the estate. Alexander Williamson to Mrs. Lincoln, December 19, 1865; Robert Lincoln to Davis, December 22, 1865, Davis Papers.

44. Mary Todd Lincoln to Mary Harlan Lincoln, n.d., Insanity File, Fort Wayne, Indiana; Daniel Butterfield to Elihu Washburne, New York, December 8, 1865, Washburne Papers, Library of Congress; Turner, *Letters,* pp. 265, 547; William McFeely, *Grant: A Biography* (New York: W. W. Norton, 1981), pp. 303, 232–33.

45. Turner, *Letters,* pp. 543, 315; U. S. Grant to N. Stafford, February 2, 1870, U. S. Grant Papers, microfilm edition, Library of Congress.

46. Turner, *Letters,* p. 307.

47. Ibid., pp. 308, 553; *Congressional Globe,* Thirty-ninth Congress, First Session, pp. 101, 104, 13, 71–72; Robert Lincoln to David Davis, December 22, 1865, Davis Papers.

48. Turner, *Letters,* p. 325; Robert T. Lincoln to David Davis, December 22, 1865, Davis Papers.

49. Turner, *Letters,* pp. 254, 323; Robert T. Lincoln to David Davis, January 15, January 25, February 8, 1866; August 6, 1867, Davis Papers.

50. David Davis to Sarah Davis, August 2, 8, 29, 1847, Davis Papers.

51. Robert T. Lincoln to Thomas Dent, September 12, 1919, Century Collection, New York Historical Society; Turner, *Letters,* pp. 260–61, 351, 353.

52. Turner, *Letters,* pp. 260, 261, 350, 351, 352, 353, 260; Norman Judd to Robert Lincoln, July 29, 1867; Judd to David Davis, n.d., Davis Papers; J. Nicholas Shriver and Shale Stiller, *How to Live and Die with Maryland Probate* (Houston: n.p., 1972); George Fiedler, *The Illinois Law Courts in Three Centuries: 1673–1973* (Berwyn, Ill.: Physicians Records, 1973).

53. Turner, *Letters,* p. 274; George M. Davis to David Davis, June 12, 1865; T. J. Coffey to David Davis, June 13, 1865; R. T. Lincoln to David Davis, June 24, 1865; David Risley to Davis, October 1866, Davis Papers; John Jay to Charles Sumner, April 29, 1865, Sumner Papers.

54. Turner, *Letters,* pp. 284, 365, 366; Brooks Kelly, "Simon Cameron and the Senatorial Nomination of 1867," *Pennsylvania Magazine of History and Biography,* vol. 83 (October 1963), pp. 375–93.

55. Turner, *Letters,* pp. 370–71, 410, 352; Leonard Sweet to Robert Lincoln, December 10, 1907; R. T. Lincoln, "Special Folder," Illinois State Historical Society.

56. Turner, *Letters,* pp. 400, 415; Robert T. Lincoln to Mary T. Lincoln, December 18, 1867, January 4, 1868, Robert Todd Lincoln Letter Press Books.

57. "Abraham Lincoln, Miss Ann Rutledge, New Salem, Pioneering, and the Poem," Broadside, 1866. The lecture was printed in William Herndon, *Abraham Lincoln, Miss Ann Rutledge, New Salem, Pioneering, and the Poem: A Lecture Delivered in the Old Sangamon County Court House, November 1866* (Springfield: Barker, 1910).

58. Herndon, *Life of Lincoln,* pp. 105–13, 180–83, 343–48; Donald, *Lincoln's Herndon,* p. 224.

59. *Chicago Tribune,* November 28, 1866, March 6, 1867; Randall, *Mary Lincoln,* pp. 395–440; Jay Monaghan, "New Light on the Lincoln-Rutledge Romance," *Abraham Lincoln Quarterly,* vol. 2 (September 1944), pp. 138–45; *New York Times,* March 9, 1867.

60. Turner, *Letters,* pp. 415, 416.

61. Ibid., p. 414; Robert T. Lincoln to David Davis, December 8, 1866; Robert Todd Lincoln to James Conkling, December 17, 1917, Robert Todd Lincoln Letter Press Books.

62. S. Weir Mitchell, *Fat and Blood: An Essay on the Treatment of Certain Forms of Nervousness* (Philadelphia: Lippincott, 1881); S. Weir Mitchell, *Lectures on Diseases of the Nervous System Especially in Women* (Philadelphia: Lippincott, 1881); George Beard, *American Nervousness: Its Causes and Consequences* (New York: Putnam's, 1881); Turner, *Letters,* pp. 462, 443.

63. Turner, *Letters,* pp. 475, 476; Dr. William Lysford, "The Origin of Bladder Problems," Chicago Historical Society; W. A. Evans, *Mrs. Abraham Lincoln: A Study of Her Personality and Influence on Lincoln* (New York: Alfred Knopf, 1932), p. 342.

64. Sarah Clarke to Caroline Dall, November 25, 1867, Caroline Dall Papers, microfilm edition, Library of Congress.

65. Turner, *Letters,* pp. 426, 451; Fanny Stone, *Racine Belle City of the Lakes and Racine County* (Chicago: Clarke, 1916), pp. 195, 318.

66. Turner, *Letters,* pp. 417, 418, 419.

67. Ibid., p. 452.

68. Ibid., p. 418.

69. Ibid., p. 434; *Illinois Journal,* September 15, 1868; Keckley, *Behind the Scenes,* pp. 272–76.

70. Keckley, *Behind the Scenes,* p. 308.

71. Turner, *Letters,* pp. 434, 435.

72. Keckley, *Behind the Scenes,* p. 294.

73. Turner, *Letters,* pp. 447, 448; Keckley, *Behind the Scenes,* p. 316.

74. *New York World,* October 5, 1867; Turner, *Letters,* p. 448; *Frank Leslie's Illustrated Weekly Newspaper,* October 13, 1867.

75. John McCalla, Jr., to John McCalla, October 19, 1867, William Perkins Library, Duke University: *New York World,* September 20–30, 1867, October 15, 1867; Keckley, *Behind the Scenes,* p. 318; Turner, *Letters,* pp. 448, 438.

76. General J. A. Early to Thomas Reynolds, December 11, 1867, Jubal Early Papers, Duke University.

77. *New York World,* September 27, October 3, 1867; Keckley, *Behind the Scenes,* p. 318; Turner, *Letters,* p. 438.

78. *New York World,* October 3, 4, 1867.

79. Turner, *Letters,* pp. 442, 438–39; *New York Commercial Advertiser,* October 4, 1867.

80. Turner, *Letters,* p. 438–40; *Columbus Georgia Advertiser,* October 4, 1867; *Cleveland*

Herald, October 6, 1867; *Columbus Georgia Sun,* October 8, 1867; *New York World,* October 7, 1867.

81. Robert T. Lincoln to Mary Harlan, October 16, 1867, quoted in Helm, *Mary, Wife of Lincoln,* p. 267; Davis to Adele Burr, July 19, 1882, Green Papers, University of North Carolina Library; *Illinois Journal,* August 7, 1868; *Boston Daily Evening Transcript,* October 23, 1867.

82. Turner, *Letters,* pp. 442, 445–46.

83. Ibid., pp. 440–44.

84. Ibid., p. 400.

85. Ibid., pp. 468, 459.

86. Ibid., p. 457; Pratt, *Personal Finances,* p. 139. Probate files of President Lincoln's Estate, Springfield, Illinois; Turner, *Letters,* pp. 457–58.

87. Pratt, *Personal Finances,* p. 136–38; Turner, *Letters,* p. 458; Robert Lincoln to David Davis, November 18, 1867, Davis Papers.

88. Turner, *Letters,* pp. 449, 428.

89. Keckley, *Behind the Scenes,* p. 326; Turner, *Letters,* pp. 469, 466.

90. Turner, *Letters,* pp. 408, 476.

CHAPTER X   EXILE AND RETURN

1. *Baltimore Sun,* September 11, October 1, October 2, 1868; *Chicago Tribune,* October 6, 1868; Charles Tilghman to "Dear ma," at sea, October 12, 1868, Tilghman Papers, privately owned.

2. *Baltimore Sun,* September 24, 25, 26, 1868; *Washington Express,* September 25, 1868; Turner, *Letters,* pp. 481, 482.

3. Turner, *Letters,* p. 485; Helm, *Mary, Wife of Lincoln,* p. 270.

4. Turner, *Letters,* p. 502.

5. Henry James, *The American* (Boston: James R. Osgood, 1877), p. 30; Turner, *Letters,* pp. 484, 550.

6. Turner, *Letters,* p. 494.

7. Ibid., p. 485.

8. Charles Tilghman to "Dear Ma," October 12, 1868, Tilghman Papers.

9. Ibid.

10. Stephen Birmingham, *Our Crowd* (New York: Harper's, 1967), pp. 122–24.

11. Turner, *Letters,* p. 495. *Frankfurter Nachrichter,* February 2, 1869.

12. Ibid., p. 534.

13. Ibid., pp. 494, 495; *New York Times,* October 26, 1870.

14. Turner, *Letters,* pp. 543, 495.

15. Sarah Orne to Charles Sumner, September 12, 1869, Sumner Papers; Turner, *Letters,* p. 495; William Murphy, "Annual Report, 1868," Consular Dispatches from Frankfurt, State Department Archives, microfilm edition.

16. *New York World,* November 13, 1869; *Portland* (Maine) *Eastern Argus,* November 10, 1869; Turner, *Letters,* p. 540.

17. Turner, *Letters,* pp. 535, 540.

18. William Murphy, Annual Reports, November 10, 1870, Consular Dispatches; Henry Gerber, *Three Centuries of Political and Economic Relations Between Frankfurt-am-Main and the United States as Well as the History of the American Consul General* (Frankfurt am Main); William Murphy to Elihu Washburne, January 10, 1868, Washburne Papers.

19. William R. Leach, "Transformations in a Culture of Consumption, Women and the

Department Store, 1890–1925," *Journal of American History* (September 1984), pp. 319–42; Turner, *Letters,* p. 494; Mary Lincoln to Mary H. Lincoln, January 26, 1871, Insanity File.

20. Mary Lincoln to Mary Harlan Lincoln, November 25, November 21, 1869, September 16, 1870. Included in this newly discovered material now in the Fort Wayne Lincoln Library, Fort Wayne, Indiana, are several other letters of Mary Todd Lincoln to Mary Harlan Lincoln, henceforth cited as Fragment, Insanity File.

21. Mary Todd Lincoln to Mary Harlan Lincoln, Fragment, Insanity File.

22. Ibid., November 21, 22, 1869.

23. Turner, *Letters,* p. 494.

24. Ibid.

25. Ibid., p. 495.

26. Ibid., pp. 496, 502, 504.

27. Adams, *The Education of Henry Adams,* p. 78.

28. Turner, *Letters,* pp. 500, 527, 579.

29. Mary Todd Lincoln to Mary Harlan Lincoln, November 22, September 4, 1869, September 16, 1870, February 22, 1869, Insanity File.

30. Sir Edward Bulwer-Lytton, *Paul Clifford* (Paris: Bandry European Library, 1838), p. 1.

31. Elizabeth Stuart Phelps, *The Gates Ajar* (Cambridge: Belknap Press, 1964), pp. 512, 129, 156.

32. Turner, *Letters,* pp. 579, 580, 515; Phelps, *The Gates Ajar,* p. 156.

33. Turner, *Letters,* pp. 524, 535.

34. Ibid., pp. 501, 502; Dr. Horatio Storer, *Southern Italy as a Health Station for Invalids* (Naples: Rhicord Marghieri, n.d.).

35. Turner, *Letters,* pp. 501–2.

36. Albert Post, "Lincoln and the Reverend Dr. James Smith," *Journal of the Illinois State Historical Society,* vol. 35 (1942), p. 397.

37. Turner, *Letters,* pp. 512, 516, 517.

38. Ibid., p. 512.

39. Ibid., p. 516.

40. Ibid.

41. Ibid., pp. 515, 513.

42. Ibid., p. 513; James Orne to Charles Sumner, Philadelphia, July 8, 1870, Sumner Papers.

43. Sally Orne to Charles Sumner, September 12, 1869, Sumner Papers.

44. Sally Orne to Charles Sumner, November 27, September 12, 1869, Sumner Papers.

45. Ibid.

46. Turner, *Letters,* pp. 527, 525, 526, 518.

47. Ibid., pp. 493, 501.

48. *Illinois Journal,* July 21, 1865; Turner, *Letters,* pp. 501, 529, 518.

49. Turner, *Letters,* pp. 498, 540, 569, 526; Thomas Belden and Marvin Belden, *So Fell the Angels* (Boston: Little, Brown, 1956), pp. 216–40.

50. Turner, *Letters,* p. 569; Obediah Wheelock to Charles Sumner, February 9, 1870; F. W. Bogen to Charles Sumner, November 23, 1868, Sumner Papers.

51. Charles Sumner to Mrs. Hamilton Fish, September 29, 1869, Hamilton Fish Papers, Library of Congress; Turner, *Letters,* p. 521.

52. *Congressional Globe,* Forty-first Congress, Second Session, pp. 3165, 4112; Report of the Commissioner of Pensions, in *House Executive Documents,* Forty-second Congress, Second Session, 1871–1872, pp. 379–419.

53. Turner, *Letters,* p. 557.

54. Lloyd Morris, *Incredible New York* (New York: Random House, 1951), pp. 55–56.

55. Turner, *Letters,* pp. 560, 564, 565.

56. "The Edmunds Report," *Senate Documents,* Forty-first Congress, Second Session, 1409, May 5, 1870.

57. *Congressional Globe,* Forty-first Congress, Second Session, pp. 4540, 5395.

58. Ibid.; Turner, *Letters,* p. 589.

59. *Congressional Globe,* Forty-first Congress, Second Session, p. 5397.

60. Ibid., pp. 5559, 5395, 5560, 5398.

61. Ibid., p. 5397.

62. Jack Northrup, "Richard Yates: Civil War Governor of Illinois" (Ph.D. dissertation, University of Illinois, 1960).

63. *Congressional Globe,* Forty-first Congress, Second Session, p. 5398.

64. Turner, *Letters,* p. 575; *Congressional Record,* Forty-first Congress, Second Session, p. 5395; F. Lauriston Bullard, "Mrs. Lincoln's Pension," *Lincoln Herald,* 1945.

65. Turner, *Letters,* p. 374; Michael Howard, *The Franco-Prussian War* (London: Rupert Hart-Davis, 1962), pp. 63, 186. For letters of Americans on the war, see T. D. Lincoln to Eliza Washburne, July 19, 1870, Washburne Papers.

66. Mary Todd Lincoln to Thomas Fowler, October 17, 1870, *The Collector* (Whole No. 716); Turner, *Letters,* pp. 531, 578, 576; Mary Todd Lincoln to Mary Harlan Lincoln, November 25, 1869, Insanity File.

67. Howard, *Franco-Prussian War,* p. 380.

68. Turner, *Letters,* p. 596.

69. Ibid., pp. 589, 583, 580; *Illinois Journal,* July 16, 17, 1865.

70. Nathaniel Hawthorne, *Our Old Home, and English Note Books* (Boston: Houghton Mifflin, 1863), pp. 59, 65; T. W. Dudley, *A Complete History of Royal Leamington* (Leamington: A. Thomas, 1896), p. 9; Ward and Lock's *Illustrated Guide to Leamington and Warwick* (Leamington: Ard and Co., 1875); Amos Middleton, *A Chemical Analysis of the Leamington Waters* (Warwick: Henry Sharpe, 1814).

71. Mary Lincoln to Mary Harlan Lincoln, n.d., Fragment, Insanity File; Michael Foster, *Baths and Medicinal Waters* (Bristol: John Wright, 1933); Sir Edward Bulwer-Lytton, *The Water Treatment* (New York: Putnam, 1849), p. 21; *Five Minutes Advice: Drinking the Waters of Leamington* (Leamington: n.p., n.d.).

72. Turner, *Letters,* p. 582; Mary Lincoln to Mary Harlan Lincoln, January 31, 1871, September 4, 1870, Insanity File; Benjamin Moran's Journal, Library of Congress; Roy Stemman, *One Hundred Years of Spiritualism* (London: British Museum, 1919).

73. Turner, *Letters,* pp. 577, 581.

74. Ibid., p. 581.

75. *New York Times,* May 11, 12, 1871.

76. Turner, *Letters,* pp. 497, 589, 587, 588, 585.

77. Anna Eastman to Mrs. Robert Lincoln, July 21, 1871, Robert Todd Lincoln Papers; Turner, *Letters,* p. 559.

78. Turner, *Letters,* p. 590.

79. Turner, *Letters,* p. 590; Louis Starr, *An American Textbook of Diseases of Children* (Philadelphia: W. B. Saunders, 1898), pp. 276–90.

80. Turner, *Letters,* p. 590; J. Lewis Smith, *A Treatise on the Diseases of Infancy and Childhood* (Philadelphia: Henry Lea, 1872), p. 507; Robert Todd Lincoln Letter Press Books, 1871, Illinois State Historical Society.

81. Thomas Cone, *A History of American Pediatrics* (Boston: Little, Brown, 1979); Robert Todd Lincoln Letter Press Books, July 2, 1871; David Davis to "my dear friend," July 12, 1871, Ward Hill Lamon Papers.

82. *Chicago Tribune,* July 17, 1871; *Lincoln Herald,* 1955.

83. Turner, *Letters*, p. 591; Mary Todd Lincoln to Mary Harlan Lincoln, Fragment, Insanity File.

84. Turner, *Letters*, p. 591; Robert Todd Lincoln to David Davis, July 18, 1871, Davis Papers; Robert Lincoln to James Hackett, September 5, 28, 1871, Robert Todd Lincoln Letter Press Books; Ruth Randall, *Lincoln's Sons* (Boston: Little Brown, 1955), p. 275.

85. Turner, *Letters*, p. 591.

86. Ibid., p. 596.

87. A. T. Andreas, *The History of Chicago* (Chicago: Andreas and Co., 1885), pp. 724–28.

88. The evidence for Mary Harlan Lincoln's alcoholism is circumstantial, though strong. Her husband never specifically names it, though he does refer obliquely to it in a number of ways. The stories about Mary Lincoln's wanting to kidnap her granddaughter, Mamie, were partly the result of the grandmother's desire to get her away from a drunken mother.

89. Maynard, *Was Abraham Lincoln a Spiritualist?*, pp. 161, 208; Ruth Pearson, *Reflections of St. Charles, Illinois, 1833–1976* (Elgin, Ill.: Brethren Press), pp. 76–97.

90. Robert Todd Lincoln to David Davis, September 21, 1871, Davis Papers; Turner, *Letters*, p. 591.

91. Turner, *Letters*, p. 600; Lillian Krueger, "Mary Todd Summers in Wisconsin,"*Journal of the Illinois State Historical Society*, vol. 34 (1941), pp. 249–53; *Waukesha Freeman*, July–August 1872; *Waukesha Plain Dealer*, September 10, 1872; *Waukesha Semi-Weekly*, July 31, 1872.

92. *New York Times*, April 21, 1869, February 25, 1872; *Argument of Eldridge Gray Before Justice Dawling on Preliminary Exam of Wm. H. Mumler Charged with Obtaining Money by Pretended Spirit Photographs, May 3, 1869* (New York: Baker, Voorhis, 1869); James Coates, *Photographing the Invisible* (London: L. N. Fowler, 1911), p. 8; Maynard, *Was Abraham Lincoln a Spiritualist?*, p. 42; *Washington Chronicle*, November 21, 1862.

93. Donald, *William Herndon*, pp. 266–78; Turner, *Letters*, p. 606; Ward Lamon, *The Life of Abraham Lincoln from His Birth to His Inauguration as President* (Boston: Osgood, 1872); Herndon, *Lincoln's Religion*, Illinois State Historical Society Broadside Supplement; *Illinois State Register*, December 13, 1873.

94. *Illinois Journal*, December 19, 1873, January 15, 1874; "Mrs. Lincoln's Denial," Massachusetts Historical Society.

95. William Jayne to William Herndon, January 19, 1874, Herndon-Weik Papers.

96. Donald, *Lincoln's Herndon*, p. 259; *Illinois Journal*, January 14, 1874; Turner, *Letters*, pp. 605, 606.

97. Basler, *Collected Works*, vol. 2, p. 10; Mary Todd Lincoln to Mary Harlan Lincoln, Fragment, Insanity File.

98. *Bucks County Intelligencer* (Doylestown, Pennsylvania), April 1, 1856; *New York Times*, September 3, 1873, September 12, 1869.

99. *St. Catharines Evening Journal*, August 29, 1873.

100. Eddie Foy, "Clowning Through Life," *Collier's*, December 18, 25, 1926.

101. Ledyard Bill, *A Winter in Florida* (New York: Wood and Holbrook, 1869).

102. Turner, *Letters*, p. 502; Mrs. A. Lincoln to Edward Isham, March 12, 1875; Mrs. A. Lincoln to Robert T. Lincoln, March 12, 1875, Insanity File.

CHAPTER XI   TRIAL AND CONFINEMENT

1. The following reconstruction is based on newspaper reports of the trial. Also Robert T. Lincoln to Leonard Swett, May 25, 1884; Leonard Swett to David Davis, May 24, 1875, Davis Papers; Leonard Swett to Ninian Edwards, June 20, 1876, Insanity File; *Chicago Inter*

Ocean, May 20, 21, 1875; *Chicago Tribune,* May 20, 21, 1875.

2. *Rules, Regulations and Price Per Day of Grand Pacific Hotel,* Chicago Historical Society; Perry Davis, "Whose City: Public and Private Places in Nineteenth-Century Chicago," *Chicago History,* vol. 12 (Spring 1983), pp. 2–27.

3. Leonard Swett to David Davis, May 24, 1875, Davis Papers.

4. Henry Hurd, *The Institutional Care of the Insane* (Baltimore: Johns Hopkins University Press, 1916); *A Compilation of the Statutes of the State of Illinois* (Chicago: Keen and Lee, 1856), p. 230; I am grateful to Mark Neely and Gerald McMurtry for allowing me to see the page proofs of their *The Insanity File: The Case of Mary Todd Lincoln* (Carbondale: Southern Illinois Press, 1986).

5. Neely and McMurtry, *The Insanity File,* pp. 1, 192, 307; *Quarterly Journal of Psychological Medicine,* vol. 1 (1867), p. 568; Harold Moyer, *Past and Present Laws Regarding Legal Restraint and Detention of the Insane* (Chicago: McCabe, 1891); Packard, *The Prisoner's Hidden Life;* Mrs. E. P. Packard, *Great Disclosures of Spiritual Wickedness: With an Appeal to the Government to Protect the Inalienable Rights of Married Women* (New York: Arno, 1974); *Mrs. Olsen's Narrative of Her One Year's Imprisonment* (Chicago: J. N. Clarke, 1868); Elizabeth Packard, *Modern Persecution, or Insane Asylums Unveiled* (Hartford: Case, Lockwood, Brainard, 1875); "Illinois Legislation Regarding Hospitals for the Insane," *American Journal of Insanity,* vol. 26 (1870), p. 204; *Illinois Journal,* January 11, 14, 25, 1867.

6. Leonard Swett to David Davis, May 24, 1875, Davis Papers.

7. Petition of R. T. Lincoln, and Application to Try the Question of Insanity, Huntington Library.

8. Inventory of the Real and Personal Estate Belonging to Mrs. Mary Lincoln, Payments to Drs. Ralph Isham, H. A. Johnson, C. G. Smith, N. S. Davis, R. J. Patterson, J. Jewell, W. Danforth, May 18, 1875, Huntington Library.

9. Leonard Swett to David Davis, May 24, 1875, Davis Papers.

10. Ibid.

11. John Duff, *A. Lincoln Prairie Lawyer* (New York: Rinehart and Co., 1960), p. 170; Basler, *Collected Works,* vol. 2, p. 81; Leonard Swett to David Davis, May 24, 1875, Davis Papers.

12. John Todd Stuart to Robert Lincoln, May 21, 1875; Elizabeth Todd Grimsley Brown to Robert Lincoln, March 16 (n.y.), May 19, 1875; Interrogations of Drs. Ralph Isham. H. A. Johnson, C. G. Smith, N. S. Davis, R. J. Patterson, J. Jewell, W. Danforth, May 1875, Insanity File.

13. *Chicago Inter Ocean,* May 20, 21, 1875; *Chicago Tribune,* May 20, 21, 1875.

14. Ibid.

15. Leonard Swett to David Davis, May 24, 1875, Davis Papers.

16. *Chicago Inter Ocean,* May 20, 21, 1875.

17. On the footstools, see Robert Todd Lincoln to Leonard Swett, May 25, 1884, Insanity File.

18. Keckley, *Behind the Scenes,* p. 123; Mary Lincoln to Mary Harlan Lincoln, n.d., Insanity File; Robert Lincoln to Horace White, December 31, 1907, Robert Todd Lincoln Letter Press Books.

19. J. J. Wilson to Robert Lincoln, n.d.; John Coyne to J. J. Wilson, March 13, 1875, Insanity File; Inventory to Mary Lincoln's Property, Huntington Library.

20. Leonard Swett to Ninian Edwards, June 20, 1876, Insanity File.

21. Ninian Edwards to Robert Lincoln, November 5, 1875, Insanity File; Robert Todd Lincoln to Leonard Swett, May 25, 1884, Insanity File. When Mary Lincoln died seven years later, her estate had increased in value from $73,000 to $84,000.

22. Oliver Sacks, *Migraine: Understanding a Common Disorder* (Berkeley: University of California Press, 1985); personal communication with Dr. William Speed, Baltimore, Maryland.

23. Leonard Swett to David Davis, May 24, 1875, Davis Papers.

24. *Annual Reports of the Commissioners and Superintendent of Indiana Hospital for the Insane* (Indianapolis: Austin Brown, 1853), p. 11.

25. Lyman J. Gage to William E. Barton, January 20, 1921, in William Barton Scrapbook, Barton Collection of Lincolniana, University of Chicago; Moyer, *Past and Present Laws Regarding Legal Restraint and Detention of the Insane*, p. 311.

26. Lyman J. Gage to William E. Barton, January 20, 1921, Barton Scrapbook.

27. *Chicago Inter Ocean*, May 20, 21, 1875; Leonard Swett to David Davis, May 24, 1875, Davis Papers.

28. *Chicago Inter Ocean*, May 21, 1875; *Chicago Times*, May 21, 1875.

29. Dr. Robert J. Patterson to Frederick Sawers, August 13, 1878; Dr. Robert J. Patterson to A. C. Babcock, July 20, 1879; Dr. Robert J. Patterson to Mrs. J. B. Grinnell, August 28, 1880, Batavia Depot Museum, Batavia, Illinois; "Speech of Dr. Patterson," Batavia Depot Museum; John Pitts, "The Association of Medical Superintendents for the Insane, 1844–1892: A Case Study of Specialism in American Medicine" (Ph.D. dissertation, University of Pennsylvania, 1979).

30. Patient Progress Reports, Batavia Depot Museum; Norman Dain, *Concepts of Insanity in the United States 1789–1865* (New Brunswick, N.J.: Rutgers University Press, 1964), pp. 131–32, 152–54; Dr. Robert Patterson to Fred Sawers, August 13, 1878, Batavia Depot Museum; *Chicago Medical Register*, 1875 (Chicago Historical Society).

31. Mary Ann Jimenez, "Changing Faces of Madness: Insanity in Massachusetts, 1700–1850" (Ph.D. dissertation, Brandeis University, 1980); John Gray, "Responsibility of the Insane," *American Journal of Insanity* (October, 1875), pp. 153–83.; Francis Gosling, "American Nervousness: A Study in Medicine and Social Values in the Gilded Age, 1870–1900" (Ph.D. dissertation, University of Oklahoma, 1976); *Sangamon Journal*, June 11, 1846; Indiana Hospital for the Insane, Indianapolis, *Reports*, 1853; Dr. George Beard, *American Nervousness: Its Causes and Consequences* (New York: Putnam's, 1881); Barbara Sicherman, "The Paradox of Prudence: Mental Health in the Gilded Age," *Journal of American History*, vol. 62 (March 1976), pp. 890–912.

32. Beard, *American Nervousness: Its Causes and Consequences*; S. Weir Mitchell, *Wear and Tear* (New York: Lippincott, 1887); *First Annual Report of the Committee and Medical Superintendent of the Indiana Central Hospital* (Indianapolis: John Defrees, 1849); Andrew Scull, ed., *Madhouses, Mad Doctors and Madmen: The Social History of Psychology in the Victorian Era* (Philadelphia: University of Pennsylvania Press, 1981).

33. David Davis to Leonard Swett, May 19, 1875, Davis Papers.

34. Patient Progress Reports, 1876–1893, Batavia Depot Museum; Dr. Gordon Staples, "Confessions of a Chloral Eater," *Belgravia* (April 1875), pp. 179–90.

35. William Goddell, *Lessons of Gynecology* (Philadelphia: D. G. Brinton, 1879), p. 37; Bellevue Patient Progress Reports, May 19, 1875, Lincoln Library, Fort Wayne, Indiania.

36. Dr. William Hammond, *On Certain Conditions of Nervous Derangement* (New York: Putnam's, 1881), pp. 231–32; Indiana Hospital for the Insane, *Reports*, No. 36 (1852), pp. 36–38; W. A. Hammond, *Spiritualism and Allied Causes and Conditions of Nervous Derangement* (New York: Putnam's, 1876).

37. Robert Lincoln to "my dear Uncle," November 17, 1875, January 17, 1876; Robert Patterson to Judge Bradwell, August 28, 1876, Insanity File.

38. My diagnosis is based on conversations with Dr. William Fitzpatrick and Dr. Melvin Prosen. See also Heinz Kohut, *The Restoration of Self* (New York: International Universities Press, 1977); Heinz Kohut, *The Analysis of Self: A Systematic Approach to the Treatment of Narcissistic Personality Disorders* (New York: International Universities Press, 1971); Joshua M. Perman, "The Search for the Mother: Narcissistic Regression as a Pathway of Mourning in Childhood," *Psychoanalysis Quarterly*, vol. 48 (1979), pp. 448–64; Karen Horney, *Neurosis*

and Human Growth: The Struggle Toward Self-Realization (New York: Norton, 1950); Karen Horney, *The Neurotic Personality of Our Time* (New York: Norton, 1937); Arnold Goldberg, with the collaboration of Heinz Kohut, *The Psychology of the Self: A Casebook* (New York: International Universities Press, 1978); Shirley Sugerman, *Sin and Madness: Studies in Narcissism* (Philadelphia: Westminster Press, 1976).

39. Mrs. A. Lincoln to Robert Lincoln, March 12, 1875, Insanity File.

40. Dr. Robert Patterson to A. B. Monard, October 20, 1876, Patient Progress Reports, Batavia Depot Museum.

41. Jiminez, "Changing Faces of Madness," pp. 80–188; U.S. Census, 1880, Tenth Census of the United States, "Insanity" p. 21; Daniel J. Rothman, *The Asylum and Its Alternatives in Progressive America* (Boston: Little, Brown, 1979); Daniel J. Rothman, *The Discovery of the Asylum: Social Order and Disorder in the New Republic* (Boston: Little, Brown, 1971); Isaac Ray, *Confinement of the Insane* (Boston: Little, Brown, 1869).

42. Dr. Charles Folsom, *Diseases of the Mind* (Boston: A. Williams, 1877), p. 277; Elgin, Illinois *Daily Carrier News,* May 22, 1875; "Bellevue Place Sanitarium," Batavia Depot Museum.

43. Bellevue Patient Progress Reports, 1875; Robert Patterson to Colonel Johnston, September 4, 1876, Batavia Depot Museum.

44. Bellevue Records, Batavia Depot Museum; Robert Patterson to O. B. Harrington, April 22, 1878, Batavia Depot Museum; *Aurora* (Illinois) *News Beacon,* December 18, 25, 1932; January 1, 1933; Bellevue Patient Progress Reports, July 10, 1875; Rodney Ross, "Mary Todd Lincoln, Patient at Bellevue Place, Batavia," *Journal of the Illinois State Historical Society,* vol. 63 (Spring 1970), pp. 5–34.

45. J. B. Andrews, "Physiological Action and Therapeutic Use of Chloral," *American Journal of Insanity,* vol. 28 (July 1871), pp. 35–56; Thomas Butler, "The Introduction of Chloral Hydrate into Medical Practice," *Bulletin of History of Medicine,* vol. 44 (March, April 1970), pp. 168–72; Bellevue Patient Progress Reports, June 27, 1875; *Chicago Journal of Nervous and Medical Diseases,* vol. 1 (1874), p. 35; Staples, "Confessions of a Chloral Eater," pp. 179–90.

46. Andrews, "Chloral," p. 40.; John Marshall to Dr. Patterson, 1883, Bellevue Records, Batavia Depot Museum; H. Wayne Morgan, *Drugs in America: A Social History, 1800–1980* (Syracuse: Syracuse University Press, 1981); David Cartwright, *Dark Paradise: Opiate Addiction in America Before 1940* (Cambridge: Harvard University Press, 1982).

47. Bellevue Patient Progress Reports, September 23, 24, 1874.

48. Dain, *Concepts of Insanity,* pp. 84–113; Rothman, *Discovery of the Asylum,* p. 94; S. P. Fullinwider, *Technicians of the Finite, the Rise and Decline of the Schizophrenic in American Thought* (Westport, Conn.: Greenwood Press, 1982), pp. 18–33; Indiana Hospital for the Insane, 1853, *Annual Reports.*

49. Robert Lincoln to Leonard Swett, June 2, 1884; Robert Lincoln to "my dear Judge," November 16, 1875, Insanity File.

50. Robert T. Lincoln to Mrs. S. M. Orne, June 1, 1875; Sally B. Orne to Robert Lincoln, August 8, 1875, Illinois State Historical Library.

51. Bellevue Patient Progress Reports, July 30, 1875; *Chicago Times,* August 23, 1875; *Chicago Post and Mail,* July 13, 1875.

52. Bellevue Patient Progress Reports, July 30, 1875.

53. Ibid., August 15.

54. Ibid., July 11, July 2, September 6, 1875.

55. *Chicago Post and Mail,* July 13, 1875; Nancy Goldner, "The Medicalization of Insanity: A Social History of McLean Asylum" (Ph.D. dissertation, Boston University, 1980).

56. Henry Blow to "my dear Mr. Lincoln," August 5, 1875, Insanity File; Bellevue Patient Progress Reports, July 29, 1875. For Robert's response to the questions of some of

these visitors, see Robert Todd Lincoln to Henry Blow, August 1875, Robert Todd Lincoln Letter Press Books.

57. Herman Kogan, "Myra Bradwell," *Chicago History,* vol. 1 (Winter 1974), p. 32; *Bradwell* v. *Illinois,* U.S. 1, 30 (1873); Robert Spector,"Woman Against the Law: Myra Bradwell's Struggle for Admission to the Illinois Bar," *Journal of the Illinois State Historical Society,* vol. 68 (June 1975), pp. 228–42.

58. Mrs. A. Lincoln to Judge Bradwell, January 17, 1874; Robert Todd Lincoln to Elizabeth Edwards, August 7, 10, 1875, Robert Todd Lincoln Letter Press Books.

59. *Chicago Times,* August 24, 1875; Dr. R. J. Patterson to Judge Bradwell, August 28, 1875; Bellevue Patient Progress Reports, August 6, 1875; *Chicago Post and Mail,* August 23, 1875.

60. Bellevue Patient Records, July 15, 1875; Myra Bradwell to Dr. Patterson, August 11, 1875; Abram Wakeman to Mrs. Myra Bradwell, August 17, 1875; Elizabeth Edwards to Robert Lincoln, August 11, 1875, Insanity File.

61. Robert Todd Lincoln to "my dear Judge [Davis]," November 16, 1875; Robert Lincoln to Horace White, December 31, 1907, Robert Todd Lincoln Letter Press Books.

62. Robert T. Lincoln to Mary Todd Lincoln, August 15, 1875, Insanity File; Robert T. Lincoln to "Aunt Lizzie," August 7, 1875, Robert Todd Lincoln Letter Press Books; Robert Lincoln to Mr. Yard, April 11, 1904, Century Collection, New York Public Library.

63. Judge Bradwell to Dr. Patterson, August 19, 1875, Batavia Depot Museum; *Chicago Post and Mail Dispatch,* clipping, Insanity File; R. J. Patterson to Myra Bradwell, August 9, 1875; Robert T. Lincoln to Dr. Robert Patterson, September 2, 1875; Robert Lincoln to "Aunt Lizzie," August 7, 1875, Insanity File; *Chicago Times,* August 19, 1875.

64. *Illinois Journal,* September 1, 1875; *Chicago Tribune,* August 30, 1875; Bellevue Patient Progress Reports, August 18, 1875.

65. Dr. Andrew McFarland to Robert Lincoln, September 8, 10, 11, 1875, Insanity File; Robert T. Lincoln, Conservatorship Records, June 1876 (copy), Huntington Library. The other consultant, Dr. A. G. McDill, may have agreed with Mary Lincoln; in any case, he apparently did not examine Mary Lincoln. Neely and McMurtry, *The Case of Mary Todd Lincoln,* pp. 71–72.

66. Octavia Roberts, *Lincoln in Illinois* (Boston: Houghton Mifflin, 1918), p. 51; Caroline O. Brown, "Springfield Society Before the Civil War," *Journal of the Illinois State Historical Society,* vol. 15 (April, July 1922), p. 479; Elizabeth Edwards to "my dear Mary," May 31, 18?, Insanity File; Elizabeth Edwards to Julia Baker, April 26, 1862 (copy), Randall Papers.

67. Mark Simmons, "1876: The Centennial Year," James Krobe, ed., *A Springfield Reader: Historical Views of the Illinois Capital* (Sangamon: Illinois State Historical Society, 1976); *Illinois Journal,* January 28, 1858, August 13, 1889.

68. Robert Todd Lincoln to "my dear Uncle," November 29, 1875; Ninian Edwards to Robert Todd Lincoln, January 5, 1876, Insanity File.

69. Elizabeth Edwards to Robert Lincoln, November 5, 1875, Insanity File.

70. Robert Lincoln to "my dear Judge [Davis]," November 16, 1875; David Davis to Robert Lincoln, November 20, 1875, Insanity File.

71. Elizabeth Edwards to Robert Todd Lincoln, November 5, 1875; Robert Todd Lincoln to "My Dear Judge [Davis]," November 16, 1875; Robert Lincoln to Leonard Swett, May 25, 1884, Insanity File; Conservator Records, Huntington Library.

72. Elizabeth Edwards to Robert, November 5, 1875; Leonard Swett to Ninian Edwards, June 20, 1876; Robert Lincoln to John Todd Stuart, November 15, 1875, Insanity File.

73. Robert Lincoln to "My dear Judge [Davis]," November 16, 1875; Robert Lincoln Todd to Ninian Edwards, November 16, 1875; Elizabeth Edwards to Robert Lincoln marked "private," n.d., Insanity File.

74. Elizabeth Edwards to Robert Lincoln, August 11, 12, September 15, 22, November 5, 1875; Ninian Edwards to Robert Todd Lincoln, November 17, 1875, Insanity File.

75. M. A. P. Corcoran to Robert Lincoln, January 11, March 9, 1876; Ninian Edwards to Robert Lincoln, January 14, 15, April 21, 1876, Insanity File.

76. Basler, *Collected Works,* vol. 6, p. 256; Ninian Edwards to Robert Todd Lincoln, December 14, 1875; Elizabeth Edwards to Robert Todd Lincoln, September 15, 1875, Insanity File.

77. Ninian Edwards to Leonard Swett, June 22, 1876; Elizabeth Edwards to Robert Lincoln, January 16, 1876, Insanity File.

78. Leonard Swett to Ninian Edwards, June 20, 1876; Robert T. Lincoln to "my dear Uncle," January 17, 1876, Insanity File; Robert T. Lincoln to Elizabeth Edwards, May 17, 1876, Robert Todd Lincoln Letter Press Books.

79. Elizabeth Edwards to Robert Todd Lincoln, private; Ninian Edwards to Robert Todd Lincoln, November 12, 17, 1875; Robert Todd Lincoln to "my dear Uncle," January 17, 1876; David Davis to Robert Lincoln, May 22, 1876, Insanity File.

80. Robert Lincoln to "my dear Uncle," April 1, 24, 25, 1876; Ninian Edwards to Robert Todd Lincoln, December 18, 1875, April 21, 1876; Elizabeth Edwards to Robert Todd Lincoln, December 1, 1875; H. C. Eames to Robert Lincoln, April 27, 1876, Insanity File.

81. Robert Todd Lincoln to John Palmer, April 20, 1876; John Palmer to Robert Todd Lincoln, December 21, 1875, April 11, 24, 1876, Insanity File; Mary Lincoln to Honorable R. M. Wallace, June 1, 1875; Ninian Edwards to David Davis, June 8, 1876; N. W. Edwards to Robert Lincoln, memo, n.d., Insanity File.

82. Photostat of records from the files of Cook County Courthouse, Illinois State Historical Library, June 15, 1876; Conservatorship Records, Insanity File.

83. Robert T. Lincoln to Ninian Edwards, June 15, 1876; Ninian Edwards to Robert T. Lincoln, June 17, 1876, Insanity File. See also Myra Bradwell's account in the *Chicago Legal News,* June 17, 1876.

84. Ninian Edwards to Robert Lincoln, June 17, 1876, Insanity File; Neely and McMurtry, *The Insanity File,* pp. 104–06.

85. *Chicago Times,* June 16, 1876.

86. Turner, *Letters,* p. 615; Robert Todd Lincoln to Mary Todd Lincoln, February 7, 1876, Insanity File.

87. Mary Todd Lincoln to Mary Harlan Lincoln, Fragment, Insanity File; Neely and McMurtry, *The Case of Mary Todd Lincoln,* pp. 160–62.

88. Leonard Swett to Ninian Edwards, June 20, July 1, 1876; Ninian Edwards to "My dear Sir," June 22, 24, 1876; Ninian Edwards to Leonard Swett, June 24, 1876; Ninian Edwards to Robert Lincoln, June 26, 1876, Insanity File.

89. Helm, *Mary, Wife of Lincoln,* p. 298.

CHAPTER XII   LAST YEARS

1. Elizabeth Edwards to Robert Lincoln, October 29, 1876, Insanity File.

2. Turner, *Letters,* p. 633.

3. Ibid.

4. Ibid., pp. 682, 633.

5. Elizabeth Edwards to Robert Lincoln, October 29, 1876, Insanity File.

6. Turner, *Letters,* p. 618.

7. Sarah Ellis, *Summer and Winter in the Pyrenees* (London: Fisher and Son, 1844); Dr. Alexander Taylor, *The Curative Influence of the Climate of Pau and the Mineral Waters of the Pyrenees* (Pau: Vignancour, 1849).

8. Turner, *Letters,* p. 546.

9. Ibid., pp. 660, 629.

10. Pierre Tucoo-Chale, *Pau's Comme Anglaise, Promenades Historiques* (Paris: Société Nouvelle d'Éditions Regionales, 1979); *Journal des Étrangers,* 1876–1880 (Pau Historical Archives, Pau, France.)

11. Turner, *Letters,* p. 627.

12. Ibid., p. 690.

13. Ibid., p. 445.

14. Ibid., pp. 699, 627, 630.

15. Ibid., p. 641.

16. Ibid., pp. 656, 679, 685, 622, 650.

17. Ibid., pp. 663, 681.

18. Ibid., p. 666.

19. Ibid., p. 687.

20. McFeely, *Grant,* p. 468; Julia Grant, *Personal Memoirs,* p. 260.

21. Turner, *Letters,* p. 690, 630.

22. Ibid., pp. 633, 694.

23. Ibid., pp. 682, 683.

24. Ibid., pp. 626, 676.

25. Ibid., pp. 633, 690, 691.

26. Ibid., pp. 633–34.

27. Elizabeth Edwards to Robert Lincoln, September (n.y.); Robert Todd Lincoln to Elizabeth Edwards, April 18, 1879, Insanity File.

28. Robert Lincoln to Mr. Yard, April 11, 1914, Century Collection, New York Historical Society.

29. Turner, *Letters,* p. 690; *New York Times,* October 31, 1880.

30. Bernhardt, *Memoirs,* p. 370.

31. *New York Sun,* October 28, 1880; July 22, 1881; *Illinois Journal,* July 10, 1881.

32. *Congressional Record,* Forty-seventh Congress, First Session, p. 653; Dorothy Meserve Kunhardt, "An Old Lady's Memories," *Life,* February 9, 1959, pp. 58–60.

33. Elizabeth Edwards to Emilie Helm, December 3, 1880, Helm Papers; *New York Times,* July 22, 1881; Randall, *Mary Lincoln,* pp. 443–44.

34. *Congressional Record,* Forty-seventh Congress, First Session; *New York Times,* July 27, 1881; Professor Edward Maumanee to Jean Baker, January 6, 1986, personal communication.

35. Robert Lincoln to Sarah Orne, June 2, 1881, Randall Papers; J. G. A. to the Editor, *New York Times,* August 4, 1881.

36. *New York Times,* July 27, 1881, August 4, 1881; *Illinois Journal,* July 10, 1881.

37. *New York Times,* November 23, 1881.

38. Ibid., November 23, July 22, August 4, 1881; Turner, *Letters,* p. 711.

39. Charles Rosenberg, *The Trial of the Assassin Guiteau* (Chicago: University of Chicago Press, 1968), p. 4.

40. Turner, *Letters,* pp. 710–16; *New York Times,* October 11, 1881; Reverend Noyes Miner, "A Vindication of Mrs. Abraham Lincoln," Illinois State Historical Society.

41. Turner, *Letters,* pp. 710, 711.

42. Reflex paralysis of the iris is sometimes associated with syphilis and has been used incorrectly as circumstantial evidence of Lincoln's syphilis. *Congressional Record,* Forty-seventh Congress, First Session, App. p. 430; No. 77; House, pp. 578, 652–53.

43. *Congressional Record,* Forty-seventh Congress, First Session, p. 430.

44. *New York Times,* July 18, 1882; "Mrs. Lincoln's Funeral," *Lincoln Lore,* November 1981, March 1965; *Illinois Journal,* May 31, June 6, July 4, 12, 17, 18, 19, 1882.

Index